The Routledge Companion to Public–Private Partnerships

A public–private partnership (PPP) is a contractual arrangement with appropriate risk sharing between public and private partners for the delivery of public infrastructure or services, which is intended to create value-for-money to the taxpayer. *The Routledge Companion to Public–Private Partnerships* provides a cutting-edge survey of the field.

PPPs remain a highly controversial subject matter globally and this comprehensive and authoritative volume provides a terrific compendium of information for students and scholars charged with understanding, critiquing and advancing this model. With sections devoted to legal aspects, institutional economics perspectives, finance and accountability, the editors draw together an impressive range of contributors from around the world.

Piet de Vries is Assistant Professor of Accounting and Finance at The University of Twente, the Netherlands

Etienne B. Yehoue is a senior economist with the International Monetary Fund, USA

Routledge Companions in Business, Management and Accounting

Routledge Companions in Business, Management and Accounting are similar to what some publishers call 'handbooks' i.e. prestige reference works providing an overview of a whole subject area or sub-discipline, and which survey the state of the discipline including emerging and cutting edge areas. These books provide a comprehensive, up to date, definitive work of reference which can be cited as an authoritative source on the subject.

One of the key aspects of the Routledge Companions in Business, Management and Accounting series is their international scope and relevance. Edited by an array of well regarded scholars, these volumes also benefit from teams of contributors which reflect an international range of perspectives.

Individually, Routledge Companions in Business, Management and Accounting provide an impactful one-stop-shop resource for each theme covered, whilst collectively they represent a comprehensive learning and research resource for researchers and postgraduates and practitioners.

Published titles in this series include:

The Routledge Companion to Fair Value and Financial Reporting
Edited by Peter Walton

The Routledge Companion to Nonprofit Marketing
Edited by Adrian Sargeant and Walter Wymer Jr

The Routledge Companion to Accounting History
Edited by John Richard Edwards and Stephen P. Walker

The Routledge Companion to Creativity
Edited by Tudor Rickards, Mark A. Runco and Susan Moger

The Routledge Companion to Strategic Human Resource Management
Edited by John Storey, Patrick M. Wright and David Ulrich

The Routledge Companion to International Business Coaching
Edited by Michel Moral and Geoffrey Abbott

The Routledge Companion to Organizational Change
Edited by David M. Boje, Bernard Burnes and John Hassard

The Routledge Companion to Cost Management
Edited by Falconer Mitchell, Hanne Nørreklit and Morten Jakobsen

The Routledge Companion to Digital Consumption
Edited by Russell W. Belk and Rosa Llamas

The Routledge Companion to Identity and Consumption
Edited by Ayalla A. Ruvio and Russell W. Belk

The Routledge Companion to Public–Private Partnerships
Edited by Piet de Vries and Etienne B. Yehoue

The Routledge Companion to Public–Private Partnerships

Edited by Piet de Vries and Etienne B. Yehoue

LONDON AND NEW YORK

First published 2013
by Routledge
2 Park Square, Milton Park, Abingdon, Oxon OX14 4RN

Simultaneously published in the USA and Canada
by Routledge
605 Third Avenue, New York, NY 10017

First issued in paperback 2021

Routledge is an imprint of the Taylor & Francis Group, an informa business

Publisher's Note
The publisher has gone to great lengths to ensure the quality of this reprint but points out that some imperfections in the original copies may be apparent.

British Library Cataloguing in Publication Data
A catalogue record for this book is available from the British Library

Library of Congress Cataloging in Publication Data
The Routledge companion to public-private partnerships / edited by Piet de Vries and Etienne B. Yehoue.
     p. cm.
   Includes bibliographical references and index.
   1. Public-private sector cooperation.   2. Public-private sector
   cooperation—Law and legislation.   I. Vries, Piet de.   II. Yehoue,
   Etienne B.
   HD3871.R68 2012
   338.8—dc23

                                                2012022073

ISBN 13: 978−1−03−224277−4 (pbk)
ISBN 13: 978−0−415−78199−2 (hbk)

DOI: 10.4324/9780203079942

Typeset in Bembo
by RefineCatch Limited, Bungay, Suffolk

Contents

Contents

Figures

Tables

Contributors

Holly Ameden holds M.S. and Ph.D. degrees in Agricultural and Resource Economics from, respectively, University of Rhode Island and University of California at Berkeley, as well as an M.A. in Economic Theory from the University of Arizona. Her areas of research include international trade and invasive species, public–private partnerships, and biotechnology. She is currently co-authoring a book on strategic public–private partnerships in research, and is serving as President of the Board of Land's Sake, a nonprofit organization in Weston, Massachusetts.

David R. Bloomgarden has served since 2005 as Lead Private Sector Development Officer responsible for the creation and management of the 'Program to Promote Public–Private Partnerships in Infrastructure for Latin America and the Caribbean' at the Multilateral Investment Fund (MIF). In addition, David is managing the programme 'Basic Services for the Poor' that provides early-stage grants for social enterprises and other non-state actors to introduce sustainable business models in health, education, energy and water and sanitation. Prior to working at the MIF, David was Deputy Manager of the office of Multilateral Development Banks responsible for US oversight of development policies and operational budgets of multilateral development institutions and has served as advisor to the US Directors on the Boards of the Inter-American Development Bank, African Development Bank and the International Fund for Agricultural Development.

Dennis A. Blumenfeld has worked as a Research Fellow and Consultant for the Multilateral Investment Fund (MIF), a member of the Inter-American Development Bank (IADB) Group, since April 2009, where he develops and manages technical assistance projects to build government capacity in public–private partnerships. Additionally, Dennis is the Lead Coordinator for the 'PPP Americas' conference, the premier knowledge event on public–private partnerships in Latin America and the Caribbean.

Ineke Boers studied Health Policy and Management at the Erasmus University, Rotterdam. After graduating, she was a researcher at the health department of the Dutch consumers' association. Since 2005 she has worked for the Netherlands Court of Audit, as (a senior) auditor in the PPS. In 2009 she was seconded to the Parliamentary Bureau for Research and Public Expenditure.

Philippe Burger is Professor of Economics and Head of the Department of Economics at the University of the Free State, South Africa. At the time of writing this chapter he was a visiting scholar at the IMF. On the topic of PPPs, he has also acted as a consultant for the OECD.

Richard Burke is a lecturer in Finance at Waterford Institute of Technology, Waterford, Republic of Ireland. His research interests include corporate governance and public–private partnership with particular reference to risk and partnership issues and he is currently completing his Doctoral thesis on PPP at Queen's University Belfast.

Maria Coelho is a Ph.D. student at UC Berkeley. At the time of writing this chapter she was a Research Assistant at the IMF's Fiscal Affairs Department, where her work focused on public expenditure reform. Previously she worked at HSBC Capital Markets as a financial analyst.

Istemi S. Demirag has been Professor of Accounting at Hull University Business School since September 2012. Previously he held a chair in accounting at Queen's University Management School, Belfast. He was co-founder and chairman of the British Accounting Association's Special Interest Group on Corporate Governance from 1998 until 2005 and currently he serves as a member on its executive group. He is an associate editor of *Accounting Forum* and the *European Journal of Finance* and serves on the editorial boards of a number of journals including the *Journal of Management and Governance*. He is the founder director and chairperson of the Early Career Accountants' Research Development Programme, funded by the European Accounting Association.

Gerhard Girmscheid (-Ing). is Full Professor at Institute of Construction and Infrastructure Management, ETH Zurich. He is a member of national boards, such as VSS and SIA/FIB. He is also member of the PPP-Experts Switzerland and board member of the Ernst Schweizer Metallbau AG. In addition, he is a member of the board of the CIB and task group coordinator of the CIB work commission 119 'Customised Industrial Construction'.

Ron Hodges is Professor of Accounting at the University of Birmingham in the UK, having held posts previously at the Universities of Sheffield and Nottingham. His research interests include the regulation of accounting, financial reporting in the public services and the audit and inspection of local government in addition to accounting for public–private partnerships and the private finance initiative. Ron was a member of the National Audit Office expert panel for their inquiry into PFI in the social housing sector in 2010. He acted as an advisor for the Communities and Local Government Committee of the House of Commons for its inquiry into local public audit and inspection in 2011. He was appointed as a member of the Financial Reporting Advisory Board (FRAB) in January 2012.

Freek Hoek studied mechanical engineering and business administration at the Technical University of Delft and Erasmus University, Rotterdam, and hospital sciences at the University of Utrecht. He was a researcher at the Institute for Applied Natural Sciences TNO. Since 1984 he has worked for the Netherlands Court of Audit, in audit fields such as health and education and for the internal policy division on the development of strategy, quality systems and audit methodology. Since 1998 he has been an audit manager/specialist of audits in the public–private sector. He is also involved in programmes for technical assistance of Supreme Audit Institutions in the African continent.

Elisabetta Iossa is Full Professor of Economics at the University of Rome Tor Vergata and Research Fellow at the CEPR and CMPO. Prior to that, she worked for 10 years at Brunel University in West London and for two years at ECARES in Brussels.

Her papers have been published in the *Economic Journal*, the *International Journal of Industrial Organization*, the *Journal of Industrial Economics*, the *Journal of Public Economics*, *Oxford Economic Papers* and the *Rand Journal of Economics*, among others. Elisabetta has worked as economic expert adviser for a number of institutions, including the UK Competition Commission, the Office of Fair Trading, the Financial Services Authority and the World Bank.

Xiao-Hua Jin (Ph.D., University of Melbourne) is Senior Lecturer at the University of Western Sydney. He was a construction project manager in China before moving to academia. Before joining UWS, he was an academic at Deakin University and the University of Melbourne. His main research interests include construction economics; risk management; infrastructure procurement; relational contracting; ICT in construction; and sustainable built environment. Dr Jin has published over 50 technical articles, many of which are in internationally renowned journals. He received a Building Research Excellence Award from the Chartered Institute of Building (CIOB). He is a Member of the Australia Institute of Project Management. He has served as an expert referee for the Australian government and is also a regular referee for many internationally renowned journals.

Izabela Karpowicz is an economist at the IMF's Office of Budget and Planning. Prior to that and at the time of writing this chapter she worked in the Fiscal Affairs Department of the IMF, on expenditure policy issues.

Iqbal Khadaroo is currently Reader and Ph.D. Director (Accounting) at the University of Essex. He was previously senior lecturer at Queen's University Belfast, visiting professor at Nottingham University Business School Malaysia, lecturer at Multimedia University Malaysia, and ACCA and CIMA freelance lecturer in Malaysia and Mauritius.

Alejandro Lopez Martinez is Business Development Specialist with OHL Construction in Madrid, Spain. He has previous experience working in the transport sector at the World Bank in Washington DC, USA.

David Martimort holds the position of Directeur d'Etudes at Ecole des Hautes Etudes en Sciences Sociales and is Professor at Paris School of Economics. He has published widely in *Econometrica*, *Review of Economic Studies*, *Journal of Economic Theory*, the *Rand Journal of Economics*, *Theoretical Economics* and the *Journal of Public Economics*.

He has been a Fellow of the Econometric Society and European Economic Association since 2005.

Claude Ménard is Full Professor of Economics at the University of Paris (Panthéon-Sorbonne). He is co-founder and past president of the International Society for New Institutional Economics, and co-founder and board member of the Ronald Coase Institute. He has published extensively in leading economic journals such as *Journal of Economic Behavior and Organization*, *World Development* and *Journal of Institutional and Theoretical Economics*.

Cor van Montfort is project manager at the Netherlands Court of Audit, visiting fellow at the Scientific Council for Government Policy and professor of 'good governance and public–private arrangements' at Tilburg University. He has also chaired national commissions on codes of good governance in childcare and higher education.

S. Ping Ho is Associate Professor of Construction Management at National Taiwan University in Taiwan. He taught at Stanford University in 2010 as endowed Shimizu Visiting Associate Professor. He is on the Editorial Board of *Engineering Project Organization Journal*. His research focuses on game theory modelling in engineering management, the internationalization of A/E/C firms, the governance of Public–Private Partnerships, strategic management, and knowledge sharing. Dr Ho has been invited by the Congress of Taiwan and the Federal Control Department of Taiwan to testify on PPP laws and policies.

Cesar Queiroz is former World Bank Highways Adviser and an international consultant on roads and transport infrastructure. His expertise includes public–private partnerships, road maintenance, financing, management and development, performance-based contracts, improving governance, quality assurance and evaluation, research, teaching and training. Cesar has published two books and more than 130 papers and articles in more than 15 countries. He holds a Ph.D. from the University of Texas, USA, M.Sc. from the Federal University of Rio de Janeiro, and B.S. in civil engineering from the Federal University of Juiz de Fora, Brazil.

Gordon Rausser is currently Robert Gordon Sproul Distinguished Professor, University of California, Berkeley, where he has taught in the Department of Agricultural and Resource Economics (ARE) for 30 years. He has won 17 national awards and honours for research and teaching and currently serves as editor of the *Annual Review of Resource Economics*.

Justin Tyson is a senior economist in the European Department at the IMF. Prior to that he worked in the Fiscal Affairs Department at the IMF, on both expenditure policy and public financial management issues; in this capacity he was involved in delivering technical assistance to member countries on how to strengthen the institutional frameworks to manage PPPs. Before joining the IMF he worked at the UK Treasury, focusing on the government's spending reviews.

Piet de Vries (Ph.D. University of Twente) is an Assistant Professor at the University of Twente, The Netherlands. He teaches public finance, institutional economic theory and health economics. His research interests concern public–private partnerships, and the economics of organization. He also lectures in managerial economics to MBA students at the Twente School of Management. He publishes on public finance issues and is versed in new institutional economics. He has published several economic research studies commissioned by the Dutch Government.

Jan Wielos studied Political Science, Economics and Public Finance. After having worked in several ministries he was employed from 1986 at the Netherlands Court of Audit, lately as a specialist in the Public Private Sector. He retired in February 2012.

Yiannis Xenidis received his Ph.D. on 'Risk Analysis of BOT projects with the Use of Fuzzy Logic' from the department of Civil Engineering in the Aristotle University of Thessaloniki (AUTH) in 2006 and, since 2009, he is a faculty member at the same department. He is the author of several peer-reviewed papers and he has contributed, upon invitation, with book chapters to several publications. His main research interests and teaching activities include: Resilient Systems, Risk Analysis and Decision-Making Theory, Infrastructure Investments and Development, Public–Private Partnerships and Risk Analysis for Infrastructure.

Etienne B. Yehoue (Ph.D., Harvard University) is a senior financial economist at the International Monetary Fund and teaches at the Georgetown University in Washington DC. His research interests include monetary and financial economics, international risk sharing, public–private partnerships in infrastructure, and governance. He was awarded the Sidney R. Knafel Prize at the Weatherhead Center for International Affairs at Harvard University in 2003 and was the Sidney R. Knafel Fellow at the Center from 2003 to 2004. He has worked for the Center for International Development and was the Policy Chair for the African Caucus at Harvard University. He has taught courses in international capital markets and development economics at the Kennedy School of Government, Harvard University, and in Operations Research at the University of Benin.

E. R. Yescombe is an independent consultant in public–private partnerships and project finance, with over 30 years' experience in structured finance. He was formerly head of project finance for Bank of Tokyo-Mitsubishi in London. Publications include *Principles of Project Finance* (2002), *Public–Private Partnerships: Principles of Policy and Finance* (2007) and (as co-author) *Public–Private Partnerships in Emerging Markets – How to Engage with the Private Sector* (2011). For further information see www.yescombe.com.

Acknowledgements

The editors would like to thank Rosemary Baron (Routledge) for her help in editing the book chapters. Her accuracy has definitely lightened their task. Many thanks also to Manon Jannink-van het Reve (University of Twente) for her secretarial support.

Introduction

Etienne B. Yehoue and Piet de Vries

Since the early 1990s, industrialized, emerging, and developing economies have witnessed a dramatic increase in Public–Private Partnerships (PPPs). The United Kingdom's 1992 launch of its Private Finance Initiative is a notorious example. More generally in Europe, between 2002 and 2006, the annual average value of PPP projects signed is estimated at 22.9 billion euros. In the United States, PPP financing in the transportation sector increased on average almost tenfold annually over 1996–2005 and 2006–2008 (Engel *et al.*, forthcoming). According to the World Bank, private sector financed about 20 per cent of infrastructure investments, amounting to about US$ 850 billion in emerging and developing countries during the 1990s.[1] Based on the World Bank's Private Participation in Infrastructure (PPI) database, Engel *et al.* (forthcoming) report that investments in PPPs in emerging and developing countries grew at an annual average rate of 28.3 per cent between 1990 and 1997 before slowing down following the East-Asian crisis, but the growth trend resumed again in 2003.

This development raises the question of why PPPs have become increasingly widespread. Inasmuch as public procurement accounts for a sizeable share of economic activity, how to deliver high-quality services at low cost to the taxpayer and user is a critical issue. The emergence of PPPs could be seen as an effort to find solutions to this issue.

While the traditional form of procurement usually exhibits some efficiency flaws and masks or fails to factor project risks into the cost of fund, PPP arrangements explicitly build them in. PPPs also have the potential to capitalize on the private sector efficiency. The delivery of public services (such as waste disposal, water management, sanitation, prison management, and public transportation), involves a variety of complex tasks ranging from erecting the infrastructure to operating it as efficiently as possible. However, the traditional form of procurement does not internalize the synergy-induced efficiency from bundling these tasks (Martimort and Pouyet, 2008). For example, to deliver a service, a government first designs the characteristics and quality attributes of the assets or infrastructure needed, second chooses a private contractor to erect the assets while retaining the ownership, and finally chooses an operator—public or private—to manage the assets and provide the service.

On the other hand, in PPP arrangements, government takes a minimalist stance, whereby it only chooses a private consortium, which will be responsible for designing the quality attributes of the assets, erecting them and managing them as efficiently as possible. Thus, PPP arrangements allow the bundling of various stages of a project, which offers the consortium the opportunity to exploit the synergies between these stages. This bundling is also the source of the complexity that characterizes PPP arrangements. Thus, while PPPs can simply be defined as long-term development and service contracts between government and a private partner, they usually exhibit various risk-sharing arrangements and governance structures.

Taking stock of PPP complexity, this volume aims at shedding some light on the recent developments of PPPs and various aspects affecting their sustainability. Its coverage ranges from the origin and history of PPPs, institutional and legal framework of PPPs, property right and corruption issues, the macroeconomic conditions, risk allocation and transaction costs, incomplete contracting and game theory, the financing and risk management in PPPs, the implications of the recent financial crisis for PPPs, to governance structure and accountability in PPPs.

General introduction to PPPs

The volume starts by offering the historical context of the emergence of the PPP phenomenon. In this regard, studying the origin and history of PPPs, Piet de Vries analyses the delineation between public and private sectors. Thus, from a political and philosophical perspective and using the organizational structure of society, he defines the concept of *public* and that of *private*. The concept of *private*, which has a straightforward relation to an individual human being or group of individuals, is simply viewed as the counterpart of *public*. In short, the distinction between public and private is part of a conceptual framework that organizes action in a social environment. This sets the scene for a historical excursion showing examples of PPP as manifestations of a specific society: the commercial society. From this, some reflection on PPPs from a theoretical point of view, where they perform a varying role resulting from deliberate economic and political choices, is offered.

Law and PPPs

PPP, as a societal phenomenon, is influenced in its development by institutional and legal frameworks. Thus, Etienne B. Yehoue highlights the importance of institutions for PPPs. He argues that institutions have the ability to influence the structure of economic incentives in a society and emphasizes the structure of property rights, contract enforceability and viability, law and order, and the presence of markets, as crucial for enabling PPPs to prosper. Establishing stable macroeconomic conditions through the adoption of appropriate economic policies is also found to be vital in affecting private sector incentives to join PPP arrangements. Ultimately, he argues, economic performance or development is shaped by the political and economic institutions. Building on Yehoue's analysis, David R. Bloomgarden and Dennis A. Blumenfeld present two case studies on Brazil and Mexico and assess the link between the institutional environment and PPPs in each of these countries.

Based on some lessons learned from successes and failures of PPPs, Cesar Queiroz and Alejandro Lopez Martinez analyse the characteristics of the legal framework that is compatible with the development of PPPs. They highlight specific laws that are important for the success of PPPs. These include public procurement, foreign investment, dispute resolution, company, insolvency, environment, competition, accounting standards, labour and tax laws.

Institutional economics and PPPs

Building on the groundwork of the institutional and legal framework section, the volume analyses the specificities of PPPs from an institutional economics perspective. Thus, Xiao-Hua Jin offers an in-depth analysis of the traditional or current practice of risk allocation in PPP construction projects and highlights its weaknesses. He then makes the case for the necessity of tackling the risk allocation issue from a transaction cost economics (TCE) perspective as it offers the possibility of integrating economics, organization theory, contract law and behavioural assumptions in an interdisciplinary and organizational framework. He shows how this approach offers a better interpretation of the mechanism that steers the risk allocation decision-making (RADM) process in a more logical and holistic way. In particular, he argues, this approach provides a useful overview of the critical determinants of the RADM.

Recognizing the complexity of PPP arrangements and its long-term nature with unanticipated events, Gordon Rausser and Holly Ameden point to incomplete contract theory as the foundation for any framework evaluating PPPs. They place control rights, the authority to make decisions in the case of both anticipated and unanticipated events, at the front and centre of PPP contracts, given their incomplete nature. They offer a three-stage framework where the public and private partners first negotiate over front-end control rights and back-end property rights—which determine the nature and scope of the partnership's production processes as well as related decision-making authority and the distribution of benefits—and make relationship-specific investments. Second, the partners bargain over management decisions in relation to the bargaining power balance agreed upon in the first stage. Third, partners terminate the partnership or renegotiate control and property-right allocations in face of an unanticipated shock. They show how the framework can be used to appropriately assign control and property rights, which align incentives and make PPPs efficient and more successful.

Analysing the difficulties associated with the complexity of PPPs, Claude Ménard emphasizes the role or responsibility of public authorities in delivering a network of infrastructures or basic public services through PPPs. He argues that this public responsibility frequently results in a 'double alignment problem'. On the one hand, a PPP is a device to set up a contractual relationship with adequately allocated property rights, inducing efficient behaviour and limiting transaction costs. Ménard refers to this as 'organizational alignment' issues addressed in neo-institutional economics. On the other hand, he discerns 'institutional alignment', that is, the institutional context that enables the public authorities to meet their societal responsibility for critical infrastructures in spite of property rights transferred to the private partner. It is this double alignment problem that Ménard identifies as a main factor explaining the difficulties and uneven spread of PPPs, notwithstanding its popularity. He uses several examples to substantiate this contention.

Against the backdrop of potential conflicts and strategic interactions between PPP promoters and governments with complicated issues such as opportunism, negotiations, competitive bidding, and partnerships, S. Ping Ho proposes an analytical and game theoretic framework to study the interaction and dynamics between the PPP stakeholders. The aim is to form proper strategies for both governments and promoters. He identifies two major opportunism problems commonly seen in PPPs—the unbalanced profit structure problem and the renegotiation/hold-up problem—which contribute to the major transaction costs related to transactional hazards and inefficiency in PPPs and whose magnitude determines whether PPPs are a suitable governance structure for a specific project. He offers two approaches aimed at resolving the opportunism-induced inefficiency in PPPs, whereby promoters send signals to the government indicating they are long-term profit-oriented type promoters and the government uses screening strategies to discourage the opportunistic, short-term profit-oriented promoters from participating in PPP projects. However, he argues that the slow learning curve of governments and the fast learning curve of promoters tend to limit the effectiveness of signalling and screening strategies, making factors that affect the propensity of opportunism in unbalanced profit structure and renegotiation/hold-up the key determinants of whether PPPs can be a good governance structure for a particular project.

The bundling of project phases into a single long-term, hence complex, contract, as well as the authority delegation required in PPPs opens the door to the principal–agent problem and corruption. Elisabetta Iossa and David Martimort argue that corruption can occur in all three stages of a PPP project: at decision stage, at tender stage and during contract execution. Emphasizing the long-term nature of a PPP contract and the likely emergence of contingencies that need to be regulated by the contract, they argue that both at tender stage and at contract negotiation stage, there is scope for corrupt deals that benefit a contractor or public officials at the expense of final users. The same holds during contract execution, given contingencies that may arise and call for a change in pricing or service conditions. They derive implications for the choice of PPP arrangements and highlight some measures that help alleviate the phenomenon.

Financing of PPPs

After tackling the various institutional angles and their economic implications for PPPs, the volume explores the financing options for the arrangements. Thus, E.R. Yescombe describes the most common method by which private finance is provided for PPP arrangements, that is, project finance—a lending technique which involves lending against the cash flow of particular projects rather than the value of any physical assets. Yescombe argues that this type of financing requires that the project to be financed must be able to stand alone, hence the need for setting up a Special Purpose Vehicle (SPV) for its execution and operation to avoid diverting resources to other activities. His contribution explains why project finance is used for PPPs, the sources of this type of finance, and the ways in which lenders evaluate PPP risks and structure loans to PPP projects.

Public sector economics and PPPs

In the section that follows, the volume studies the interplay between the public and the private sectors in PPP arrangements from a risk—sharing perspective. In particular, the implications of government commitments or obligations in PPP arrangements are examined. In this regard Piet de Vries in another contribution highlights the fiscal-sustainability risk PPPs may entail. Comparing PPP-specific accounting standards to the budget general norms, he points to the existence of an anomaly. The specific PPP norms appear not to be fully under the umbrella of the general public-budget norms. For example, even though PPP liabilities impact the fiscal sustainability through public-funding obligations for years to come, the PPP-tailored accounting standards may classify PPP liabilities as private. He argues that the issue of the demarcation of public versus private is at the core of this anomaly, which may harm the required transparency for a sound public finance practice. He makes the case that a private-financing component of a PPP that results in prospective taxation amounts to public debt and is relevant to the calculation of any public-sector deficit, and should be reflected in the government-budget constraint.

Gerhard Girmscheid, providing an in-depth analysis of the practice of risk allocation in PPPs, points to some differentiation depending on the types of risk. He argues that certain risks are allocated based on the legal conditions, while others are free of such restrictions and their allocation is driven by past experiences and opportunistic factors. As such, they reflect the negotiating strength of the partners. Thus, transparent and standard based risk-allocation criteria that would deliver efficiency in PPPs are yet to be established. Girmscheid argues that optimal risk allocation for the public sector would reflect both the general legal conditions and the competency and financial capacity of both partners involved. He then presents a multi-dimensional risk allocation model, which takes account not only of the professional competency and options available to the two partners, but also of the financial risk coverage capacity of each risk-taker. His model offers a risk distribution that aligns efficiency with the need to safeguard fiscal sustainability. In particular, risks in PPPs can be allocated in a manner that incentivizes private sector's efficiency, while guaranteeing the public budget safety as well as the quality of the public sector services to be delivered.

Recent financial crisis and PPPs

PPPs are usually mega projects requiring significant financing, which requires financial intermediation. As the recent financial crisis had threatened to close down financial markets around the world, the volume also analyses its implications for PPP arrangements. Thus, Philippe Burger and his co-authors examine the channels through which the crisis may have affected PPPs and point to cost of and access to finance as the main channels. They focus on government responses with the aim of pinning down the circumstances under which providing support to new and existing projects could be justified. The possible government measures that their analysis suggests include contract extensions, output-based subsidies, revenue enhancements and step-in rights.

Etienne B. Yehoue, in another contribution, takes a close look at the effective impacts of the crisis on PPPs. His empirical analysis suggests that these impacts are somewhat weak and short term, suggesting that PPP markets were resilient. He attributes this resiliency to re-adjustments of PPP market structure during the course of the crisis. The readjustments, he argues, mainly occur along two dimensions—PPP financing structure and PPP schemes—which increase some types of risk for the private sector but also call for an increased role for public entities. Beyond the recent global financial crisis, Yehoue's contribution also offers an assessment of the effects of the ongoing eurozone sovereign debt crisis. His finding suggests that the Euro area sovereign debt crisis that began in 2011 and is still ongoing has had a much bigger impact on PPPs in 2011 than the 2007–9 financial crisis. This results primarily from the enhanced role for the public sector in the new crisis-induced PPP market structure.

Governance of PPPs

As PPPs are complex undertakings, involving various stakeholders, their governance structure is a key determinant for their success, as it can affect efficiency. But PPP governance structure is influenced by the specific type of partnership between stakeholders. Istemi Demirag and Richard Burke argue that just focusing on the relationship between the public and private sectors is not enough to tackle the issue of governance in PPPs. Instead, for each PPP project, they suggest exploring the relationship between the public sector bodies responsible for the project, between the procuring authorities and the SPV set up for the execution and operation of the project, and between the SPV members. They argue that for a successful PPP, the governance structure must internalize partnerships across these three different levels.

Yiannis Xenidis identifies two interrelated fields that shape PPP governance structure and are decisive for successful partnerships, namely, the legal and appropriate contractual frameworks. Thus, formulating a comprehensive context mapping the different perceptions over the legal, contractual, political and social risks that have a strong impact on the success of PPPs is crucial. This step should be followed by exploring the legal tools that may advance the pursuit of PPPs from achieving viable projects to achieving viable partnerships, which in turn will foster a governance structure conducive to the success of PPPs. This procedure will result in a range of well-identified PPP contracting issues such as renegotiations, standardization, bundling/unbundling and contract durations, which the legal framework should address. Xenidis' research also points to short-term contracts as a tool to advance the viability of PPPs.

Accountability, auditing and assessment of PPPs

Without accountability, the defining characteristic of PPPs, that is, the delivery of value for money (VFM)—which requires improving productivity and cutting costs—may not materialize. The effectiveness of accountability requires its understanding and appropriation by taxpayers. Istemi Demirag and Iqbal Khadaroo offer a framework articulated around four themes—answerability, liability, blameworthiness, and attributability—that help to better comprehend the concept and equip taxpayers in their quest for accountability in the delivery of public infrastructure or basic services.

Beyond the notion of accountability related to the desire to achieve VFM, Ron Hodges, in his contribution, focuses on PPP accounting as another element of accountability. He provides an overview of the importance of PPP accounting and highlights some challenges that regulators face in the development of PPP accounting financial reporting rules. Reflecting on current international developments in PPP accounting, he offers an assessment of the recent proposals of the International Public Sector Accounting Standards Board.

Auditing is a key instrument for the effectiveness of accountability. It helps to evaluate and to situate responsibility. Ineke Boers and her co-authors analyse the findings on PPPs from the audits performed by various national and regional audit offices. Two types of audits were performed: (i) financial and regulatory audits, which relate to government accounts; and (ii) VFM audits, which relate to efficiency, effectiveness, policies, and institutions of government. From the various audits, it emerges that shortcomings are present in both planning and execution of contracts and, more importantly, changes made during the course of a project place VFM under pressure.

Note

1   World Bank, 2002, 'Building Institutions for Markets' *World Development Report, 2002* (Washington: World Bank) Chapter 8

References

Engel, Eduardo, Ronald Fischer, and Alexander Galetovic, forthcoming, 'The Basic Public Finance of Public–Private Partnerships' *Journal of the European Economic Association*
Martimort, David and Jerome Pouyet, 2008, 'To Build or not to Build: Normative and Positive Theories of Public–Private Partnerships' *International Journal of Industrial Organization*, Volume 26, pp: 393–411.
World Bank, 2002, 'Building Institutions for Markets' *World Development Report, 2002* (Washington: World Bank), Chapter 8 on Regulatory of Infrastructure, pp: 151–67.

Part I

General introduction to public–private partnerships

The modern public–private demarcation

History and trends in PPP

Piet de Vries[1]

1.1 Introduction

Public–private partnership (PPP) relates to risk-transferring and long-term cooperation between the State and a private institution to realize a public facility and/or service. Two main forms profile the history of this goal-oriented cooperation; the concession (charter) and the project agreement. Public authorities make use of private-sector skills to provide facilities that the market would have less incentive to provide; for instance, to exploit an infrastructural facility, or to revitalize an urban area. It is a widespread phenomenon, and has a long history. This chapter deals with the origin and the nature of PPP, and presents some historical patterns in the vicissitudes of the phenomenon. It focuses on addressing two themes: the societal turn enabling the rise of PPPs, and a history of PPPs through examples and reflecting their patterns.

The chapter is organized as follows. In a historical perspective, section 1.2 presents PPP as straightforwardly related to the rise of the modern society: the *modern economy*. This societal turn results from a basic change in the relation between 'public' and 'private'. Simultaneously, PPPs emerge as a manifestation of the modern economy. The modern economy offers unprecedented opportunities for mutually beneficial cooperation between public authorities and (private) individuals. The Dutch Republic during the seventeenth century is seen as the first full-blown modern economy, succeeded by Britain and the USA in the eighteenth and nineteenth centuries. Section 1.3 presents the early PPP history. The historical sequence of modern economies structures this section furnishing several early examples of PPP. It discusses seventeenth-century PPPs in forerunner Holland, eighteenth- to nineteenth-century examples in Britain, and early nineteenth-century PPPs in the USA. Section 1.4 reflects on the early trends and key features of the traditional PPPs. Section 1.5 presents recent developments and modern characteristics of PPPs. A final section concludes.

1.2 The modern public–private dichotomy

Private is the counterpart of public. In a common-sense meaning the concepts will refer to intimacy versus openness. In the PPP context they refer to the public and the private *sector*, i.e. sectors of societal (economic) activity. During the sixteenth and seventeenth centuries Western-European societies showed a gradual change in societal relations and in organizing activities. Increasingly, it was the commoner, a civilian without social rank, who thanks to his economic success acquired a certain position in the society. Civilians' economic merits replaced birth privilege or family prestige as a decisive variable in social relations and organizing social activities. Gradually, a society was emerging, in which individuals driven by self-interest traded and exchanged with others, who were likewise self-interested.

In such a society, mutually beneficial relations constitute the social fabric. It is the modern economy obviously emerging during the seventeenth century. This modern economy brings about another modern phenomenon. In the pre-market society 'court rationality' prevails (Elias 1969: 111). Station, prestige and clientelism form instruments of societal power; public and private interests are intermingled. Contrariwise, in the modern economy it is definitely not done to mix personal relations with calculating self-interest. Commercial, and in the same manner, bureaucratic relations ought to be freed of friendship and other personal ties. It follows that personal feelings and in particular friendship in the modern commercial society is an entirely separate domain (Silver 1997). Calculating friendship isn't friendship at all. The modern economy gives the concepts 'public' and 'private' an instrumental and normative feature. The public interest government bears responsibility for, should not be mixed with private interests of the public authorities. In the same manner, the private commercial relations should be based on impersonal, unprivileged calculation. It results in a new, modern public–private dichotomy. On the one hand, a private sector profiles the society in which the individual and his commercial self-interest play a pivotal role. On the other, in the public sector, government protects the public interest, in a manner removed from private windfalls.

A few references to Adam Smith may recap the emergence of the modern economy and the corresponding public–private dichotomy. 'Every man thus lives by exchanging, or becomes in some measure, a merchant, and the society itself grows to be what is properly a commercial society' (Adam Smith 1776: 25). At the same time, the evolution of a private sector makes clear that for some goods the mutually beneficial commerce does not function. Smith refers to protecting the society from violence, public works, educational institutions, and protection from injustice, as 'tasks the Sovereign should take care of' (Smith 1776: 459–61).

It is this commercial society that constitutes the breeding ground for PPPs. Inevitably, the merchant will see beneficial opportunities for which he might require some help or admittance from the public authorities. On the other hand, the public authorities may observe opportunities to make the private self-interest subservient to the public interest. PPP is a natural consequence of the modern economy, an equally modern phenomenon. In the same way, PPP entails the normative implications, underlining the normative feature of the modern public–private dichotomy.

1   PPP is a device to foster the public interest, e.g. value-for-money for the taxpayer, using private self-interest to organize the social activity, i.e. tasks the sovereign should take care of.

2   The modern dichotomy makes clear that economic relations should be based on mutual self-interest; impersonal, unprivileged calculation results in commercial relations. It follows from this that PPPs should not be contaminated with clientelism and favouritism. A PPP ought to be based on contractual relationships defining 'tit-for-tat' arrangements; instruments to meet a well-defined public interest by means of partnerships with private agents fuelled by self-interest.

3 Public access to information concerning a PPP project, accountability, is aimed at demonstrating that the private interests are subordinated to the public interest of the project.

These normative notions of the public–private dichotomy will repeatedly emerge in any historic overview of the PPP. And these norms turn out to be valid to this very day. This overview starts with the rise of the commercial society.

1.3 The emergence of the modern economy and PPP

Frequently, Adam Smith in his *Wealth of Nations* refers to Holland as the model commercial society he was analysing. Even a hundred years after its Golden Age, Smith described the state of the Dutch economy of his day as a kind of general equilibrium, with normal ('clear') profits and low interest rates; 'a country which had acquired its full complement of riches' (Adam Smith 1776: 107–8). On the other hand, prominent students of economic history such as Joel Mokyr and David Landes consider the Dutch Golden Age as an interesting period of merely accidental economic growth; a curious phenomenon that will disappear in the same unexpected manner as it appeared (Landes 1998: 408; Mokyr 2002: 31). According to these and many other authors, it is the French political and the English industrial revolution that constitute the real dividing line between the traditional and the modern; before this line a society with social stratification that rules social action and relations, and behind that line a meritocracy with social action and relations based on tit-for-tat. A recent example of this position is Douglas Allen's *The Institutional Revolution*, claiming that before the British Industrial Revolution (1760–1850) the society, throughout Europe, was grounded on 'pre-modern institutions based on patronage, purchase, and personal ties' (Allen 2012: jacket text).

At the same time, Douglass North, for example, assesses the Low Countries economy of those days of 'unparalleled importance of industry and commerce'. North concludes: 'The Netherlands as a result [of enforcing property rights] became the first country to achieve sustained economic growth' (North 1980: 152, 154). And, Immanuel Wallerstein sees (the Dutch Republic of) 'the United Provinces in the mid-seventeenth century as the first of the only three instances of hegemony'; succeeded by 'the United Kingdom in the mid-nineteenth, and the United States in the mid-twentieth' (Wallerstein 1984: 39–40).

The Dutch Republic of the seventeenth century exhibits the 'genetic features' of a modern economy; reasonably free and pervasive markets, for both commodities and production factors; agricultural productivity supporting far-reaching division of labour; a State attentive to property rights; and technology and organization capable of sustained development (De Vries and Van der Woude 1997: 693). These genetic features are applicable to all modern economies ever since. During the seventeenth century these features result in an unprecedented sustained economic growth of the Dutch economy. And these features constitute the seed-bed for all kinds of PPP.

For that matter, it must be stressed that the focus on the Dutch republic as a modern-economy paragon definitely does not imply that similar modern genetic features are absent in other European countries or regions, such as England, France, Portugal or Scandinavia. Moreover, earlier urban economies such as Florence and Venice exhibited modern, commercial genes. At the same time, it is hegemony on the world market that may justify seeing Holland as the area where modern public–private demarcation emerged clearly. It is Wallerstein's position regarding instances of hegemony that is followed in presenting a historical view of PPP in trendsetting modern economies; in succession: Holland, Britain and the

USA. Subsection 1.3.1 presents some early Dutch PPP examples. Subsections 1.3.2 and 1.3.3 deal with early British and US examples respectively.

1.3.1 PPP in the modern economy of the Dutch Republic

The modern-economic development of the Dutch society brings about PPP as a natural consequence. For instance, the conspicuous economic growth of Amsterdam during the seventeenth century posed the urban authorities some challenging town-planning issues. On a limited scale the authorities succeeded in organizing financial participation of the civilians who benefited from the new urban extensions. For instance, in January 1613 the Amsterdam urban authorities organized an auction of canal lots to be issued. In the city hall the project documents had been available for inspection. The new area was parcelled out in uniform lots, and all conditions made public preceding the auction. In these conditions some PPP elements may be found. In this respect, part of the obligation of the new lot owners was to co-finance infrastructural facilities such as bridges, quay walls and parts of the canal-digging activities (Abrahamse 2010: 97). However, full-blown Dutch PPP examples during the seventeenth century may be found in land-reclamation projects, dealt with in the rest of this section.

'God created the world, Holland is created by the Dutch themselves', immigrant René Descartes observed. The Dutch crusade against the water knows many forms, with dikes and polders as main weapons. These infrastructural works form a rich source of PPP examples referring to a period that spans from the sixteenth till the twentieth century. Water works exhibit prominent collective-good aspects that all but inevitably result in public authorities' involvement. It is in particular the regional authorities of the water-board district and the provincial State that played a dominant role in the dramatic change of the landscape and the map of Holland during those past four centuries. At the same time, private initiatives, and involvement in construction and exploitation by the private sector at its own risk profile this history. The land reclamation history shows the evolution of interaction between private actors and public authorities to full-fledged forms of PPP. The projects develop to more complex systems, both in the technical and in the institutional respect. It refers to three phases that may be discerned (Stol 2002: 109–34).

1 Diking-up of mud flats. This refers to the first type of land reclamation. The first successful diking-up, of 6,500 ha, was in North-Holland (Zijpe). It was a State initiative, in particular as a protection against storm tides. Consequently, it initiated private requests for concessions to dike-up adjacent mud flats, resulting in the Wieringerwaard (a 1,600 ha polder), finally in 1611. It concerned a mutually beneficial project; the private investors acquired new farmland to be leased out, and a period of tax exemption; the public authorities future fiscal opportunities. The restricted period of tax exemption formed an incentive to complete the project as soon as possible. For that matter, several setbacks, such as a weak base to the dikes, led to several renewals of the concession. Moreover, two episodes of gale damage to the dikes brought new patents for the private investor and new fiscal privileges for a limited period of time (Stol 2002: 110). This may be interpreted as an example of risk-sharing between the public and the private partners.
2 Pumping dry of (natural) lakes and expanses of water. Technically more challenging than diking-up sea-clay flats above normal sea level is a polder below sea level, outside the dike or natural lakes inside. It requires the pumping-dry of the lake and permanent drainage of the new polder. The first examples of pumping dry of lakes happened in 1533 (35 ha)

and 1564 (686 ha) in North Holland; small-scale experiments initiated by the local nobility (Stol 2002: 111). In the seventeenth century it became the domain of enterprising merchants. The new windmill technology offered up-scaling opportunities. As a consequence, in the course of the seventeenth century the size of projects started exceeding the financial strength of a small group of individual investors. The solution was found in project financing by a kind of Special Purpose Vehicle, an 'opportunity combination' (*gelegenheidscombinatie*) (Stol 2002: 111). Actually, it involves a company that provides financing in the investment and the dispersion of the entrepreneurial risks. In particular in the seventeenth century the polder was an attractive long-term investment for surplus capital of the urban Dutch civilians. The North-Holland Beemster polder (7,100 ha) is the first commercial example. The polder turned out to be an interesting business case for a concession company; it finances the investment of land reclamation, partitions the lots in proportion to the financial participation in the initial investment, and finally aims to succeed in achieving a positive financial result of its funding by leasing out the new lots and premises. The public side firstly concerns the concession granted, and secondly a water board district that takes care of the collective-good features of the project, i.e. drainage and maintenance of the drainage system, empowered to charge the new landowners. In the short period of 1610 to 1640 the map of North Holland changed radically. Prominent Amsterdam merchants and other urban investors invested at least ten million guilders in concession projects for 26,000 ha land reclamation in the northern quarter of Holland – rather risky enterprises as the financial returns were straightforwardly dependent on variables such as economic growth and food prices (De Vries and Van der Woude 1997: 29).

3 Pumping dry of lakes created by the digging-out of peat. Peat was the main fuel in the Dutch Republic and economic growth and population growth caused strong increase in demand for this energy source. A side effect was the undesirable creation of lakes and sheets of water. This induced, for instance, in 1680 water-board district Rijnland in Southern Holland to set up a guarantee fund financing the land reclamation of the water flats created by the digging-out. The concessionaire of the peat bog was obliged to feed this fund controlled by the board district. Another device was the concession condition to create a land reclamation fund, fed and controlled by the peat-digging firm itself, to guarantee its financial affordability to meet its concession obligation to change immediately the new created wetland into a polder; a practice that lasted until the end of the nineteenth century. In Friesland together with South Holland it resulted in 23,000 ha land reclamation (Stol 2002: 128–9).

Public authorities' involvement is evidently present, but limited to front- and end-stage. The private partners bear the risks, and have the incentives to invest efficiently. Prominent are the commercial risks exclusively borne by the private partners. At the same time, force majeure and other unknown risks may be shared by both the public and the private partners. Mutual interests feature the land reclamation PPPs. Negative externalities stemming from earlier concessions, such as reduced overflow capacity and setting problems were lessons for new concessions. For instance, the concession for Schermer-polder (1633) conditioned the private company to dig two drainage channels for overflow control (Stol 2002: 113). All in all, De Vries and Van der Woude conclude, 'it is clear that one motivation dominated this multifaceted movement: profit' (De Vries and Van der Woude 1997: 30). Complementary to this profit-seeking behaviour is public authorities' facilitating attitude and their attentiveness to property rights.

Piet de Vries

1.3.2 PPP and the British Industrial Revolution

It is a broad cultural and sociological change in Western Europe that announces the modernity of the public–private demarcation described above. It is this long-term economic and social evolution 'from the late sixteenth century, particularly in relation to agricultural development, overseas trade, the emergence of more consumer-oriented industries and market awareness' that forms the multifaceted prelude to the period beyond 1750, the Industrial Revolution. A clear 'moment of transition' in this British scheme of economic evolution refers to the several enclosure periods, such as the parliamentary enclosure during the eighteenth century (Hoppit 1987: 213). The turnpike trust reflects the same British transition from common property and responsibility, to private property and private initiatives. A logical consequence is PPP. Three PPP applications will be dealt with: the turnpike trusts; the Canal Mania; and the emergence of railways.

1.3.2.1 The turnpike trust

Since the Middle Ages maintaining the king's highway was a local responsibility in Great Britain. It was a common-law obligation based on coerced labour on the roads for which the parishes were liable. Increasing through traffic during the seventeenth and eighteenth centuries exerbed enormous pressure on this system. During the seventeenth century various solutions had been tried such as a temporary permission to levy toll. Finally, from 1714 a legal novelty, the trustee, was used to maintain roads in good order. The trustee was a public authority enabled by the parishes to collect tolls and to borrow money, mortgage the toll yield, divert the course of the road, and do most other things necessary for maintaining and improving a road. The management was placed in the hands of appointed trustees, mainly landowners, but also merchants or local alderman acting ex-officio (Albert 1983: 44). From 1750 turnpikes spread rapidly to most parts of Britain, over 500 trusts being formed to cover more than 15,000 miles (Albert 1983: 42). The turnpike history offers two elements of PPP: toll collection; and financing.[2]

An evident PPP element applied by the turnpike trustees concerns the private-sector involvement in toll collection. The collection of tolls was a main occupation of the trustees, which caused several problems. The charge system was highly itemized and complex. It was extremely difficult to guard against toll evasion and fraud. Therefore, 'many trustees resorted to leasing, or "farming", gates for a fixed yearly sum' (Albert 1983: 47). The lessee could acquire the toll collection rights by an auction. The fixed sum transferred the demand risk to the private farmer, and strongly incentivized him to prevent fraud and evasion. The trustee as a public authority deployed private actor's incentives to realize its (public) aim, i.e. funding by an efficient toll collection.

The second PPP element the turnpike history performs, involves the private financing practices of the trustees. In contrast with canals and railways, turnpikes by that time did not usually require large amounts of capital expenditure. The modest finance needs were provided by civil lenders. Legislation by the 1760s enforced loan subscription. Often the loan was subdivided into small denominations, which broadened the base of financial support: 'There was an increase in funds from merchants, manufacturers, artisans and shopkeepers' (Albert 1983: 53). Investors with modest resources saw the trusts as a secure investment, whereas merchants and landed interests had much to gain directly from the investment in better roads. This private-financing involvement may be seen as a PPP element, in spite of the public feature of the trustee. The trustee evolved as a device

14

meeting a public responsibility by private financing and funding; actually, a genuine off-public-budget route.

1.3.2.2 The canal mania

Navigable water has always been an important location factor for economic activity and trade. Early economic centres stood on or near navigable water. Improvements of navigation were locally organized projects, preferably private investments. The steady increase in economic growth and trade in Britain since the mid-eighteenth century raised an unprecedented need for efficient conveyance of goods. After 1760 the time was ripe for promotion of the construction of waterways *ex nihilo*: canals (Duckham 1983: 101). In an increasing degree, economic growth had made mere improvement of the river navigability insufficient. The particular needs of the localities, merchants, businessmen and industrialists, formed the deciding factor in promotion of inland navigation Acts (Duckham 1983: 105). Private initiatives induced public authorities to enact concessions for new navigation schemes. 'The mileage of inland waterway in England and Wales rose from 1,398½ in 1760 to 3,875½ in 1830' (Duckham 1983: 109). Between 1790 and 1794 there was a canal mania, during which 51 Acts for canal projects were passed.

The canal investments performed several PPP features. First, all the inland navigation projects concerned a concession PPP. Second, the usual finance vehicle of the canal investment was a joint-stock company. The stock company invested a legally stated sum of equity shares issued, and additionally an amount borrowed. It was empowered to levy tolls. The company bore all the risks, inclusive the major up- and down-side risks of construction and demand with resulting high return amplitude. Therefore, 'the concern's enabling Act also furnished a schedule of maximum tolls aimed to strike an appropriate balance between reasonable returns on capital and the public good' (Duckham 1983: 114). Apparently, the legislator was navigating between public and private interests, being well aware of the natural-monopoly nature of the inland navigation works. For that matter, the returns on the canal investments varied widely (Duckham 1983: 122). Third, in some cases (local) public authorities supported canal projects by cheap loan facilities, or even directly by poured-over money. So, public-authorities' involvement in the canal projects varied from just enacting the concession conditions to sharing risks by a financial stake in a project.

The private lead features the canal PPPs. Localities took promotional initiatives to develop new inland navigation. 'Like most other economic developments in eighteenth-century Britain, canals were a form of self-help which sprang from local initiatives' (Duckham 1983: 114). Moreover, the financing of the canal companies mainly relied on local resources. It might denote the modest role of the State in the economy at that time. At the same time, the British canal history shows public-authorities' awareness of the fragile balance between private-finance interests and the interests of the society at large. This awareness is the very base of PPP, shown by a municipal financial stake in a canal project as much as by toll and return-on-investment restrictions imposed on the concessionaires.

1.3.2.3 British railways in the nineteenth century: a regulated industry versus PPP

The British railway take-off in the 1830s and 1840s was a private-sector affair; a number of new competing stock companies emerged. Public authorities' involvement was limited to granting the rights of way to the companies. Spontaneous private initiatives served private interests. In the period 1825–35, 54 railway Acts had gone through Parliament. The railway mania continued during the two years 1836–7 when 39 railway bills for new lines received royal assent (Clapham 1930: 387). Numerous joint-stock railway companies were founded. The tremendous increase in mileage, to more than 1,900 in 1843, gradually created a network challenging market efficiency. From this point on, government regulation may be observed in the early railway histories; so in the British. Networks raise natural-monopoly issues. Therefore, railways legislation 'was primarily concerned with avoiding monopolistic behaviour' (Foreman-Peck and Millward 1994: 14). Parliament aimed at separating ownership of infrastructure from carriage owners using it. The track required anti-monopoly regulation, while the transport service remained competitive. However, this policy did not forestall monopoly power. Particular lines required specific carriage material, and it turned out that enforcement of the right to run traffic independent of the railway company was non-existent. For instance, it was an easy job for the track company to hinder a carriage company by non-cooperation in signalling and the provision of sidings. Moreover, Parliamentary maximum tolls were fixed too high for potential carriage competition (Foreman-Peck and Millward 1994: 15). Price- and profit-regulation form obvious alternatives to the divided ownership policy. However, the British railway policy of the nineteenth century in particular relied on the market test; the most efficient monopolist should survive. Before entering the market a company needed a private Act of Parliament. In this respect, Foreman and Millward infer that the parliamentary consideration of railway schemes was not really impartial. For instance, the Committee of the House of Commons evidently protected the interests of the Great Northern Railway from potential competition. 'The competitive process was worked out as much in the legislature . . . as in the open market' (Foreman-Peck and Millward 1994: 17). Competition for railway services was confined to those few points where alternatives were available. New entrants feared head-on competition from existing companies. In 1843, 70 companies controlled 2,000 miles of track. Twenty years later the much larger network (11,451 miles) was controlled by almost the same number, 78 (Foreman-Peck and Millward 1994: 18).

The early history of the British railways reflects a recurring tension between the railway companies driven by private interests, and the public authorities, supposed to safeguard the public interests. It stands midway between PPP and regulation. On the one hand, this railway history may be seen as a heap of PPP contracts; a number of concessions granted to separate private stock companies governed by concession conditions concerning safety, timetables and market power restrictions. In this perspective, the history exhibits usual PPP issues. For example, the monopoly remedies by separation of ownership lacked enforcement due to information asymmetries and incomplete contracting. Moreover, the competition-enhancing policy was hit by public authorities prone to bribery by their private partners; a case of non-market failure. A common PPP feature is that it refers to specific contractual relations between public authorities and private companies. On the other hand, the railway history evolved as a regulation issue. For instance, the 1844 Railway Act limited the laissez-faire policy intending to control the railway industry as a whole (Foreman-Peck and Millward 1994: 20). For that matter, the PPP versus regulation distinction underlines the limited scope of the PPP concept. The concessionaire/railway company fits into the PPP definition, while the access permits for the carriage companies concern a regulation item; a market-oriented form of regulation protecting the public interest against concessionaire's market power.

1.3.3 PPP in the early history of the USA

The PPP history of the nineteenth-century USA shows similarity with the British. The American 'Turnpike Era', lasting from 1790 until 1845, was a manifestation of a newly grown-up civil society in which civilians saw profit opportunities (Klein and Majewski 2010: 1). After the Turnpike Era comes the private-sector involvement in American railroad construction. The rise of PPP in the newborn Republic of the USA may be seen as a manifestation of the American version of the modern public–private dichotomy. At the municipal level the nineteenth century exhibited an extensive practice of private sector involvement in public utilities such as gas and water. The following section considers turnpikes and public utilities.

1.3.3.1 Turnpikes in nineteenth-century USA

Prior to 1790 roads were built and maintained mainly by local authorities, and there was a compulsory road labour tax. For instance, 'the State of New York assessed eligible males a minimum of three days of roadwork under penalty of fine of one dollar' (Klein and Majewski 2010: 1). This system is commensurable with the British and, like in Britain, it was appropriate neither to safeguard road conditions, nor to facilitate through traffic. Labourers' involvement in the road maintenance activities was very weak. Financially, the system depended in particular on the unstable stream of fines and commutations. Another issue was the regional coordina-tion between townships. For instance, when a road passed unsettled land it was difficult to mobilize labour, 'because assessments could be worked out only in the district in which the laborer resided' (Klein and Majewski 2010: 1). Public authorities acknowledged being unable to maintain road conditions, and particularly in developing a network of roads. The turnpike charter brought a solution.

From the outset, the American turnpike history was a private-sector affair, in contrast to the British with its public trustees. The American legislation commissioned business corporation charters to build and maintain a road for the right to collect fees from travellers. In 1792 Pennsylvania chartered the first private turnpike in the USA; a 62 mile road between Philadelphia and Lancaster. Soon it attracted the attention of merchants and lawmakers in other states as a turnpike opened new markets and commerce away from their direct environment. The Pennsylvania turnpike initiated a turnpike era that lasted until 1845. In the period 1792–1845, 1,562 turnpike incorporations were founded (Klein and Majewski 2010: Table 2). Some states subsidized the private turnpike corporations but most turnpikes were financed solely by private stock capital and structured to pay dividends (Klein and Majewski 2010: 2). Although it concerned private enterprises, the private property rights of the turnpike corporations were definitely curtailed; on the one hand, by regulation limiting potential monopolistic behaviour, and free-riding by toll evasion on the other. Additionally, legislators exempted numerous groups from toll payments. Therefore, it is not surprising that the attenuated property rights resulted in limited success of the turnpike corporations in terms of financial return. In this context, their success in raising sufficient finance and in service performance is all the more striking. In a publication of 1934 George Taylor pointed out that the organizational advantages of turnpike companies 'not only generated more road mileage, but also higher quality roads', relative to government roads (Taylor 1934: 334; cit. in Klein and Majewski 2010: 4). According to Klein and Majewski this remarkable combination in the American turnpike history demonstrates 'how Americans integrated elements of the modern corporation – with its emphasis on profit-taking residual claimants – with non-pecuniary motivations such as use and esteem' (Klein and Malewski 2010: 1).

The American turnpike era presents a PPP era. Its form is a concession. The private corporation in most cases bears all the risks, while the public authorities safeguard the public interest by a number of regulations. There is some evidence that the residual claimant role of the private sector guaranteed good quality of the roads. At the same time, the turnpike era shows that the role of private property rights and the residual claimant focused on capturing these rights must have been limited. The return on investment can hardly explain private-finance involvement; the turnpikes were not really promising in terms of dividends. Turnpikes facilitated trade and traffic, beneficial to merchants, landowners and ordinary residents. It must have been the indirect, societal benefits that have encouraged this long-term financial involvement in the private turnpike corporation. A 'civic-minded culture' induced investors to pay for long-term community gain. In this respect, Klein and Malewski refer to Alexis de Tocqueville. 'Having no particular reason to hate others, since he is neither their slave nor their master, the American's heart easily inclines towards benevolence' (de Tocqueville cit. in Klein and Majewski 2010: 3). This reference straightforwardly relates to the modern public–private demarcation already dealt with. It underlines the relevance of that basic societal-cultural turn to the understanding of the PPP phenomena.

1.3.3.2 Municipal utility franchises

As early as the 1820s New York City introduced a franchise contract for gas, followed in the 1830s by one for street railway transportation. Through the early decades of the twentieth century in many states municipalities granted franchises: 'virtually all services benefited by the use of public rights-of-way: gas, electricity, water, sewer, street railways, telegraph, and separately, telephone, subways, railroad terminals, ferries, private bridges, tunnels and toll roads' (Priest 1993: 302). Private companies finance the initial and subsequent investments, and provide the services running the assets. It concerns asset-and-service contracts between (local) authorities and an independent entrepreneur who bore all responsibilities and risks of capital investment and, at times of subsequent renewal, a firm that owned the capital plant then providing current service to local citizens (Priest 1993: 306).

This local franchise practice is a rich source of PPP examples in the USA, as the enumeration of applications shows. It is a mutually beneficial deal. The public authorities offer the utility company the public right-of-way that enables the company to avoid the transaction costs of negotiating with individual landowners. The authorities may limit the market power and (natural) monopoly returns by specifying price and quality in return for the public right-of-way (Priest 1993: 306). Priest surveys a number of principal provisions that the American nineteenth-century utility franchise contracts generally had in common:

1 *Franchise duration*. Duration of 20, 30, or even 50 years was not uncommon. The lengthy duration may suggest concerns about returns on investment, or be meant as a stimulus for continuing investment during the exploitation period. At the same time, such a length complicates specification of service quality and price-structure provisions.
2 *Price*. The Duluth electricity franchise of 1888 was required to provide electricity 'at reasonable prices'. The Erie Gas Light Co should set prices by reference to external indices. Increasingly over time, utility franchises introduced techniques for greater rate flexibility.
3 *Quality of service*. Following initial broad and general standards, franchise provisions became increasingly detailed. Later, mature franchises returned to general standards, delegating detailed requirements to arbitration or a commissioner.
4 *Adjustment over time*. Frequently, the local authorities would secure renegotiations of the franchise provisions. For instance, the Saginaw, Michigan, gas contract (1886) provided

for the city council to review and reset prices every five years. Another renegotiation base was a consolidation with another utility.

5 *Exclusivity and competition.* The 1833 franchise to the Manhattan Gas Light Co was expressively non–exclusive.

6 *Cross subsidization.* Virtually all local authorities negotiated for free service for city departments and other public facilities (Priest 1993: 312–313).

On the one hand, these provisions aim to limit the potential monopoly power passed to the utility company. On the other, they reflect authorities' intention to consider contingencies forestalling hold-ups. Obviously, the enumeration of these contract practices underlines the complicated nature of a partnership of public authorities and a private company in an asset-and-service contract. These nineteenth-century contract practices constitute a gold-mine for twentieth-century economists who consider contracts as exchanges of property rights between more-or-less ill-informed, rent-seeking agents.

1.4 Early trends and features of PPPs

PPP may help to remedy the deviations from the (Paretian) welfare optimum, due to public-good, external-effect, and natural-monopoly phenomena. The Dutch polder history exhibits PPPs providing public goods. For instance, the concession for the Schermer-polder (1633) conditioned the private company to dig drainage channels for overflow control. Other examples may substantiate the role of PPP remedying public-good and externality inefficiencies. However, it is evident in the history of modern economies that PPP finds its obvious application in natural monopolies. History shows numerous PPP projects for network facilities by franchise/concession contracts; infrastructure seems to be the natural habitat for PPP. In particular, the British Industrial Revolution (1760–1850) opened unprecedented opportunities for PPPs providing waterways, railways and municipal utilities in the new industrializing economies. Subsection 1.4.1 presents some trends in the PPP history, extending from the early seventeenth century until the 1970s. Subsection 1.4.2 summarizes some characteristics of the traditional PPPs.

1.4.1 Some trends in early PPP history

The modern economy unfolding since the mid-sixteenth century has been a private affair by nature. The role of the sovereign was focused on law, political order and military power. As shown above for the Dutch Republic, this traditional role of the State has enabled it to create an institutional order facilitating the new social order. The new-born modern economy offers unprecedented investment opportunities challenging the commercial ambitions of the citizens. At the same time, market-failure aspects necessitate some assistance by the State. The public authorities are attentive to these ambitions. This supportive aspect of governments is reflected in the international seventeenth-century practice of governments supporting worldwide trade: incentives policy *avant la lettre*. The broad international rise of global-trade companies illustrates government's lead in this respect. Infrastructure, investment-and-service projects, is the second, relatively more important PPP field in the early days of the modern economy. Until the end of the nineteenth century this picture did not change. In a broad international perspective, two directions of investment substantiate this claim: trade companies and infrastructure.

Trade companies. Private initiatives entered into the new commercial challenges that the new navigation technologies offered. The public authorities provided support by assembling these initiatives in a monopoly company granted public powers. The public involvement raised positive externalities. Private financiers were the first movers. For instance, in Holland several separate East-Indian initiatives preceded the 1602 foundation of the *Verenigde Oostindische Compagnie* (VOC; known in English as the Dutch East India Company). Comparable public–private cooperation emerged in England (1600), Denmark (1616) and France (1607, 1664).

Infrastructure. Public authorities' help for infrastructure investments consists primarily in granting the public right-of-way. As shown, infrastructure is a main field of public authorities' involvement in investments and services. Their role may vary, and the private-versus-public lead in it varies in tandem. The following may show this variation:

- Infrastructural investments might be used as a basic stimulus for developing a modern economy. It is France in particular that exhibited examples of such purposive investments during the seventeenth century. For instance, the Briare canal was initiated by the Duc de Sully, with support from Henri IV, in order to develop the grain trade, and to reduce food shortages. Its construction started in 1604 and was completed in 1642. Like the later constructed Midi canal (1666) it involved concessions, financed and maintained by private enterprises: the PPP model frequently used in France.
- In Britain and the USA private initiatives were prevalent. In particular the American turnpike history of the early nineteenth century exhibited this prevalence. Both in Britain and in the USA new commercial opportunities, access to new markets, generated private finance at risk on return. Public authorities facilitated this by granting public right-of-way, and empowering the concessionaire with tolling right. New industries, railways, gas and electricity introduced a new 'competitive era', lasting from 1820 until the 1860s (Foreman-Peck and Millward 1994: 6).
- The predominance of the private sector in infrastructural facilities entailed slowly but surely an increasing involvement of the public authorities. This involvement involved coordination of the networks, regulation of safety measures, and mitigation of concessionaires' market power. An autonomous variable in this respect is politicians' political agenda; e.g. railway investments for military purposes. During the second half of the nineteenth century, a shift took place from private to public dominance in network facilities. Regulation by parliament and commissions replaced regulation by concession (franchise) contract. In particular, municipal utility enterprises replaced the concession firms, partly induced by the return on investment as a welcome stable financial base for the municipalities. The concession PPP went out of fashion by the end of the nineteenth century. It may be seen as an accompanying phenomenon of Adolph Wagner's *Gesetz der ausdehnenden Staatlichkeit*. By the end of the nineteenth century, Wagner observed 'a "law" of "growing public and state activities" as a general consequence of cultural development' (Reich 1996: 846).
- Finally, the dominance of the State culminated in the post-war nationalization era that lasted until the 1980s. In Britain it was the success of wartime planning that induced the Labour administration to nationalize railway, gas, electricity and heavy industries (Foreman-Peck and Millward 1994: 6). This was a tendency observable in several Western industrialized economies.

1.4.2 Features of traditional PPPs

Four aspects characterize the traditional PPP: private versus public initiative; private financing and funding; risk allocation; and degree of regulation.

- The private initiative is dominant in the early PPPs. Citizens see opportunities for profitable enterprises such as land reclamation or the construction of turnpikes, waterways and railways. The public authorities are attentive to these opportunities, and play a facilitating role. Exception in this respect is the leading role of European governments in organizing trade companies.
- Private investors are prominent both in financing and funding in the PPPs. Seventeenth-century SPVs in Holland and eighteenth-century trustees in Britain form institutional devices organizing private financing *and* private funding. The private stock corporation finds application in combination with the franchise model, in particular for network facilities. Usually, the public part of the partnership is concerned with the enactment of the concessions. Subsidization by public authorities is limited and always well-defined.
- The combination of private financing and private funding results in a transfer of the main risks to the private partner. Private financing means that the private partner bears demand risk, i.e. main risk for infrastructure facilities.
- During the nineteenth century the public authorities' involvement in PPPs was increasing. In particular, it is the network nature of railways and municipal utilities that induced public authorities to massively regulate the private concessionaires. During the first half of the twentieth century this public-sector involvement in the natural monopolies ended in public enterprises.

Authorities' modest fiscal capacity may explain the prominent significance of private finance and initiatives as marked features of the early PPPs. At the same time, the prominent private-sector stake in infrastructural networks raised market-power issues, causing an increase in intervention by the public authorities'.

1.5 Recent trends and features of PPPs

The first half of the twentieth century consolidated the increasing public authorities' dominance in PPPs that started at the end of the nineteenth century. PPPs were heading downhill, making way for public enterprises of nationalized concessionaires. Illustrative in this respect is the intellectual climate among outstanding economists in the first decades after the Second World War, as sketched by Shleifer (Shleifer 1998). Future Nobel Prize winners Allais and Meade argued the nationalization of industries such as iron and steel and chemicals. And libertarian economists such as Herbert A. Simon, Pigou, and Lionel Robbins were not too opposed to state ownership of all industries 'in which it is impossible to maintain effectively competitive conditions' (H.A. Simon, cited in Shleifer 1998: 134). Apparently, the focus is on market morphology, while the role of property rights seems to be a non-issue. It is in line with the intellectual climate that the PPP option does not play a role in considering the allocation branch of public finance and policy. Finally, it is likely that the post-war success of the Keynesian stabilization policy has contributed to the positive opinion about state ownership in addressing allocation issues. By the end of the 1970s change was pending.

At the beginning of the 1980s, stagflation, derailed public finance, and excessive tax- and social-premium burdens characterized the economic situation in almost all Western industrialized countries. It induced a turn in the intellectual climate sketched above targeting the role of the public sector in the economy. The diagnosis of the miserable economic situation was that the public sector had become too large. This sector no longer offered solutions. On the contrary, it was seen as the actual problem. The generous social-security system frustrated the efficiency of the labour market. Moreover, labour unions passed on tax- and social-premium increments to employers, safeguarding real wages. As a consequence, profits were squeezed, cutting down investments and causing new unemployment. Shortly, it was time for a shift in attention; away from stimulating the demand side of the economy and directing the focus to the supply side. Structural changes appeared on the economic-policy agendas of governments and international organizations.

The reorientation towards the supply side of the economy causes their governments to start reconsidering their own supply. The diagnosis recommends downsizing the public sector, with unpopular effects on politicians' position in their constituency. The privatization option seems to offer the best of both worlds: public-sector austerity while keeping up the level of provisions. In particular, PPP may offer an attractive practice: the off-public-budget-financing route. A PPP may occasion private financing of the capital expenditure of an investment, until then part of the public budget. PPP is the politician's dream solution: austerity and persistent generosity. This is the first explanation for the growing popularity of PPP since the 1980s.

Second, produced by part of the supply focus is the attention to the public-sector perform-ance, in particular compared to that of the private sector. A new item is the relative efficiency of the public-sector versus the private-sector supply. This newly regained comparative analysis offers an unprecedented grand field of application for a ready-made new direction in economic theory: the new institutional economics. In this approach public-versus-private ownership, property rights, matter. Aforementioned post-war attention to prices is redirected to ownership. The new institutional economics constitutes the intellectual base for rethinking government and policies that favour PPP and other forms of public–private arrangements. Recapped as privatization, the efficiency issue is often seen as a result of a political turn inex-tricably bound up with Margaret Thatcher and Ronald Reagan. However, considering the global adoption of public–private initiatives – advocated by international organizations such as the World Bank, OECD and IMF – it seems to be more appropriate to see PPP and the like, first of all, as a result of an intellectual turn. Subsection 1.5.1 presents some recent PPP trends. Subsection 1.5.2 identifies some recent features in PPP.

1.5.1 Recent trends in PPP

The adoption of PPP is widespread, applied in Western industrial economies, in emerging economies and in less-developed countries. Between 1985 and 2004, there were about 3,000 PPP projects worldwide with a total capital value of nearly US$900 billion (Kwak et al. 2009: 56). The fields of application of PPP are also very diverse. It is outside the Scope of this chapter to give an overview of the global application in such a diversity of areas. A sketch follows of some trends that showed up during the past decades; it is limited to PPP examples for investment-and-service projects. The discussion refers to some developed and some emerging economies and to the PPP policy of some international organizations. Point by point:

- Application of PPP is diverse. However, a sector breakdown by value shows that the trans-port sector accounts for the lion's share. For instance, for 2011 (first half) the transport sector accounted for 55 per cent of the European PPP market value. The remainder of the applications concern public order and safety, environment, healthcare, general public service, education and telecom (as categorized by European PPP Expertise Centre) (EPEC 2011: 3).
- The modern PPP is first and foremost a public authorities' concern. It stems from rethinking government's role, and forms the opposite of the private prominence in PPP

phenomena in the eighteenth and nineteenth centuries. Concerning the public-sector lead in PPP, the United Nations present a three-stage model of developing PPP:

i   Government defines policy framework, tests legal viability, identifies projects, develops evaluation of projects and procurement process, and develops a national market place for PPP.
ii Government establishes a dedicated PPP unit, consolidates the legal framework and continues to foster PPP. The OECD counts 17 member countries that have a dedicated PPP unit (OECD 2010: 11).
iii Final outcome is that the government has developed a fully comprehensive system, and removed the legal impediments for PPP; 'use of a full-range of funding sources while drawing upon pension funds and private equity funds' (United Nations 2007; cited in OECD 2010: 14).

• State guarantees are usually provided in connection with PPPs (IMF 2006: 56). It is the norm for governments to entice financiers to participate in PPP projects. In a state guarantee the public authorities bear all or part of the downside risks of a PPP: a contingent liability. Since the credit crisis in 2008, the use of state guarantees has 'become more prevalent and varied in nature' (EPEC 2011a: 5). For instance, an EU Project Bond Initiative is under construction at the time of writing (May 2011) to attract private sector financing for large-scale infrastructure projects such as the Trans-European-Transport-Network projects.

• Public sector accounting and budgeting systems may create a bias in favour of guarantees over other forms of spending. At the same time, State guarantees pose significant fiscal risks. Therefore, it is relevant to create transparency about guarantees. In a sample of 30 countries, 60 per cent 'note their contingent liabilities in budget documentation presented to the Legislature' (Velloso 2008: 11).

It is rather complicated to sketch a global overview of PPP developments during the last two decades. In many ways, data are incomparable due to differences in definition and sectors included. Therefore, the following figures give an overall impression of the (absolute) magnitude of PPP in parts of the world.

• In Europe the value of PPP transactions increased from €17 billion in 2002 to almost €30 billion in the top year, 2007. Since the financial crisis of 2008 the volume dropped back below €20 billion. Spain, the United Kingdom and France are prominently present in these figures. In 2010 eight projects involved deals exceeding €500 million in value. European PPPs rely more and more on funding and financial support by governments and public international financial institutions (EPEC 2011b: 2–3). The sectors included in the EPEC figures involve: transport, public order and safety, environment, healthcare, general public service, education and telecom. In 2010 transport accounted for 50 per cent of total PPP value.

• The United States Department of Transport (USDOT) 'encourages the consideration of public–private partnerships (P3s) in the development of transportation improvements' (FHWA/ IPD). The US Federal Government applies two instruments promoting PPP: Private Activity Bonds (PAB) and the Transportation Infrastructure Finance and Innovation Act (TIFIA).

    PAB provide private developers and operators with access to tax-exempt interest rates. As of October 2011, PAB allocations approved by USDOT totalled nearly $8.1 billion.

The law limits the total amount of such bonds to $15 billion, to be allocated among qualified facilities (FHWA/ IPDa).

'The TIFIA program provides Federal credit assistance in the form of direct loans, loan guarantees, and standby lines of credit to finance surface transportation projects of national and regional significance.' 'Each dollar of Federal funds can provide up to $10 in TIFIA credit assistance – and leverage $30 in transportation infrastructure investment.' From 1999 until December 2011 the TIFIA programme amounts to $33.1 billion total project costs, supported by TIFIA assistance of $8.7 billion (FHWA/ IPDb).

- Australia has developed a substantial PPP market. 'In 2004 the National PPP Forum estimated that at that time, over $9 billion in PPP projects were already contracted.' Australian State Infrastructure Plans (2007) project an investment of over $350 billion in infrastructure over the next decade. PPP share in these investments is 10–15 per cent. The Allen Group optimistically report figures as $100 billion PPP market for the decade up to 2018; with increased PPP share to 25 per cent of projected investments of $400 billion. (Allen Consulting Group 2007: 12) It underlines the potential size of the modern PPP market.
- The World Bank Group, in particular the Public–Private Infrastructure Advisory Facility (PPIAF), is a rich source of information about PPP trends in low- and middle-income countries. PPIAF figures involve four sectors: energy, telecom, transport, water and sewerage. The World Bank PPP definition includes subdivisions: concession, divestiture, greenfield project, and new projects. As far as a divestiture concerns 'a 100% transfer of the equity in the state-owned company to private entities', figures do not correspond to the PPP definition (PPIAFa 2011). Some trends are as follows:

i   Private infrastructure investments in Sub-Saharan Africa 'implemented in the 1990–2009 period attracted US$11.1 billion', primarily greenfield projects (PPIAFb 2011: 1).
ii Infrastructure projects in Latin America and the Caribbean 'implemented in the 1990–2009 period attracted new investment of US$21.9 billion, bringing total investment in infrastructure to US$34.2 billion in 2010' (PPIAFc 2011: 1).
iii Infrastructure projects in East Asia and Pacific 'implemented in the 1990–2009 period attracted new investment of US$4.3 billion, bringing total investment commitments to infrastructure in the region to US$15.2 billion in 2010' (PPIAFd 2011: 1).
iv Additional information about private investment participation may be found on the PPIAF website referred to; e.g. concerning Europe and Central Asia, Middle East and North Africa. Common in all these data is the cutback in private participation after the 2008 financial crisis.

The worldwide application of PPP forms a part of the 'increasing use of markets to allocate resources'. In 2001 Megginson and Netter observed that 'privatization now appears to be accepted as a legitimate – often a core – tool of statecraft by governments of more than 100 countries' (Megginson and Netter 2000: 321). Apparently, the time was ripe for change by the end of the 1970s when privatization came into vogue; the trend then moved away from the post-war nationalization mode.

1.5.2 Features of recent PPPs

The shift from government provision of functions and services to provision by the private sector revisits the privatization agenda embraced since the 1980s for the greater part of the world. Privatization reconfirms the individual's primacy in society. Therefore, ownership- and property-rights issues identify the privatization. At the same time, privatization is a normative notion. It should establish an individual's primacy within a fragile institutional setting, rewarding the public interest of social welfare. PPP is an intermediate form of privatization. It partly profiles the recent PPPs:

- Public authorities actively promote PPP initiatives.
- The private-financing element forms an important public-sector drive for PPPs. Consequently, this induces public authorities concerned about sound public-finance practices to formulate PPP-tailored public-budget norms.
- Bundling of investment and service may incentivize the private partner to economize on a project's lifetime costs. An additional feature will be the long-term PPP contract, matching the economic life of the assets.
- Usually an SPV will be the legal body of the private partner, forestalling contamination with investors' other business activities.
- The SPV applies project finance, wielding financing and funding together. The usually high debt–equity ratio will incentivize the project control of the debt lenders. The very base of project finance is a project's cash flow. This cash-flow base of project finance stems from the asset-specific nature of the investment, prevailing in infrastructure. The sunk-cost nature of the infrastructure investment renders it unfit as a collateral. Therefore, key factor in project finance is the security package for the debt lenders. Non-market risks such as the construction and completion risks may be passed down to subcontractors. Finally, the cash flow is the lender's pledge in financing a SPV. In project finance 'CADS' is the basic ratio; i.e. cash flow available for debt service.
- Public-sector guarantees render PPPs feasible. It is in particular the market risk of demand the private debtors will deter. SPVs' risk-exposure capacity is limited, definitely in relation to the massive commercial risks infrastructure projects may entail. In the PPP context the obvious solution is that the public sector retains the market risk, guaranteeing stable cash flows; frequently by straightforward public funding.
- PPP's basic feature is the transfer of risks to the private partner. However, the transfer prospects are limited. Moreover, commonly PPP projects are 'too important to fail'. Finally, government turns out to be the partner of last resort.

In the recent PPPs government takes the lead. It is the retrenchment policy, dominating economic policy since the 1980s, that considers PPP as an inviting route that should be fostered. Moreover, PPP may bring in the famous private sector drive for efficiency the public sector is lacking. These have formed important drivers for PPP's worldwide interest during the recent decades. At the same time, government retains its responsibility, its retrenchment will be limited. And efficiency gains require appropriate checks and balances.

1.6 Some conclusions

It goes without saying that PPP presupposes a private and a public sector. However, a specific approach to what is 'public' and what 'private' makes clear that PPP is straightforwardly related to a specific society, i.e. the modern, commercial economy. The modern economy is a normative concept that gives primacy to the individual and his self-interest. It frees the economic relations of personal ties and favouritism. At the same time, the commercial agent is framed within an institutional setting by which the self-interest acquires meaning. The modern economy unfolding since the sixteenth/seventeenth century entails new social relations. Strictly private human relations are no longer contaminated with commercial interests and strategic behaviour, and the commercial relations become instrumental. This societal change has immediate implications for PPP. Favouritism and clientelism are no longer part and parcel of the relations between public authorities and civilians. Transparency and accountability become a rule of law.

The reality of market and non-market failures results in the emergence of PPP phenomena in the first modern economies. Markets fail in organizing fortification, urban planning and public order. Often in the commercial society, a call for a visible hand may be heard. Therefore, the role of the State in this society is not restricted to establishing the institutional setting. The public sector itself is involved in societal activities such as investment and production. Here, the PPP theme comes within sight. Actually, PPP results from a pendulum motion. It is a myth that the invisible hand of the market realizes a welfare optimum. The private sector fails to attain social optimal solutions. The public authority is the safeguard of the public interest, and aims to remedy the private-sector deficiencies. However, it is a myth too that the public authority may succeed in repairing these deficiencies efficiently. Governments are not famous for efficiency. For instance, self-interested bureaucrats may harm the public interest. This observation brings the public authorities back to the private sector with a request for assistance promoting the public interest. Finally, a PPP may result.

The initial PPPs predominantly resulted from private initiatives. Private agents noticed opportunities such as land reclamation and the construction of turnpikes and railways. Extension of the network facilities challenged market efficiency. Public sector intervention replaced the private-sector lead at the end of the nineteenth century. The twentieth century substantiated Wagner's *Gesetz der ausdehenenden Staatlichkeit*.

The 1980s brought a turn in the intellectual climate in the industrialized Western world entailing a twist in the economic policy of Western countries: a reassessment of the role of the State in the economy. Public versus private ownership becomes the basic issue. It is a renewal of the modern public–private dichotomy, a reorientation on the primacy of the individual and his self-interest. Private initiatives and incentivizing self-interest should be mobilized to prompt efficiency and social welfare. Privatization and PPP form a normative agenda, whose success depends on the quality of the institutional setting. In recent PPPs the public sector takes the lead, and government guarantees seem to be indispensable.

Notes

1   I am indebted to John Groenewegen, Peter M. Hommes and Etienne B. Yehoue for their useful comments on the draft version of this chapter.
2   *Financing* refers to acquiring loans, equity and hybrid capital titles to pay for a certain investment. It concerns the liabilities side for all assets invested in at a certain point in time. The balance sheet reflects that position; a 'snap shot'. *Funding* refers to the recovery of all costs incurred to provide a product during a certain period. It is reflected in the income statement. The user charges paid for the services constitute (part of) the funding.

References

Abrahamse, J.E. (2010) *De grote uitleg van Amsterdam*, Bussum: Uitgeverij Thoth.
Albert, W. (1983) The Turnpike Trust, 31–63, in D. Aldcroft and M. Freeman (eds) *Transport in the Industrial Revolution*, Manchester: Manchester University Press.
Allen Consulting Group (2007) *Performance of PPPs and Traditional Procurement in Australia*, Melbourne: The Allen Consulting Group Ltd.

Allen, D.W. (2012) *The Institutional Revolution*, Chicago: The University of Chicago Press.

Clapham, J.H. (1930) *An Economic History of Modern Britain; the Early Railway Age*, Cambridge: Cambridge University Press.

Duckham, B.F. (1983) Canals and River Navigations, 100–41, in D. Aldcroft and M. Freeman (eds) *Transport in the Industrial Revolution*, Manchester: Manchester University Press.

Elias, N. (1969) *The Court Society*, New York (1983): Pantheon.

European PPP Expertise Centre (EPEC) (2011) *Market Update; H1 2011*. http://www.eib.org/epec/ resources/epec-market-update-h1-2011.pdf (accessed Dec. 15, 2011).

European PPP Expertise Centre (EPEC) (2011a) *State Guarantees in PPPs*. http://www.eib.org/epec/ resources/epec-state-guarantees-in-ppps-public.pdf (accessed Dec. 15, 2011).

European PPP Expertise Centre (EPEC) (2011b) *Market Update; 2010*. http://www.eib.org/epec/resources/ epec-market-update-2010-public.pdf (accessed Dec. 15, 2011).

Federal Highway Administration/ Innovative Program Delivery (FHWA/ IPD) http://www.fhwa. dot.gov/ipd/p3/index.htm (accessed Dec. 19, 2011).

FHWA/IPDa http://www.fhwa.dot.gov/ipd/finance/index.htm (accessed Dec. 19, 2011).

FHWA/IPDb http://www.fhwa.dot.gov/ipd/tifia/index.htm (accessed Dec. 19, 2011).

Foreman-Peck, J. and R. Millward (1994) *Public and Private Ownership of British Industry 1820–1990*, Oxford: Clarendon Press.

Hoppit, J. (1987) 'Understanding the Industrial Revolution (Review)', *The Historical Journal* 30, 211–24.

IMF (2006) R. Hemming, *Public–Private Partnerships, Government Guarantees, and Fiscal Risks*, Washington DC: International Monetary Fund.

Klein D.B. and J. Majewski (2010) Turnpikes and Toll Roads in Nineteenth-Century America, *EH Net Encyclopedia*. http://eh.net/encyclopedia/article/klein.majewski.turnpikes (accessed Nov. 20, 2011).

Kwak, Y.H., Y.Y. Chih and C.W. Ibbs (2009) 'Towards a Comprehensive Understanding of Public Private Partnerships for Infrastructure Development', *California Management Review* 51, Vol. 2.

Landes, D.S. (1998) *The Wealth and Poverty of Nations*, New York: W.W. Norton.

Megginson, W.L. and G.M. Netter (2001) 'From State to Market; a Survey of Empirical Studies on Privatization', *Journal of Economic Literature* Vol. XXXIX, 321–89.

Mokyr, J. (2002) *The Gifts of Athena*, Princeton: Princeton University Press.

North, D.C. (1980) *Structure and Change in Economic History*, New York: W.W. Norton.

Organisation for Economic Co-Operation and Development (OECD) (2010) *Dedicated Public–Private Partnership Units*, Paris: OECD.

PPIAFa (2011) *Private Participation in Infrastructure Database*, Glossary, http://ppi.worldbank.org/ resources/ppi_glossary.aspx#divestiture (accessed Dec. 15, 2011).

PPIAFb (2011) *Private Participation in Infrastructure Database* http://ppi.worldbank.org/features/ September-2011/2011-Sub-Saharan-Africa-PPI-infrastructure-Note.pdf (accessed Dec. 15, 2011).

(PPIAFc 2011) *Private Participation in Infrastructure Database* http://ppi.worldbank.org/features/ September-2011/2011-Latin-America-PPI-infrastructure-note.pdf (accessed Dec. 15, 2011).

(PPIAFd 2011) *Private Participation in Infrastructure Database* http://ppi.worldbank.org/features/ September-2011/2011-East-Asia-and-Pacific-infrastructure-Note.pdf (accessed Dec. 15, 2011).

Priest, G.L. (1993) 'The Origins of Utility Regulation and the "Theories of Regulation" Debate', *Journal of Law and Economics* Vol. 36, No. 1, Part 2, 289–323.

Reich, H. (1996) Wagner, Adolph Heinrich Gotthelf', in J. Eatwell, M. Milgate and P. Newman (eds) *The New Palgrave; a Dictionary of Economics*, Volume 4, London: The Macmillan Press Limited.

Shleifer, A. (1998) 'State versus Private Ownership', *Journal of Economic Perspectives* 12, 133–50.

Silver, A. (1997) Two different sorts of commerce, friendship and strangership in civil society, in J. Weintraub and K. Kumar (eds) *Public and Private in Thought and Practice*, Chicago: The University of Chicago Press.

Smith, A. (1776) *The Inquiry into the Nature and Causes of the Wealth of Nations*, Volume I, London (Reprint 1904): Grant Richards.

Stol, T. (2002) De leeuw en zijn longen: 109–34, in Th. De Nijs en E. Beukers, *Geschiedenis van Holland Deel II, 1572 tot 1795*, Hilversum: Uitgeverij Verloren BV.

Taylor, G. (1934) *The Transportation Revolution, 1815–1860*, New York (1951): Rinehart.

United Nations (2007) *Guidebook on Promoting Good Governance in Public–Private Partnerships*, New York: United Nations.

Velloso, R. (2008) *Good Practices in Fiscal Risks Disclosure; International Experiences*, October 28–9, 2008. http://www.imf.org/external/np/seminars/eng/2008/fiscrisk/pdf/velloso.pdf (accessed Dec. 16, 2011).

Vries, J. de and A. van der Woude (1997) *The First Modern Economy*, Cambridge: Cambridge University Press.

Wallerstein, I. (1984) *The Politics of the World-Economy*, Cambridge: Cambridge University Press.

Weintraub, J. and K. Kumar (eds) (1997) *Public and Private in Thought and Practice*, Chicago: The University of Chicago Press.

Part II

Law and public–private partnerships

2

Institutional setting, macroeconomic stability and public–private partnerships

Etienne B. Yehoue

2.1 Introduction

While not new, the concept of public–private partnerships (PPPs) has become more widespread since the 1980s. Governments have increasingly come to view PPPs as alternative or complementary ways to finance and manage complex projects.

PPPs are gaining importance as vehicles to finance much-needed public infrastructure across various regions of the globe. Their primary goal is to reduce the sources of inefficiency in public organizations and allow the public sector to leverage more financial resources by using the private sector as an intermediary. PPP arrangements allow the public sector to consider otherwise unaffordable projects. As such, PPPs help fill the infrastructure gap between what the government can afford and what people need. The concept also aims at freeing limited public financial resources and enabling the public sector to allocate them to other worthy—albeit less commercially viable—projects (Hammami *et al.*, 2006; Kopp, 1997; Williams, 1992).

Public private partnerships (PPPs) are contractual arrangements by definition. In this regard, institutions for contract enforceability are critical for the success of PPPs. Broadly speaking, institutions have long been recognized as important for economic outcomes by many scholars including John Locke, Adam Smith, John Stuart Mill, Douglass North and Robert Thomas. In particular, North (1990) brought the concept to the centre stage of economic development literature. North (1990: 3) defines institutions as 'The rules of the game in a society or, the humanly devised constraints that shape human interaction.' The implications according to North (1990) are that 'Institutions structure incentives in human exchange, whether political, social, or economic.' Ultimately, economic performance or development is shaped by the political and economic institutions.

Of particular importance to PPPs are the economic institutions, such as the structure of property rights, contract enforceability and viability, law and order, and the presence and perfection of markets. Economic institutions and their impacts on economic outcomes have been the focus of many subsequent studies in the late 1990s and early 2000s.[1] Daron Acemoglu *et al.* (2005a) highlight the importance of economic institutions via their ability to influence the structure of economic incentives in a society. Institutions incentivize the development of the private sector and the adoption of more efficient technologies.

Institutions particularly matter for economic outcomes because along with the technology employed, they determine the transaction and the transaction costs that add up to the costs of production (Coase, 1960; North, 1994). This is particularly relevant for PPP arrangements. Since bargaining between public and private actors is generally not costless, arrangements that maximize aggregate income will always be sensitive to institutional framework. In other words, institutions matter because it is generally costly to transact.

For example, due to institutional flaws, the results of the first PPP experiments in the infrastructure sector in Africa, though difficult to assess as yet, appear to be disappointing. In many cases political problems and contract renegotiations—which are often the results of weak institutions—have led to the surrender or non-renewal of contracts, thereby undershooting the very service-improvement objectives for which the PPP arrangement was initiated. In fact, the weak institutional environment in Africa gives rise to various forms of predatory behaviour, and as a consequence undermines the trust of investors.

Equally important are the macroeconomic conditions characterized by adequate tariff regimes, appropriate price levels, a track record of honouring commitments, and reasonable economic policies. In this chapter, the extent to which institutional setting and macro-economic stability could influence the dynamics of PPPs both in terms of project count and total dollar investment is explored. Are countries with strong institutions and macro-economic stability reducing uncertainties and thus able to attract more PPP projects and more PPP dollar investment?

Institutions as constraints could be categorized into formal institutions (rules, laws, constitutions) and informal institutions (norms of behavior, conventions, and self-imposed codes of conduct). While recognizing the cultural or informal dimension of institutions, the empirical analysis in this chapter emphasizes the formal constraints, as cross-country quantitative assessments are readily available on them.

The contention is that political commitment and good governance are prerequisites for success in PPPs. The assurance that the political apparatus is fully committed to private involvement is crucial to secure private participation, as a PPP is a major commitment on the part of the private sector, and this goes beyond the term of one government. Any uncertainty patterning to less political commitment would give rise to political risk that is not conducive to long-term business decision making (IMF, 2004).

Institutions limiting corruption and guaranteeing equity and fairness of government in dealing with private partners are helpful for successful PPPs. Existence and effectiveness of such institutions will assure the private sector that the government will meet its commitment under PPP arrangements. Corruption has proven to be an obstacle for successful privatization (Lora and Panizza, 2003). More generally, widespread corruption in government would be a serious impediment for successful PPPs.

Bureaucracy quality or expertise in government may also facilitate contract negotiations and contribute to successful PPPs. This includes a full range of skills necessary to manage a PPP programme. For example, in the United Kingdom, which arguably has the best-developed Private Finance Initiative (PFI)[2] programme, a specialized government agency, Partnerships UK, has the responsibility to promote PFI projects within government. Partnerships UK performs its function by providing legal, financial and other technical assistance to support contract negotiations and procurement.

To account for these various types of institutions, the chapter makes use of the *International Country Risk Guide* (ICRG) rating. The advantage of this rating is that it covers a wide range of variables capturing political, economic and financial risk. The composite country risk is an index comprising 22 variables classified in three categories: political, economic and financial (The Political Risk Services (PRS) Group, 1992). The analysis considers not only the composite risk index, but also its components as well as their subcomponents. It is shown that institutions matter for PPPs either directly or through their impacts on GDP growth.

The rest of the chapter is organized as follows. The next section presents a general overview of the institutional and macroeconomic environments for PPPs. Section 2.3 provides details on the ICRG rating indexes as well as on the PPP data. Section 2.4 highlights the framework for analysing the impact of the institutional and macroeconomic variables on PPPs. Section 2.5 presents the results and offers some analyses. Section 2.6 concludes the chapter.

2.2 Institutional and macroeconomic environment for PPPs: a general overview

Inefficiencies in public institutions or enterprises are common and result from distortionary government interventions as well as States' organizational structures, which are typically highly bureaucratic. These inefficiencies are at the core of the emergence of the New Public Management in the UK (under Margaret Thatcher) and in other countries. The main goal of this innovation was to introduce implicitly in public administrations the functioning principles of private firms (Hammami *et al.*, 2006). Attracting private organizations to set up PPP arrangements requires that appropriate institutions are in place. Institutions help to create the environment for PPPs.

The quality of these institutions matters and influences country risk. As PPP arrangements are contractual arrangements by nature, a well-functioning institutional environment is vital for their success. The sustainability of PPP arrangements depends critically on the regulatory environment, which in turn is shaped by the quality of institutions. Crucial elements for this regulatory environment include specific and transparent PPP law, clear mechanisms for litigation and early termination, guidelines for risk allocation, and formal rules on accounting.

An important characteristic of the institutional environment is the effectiveness of the rule of law. As Pistor *et al.* (2000) point out, the effectiveness of legal institutions has a much stronger impact on the availability of external finance than do laws on the books. Thus, strong institutions and effective rule of law are important for securing PPP arrangements.

Specialized institutions are also important to develop and implement PPP projects. They help to protect public interest, maximize value added and determine the most effective type of PPP for a given project. They provide oversight for PPP projects. With the right guidelines and expertise, they facilitate the implementation of PPPs. For example, a transparent competitive procurement process with a clear bidding parameter and a policy of handling single or unsolicited proposals facilitates the contractual aspect of PPPs, which is crucial for their success. One example of specialized institutions is the European PPP Expertise Centre (EPEC) jointly set up by the European Investment Bank and the European Commission. The collaborative initiative aims to enable public authorities in the European Union and candidate countries to become more effective participants in PPP transactions. EPEC's main task is to help the public sector to overcome shortfalls in PPP expertise. EPEC's team of experts shares experience and information with its members, helping to reduce transaction costs and increase the European PPP deal flow.

Beyond the institutional setting, macroeconomic indicators are important for the success of PPP arrangements. Market conditions affect the incentives of private firms to participate in any PPP arrangements. Demand for the services to be provided and the size of the market affect private sector participation in PPPs. Infrastructure services provided to a large number of consumers paying market prices would generally be more profitable and allow a faster recovery of sunk costs usually required by infrastructure projects. Moreover, the level of income—or purchasing power—of potential customers is also important as it indicates their ability to pay for services at market prices.

Establishing stable macroeconomic conditions, adequate tariff regimes, a track record of honouring commitments, and reasonable economic policies, affect private sector incentives to join PPP arrangements. Governments that manage to improve macroeconomic conditions—as reflected, for instance, in sovereign debt ratings given by various rating agencies—are better able to attract private investors and efficient infrastructure service providers. Of particular importance for the private sector to join PPP arrangements is exchange-rate risk. Most infrastructure projects in developing countries are financed with significant amounts of foreign capital through equities or loans, making investors vulnerable to currency risks. Debt repayments, as well as dividend payments, require foreign currencies while revenues accrue in local currency. Thus, unexpected devaluations can alter the profitability of a project. Firms could hedge against currency risks, but it would involve additional costs (Dailami and Klein, 1997; Hammami et al., 2006).

2.3 Data

The sample covers 94 emerging and developing countries for which data are available, with some missing data in some cases. The PPP data are extracted from the World Bank's *Private Participation in Infrastructure* (PPI) project database. An examination of the PPI data shows that PPP projects are more important in the energy sector with 1,669 projects. The transportation sector comes in second position with 1,169 projects followed by the telecommunication sector (815 projects) and water and sewerage sector (684 projects) (Table 2.1). The data also reveal that the most common mode of entry into the energy and telecommunication sectors is through greenfield investments, while the most common mode of entry in transportation is through concessions. For water and sewerage the entry mode seems to be equally distributed between greenfield investments and concessions (Table 2.1).

Figure 2.1 displays the range of contract types used in PPP projects. The most common for PPPs appears to be build–operate–transfer with 24.2 percent of all projects, followed by build–own–operate with 14.3 percent. Merchant and partial divesture come in joint third position with 13.9 percent each. These four categories represent about two-thirds or 66.3 percent of all projects (Figure 2.1).

Table 2.1 Number of PPP projects in infrastructure by industry and mode of entry, 1985–2008

Industry sector	Concession	Divesture	Greenfield	Other mode	Total number of projects
Energy	103	490	1,042	34	1,669
Telecommunications	11	198	600	6	815
Transportation	632	71	398	68	1,169
Water and sewerage	272	31	271	110	684
					4,337

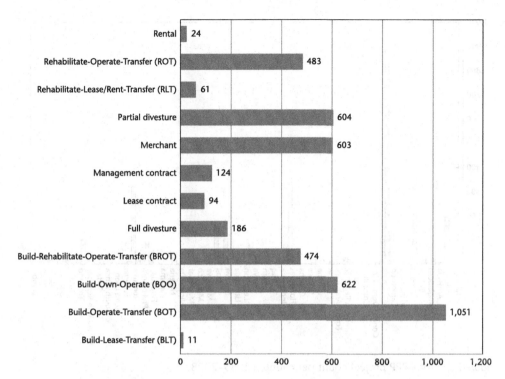

Figure 2.1 Number of PPP projects by types of contract, 1985–2008
Source: World Bank's PPI database

Public–private partnerships exhibit great variations over time as well as from one country to another, both in terms of project count and total investments (Figures 2.2 and 2.3). To explain such variations, two dependent variables are considered: project count (number of PPP projects) and PPP total dollar investment. The data cover the period 1985–2008. Project count ranges from zero to 152. On a per-country cumulative basis, total project count per country over the period 1985–2008 ranges from 1 to 886. Total PPP dollar investment ranges from zero to US$46,585 billion (May 2011). Total PPP investment per country over 1985–2008, on a per-country cumulative basis, ranges from zero to US$220,265 billion (May 2011).

The focus of this chapter is to explore to what extent institutional setting and macroeconomic stability contribute in explaining the PPP variations highlighted earlier. Given the qualitative nature of the institutional variables, the chapter relies on the *International Country Risk Guide* (ICRG) ratings for these variables. These ratings are from Political Risk Services (PRS), a private company which assesses the risk that investments will be exposed to in different countries. For ease of comparison, economic variable ratings from the same source are also used; though in some cases per capita real GDP and population are appropriately used as control variables or to check robustness. The GDP and population data are from the World Bank's *World Development Indicators* (WDI).

The ICRG indexes comprise mainly political risk, economic risk and financial risk ratings.

The political risk rating ranges from zero to 100 and combines factors such as government stability, socioeconomic conditions, investment profile, internal conflict, external conflict, corruption, military in politics, religious tensions, law and order, ethnic tensions, democratic

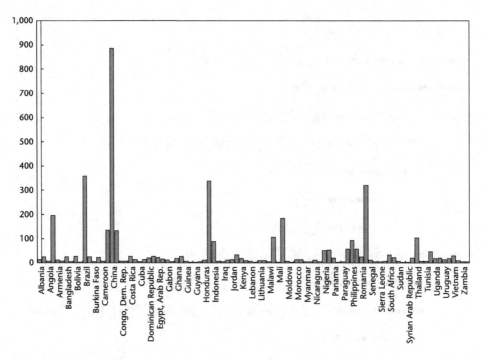

Figure 2.2 Total PPP project count per country, 1985–2008

Source: World Bank's PPI database

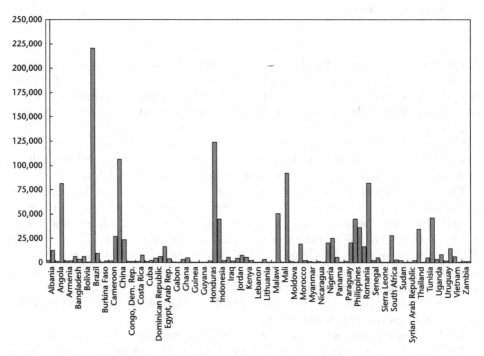

Figure 2.3 Total PPP investment (US$ millions) per country, 1985–2008

Source: World Bank's PPI database

accountability and bureaucracy quality. To each of these factors a score is appropriately assigned and the sum determines the political risk rating.

The economic risk rating is scaled from zero to 50. It rates risk related to factors such as GDP per capita, real GDP growth, annual inflation rate, budget balance as a percentage of GDP, and current account as a percentage of GDP. Various scores are appropriately attributed to capture the risk related to these factors and the sum determines the economic risk rating.

The financial risk rating also ranges from zero to 50. It is based on factors such as foreign debt as a percentage of GDP, foreign debt service as a percentage of exports of goods and services (XGS), current account as a percentage of XGS, net international liquidity as months of import cover, and exchange rate stability. These factors receive various scores to capture their risk and the sum determines the financial risk rating.

A composite risk rating, which captures political, economic, and financial risk all together, is also used. It is scaled from zero to 100 and broken into categories from very low risk (80 to 100 points) to very high risk (zero to 49.9 points). For all of these ratings a low rating point indicates high risk, while a high rating point indicates low risk.

2.4 Framework for the analysis of institutional and macroeconomic determinants of PPPs

To assess to what extent the institutional setting and macroeconomic stability might impact the dynamics of PPPs, a series of regressions is performed. There are two sets of regressions. One relates to cross-country regressions where total PPP project number or total dollar investment per country over the period 1985–2008 is considered as the dependent variable. The other is related to a panel analysis. For each set of regressions both project count and dollar investment are considered. PPP project count is a discrete variable. The discrete and limited nature of this dependent variable requires an intrinsically nonlinear model commonly known as limited dependent variable (LDV) models.

To make the LDV models linear, a transformation is done on the dependent variable. In logit regressions, the transformation is the logit function, which is the natural log of the odds. In probit models, the function used is the inverse of the standard normal cumulative distribution also known as a z-score. In this analysis, project count is not binomial, but multinomial, so for all the regressions related to PPP project count, an ordered probit model is used. The LDV model is estimated using maximum likelihood, which unlike the method of least squares, is not based on minimizing error variance. This means there is no measure of the model 'fit' directly comparable to the R-squared in OLS, and as a result, model assessment is largely restricted to testing the joint significance of all model variables (as is done in OLS using an F-test of overall model significance). In a probit model, this is carried out via a chi-squared-test.

In an earlier work (Hammami et al., 2006) various econometric techniques were used to explore the possible determinants of PPPs in infrastructure. The results were not qualitatively much different from one technique to another. In this chapter, ordered probit and GLS were appropriately used depending on the type of the regression. In addition, the focus here is narrowed to institutional and macroeconomic stability determinants. Thus, contrary to Hammami et al. (2006), this chapter provides an in-depth and more rigorous analysis of the institutional determinants.

In particular, the empirical strategy consists of starting from the aggregate or composite country risk to more disaggregated risks in order to pin down specific risk factors. More precisely, for each set of regressions, the composite country risk is first considered as an independent variable combined with appropriate control variables such as population and real

GDP. The composite country risk is subsequently replaced in the following regressions by its components; that is, political risk, economic risk, and financial risk. These components are in turn replaced by their subcomponents depending on their significances. Non-significant variables are progressively and appropriately dropped in subsequent regressions in order to pin down the key risk factors affecting the variation of PPP project count or dollar investment.

In the panel analysis where there are time variations, past experiences of PPP are also considered. This is important for both the public and private sectors seeking to enter into a PPP agreement. Government's reputation and the private sector's experience in PPP projects could facilitate the negotiations. Owing to the particular nature of PPP agreements, past experience in running these projects could be a key predictor of successful future arrangements, hence the need to control for this variable. In the cross-section analysis there are no time variations and lagged PPP could not be considered.

2.5 Estimates of PPP equations

2.5.1 Overview

To get an initial estimate of how institutional setting and macroeconomic stability might affect PPPs a cross-country analysis is carried out. Tables 2.2 and 2.3 present the results. The analysis is later deepened in panel estimations and Tables 2.4 and 2.5 report the results. For the PPP project count estimates where ordered probit is used, model significance is indicated by the significance ($p<0.05$) of the likelihood ratio chi-squared statistic, which tests the model considered against an intercept only model. The likelihood ratio chi-square for each of the project count estimations is high enough to guarantee the model's significances (Tables 2.2 and 2.4). The corresponding p-value of 0.000 suggests that each model as a whole is statistically significant at the 1 percent level. Overall, the findings indicate that institutional setting and macroeconomic stability indicators affecting risk through political, economic or financial channels are critical in determining the number as well as the size of investment in PPP projects.

2.5.2 Preliminary results: cross-country analysis

2.5.2.1 PPP project count

In Model 1 (Table 2.2) composite country risk enters the regression with control variables such as population and GDP per capita expressed in purchasing power parity, constant 2005 international dollars. Population and GDP per capita are used to control for country size as well as purchasing power. The coefficient of composite country risk is significant at 1 percent with a positive sign. The significance of GPD per capita suggests that purchasing power matters for PPPs. These are preliminary results; as the analysis gets deeper using panel estimations, marginal effects will be appropriately computed.

In Model 2 (Table 2.2), GDP per capita in purchasing power parity is substituted by real GDP per capita expressed in 2 U.S. dollars of 2000. The results are very similar to those in Model 1. The analysis then reverts to GDP per capita in purchasing power terms and replaces the composite country risk by its components, that is, political risk, economic risk, and financial risk (Model 3). In this model only the control variables are significant. The components political risk, economic risk, and financial risk are not significant.

In Model 4, the political, economic, and financial risks are each replaced by their various components. Other than population and risk for debt service, none of the variables is

Table 2.2 Probit cross-country regressions for PPP project count

	(1)	(2)	(3)	(4)	(5)	(6)	(7)	(8)	(9)	(10)	(11)
Bureaucracy quality (risk)				0.137	0.217	0.0981					
				(0.536)	(0.893)	(0.440)					
Corruption (risk)				0.295	0.253	0.127	0.156				
				(1.501)	(1.314)	(0.776)	(0.956)				
Democratic accountability (risk)				-0.15	-0.226						
				(-0.882)	(-1.539)						
Government stability (risk)				-0.104	-0.132						
				(-0.626)	(-0.866)						
Investment profile (risk)				0.0359							
				(0.205)							
Debt service (risk)				-0.255**	-0.300**	-0.280**	-0.274**	-0.298**	-0.297**	-0.267**	
				(-2.071)	(-2.315)	(-2.189)	(-2.076)	(-2.392)	(-2.262)	(-2.379)	
Exchange rate stability (risk)				0.413*	0.423**	0.355*	0.366*	0.306***	0.268**	0.355***	
				(1.920)	(1.976)	(1.851)	(1.914)	(2.632)	(2.432)	(3.296)	
Foreign debt (risk)				0.0359	0.0298	0.0298					
				(0.408)	(0.354)	(0.368)					
Budget balance (risk)				0.0815	0.077						
				(0.594)	(0.520)						
GDP growth (risk)				-0.0915	-0.0719	-0.0649	-0.0519				
				(-0.494)	(-0.411)	(-0.414)	(-0.353)				
Inflation (risk)				-0.134*	-0.173**	-0.158**	-0.153**	-0.144**	-0.132*	-0.144**	
				(-1.726)	(-2.253)	(-2.136)	(-2.023)	(-1.990)	(-1.836)	(-2.173)	
GDP per capita (risk)				0.304	0.181	0.262	0.321	0.399		0.517**	
				(0.821)	(0.521)	(0.814)	(1.19)	(1.476)		(2.392)	
GDP per capita (PPP, constant)	0.000139***		0.000122***	5.88e-05	5.31E-05	4.31E-05	4.85E-05	4.53E-05	8.84e-05***		
	(3.832)		(2.872)	(1.023)	(1.055)	(0.991)	(1.231)	(1.179)	(2.641)		
Population	6.37e-09***	6.51e-09***	5.89e-09***	7.03e-09***	7.19e-09***	6.95e-09***	7.15e-09***	7.00e-09***	7.02e-09***	6.70e-09***	
	(3.368)	(3.331)	(3.292)	(3.065)	(3.144)	(3.216)	(3.336)	(3.519)	(3.512)	(3.495)	

(Continued overleaf)

Table 2.2 Continued

	(1)	(2)	(3)	(4)	(5)	(6)	(7)	(8)	(9)	(10)	(11)
Economic risk			-0.0188								
			(-0.489)								
Financial risk			0.057								
			(1.395)								
Political risk			-0.0075								
			(-0.457)								
Composite risk	0.00269***	0.00281***									
	(5.154)	(4.423)									
Contract viability (risk)					-0.0553						
					(-0.191)						
Payment delays (risk)					0.455*	0.350*	0.348*	0.386**	0.478***	0.429**	
					(1.803)	(1.726)	(1.705)	(2.030)	(2.576)	(2.425)	
GDP per capita (constant)		0.000308***									
		(4.116)									
Log debt service (risk)											-1.749**
											(-2.555)
Log exchange rate stability (risk)											1.442*
											(1.761)
Log inflation (risk)											0.182
											(0.461)
Log GDP per capita PPP (constant)											0.537***
											(3.697)
Log payment delays (risk)											0.948**
											(2.466)
Log Population											1.043***
											(9.493)
Wald χ^2	77.41	77.1	79.23	98.93	97.91	91.72	91.18	92.45	119.14	119.7	136.83
Observations	90	91	89	89	89	89	89	89	89	93	89

Robust z-statistics in parentheses   *** $p<0.01$, ** $p<0.05$, * $p<0.1$

significant at 5 percent. In Model 5, the investment profile risk index is replaced by some of its key subcomponents (contract viability risk index and payment delay risk index).[3] Inflation risk index and exchange rate stability risk index then become significant at 5 percent, with population and debt service risk index keeping their significances. In Model 6, risk for democratic accountability, risk for government stability, risk for budget balance, and risk for contract viability are dropped and the pattern of significance remains the same overall.

In Model 7, risk for foreign debt and risk for corruption are dropped and in Model 8, risk for GDP growth is dropped, making the risk for payment delay to become significant at 5 percent. In Model 9, risk for GDP per capita is dropped, making the constant GDP per capita in purchasing power parity terms to become significant. In Model 10, the GDP per capita in purchasing power parity terms is replaced by the ICRG risk index for GDP per capita, which becomes significant. Notice that when both the ICRG risk index for GDP per capita and the real GDP per capita in purchasing power parity terms enter together, neither of them is significant (Models 4–8). However, when they enter separately, both are significant, suggesting they substitute for one another.

In Model 11, equation 9 is re-estimated with the independent variables in log terms. In log terms, risk index for debt service, the purchasing power parity GDP per capita, risk index for payment delay, and population all retain their significance at 5 percent or stronger. However, the significance of the risk index for exchange rate stability weakens to 10 percent and the risk index for inflation loses its significance completely.

2.5.2.2 PPP total investment

The chapter now examines whether the dollar value of PPP projects is also affected by institutional setting and macroeconomic stability variables. The GLS estimator with robust standard error is used to perform the regressions. In a similar manner as above, the composite country risk index first enters with population and the purchasing power parity GDP per capita as control variables (Model 1, Table 2.3). The composite country risk index is not significant, but the control variables are. The significance along with the positive sign of both population and GDP per capita suggests that, everything else being equal, bigger countries—in terms of population or aggregate GDP—are more likely to attract more PPP dollar investment.[4] The significance along with the positive sign of GDP per capita also suggest that countries with higher purchasing power are more likely to attract more PPP investment. In Model 2 (Table 2.3), the GDP per capita in purchasing power parity terms is substituted by real GDP per capita expressed in US dollars of 2000 and the results are similar to those in Model 1. Thus, GDP per capita in purchasing power parity terms is adopted throughout the remaining regressions of this subsection.

In Model 3 (Table 2.3), the composite country risk index is replaced by its component's political, economic and financial risk indexes. None of these variables is significant. In Model 4 (Table 2.3), each of these variables is replaced by their subcomponents, seldom significant. In Model 5 (Table 2.3), investment profile, which was not significant in the previous model, is replaced by the subcomponents contract viability risk index and payment delay risk index. Corruption risk index, democratic accountability risk index, government stability risk index (Model 6), contract viability risk index (Model 7), exchange rate stability risk index, budget balance risk index (Model 8), inflation risk index (Model 9), foreign debt risk index, GDP growth risk index, and GDP per capita risk index (Model 10) will subsequently be dropped (Table 2.3). These progressive drops leave GDP per capita and population strongly significant at 1 percent with the right positive sign. On the other hand, bureaucracy quality risk index is only weakly significant at 10 percent, though with the right positive sign, suggesting that low

Table 2.3 Cross-country regressions for PPP total investment

	(1)	(2)	(3)	(4)	(5)	(6)	(7)	(8)	(9)	(10)	(11)[a]
Bureaucracy quality (risk)				6,810 (1.183)	7,238 (1.290)	5,881 (1.391)	5,923 (1.380)	5,755 (1.387)	4,961 (1.311)	7,757* (1.964)	
Corruption (risk)				-833.5 (-0.209)	-1,668 (-0.423)						
Democratic accountability (risk)				-70.23 (-0.0216)	-1,391 (-0.420)						
Government stability (risk)				-488.4 (-0.153)	-783.3 (-0.256)						
Investment profile (risk)				-1,483 (-0.462)							
Debt service (risk)				-6,978* (-1.860)	-7,531* (-1.890)	-7,141* (-1.929)	-7,157* (-1.922)	-6,862* (-1.951)	-7,098* (-1.892)	-6,718* (-1.939)	
Exchange rate stability (risk)				-1,192 (-0.412)	-1,385 (-0.467)	-1,214 (-0.502)	-1,215 (-0.505)				
Foreign debt (risk)				1,239 (0.731)	1,135 (0.701)	1,051 (0.690)	1,048 (0.703)	779.4 (0.612)	511.3 (0.439)		
Budget balance (risk)				-1,691 (-0.696)	-2,115 (-0.812)	-2,278 (-0.793)	-2,288 (-0.786)				
GDP growth (risk)				3,897 (1.045)	3,263 (0.985)	2,839 (0.958)	2,867 (0.948)	1,103 (0.612)	117.7 (0.076)		
Inflation (risk)				-1,987 (-0.879)	-2,628 (-1.053)	-2,578 (-1.141)	-2,575 (-1.145)	-2,822 (-1.324)			
GDP per capita (risk)				9,298 (1.642)	6,302 (1.245)	6,091 (1.191)	6,084 (1.206)	6,027 (1.230)	6,076 (1.243)		
GDP per capita (PPP, constant)	3.047*** (3.059)		3.240** (2.517)	1.351 (1.303)	1.422 (1.491)	1.412 (1.611)	1.411 (1.613)	1.179 (1.382)	1.535 (1.538)	2.277*** (2.637)	
Population	0.00012*** (4.874)	0.00012*** (4.796)	0.00013*** (4.351)	0.00011*** (5.581)	0.00012*** (5.743)	0.00012*** (5.798)	0.00012*** (5.798)	0.00012*** (5.738)	0.00012*** (5.546)	0.00012*** (5.823)	

Variable	(1)	(2)	(3)	(4)	(5)	(6)	(7)	(8)	(9)	(10)	(11)
Economic risk			-376 (-0.574)								
Financial risk			-434.3 (-0.548)								
Political risk			256.1 (-0.597)								
Composite risk	0.465 (0.0903)	1.327 (0.286)									
GDP per capita (constant)		7.118*** (2.989)									
Contract viability (risk)				255.2 (0.050)	235.3 (0.044)						
Payment delays (risk)				4,567 (0.781)	3,475 (0.608)	3,609 (0.861)	3,383 (0.826)	1,353 (0.368)			
Log GDP per capita PPP (constant)											0.869*** (8.444)
Log population											1.049*** (19.200)
Log democratic accountability (risk)											0.484** (1.989)
Log debt service (risk)											-0.750* (-1.702)
Constant	-4,358 (-1.623)	-2,926 (-1.214)	4,920 (0.291)	47,674 (1.288)	55,293 (1.397)	45,203 (1.542)	45,499 (1.555)	38,859 (1.563)	34,365 (1.463)	38,919 (1.618)	-15.15*** (-9.573)
Observations	90	91	89	89	89	89	89	89	89	89	89
R-squared	0.44	0.46	0.45	0.55	0.55	0.55	0.55	0.54	0.53	0.52	0.84

Robust t-statistics in parentheses   *** p<0.01, ** p<0.05, * p<0.1   [a] The dependent variable for this regression is Log(Total PPP Investment)

bureaucracy quality risk, that is, high quality bureaucracy, is associated with higher PPP investment size. Debt service risk index is also weakly significant at 10 percent, but with a negative sign.[5]

In Model 11 (Table 2.3), equation 10 is re-estimated in log terms, where the log of the PPP total investment is regressed against the log of the independent variables of Model 10. In this estimation, while other variables kept their significance, the bureaucracy quality risk index, whose significance was weak, completely loses its significance. Bureaucracy quality risk index is then dropped and replaced by democratic accountability risk index, which becomes significant at 5 percent with the right positive sign (Model 11, Table 2.3). Perhaps high democratic accountability acts as a discipline mechanism on government, which in turn reassures the private sector and positively affects the size of PPP investment. In log terms, the significance of debt service risk index remains weak at 10 percent, confirming that no firm inference can be drawn with regard to the impact of risk for debt service on PPPs.

2.5.3 Results for panel data analysis

In order to account for both time and cross-variations of PPPs that are explained by institutional setting and macroeconomic stability indicators, the chapter considers a panel analysis. Here again both PPP project count and PPP total investment are considered as dependent variables. The same set of independent variables used above is also considered in this section. Tables 2.4 and 2.5 report the results. In addition, because the panel allows for a time dimension, past PPP experience is added to the independent variables.

2.5.3.1 PPP project count

The strategy is similar to the one used above. Composite country risk first enters the regression along with population and constant GDP per capita in purchasing power parity terms. In addition, past PPP experience is controlled for (Model 1, Table 2.4). Composite country risk is not significant, but population, GDP per capita, and past PPP experience are all significant at 1 percent.

In Model 2 (Table 2.4), composite country risk is replaced by its components. None of these components, political risk, economic risk, and financial risk is significant. In Model 3 (Table 2.4), these components are replaced by their subcomponents. In this Model 3, GDP per capita loses its significance, but the ICRG GDP per capita risk index is significant at 1 percent. In Model 4 (Table 2.4) where GDP per capita is dropped as well as the risk index of law and order, the ICRG GDP per capita risk index retains its significance. In Model 5 (Table 2.4), the ICRG GDP per capita risk index is dropped and GDP per capita re-enters the regression. GDP per capita now becomes significant at 1 percent, suggesting that the substitutability between the ICRG GDP per capita risk index and GDP per capita is also confirmed in the panel analysis.

In Model 6 (Table 2.4), the ICRG GDP per capita risk index is adopted and GDP per capita dropped. In addition investment profile is replaced by its subcomponents, contract viability risk index, payment delay risk index, and profit repatriation risk index, and none of them is significant.

In Model 7 (Table 2.4), bureaucracy quality risk, corruption risk, democratic accountability risk, government stability risk, exchange rate stability risk, foreign debt risk, budget balance risk, inflation risk, contract viability risk, payment delay risk, and profit repatriation risk indexes are all dropped. This leaves GDP growth risk index, GDP per capita risk index,

Table 2.4 Probit panel regressions for PPP project count

	(1)	(2)	(3)	(4)	(5)	(6)	(7)		(8)	
							Regression	Marginal effects order 5	Regression	Marginal effects order 5
Bureaucracy quality (risk)			0.0878	0.094	0.114	-0.079				
			(1.170)	(1.293)	(1.547)	(-0.564)				
Corruption (risk)			0.00831	-0.0168	0.0482	0.0315				
			(0.148)	(-0.309)	(0.917)	(0.303)				
Democratic accountability (risk)			0.0481	0.0609	0.0334	-0.071				
			(1.077)	(1.443)	(0.760)	(-1.031)				
Government stability (risk)			0.0465*	0.0292	0.0227	-0.00494				
			(1.655)	(1.086)	(0.833)	(-0.100)				
Investment profile (risk)			-0.0672*	-0.0557	-0.0655*					
			(-1.915)	(-1.636)	(-1.856)					
Law and order (risk)			-0.0654							
			(-1.285)							
Debt service (risk)			-0.038	-0.0428	-0.0594*	-0.0907*	-0.0548*	-0.0025*		
			(-1.116)	(-1.262)	(-1.663)	(-1.672)	(-1.761)	(-1.68)		
Exchange rate stability (risk)			-0.00508	0.00452	-0.0262	-0.0433				
			(-0.175)	(0.161)	(-0.947)	(-0.770)				
Foreign debt (risk)			0.0533*	0.0528*	0.0898***	0.0146				
			(1.795)	(1.852)	(3.167)	(0.337)				
Budget balance (risk)			-0.0101	0.00559	-0.000786	0.0682				
			(-0.301)	(0.172)	(-0.0229)	(1.385)				
GDP growth (risk)			0.0691**	0.0705**	0.0156	0.0766	0.0600**	0.0027**		
			(2.302)	(2.359)	(0.541)	(1.123)	(2.179)	(1.94)		
Inflation (risk)			0.0404	0.0227	0.0519	0.105*				
			(1.212)	(0.736)	(1.601)	(1.670)				
GDP per capita (risk)			0.372***	0.383***		0.337***	0.439***	0.0201***		
			(4.828)	(6.554)		(3.002)	(8.882)	(4.44)		

(Continued overleaf)

Table 2.4 Continued

	(1)	(2)	(3)	(4)	(5)	(6)	(7)		(8)	
							Regression	Marginal effects order 5	Regression	Marginal effects order 5
GDP per capita (PPP, constant)	0.000105*** (7.845)	8.46e-05*** (5.027)	2.08E-05 (1.000)		7.83e-05*** (4.761)					
Lag (−1) Project Count	0.0375*** (3.251)	0.0375*** (3.315)	0.0625*** (5.752)	0.0649*** (5.999)	0.0596*** (5.339)	0.0393** (2.192)	0.0390*** (3.742)	0.0018*** (3.09)	0.0375*** (3.671)	0.0016*** (3.06)
Population	1.97e-09*** (6.353)	1.81e-09*** (6.058)	1.89e-09*** (5.838)	1.73e-09*** (5.641)	1.79e-09*** (5.627)	4.15e-09*** (7.762)	2.10e-09*** (6.109)	9.61e-11*** (3.87)		
Economic risk		0.0147 (1.032)								
Financial risk		0.0158 (1.169)								
Political risk		0.00529 (0.745)								
Composite risk	0.000333 (0.117)									
Contract viability (risk)						0.0926 (0.565)				
Payment delays (risk)						0.106 (0.691)				
Rapatriation (risk)						−0.0558 (−0.456)				
Log debt service (risk)									−0.309* (−1.939)	−0.0132* (−1.73)
Log GDP growth (risk)									0.413** (2.411)	0.0176** (2.00)
Log GDP per capita (risk)									0.546*** (6.777)	0.0233*** (3.68)
Log population									0.449*** (8.352)	0.0192*** (3.79)
Wald χ²	151.97	189.72	199.35	191.31	161.84	149.65	124.67		179.61	
Observations	502	501	488	497	488	229	501		390	

past PPP experience, and population significant at 5 percent or stronger. Debt service risk index is weakly significant at 10 percent. In order to draw possible inferences from these ordered probit regressions, the marginal effects are computed. The results for marginal effects of order 5 are reported based on Model 7 (Table 2.4).[6] The results show that the marginal effects for GDP growth risk index, GDP per capita risk index, past PPP experience, and population are all significant at 5 percent or stronger, with the right positive sign. The marginal effect of debt service risk index is weakly significant at 10 percent with a negative sign and no firm inference can be drawn from it.

In Model 8 (Table 2.4), equation 7 is re-estimated with the independent variables in log terms. Qualitatively, the results are very similar to the ones from Model 7 (Table 2.4), with the independent variables keeping the same signs and same level of significance as in Model 7. The marginal effects of order 5 based on this Model 8 are reported (Table 2.4). Again, qualitatively the results are very similar to those obtained using Model 7. This is an indication of the robustness of the results. The strong and consistent significance of past PPP experience and of its marginal effect confirms that, in addition to other determinants, past PPP experience matters for attracting new PPPs.

2.5.3.2 PPP total investment

The PPP total dollar value is now considered as the dependent variable. The results are reported in Table 2.5. In Model 1 the dependent variable is regressed against composite country risk index, population, constant GDP per capita and lag total PPP investment. Composite country risk is not significant and is replaced by its components in Model 2. Overall, these components are not significant; with the exception that economic risk index is weakly significant at 10 percent. They are all then replaced by their subcomponents (Model 3, Table 2.5). In this model, GDP per capita loses its significance as the economic risk index is explicitly replaced by its subcomponents. On the other hand, the ICRG GDP per capita risk index appears strongly significant at 1 percent. Thus, in Model 4, GDP per capita is dropped.

In Model 5 (Table 2.5), investment profile, which was not significant, is replaced by its subcomponents contract viability risk index, payment delay risk index, and profit repatriation risk index. In Model 6 (Table 2.5), corruption, government stability, law and order, exchange rate stability, foreign debt, budget balance, inflation, contract viability, and profit repatriation risk indexes were dropped. In Model 7 (Table 2.5) bureaucracy quality and payment delay risk indexes were dropped. This leaves GDP growth risk index, GDP per capita risk index, past PPP experience, and population significant at 5 percent or stronger, all of them with the right positive sign. Democratic accountability risk index and debt service risk index remain non-significant. They are subsequently dropped in Model 8 (Table 2.5). In this Model 8, while GDP growth risk index, GDP per capita risk index, and past PPP experience maintain their significance, the significance of population weakens to 10 percent.

In Model 9 (Table 2.5), equation 8 is re-estimated in logarithm terms. That is, the logarithm of PPP total investment is regressed against the logarithm of the independent variables of Model 8. In the regression all the independent variables (including population) are significant at 1 percent, with the right positive sign. Model 9 is later extended to include the logarithm of democratic accountability risk index (Model 10, Table 2.5). This log appears strongly significant at 1 percent with the right positive sign, confirming the earlier cross-country finding relative to this determinant.

Table 2.5 Panel regressions for total PPP investment

	(1)	(2)	(3)	(4)	(5)	(6)	(7)	(8)	(9)[a]	(10)[a]
Bureaucracy quality (risk)			-58.28 (-0.713)	-76.15 (-0.984)	-144.9 (-1.542)	-138.5 (-1.485)				
Corruption (risk)			31.45 (0.701)	28.2 (0.596)	16.03 (0.216)					
Democratic accountability (risk)			86.50* (1.892)	82.69* (1.941)	95.16* (1.816)	93.46* (1.819)	51.38 (1.131)			
Government stability (risk)			26.79 (0.834)	19.79 (0.651)	-12.57 (-0.365)					
Investment profile (risk)			-34.15 (-1.181)	-29.42 (-0.967)						
Law and order (risk)			-81.66 (-1.569)	-81.67 (-1.568)	-45.97 (-0.890)					
Debt service (risk)			-52.05 (-1.108)	-52.94 (-1.239)	9.66 (0.267)	22.1 (0.732)	-55.2 (-1.270)			
Exchange rate stability (risk)			17.52 (0.397)	28.07 (0.680)	17.68 (0.387)					
Foreign debt (risk)			39.94** (1.981)	40.40** (2.066)	12.3 (0.656)					
Budget balance (risk)			-66.13 (-1.338)	-62.08 (-1.299)	7.042 (0.215)					
GDP growth (risk)			131.4*** (3.928)	126.1*** (3.891)	137.0*** (3.847)	115.0*** (3.193)	109.0*** (3.509)	104.2*** (3.379)		
Inflation (risk)			1.132 (0.050)	-5.816 (-0.244)	-23.52 (-0.809)					
GDP per capita (risk)			280.7*** (3.042)	309.8*** (3.147)	157.1 (1.468)	157.7* (1.651)	272.1*** (2.911)	269.8*** (2.976)		
Lag (-1) total investment	0.788*** (4.576)	0.789*** (4.602)	0.769*** (4.495)	0.772*** (4.619)	0.865*** (10.460)	0.869*** (10.300)	0.773*** (4.637)	0.789*** (4.774)		
GDP per capita (PPP, constant)	0.0591** (1.977)	0.0489* (1.698)	0.0146 (0.517)							

	(1)	(2)	(3)	(4)	(5)	(6)	(7)	(8)	(9)	(10)
Population	2.02e-06*	1.93e-06*	2.28e-06*	2.25e-06**	0.00000205	0.00000203	2.28e-06**	1.88e-06*		
	(1.885)	(1.862)	(1.890)	(1.966)	(1.618)	(1.630)	(1.996)	(1.898)		
Economic risk		17.73*								
		(1.711)								
Financial risk		1.805								
		(0.169)								
Political risk		0.34								
		(0.070)								
Composite risk	0.833									
	(0.359)									
Contract viability (risk)					-27.97					
					(-0.243)					
Payment delays (risk)					25.94	-25.5				
					(0.2)	(-0.277)				
Rapatriation (risk)					-34.35					
					(-0.477)					
Log GDP growth (risk)									0.452***	0.456***
									(4.021)	(4.296)
Log GDP per capita (risk)									0.253***	0.156*
									(3.497)	(1.828)
Log Lag (–1) total investment									0.577***	0.481***
									(16.3)	(12.87)
Log population									0.396***	0.470***
									(8.24)	(7.079)
Log democratic accountability (risk)										0.517***
										(4.23)
Constant	-140.5	-709.1	-768.7	-660.2	-1,176*	-1,278***	-703.5*	-917.4***	-5,037***	-6,434***
	(-0.832)	(-1.621)	(-1.336)	(-1.267)	(-1.734)	(-3.128)	(-1.693)	(-3.456)	(-7.117)	(-6.339)
Observations	1,032	1,031	1,019	1,050	626	658	1,054	1,062	672	669
Number of country	90	89	89	93	87	92	93	93	73	73
Overall R-squared	0.64	0.64	0.65	0.65	0.75	0.75	0.65	0.65	0.7	0.71

Robust z-statistics in parentheses   *** $p<0.01$, ** $p<0.05$, * $p<0.1$ [a] The dependent variable for these two regressions is Log(Total PPP Investment)

2.5.4 Discussion

It appears from this empirical investigation that factors affecting institutional setting such as bureaucracy quality, government stability, and corruption, impact PPPs via their impacts on GDP growth. In the literature these factors are known to affect economic growth and the analysis in this chapter reveals the risk to GDP growth or GDP growth prospect to be an important determinant for PPPs especially in the panel analysis. These factors are individually significant in basic PPP regressions when GDP growth risk index is not included. The finding that GDP growth risk index is significant in the panel analysis and not in the cross-country analysis seems to suggest that this is driven by the within or time dimension and not the between dimension. This implies that as countries' growth performance improves over time, they are more likely to attract more PPPs.

The emergence of economic growth prospect as a key driving factor for the formation of PPPs also underscores the importance of macroeconomic stability. In the absence of such stability, the risk for economic growth increases, weakening the prospect for economic growth and thereby negatively affecting PPPs. Macroeconomic stability lowers the risk for economic growth and increases the ICRG rating score for growth index, which positively affects PPPs. In other words, macroeconomic stability enhances the prospect of economic growth and facilitates PPPs.

Democratic accountability appears to affect the size of the dollar PPP investment. This finding emerges in both cross-country and panel analyses. Countries with strong democratic accountability are more likely to attract bigger PPP investment. Also, improvement over time of democratic accountability is associated with bigger size of PPPs. Perhaps strong democratic accountability contributes to strengthening investors' confidence and positively affects the dollar value of PPP investment.

It also emerges from the analysis that payment delay risks shake investors' confidence and thereby affect the number of PPP projects. This is found especially in the cross-country analysis, suggesting that countries with high risks of payment delays are less likely to attract more PPP projects. The fact that this does not emerge in the panel analysis might be an indication that once a country has exhibited payment delays, it takes time to change such a reputation. In addition, the time period here (1985–2008) might not be enough for such a change to materialize.

Throughout the analysis, GDP per capita appears as a strong determinant for PPPs, both in terms of number of projects and of dollar investment. This suggests that purchasing power matters in attracting PPPs. Population has also been consistently significant, suggesting that a country's size is an important determinant for PPPs.

Another important determinant that deserves to be highlighted is past PPP experience. Such experience certainly makes new PPP arrangements easier for both the public and private sectors. Past successful PPP experience in a country could boost investors' confidence, and at the same time improving the negotiation skills of the public sector, thereby facilitating agreement between the private and public sectors.

2.6 Concluding remarks

PPPs involve private sector supply of capital, services or management that can ease fiscal constraints on infrastructure and increase efficiency (IMF 2004). In as much as such partnerships can be beneficial for the government by easing fiscal constraints and improving efficiency, they also have to be profitable for private firms, which after all care about making money. Thus, too many risks assumed by governments will likely put unjustified pressures on taxpayers; too few will prevent potential private investors from participating in the venture (Hammami *et al.*, 2006). Strong institutions may incentivize private participation in the venture. Institutions are useful in determining the extent to which commitments from both the public and private sector can be honoured.

This chapter explores the link between institutional setting, macroeconomic stability, and PPPs. The analysis uses cross-country and panel data based on the ICRG political, economic and financial risk indexes. It goes further and identifies specific factors affecting these three indexes that hamper PPPs or prevent them from taking place.

The evidence suggests that larger market size and higher customers' purchasing power are crucial determinants of PPPs. This relates to demand risk, often perceived as the most important risk incurred in PPPs and confirms Hammami *et al.*'s (2006) finding, which was based on a shorter time period, 1990–2003.

Institutional factors affecting bureaucracy quality, government stability, and corruption are important for PPPs via their impacts on GDP growth. More broadly, all factors contributing to GDP growth seem important for PPPs, as growth in itself is a key determinant for PPPs. Private investors seem more attracted to projects initiated by countries with high and sustained GDP growth. In addition, democratic accountability, which fosters discipline in politicians and the obligation to deliver results, appears to have a direct and positive impact on PPPs.

Past PPP experience also appears to be conducive to attracting more PPPs. It is conceivable that past PPP experience improves government's expertise in dealing with future PPPs and facilitates contract negotiations. Finally, the analysis also seems to suggest that countries with difficulties in servicing their debt might find it attractive to initiate PPP projects, as this could help to move public investment off the budget and debt off the government balance sheet. This latter finding, however, is not robust, and more empirical work would be needed for confirmation. Also, even if it is attractive for the governments of these countries to initiate PPP projects, private firms may not find it attractive to enter into such partnerships.

From the findings in this chapter, countries aspiring to attract PPPs should pay particular attention to factors affecting their economic growth potential. In particular, controlling corruption, improving the quality of the public administration, and accountability or the obligation to achieve results should be prioritized in their reform agenda.

Notes

1   See among others Daron Acemoglu (1995, 2003); Daron Acemoglu *et al.* (2002, 2005b); La Porta *et al.* (1998).
2   In the United Kingdom, PPP is known as PFI.
3   Profit repatriation risk index is also a component of investment profile risk index, but is not significant in the regressions and was dropped early on.
4   Notice that the aggregate GDP is simply determined by GDP per capita multiplied by population.
5   This could possibly suggest that countries experiencing difficulties in the sustainability of their debt might find it attractive to resort to PPPs, everything else being equal, but again the significance here is too weak and no firm inference can be drawn.
6   Many of the marginal effects for order lower than five were not significant.

References

Acemoglu, D. (1995) 'Reward Structure and the Allocation of Talent', *European Economic Review*, 39: 17–33.

Acemoglu, D. (2003) 'Why Not a Political Case Theorem?', *Journal of Comparative Economics*, 31: 620–52.

Acemoglu, D., Johnson, S. and Robinson, J. (2002) 'Reversal of Fortune: Geography and Institutions in the Making of the Modern World Income', *Quarterly Journal of Economics*, 118: 1231–94.

Acemoglu, D., Johnson, S. and Robinson, J. (2005a) 'Institutions as the Fundamental Cause of Long-Run Growth', in P. Aghion and S. Durlauf (eds), *Handbook of Economic Growth*, Amsterdam: Elsevier.

Acemoglu, D., Johnson, S. and Robinson, J. (2005b) 'The Rise of Europe: Atlantic Trade, Institutional Change and Economic Growth', *American Economic Review*, 95(3): 546–79.

Coase, R.H. (1960) 'The Problem of Social Cost', *Journal of Law and Economics*, 3: 1–44.

Dailami, M. and Klein, M. (1997) 'Government Support to Private Infrastructure Projects in Emerging Markets', Policy Research Working Paper, No. 1688, Washington: World Bank.

Hammami, M., Ruhashyankiko, J-F. and Yehoue, E. (2006) 'Determinants of Public Private Partnerships in Infrastructure', IMF Working Paper 06/99.

International Monetary Fund (2004) 'Public Private Partnerships', Washington DC: International Monetary Fund. Online available HTTP: <http://www.imf.org/external/np/fad/2004/pifp/eng/031204.htm> (accessed 12 March 2004).

Kopp, J. C. (1997) 'Private Capital for Public Works: Designing the Next-Generation Franchise for Public–Private Partnerships in Transportation Infrastructure', (Master's Thesis; Evanston, IL: Department of Civil Engineering, Northwestern University), May.

La Porta, R., Lopez-de-Silanes, F., Shleifer, A. and Vishny, R. (1998) 'Law and Finance', *Journal of Political Economy*, 106: 1113–55.

Lora, E. and Panizza, U. (2003) 'The Future of Structural Reforms', *Journal of Democracy*, 14: 123–37.

North, D. C. (1990) *Institutions, Institutional Change, and Economic Performance*, New York: Cambridge University Press.

North, D. C. (1994) 'Economic Performance through Time', *American Economic Review*, 84 (3): 359–68.

Pistor, K., Raiser, M. and Gelfer, S. (2000) 'Law and Finance in Transition Economies', *Economics of Transition*, 8 (2): 325–68.

The Political Risk Services Group (1992) *International Country Risk Guide Methodology*, HTTP: <http://www.prsgroup.com/>.

Williams, C. (1992) 'Public–Private Partnerships in Transportation: Lessons Learned by a Public-Sector Entrepreneur', *Public Works Financing* (March): 22–25.

3

The institutional environment for public–private partnerships

The case of Mexico and Brazil[1]

David R. Bloomgarden and Dennis A. Blumenfeld

3.1 Introduction

Developing countries in the mid-1980s, especially in Latin America and the Caribbean, began to allow for private provision of infrastructure services as a component of widespread market reforms. Prior to that, services were predominantly provided by the public sector, but increasingly governments began to partner with the private sector. Otherwise, inadequate budgetary resources and competing investment needs made it difficult for governments to secure needed investments for improvements to infrastructure and service provision (Guasch 2004: 23).

As Nellis (2003) points out, when OECD countries are not included, privatization spread faster and deeper in Latin America than in any other region of the world and sales there raised more revenue than elsewhere.[2] The earliest privatizations involved the sale of state firms in competitive markets (Nellis 2003: 5). Initially, ownership changes occurred in Mexico, Chile and Colombia and then the trend spread to other countries in the region (Vassallo Magro and de Bartolomé 2010: 283). In the utilities sector, management, operation, finance and in some cases ownership was transferred from the public sector to private enterprises (Nellis 2003: 5).

Studies have supported the conclusion that private participation has contributed to increased investment and efficiency, improved service quality and greater coverage (Guasch 2004: 141). Of course, this has not always been the case. At times, transactions have been tainted by collusion or fraud (Nellis 2003: 8). More commonly users have not directly benefited from efficiency gains made through private involvement. In many countries, poorly structured contracts have led to renegotiation and disputes. Problems have arisen from ineffective regulations (Guasch 2004: x–xi).

This chapter focuses on PPPs in Latin America and the Caribbean and more specifically presents case studies on the institutional framework for PPPs in Mexico and Brazil. The chapter is organized as follows. The next section discusses the political environment for private participation in infrastructure and service provision in Latin America and the Caribbean. We recognize the importance of political leadership and assess the influence of public opinion in the successful implementation of private participation in infrastructure.

Furthermore, we maintain that in many countries in Latin America and the Caribbean policymakers' support for PPPs stems from recognition of limited fiscal resources and the need to secure additional financing. As will be further explained, through PPPs the private sector usually provides financing to develop public infrastructure and services. Previously, policymakers were less supportive of PPPs because of a belief that the provision of public infrastructure and services should be the responsibility of the State, despite arguable benefits from private participation.

In section 3.3 we provide a working definition for 'public-private partnership' and afterward explain the origin, structure and purpose of the Infrascope, an interactive benchmarking index and learning tool that analyses PPP capacity in 19 countries in Latin America and the Caribbean. Much of the analysis in this paper is based on the Infrascope. Later, in section 3.4, we summarize how PPPs in infrastructure and basic services are becoming widespread both worldwide and in Latin America and the Caribbean. Generally, in the midst of the more cautious financing environment following the recent financial crisis, there has been a tendency to invest in fewer projects overall and investment was concentrated disproportionately in larger projects. In Latin America and the Caribbean, PPP project development has increased, which reflects the relative effectiveness of the region in weathering the financial crisis. In this section, we also assess the Mexican and Brazilian economies and the rate and composition of PPP project development in both countries during the last decade.

The experience of Mexico in PPPs began primarily to develop the country's highway system. Section 3.5 recounts this experience. The Mexican highway concession programme of the 1990s experienced problems largely due to the Peso Crisis. Since this time, the country has adjusted its approach to PPPs for more effective project development and implementation. In section 3.5, we describe the legal, regulatory and institutional framework for PPPs in Mexico and bidding, award and contractual practices. We analyse these factors relative to the Infrascope rankings assigned to them. As in Mexico, the development and implementation of PPPs in Brazil began primarily for highways. In section 3.6, we assess the legal, regulatory and institutional framework for PPPs in Brazil and bidding, award and contractual practices. Again we analyse these factors relative to their corresponding Infrascope rankings. Finally, section 3.7 provides a comparative analysis of the legal, regulatory and institutional framework for PPPs in Mexico and Brazil and briefly relates these factors to per capita PPP investment.

3.2 The political environment for private participation in infrastructure in Latin America and the Caribbean

An important factor that affects the ability to attract long-term private sector investments in PPPs is political will. This refers to the level of political consensus to involve the private sector in infrastructure development and the willingness to implement institutional frameworks that encourage private sector engagement. Across Latin America, governments' willingness to support private provision of infrastructure and services varies significantly. Of course, levels of public support influence this willingness. Benefits from private participation in infrastructure can be spread throughout the public. Those that do benefit from increased coverage or lower tariffs might not associate these improvements with private sector participation. As a result, there is rarely organized public support for PPPs. The voices of those opposed to private involvement, such as public sector unions, for example, are often more concentrated, more visible and louder. Often, union members are opposed to private participation or privatization for fear of losing their job. Additionally, the beneficiaries of extended coverage of certain services resulting from private sector involvement, such as water and sanitation and electricity, have often been the poor who are relatively less organized than the rest of society (Nellis 2003: 17–19).

According to Latinobarómetro, a polling firm, a majority of people in the region support a market economy and believe in the importance of the private sector for economic development (Corporación Latinobarómetro 2010: 106).[3] Yet, many believe that the experience of privatization has not been good for their country. Similarly, many are unsatisfied with private provision of services (Corporación Latinobarómetro 2010: 104–6).[4] One would expect that such sentiment is in part a response to incidences of rapid tariff increases and collusion or fraud, often resulting from poor contractual or project oversight.

Indeed, in some instances, the onset of private participation in infrastructure was accompanied by rapid tariff increases (Nellis 2003: 8). One reason for this is related to the fact that under State control governments set tariffs at levels that did not cover costs, which resulted in scarcity or rationing. Additionally, there was a lack of resources for capital investments. Therefore price increases were often needed for firms to invest in order to modernize and expand output. Nevertheless, it is important that price increases are gradual and do not overburden society, especially lower income users (Nellis 2003: 11–12). An often-cited example of unreasonable tariff increases is the water concession in Cochabama, Bolivia, in which water prices increased by an average of 43 per cent for consumers within a short period of time. Following widespread social unrest in 2000, amidst concerns about access to water, the concession contract was terminated. A key issue in Latin America and the Caribbean continues to be retail pricing for socially sensitive products such as water (Nellis 2003: 26).

Increasingly, policy prescriptions are influenced by practical considerations rather than ideological views. However, it is conceivable that views on private provision of services may have been influenced by ideology. In Latin America, some strongly believe that service provision should be a responsibility of the state and that universal access to these services is an unquestionable right. Yet, those concerned with service provision from a practical policy perspective understand that this cannot occur in light of limited resources and investment capacity. In Latin America and the Caribbean, an increasing percentage of people believe the state plays an important role in improving life conditions through public policy (Corporación Latinobarómetro 2010: 82).[5] Many are concerned with how private sector efficiency and financing can be harnessed in a way that leads to increased and improved access for users while avoiding the problems of the 1990s during which there was insufficient institutional development for effective state oversight of private provision of services. Concurrently, there is a more widespread recognition that the state should play an important role in ensuring that populations have adequate, efficient and equitable access to basic services such as water and sanitation and electricity. This combination of private provision and governmental regulation and oversight is central to public–private partnerships.

Thus, in many countries, policies are enacted to lessen negative effects on the poor from utility price increases. While government subsidies can serve an important role in increasing access to basic services for low-income users, it is important that support effectively and reliably targets lower income households. Uniform subsidies that benefit both wealthier and poor households are an inefficient use of government resources but are not uncommon.

3.3 Institutional characteristics for PPPs in Latin America and the Caribbean and the Infrascope

Yehoue (Chapter 2 of this volume) and Queiroz and Martinez (Chapter 4 of this volume) have provided a general overview of the institutional and legal environment for PPPs. In this section, we focus on some specific institutional characteristics for PPPs in Latin America and the Caribbean.

We begin by defining the type of PPPs that are the focus of this chapter. We refer to PPPs as projects that entail a long-term contract between a public sector body and a private sector entity for the design, construction or upgrading, operation and maintenance of public infrastructure. Finance is usually provided by, and significant construction, operation and maintenance risks are transferred to, the private sector, which also bears demand risk. However, the public sector is responsible for policy oversight and regulation and, generally, the infrastructure reverts to public sector control at the end of the contract term. Using this definition, we include concessions and greenfield projects but exclude management and lease contracts as well as divestitures by the private sector, which share some but not all the characteristics of PPPs under this definition.

When structured and executed correctly, PPPs can harness private sector management efficiency and needed financing. However, PPPs have not been immune to problems. These include poorly designed tariff structures and contract disputes and renegotiations. These problems are not a symptom of the PPP model itself but rather can be prevented through effective PPP design and implementation (Guasch 2004: x–xi).

Our analysis of specific institutional characteristics for PPPs in Latin America and the Caribbean is based on the Infrascope. The Infrascope is an interactive benchmarking index and learning tool accompanied by a summary report, which analyses PPP capacity in 19 countries in Latin America and the Caribbean. The Multilateral Investment Fund (MIF), a member of the Inter-American Development Bank Group, commissioned The Economist Intelligence Unit (EIU) to develop the Infrascope. This index and learning tool analyses 19 countries in Latin America and the Caribbean according to their relative capacity to develop and implement PPPs in water and sanitation, transportation and energy (specifically, electricity generation). The analysis in this chapter is based on these sectors in particular, but many of the conclusions apply across sectors. The Infrascope is an independent assessment of the laws, regulations, institutions and practices that affect the environment for PPPs (EIU 2010a). Quantitative data sources were used in the development of the tool, but in large part the Infrascope was developed through qualitative methods including expert interviews and review of primary legal and secondary sources.[6] As mentioned, it serves as a learning tool rather than a financial index. Therefore the Infrascope is not meant to guide investment or show a definitive relationship between PPP investment and the environment and capacity of countries to develop and implement PPPs. Yet, it is strongly believed that the legal, regulatory and institutional framework for PPPs, and governments' capacity to manage PPP transactions, influences PPP investment and the effectiveness of contract development and management. This belief guides this chapter as well as the work the MIF does to promote the development of PPPs to develop infrastructure and support service provision. The MIF works with interested governments in the region to strengthen institutions and build capacity to develop, implement and oversee PPP projects and programmes through training and advisory services. The Infrascope, as an independent assessment, serves as an important reference for dialogue and a learning tool for MIF and countries in Latin America and the Caribbean to develop PPP programmes.[7]

The Infrascope analyses PPP capacity based on six country-level categories: the *Legal and Regulatory Framework* for PPP projects; the *Institutional Framework* for PPP projects; *Operational Maturity* or the extent to which PPP-related laws and regulations are upheld as well as the number and level of success of past projects; the *Investment Climate; Financial Facilities* for funding infrastructure; and a *Sub-National Adjustment* indicator, which was added to the most recent edition of the Infrascope to take into consideration intra-State differences in PPP capacity in a particular country. For each category, countries receive an assessment based on the evaluation of underlying indicators. In addition to assessments specific to each category, based on the weighted sum of these assessments, the developers of the Intrascope derived overall country evaluations.

This chapter focuses on the institutional environment for PPPs in Mexico and Brazil. For this focus, our analysis is based on the *Institutional Framework* and *Legal and Regulatory Framework* categories of the Infrascope. The *Institutional Framework* category is composed of two indicators: *Quality of Institutional Design* and *PPP Contract, Hold-Up and Expropriation Risk* (see Table 3.1). *Quality of Institutional Design* refers to the existence or lack thereof of agencies at the federal level for effective PPP project oversight as well as the role and oversight of budget and planning offices. This indicator concerns whether or not there is comprehensive and coordinated oversight and whether agencies are accountable and independent with well-defined structures and roles. *PPP Contract, Hold-Up and Expropriation Risk* refers to the effectiveness of property rights, arbitration rulings and contract rulings as well as the existence of mechanisms to protect creditors' rights.

The *Legal and Regulatory Framework* category is composed of four indicators: *Consistency and Quality of PPP Regulations, Effective PPP Selection and Decision-Making, Fairness and Openness of Bids and Contract Changes*, and *Dispute Resolution Mechanisms* (see Table 3.2). *Consistency and Quality of PPP Regulations* concerns whether or not PPP laws and regulations are clear and comprehensive across sectors, different project stages and different levels of government. Additionally, the indicator concerns whether or not laws and regulations establish adequate mechanisms that regulate risk allocation and, when appropriate, compensation for contractual changes. *Effective PPP Selection and Decision-Making* concerns whether or not effective planning, accounting and cost-benefit methods are in place. *Fairness and Openness of Bids and Contract Changes* relates to whether or not bidding procedures are clear, competitive and efficient. The indicator concerns initial bidding, bidding for additional work and renegotiations. Finally, the *Dispute Resolution Mechanisms* category assesses whether or not such mechanisms are clear and transparent. Additionally, under consideration is whether or not conciliation schemes are effective and sufficient.

Table 3.1 Infrascope: institutional framework: explanation of indicators

Indicators

Quality of institutional design
Evaluates the existence and role of various agencies necessary for proper project oversight and planning at the federal level, such as a PPP board at ministerial level, a State Contracting Agency and a PPP Advisory Agency and a Regulatory Agency for enforcement of project standards. Also considers the oversight role and involvement of government budget and planning offices.

PPP contract, hold-up and expropriation risk
Does the judiciary enforce property rights and arbitration rulings? Does the judiciary uphold contracts related to cost recovery? Can investors appeal against rulings by regulators, expedite contract transfer for project exit and obtain fair compensation for early termination? Also considers whether the state has an expedite mechanism for replacing failed operators, to protect creditors' rights.

Source: 2010 Infrascope Index for Latin America and the Caribbean

Table 3.2 Infrascope: legal and regulatory framework: explanation of select indicators

Indicators

Consistency and quality of PPP regulations
How consistent are PPP laws and regulations at different levels of government and across sectors? Do regulations establish clear requirements and oversight mechanisms for project implementation (project preparation, bidding, contract awards, construction and operation)? Must risk be allocated to different parties according to ability to manage them? Is there a clear system for compensating the private sector for acts of authority that change sector-specific economic conditions not foreseen during bidding? Also considers if regulations avoid open-ended compensation rights for changes in financial equilibrium so that the State only assumes explicitly written commercial contractual contingent liabilities.

Effective PPP selection and decision-making
Do regulations establish efficient planning frameworks and proper accounting of contingent liabilities? Have regulators determined appropriate project planning and cost-benefit analysis techniques to ensure that a PPP is the optimal project financing and service-provision option? Does the Budget Office systematically measure contingent contractual liabilities and account for delayed investment payments in a way consistent with public investment accounting?

Fairness/openness of bids, contract changes
Do regulations unfairly favour certain project bidders over others? Do regulations require and establish competitive bidding (i.e. use of objective criteria during the selection process, requiring the publishing of necessary bidding documents, contracts and changes in contracts)? Do regulations require bidding for any significant, additional work necessary? Is a system established for independent oversight of such renegotiation procedures and conditions?

Dispute-resolution mechanisms
Are there fair and transparent mechanisms for solving controversies between the State and the operator? Does the law provide technically adequate and efficient conciliation schemes? Must arbitration rulings proceed according to law and to contracts, without lengthy appeals?

Source: 2010 Infrascope Index for Latin America and the Caribbean

In this chapter, we will analyse the factors considered under these indicators in the Mexican and Brazilian contexts. The indicator rankings for each country will be included as an aggregate of these factors and a representation of the state of the institutional, legal and regulatory framework for PPPs in each country. Before tackling the Mexican and Brazilian cases, we first present the market for PPP worldwide and in Latin America and the Caribbean in particular.

3.4 The market for public–private partnerships

Worldwide, from 2000 to 2009, there were 1,680 PPP projects or an average of 168 new projects per year.[8] In 2009, there were 201 projects, which is the least since 2005 (see Figure 3.1 below). The largest annual increase during this period, in terms of projects, occurred between 2005 and 2006 when the number of projects jumped 36 per cent from 179 to 243. Investment in PPP projects from 2000 to 2009 totalled US$ 376.4 billion or an average of US$ 37.6 billion per year.[9] By sector electricity projects outnumbered transport and water and sanitation projects in terms of both number of projects and level of investment. Between 2000 and 2009, 40 per cent of total projects and 53 per cent of total investment was in electricity (Private participation in Infrastructure Project Database 2011).

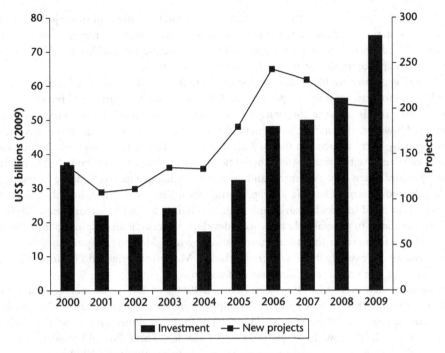

Figure 3.1   Worldwide PPP Project Development, 2000–09
Source: Private Participation in Infrastructure (PPI) Project Database

Despite the financial crisis, annual investment in 2009 was US$ 74.5 billion, which is greater than in any of the nine years prior and a 32 per cent increase from 2008 (Private participation in Infrastructure Project Database 2011). This figure, however, includes divestitures and management and lease contracts in all infrastructure sectors. Excluding divestitures and management and lease contracts that do not fit the definition of PPPs in this chapter, and focusing on the water and sanitation, transportation and electricity sectors, there was actually a 7 per cent decrease in investment from 2008 through 2009 (PPIAF December 2010: 1–2). Worldwide, approximately 0.5 per cent of total concession and green-field projects in the sectors considered were cancelled or distressed in 2008, which is below the annual average of 3.6 per cent between 2000 and 2008.[10] During this period, the highest annual rate of project cancellation and distress occurred in 2001 at approximately 9.4 per cent (Private participation in Infrastructure Project Database 2011). For the entire period under consideration, 2.8% of projects were recorded as cancelled or distressed (Private participation in Infrastructure Project Database 2011).

In Latin America and the Caribbean, between 2000 and 2009, there was a total of 537 PPP projects or an average of 54 new PPP projects each year. In 2009, there were 68 new PPP projects in the region, which is the most since 2000. During this period, investment totalled US$ 133.5 billion or US$ 13.4 billion per year. From 2000 to 2009, the region accounted for 32 per cent of total worldwide PPP projects and 36 per cent of total worldwide PPP project investment (Private participation in Infrastructure Project Database 2011). In the region, projects in the electricity industry outnumbered those for water and sanitation and transport. During the 10-year period, almost half of projects were for electricity. Approximately

33 per cent of projects were in transport, and approximately 18 per cent of projects were for water and sanitation. Approximately 4 per cent of total projects in the region were recorded as cancelled or distressed during this period, which is above the worldwide rate of 2.8 per cent (Private participation in Infrastructure Project Database 2011).

Mexico's economy, highly linked to that of the United States, contracted 6.5 per cent in 2009 but was forecast to grow 4.2 per cent in 2010 partly due to a partial US recovery (IMF 2010: 58–61). In Mexico, the corporate debt market remains small relative to the size of the economy. However, the market has benefited from 2008 reforms of regulations governing investments by Mexican pension funds. This has provided more financing for infrastructure projects combined with funding from the National Infrastructure Fund (Fonadin) that offers a mix of subordinated debt guarantees and subsidies. Exchange rate risk hedging instruments are largely short term. There is a deep, liquid, local currency denominated, fixed-rate, medium-term bond market in marketable debt but mainly for public sector issues. Cautious credit policies and, in general, relatively well-developed oversight are helping to mitigate the impact of the financial crisis and economic slowdown in Mexico. Despite cautious credit policies and an increasingly developed credit market, Mexico experienced a decline in overall PPP activity in line with a reduction in economic growth.

In Mexico, there were 64 PPP projects between 2000 and 2009 or an average of about six projects per year. For the period, project development in Mexico accounted for 12 per cent of projects in the region and 4 per cent worldwide. The four new projects recorded in both 2008 and 2009 are slightly below the annual average for Mexico. This follows 13 projects recorded in 2007, which is the largest amount in a single year between 2000 and 2009.

During the period considered, total PPP investment in Mexico was approximately US$ 22.5 billion or 17 per cent of the total for Latin America and the Caribbean and 6 per cent of the total worldwide. In 2009, there was a significant decrease in investment compared to the annual average of US$ 2.2 billion over the ten-year period, reflecting the impact of the financial crisis in private investment. For 2009, there was US$ 0.4 billion in investment. Approximately 56% per cent of PPP projects during this period were for electricity (Private participation in Infrastructure Project Database 2011).

With regard to Brazil, the economy contracted in 2009 (−0.2 per cent growth). Yet, the country rebounded in 2010 during which growth estimates were forecast at 5.5 per cent. The economic improvement in Brazil was mainly due to significant investment and healthy levels of private consumption (IMF 2010: 58–61). The country has deep and liquid capital markets providing firms with the ability to issue bonds in local and foreign currency and increasing access to interest rate and exchange rate hedging instruments. Reforms in recent years have also given rise to the growth of insurance and pension funds. A major source of medium- to long-term infrastructure financing is the National Bank for Social and Economic Development (BNDES), a publicly owned national development bank, which is committed to financing PPPs. Domestic capital markets are gradually deepening and becoming more competitive even though local currency loans are expensive and short term. Large private banks are well managed, profitable and capitalized. Deep and liquid capital markets and a well-capitalized national development bank have enhanced the capacity to finance PPPs in Brazil even as developed economies are facing more adverse financial conditions.

Today, to say that the PPP market in Brazil significantly contributes to that of the region, and that of emerging markets worldwide, is somewhat of an understatement. From 2000 to 2009, there were approximately 275 PPP projects in Brazil accounting for approximately 51 per cent of projects in the region and 16 per cent worldwide. In terms of PPP investment, that of Brazil, at US$ 50.9 billion, accounted for approximately 38 per cent of the regional total and 14 per cent worldwide. By sector, electricity projects have been most prominent. Seventy per cent of total projects were for electricity during the period under consideration.

3.5 The National Highways Concessions Program and the institutional framework for public-private partnerships in Mexico

The development and implementation of PPPs in Mexico began much earlier than in Brazil and primarily to develop the country's highway system. In 1952, the Mexico City–Cuernavaca toll road was the first transport project in Mexico constructed through a PPP. At this time, the government created the Federal Roads and Bridges authority (CAPUFE) to manage and regulate toll road concessions. The level of PPP development in Mexico fluctuated with the overall state of the economy. For example, in the 1970s, with rising oil revenues, the Mexican government decided to construct toll roads using conventional public sector procurement processes rather than through PPPs. In the late 1980s, the Mexican economy was in recession and the country's highways were in bad condition. Up until this time, the Secretary of Communications and Transport (SCT) was the sole authority responsible for the design, construction, operation and maintenance of highways in Mexico. The Mexican government again began to concession toll roads, and along with Banobras, a government-owned public works bank, provided subsidies for toll road construction. Following the successful concession of three highways, in 1989, the government approved the National Highways Concessions Program for the construction, finance, maintenance and operation of 4,000 km of toll roads (Vassallo Magro and de Bartolomé 2010: 244–5).

Since the concession period for many projects under the programme was relatively short (typically 5 to 12 years), tolls were worrisomely high, which triggered concerns about traffic demand levels. Under the programme there were conditions under which the State was required to compensate the concessionaire by lengthening the term of the concession contract. Specifically, these conditions included: if traffic volumes were below forecast levels, if construction costs increased 15 per cent or more above cost estimates, or if there were delays due to government contract modifications. By 1993 many highway concessions were in crisis and, following concessionaires' requests, the government undertook a re-evaluation of the programme. It was concluded that eight highways needed additional funding. Tolls were reduced on highways with high traffic volume. For most projects, the contract period was extended up to 30 years. Furthermore, contracts were financially restructured. The State was required to pay the concessionaire if toll income was insufficient for debt servicing. The situation worsened with the Peso Crisis, especially because many projects were financed with foreign currency debt. In 1997, the government rescued 23 of 53 previously concessioned highways. Project debt was assumed by the government, restructured and transferred to the government guaranteed Trust for Supporting the Recovery of Licensed Highways (FARAC). Ultimately, under the National Highways Concession Program, 5,316 km of high-speed roads, 14 beltways and 6 transnational bridges were constructed at a cost of US$ 6 billion for Mexican taxpayers (Vassallo Magro and de Bartolomé 2010: 245–7).

Currently, Mexico does not have a council of government or assigned agency for establishing national policies and overseeing the entire PPP system. Each level of government is responsible for planning, implementing and supervising projects. Institutional fragmentation in Mexico has affected the development of comprehensive project planning, development and oversight capacity among those organizations involved in the PPP process. Therefore organizational oversight is not comprehensive. Largely due to this factor Mexico receives a somewhat reduced ranking for the Quality of Institutional Design indicator in the Institutional Framework category of the Infrascope. Specifically, two out of a possible four points (see Table 3.3).

Agencies exist to support PPPs in Mexico and have adequate technical capacity. Capacity to plan and develop PPP projects exists in the Secretary of Communications and Transport (SCT) and Banobras, the government-owned public works bank. Separately, the Ministry of

Table 3.3 Institutional framework, Mexico

Institutional Framework	0–100, 100 = best	58.3
Quality of institutional design	**0–4, 4 = best**	**2.0**
	0 = PPP-specific agencies or boards do not exist and relevant institutions in this sector lack accountability and independence from rent seekers; 1 = Some oversight and checks and balances exist, but these are not comprehensive and agencies are highly prone to political distortion; 2 = Agencies exist and are fairly technical in nature, but do not play all necessary roles for comprehensive sectoral oversight; 3 = The necessary agencies exist and generally fill all necessary roles for sector oversight, although their structure and roles could be improved; 4 = The institutional design establishes satisfactory oversight and planning agencies, and incorporates checks and balances so as to ensure effective planning, regulation and increase accountability.	
PPP contract, hold-up and expropriation risk	**0–4, 4 = best**	**2.0**
	0 = The judiciary is a poor enforcer of private operator and investor rights and arbitration rulings, and there is no effective appeals process; 1 = The judiciary occasionally upholds PPP operator and investor rights and arbitration rulings, but in an inefficient manner; 2 = The judiciary usually upholds contracts, PPP operator and investor rights and arbitration rulings, but hold-ups are common; 3 = The judiciary consistently and effectively upholds contracts and allows for appeals to regulator rulings, ensures fair compensation for early termination and transfer of contracts, although delays occur and can generate hold-up risk; 4 = The judiciary effectively enforces PPP operator and investor rights and arbitration rulings, allowing for expedited contract transfers and ensuring that early termination occurs only in exceptional public-interest circumstances, with fair compensation to the operator and protection to creditors.	

Source: 2010 Infrascope Index for Latin America and the Caribbean

Notes: Category scores, in this case 'Institutional Framework', are the weighted sum of indicator scores (e.g. consistency and quality of PPP regulations) converted to a 0–100 scale.

Finance and Public Credit is responsible for the evaluation of public investments and concessions and has established a public sector comparator methodology for value for money analysis, though it is not required in all PPP evaluations. While there are alternatives to value-for-money analysis, what is important is that an effective method exists for assessing whether traditional public procurement or a PPP project would be more beneficial for government and society as a whole. The Ministry of Finance is currently analysing PPP best practices as part of a broader initiative to improve the efficiency and effectiveness of public expenditure. Capacity for project planning, design and financial analysis is relatively strong. There is less capacity for overseeing service standards under PPP contracts and relatively fewer resources devoted to project oversight. This may change as there are now conscious efforts within government, mainly in the Ministry of Transport and Banobras, to enhance PPP capacity. Several Mexican states have established programmes with the Multilateral Investment Fund of the Inter-American Development Bank to create government units with improved capacity to plan, implement and supervise PPP projects at the state level.

Although Mexico does not currently have a national PPP law, the Calderón government proposed such a law, under consideration at the end of 2010, designed to enhance the regulatory framework. As of December 2010, the proposal had not been enacted into law. A national PPP law would improve the allocation of commercial risks by specifying that those commercial risks assumed by the state should be explicitly set out in project-bidding documents and contracts. The law would facilitate contract adjustments, when needed, due to government actions that adversely affect project viability. Presently, rules for PPP project oversight, risk-allocation and compensation of private sector bidders are part of the country's legal framework but are not fully defined.

The power to issue concessions lies with different legal bodies and levels of government depending on the sector. State governments have their own legislation and procedures for PPPs. In transportation, the federal government is involved in PPPs for inter-state roads, airports and seaports. State and local governments are responsible for local roads. Water concessions are also a responsibility at the state and local level. In energy, the government is involved in power purchase agreements through the Federal Commission of Electricity, which has a constitutional role in generating electricity. Private operators, however, can generate electricity designated for export. The system, however, remains essentially State operated and is vertically integrated. The heterogeneous legal framework affects the ability to promote PPPs on a national basis. This is the main factor that explains why Mexico receives a score of two out of a possible four in the Infrascope in the *Consistency and Quality of PPP Regulations* indicator under the *Legal and Regulatory Framework* category (see Table 3.4).

Since the 1989–94 Highway Concessions Program, the PPP system for highways in Mexico has been reformulated. Three PPP models are used for highways: service project provision (PPS), asset utilization and concessions. Under PPS projects, the SCT offers contracts for a period of 15 to 30 years to design, finance, build, maintain and operate a road. According to these contracts, the private firm provides services in exchange for periodic payments from the government. The net present value of these future payments from the State is determined as part of the tendering process with the lowest net present value of payments used as the decision criterion to award the concession, provided that the winner complies with technical, legal and financial requirements. Each bidder requests a periodic payment based on construction, maintenance and operating costs; rate of return on equity; estimated annual traffic; and the duration of the contract. The government has developed regulations based on the Public Acquisitions Law of 1983 that allows these future payment commitments for PPS projects. The government has sought to work around

David R. Bloomgarden and Dennis A. Blumenfeld

Table 3.4 Legal and regulatory framework, Mexico

Regulatory Framework	0–100, 100 = best	56.3

Consistency and quality of PPP regulations — 0–4, 4 = best — **2.0**

0 = The legal framework is so cumbersome or restrictive that in practice national-level concessions are extremely difficult to implement;
1 = The legal framework allows national-level concessions, but it is ill defined and risk allocation and compensation is unclear and inefficient;
2 = The legal framework allows national-level concessions and also establishes general, open ended oversight, risk-allocation and compensation rules;
3 = The legal framework is generally good and coherent, addressing risk-allocation issues while leaving some ambiguity with regard to compensation schemes and project implementation;
4 = The legal framework is comprehensive and consistent across sectors and layers of government, addresses risk-allocation and compensation issues according to strict economic principles and establishes sophisticated and consistent oversight of project implementation.

Effective PPP selection and decision making — 0–4, 4 = best — **2.0**

0 = Decision-making processes are not defined–they are erratic and subject to change, without accounting for liabilities;
1 = Decision-making processes are defined, but are only occasionally followed, and accounting for liabilities is not well established;
2 = Decision-making processes are defined and upheld, but accounting practices are not adequate;
3 = Proper decision-making is both defined and used for PPP project decisions, although accounting for liabilities should be improved for more consistent decisions;
4 = PPP project selection is a consistent result of various efficiency, cost benefit and social-evaluation considerations required by law and accompanied by rigorous accounting practices.

Fairness/openness of bids, contract changes — 0–4, 4 = best — **2.0**

0 = Regulations unfairly favour certain bidders over others, transparency requirements are not in place and contracts are changed in discretionary manner;
1 = Regulations introduce some bias towards particular parties, and bidding, transparency and renegotiation schemes are poor;
2 = Project bidding is fair and transparent, but renegotiations and expansions are regulated poorly;
3 = Regulations generally define a fair playing field, with considerations for contract expansion, renegotiation and adjustments;

64

4 = Regulations establish fair and transparent bidding procedures, set limits to renegotiations and adjustments and require independent oversight of post-award procedures.

Dispute resolution mechanisms	0–4, 4 = best	3.0

0 = Dispute resolution systems for PPPs are undefined and insufficient;
1 = Dispute resolution mechanisms exist but these are not transparent or efficient;
2 = Adequate dispute resolution mechanisms exist but arbitration and appeals are lengthy and complex;
3 = Comprehensive, effective dispute resolution mechanisms exist, incorporating necessary technical considerations;
4 = Effective and efficient dispute resolution mechanisms establish independent arbitration according to law and contracts, without lengthy appeals and with accompanying viable prejudicial reconciliation options.

Source: 2010 Infrascope Index for Latin America and the Caribbean

Note: Category scores, in this case 'Regulatory Framework,' are the weighted sum of indicator scores (e.g. consistency and quality of PPP regulations) converted to a 0–100 scale.

the absence of a national framework for PPPs by establishing trusts for projects to guarantee future payments.

Under the asset utilization model, SCT packages toll roads for bidding (SCT 2010). This includes both new projects and projects rescued under the Highways Concessions Program (Vassallo Magro and de Bartolomé 2010: 247). For a previously rescued highway to be procured under the asset utilization model along with new projects, it must have ten years of continuous operation under FARAC. Under the contract, the winning bidder is responsible for operating, maintaining, and collecting toll revenues on the existing toll roads as well as for building and later operating new highways.

For projects under the concessions model, the winning bid is based on the minimum amount of financing requested from the public sector. Through the National Infrastructure Fund (FONADIN), a trust in Banobras, the government provides initial financing to the concessionaire. Also, the government provides a minimum revenue guarantee to attract private lending. An assessment of the government's contribution is derived from the initial financing provided and the net present value of the minimum revenue guarantee. When government funding is not needed, the largest monetary bid offered to the government and compliance with legal, technical and financial criteria are used to determine the winner (SCT 2010).

In Mexico, options for project modifications are limited and PPS contracts are for a fixed term. Fixed terms can result in unexpectedly high or low profits if demand is higher or lower than expected. In response, the government has aimed to improve planning capacity during bidding, and in the case of highway packages under FARAC, reduce the size in order to increase competition. Indeed, the government is taking positive steps to improve project planning. Yet, additional flexibility in allowing project modifications, assuming such flexibility is well regulated, would prove beneficial. Due to a lack of such flexibility, Mexico receives a score of two out of a possible four for the *Fairness and Openness of Bids and Contract Changes* indicator.

In Mexico, the judiciary usually upholds contracts and the rights of PPP operators and investors. By constitutional requirement, disputes between the private sector and the federal government must be resolved by the Contenscioso-Administrative tribunal, which enjoys relative independence. The general legal framework and the Constitution protect property rights and generate a reasonable level of legal security. The Mexican government has a good record of honouring its obligations and uses a fidecomiso, an independent trust, by which it fulfils its future payments to PPP projects. Comprehensive and effective dispute resolution mechanisms exist. In practice, many disputes are resolved by direct negotiation. When this is not the case, hold-ups in the courtroom and arbitration panels are common which is the principal factor explaining why Mexico receives a score of three out of a possible four for the *Dispute Resolution Mechanisms* indicator.

Sound economic and monetary policies will ensure that Mexico can attract financial flows despite the slow pace of advancing reforms and the economic slowdown. Although the experience with the first generation of PPP investment demonstrated that the State did not successfully transfer risk to the private sector, and many projects had to be re-concessioned under FARAC, the government retains a strong political commitment to PPPs to meet its infrastructure investment objectives.

3.6 The institutional framework for public private partnerships in Brazil

In the mid-1990s, public–private partnerships began in Brazil after development and implementation started in Chile, Mexico and Colombia. The motivation for PPPs grew from the deterioration of highways following a period of scarce public resources and lack of financing to invest in construction and maintenance. Between 1995 and 2010 Brazil developed more than 13,000 km of highway through PPPs (Vassallo Magro and de Bartolomé 2010: 283).

Today, Brazil has a high-level ministerial council that approves federal projects and tendering. A unit in the Ministry of Planning chairs the council. Sector ministries present projects to the council for approval. A unit in the Ministry of Finance evaluates the fiscal impacts and contingencies of projects, ensuring that fiscal allocations and limits are set on future budget commitments. Bidding, supervision and execution of projects are the responsibility of sector ministries following the launch of tenders. Generally, government institutions provide comprehensive sector oversight. This is largely why Brazil receives a score of three out of a possible four points for the *Quality of Institutional Design* indicator in the *Institutional Framework* category (see Table 3.5).

According to research conducted to develop the Infrascope, an insufficient availability of technical capacity at the national and sub-national levels has had a negative effect on the development of PPP projects. BNDES, the publicly owned national development bank, has acted as a technical consultant to the government for the preparation of PPP projects. The national government, as well as some States, has engaged multilateral development institutions, including the MIF, a member of the Inter-American Development Bank (IADB) Group, and the International Finance Corporation (IFC), to improve PPP planning and technical capacity through training and advisory services. There is also a need to enhance supervisory capacity.

The legal framework, established in the 2004 Public Private Association law, governs PPP activities at all levels of government along with various other laws and regulations including the 1995 Lease Law, the Public Contracting Law of 1986, and the Public Tendering Law of 1993. The federal government is responsible for projects in the power sector, inter-state roads,

Table 3.5 Institutional framework, Brazil

Institutional Framework	0–100, 100 = best	75.0

Quality of institutional design	**0–4, 4 = best**	**3.0**
	0 = PPP-specific agencies or boards do not exist and relevant institutions in this sector lack accountability and independence from rent seekers; 1 = Some oversight and checks and balances exist, but these are not comprehensive and agencies are highly prone to political distortion; 2 = Agencies exist and are fairly technical in nature, but do not play all necessary roles for comprehensive sectoral oversight; 3 = The necessary agencies exist and generally fill all necessary roles for sector oversight, although their structure and roles could be improved; 4 = The institutional design establishes satisfactory oversight and planning agencies, and incorporates checks and balances so as to ensure effective planning, regulation and increase accountability.	
PPP contract, hold-up and expropriation risk	**0–4, 4 = best**	**3.0**
	0 = The judiciary is a poor enforcer of private operator and investor rights and arbitration rulings, and there is no effective appeals process; 1 = The judiciary occasionally upholds PPP operator and investor rights and arbitration rulings, but in an inefficient manner; 2 = The judiciary usually upholds contracts, PPP operator and investor rights and arbitration rulings, but hold-ups are common; 3 = The judiciary consistently and effectively upholds contracts and allows for appeals to regulator rulings, ensures fair compensation for early termination and transfer of contracts, although delays occur and can generate hold-up risk; 4 = The judiciary effectively enforces PPP operator and investor rights and arbitration rulings, allowing for expedited contract transfers and ensuring that early termination occurs only in exceptional public-interest circumstances, with fair compensation to the operator and protection to creditors.	

Source: 2010 Infrascope Index for Latin America and the Caribbean

Notes: Category scores, in this case 'Institutional Framework,' are the weighted sum of indicator scores (e.g. consistency and quality of PPP regulations) converted to a 0–100 scale. In the Infrascope, there are 19 indicators (15 qualitative, 4 quantitative).

railroads, airports and seaports. Congress must approve projects with mixed public–private finance where the state contributes more than 70 per cent of resources to the project. The legal framework requires that the government compensate concessionaires due to external changes that affect the financial equilibrium of projects, having the effect of transferring some commercial risk back to the State. Specifically, an 'honest service' principle, set out in the

David R. Bloomgarden and Dennis A. Blumenfeld

public tendering law of 1993, requires the government to provide compensation to private participants in anticipation of adverse external conditions affecting a transport or a water and sanitation project. Compensation has often been provided ex-post, which allows for private sector opportunism. Because the Brazilian legal framework generally provides for effective risk-allocation, but does not always effectively address compensation issues, Brazil receives three out of a possible four points in the *Consistency and Quality of PPP Regulations* indicator in the *Legal and Regulatory Framework* category (see Table 3.6 below). At the same time, the possibility of private sector opportunism is buffered by fiscal regulations that prevent the state from assuming contingent liabilities or using PPPs to improve the outlook of fiscal balances. Indeed, the law also establishes limits on future fiscal commitments, at all levels of

Table 3.6 Legal and regulatory framework, Brazil

Regulatory Framework	0–100, 100 = best	71.9
Consistency and quality of PPP regulations	0–4, 4 = best	**3.0**
	0 = The legal framework is so cumbersome or restrictive that in practice national-level concessions are extremely difficult to implement; 1 = The legal framework allows national-level concessions, but it is ill defined and risk allocation and compensation is unclear and inefficient; 2 = The legal framework allows national-level concessions and also establishes general, open ended oversight, risk-allocation and compensation rules; 3 = The legal framework is generally good and coherent, addressing risk-allocation issues while leaving some ambiguity with regard to compensation schemes and project implementation; 4 = The legal framework is comprehensive and consistent across sectors and layers of government, addresses risk-allocation and compensation issues according to strict economic principles and establishes sophisticated and consistent oversight of project implementation.	
Effective PPP selection and decision making	0–4, 4 = best	**3.0**
	0 = Decision-making processes are not defined–they are erratic and subject to change, without accounting for liabilities; 1 = Decision-making processes are defined, but are only occasionally followed, and accounting for liabilities is not well established; 2 = Decision-making processes are defined and upheld, but accounting practices are not adequate; 3 = Proper decision-making is both defined and used for PPP project decisions, although accounting for liabilities should be improved for more consistent decisions; 4 = PPP project selection is a consistent result of various efficiency, cost benefit and social-evaluation considerations required by law and accompanied by rigorous accounting practices.	

Fairness/ openness of bids, contract changes	0–4, 4 = best	2.0
	0 = Regulations unfairly favour certain bidders over others, transparency requirements are not in place and contracts are changed in discretionary manner; 1 = Regulations introduce some bias towards particular parties, and bidding, transparency and renegotiation schemes are poor; 2 = Project bidding is fair and transparent, but renegotiations and expansions are regulated poorly; 3 = Regulations generally define a fair playing field, with considerations for contract expansion, renegotiation and adjustments; 4 = Regulations establish fair and transparent bidding procedures, set limits to renegotiations and adjustments and require independent oversight of post-award procedures.	
Dispute resolution mechanisms	0–4, 4 = best	3.0
	0 = Dispute resolution systems for PPPs are undefined and insufficient; 1 = Dispute resolution mechanisms exist but these are not transparent or efficient; 2 = Adequate dispute resolution mechanisms exist but arbitration and appeals are lengthy and complex; 3 = Comprehensive, effective dispute resolution mechanisms exist, incorporating necessary technical considerations; 4 = Effective and efficient dispute resolution mechanisms establish independent arbitration according to law and contracts, without lengthy appeals and with accompanying viable prejudicial reconciliation options.	

Source: 2010 Infrascope Index for Latin America and the Caribbean

Note: Category scores, in this case 'Regulatory Framework,' are the weighted sum of indicator scores (e.g. consistency and quality of PPP regulations) converted to a 0–100 scale.

government, not to exceed 1 per cent of government revenues on an annual basis. The Treasury supervises compliance with this regulation and can stop a PPP project if the limit is exceeded.

Sector-specific laws have established regulatory regimes at the federal level. In transport, the National Transport Regulating Agency supervises project operations, and the Ministry of Transport is responsible for project planning and design. The Ministry of Transport carries out a social evaluation and comparison between PPPs and public investment alternatives. The executive branch created a managing agency, the Comité Gestor de Parceria Publico-Privado (GCP), which functions under the Ministry of Planning, Budget and Management. The agency judges bid proposals according to the lowest rate, best technical proposal and lowest instalment payments by the public sector. The government may also require evidence of social responsibility. The National Aquatic Transport Agency is responsible for inter-State water transportation. In electricity the State is responsible for most transmission, distribution and generation capacity, although private power plants can be developed for large industrial users and the spot market. Responsibility for PPPs in water and sanitation and in urban and State roads lies at the municipal and State levels.

The 1988 constitution permits contracting public services to the private sector. The GCP publishes information on PPPs, but the PPP law does not establish limits for independent review of changes to the original contract, contract changes or bidding for additional works. Brazilian companies receive preferential treatment in bidding that favours partnerships between international bidders and local companies. Due in large part to a non-comprehensive legal framework for contract changes and bidding for additional works, as well as for the preferential treatment given to Brazilian companies, Brazil is assigned two out of a possible four points for the *Fairness and Openness of Bids and Contract Changes* and the *Effective PPP Selection and Decision-Making* indicators in the *Legal and Regulatory Framework* category. Dispute resolution is available under the PPP law; however, arbitration proceedings are not regulated, which favours a more consensus-based approach and a tendency to resolve conflicts bilaterally.

The track record of the Brazilian government for making payments is good. A guarantee fund was created at the federal level as part of the 2004 PPP law. Sound economic management has been maintained throughout the financial crisis and reduced vulnerability to external shocks. Increased interest in PPPs among some government officials has been driven by political rather than technical considerations. Additionally, political support for PPPs is greater in the water and sanitation and transport sectors than in electricity. Even though the political commitment to private participation in infrastructure at the federal level has been mixed in recent years, its investment grade rating combined with sound economic management and access to finance has enabled Brazil to maintain its role as the largest and most active market for PPP investment in the region.

3.7 Institutional environment in Brazil and Mexico: a comparative analysis

While the administration of Luiz Inácio Lula da Silva did not prioritize private participation in infrastructure to the same extent as the preceding administration, Brazil maintained an effective legal and institutional environment for PPPs that encourages private investment. By contrast, Mexico lacks an overall legal framework and a fully comprehensive institutional arrangement for PPPs, but has a strong level of support for PPPs at the national and subnational levels and is making important strides toward developing a more conducive legal and institutional environment as evidenced by the establishment of an infrastructure fund that can finance PPPs for national and local projects and the presentation of a new PPP law to Congress. While in Mexico options for project modifications are limited and PPS contracts are for a fixed term, in Brazil the PPP law does not establish limits for contractual changes. Therefore in both countries the legal framework for contract adjustments could be improved.

In both Brazil and Mexico, the development and long-term success of PPPs could be enhanced through increased technical capacity at the national and sub-national levels, especially in terms of project oversight. As mentioned, in Brazil BNDES has provided technical assistance in order to enhance government capacity for PPPs. The Mexican government, with the support of multilateral organizations, is coordinating initiatives to enhance PPP capacity.

As mentioned, while there are alternatives to value-for-money analysis, what is important is that an effective method exists for assessing whether traditional public procurement or a PPP project would be more beneficial for government and society as a whole. The utilization of the public sector comparator and value-for-money analysis is more common in Brazil because the Ministry of Transport has an established role in carrying out these assessments. Assessments of project bids, conducted by the GCP, consider both technical and financial considerations. In Mexico, under PPS contracts, deferred payments from the State are not properly accounted for as debt. Lack of competition in the electricity industry limits the importance of accounting and financial criteria for project bidding and selection.

There are important distinctions when one compares the organizational framework for the electricity industry in Mexico and Brazil. In Mexico, the independent regulatory role of the Comisión Reguladora de Energía (CRE, the energy regulator) is hindered because in practice all energy purchases are first approved by the CFE. In Brazil, private participation in the industry is somewhat more competitive, especially after reforms were put in place in 1996 that supported private sector participation in generation, transmission and distribution. More recently the development of bidding schemes for long-term contracts has increased the willingness of the private sector to participate in electricity projects. Yet, political will for private participation in electricity is low in comparison to the transport and water and sanitation sectors.

Generally, Brazil and Mexico have a relatively favourable institutional environment for the development and implementation of PPPs as evidenced by the *Legal and regulatory framework, Institutional Framework*, and overall Infrascope scores (see Table 3.7). Legal, regulatory and institutional factors have an important influence on the readiness and capacity of countries to carry out PPPs and have affected PPP development in Brazil and Mexico. Indeed, the favourable Infrascope rankings of Brazil and Mexico correspond with relatively high rates of per capita PPP investment when compared with other countries in the region (see Figure 3.2). Furthermore, those countries with higher Infrascope scores tend to have relatively higher rates of per capita PPP investment. We maintain that those legal, regulatory and institutional

Table 3.7 Overall Infrascope scores

Rank	Country	Score/100
1	Chile	79.3
2	Brazil	73.2
3	Peru	67.2
4	Mexico	58.1
5	Colombia	53.7
6	Guatemala	42.4
7	Panama	34.6
8	Costa Rica	32.3
9	Uruguay	31.8
10	El Salvador	30.6
11	Trinidad & Tobago	29.9
12	Argentina	27.5
13	Jamaica	25.4
14	Honduras	24.6
15	Paraguay	24.5
16	Dominican Republic	23.7
17	Nicaragua	16.0
18	Ecuador	14.2
19	Venezuela	4.2

Source: 2010 Infrascope Index for Latin America and the Caribbean

Note: Each Infrascope category is scored on a scale of 0–100 and weighted to produce the overall Infrascope scores.

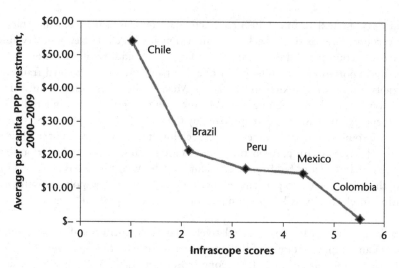

Figure 3.2 Per capita PPP investment and Infrascope scores

Sources: 2010 Infrascope Index for Latin America and the Caribbean, World Development Indicators 2011

Notes:

Per capita PPP investment in current US$ millions.
Infrascope rankings 1–5, where 1 = best.

factors that have supported a PPP enabling environment in Brazil and Mexico have positively affected PPP investment.

3.8 Conclusion

An appropriate legal framework, political will and a well-functioning institutional environment characterized by clear channels of responsibility and accountability to plan, design and oversee projects is necessary for a successful PPP programme. This chapter has presented case studies of Mexico and Brazil, two of the stronger performers in Latin America and the Caribbean in terms of PPPs according to the Infrascope. While Brazil under the administration of Luiz Inácio Lula da Silva did not prioritize private participation in infrastructure as much as its predecessor, it maintained a cohesive and well established institutional and legal environment that encourages private investment in PPPs. Mexico lacks an overall legal framework and has a fragmented institutional arrangement, but has a strong level of political support at the national and sub-national levels. In conclusion, the institutional factors presented in this paper are associated with the outcomes of PPP programs but no one size fits all. The degree to which individual institutional factors affect successful PPP programs will depend on the political, social, and economic context of each country.

Notes

1 The views and opinions expressed here are solely those of the authors and do not reflect the views and opinions of the Multilateral Investment Fund or the Inter-American Development Bank, its Management or Board of Directors.
2 The statement on the spread and extent of privatizations in Latin America also excludes the number of firms divested in post-communist transition states. Here privatization refers both to private sector

equity ownership as well as arrangements, such as concessions, in which ownership usually remains or returns to the state but assets are under the control of private partners.

3 In 2010, at the regional level, 58 per cent of respondents strongly agreed or agreed with the statement, 'The market economy is the single system in which (country) can become developed.' This was up from 47 per cent in 2009. In 2010, at the regional level, 71 per cent of respondents strongly agreed or agreed with the statement, 'Private enterprise is indispensable to the development of the country.' This was up from 61 per cent in 2009.

4 In 2010, 36 per cent of respondents strongly agreed or agreed that, 'Privatization of State enterprise has been beneficial for the country.' The percentage of those in agreement dropped significantly from 46 per cent in 1998 to 22 per cent in 2003. Since 2003, the percentage in agreement has consecutively increased even during the recent financial crisis.

In 2010, 30 per cent of respondents answered 'very satisfied' or 'satisfied' to the question, 'Now that we have privatized State-owned services, water, electricity, etc., taking into account price and quality are you now "a lot more satisfied, more satisfied, less satisfied or a lot less satisfied with the privatized services?' " This indicator increased from 19 per cent in 2004 to 35 per cent in 2008 before decreasing to 34 per cent in 2009 and 30 per cent in 2010.

5 In 2010, 44 per cent of those polled answered 'some' or 'a lot' to the question, 'How much do you think that public policies conducted by the government improve the life conditions of the (nationals)?'

6 In the Infrascope, there are 19 indicators (15 qualitative, 4 quantitative). Quantitative information is primarily taken from World Bank, PPIAF and EIU sources. Sources for qualitative information include primary sources (legal documents, government websites, press articles, interviews) as well as secondary reports.

7 At the time of writing the Asian Development Bank was piloting the Infrascope in Asia which was released in May 2012.

8 Project data is primarily for medium- and large-size projects reaching financial or contractual closure in low-income and middle-income countries as classified by the World Bank. Due to lack of information, data for small-size projects is unavailable and therefore not included. In this chapter, we examine only concession and greenfield projects in transport, water and sanitation, and electricity.

Financial or contractual closure takes place when private sponsors commit legally to provide funding or services. For concession projects, contractual closure occurs when the concession agreement is signed and a date is established for taking over operations. Financial closure for greenfield projects occurs when a legally binding agreement exists between equity holders or debt financiers to provide or mobilize funding for the full cost of a project. In cases where construction of a greenfield project begins with partial funding, the project is accounted for as having reached closure if 25 per cent or more of project construction has been completed.

9 Investment figures are provided in millions of current US dollars, which have been converted to billions of constant US dollars (2009).

10 Figures are for projects that become distressed or cancelled after having reached financial or contractual closure.

References

Corporación Latinobarómetro (2010) *2010 Report*, Santiago: Corporación Latinobarómetro. Online. Available at: <http://www.latinobarometro.org/latino/latinobarometro.jsp> (accessed 30 January 2011).

Economist Intelligence Unit (2010a) *Evaluating the Environment for Public–Private Partnerships in Latin America and the Caribbean: the 2010 Infrascope: a guide to the index and methodology*, London: Economist Intelligence Unit.

—— (2010b) '2010 Infrascope Index for Latin America and the Caribbean.' Available at: <http://www.iadb.org/document.cfm?id=35434951> (accessed 10 November 2010).

Fitch Ratings (2010) 'Sovereign review and outlook: contrasting credit outlook – negative for "advanced economy" sovereigns; positive for emerging markets.' Fitch Ratings. Online. Available at (with login): <http://www.fitchratings.com/creditdesk/reports/report_frame.cfm?rpt_id=593329> (accessed 6 January 2011).

Guasch, J.L. (2004) *Granting and Renegotiating Infrastructure Concessions: doing it right*, Washington, DC: World Bank.

International Monetary Fund (2004) 'Public Private Partnerships,' Working Paper, Washington, DC.
—— 2010. *World Economic Outlook April 2010: rebalancing growth*, Washington, DC: International Monetary Fund. Online. Available at: <http://www.imf.org/external/pubs/ft/weo/2010/01/pdf/text.pdf> (accessed 6 January 2011).
Lucioni, L. (2009) *La provisión de infraestructura en América Latina: tendencias, inversiones y financiamiento*, Santiago: United Nations. Online. Available at: <http://www.cepal.org/publicaciones/xml/0/35300/lcl2981e.pdf> (accessed 7 January 2011).
Moody's Investors Service (2010) 'Latin America and Caribbean sovereign outlook,' New York: Moody's Investors Service. Online. Available at (with login): <http://www.moodys.com/researchdocumentcontentpage.aspx?docid=PBC_126238> (accessed 6 January 2011).
Nellis, J. (2003) 'Privatization in Latin America.' Center for Global Development Working Paper 31, Washington, DC: Center for Global Development. Available at: <http://www.cgdev.org/files/2759_file_cgd_wp031.pdf> (accessed 11 May 2009).
Sanghi, A., Sundakov, A. and Hankinson, D. (2007) 'Designing and using public–private partnership units in infrastructure: lessons from case studies around the world.' Gridlines Note No. 27, Washington, DC: Public–Private Infrastructure Advisory Facility. Available at: <http://www.ppiaf.org/ppiaf/sites/ppiaf.org/files/publication/Gridlines-27-PPP%20Units%20in%20Infra%20-%20ASanghi%20A%20Sundakov%20DHenkinson.pdf> (accessed 29 December 2009).
SCT, General Directorate of Road Development (2010) 'Public–private partnerships for highways in Mexico.' Conference presentation (unknown).
Vasallo Magro, J.M. and Izquierdo de Bartolomé, R. (2010) *Infraestructura pública y participación privada: conceptos y experiencias en América y España*, Caracas: Andean Development Corporation.
—— (2007) *Public–Private Partnership Units: lessons for their design and use in infrastructure*, Washington, DC: World Bank.
—— (2010) 'Private activity in infrastructure remains at peak levels but is becoming more selective.' PPI Date Update Note 42, Washington, DC: World Bank. Available at: <http://ppi.worldbank.org/features/December2010/Global-update-note-2010.pdf> (accessed 8 January 2011).
—— PPI Project Database. Available at: <http://ppi.worldbank.org> (accessed 6 January 2011).
—— World Development Indicators. Available at: http://data.worldbank.org/indicator (accessed 1 December 2011).

4

Legal frameworks for successful public–private partnerships

Cesar Queiroz and Alejandro Lopez Martinez

4.1 Introduction

Many governments do not have all the financial resources required to expand, maintain and operate their country's transport networks and other forms of infrastructure. While the overall resources needed are enormous, it is well recognized that the quality of physical infrastructure affects a country's productivity, competitiveness in export markets, and ability to attract foreign investment (Akitoby *et al.* 2007).

In many developed and developing countries, the private sector has been involved in financing infrastructure through concessions under a public–private partnership (PPP or P3) programme. Interest in PPP has grown in several countries and regions. As an example, a recent European Parliament resolution stressed that the Europe 2020 strategy can only be credible if it is adequately funded, and emphasized that 'greater reliance on Public Private Partnerships (PPP) can be an effective approach, without being a "one-size-fits-all" solution' (European Parliament 2010).

Public–private partnerships are long-term associations between the public and private sectors that usually involve the private sector undertaking investment projects that traditionally have been executed (or at least financed) and owned by the public sector. The central feature of a PPP is that the public sector purchases (directly or through user charges) a flow of services rather than building or procuring the physical assets and employing the personnel for its maintenance and operation.

The archetypical PPP is a Build-Operate-Transfer (BOT) project, where a private sector company or consortium (the 'concessionaire') builds, operates and transfers the asset back to the public sector at the end of the concession life. The concessionaire sells the final service to the public sector or to the public (i.e. the users) under a government concession. Broadly defined, a concession is a legal arrangement in which a firm obtains from the government the right to provide a particular service (Kerf 1998). The transfer of risks to the private sector is a key requirement of PPP to fuel the private sector's drive for efficiency. Where commercial risks are shifted to the private sector, private participation will deliver better results than credible alternatives, such as attempts to strengthen public provision (Harris 2003).

PPP projects, however, are somewhat underutilized in transition and developing economies, where the potential financing gaps are significant and growing, and there seems to be an enormous potential for more private sector involvement in the financing and operation of infrastructure assets in these countries. Since the 1990s, governments remain the main source of infrastructure financing in such countries, providing 78 per cent of the total investments, while the private sector has contributed only 22 per cent (PPIAF/World Bank 2010).

With many developing countries increasingly interested in attracting private capital to infrastructure projects, partial risk guarantees (and other forms of guarantees or insurance) are particularly relevant in the context of seeking more private involvement in the financing of infrastructure, especially in the case of large transport infrastructure projects.

This chapter reviews the required legal framework (for example, concession law) for attracting private capital for PPP projects, potential applications of partial risk guarantees, possible steps for a country to launch a programme of private participation in infrastructure, the concept of greenfield and infrastructure maintenance concession programmes, and the treatment of unsolicited proposals. It also reviews the requirements for good governance in PPP projects. Because such projects in infrastructure tend to have monopolistic features, good governance in managing them is essential to ensure that the private sector's involvement yields the maximum benefit for the public. Seemingly non-legal issues, such as a risk matrix and procurement procedures, are also discussed because they are relevant to an enabling legal PPP framework.

There has been so far relatively low private financing of road infrastructure in transition and developing economies. The reasons for this include lack of appropriate legal framework, economic and political instability and consequent high perception of risks, and relatively low demand for infrastructure services. As appropriate legislation is enacted (Russia, India, Brazil and Serbia are good examples), institutions and economic growth become more sustainable (China and India, as an example, have grown steadily over the last several years), and there is higher demand for infrastructure (for example, traffic has increased substantially on key roads and corridors), it seems fair to expect that the sector will become more attractive to private investors. High economic growth figures dramatically reduce the demand risks faced by private sector investors, thus reducing the need for minimum revenue guarantees.

Nevertheless, appropriate legal structures are a key success factor. Promoting sound and well-functioning legal systems minimizes risk and assists the development of an attractive investment climate (EBRD 2010a).

4.2 Factors for successful PPP projects

A World Bank analysis of the experience with motorway development in Hungary, the Czech Republic, Poland, Slovenia, Croatia, Romania and Serbia showed that any PPP project, in order to be successful, requires strong government support and long-lasting political will and engagement (World Bank 2004a). A study conducted by the European Parliament highlights the following key success factors for PPP projects (European Parliament 2007):

1   *Political commitment and a clear policy.* The experience in successful PPP countries illustrates the importance of political will to implement PPP. For example, in the UK and in the Netherlands, the personal effort by high-level government officials led to the successful implementation of PPP in several sectors, including roads, rail, schools, urban development and government accommodation.

2   *A competent public administration and transparent institutional framework.* To ensure efficient and effective transactions it is crucial that the public administration is well trained, that PPP activities are coordinated, and that guidance to PPP is provided to all stakeholders. For these purposes, mainly, many governments have established central PPP units following the practice in the UK, as discussed later in the chapter.

3   *Availability of both public and private capital and willingness to invest by the private sector.* In general there is a large amount of private capital available for infrastructure projects, mainly from international banks but also locally (both public and private) in several countries (e.g. Brazil, Russia, India).

4   *A legislative framework to enable PPP.* In many countries the legislative system may not support the concept of PPP, such as the transfer of the responsibility to have a private entity provide a public service, and the suitability of procurement legislation for PPPs. Countries such as Ireland, Spain, Portugal are successful PPP countries and all have specific PPP legislation in place. A study by the European Bank for Reconstruction and Development (EBRD) illustrates that several countries, where concession legislation has low to medium compliance with international standards, have limited or no successful PPP programmes (EBRD 2010b). In addition to an enabling legislation for public authorities to enter into PPPs, it may also be necessary to ensure that investors can take security over project revenues. The next section elaborates on what is meant by an adequate concession law. An appropriate legal framework may reduce the need for public sector guarantees, thus facilitating the transfer of risks to the private sector, which is a key feature of PPPs.

4.3 Legislative framework

As described in detail in the Toolkit for PPP in Roads and Highways (PPIAF/World Bank 2009), the legislative framework includes two different types of law: 1) the laws that make PPP possible, also called the enabling law or framework, such as a country concession law or PPP law; and 2) the laws that may have an impact on a PPP project, which are numerous because PPPs are large and complex multi-faceted projects. While the Toolkit was developed specifically for the road sector, most of its components, *mutatis mutandis*, also apply to other infrastructure sectors.

The enabling law could either be general or sector-specific, including concession and PPP laws and sector-specific laws. Examples of laws that typically would have substantial impact on a PPP project in infrastructure include:

- public procurement;
- foreign investment laws;
- property laws;
- dispute resolution;
- company laws;
- security and insolvency laws;
- tax laws;
- accounting standards;
- labour laws;
- intellectual/industrial property laws;
- environment laws;
- competition laws;
- tort laws.

The focus of this chapter is on PPP-enabling law, and several related issues such as risks and procurement procedures.

4.4 PPP-enabling laws

According to a study commissioned by the European Parliament, a good PPP law can serve as a communication and a marketing tool for investors (European Parliament 2007). Most details should be delegated to specific regulations. In case of conflict with existing laws, such laws should be updated or repealed accordingly.

An appropriate concession law is fundamental for a country to establish an enabling environment for PPPs. It should apply to construction, expansion, rehabilitation and maintenance of assets providing a public service, aiming at improving the efficiency and modernization of public services.

A concession law can be kept relatively simple and general, while specific regulation (e.g. the way in which the procurement process will be conducted, award criteria, selection committees) should be documented in operational guidelines (or decrees). A separation between law and regulation provides more flexibility for amendments during the implementation of a PPP programme.

Public disclosure of concession agreements is highly desirable (Queiroz and Kerali 2010). This has several benefits, including: 1) it provides a further check on corruption, which in addition to its direct benefits can enhance the legitimacy of private sector involvement in often sensitive sectors; and 2) when the concession agreement relates to the provision of services to the public, it provides consumers with a clearer sense of their rights and obligations, and can facilitate public monitoring of concessionaire performance. The lack of transparency in concession agreements may lead to serious public concerns, as highlighted in a report by Transparency International (Transparency International 2005).

Concession laws should establish clear mechanisms for renegotiation and amendments (as a way to minimize contract distress and cancellation). The renegotiation of projects is not an unusual occurrence (Harris *et al.* 2003). In fact, about half of all concessions become subject to renegotiation, often due to unrealistic cost and revenue assumptions (Amos 2004). While not all renegotiation is undesirable, opportunistic renegotiation should be discouraged in both existing and future concessions. The appropriate behaviour for governments is to uphold the contractual obligations resulting from the competitive bidding process, and not to concede to opportunistic requests to renegotiate. Improving concession design and establishing credible regulations can lower the incidence of renegotiations (Guasch 2004: 38, 96).

Concession laws typically identify the government agency (or agencies) responsible for overseeing the bidding, construction and operation of the authorized projects and set parameters for each. Laws vary as to the rules of tender, but frequently involve a two-stage process, following pre-qualification.

In a two-stage bidding procedure, first, unpriced technical proposals on the basis of a conceptual design or performance specifications are invited. Such proposals are subject to technical as well as commercial clarifications and adjustments. Then, as a second stage, amended bidding documents are issued and the final technical and priced bids are submitted (World Bank 2010a).

The exact terms of the concession are then negotiated between the preferred bidder and the government before the concession is signed. The concession law will also usually address the methods of financing, in some cases including state funding as part of the concession.

Some details, however, may be better placed in a Model Concession Agreement (MCA), as is the case of India (India 2009), than included in a Concession Law. These may include standards and methods of user fee collection, technical specifications for the physical structure, and the State's obligations toward the concessionaire with respect to land acquisition. Standardization in this respect, however, is not the preferred approach in several countries.

Some key terms of concession legislation include the project structure (e.g. build-operate-transfer or BOT, design-build-finance-operate or DBFO, availability fee or annuity), the concession life, required percentage of domestic participation (more likely in less developed countries), and possibly limitations on the transfer of shares to third parties until the project completion.

A study carried out by the European Bank for Reconstruction and Development (EBRD 2010b), on the compliance of transition economies with international practices regarding concession legislation, indicates that only a few countries in the region studied (i.e. East Europe and Central Asia) show a high degree of compliance, thus indicating there is a need for an improved legal framework in several countries. Nevertheless, there have been recent improvements including, for example, legal reforms in Russia in response to the global financial crisis (Stubbs and Higgins 2010).

A PPP framework law (or enabling law) is not essential for a successful PPP programme. The United Kingdom, for example, which is the European country with the most developed PPP market, does not have a specific PPP law (which may be related to the UK jurisprudence and common law tradition). It relies on its commercial laws for the implementation of PPP projects. However, there are a number of countries where existing laws of a host country may need to be modified to allow for successful infrastructure PPP projects, such as enabling the grant of step-in rights to lenders and requiring open and fair procurement processes. These modifications may be embodied in sector-specific law, or in the case of procurement, a procurement or competition law. Or they can be included in a general concession or PPP law. Guidance on drafting PPP/Concession laws, including sample enacted PPP laws, is provided under the World Bank website on 'PPP Laws/Concession Laws' (World Bank 2010b).

A study by the EBRD (2005) reviewed the implementation of PPP programmes in a sample of common law countries (Australia and UK) and civil law countries (Croatia, Czech Republic, Hungary, Netherlands, Portugal and Romania). The study found that the opportunities for innovation and for fast implementation of PPP schemes enabled by the freedom inherent to the structure of common laws have resulted in more use of PPPs' potential. However, the greater flexibility in common law requires more safeguards, as it is more open to misuse and less predictable consequences. For less developed and emerging economies, a PPP-enabling legal framework may help attract broader interest from private sector investors.

Many countries or states have also adopted laws specifically governing the granting of concessions in specific sectors. This is the case, for example, in the UK, Poland, France, Ukraine, States of California and Virginia in the USA, which have specific laws for toll road concessions. In such cases, the distinction between common law and written law countries seems to be irrelevant.

4.5 Constraints of private sector involvement

Public–private partnerships involve two agents whose objectives are different, who are in possession of different levels of information (informational structure) and who are rational economic agents trying to maximize their objectives with minimum effort (Macário 2010). Such complexities pose some constraints to private sector involvement in infrastructure projects.

When a government is considering whether to launch a PPP project, several constraints should be considered. The World Bank 'PPP in Infrastructure Resource Center for Contracts, Laws and Regulation' (World Bank 2010c) provides a good description of such constraints, which can be summarized as:

1   The private sector will do what it is paid to do and no more than that – therefore incentives and performance requirements should be included in the contract.
2   There is a cost attached to debt – while the private sector can make it easier to get finance, finance will only be available where the operating cash flows of the concessionaire are expected to provide an acceptable return on investment, i.e. the cost has to be borne either by the users or the government (through, for example, subsidies, shadow tolls, annuities). Care should be taken, however, in providing such government support to avoid harming the transfer of risks feature of PPP.
3   Bidding costs in PPP projects are likely to be greater than for traditional government procurement processes – the government should therefore determine whether the greater costs involved are justified (UK PFI 2008).
4   There is no unlimited risk bearing – private firms will be cautious about accepting major risks beyond their control, such as exchange rate risks, risk of existing assets and some demand risks. If they bear these risks then their price for the service will reflect this. Private firms will also want to know that the rules of the game are to be respected by government as regards undertakings to increase tariffs and fair regulation. The private sector will also expect a significant level of control over operations if it is to accept significant risks.
5   Government responsibility continues – citizens will continue to hold government accountable for the quality of the facility and services provided. The government will also need to retain sufficient expertise, whether itself or via a regulatory body, to be able to monitor performance of the private sector and enforce its obligations.
6   A clear legal and regulatory framework is crucial to achieving a sustainable PPP programme.

A country's legal framework may also include requirements for carrying out a public sector comparator and a competitive selection of the private concessionaire, as discussed further in the chapter.

4.6 PPP value added

Several countries require that PPP should only be considered if it can be demonstrated that they will achieve additional value compared with other approaches, if there is an effective implementation structure and if the objectives of all parties can be met within the partnership. Regarding additional value, as an example, the UK government has developed a value for money (VfM) framework, the application of which (including a 'Quantitative Evaluation' tool) is mandatory for all PPP projects proposed in the UK (UK HM Treasury 2006).

A usual way to estimate the value for money of a PPP project is to carry out a Public Sector Comparator (PSC) exercise. PSC plays a key role in project development in such countries as Australia, Canada, the Netherlands, South Africa, as well as the United Kingdom, the country where it originated in the early 1990s. The PSC main objective is to help ensure that PPP projects clearly demonstrate a viable alternative and value for money before public partners enter into PPP contracts. The PSC method consists in conducting a quantitative comparison between a PPP project and a public sector project that would deliver the same services.

The PSC can be interpreted as a risk-adjusted financial model of the hypothetical public sector project. It estimates the total costs to the government of achieving the targeted outputs, assuming that the project is handled in the 'normal' way, with reasonably foreseeable efficiency improvements. The comparison is typically made before bids are received – to determine whether to proceed with the expensive PPP procurement process. In this case, the comparison is made with a hypothetical PPP project, a risk-adjusted financial model that estimates the total cost to government of having a private company deliver the targeted outputs. In some cases the comparison is also made after bids are received to refine the comparison when the private sector financial proposals are known. However, the usefulness of such refinement is debatable, as a commitment to involve the private sector may have already been made at this stage.

When public funding is unavailable to implement a project without private financing, the PSC is largely irrelevant. For example, in Australia, the Fitzgerald Report (Fitzgerald 2004) recommended against carrying out the PSC comparison where public sector provision is not a reasonable option.

In view of the subjectivity of the PSC estimates (e.g. small adjustments for risks or discount rate can have dramatic effects on cost estimates), Leigland has appropriately suggested that it might be sensible to use the PSC more as a way to achieve consensus among stakeholders about what features a project should have than as an expert judgement for convincing stakeholders that a project offers value for money (Leigland 2006).

4.7 Steps to launch a PPP programme in infrastructure

A first step in launching a PPP programme in infrastructure in a country is to define the priority projects where the government envisages soliciting private investors financing of the total or partial cost of the project. Several countries have prepared such project lists. In the case of Russia, for example, several high-priority projects for potential PPP in highways have been identified, such as Moscow–St Petersburg motorway, outer Moscow ring road, Moscow–Minsk highway, access to Domodedovo airport, St Petersburg Western High-speed Diameter Motorway, bridge on Volga river at Volgograd.

Other steps to launch a PPP programme would include (some of these steps can be done in parallel):

1 Enact relevant legislation (as discussed earlier).
2 Carry out feasibility study of priority projects. Employ reputable consultants, using well-prepared terms of reference. Identify/quantify social and economic benefits; carry out financial assessment to help check the potential for attracting private capital (for example, relatively high overall project financial rate of return and return on equity).
3 Carry out environmental and social assessment, including development of mitigation plan and land acquisition plan for the right of way.
4 Assess the willingness of users to pay; review tolling/payment options (for example, actual tolls, shadow tolls, vignette system, availability fee or annuity).
5 Define performance standard for the new investment and the service standards during the operation period.

4.8 Selection of the strategic private investor or concessionaire

Open and transparent competitive bidding is usually perceived as a prerequisite to ensuring the efficient allocation and use of scarce public resources. The World Bank Procurement Guidelines recommend the use of international competitive bidding (ICB) to select the concessionaire or entrepreneur under BOO (Build, Own, Operate), BOT (Build, Operate, Transfer), BOOT (Build, Own, Operate, Transfer) or similar type of concessions for projects such as toll roads, tunnels, harbours, bridges (World Bank 2004b). The Guidelines state that the ICB procedures may include several stages in order to arrive at the optimal combination of evaluation criteria, such as the cost and magnitude of the financing offered, the performance specifications of the facilities offered, the cost charged to the user, other income generated by the facility, and the period of the facility's depreciation. Competition can help to reduce prices and expand access, and should be used to the maximum extent possible (Harris 2003). In order to facilitate bid evaluation, it is highly recommended that a simple criterion be applied to compare the price proposals. Examples of such criterion include minimum toll rate to be charged to the users, minimum annuities to be paid by the government to the concessionaire, or maximum present value of the payments to be made by the concessionaire to the government during the concession life.

The European Union encourages the use of the 'competitive dialogue procedure' for major projects (Freshfields Bruckhaus Deringer 2005). Such competitive dialogue is somewhat similar to the World Bank ICB procedure that involves several stages (World Bank 2004b).

Steps in the selection process are likely to include:

1 *Advertising.* A notice requesting expressions of interest to pre-qualify should be published in at least one international newspaper and one of national circulation and should include the scheduled date for availability of pre-qualification documents.
2 *Investor feedback.* Meeting with selected potential investors/concessionaires to solicit feedback on the options being analysed as well as on the key parameters and assumptions underpinning the conclusions of financial feasibility.
3 *Public information.* Implement an appropriate programme to disseminate information to the public on the financing and construction of the proposed facility (or project).
4 *Pre-qualification of concessionaires.* Develop operational and financial criteria to be used in judging the suitability of prospective bidders, and conduct a transparent pre-qualification process. Pre-qualification ensures that invitations to bid are extended only to those who have adequate capabilities and resources. Pre-qualification will be based entirely upon the capability and resources of prospective bidders to perform the particular concession contract satisfactorily, taking into account their i) experience and past performance on similar contracts, ii) capabilities with respect to personnel, equipment and construction, and iii) financial position. All bidders that pass this stage are by definition qualified and should be considered for the next phase.
5 *Inviting pre-qualified firms/consortiums to submit bids.* Define the procedures for the pre-qualified bidders to carry out their own due diligence of the proposed project. In addition, a Data Room prepared by the client should be made available to potential investors, to enable them to fully assess the investment opportunity.
6 *Bidders' review and comments.* In order to minimize opportunities for post-bid negotiations on substantive issues with the winning bidder, major transaction documents (such as concession contract, shareholders' agreement) should be circulated to the bidders for

review and comments before bids are submitted. The clear understanding to bidders should be that the period designated for review and providing comments will be their only opportunity to influence the terms of the bidding process.

7 *Competitive bidding process.* Once the structure of the transaction has been approved, organize a competitive bidding process to award the concession contract to a strategic investor. Steps in the bidding process include preparation of the tender documents, administering the offer period for bidders' due diligence, and preparing the bid procedures and selection criteria.

8 *Bid evaluation.* Evaluate the bids received based on the agreed, transparent selection criteria, and recommend award to the best-evaluated bidder. As an example, in the case of road projects, typically the final selection criterion is based on: a) the minimum toll rate proposed by the bidders; or b) the minimum public contribution, or subsidies, to the construction cost of the project, which is required by the bidders; or c) the minimum availability fee or annuity proposed by the bidders.

9 *Transaction closure.* The principal parties complete and execute the concession contract, shareholders' agreement and other documents necessary for the satisfactory closing of the transaction.

10 *Public disclosure of the concession agreement.* By providing a further check on corruption, this can enhance the legitimacy of private sector involvement.

The selection process described above follows general international good practice. However, in cases where competition is perceived to be relatively limited and the country environment is prone to collusion of prospective bidders, some innovative approach in the procurement process may lead to better results. A good example is provided in the selection of concession-aires under the second phase of the Brazilian federal road concession programme. The first phase, in the 1990s, had followed a more traditional approach, which led to relatively high toll rates. In the second phase, around 2008, the selection was carried out by the Sao Paulo Stock Exchange (BOVESPA) through an auction (Amorelli 2009). The process consisted of the following main steps:

1 Public consultation on the draft bidding documents.
2 Preparation of the final bidding documents.
3 Adopting as the selection criterion the lowest toll rate (as in the first concession phase).
4 BOVESPA held a simultaneous auction for seven road concessions, without pre-qualification, defining the bidder offering the lowest toll rate for each project road, including foreign firms.
5 The bid evaluation committee reviewed compliance of the technical offer and bid guar-antee of the best-ranked candidate for each project, while other technical offers were not opened.
6 Award of each concession contract to the respective lowest bidder, without negotiations.

Compared to the first phase of road concessions, the innovative approach used in the second phase showed considerable advantages, by a) reducing the time between invitation to bid and contract signing, and b) leading to substantially lower toll rates, with an average of about US$0.02/car-km, compared to about US$0.04/car-km in the first phase. Additionally, the sequencing of bidding steps (financial offer first, technical second) limited the impact of judicial recourses – a critical factor in traditional tendering processes in Brazil (Véron and Cellier 2010).

While this innovative approach worked well for these relatively simple projects, it is likely that the traditional approach, including pre-qualification, will be the most appropriate for more complex projects.

Nevertheless, the above example illustrates that even in a country with a well-established legal framework it is important to keep some flexibility for applying innovative solutions to specific problems (such as collusion of potential concessionaires).

4.9 Unsolicited proposals

Unsolicited proposals, which seem attractive to some governments in their wish to accelerate the implementation of infrastructure projects in the country, tend to be so controversial (usually involving allegations of corruption), that in fact they usually take longer to award than an open, competitive tender procedure. In theory, unsolicited proposals could generate beneficial ideas; in practice, there have been a number of unfavourable experiences, mostly as a result of exclusive negotiations behind closed doors. There have been cases where a contract signed between a government and a private company included a clause that prohibits any leakage of the signed contract.

Several countries have adopted specific legislation to deal with such proposals, while some governments have simply forbidden unsolicited proposals to reduce public sector corruption and opportunistic behaviour by private sector companies. The general experience with unsolicited proposals is often negative, reflecting the fact that projects of this type have usually represented poor value for money, and were frequently incompatible with the actual development needs of the countries, and their ability to pay. They also often lead to allegations of corruption. Corruption has been shown to be associated with the lack of adequate transport infrastructure in a country, as well as a low degree of economic development (Queiroz and Visser 2001). It is essential to eliminate or minimize the perception, as well as the reality, of corruption in PPP programmes so that such programmes can best contribute to a country's economic development.

Some governments have adopted procedures to transform unsolicited proposals for private infrastructure projects into competitively tendered projects. Such countries include Chile, the Republic of Korea, the Philippines and South Africa (Hodges 2003a, 2003b). How to respond to unsolicited bids so as to protect transparency in the procurement process and recognize the initiative of the proponent, is typically difficult. The World Bank considers that unsolicited proposals should be handled with extreme caution and does not permit the use of unsolicited proposals in World Bank-funded projects.

A number of approaches on managing unsolicited proposals are available on the World Bank website at 'World Bank PPP in Infrastructure Resource Center for Contracts, Laws and Regulation' (World Bank 2010b). Such approaches include:

- UNCITRAL Approach. UNCITRAL sets out suggested legislative language in provisions 20 to 23 of its Model Legislative Provisions (UNCITRAL 2004). Whenever a host authority receives an unsolicited bid, UNCITRAL recommends that the authority first consider whether the proposal is potentially in the public interest. If so, the authority then requests further information from the proponent in order to make a full evaluation. If the authority decides to go ahead with the project, it determines whether the project involves intellectual property, trade secrets or other exclusive rights of the proponent. For projects that do not involve these rights, a full selection procedure is followed, with the proponent being invited to take part in the selection. If it does involve the proponent's intellectual property, a full selection procedure does not need to be followed. In this case, the contracting authority may request the submission of other proposals, subject to any incentive or other benefit that may be given to the person who submitted the unsolicited proposal.

- Chilean law approach. Chile has adopted an approach whereby the project proponent is required to take part in a fully competitive tender process, but is given bonus points in relation to the evaluation (Chile 1997).

In view of the risks involved with unsolicited proposals, it seems essential that the legal framework in each country includes a clear provision to deal with these types of offer.

4.10 Risk management

Risks associated with PPP programmes should be adequately managed. The main risks of PPP projects, in addition to changes in design during construction, which can lead to significant cost increases, are those that affect gross revenue. Revenue-related risks usually reflect uncertainty in both the predictability of future demand (e.g. traffic volumes) and the willingness of users to pay tariffs. In the particular case of roads, Bain compiled a database of predicted and actual traffic usage for over 100 international, privately financed toll road projects. Bain's findings suggest that toll road traffic forecasts are characterized by large errors and considerable optimism bias. As a result, financial engineers need to ensure that transaction structuring remains flexible and retains liquidity such that material departures from traffic expectations can be accommodated (Bain 2009).

A study of 67 toll road cases by Standard & Poor's found that actual traffic, on average, was 70 per cent of the forecast volume, with a spread of 18 per cent to 146 per cent (Standard & Poor's 2002). For countries without previous tolling experience, the average actual traffic was only 56 per cent of the forecast, compared with 87 per cent for those with previous experience.

Particularly helpful PPP resource guidance, including risk issues, can be found in: 'Public and Private Sector Roles in the Supply of Transport Infrastructure and Services: Operational Guidance for World Bank Staff' (Amos 2004); and 'Guidelines for the Development of Successful Public–Private Partnerships' (European Commission 2003).

The European Commission, recognizing that Accession Countries and Member States can potentially benefit from the PPP approach to reform and upgrade infrastructure and services, has published, in addition to the Guidelines, a 'Resource Book' with a number of PPP case studies across countries and sectors (European Commission 2004).

Risks should be identified for each stage of a project, and responsibility should be allocated for the identified risks. More detailed discussions of the risks involved in a PPP project, as well as their allocation, are provided, for example, by Delmon in the 'Private Sector Investment in Infrastructure: Project Finance, PPP Projects and Risks' (Delmon 2009) and Irwin in the 'Government Guarantees for Private Infrastructure' (Irwin 2007).

As PPP are legally long-term contractual agreements, responsibilities should be clearly defined as they will determine the costs that the public and private partners will ultimately pay. For example, construction risk is usually transferred to the private sector, which means that it will be responsible (and will not be able to claim additional compensation) for delays and cost-overruns in completing the works. The best approach is not to try to transfer all risks to the private sector, as this would result in less interest (or no interest) by the private sector or a much higher cost to the public sector. As a result, risk allocation is a very important component in the assessment of any PPP project (Queiroz and Kerali 2010).

A good practice in preparing risk matrices is to adopt the following structure for each stage of the project:

- description of the risk;
- proposed allocation of the risk (usually two columns – 'Grantor' and Concessionaire' – and one of them gets checked for a particular risk);
- comments.

The general rule is that risks need to be allocated to the party that is best capable to manage them. This means that the government would need to take some risks that it can manage better or because the costs of the private sector assuming such risks would be too high. The private sector will price the risk of the project based on how individual risks are allocated, their likelihood of occurrence, and impact. If the private sector has transferred to it a risk that it cannot control (for example, inflation being higher than forecast) it will either take a very conservative scenario (such as assuming a very high inflation rate) or simply not accept it (and therefore will not make any proposal, thus reducing competition). The risk allocation exercise requires a very good understanding of the market and project finance principles in order to allocate the risk in a way that balances the public and private sector concerns and interests.

The preparation of a risk matrix would help the government to decide which risk should be allocated to which party. Risk framework is a useful tool that provides the basis for discussions on potential structuring of the transaction and relevant policy choices, and allows the government team preparing the project to discuss with the decision makers the proposed risk allocation and obtain approvals for moving ahead with the transaction. The risk matrix should be prepared with a legal perspective in mind because it should provide the basis for drafting the PPP legal agreement/concession agreement.

Potential bidders will carefully examine the risks and proposed risk allocation and will prepare their bids based on their perceived risks and how comfortable they are with taking on some of the risks. In view of the volatility of the market resulting from the current global economic crisis, and the limited experience with PPP in some countries, it is likely that the investors will be uncomfortable with assuming many risks that are usually borne by the private sector in established economies with a good track record of PPP projects.

The risk allocation matrix should be updated and refined as project preparation evolves. It is usually prepared with the support of transaction experts and in consultation with potential bidders. Ultimately the risk allocation will determine if a PPP project is financeable (i.e. lenders will not finance it if they believe the risk allocation is not appropriate), so the public sector should remain flexible when designing such a matrix.

Countries with limited PPP experience, in particular, may be seen as risky environment for private investment, and the use of risk mitigation instruments can help reduce the risk perception and facilitate private sector investment.

Regarding risk mitigation, several instruments can be used to facilitate the mobilization of private capital to finance PPP projects, particularly in those infrastructure sectors in which financing requirements substantially exceed budgetary or internal resources. Risk mitigation instruments are financial instruments that transfer certain defined risks from project financiers (lenders and equity investors) to creditworthy third parties (guarantors and insurers) that have a better capacity to accept such risks. These instruments are especially useful when the public partner is not sufficiently creditworthy or does not have a proven track record in the eyes of private financiers to be able to attract private investments without support. The advantages of such instruments are multifaceted (Matsukawa and Habeck 2007):

- The public sector is able to mobilize domestic and international private capital for infrastructure implementation, supplementing limited public resources.
- Private sector lenders and investors will finance commercially viable projects when risk mitigation instruments cover those risks that they perceive as excessive or beyond their control and are not willing to accept.
- Governments can share the risk of infrastructure development using limited fiscal resources more efficiently by attracting private investors rather than having to finance the projects themselves, assuming the entire development, construction and operating risk.

Commonly used risk mitigation instruments include guarantees and insurance products (Matsukawa and Habeck 2007). Guarantees typically refer to financial guarantees of debt that cover the timely payment of debt service. Procedures to call on these guarantees in the event of a debt service default are usually relatively straightforward. In contrast, insurance typically requires a specified period during which claims filed by the insured are to be evaluated, before payment by the insurer. Examples of risk mitigation instruments available include (Matsukawa and Habeck 2007):

- Credit Guarantees, which cover losses in the event of a debt service default regardless of the cause of default (that is, both political and commercial risks are covered with no differentiation of the source of risks that caused the default).
- Political Risk Guarantees or Insurance, which cover losses caused by specified political risk events. They are typically termed Partial Risk Guarantees (PRGs), which may be termed as Political Risk Guarantees (PRGs), or Political Risk Insurance (PRI) depending on the provider.

Partial Risk Guarantees cover commercial lenders in PPP infrastructure projects. They typically cover the full amount of debt. Payment is made only if the debt default is caused by risks specified under the guarantee. Such risks are political in nature and are defined on a case-by-case basis. PRGs are offered by multilateral development banks (World Bank 2010d) and some bilateral agencies. Figure 4.1 provides an illustration of how a partial risk guarantee

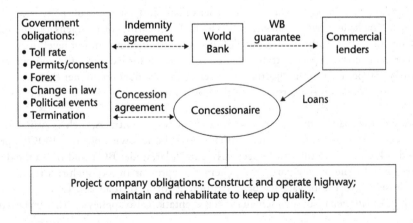

Figure 4.1   Structure of a highway concession contract and World Bank guarantee

Source: Figure 3 of Queiroz (2006)

can apply to a highway concession contract. *Mutatis mutandis*, such illustration also applies to other infrastructure sectors.

4.11 Public sector financial support

Governments should seek to minimize the need for public financial support for infrastructure projects in order to maximize the benefits of concessioning relative to its costs. However, public financial support may be appropriate if it helps ensure the mobilization of large amounts of private capital. Governments involved in toll road projects should also seek to limit their contingent liabilities, such as minimum traffic and revenue guarantees, as well as their direct financial contributions.

Overall, the type and level of government financial contribution to the concession project should be limited to the extent required to attract private financing and promote a successful project. A commitment by the government to repay the project's debt is called a government guarantee (Irwin 2005). If public financial support is appropriate, several mechanisms can be used to support private financing. Fishbein and Babbar (1996: 26–27) illustrate, for the case of road projects:

1 *Equity guarantees*, under which the concessionaire is granted an option to be bought out by the government with a guaranteed minimum return on equity. Although equity guarantees entail no public cost as long as the project generates the minimum return on equity, the government essentially assumes all of the project risks, and the private sector performance incentives are severely reduced.
2 *Debt guarantees*, under which the government provides a full guarantee or a cash-flow deficiency guarantee for repayment of loans. As in the above case, there is no public cost under this arrangement as long as sufficient cash flow is generated to service debt; the private sector performance incentives are also reduced.
3 *Shadow toll*, which is paid to the concessionaire by the government, not charged to motorists, on the basis of volume and composition of traffic. The concept was created for DBFO (Design, Build, Finance and Operate) roads in the UK, and is also used in other countries (e.g. Finland, Portugal).
4 *Availability fee or annuity*, which is paid to the concessionaire by the government based on the availability of required capacity (number of lanes), irrespective of the traffic volumes.
5 *Minimum traffic or revenue guarantees*, in which the government compensates the concessionaire in cash if traffic or revenue falls below a specified minimum level (for example, 90 per cent of the expected traffic volume). In Spain, for example, the compensation is based on 50 per cent of the shortfall. Conversely, if revenues are higher than forecast, the concessionaire shares the surplus with the government, also on a 50 per cent basis.

In the case of the road sector, different forms of concession contracts, such as availability fee, shadow tolls, build-operate-transfer (BOT), and build-own-operate (BOO), provide increased risk transfers to the private sector. In particular, under BOT and BOO the demand risks are borne by the private partner. A schematic representation of such risk transfers from the public sector to the private sector, for different forms of road concessions, is given in Figure 4.2. *Mutatis mutandis*, such schematic representation also applies to other infrastructure sectors.

The cost of public sector risk bearing is an important element to consider when evaluating PPP proposals and should be used in the evaluation of PPP programmes. One of the key

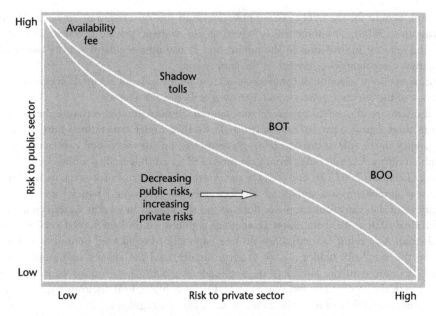

Figure 4.2 Schematic allocation of risks by forms of road concessions

Source: Adapted from Figure 1 of Queiroz (2006)

premises that should be considered using PPPs is the optimum allocation of project risks to the partner that is best able to manage them cost effectively. Consequently, to truly assess the impact of private sector involvement, governments need to adopt an approach to quantify the short-term impacts of the project on the public budget and the long-term potential cost of the risks the government chooses to retain (Aldrete *et al.* 2010).

Greenfield PPP projects include investment in new construction by the concessionaire, while in maintenance/rehabilitation/operation (MRO) concessions the concessionaire agrees to assume responsibility for an existing facility (e.g. a road or part of a road network). Several concession options are available and each country should select the most appropriate for its specific needs. Through the most common forms of concession, a country can transfer to the private sector the responsibility to: 1) build, operate and transfer (BOT) back to the public sector (at the end of the concession period) a facility (for example, a motorway, bridge, tunnel), or 2) maintain, rehabilitate, operate (MRO concessions) an existing facility.

When the main purpose of the concession is to obtain additional funds to those available in the country's budget, or release limited public funds for use on other infrastructure facilities (for example, secondary and rural roads), shadow-tolls (whereby payments to concessionaires are made out of the budget, based on traffic volumes and classification) and availability fees (whereby payments to concessionaires are made out of the budget, based on lane availability) would not be feasible options, except insofar as they postpone the budgetary burden.

4.12 Good governance in PPP projects

Because PPP projects in infrastructure tend to have monopolistic features, good governance in managing them is essential to ensure that the private sector's involvement yields the maximum benefit for the public. Good governance in this case requires, *inter alia* (Queiroz and Izaguirre 2008), 1) competitively selecting the strategic private investor, 2) properly disclosing relevant information to the public, and 3) having a regulatory entity oversee the contractual agreements over the life of the concession.

The competitive selection of concessionaires, usually considered essential for economy and efficiency of the selection process, was discussed earlier in the chapter.

Full disclosure of concession agreements, an indication of good governance, helps ensure that the users know what to expect from the facility under concession, thus increasing transparency in the role of the regulator. Nevertheless, not all concession contracts are open to public scrutiny. Excuses range from a claimed need for confidentiality to the cost of photocopying (*Economist* 2007). In one country in Central and Eastern Europe, the main text of a concession agreement was published but key annexes including financial and technical obligations of the concessionaire were not open to the public. In a Latin American country, the full final draft of the concession agreements is published, but the signed version is kept confidential. As a result, potential last-minute negotiations conducted behind closed doors between the successful bidder (i.e. the concessionaire) and the agency responsible for the project, if inserted in the contract, are not made available to the public or to the other contenders in the competitive bidding process (Queiroz 2009). Full disclosure, in every case, increases accountability of both the concessionaire and the regulator.

Many countries have established regulatory agencies that monitor the performance of infrastructure facilities under concession. For example in 2001 Brazil established the National Agency for Land Transport, which, *inter alia*, monitors federal road concessions (Brazil 2001).

Roads and other infrastructure concession contracts typically include required standards for construction, operation, maintenance, and toll (or fee) collection. For monitoring the quality of the facility during the life of the concession, several indicators of condition are usual. In the case of roads, such indicators include surface roughness, skid resistance, luminescence of pavement markings, and the presence and condition of signs, lighting and other safety features. Performance on these indicators that falls outside the boundaries of acceptability may lead to penalties for the concessionaire. Enforcing such standards helps the government and the users to reap maximum benefits of road concessions.

4.13 Conclusions

This chapter has presented a review of the legal framework required for attracting private capital for PPP projects, PSC, possible steps for a country to launch a programme of private participation in infrastructure, different forms of concessions, and the treatment of unsolicited proposals, risks, and government support. It has also summarized the requirements for good governance in PPP projects. Because such projects in infrastructure tend to have monopolistic features, good governance in managing them is essential to ensure that the private sector's involvement yields the maximum benefit for the public. Good governance in this case requires, *inter alia*, 1) competitively selecting the strategic private investor, 2) properly disclosing relevant information to the public, and 3) having a regulatory entity oversee the contractual agreements over the life of the concession. Seemingly non-legal issues, such as a risk matrix and procurement procedures, are also discussed because they are also relevant to an enabling legal PPP framework.

There has been, so far, relatively low private financing of roads and other infrastructure in transition and developing economies. The reasons for this include lack of appropriate legal framework, economic and political instability and consequent high perception of risks and relatively low demand for infrastructure services. As appropriate legislation is enacted, institutions and economic growth become more sustainable, and there is higher demand for infrastructure (for example, traffic has increased substantially on key roads and corridors), it seems fair to expect that the sector will become more attractive to private investors. High economic growth figures dramatically reduce the demand risks faced by private sector investors, thus reducing the need for minimum revenue guarantees.

Nevertheless, appropriate legal structures are a key success factor. Promoting sound and well-functioning legal systems minimizes risks and assists the development of an attractive investment climate in a country.

Acknowledgements

The authors benefited from comments by Piet de Vries. This chapter reflects only the authors' views, and should be used and cited accordingly. The findings, interpretations, and conclusions are the authors' own.

References

Akitoby, Bernardin, Hemming, Richard and Schwartz, Gerd. 2007. 'Public Investment and Public–Private Partnerships.' *Economic Issue No. 40*, International Monetary Fund, Washington, DC. http://www.ebrd.com/downloads/legal/concessions/pppimf.pdf (accessed 3 September 2010).

Aldrete, R., Bujanda, A. and Valdez-Ceniceros, G.A. 2010. *Valuing Public Sector Risk Exposure in Transportation Public-Private Partnerships*. University Transportation Center for Mobility. Texas Transportation Institute, Texas. http://utcm.tamu.edu/publications/final_reports/Aldrete_08-41-01.pdf (accessed 15 November 2010).

Amorelli, Lara. 2009. *Brazilian Federal Road Concessions: New challenges to the regulatory framework*. Institute of Brazilian Business and Management Issues, Minerva Program, George Washington University, Washington, DC. http://www.gwu.edu/~ibi/minerva/Spring2009/Lara.pdf (accessed 30 June 2010).

Amos, Paul. 2004. 'Public and Private Sector Roles in the Supply of Transport Infrastructure and Services: Operational Guidance for World Bank Staff.' *World Bank Transport Paper No. 1*. The World Bank, Washington, DC. http://siteresources.worldbank.org/INTTRANSPORT/214578-1099319223335/20273720/tp-1_pp-roles.pdf (accessed 2 August 2010).

Bain, Robert. 2009. 'Error and Optimism Bias in Toll Road Traffic Forecasts.' *Transportation*, Volume 36, Number 5, September 2009. Springer, The Netherlands. http://www.springerlink.com/content/p8306526tn94515m (accessed 10 November 2010).

Brazil. 2001. National Agency for Land Transport. Brazil. http://www.antt.gov.br (accessed 29 October 2010)

Chile. 1997. *Chile Concession Regulation No. 956*. Ministerio de Obras Publicas. Santiago, Chile. http://siteresources.worldbank.org/INTINFANDLAW/Resources/Chileanconcessionregulations.pdf (accessed 21 September 2010).

Delmon, Jeffrey. 2009. *Private Sector Investment in Infrastructure: Project Finance, PPP Projects and Risks*. Co-publication of the World Bank and Kluwer Law International.

EBRD. 2005. *Update on Best International Practices in Public Private Partnership with Regards to Regional Policy Issues – Executive Summary of the Review Report*, November 2005. London. http://www.ebrd.com/downloads/legal/concessions/execsumm.pdf (accessed 2 November 2010).

EBRD. 2010a. *Legal Transition Programme*. European Bank for Reconstruction and Development, London, UK. http://www.ebrd.com/pages/sector/legal.shtml (accessed 3 September 2010).

EBRD. 2010b. *Legal Transition Programme: Legal Reform Projects, 1996 to April 2010*. European Bank for Reconstruction and Development, London, UK. http://www.ebrd.com/downloads/legal/corporate/ltprojects.pdf (accessed 10 November 2010).

The Economist. 2007. 'Who Benefits from the Minerals?' Volume 384, Number 8547, September 22, p 62. London.

European Commission. 2003. *Guidelines for the Development of Successful Public-Private Partnerships*. Brussels, Belgium. http://ec.europa.eu/regional_policy/sources/docgener/guides/ppp_en.pdf (accessed 8 November 2010).

European Commission. 2004. *Resource Book on PPP Case Studies*. Brussels, Belgium. http://ec.europa.eu/regional_policy/sources/docgener/guides/pppresourcebook.pdf (accessed 8 November 2010).

European Parliament. 2007. *New Financial Instruments for European Transport Infrastructure and Services*. Directorate General Internal Policies of the Union. Report preparared by ECORYS Nederland BV, June 2007, pp 20–22. http://www.pedz.uni-mannheim.de/daten/edz-ma/ep/07/pe379.207_en.pdf (accessed 23 March 2011).

European Parliament. 2010. *Resolution of 16 June 2010 on economic governance. Paragraph 25*. http://www.europarl.europa.eu/sides/getDoc.do?type=TA&reference=P7-TA-2010-0224&format=XML&language=EN (accessed 20 September 2010).

Fishbein, G. and Babbar, S. 1996. *Private Financing of Toll Roads*. World Bank. Washington, DC. http://rru.worldbank.org/Documents/Toolkits/Highways/pdf/05.pdf (accessed 15 October 2010).

Fitzgerald, Peter. 2004. *Review of Partnerships Victoria Provided Infrastructure*. Final Report to the Treasurer, State Government of Victoria, Australia. Appendix A List of recommendations. http://www.partnerships.vic.gov.au/CA25708500035EB6/WebObj/PPPFinalFitzgeraldJan2004Review/$File/PPP%20Final%20Fitzgerald%20%20Jan%202004Review.pdf (accessed 6 March 2011).

Freshfields Bruckhaus Deringer. 2005. *Competitive dialogue: the EU's new procurement procedure*. http://www.freshfields.com/publications/pdfs/2005/13494.pdf (accessed 6 March 2011).

Guasch, J. Luis. 2004. *Granting and Renegotiating Infrastructure Concessions – Doing It Right*. World Bank Institute Development Studies. The World Bank. Washington, DC. http://www-wds.worldbank.org/servlet/WDSContentServer/WDSP/IB/2004/05/06/000090341_20040506150118/Rendered/PDF/288160PAPER0Granting010renegotiating.pdf. (accessed 30 August 2010).

Harris, Clive. 2003. *Private Participation in Infrastructure in Developing Countries: Trends, Impacts, and Policy Lessons*. World Bank Working Paper No. 5. p25. The World Bank. Washington, DC. http://rru.worldbank.org/Documents/PapersLinks/1481.pdf (accessed 23 March 2011).

Harris, C., Hodges, J., Schur M. and Shukla, P. 2003. *Infrastructure Projects: A Review of Canceled Private Projects*. Public Policy for the Private Sector, Note No. 252. The World Bank. Washington, DC. http://rru.worldbank.org/Documents/PublicPolicyJournal/252Harri-010303.pdf (accessed 2 August 2010).

Hodges, J. 2003a. *Unsolicited Proposals – Competitive Solutions for Private Infrastructure*. Public Policy for the Private Sector, Note No. 258. The World Bank. Washington, DC. http://rru.worldbank.org/Documents/PublicPolicyJournal/258Hodge-031103.pdf (accessed 22 September 2010).

Hodges, J. 2003b. *Unsolicited Proposals – The Issues for Private Infrastructure Projects*. Public Policy for the Private Sector, Note No. 257. The World Bank. Washington, DC. http://rru.worldbank.org/Documents/PublicPolicyJournal/257Hodge-031103.pdf (accessed 22 September 2010).

India. 2009. *Public Private Partnership in State Highways: Model Concession Agreement*. Planning Commission, Government of India, 2nd edn, April 2009. New Delhi, India.

Irwin, Timothy. 2005. *Government Guarantees for Private Infrastructure*. Presented at the Workshop on Public–Private Partnerships in Highways: Institutional, Legal, Financial and Technical Aspects, October 6, 2005. The World Bank. Washington, DC. http://web.worldbank.org/WBSITE/EXTERNAL/TOPICS/EXTTRANSPORT/0,,contentMDK:20676743~pagePK:148956~piPK:216618~theSitePK:337116,00.html (accessed 5 November 2010).

Irwin, Timothy. 2007. *Government Guarantees: Allocating and Valuing Risk in Privately Financed Infrastructure Projects*. World Bank, Washington, DC. http://siteresources.worldbank.org/INTSDNETWORK/Resources/Government_Guarantees.pdf (accessed 10 November 2010).

Kerf, Michel, et. al. 1998. *Concessions for Infrastructure: A Guide to Their Design and Award*. World Bank Technical Paper No. 399, p.10. World Bank, Washington, DC. http://rru.worldbank.org/Documents/Toolkits/concessions_fulltoolkit.pdf (accessed 22 March 2011).

Leigland, James. 2006. *Is the Public Sector Comparator Right for Developing Countries? Appraising Public–Private Projects in Infrastructure*. Public–Private Infrastructure Advisory Facility and the World Bank: Washington DC. http://www.ppiaf.org/ppiaf/sites/ppiaf.org/files/publication/Gridlines-4-Is%20the%20Public%20Sector%20Comparator%20-%20JLeigland%20CShugart.pdf (accessed 15 September 2010).

Macário, Rosário. 2010. *Critical issues in the design of contractual relations for transport infrastructure development*. Research in Transportation Economics. Elsevier. Amsterdam. http://www.elsevier.com/locate/retrec (accessed 18 November 2010).

Matsukawa, Tomoko and Odo Habeck. 2007. *Review of Risk Mitigation Instruments for Infrastructure Financing and Recent Trends and Developments*. Trends and Policy Options No. 4, Public–Private Infrastructure Advisory Facility (PPIAF) and the World Bank: Washington DC. http://www.ppiaf.org/ppiaf/publications/Trends%20and%20Policy%20Options (accessed 20 September 2010).

PPIAF/World Bank. 2009. *Toolkit for PPP in Roads and Highways*. World Bank and Public–Private Infrastructure Advisory Facility (PPIAF). Washington, DC. http://www.ppiaf.org/ppiaf/sites/ppiaf.org/files/documents/toolkits/highwaystoolkit/4/4-22.html (accessed 3 September 2010).

PPIAF/World Bank. 2010. *The PPI Database*. World Bank and Public–Private Infrastructure Advisory Facility (PPIAF). Washington, DC. http://www.worldbank.org/ppi (accessed 17 November 2010).

Queiroz, Cesar. 1999. *Highway Concessions and World Bank Guarantees*. International Road Federation Regional Conference on European Transport and Roads. Lahti, Finland, 14–16 June 1999.

Queiroz, Cesar. 2006. *The Potential of Private Financing to Enhance Road Infrastructure in the Baltic States*. 26th International Baltic Road Conference, Kuressaare (Saaremaa), Estonia, 28–30 August 2006. http://www.bjrbe.vgtu.lt/news/news002.php.

Queiroz, Cesar. 2007. 'Public–Private Partnerships in Highways in Transition Economies: Recent Experience and Future Prospects.' *Transportation Research Record: Journal of the Transportation Research Board*, Issue Number 1996, pp 34–40. US National Research Council, Washington, DC. http://pubsindex.trb.org/view.aspx?id=801043 (accessed 12 October 2010).

Queiroz, Cesar. 2009. *Financing of Road Infrastructure*. Proceedings of the 5th Symposium on Strait Crossings, June 21–24, 2009, pp45–57. ISBN 978-82-92506—69-1. Trondheim, Norway. http://www.straitcrossings.com (accessed 25 October 2010).

Queiroz, Cesar and Visser, Alex. 2001. *Corruption, Transport Infrastructure Stock and Economic Development*. Infrastructure and Poverty Briefing for the World Bank Infrastructure Forum, CD-ROM. World Markets Research Centre Ltd. The World Bank. Washington, DC. http://www2.udec.cl/~provial/expo/WB%20Infrast%20Forum%20May%202001%20TranspInfra&Corrup%20CQ%20AV.pdf (accessed 20 September 2010).

Queiroz, Cesar and Izaguirre, Ada Karina. 2008. *Worldwide Trends in Private Participation in Roads: Growing Activity, Growing Government Support*. Gridlines series, no. 37, Public–Private Infrastructure Advisory Facility-PPIAF, Washington, DC. http://www.ppiaf.org/ppiaf/sites/ppiaf.org/files/publication/Gridlines-37-Worldwide%20Trends%20in%20Private%20-%20CQueiroz%20AIzaguirre.pdf (accessed 22 September 2010).

Queiroz, Cesar and Kerali, Henry. 2010. *A Review of Institutional Arrangements for Road Asset Management: Lessons for the Developing World*. World Bank Transport Paper No. TP-32. Washington, DC. http://go.worldbank.org/6HDCYBMRT0 (accessed 8 November 2010).

Standard & Poor's (S&P). 2002. *Traffic Risk in Start-Up Toll Facilities*. London.

Transparency International. 2005. *Granting a Concession for the Trakia Motorway: Interim Report*. Sofia, Bulgaria. Http://www.transparency-bg.org/?magic=0.5.71.2 (accessed 10 November 2010).

Stubbs, Timothy and Higgins, Mary Faith. 2010. *Creditors' rights: the Russian revolution*. In Law in Transition 2010. European Bank for Reconstruction and Development, London. http://www.ebrd.com/downloads/research/law/lit10e.pdf (accessed 17 November 2010).

UK HM Treasury. 2006. *Value for Money Assessment Guidance*, pp15–19. London. http://www.hm-treasury.gov.uk/d/vfm_assessmentguidance061006opt.pdf (accessed 26 October 2010).

UK PFI. 2008. *Public Private Partnerships, Private Finance Initiative*. London. http://webarchive.nationalarchives.gov.uk/+/http://www.hm-treasury.gov.uk/documents/public_private_partnerships/ppp_index.cfm (accessed 4 November 2010).

UNCITRAL. 2004 *Model Legislative Provisions on Privately Financed Infrastructure Projects*. United Nations, New York. http://www.uncitral.org/pdf/english/texts/procurem/pfip/model/03-90621_Ebook.pdf (accessed 20 September 2010).

Véron, Adrien and Cellier, Jacques. 2010. *Private Participation in the Road Sector in Brazil: Recent Evolution and Next Steps*. World Bank Transport Paper No. TP-30. Washington, DC. http://go.worldbank.org/6HDCYBMRT0 (accessed 1 November 2010).

World Bank. 2004a. *Reducing the 'Economic Distance' to Market: A Framework for the Development of the Transport System in South East Europe*. Washington, DC. http://wbln0018.worldbank.org/ECA/

Transport.nsf/ECADocByLink/BEF3FC761FF49D0785256FB200508860?Opendocument (accessed 8 November 2010).

World Bank. 2004b. *Guidelines: Procurement under IBRD Loans and IDA Credits.* May 2004 (Revised October 2006 and May 2010). The World Bank. Washington, DC. http://go.worldbank. org/1KKD1KNT40 (accessed 8 November 2010).

World Bank. 2010a. *Guidance Note: Procurement arrangements applicable to Public-Private Partnerships (PPP) contracts financed under World Bank projects.* Washington, DC.

World Bank. 2010b. *PPP Laws/Concession Laws.* Washington, DC. http://go.worldbank.org/ JXBNHBLKB0 (accessed 10 November 2010).

World Bank. 2010c. *PPP in Infrastructure Resource Center for Contracts, Laws and Regulation (PPPIRC).* Washington, DC. http://www.worldbank.org/pppiresource (accessed 10 November 2010).

World Bank. 2010d. *World Bank Guarantee Program.* Washington, DC. http://web.worldbank.org/ external/default/main?menuPK=64143540&pagePK=64143532&piPK=64143559&theSitePK= 3985219 (accessed 10 November 2010).

Part III

Institutional economics and public–private partnerships

Risk allocation, transaction cost economics and PPP

Xiao-Hua Jin

5.1 Introduction

The level of infrastructure provision is a major factor in the attractiveness of a country or region for overseas investment. The impact of infrastructure on economy, environment and the provision of services collectively promote the quality of life. There have been increasing demands for the delivery of new infrastructure and the maintenance of existing assets. Conventionally, infrastructure has been provided and funded by governments. However, the performance in delivering public sector projects remains poor. In addition, conventional provision method has subjected infrastructure development to the availability of governmental funds. Such fiscal stresses experienced by governments have been exacerbating investment needs. Over recent years, governments around the world have redefined their role by restructuring, corporatizing or privatizing some areas of government activity that had been deemed core in the past. The concept of providing concessions for financially unattractive projects has enabled governments to maintain a strategic interest in the infrastructure and has led to a range of PPP arrangements.

Although appropriate risk allocation is a great driver of value for money (VFM) in PPP projects, the complexity of the arrangements and incomplete contracting nature of PPPs have led to increased risk exposure for all the parties involved (Jin 2010a). Therefore, the decision-making on efficient risk allocation in PPP projects is no easy job. How do public and private partners allocate risks between themselves? In particular, why is a particular risk is transferred to a private consortium in one project while retained by government or shared in another? Most importantly, is there any mechanism guiding the formation of risk allocation strategies? The answers to these questions are critically important to the success (or failure) of PPP projects (Jin 2010a).

In this chapter, we will take a close look at the current or traditional risk allocation in construction and, in particular, PPP projects. We will examine the risk allocation practice in three Australian PPP projects based on the principles of optimal risk allocation. The weaknesses of the traditional risk allocation practices, which are mainly (organizational) risk management (RM) capability-oriented, will thus be highlighted. We will later make the case for the necessity of tackling risk allocation decision making (RADM) from a perspective of transaction cost economics (TCE) augmented with organizational capability (in particular resource-based view (RBV)). It is because TCE integrates economics, organization theory, contract law and behavioural assumptions in an interdisciplinary framework of organizational phenomena and takes account of the role of transaction costs and informational issues that the self-interested economic agent faces, that we claim and adopt the TCE plus RBV approach as one suitable to the study of risk allocation. After a brief introduction to the TCE theories, we will discuss and analyse the risk allocation decision-making process from the perspective of TCE. From a TCE perspective, the RADM process could actually be viewed as the process of deciding the proportion of risk management responsibility between internal and external organizations (i.e. public and private partners in PPP projects) based on a series of characteristics of the risk management service transaction in question. Finally, this chapter is concluded with recommendations for further study on risk allocation in PPP projects using TCE.

5.2 Risk allocation in PPP projects: current or traditional practices

While risk transfer is one of the major drivers for VFM in PPPs, it is also an area criticized as problematic and controversial. Therefore, current or traditional risk allocation in PPP projects is discussed in this section. Risk allocation practice in Australia is examined using a number of PPP projects as empirical evidence. While weakness and problems of traditional risk allocation are revealed, it is acknowledged that traditional risk allocation is mainly based on organizational capability, which is an essential consideration of the principles for optimal risk allocation.

5.2.1 Risk allocation in PPP projects

Joint Australia/New Zealand standards AS/NZS 4360:2004 defined risk as 'the chance of something happening that will have an impact upon objectives' (AS/NZS 2004: 2). In the context of PPPs, a risk is 'the chance of an event occurring which would cause actual project circumstances to differ from those assumed when forecasting project benefit and costs' (DTF 2001: 16). To the public sector, a risk may be 'any event which jeopardizes the quality or quantity of service that they have contracted for' whilst to the private sector it may be 'any event which causes the cash flow profile of the project to depart from the base case and jeopardize the debt servicing ability of the project or its ability to generate a dividend stream for shareholders' (Arndt 1999: 3). Risks emerge over time, are indeterminate and often endogenous. Given the complexity, longevity and large size of PPP projects, there is a wide range of potential risks that can affect expected outcomes. These risks have been identified in previous research such as Thomas *et al.* (2003).

It is well known that the allocation of risks to contracting parties significantly influences the behaviour of the project participants and has a substantial impact on project performance. Improper allocation of risks among stakeholders leads to sub-optimality and higher-than-necessary prices for risk transfer (Jin 2010a). In traditional public projects, the public sector purchases an asset from private sector contractors and consultants whose liability is limited to the design and construction of the asset. Financial and operational risks remain with the public sector. Risk allocation in PPP projects is fundamentally different. The PPP model involves the purchase of a relatively risk-free long-term service. The government bears little or no asset-based risk and is entitled to reducing payments, abatements and compensation if the service is not delivered to the specified standards.

Major risks are allocated among project participants mainly through contracts, e.g. through payment mechanisms and disclaimer clauses. A contract has been deemed an efficient and effective instrument to define the duties and responsibilities of each party and assign risks between them. However, due to the fact that not all the risks are foreseeable and not all the project information is available at the outset, effective risk allocation cannot be achieved through contract conditions alone (Rahman and Kumaraswamy 2002). Unfortunately, risk transfer is often handled poorly in PPP projects. Many studies have suggested that there is a disparity in perceptions on both actual and preferred risk allocation, both within and between different contracting parties (see e.g. Kangari 1995; Ahmed *et al.* 1999; Rahman and Kumaraswamy 2002). Sometimes risks will inevitably be allocated to the party least able to refuse them rather than the party best able to manage them, especially when the government maintains maximum competitive tension. This has been found to have major limitations. Therefore, inappropriate risk allocation can damage the VFM proposition of a PPP arrangement; and government should aim to transfer risks only to the party who can manage them best and minimize the overall cost of a project.

5.2.2 Optimal risk allocation

Optimal risk allocation seeks to minimize not only project costs but also the risks to the project by allocating particular risks to the party in the best position to control them. This is based on the principle that the party in the strongest position of control or possessing the best capability of management with respect to a particular risk has the best opportunity to reduce the likelihood of the risk eventuation and to control the consequences of the risk if it materializes, and thus should assume it (Rahman and Kumaraswamy 2002; Thomas *et al.* 2003). Allocating the risk in line with those opportunities creates an incentive for the controlling party to use its influence to prevent or mitigate the risk and to use its capacity to do so in the overall interests of the project. Optimal risk allocation will also lead to lower risk premiums and therefore reduces overall project costs.

In order to achieve an optimal risk allocation, a number of rules and principles have been established. The two most important are: 1) a risk should be borne by the party who possesses the best capability; and 2) a risk should be borne by the party who presents willingness or commitment. Nonetheless, one serious problem in the construction industry is that, although decisions have to be made about allocating risks, very little consideration has been given to basic risk allocation principles when negotiating contracts. Although many governments now recognize that privatization is a partnership in which they must retain some risk, the principle of optimal risk allocation is often not followed in many PPP infrastructure projects (Faulkner 2004; Jin 2009; Thomas *et al.* 2003).

Risk allocation practices in PPP projects have been found to be highly variable, intuitive, subjective and unsophisticated (Ng and Loosemore 2007). Discussions about which categories of risk should generally be accepted or transferred by governments are currently ongoing. Given its critical importance in PPP projects, a number of studies have been conducted to explore how to achieve optimal risk allocation, such as Arndt (1999), Thomas *et al.* (2003), and Ng and Loosemore (2007). Nonetheless, these studies either oversimplify the risk allocation process as one that is only affected by agents' risk attitudes or management capabilities; or lack theoretical foundations and/or empirical evidence to support their submissions.

5.2.3 Risk allocation practice in PPP projects – three cases in Australia

In this section, three recent infrastructure projects in Australia using PPP procurement methods are selected to critically investigate the current risk allocation practice adopted in

Australian PPP projects. The projects are: 1) the Southern Cross Station redevelopment (SCS) project in Melbourne, Victoria; 2) the Cross City Tunnel (CCT) project in Sydney, NSW; and 3) the Royal Children's Hospital (RCH) redevelopment project in Melbourne, Victoria. The information about the three projects is summarized in Table 5.1. Each project is used to examine the risk allocation practice regarding different risk categories, as shown in the last row of Table 5.1. For each risk category, information about the relevant project is briefly introduced. Based on the information, possible reasons for appropriate or problematic decision on risk allocation are discussed.

5.2.3.1 Allocation of financial risks

Financial risks are the risks that prevent or frustrate the financiers or financial sponsors from fulfilling their contractual obligations to the project (DFA 2005; DTF 2001), such as private consortium's financial failure or delay, and adverse change in interest rates or tax.

Table 5.1 Information about three selected PPP projects

	Project		
	SCS	CCT	RCH
State	Victoria	New South Wales	Victoria
Value	AUS$700 million	AUS$700 million	AUS$946 million
Concession period	30 years	30 years	25 years
Public agency	State Rail Authority of Victoria	Roads and Traffic Authority (RTA) of NSW	Victorian Department of Health
Private contractor (consortium)	Civic Nexus	CrossCity Motorway Pty Limited	Children's Health Partnership
Private sponsors	ABN AMRO	Bilfinger Berger AG, Baulderstone Hornibrook Pty Limited, and Deutsche Bank AG	Babcock & Brown International Pty Ltd
Design and construction contractor	Leighton Contractors	Baulderstone Hornibrook Bilfinger Berger Cross City Tunnel Joint Venture (BHBB JV) (formed by Bilfinger Berger AG and Baulderstone Hornibrook Pty Limited)	Bovis Lend Lease Pty Ltd
Operation/ Maintenance contractor	Leighton Contractors	Baulderstone Hornibrook Pty Limited	Spotless P&F Pty Ltd
Design consultants	Daryl Jackson Architects associated with Grimshaw Architects	Connell Wagner and Hyder	Billard Leece, Bates Smart and HKS
Risk categories discussed	Financial risks; planning and design risks; construction risks; and market risks	Political, legislative and regulative risks	Operating risks

The allocation of financial risks is investigated by studying the Southern Cross Station redevelopment (SCS) project.

The SCS project is one of the largest infrastructure projects in Victoria that adopted *Partnerships Victoria* policy. The Civic Nexus consortium won the bid in July 2002. The government would pay Civic Nexus AUS$34 million per annum for 30 years. In return, Civic Nexus would be responsible for maintaining the facility. Afterwards, the ownership of the station will be transferred to the government. This payment stream was equivalent to a net present value (NPV) of AUS$309 million at a nominal pre-tax discounting rate of 8.65 per cent and involved a saving against the risk-adjusted cost of the Public Service Comparator (PSC) at 5 per cent. In addition, Civic Nexus would pay the government AUS$66 million for commercial development rights via a 99-year lease for the properties adjacent to the station.

In order to finance the construction, Civic Nexus issued three tranches of bonds, including an AUS$135 million indexed bond with a 30-year maturity, an AUS$200 million fixed-rate bond with a 12-year maturity, and a US$73.9 million bond with a 12-year maturity specifically targeted at US investors. ABN AMRO was the underwriter and provided a 12-year cross currency swap to mitigate the currency risk. In addition, Leighton Contractors provided AUS$60 million in case there would be construction overruns or failure. Due to the existence of a series of mechanisms to cover risks, both bonds attracted investors. In December 2003, ABN AMRO announced that it had formed a Social Infrastructure Strategic Alliance with Development Australia Fund Management Ltd. (DAF) to acquire and manage Social Infrastructure investments for superannuation funds. As a result, DAF gained a 75 per cent equity stake in the project. The financial structure of SCS is illustrated below in Figure 5.1.

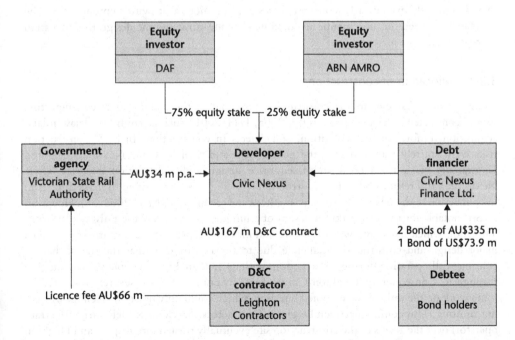

Figure 5.1 Financial structure of Southern Cross Station redevelopment project

In SCS, financial risks such as Civic Nexus' financial failure or delay were appropriately allocated to Civic Nexus and thus well managed and mitigated. The information presented above revealed the main characteristics of the allocation of financial risks, such as Civic Nexus' strong financial capacity, mature and stable financial and insurance markets, appropriate financing tools utilized, stable legislative and regulatory system and strong regional economy in which SCS was developed. The appropriate match between these characteristics and the adopted risk allocation strategy might contribute to the risk management success.

5.2.3.2 Allocation of planning and design risks

Planning and design risks are the risks that the planning and design processes of the facility could generate on the contracted service delivery (DFA 2005; DTF 2001), such as output specification changes and design defects. In SCS, the private party was responsible for design risk. However, the government paid Leighton Contractors $32.25 million to cover time and cost overruns resulting from contract variations, including a new tram superstop and a new train refuelling facility. This was because, according to *Partnerships Victoria*, the public party will be responsible for design risk 'where an express Government mandated change has caused the design defect' (DTF 2001). It is hard to imagine that the government did not anticipate such needs and include them in the project specifications before the contract was signed. As the government did not possess the expertise of conceptual design, it might have been   better if they had the performance requirements and parameters determined after selecting a particular urban or architectural design. Although SCS bears high technical novelty, generally design-specific investment is relatively small. Considering these characteristics, would it be better if this design risk were also transferred to the private sector? It is evident that design risk, particularly conceptual design, was not dealt with appropriately. The mismatch between the aforementioned design-related features and the design risk allocation strategy might be a major reason.

5.2.3.3 Allocation of construction risks

Construction risks refer to the construction processes of the facility adversely impacting on the contracted service delivery (DFA 2005; DTF 2001), such as failure or delay in land acquisition, unforeseen site condition, and defects in construction. In SCS, construction risks were entirely transferred by the government and then by Civic Nexus to Leighton Contractors via a fixed term and fixed price design and construction contract. Civic Nexus took full responsibility for construction risks and was 'not entitled to make any claim in connection with construction means, methods and techniques' (AAR 2002: 58). However, SCS is notable for the architectural design of a unique roof to cover the railway platforms. This roof, which has a two-way curvature and measures a massive 4.2 hectares, presented a major design and construction challenge due to the requirement that the station had to continue full operation during construction, with more than 30,000 people per day moving through it. Consequently, Leighton Contractors' operating time was severely restricted by some work on the unique wave-roofed building, which could only be done when trains were not running. This conflict between Leighton Contractors and Connex Melbourne (the train operator) over the access to the construction site eventually turned into dispute and Leighton Contractors made a claim on the resultant losses (Tomazin and Myer 2006).

Apparently, construction risks in SCS were not dealt with appropriately. One important reason might be that fully transferring construction risks to the private partner was not suitable for the construction-related characteristics in SCS, such as complex design and construction methods, ineffective communication between designer, constructor and operator, and the private partner's reluctance to fully burden construction risks (although forced to). A more efficient risk allocation strategy might be the government sharing a particular amount of construction risks, such as those caused by unforeseen issues, just as the Victorian government finally did by compensating Leighton Contractors for the cost and time overruns.

5.2.3.4 Allocation of market risks

Market risks are the risks that cause demand and/or price for a service to vary adversely from the initially projected amount so that the total revenue over the project term varies from initial expectations (DFA 2005; DTF 2001). Market risks include, but are not limited to, demand and revenue below anticipation, unanticipated economic downturn, adverse demographic change, and unanticipated inflation. In particular, inflation is a key market risk. *Partnerships Victoria* specifies that private party 'seeks an appropriate mechanism to maintain real value' and 'takes risk on the methodology adopted to maintain value' (DTF 2001). However, in SCS, the Victorian government bears the inflation risk by paying AUS$34 million per annum plus inflation over 30 years. A possible explanation is that the government might reckon that they are more capable of tackling inflation than the private partner. With regard to risk allocation, such arrangement might be more suitable for efficiently managing inflation risk, which is highly unstable in nature.

5.2.3.5 Allocation of political, legislative and regulatory risks

Political, legislative and regulatory risks refer to the risks that are caused by changes in legislation, regulation or policy, and prevent or frustrate the facility or related services from delivery (DFA 2005; DTF 2001). A change in law, policy or regulation that could not be anticipated at contract signing may bring about substantial cost or revenue effects. The Cross City Tunnel (CCT) project in Sydney, Australia is a recent example of the disastrous impact of such risks.

The private sector financed, designed and constructed the CCT project; and will own and operate it until December 2035 when the facilities are passed into public ownership. The tunnel opened to traffic four months ahead of schedule in August 2005 and the original toll was AUS$3.53. The high toll had been blamed for keeping patronage at barely a third of the 90,000 daily trips forecast and increasing chaos on surface roads. From March 2006, the toll was thus halved for three months to encourage motorists to use the tunnel. With the situation not improved, however, the government forced surface alternative road closures to funnel motorists into the tunnel probably because they were trying to increase patronage to the forecast level and shake off the electoral disadvantage of the CCT project on the upcoming election. The resultant anger by motorists and residents over this governmental action forced the government to reverse the changes in June 2006. Unfortunately, the reversal by the government over road changes set out in the CCT contract without the consent of the operator exposed the government to a multi-million-dollar damages claim. The CCT project went into receivership in December 2006 because it was unable to service AU$580 million in debts. In June 2007, the CCT project was sold to a consortium made up of ABN AMRO and Leighton Contractors for about AUS$695 million.

In this case, the occurrence of policy and regulation changes materialized the political and regulatory risks and further exacerbated the operation risks. Whether the private partner or the government should bear the consequences is still controversial, at least to the private sector. Some argue that government is more capable of and subsequently responsible for mitigating such risks by excluding such changes while others think private party is liable to assess legal, political and regulatory system before entering into the contract. In this chapter, in what scenario it is better for the government to retain, share or transfer this category of risks is of the most concern.

5.2.3.6 Allocation of operating risks

Finally, operating risks are the risks that adversely affect the process of contracted service delivery so that the contractor fails to deliver the contracted services (DFA 2005; DTF 2001), such as operation failure or delay, excessive maintenance and refurbishment, and adverse impact of core services delivery. The new Royal Children's Hospital (RCH) project is used to examine the allocation of operating risks and to demonstrate possible impact.

The new RCH project is the largest hospital redevelopment to be undertaken by the Victorian State Government, with a cost of AUS$946 million including both construction costs and facilities maintenance costs over 25 years, which is 6.9 per cent below the PSC. Project brief was released to bidders in October 2006. In November 2007, the Children's Health Partnership (CHP) was announced as the preferred private partner. The private partner will deliver the design and construction of a new facility adjacent to the existing site, with retention of two existing buildings; and provide facilities maintenance services for 25 years. Although it was stated that the Victorian government will continue to operate the hospital and provide all core clinical services, staffing, teaching, training and research, significant issues, including operating risks that may cause negligence and chaos in the routine service, have been in the spotlight. Government's transparency of decision-making, control capability, and relationship with private partner are among the most important factors that are deemed critical to the project success. In spite of the proposals that the health system needs to integrate more private participation, the question 'who should be responsible for operating risks' has aroused a lot of concerns and discussion in RCH.

5.2.4 Focus on organizational capability – necessary but insufficient

Based on the above examination on the risk allocation practice regarding different risk categories in several Australian PPP projects, it is apparent that the decisions on the allocation of some risks have generated positive outcome, such as those of financial, inflation and operating risks. Meanwhile, the decisions on the allocation of the other risks are deemed problematic, such as those of design, construction and regulatory risks. To a large extent, those problematic decisions on risk allocation were made with sole consideration of organizational capability in managing a relevant risk. In contrast, those successful decisions on risk allocation were reached with consideration not only of partners' risk management capability but also of other features revolved around the management of the relevant risk.

Therefore, the above discussion has made it clear that, in PPP projects, partners' organizational capability in risk management has been consistently considered during the risk allocation decision-making process and deemed as a major determinant of who should be responsible for various risks. This should be acknowledged with acclamation because the consideration of organizational capability is necessary for optimal risk allocation (and seems missing in the TCE approach, as discussed later). However, a sole consideration of partners' risk management capability does not seem to always work well. When other features of the relevant risk and its management are considered during the risk allocation decision-making process, there seems to be a greater chance of success in managing the risk, probably due to a better allocation strategy for the risk. These features are closely related to those of a transaction considered in the TCE approach, as described in later sections.

A number of theories have been established to address how firms may develop organizational capabilities. They primarily include the resource-based view (RBV) (Barney 1991; Wernerfelt 1984), dynamic capabilities (Teece *et al.* 1997), evolutionary economics (Nelson and Winter 1982), and the emerging knowledge-based view (KBV) (Conner and Prahalad 1996; Grant 1996; Kogut and Zander 1996). Among these theories, the RBV has more complementarities with the TCE due to their common focus on asset specificity (Rao 2003).

The RBV explains competitive heterogeneity based on the premise that close competitors differ in their capabilities and resources (i.e. the factors of production) in important and durable ways. Two basic conditions have been highlighted in the RBV. The first is that firms are largely heterogeneous in terms of their resources and capabilities. The second is that some of these resources and capabilities are limited in supply or costly to imitate. Such heterogeneity in turn affects competitive advantage and disadvantage. Therefore, non-imitable and non-substitutable organizational capabilities (and resources) are a key source of inter-firm performance differences. Less capable organization would incur more investments of time and resources to improve its capabilities to meet the requirements.

While greater risk management experience may be a necessary and important condition for organizations to build risk management capability, it may not be sufficient. Experience is only a crude approximation of the mechanisms that lie at the foundation of building organizational capability. Risk management capability would also rest upon how effectively the organization is able to capture, share, and disseminate the risk management know-how associated with prior experience. To the extent that organizations engage in risk management practices in a reasonably stable and repetitive pattern, these practices can be viewed as the management routines that form the basis for a risk management capability. Importantly, management routines also have implications on the asset specificity of a transaction, which is the most important characteristics of the TCE theory (which will be discussed in greater details in later sections). Therefore, the RBV plays a critical role in economic theory by providing one means to analyse the effect of organizational capabilities on governance decisions.

The TCE theory has been successfully employed to describe how transaction conditions affect the optimal form of governance. However, it has been found that decisions regarding governance structures are strongly influenced by both exchange conditions at the transaction level and organizational capabilities at the firm level (Jacobides and Winter 2005). Unfortunately, the TCE approach has historically neglected the differences in organizational capabilities by holding the constraint that firms maintain homogeneous capability (Jacobides and Hitt 2005). A more complete understanding of the organization of economic activity thus requires a greater sensitivity to the interdependence of production and exchange relations. It is believed that by relaxing this constraint and being integrated with the RBV, the TCE will provide a more logical and holistic understanding of governance decision.

In conclusion, it is expected that an optimal risk allocation is only achievable when partners' risk management capability and other features of the risk and its management, in particular those associated with the transaction of risk management services, are both fully considered. That is, the theories associated with both organizational capability in producing a good or service (in this case, the risk management service) and the transaction of the good or service need to be considered. Next, we will have a review on the transaction cost economics, which has not been carefully considered in association with risk allocation. Contrarily, the theories of organizational capability have been well examined in the pursuit of optimal risk allocation.

5.3 Transaction cost economics

The discussion and analysis in the previous section reveals that the current theoretical and practical basis, on which risk allocation strategies are formed, is organizational capability oriented. However, the design of risk allocation must also be judged on a cost-benefit basis due to the law of diminishing returns. This is because, when devising risk allocation strategies, at a certain point the costs of acquiring additional information or gaining further control over risks will exceed the extra value that can be created and thereby negative return occurs. Unfortunately, research in risk management has been concerned mainly with process (such as the four-step risk management process) and technique (such as various risk assessment tools based on probability or possibility). The part related to economics has not been incorporated yet. While both process and technique aspects aim at increasing efficacy, neither is successful in understanding what kind of existing governance structures best suits a particular project in terms of efficiency and why.

Transaction cost economics (TCE) can contribute to this. From a TCE perspective, the risk allocation decision-making (RADM) process could actually be viewed as the process of deciding the proportion of risk management responsibility between internal and external organizations (i.e. public and private partners in PPPs) based on a series of characteristics of the risk management service transaction in question (Jin and Doloi 2008). Moreover, the TCE theory can allow an examination of the relationship between organizational capability and the TCE approach to organizational governance to establish whether each enriches the other to further consolidate risk management and project management theory.

In this section, before we propose a theoretical framework for risk allocation decision-making in PPP projects based on TCE and RBV, major aspects of TCE will be briefly reviewed and discussed in the context of PPPs and risk allocation. These aspects include transaction costs, transaction dimensions (i.e. asset specificity, transaction frequency, and uncertainty), and transaction governance (i.e. 'market', 'hybrid' and 'hierarchy').

5.3.1 Background

The TCE approach was developed out of the institutional economics, which focuses on understanding the role of the evolutionary process and the role of institutions (e.g. individuals, firms, states, social norms) in shaping economic behaviour. This approach emerged from the economist Coase's seminal work, in which he argued that, in the absence of transaction costs, there is no economic basis for the existence of the firm (Coase 1937). TCE recognizes that the costs of using the pricing system give rise to various forms of economic organizations (Coase 1988). It represents a major attempt to combine economic and sociological perspectives on industrial organizations. This analysis supersedes neoclassical economic analysis, which assumes that economic activities can be coordinated costlessly by a system of prices and tells nothing about the organizational structure (Hart 1990).

TCE adopts a contractual approach to the study of economic organization (Williamson 1996). The essential insight of TCE is that in order to economize on the total costs of producing a good or providing a service, both 1) production costs, which are the costs of producing a good or providing a service by adopting a certain production technique without governance requirements, and 2) transaction (or governance) costs, which are the costs of governing the transactions inherent in that choice of production technique, must be taken into account (Williamson 1985, 1996). A production technique that has the lowest production costs might not be the economizing choice if transaction costs are also taken into account (Winch 2001). While a traditional economic analysis can identify the most efficient choice of production technique, it cannot explain the most effective use of that production technique (Winch 2006).

The TCE approach is suitable to the study on PPPs because TCE integrates economics, organization theory, contract law and behavioural assumptions in an interdisciplinary study of organizational phenomena (Williamson 1981). The comparative institutional approach adopted in TCE facilitates analysis in which the absolute amount of costs is difficult to collect (Williamson 1985). Making a transaction as the basic unit of analysis and using the 'governance structure' to include the organizational approaches required to regulate and control activities, Williamson (1981) generalized that the governance structures that have better transaction cost economizing properties prevail in the long run.

5.3.2 Transaction costs

Bounded rationality and *opportunism* are the two behavioural assumptions that support the TCE approach (Williamson 1981). *Bounded rationality* is in contrast to the traditional assumptions of economics of the perfectly rational being in that people act rationally but are limited by their analytical and data-processing capabilities. Similarly, in a situation where completeness is limited to a small number of entities, there is likely to be opportunistic exploitation of the situation or 'self-interest seeking with guile' (Williamson 1985: 47). When bounded rationality and asset specificity are joined with opportunism, the organization is compelled to 'organize transactions so as to economize on bounded rationality while simultaneously safeguarding them against the hazards of opportunism' (Williamson 1985: 32). Opportunism thus leads to the need for internal mechanisms such as administrative governance and ordering forces. The establishment and implementation of these mechanisms incur transaction costs.

Williamson (1985) described transaction costs as drafting and negotiating agreements, set-up and running costs of the governance structure which monitors and settles disputes, haggling costs, and bonding costs of effecting secure commitments. Regarding risk allocation, if a risk is improperly allocated, possible resultant transaction costs may include, among others: 1) the extra costs for clients of a higher contingency (or premium) included in the bid price from contractors; 2) the extra costs for clients of more resources for monitoring the risk management (RM) work; 3) the extra costs for clients and/or contractors of recovering lower quality work (i.e. the materialized or deteriorated risk) for a given price; 4) the extra costs for contractors of increasing safeguards (both *ex ante* and *ex post*) against any opportunistic exploitation of one's own risk management service-specific assets by other parties; 5) the extra costs for contractors of the resources dedicated to lodging claims related to the misallocated risk; 6) the extra costs for both parties of dealing with the disputes or litigation related to the misallocated risk.

5.3.3 Dimension of transaction

A transaction occurs whenever 'a good or service is transferred across a technologically separable interface' and 'one stage of activity terminates and another begins' (Williamson 1981: 552). The principal dimensions on which TCE presently relies for purposes of describing transactions are: 1) the frequency with which they occur; 2) the degree and type of uncertainty to which they are subject; and (3) the condition of asset specificity. The appropriate choice of transaction governance mode occupies a three-dimensional space as a function of the three features. These features are only troublesome in interaction with each other (Winch 2001). Without asset specificity, for example, any negotiations to handle unforeseen events can be made when they occur. Without uncertainty, complete contracts can be written in advance to foreclose opportunistic behaviour that arises from asset specificity. Without frequency, it would be difficult to determine whether or not there is any return on investing in transaction-specific governance modes.

5.3.3.1 Asset specificity

Asset specificity refers to 'the degree to which an asset can be redeployed to alternative uses and by alternative users without sacrifice of productive value' (Williamson 1996: 59). The full implications of asset specificity become evident only in the context of incomplete contracting (Williamson 1975). Asset specificity can take many forms and Williamson (1996) described six kinds of asset specificity, including: 1) site specificity; 2) physical asset specificity; 3) human asset specificity; 4) dedicated assets; 5) brand name capital; and 6) temporal specificity. In construction projects, the physical and human asset specificities bear the most relevant and influential ramifications, although the other types of specificity may exist in a more general and common sense (Winch 1989).

Regarding physical asset specificity, problems arise post-contract, especially during post-contract negotiations over variations and claims (Winch 2001). In PPP projects, the necessity to make huge capital investments of limited alternative usage rapidly leads to a situation where a supplier cannot withdraw due to such transaction specific investments. However, once a supplier has started work, typically the costs of replacing that supplier are quite high, both in financial and project progress terms (Winch 1989). A particular problem is 'temporal specificity', i.e. the ability of suppliers to hold up the project programme and hence disrupt the production (Masten et al. 1991). Clients are thus exposed to the costs of opportunistic behaviour up to the full replacement cost of the supplier or, conversely, suppliers may risk writing off their transaction-specific investments if they abandoned the project (Winch 2002). In comparison, human asset specificity is more widely relevant because detailed knowledge is usually held by a relatively small number of people in a firm (Walker and Chau 1999). From the viewpoint of risk management in PPP projects, the human asset, particularly the behaviour patterns developed and constantly refined by firms in the course of their ordinary productive activities, should be treated as the most relevant and important assets (Jin and Doloi 2008).

5.3.3.2 Transaction frequency

TCE holds that whether *ex post* competition is fully efficacious or not depends on whether the good or service in question is supported by durable investments in transaction-specific assets (Williamson 1996). Contracting in which pair-wise identity of the parties matters thus displaces faceless contracting. Typically, transaction frequency is low in construction, often effectively unity for most client–supplier dyads (Winch 2002). However, this is one of the areas in which many clients are making changes with the aim of achieving learning benefits. In particular, PPP *per se* indicates a higher level of transaction frequency due to its long-term commitment (Jin and Doloi 2008). Therefore, the difference in transaction frequency, though probably not great and clustering within the low range, is expected to influence the governance over risk management service transaction.

5.3.3.3 Uncertainty

PPP projects usually bear the feature of much prolonged uncertainty due to their decades of lifecycle and the difficulty in foreseeing future uncertainties, especially those inherent in later stages. Uncertainties, on the one hand, may arise from changes in the external environment affecting a system (Rao 2003). Environmental uncertainty hinders exchanges via increased opportunism (Williamson 1975, 1985). When a partnership operates in a complex and uncertain environment, such an environment impedes inter-party collaborations, attachment building, resource sharing and collective commitments, and thereby increases the transaction costs over the project lifecycle (Luo 2007; Winch 1989). On the other hand, strategic features such as non-disclosure, disguise or distortion of information are unavoidably presented when parties are joined in a condition of bilateral dependency. Such strategic behavioural uncertainty arises when incomplete contracting and asset specificity are joined and contributes to compounded uncertainty effects (Rao 2003).

According to the logic of comparative governance, partnership is potentially among better governance forms when external or environmental uncertainty is high (Williamson 1991). Compared to other forms, partnership is superior in exploring and exploiting opportunities in a highly uncertain context because of risk-sharing and resource-sharing effects. In current PPPs, though the non-recourse financing mode and the public sector's risk-averse attitude inhibit a risk-sharing structure, complementary resources pooled from all parties consolidate a partnership's collaborative competitive advantages in a volatile market.

However, partnerships may suffer a greater internal or behavioural uncertainty due to increased opportunistic acts by individual parties (Williamson 1985). Inter-party differences in strategic objective, corporate culture and managerial style, and inter-party asymmetries in bargaining power, equity ownership and parent control, all help explain why opportunism occurs (Luo 2007). Moreover, it is often impossible to fully specify a partnership contract due to unanticipated contingencies and environmental changes. An incomplete contract creates leeway for opportunism and generates moral hazards for a cooperative relationship. Consequently, opportunism may hold back collaborative incentives and unilateral commitment and undermine confidence development and trust building.

5.3.4 Efficient transaction governance

TCE maintains that 'Efficiency purposes are served by matching governance structures to the attributes of transactions in a discriminating way' (Williamson 1985: 68). Governance structures differ in their capacities to respond effectively to disturbances when confronted by the need to tackle both bounded rationality and opportunism. Market, hybrid and hierarchy are the three governance structures considered in TCE. Markets and hierarchies are polar modes. The hybrid mode is more elastic than the former and more legalistic than the latter. By preserving ownership autonomy, the hybrid governance promotes stronger incentives for trading than hierarchy and encourages the A (autonomy) type adaptations. By added contractual safeguards and administrative apparatus, the hybrid mode facilitates the C (cooperation) type adaptations, though decreasing incentives for trading compared to markets.

Williamson's classical comparative illustration of production and governance costs discloses that: 1) when asset specificity is slight, market procurement enjoys the advantages of both scale economy and market governance; 2) when asset specificity is substantial, internal organization has the advantage of hierarchy governance and, in contrast, the market realizes few economy benefits and suffers inadaptability to disturbance; 3) when asset specificity is intermediate, non-standard contracting (in comparison with classical contracting of market governance) may arise to serve hybrid governance (Williamson 1985). Williamson (1996) further added the governance costs of hybrid mode into the analysis and reveals that over some intermediate range of asset specificity, the mixed adaptation (both A and C types) that hybrids afford could well be superior to the type A-favouring or type C-favouring adaptations supported by markets and hierarchies, respectively.

5.4 A theoretical framework for risk allocation decision-making in PPP projects drawing on TCE combined with RBV

The works of Williamson and his colleagues have been well received by theorists in construction management and economics. This is because, generally, the organization of the construction industry is of a set of projects initiated and financed by clients to which contractors allocate resources according to their individual contracts with the client (Winch 1989). The firms within each project are structured on the basis of sequential interdependence through a series of market transactions and bound together by the terms of contracts. That is, each project consists of multiple transactions between firms (Fellows *et al.* 2002). However, it has been found that many works focus on the type of transaction in traditional construction projects, such as those between client and main contractor and between main contractor and subcontractor. They did not take into account the special characteristics of PPP projects, in particular risk allocation in PPP projects, given that the criticality of optimal RA to PPP success has been widely acknowledged. Fewer studies have sought to investigate how various RA strategies are formed and how optimal or efficient RA can be achieved in PPP projects. This knowledge gap justifies a systematic study on how to optimize RA practice in PPP projects. As a result, it is believed that the TCE theory, when integrated with the RBV of organizational capability, can be utilized to interpret the mechanism that steers the RADM process in a more logical and holistic way. In particular, these theories provide a useful overview of the critical determinants of the RADM. In this section, a theoretical framework for RADM in PPP projects is introduced. The framework is not only an extension of the TCE theory but also an integration of the RBV theory into the TCE theory.

5.4.1 The theoretical framework

From the point of view of the TCE theory, the RADM process could actually be viewed as the process of deciding the proportion of risk management responsibility between internal and external organizations based on a series of characteristics of risk management service transaction in question (Jin and Doloi 2008). A theoretical framework for RADM is shown in Figure 5.2.

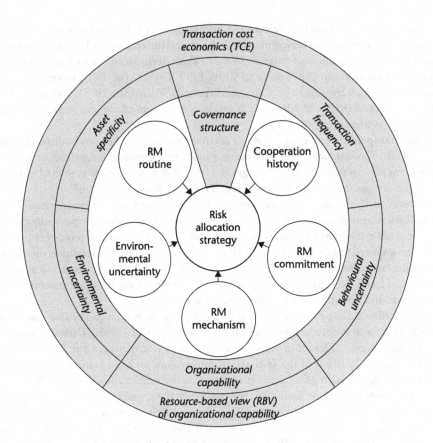

Figure 5.2 Theoretical framework of RADM process

Following TCE and RBV, the determinants of RADM, i.e. the characteristics of a risk management service transaction, can be categorized into:

1 Private partner's risk management routines, which embody competence in carrying out risk management activities and indicate that alternative uses could have been achieved without sacrificing productive value. That is, the longer the history of a RM routine, the more productive activities have been carried out, which means more alternative use has been made of the asset, and accordingly, the less specific the RM routines become (Jin and Doloi 2008). It reversely approximates to asset specificity of TCE.

2 Partners' cooperation history, which approximates to transaction frequency of TCE. One of the most important factors in partnership success is previous partnership experience (Jin and Ling 2005). Unlike existing goods, efficient risk management in PPP projects cannot be obtained by a one-off transaction and requires time to develop. The interaction among partners during that time necessitates communication and governance. Partners could better address such challenges if they have more transactions in the past because such relationship serves as a brake on opportunism for both partners (Dyer 1994, 1996; Williamson 1983).

3 Partners' risk management commitment, including both public and private partners' risk management commitment, reversely matches behavioural uncertainty of TCE. Organizational commitment is a willingness of partners to make short-term sacrifices to realize long-term benefits in the relationship (Anderson and Weitz 1992; Dwyer *et al.* 1987; Holm *et al.* 1999). Opportunism, which triggers behavioural uncertainty (Williamson 1975), and commitment are reversely related (Kim and Mahoney 2006) because commitment can serve as a brake to opportunism (Williamson 1983).

4 Risk management environmental uncertainty, which matches environmental uncertainty of TCE. Environmental uncertainty is a multidimensional concept and its effects on organizations are context-specific (Bourgeois 1980; Milliken 1987). It is related with both micro and macro business environment (Dess and Beard 1984; Miller 1987).

5 Partners' risk management mechanism, which approximates the organizational capability in RBV. Capabilities are more likely to develop effectively when purposefully designed mechanisms are established to accumulate, store, integrate and diffuse relevant organizational knowledge acquired through experience (Kale *et al.* 2002). These integrative mechanisms act as an important locus of firm learning (Pisano 1994). Risk management is a systematic mechanism. Thus, RM capability would rest upon how effectively the organization is able to capture, share and disseminate the RM know-how.

Risk allocation is the process of dividing and assigning the responsibility associated with a particular risk for a variety of hypothetical circumstances (Uff 1995). Different allocation strategies thus specify different governance structures of risk management. TCE holds that with a certain combination of the transaction dimensions, an organization will respond to them by adopting a certain governance structure to economize transaction cost (Williamson 1985). The structures include hierarchy (internal or 'make'), market (external or 'buy'), and hybrid (both 'make' and 'buy') mode (Williamson 1996). Correspondingly, for a given combination of the status of the abovementioned characteristics, a specific risk-allocation strategy, i.e. a specific proportion of a given risk to be transferred from public partner to the private partner, will be agreed by partners in order to economize transaction cost. This proportion or strategy can be 100 per cent (entirely transfer or 'buy'), 0 per cent (entirely retain or 'make'), or somewhere in-between ('make and buy'), e.g. 50 per cent (bear equally). With the TCE assumption of transaction cost economizing purpose, the inherent mechanism, which assigns different RM transactions to different governance structures (transfer proportions), attracts major attention in this chapter.

5.4.2 Asset specificity for providing risk management service (based on TCE)

As discussed before, the principal factor to explain TCE is asset specificity, which 'increases the transaction costs of all forms of governance' (Williamson 1996: 106). Without it, not only can production be economized by an external supplier due to economies of scale and scope, but governance costs are negligible due to the absence of transaction-specific interest in the continuity of the trade. As a result, markets have good economizing properties.

In traditional TCE analysis, comparative production and governance costs, i.e. the difference of these costs, were examined. In order to interpret and understand TCE more logically and holistically, production costs (based on RBV) and governance costs (based on TCE) of different governance structures have been adopted for the analysis in this study. With this method, the TCE analysis is extended and the knowledge body enriched, which is one of the major contributions of this study. As such, the analysis of production and governance costs of market, hybrid and hierarchy is combined and reinterpreted in Figure 5.3.

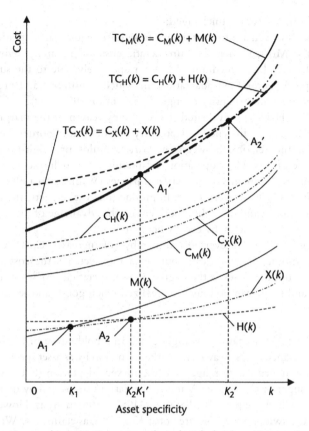

Figure 5.3 Production and transaction costs of market, hybrid and hierarchy

Similar to Williamson (1985), let:

1 k be an index of asset specificity;
2 $H(k)$ be the costs of hierarchical governance (namely entirely retaining a risk);
3 $X(k)$ be the costs of hybrid governance, i.e. both producing internally and procuring in the market (namely sharing a risk);
4 $M(k)$ be the costs of market governance (namely entirely transferring a risk);
5 $C_H(k)$ be the steady state production cost under a hierarchical governance (according to Williamson (1985: 92), steady state production refers to the situation where production output (i.e. risk management performance) is held unchanged across different governance modes);
6 $C_X(k)$ be the steady state production cost under a hybrid governance;
7 $C_M(k)$ be the steady state production cost under a market governance;
8 $TC_H(k) = C_H(k) + H(k)$ and be the total cost under a hierarchical governance;
9 $TC_X(k) = C_X(k) + X(k)$ and be the total cost under a hybrid governance; and
10 $TC_M(k) = C_M(k) + M(k)$ and be the total cost under a market governance.

Further assume that, according to Williamson (1985: 91–92, 1996: 108):

1 the output of a transaction is unchanged;
2 uncertainty is present in a sufficient degree to require sequential adaptations;
3 H(0) > X(0) > M(0), in that the bureaucratic costs of hierarchy, hybrid, and market modes are relatively high, medium and low, respectively, due to the superiority of the market in type A (autonomy) adaptation, in which consumers and producers respond independently to parametric price changes (Williamson 1996: 102);
4 $M(k)' > X(k)' > H(k)' > 0$ evaluated at every k, by reason of the marginal disability of these governance modes in type C adaptability in a descending order, i.e. as the bilateral dependency of the relation between the parties builds up, high-powered incentives impede the ease of type C (cooperation) adaptation, in which uncontested coordinated investments and realignments occur between parties (Williamson 1996: 103);
5 $C_H(k) > C_X(k) > C_M(k)$ at every k, i.e. in production cost respects, the market is everywhere at an advantage and the hybrid both enjoys the advantage of the market and suffers the disadvantage of the hierarchy everywhere; and
6 $C_M(k)' > C_X(k)' > C_H(k)'$ at every k and thereby as k increases, $C_H(k)$, $C_X(k)$, and $C_M(k)$ approach one another asymptotically but never intersect, i.e. the cost advantage of the market remains but decreases as the degree of asset specificity increases until the economies of scale and scope can no longer be realized when goods and services become very close to unique.

The economized total cost against k is highlighted in a bold curve in Figure 5.3. It can be seen that the cost balance shifts away from market to hierarchy as asset specificity (k) increases and that over some intermediate range of k, the mixed adaptation (both type A and C) of hybrids could be superior to the type A and C adaptations supported by markets and hierarchies, respectively, which supports Williamson's (1985, 1996) analysis. However, it is argued in this study that the switchover values are not at K_1 and K_2, as claimed by Williamson (1996). Instead, they occur at K_1' and K_2', which are higher specificity values than K_1 and K_2, respectively. Moreover, the range between K_1' and K_2' is arguably greater than that of K_1 and K_2. These are the results of considering the advantage of markets in terms of production costs due to the economies of scale and scope that are realized by markets. This advantage serves to offset to some degree the type C inadaptability suffered by markets. Therefore, both markets and hybrids enjoy a wider range of asset specificity values than would be observed if only governance costs are taken into consideration. Therefore, the rule for efficient risk allocation in a PPP project is for the government to transfer the risk to the private partner (i.e. to procure in market) for $k < K_1'$, to share the risk with the private partner (i.e. to use hybrid contracting) for $K_1' < k < K_2'$, and to retain the risk (i.e. to produce internally) for $k > K_2'$.

5.4.3 Capability to manage a risk (based on RBV)

The TCE approach regards the economics of production as important but already well understood. Instead, it focuses on understanding the drivers of the costs of governing the transactions inherent in that choice of production technique (Williamson 1985, 1996). Thus production costs are sometimes neglected in TCE analysis. Moreover, the goods and services to be transacted and their production costs have often been assumed as 'mature' and in a 'steady state', respectively, to avoid the need for adaptation. Meanwhile, the advantage in production costs respects has been ascribed to the economies of scale and/or scope only (see e.g. Williamson 1985, 1996). These constraints need to be relieved because non-imitable and non-substitutable organizational capabilities are a key source of inter-firm performance differences. Accordingly, the RBV of organizational capability, on which production costs are greatly contingent, was considered as a crucial construct of the framework.

First, consider the situation in which the private partner's RM capability has been improved to a non-trivial degree, i.e. the production costs of markets and, correspondingly, the production costs of hybrids have been reduced. The costs of production and governance and their summation before and after the capability improvement are shown in Figure 5.4. The optimal supply is highlighted in a bold curve.

Let:

1 $RC_X(k)$ be the reduced production cost of hybrid;
2 $RC_M(k)$ be the reduced production cost of market;
3 $RTC_X(k) = RC_X(k) + X(k)$ and be the reduced total cost under a hybrid governance; and
4 $RTC_M(k) = RC_M(k) + M(k)$ and be the reduced total cost under a market governance.

Keeping other assumptions unchanged, assume that:

$C_M(k) - RC_M(k) > C_X(k) - RC_X(k)$ at every k, i.e. in production cost reduction respects, the market is everywhere at an advantage and the hybrid suffers the disadvantage of the hierarchy everywhere.

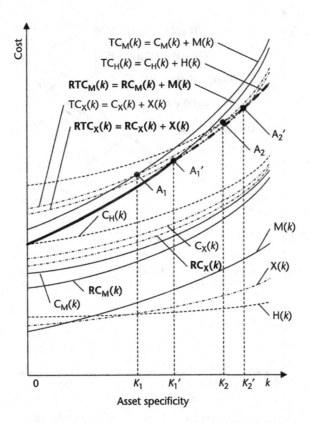

Figure 5.4 Production and transaction costs of market, hybrid and hierarchy when private partner's RM capability improves (decreasing C_M)

It can be seen clearly that markets enjoy a wider range of asset specificity values (between 0 and K_1') after capability improvement than before (between 0 and K_1). In contrast, hierarchies retreat to a smaller range of k values with a reduction of $K_2' - K_2$. The range of k values for hybrids is also reduced, although the reduction is smaller than that of hierarchies. Therefore, the rule for efficient risk allocation in a PPP project after a non-trivial reduction in production costs of market is for the government to transfer the risk to the private partner (i.e. to procure in market) for $k < K_1'$, to share the risk with the private partner (i.e. to use hybrid contracting) for $K_1' < k < K_2'$, and to retain the risk (i.e. to produce internally) for $k > K_2'$. It can be argued that the effects of the public partner's deteriorated RM capability are similar to those of the private partner's improved RM capability.

Next, consider the situation in which the public partner's own RM capability has been improved to a non-trivial degree, i.e. the production costs of hierarchy and, correspondingly, the production costs of hybrids have been reduced. The costs of production and governance and their summation before and after the capability improvement are shown in Figure 5.5. The optimal supply is highlighted in a bold curve.

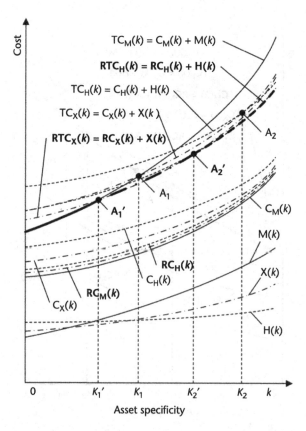

Figure 5.5 Production and transaction costs of market, hybrid and hierarchy when public partner's RM capability improves (decreasing C_H) (a)

Let:

1 $RC_H(k)$ be the reduced production cost of hierarchy;
2 $RC_X(k)$ be the reduced production cost of hybrid;
3 $RTC_H(k) = RC_H(k) + H(k)$ and be the reduced total cost under a hierarchy governance; and
4 $RTC_X(k) = RC_X(k) + X(k)$ and be the reduced total cost under a hybrid governance.

Keeping other assumptions unchanged, assume that:

$C_H(k) - RC_H(k) > C_X(k) - RC_X(k)$ at every k, i.e. in production cost reduction respects, the hierarchy is everywhere at an advantage and the hybrid suffers the disadvantage of the market everywhere.

It can be observed that hierarchies enjoy a wider range of asset specificity values (from K_2' onwards) after capability improvement than before (from K_2 onwards). In contrast, markets retreat to a smaller range of k values between 0 and K_1'. The range of k values for hybrids also reduces although the reduction is smaller than that of markets. Therefore, the rule for efficient risk allocation in a PPP project after a non-trivial reduction in production costs of hierarchy is for the government to transfer the risk to the private partner (i.e. to procure in market) for $k < K_1'$, to share the risk with the private partner (i.e. to use hybrid contracting) for $K_1' < k < K_2'$, and to retain the risk (i.e. to produce internally) for $k > K_2'$. It can be argued that the effects of the private partner's deteriorated RM capability are similar to those of the public partner's improved RM capability.

Further, a situation extended from the above one is considered. As above, it is assumed that $C_H(k) > C_M(k)$ at every k. Regarding RM in PPP projects, however, it is not uncommon that the public partner is sometimes more competent in managing some risks. Therefore, this assumption needs to be relieved in such situations, in which the public partner's RM capability is so superior to the private partner's that the production cost savings are able to offset the added bureaucratic costs when $k = 0$, that is:

1 $C_M(k) > C_H(k)$ at every k;
2 $H(0) - M(0) = C_M(0) - RC_H(0)$; and consequently
3 $RTC_H(0) = TC_M(0)$.

The costs of production and governance and their summation before and after the capability improvement are shown in Figure 5.6. The optimal supply is highlighted in a bold curve.

It can be seen that hierarchies enjoy the whole range of asset specificity after capability improvement. In contrast, markets and hybrids suffer disadvantage in total costs respects throughout although they are advantageous in governance costs respects within a certain range of asset specificity. Therefore, after a significant reduction in production costs of hierarchy, the rule for efficient risk allocation in a PPP project is for the government to retain the risk and provide risk management service internally (i.e. to produce internally) all the time.

5.4.4 Frequency of risk management service transaction (based on TCE)

One of the most important factors for partnership success is previous partnership experience (Jin and Ling 2005). Unlike existing goods, efficient risk management in building and construction projects cannot be obtained by a one-off transaction and requires time to

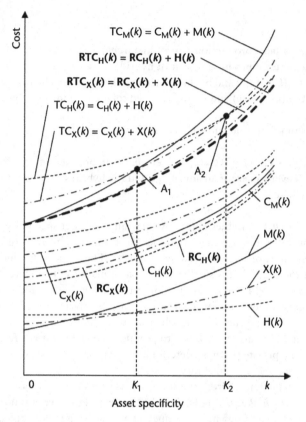

Figure 5.6 Production and transaction costs of market, hybrid and hierarchy when public partner's RM capability improves (decreasing C_H) (b)

develop. During that time, the buyer and supplier of risk management service – in this study, the public partner and the private partner or the public partner's internal divisions – must interact to develop mutually acceptable specifications. This interaction necessitates communication and governance. Partners could better address challenges of communication and governance if they have more similar transactions in the past. Because the cost of managing relationships is also a type of governance cost, transaction frequency must also be considered in risk management service transactions.

According to Williamson (1996), transaction frequency matters only when asset specificity deepens and consequently bilateral dependency builds up. This is because the buyer must persuade potential suppliers to make similar specialized investments should the buyer seek least-cost supply from an outsider and the supplier would be unable to realize equivalent value should the specialized assets be redeployed to other uses (Williamson 1996). The added costs of such non-standard contracting may be recovered by frequent transactions (Williamson 1985).

Taking the situation illustrated in Figure 5.3 as the initial state, first consider the situation in which the partners' risk management service transaction frequency has increased to a non-trivial degree, i.e. only the governance costs of hybrids have been reduced because little bilateral dependency arises in markets and hierarchies and frequency thus lacks relevancy. The costs of production and governance and their summation before and after the frequency increase are shown in Figure 5.7. The optimal supply is highlighted in a bold curve.

118

Let:

1   RX(k) be the reduced governance cost of hybrid; and
2   RTC$_X$(k) = C$_X$(k) + RX(k) and be the reduced total cost of hybrid.

Keeping other assumptions unchanged, assume that:

1   RX(0) = X(0), by reason that frequency matters only when asset specificity is non-trivial; and
2   RX(k) < X(k) at every k except at k = 0 because higher frequency serves to reduce governance costs.

It can be seen that the hybrid mode enjoys a wider range of asset specificity values (between K_1' and K_2') after the increase in transaction frequency than before (between K_1 and K_2) although the shift may not be significant. In contrast, markets and hierarchies retreat to a smaller range of k values, i.e. between 0 and K_1' and K_2' onwards, respectively.

In comparison, consider the situation in which the partners' transaction frequency has decreased to a non-trivial degree, i.e. added governance costs of hybrids have been introduced. The costs of production and governance and their summation before and after the frequency decrease are also shown in Figure 5.7.

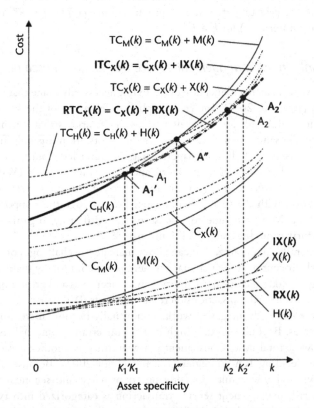

Figure 5.7   Production and transaction costs of market, hybrid and hierarchy when transaction frequency changes (changing (i.e. increasing or decreasing) X(k))

Let:

1 IX(k) be the increased governance cost of hybrid; and
2 $ITC_X(k) = C_X(k) + IX(k)$ be the increased total cost of hybrid.

Keeping other assumptions unchanged, assume that:

1 IX(0) = X(0); and
2 IX(k) > X(k) at every k except at k = 0.

It is observed that the hybrid mode retreats to a much smaller range of k values if transaction frequency decreases. At $k = K''$, if frequency further decreases (e.g. a one-off transaction), the hybrid mode will be disadvantageous throughout and, consequently, it will not be considered as a governance alternative. Accordingly, markets and hierarchies enlarge the range of k values that they occupy until they become the only two alternatives.

Consequently, the rule for efficient risk allocation in a PPP project is very complicated when transaction frequency changes. When the transaction frequency is comparatively high, the rule is for the government to transfer the risk to the private partner (i.e. to procure in market) for $k < K_1'$, to share the risk with the private partner (i.e. to use hybrid contracting) for $K_1' < k < K_2'$, and to retain the risk (i.e. to produce internally) for $k > K_2'$. On the other hand, when the transaction frequency is substantially low, the rule is for the government to transfer the risk to the private partner (i.e. to procure in market) for $k < K''$, and to retain the risk (i.e. to produce internally) for $k > K''$.

5.4.5 Uncertainty in risk management service transaction (based on TCE)

Past transactions with a partner alone, however, do not necessarily make that partner the most attractive choice (Jin *et al.* 2007). Internal suppliers offer many of the same advantages as long-term suppliers, although for different reasons. TCE argues that when the buyer and supplier belong to the same organization, governance costs are mitigated due to distinctive governance mechanisms, including managerial fiat, a greater legal burden on employees to disclose information than contracting partners, and judicial forbearance (Williamson 1991). Belonging to the same organization can also reduce communication costs because an individual's identification with the firm generates social knowledge that supports coordination and communication. Moreover, due to a sense of shared destiny, organizational integrity leads to better information disclosure (Williamson 1985).

Therefore, generally, an organization can better manage the challenges of communication and governance that occur over the risk management process internally than with an external supplier. Although weaker technical capability, lower incentives and greater bureaucracy that occur in intra-organizational transactions increase total costs (Williamson 1985), the communication and governance advantages of working internally become increasingly apparent as uncertainty increases. Beyond a certain high level of uncertainty, internal risk management may offer the lowest total cost. Consequently, uncertainty is another critical factor to be considered when deciding RA strategies (Jin and Doloi 2007). Because TCE practically recognizes behavioural uncertainty in addition to primary and secondary uncertainties, uncertainty in a risk management service transaction is categorized into two distinct but related groups, i.e. project environmental uncertainty and partner's behavioural uncertainty (Jin and Doloi 2008).

Generally, the efficiency of all forms of governance may weaken in the presence of greater uncertainties. Williamson (1996) argued that the effects of greater uncertainties are especially pertinent for those uncertainties for which mainly or strictly coordinated responses are required. As a result, when facing greater uncertainties, the hybrid mode is the most easily affected. This is because hybrid adaptations cannot be made unilaterally as in markets or by fiat as in hierarchies. They necessitate mutual consent and coordinated actions.

Therefore, the situation in which transaction-related uncertainties become greater should be considered, i.e. the governance costs of all governance forms have been increased and particularly those of hybrids. The costs of production and governance and their summation before and after the uncertainty increase are shown in Figure 5.8. The optimal supply is highlighted in a bold curve.

Let:

1   $IM(k)$ be the increased governance cost of market;
2   $IH(k)$ be the increased governance cost of hierarchy;
3   $ITC_M(k) = C_M(k) + IM(k)$ be the increased total cost of market; and
4   $ITC_H(k) = C_H(k) + IH(k)$ be the increased total cost of hierarchy.

Keeping other assumptions unchanged, assume that:

1   $IM(0) = M(0)$ because uncertainty matters only when asset specificity is non-trivial;
2   $IX(0) = X(0)$ because uncertainty matters only when asset specificity is non-trivial;
3   $IH(0) = H(0)$ because uncertainty matters only when asset specificity is non-trivial;
4   $IM(k) > M(k)$ at every k except at $k = 0$ because greater uncertainty increases governance costs;
5   $IX(k) > X(k)$ at every k except at $k = 0$ because greater uncertainty increases governance costs;
6   $IH(k) > H(k)$ at every k except at $k = 0$ because greater uncertainty increases governance costs; and
7   $IX(k) - X(k) > IM(k) - M(k) > IH(k) - H(k)$, in that hybrids are the most susceptible.

It can be seen that the hybrid mode retreats to a much smaller range of k values (between K_1' and K_2') as uncertainties become greater. In contrast, markets and hierarchies enjoy a wider range of k values. It arguably obtains that if uncertainty further increases, the hybrid mode will be disadvantageous throughout and consequently will not be considered as a governance alternative. Accordingly, markets and hierarchies then become the only two options.

Therefore, the rules for efficient risk allocation in a PPP project are very complicated when environmental and/or behavioural uncertainty changes. When the uncertainty is substantially low, the rule is for the government to transfer the risk to the private partner (i.e. to procure in market) for $k < K_1$, to share the risk with the private partner (i.e. to use hybrid contracting) for $K_1 < k < K_2$, and to retain the risk (i.e. to produce internally) for $k > K_2$. When the uncertainty is comparatively high, the rule is for the government to transfer the risk to the private partner (i.e. to procure in market) for $k < K_1'$, to share the risk with the private partner (i.e. to use hybrid contracting) for $K_1' < k < K_2'$, and to retain the risk (i.e. to produce internally) for $k > K_2'$. When the uncertainty is substantially high, the rule is for the government to either transfer the risk to the private partner (i.e. to procure in market) or retain the risk (i.e. to produce internally).

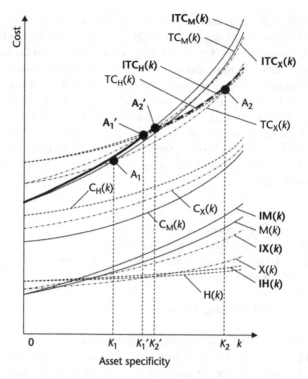

Figure 5.8 Production and transaction costs of market, hybrid and hierarchy when uncertainty increases (increasing $X(k)$, $M(k)$, and $H(k)$)

5.5 Application of the theoretical framework

In this section, the TCE-RBV-based theoretical framework is applied to the RADM process for 'Defects in design risk' of the New Schools PPP Project (Project 1) (referred to as the Project hereafter) in Sydney, New South Wales (NSW), Australia. The Project was the first project delivered under the NSW Government's *Working with Government: Guidelines for Privately Financed Projects* (NSW Audit Office 2006). It was also the first privately financed social infrastructure project in NSW and the first privately financed schools project in Australia (NSW Treasury 2005). Private sector firms, which include Axiom Education Pty Limited (Contractor), supported by ABN AMRO Australia Limited (Bond Manager), Hansen Yuncken Pty Limited (Construction Contractor), St Hilliers Contracting Pty Limited (Construction Contractor), Spotless Services Australia Limited (Operator), financed, designed and constructed nine new public schools in new urban release areas across NSW. Four schools opened in 2004 and five in 2005. Additionally, the private sector provides cleaning, maintenance, security, safety, utility, furniture, equipment and grounds main-tenance and other services for these school buildings until 31 December 2032, when the buildings will be handed over to the Department of Education and Training (DET), in return for performance-based monthly payments by the DET during the operational phase of the project (NSW DET 2003).

Based on collected data, it has been found that collaboration history between the two partners is not long. The private partner needed to invest in highly specific assets in order to manage the design risk. Neither partner's capability to tackle the design risk is strong enough. However, partners from both sectors, particularly the public partner, showed strong willingness and commitment to managing the risk probably because the general environment for managing the risk is relatively stable. That is, the level of both behavioural and environmental uncertainty is very low. Under such circumstances (namely high asset specificity, low uncertainty, low transaction frequency, and low capability), according to the theoretical framework, entirely transferring design risk to the contractor (namely adopting market governance), as is the case for many PPP projects, would result in a higher price to manage the risk and even create additional significant risks for both parties.

The theoretical framework therefore suggests that government bear most or all of design risk (namely adopt hierarchy or hybrid governance). This is exactly the strategy that was adopted in the Project. That is, the proportion of design risk transferred to the private sector was relatively low (NSW Audit Office 2006). There was an expectation that the private sector would introduce innovative solutions to reduce the whole of life cost of the schools. In reality, this was not reflected in the development process of the Project. Only the current school buildings specifications were observed, which had been set as the minimum requirement by the DET. The DET's specifications detailed the required school facilities room by room, including size requirements, finishes, number of power points etc. (NSW DET 2003). The DET saw these specifications as ensuring that the provision of school facilities remains equitable (NSW Treasury 2005). Because they are subject to regular reviews to achieve efficiency in design, innovation and cost effectiveness, they provide greater certainty in relation to the final product. Therefore, there was little innovative design in the way. The recent audit report thus found that the DET clearly defined its requirements from the outset and scoped the project to maximize its prospects of achieving value for money (NSW Audit Office 2006).

5.6 Conclusion

Public–Private Partnership is rapidly becoming the preferred way to provide public infrastructure and services in many countries. Although appropriate risk allocation is a great driver of value for money in PPP projects, the decision-making on efficient risk allocation in PPP projects is no easy job. Implementing optimal risk allocation strategies is critically important to the success of PPP projects. In this chapter, risk allocation decision-making in PPP projects has been discussed. Some recent PPP projects are reviewed to examine the risk allocation practice. It has been found that partners' capabilities in risk management have been consistently considered when current risk allocation strategies are formed. While having their merits as a necessity of achieving optimal risk allocation, such risk allocation strategies may fail to take economic aspects into account and thus do not always contribute to project success and usually undermine value-for-money. Such failure is evident in some of the risk allocation decisions in the case study PPP projects.

In order to tackle this problem, transaction cost economics (TCE), augmented with the resource-based view (RBV) of organizational capability, is adopted to build a theoretical framework to guide the risk allocation decision-making (RADM) process. The framework is based on the view that the RADM process could actually be viewed as the process of deciding the proportion of risk management responsibility between internal and external organizations based on a series of characteristics of risk management service transaction in question. Following TCE and RBV, the determinants of RADM, i.e. the characteristics of a risk management service transaction, are categorized into: 1) Private partner's risk management routines, which reversely approximates to asset specificity of TCE; 2) Partners' cooperation history, which approximates to transaction frequency of TCE; 3) Partners' risk management commitment, which reversely matches behavioural uncertainty of TCE; 4) Risk management environmental uncertainty, which matches environmental uncertainty of TCE; and 5) Partners' risk management mechanism, which approximates the organizational capability in RBV. For a given combination of the status of the abovementioned characteristics, a specific risk allocation strategy, i.e. a specific proportion of a given risk to be transferred from public partner to the private partner, will be agreed by partners in order to economize transaction cost. With the TCE assumption of transaction cost economizing purpose, the inherent mechanism assigns different RM transactions to different governance structures (transfer proportions). The established framework is applied to a real PPP project to demonstrate its validity and value in risk allocation decision-making. Various further applications using empirical data have been undertaken and reported in a series of publications including Jin (2009, 2010a, b, 2011), Jin and Doloi (2008, 2009) and Jin and Zhang (2011).

References

AAR (2002) *Deed of Variation – Spencer Street Station Transport Interchange Facility – Services and Development Agreement*, Melbourne, Australia: Allens Arthur Robinson.

Ahmed, S.M., Ahmad, R. and Saram, D.D.D. (1999) 'Risk management trends in the Hong Kong construction industry: a comparison of contractors and owners perceptions'. *Engineering, Construction and Architectural Management*, 6(3): 225–34.

Anderson, E. and Weitz, B. (1992) 'The use of pledges to build and sustain commitment in distribution channels'. *Journal of Marketing Research*, 29: 18–34.

Arndt, R. (1999) 'Optimum risk transfer in Build-Own-Operate-Transfer projects: the challenge for governments'. *Transactions of Multi-disciplinary Engineering, Australia*, GE 22: 1–8.

AS/NZS (2004) *AS/NZS 4360:2004 – Risk Management*, 3rd edn, Sydney, NSW, Australia; Wellington, New Zealand: Standards Australia/Standards New Zealand.

Barney, J.B. (1991) 'Firm resources and sustained competitive advantage'. *Journal of Management*, 17(1): 99–120.

Bourgeois, L. (1980) 'Strategy and environment: conceptual integration'. *Academy of Management Review*, 5: 25–39.

Coase, R.H. (1937) 'The nature of the firm'. *Economica*, 4: 386–405.

Coase, R.H. (1988) *The Firm, the Market and the Law*, Chicago: The University of Chicago Press.

Conner, K. and Prahalad, C. (1996) 'A resource-based theory of the firm: knowledge versus opportunism'. *Organization Science*, 7(5): 477–501.

Dess, G. and Beard, D. (1984) 'Dimensions of organizational task environments'. *Administrative Science Quarterly*, 29: 52–73.

DFA (2005) *Public private partnerships: Guideline: Commonwealth policy principles for the use of private financing: Risk management*, Canberra, Australia: Australian Department of Finance and Administration (DFA).

DTF (2001) *Partnerships Victoria Guidance Material: Risk Allocation and Contractual Issues*, Melbourne, Australia: Victorian Department of Treasury and Finance (DTF).

Dwyer, F.R., Schurr, P.H. and Oh, S. (1987) 'Developing buyer-seller relationships'. *Journal of Marketing*, 51(2): 11–27.

Dyer, J.H. (1994) 'Dedicated assets: Japan's manufacturing edge'. *Harvard Business Review*, 72(6): 174–9.

Dyer, J.H. (1996) 'Specialized supplier networks as a source of competitive advantage: evidence from the auto industry'. *Strategic Management Journal*, 17(4): 271–91.

Faulkner, K. (2004) 'Public–Private Partnerships', in Ghobadian, A., Gallear, D., O'Regan, N. and Viney, H. (eds) *Public–private partnerships: policy and experience*, 65–70, Houndmills, England; New York: Palgrave Macmillan.

Fellows, R., Langford, D., Newcombe, R. and Urry, S. (2002) *Construction Management in Practice*, 2nd edn, Oxord: Blackwell.

Grant, R. (1996) 'Toward a knowledge-based view of the firm'. *Strategic Management Journal*, 17(Winter Special Issue): 109–22.

Hart, O. (1990) 'An economist perspective on the theory of the firm', in Williamson, O.E. (ed.) *Organization Theory*, Oxford: Oxford University Press.

Holm, D.B., Eriksson, K. and Johanson, J. (1999) 'Creating value through mutual commitment to business network relationships'. *Strategic Management Journal*, 20(5): 467–86.

Jacobides, M.G. and Hitt, L.M. (2005) 'Losing sight of the forest for the trees? Productive capabilities and gains from trade as drivers of vertical scope'. *Strategic Management Journal*, 26(13): 1209–27.

Jacobides, M.G. and Winter, S.G. (2005) 'The co-evolution of capabilities and transaction costs: explaining the institutional structure of production'. *Strategic Management Journal*, 26(5): 395–413.

Jin, X.-H. (2009) 'Allocating risks in Public–Private Partnership projects using a transaction cost economics approach – A case study'. *Australasian Journal of Construction Economics and Building*, 9(1): 19–26.

Jin, X.-H. (2010a) 'Determinants of efficient risk allocation in privately financed public infrastructure projects in Australia'. *ASCE Journal of Construction Engineering and Management*, 136(2): 138–50.

Jin, X.-H. (2010b) 'Neuro-fuzzy decision support system for efficient risk allocation in public-private partnership infrastructure projects'. *ASCE Journal of Computing in Civil Engineering*, 24(6): 525–38.

Jin, X.-H. (2011) 'A model for efficient risk allocation in privately financed public infrastructure projects using neuro-fuzzy techniques'. *ASCE Journal of Construction Engineering and Management*, 137(11): 1003–14.

Jin, X.-H. and Doloi, H. (2007) 'A conceptual risk-allocation framework for Public–Private Partnership projects in Australia', in London, K., Thayarapan, G. and Chen, J. (eds) *Proceedings of CIB Working Commissions W92 Built Environment Procurement International Conference – Interdisciplinarity and Multidisciplinary Intersections in Built Environment Procurement*, 23–26 September 2007, Hunter Valley Gardens, NSW, Australia: 64–75.

Jin, X.-H. and Doloi, H. (2008) 'Interpreting risk allocation mechanism in public-private partnership projects: an empirical study in a transaction cost economics perspective'. *Construction Management and Economics*, 26(7): 707–21.

Jin, X.-H. and Doloi, H. (2009) 'Modelling risk allocation in privately financed infrastructure projects using fuzzy logic'. *Computer-Aided Civil and Infrastructure Engineering*, 24(7): 509–24.

Jin, X.-H., Doloi, H. and Gao, S.-Y. (2007) 'Relationship-based determinants of building project performance in China'. *Construction Management and Economics*, 25(3): 297–304.

Jin, X.-H. and Ling, F.Y.Y. (2005) 'Constructing a framework for building relationship and trust in project organizations: two case studies of building projects in China'. *Construction Management and Economics*, 23(7): 685–96.

Jin, X.-H. and Zhang, G. (2011) 'Modelling optimal risk allocation in PPP projects using artificial neural networks'. *International Journal of Project Management*, 29(5): 591–603.

Kale, P., Dyer, J.H. and Singh, H. (2002) 'Alliance capability, stock market response, and long-term alliance success: the role of the alliance function'. *Strategic Management Journal*, 23(8): 747–67.

Kangari, R. (1995) 'Risk management perceptions and trends of U.S. construction'. *Journal of Construction Engineering and Management, ASCE*, 121(4): 422–9.

Kim, S.M. and Mahoney, J.T. (2006) 'Mutual commitment to support exchange: relation-specific IT system as a substitute for managerial hierarchy'. *Strategic Management Journal*, 27(5): 401–23.

Kogut, B. and Zander, U. (1996) 'What do firms do? Coordination, identity, and learning'. *Organization Science*, 7(5): 502–18.

Luo, Y. (2007) 'Are joint venture partners more opportunistic in a more volatile environment?'. *Strategic Management Journal*, 28(1): 39–60.

Masten, S.E., Meehan, J.W. and Snyder, E.A. (1991) 'The costs of organization'. *Journal of Law, Economics and Organization*, 7: 1–25.

Miller, D. (1987) 'The structural and environmental correlates of business strategy'. *Strategic Management Journal*, 8(1): 55–76.

Milliken, F.J. (1987) 'Three types of perceived uncertainty about the environment: state, effect, and response uncertainty'. *Academy of Management Review*, 12: 133–43.

Nelson, R.R. and Winter, S.G. (1982) *An Evolutionary Theory of Economic Change*, Cambridge, MA: Belknap Press of Harvard University Press.

Ng, A. and Loosemore, M. (2007) 'Risk allocation in the private provision of public infrastructure'. *International Journal of Project Management*, 25(1): 66–76.

NSW Audit Office (2006) *Auditor-General's report: Performance audit: the New Schools Privately Financed Project*, Sydney, Australia: The Audit Office of New South Wales.

NSW DET (2003) *Summary of contracts: New South Wales New Schools Privately Financed Project*, Sydney, Australia: The New South Wales Department of Education and Training (DET).

NSW Treasury (2005) *Research and information paper: New Schools Privately Financed Project post implementation review*, Sydney, Australia: Office of Financial Management, New South Wales Treasury. [Available online from http://www.treasury.nsw.gov.au/]

Pisano, G. (1994) 'Knowledge, integration, and the locus of learning: an empirical analysis of process development'. *Strategic Management Journal*, 15(3): 85–101.

Rahman, M.M. and Kumaraswamy, M.M. (2002) 'Risk management trends in the construction industry: moving towards joint risk management'. *Engineering, Construction and Architectural Management*, 9(2): 131–51.

Rao, P.K. (2003) *The Economics of Transaction Costs: Theory, Methods and Applications*, New York: Palgrave MacMillan.

Teece, D.J., Pisano, G. and Shuen, A. (1997) 'Dynamic capabilities and strategic management'. *Strategic Management Journal*, 18(7): 509–33.

Thomas, A.V., Kalidindi, S.N. and Ananthanarayanan, K. (2003) 'Risk perception analysis of BOT road project participants in India'. *Construction Management and Economics*, 21(4): 393–407.

Tomazin, F. and Myer, R. (2006) 'Spencer St dispute lead to $33m bill', in *The Age*, 4 August, Melbourne, Australia.

Uff, J. (1995) *Risk, Management and Procurement in Construction*, London: Centre of Construction Law and Management.

Walker, A. and Chau, K.W. (1999) 'The relationship between construction project management theory and transaction cost economics'. *Engineering, Construction and Architectural Management*, 6(2): 166–76.

Wernerfelt, B. (1984) 'The resource-based view of the firm'. *Strategic Management Journal*, 5(2): 171–80.

Williamson, O.E. (1975) *Markets and Hierarchies, Analysis and Antitrust Implications: A Study in the Economics of Internal Organization*, New York: Free Press.

Williamson, O.E. (1981) 'The economics of organization: the transaction cost approach'. *American Journal of Sociology*, 87: 548–77.

Williamson, O.E. (1983) 'Credible commitments: using hostages to support exchange'. *American Economic Review*, 73(4): 519–40.

Williamson, O.E. (1985) *The Economic Institutions of Capitalism: Firms, Markets, Relational Contracting*, New York: Free Press.

Williamson, O.E. (1991) 'Comparative economic organization: the analysis of discrete structural alternatives'. *Administrative Science Quarterly*, 36(2): 269–96.

Williamson, O.E. (1996) *The Mechanisms of Governance*, New York: Oxford University Press.

Winch, G.M. (1989) 'The construction firm and the construction project: a transaction cost approach'. *Construction Management and Economics*, 7(4): 331–45.

Winch, G.M. (2001) 'Governing the project process: a conceptual framework'. *Construction Management and Economics*, 19(8): 799–808

Winch, G.M. (2002) *Managing Construction Projects: An Information Processing Approach*, Oxford: Blackwell.

Winch, G.M. (2006) 'Forum: Towards a theory of construction as production by projects'. *Building Research and Information*, 34(2): 164–74.

Incomplete contracts and public–private partnerships

Gordon Rausser and Holly Ameden

6.1 Introduction

A contract is incomplete if there is a set of events that can influence the partnership that have not been anticipated and addressed in the initial contract. Incomplete contracting theory provides the foundation for any framework evaluating PPPs. PPPs are, by definition, an incomplete contract due to the complexity of such a partnership and its long-term unantici- pated events. Control rights, the authority to make decisions in the case of both anticipated and unanticipated events, are a key consideration in incomplete contracting and in particular, for PPP contracts. The allocation of control rights through a PPP contract can determine whether a partnership achieves efficiency as well as an equitable distribution of partnership benefits.

Contracts for PPPs come in many forms, ranging from large, multi-project, multi-year alliances to small-scale projects. In this chapter, we present a three-stage operational frame- work to analyse the process of forming PPP contracts. This structure is based on control rights that stem from contingencies in the partnership's production process and are embedded in the contract. A pre-contract partner-selection process sets the bargaining space. In Stage 1, the public and private partners negotiate over front-end control rights and back-end property rights (i.e., control rights over partnership output), and make relationship-specific invest- ments.[1] The front-end control rights determine the nature and scope of the partnership's production processes as well as decision-making authority over these processes. Back-end property rights determine how the benefits of the partnership will be distributed. In Stage 2, the partners bargain over management decisions given the bargaining power balance negoti- ated in Stage 1. The equilibrium outcome of Stage 2 is either a non–cooperative decision (i.e., default outcome or disagreement payoff) or a cooperative solution that maximizes joint benefit. In Stage 3, there is an unanticipated shock, causing partners either to terminate the partnership or to revisit and renegotiate control- and property-rights allocations.

This chapter is organized as follows. Section 6.2 reviews the theoretical research on incomplete contracts relating to PPPs, with a particular focus on how this literature informs the optimal allocation of control rights. Section 6.3 presents findings from illustrative applications (e.g., empirical, quantitative, case study, and survey analyses) of a broad range of contracts research (incomplete contracts research, relational contracts research, general contracts research), again with a focus on findings relevant for control-rights allocations. Section 6.4 synthesizes both the theoretical and illustrative findings into an operational framework for assessing PPPs. Section 6.5 applies the proposed operational framework to R&D PPPs and to an assessment of specific transportation infrastructure PPPs. Section 6.6 provides some concluding remarks.

6.2 Incomplete contracting theory and PPPs

Any framework for evaluating PPPs must be rooted in the incomplete-contracting-theory literature and analyses of decision or control rights (Hart and Moore 1988; Aghion and Bolton 1992; Aghion *et al.* 1994; Dewatripont and Maskin 1995; Hart 1995; Aghion and Tirole 1997; Hart *et al.* 1997; Hart and Moore 1999; Tirole 1999; Hart 2003). At the heart of the concept of control rights and PPPs is the designation of the nature of the partnership output. PPP output can be designated as a private, public or an impure good.

6.2.1 Optimal control-rights allocation and private good

Grossman and Hart (1986), who provide a foundation for this incomplete contracting research, focus on the ownership of residual rights in a two-period model of integration of two private firms where the product of the relationship is a private good. In period 1, the firms form a contract that allocates control rights and allows each firm to make relationship-specific investments. In period 2, each firm makes production decisions based on the control rights designated under the contract. The production decisions and market outcomes determine the partnership value for each partner. In the first period, the investments and the production decisions are uncontractible. The firms make the relationship-specific investments non-cooperatively. The investments are observed, the second period begins and the control rights allocated by the first-period contract are exercised. The production decisions can be non-cooperative or cooperative through costless renegotiation (the production decision becomes contractible in period 2). Because the partnership's value is unlikely to be maximized with non-cooperative decisions, the firms benefit from renegotiation in period 2 after observing investments. Assuming symmetric information, renegotiation will lead to an efficient *ex post* allocation. The distribution of *ex post* surplus, however, depends on the initial allocation of ownership rights, and thus distorts *ex ante* investment decisions. If the firms are assumed to divide the partnership surplus symmetrically, both firms under-invest, failing to achieve efficiency. This finding is supported by Hart and Moore (1990).

Grossman and Hart (1986) find that if the first-period investment of one firm has a larger effect on the partnership's value than that of the other firm, the contract should assign the firm with the more valuable investment full control rights over decision making in the second period, giving this firm an incentive to invest optimally, thus maximizing the partnership's value. Therefore, in the case of a jointly produced private good, assignment of control rights to agents based on the value generated by investments can help prevent under-investment.

6.2.2 Optimal control-rights allocation and public good

Besley and Ghatak (2001) use incomplete contracting theory to evaluate a partnership that produces a public good, i.e., a product that is presumed to be non-rival and non-excludable. In their model, two agents make relationship-specific investments. The benefits of the relationship are public and are dependent on the investment decisions. The two agents are assumed to have different valuations of the project. With no contracting problems, the agents choose investments that maximize joint surplus. If the contract is incomplete in that the investments cannot be specified *ex ante*, each party holds bargaining power after investments have been made and the first-best levels of investment are generally not reached. Besley and Ghatak (2001) show, however, that by allocating full ownership, and thus all control rights, to the partner with the highest valuation of the project, joint surplus will be maximized. Given this assignment of authority, the high-valuation partner has the incentive and ability to invest optimally. Accordingly, when a public good is generated by a partnership, the allocation of control rights should be based on the agents' valuation of the partnership output, not the relative value of their investment (as found by Grossman and Hart (1986) for private goods).

6.2.3 Optimal control-rights allocation and impure goods

Much of the contracting and control-right literature focuses on the allocation of control rights within a partnership assuming either a private or public good is generated. While providing important insights, this literature does not provide a full framework for evaluating most PPPs which generate impure goods. For example, in the area of natural resources, PPPs produce impure goods such as environmental remediation, water sanitation, infrastructure, or scientific research. Francesconi and Muthoo (2006) were the first to develop a framework for evaluating PPPs that generate an impure good. Moreover, in contrast to Grossman and Hart (1986) and Besley and Ghatak (2001), this model allows control rights to be shared between two partners. In the first stage, two agents choose the allocation of control rights. After the initial allocation, the two agents invest in the project. Once the investment decisions are made, the partners can make unilateral or joint decisions through cooperative bargaining, rather than invoking the control rights, and a surplus results. If the partners do not cooperate, the project's value, as determined by the allocated control rights, will be less than if they cooperated. Thus, the *ex post* bargaining affects the marginal returns to investment for each partner, which are influenced, in turn, by the disagreement payoffs coming from the *ex ante* allocated control rights. The partners bargain over whether the decisions are to be made cooperatively or non-cooperatively and what, if any, transfers are to be made.

Francesconi and Muthoo (2006) find that when the level of impurity is small (i.e., the partnership product is primarily a public good), control rights should go to the partner that values the results of the partnership the highest, following Besley and Ghatak (2001). When the degree of impurity is large (i.e., the partnership product is primarily a private good), control rights should be allocated to the largest investor, as in Grossman and Hart (1986). If the degree of impurity is large and investments are roughly equal, it is optimal for control rights to be shared, with a relatively greater share going to the low-valuation partner. If the degree of impurity is neither small (i.e., public good) nor large (i.e., private good) and the investments are of similar importance, the low-valuation partner should be allocated all control rights. Allocating control rights to the low-valuation partner is optimal in these cases because the high-valuation partner already has an incentive to invest and the low-valuation partner will be more willing to invest if they hold a greater share of the control rights.

The major results regarding the assignment of control rights in the academic theoretic literature are presented in Table 6.1. The efficient assignment depends on the type of good or value generated (private, public, degree of impurity) and the choices/attributes of the parties entering into the partnership.

Table 6.1 Optimal allocation of control rights in a PPP

Type of good	To partner(s) with the most valuable investment	To partner(s) with the highest valuation of output	Shared, with greater share to low-valuation partner (output)	All rights to low-valuation partner (output)
Private good (Grossman and Hart 1986; Hart and Moore 1990)	X			
Public good (Besley and Ghatak 2001)		X		
Impure good (Francesconi and Muthoo 2006)				
• Impurity large (i.e., private good), unequal investment	X			
• Impurity small (i.e., public good)		X		
• Impurity large (i.e., private good), equal investment			X	
• Impurity neither large nor small, equal investment				X

6.2.4 Evaluating research on PPP contracting

The broad themes developed in these papers are addressed by research evaluating specific types of PPPs, such as the contracting out of public services. Hart *et al.* (1997) evaluate a government's decision whether to provide a service in-house, thereby retaining residual control rights over non-human assets generated by the partnership (e.g., a prison), or whether to contract out to a private firm, giving the private provider residual control rights. These residual control rights assign authority to make changes given unforeseen contingencies. The service provider chooses investment in quality improvement and cost reduction. The Hart *et al.* (1997) model shows that while the private provider has stronger incentives than a government employee for both quality improvement and cost reductions, the cost-reducing incentives are too strong, sacrificing quality. Thus, private provision may be preferred when cost reductions do not have a strongly negative effect on quality or when these cost reductions can be controlled through contracts, and when quality innovations are a priority. Hart *et al.* (1997) present the example of prisons as a case of private contractors reducing costs to an extent that can cause quality to deteriorate. The authors cite data that indicate that the level of violence is higher in private prisons. They conclude that although some of this concern about quality can be addressed by adopting standards or 'best practices', contractual incompleteness remains. As a result, their theoretical model makes a case against privatization of prisons.

Building on this research, Hart (2003) evaluates a PPP that creates infrastructure to be constructed and operated privately. The government can 'bundle' the construction and operation by forming a partnership with a private firm or 'unbundle' the project using different firms, one to construct and another to operate the infrastructure. The advantage of bundling is that the private firm internalizes the benefits of investments made during construction. A firm that manages a bundled project (i.e., the firm holds control rights) will be more willing to make quality investments in construction that lead to more efficient operation than a firm that is responsible for construction alone. At the same time, Hart argues, the firm of the bundled project has an incentive to make investments that reduce cost but harm quality of service. Hart concludes that if the quality of the building can be specified, but the quality of service cannot be specified (e.g., prisons or schools), unbundling, or separate provision, may be preferred. Alternatively, if the quality of the infrastructure cannot be specified in the contract, but the quality of the service can be (as may be the case with a hospital), a PPP could provide the best incentives for the private firm to invest optimally in construction.

Bennett and Iossa (2006) also evaluate bundling the construction and management of a facility and whether private or public ownership is optimal. The project may affect social benefit, management costs and residual value of the facility. Under private ownership, the owner has the power to implement an innovation unilaterally. Under public ownership, re-negotiation between the firm/consortia and the public authority must take place before an innovation is implemented. An innovation that increases social benefit may either decrease cost at the management stage (bundling results in a positive externality, so bundling is optimal) or increase management costs (bundling results in a negative externality, so unbundling may be optimal). Bennett and Iossa find that with a positive externality, ownership by the consortia (i.e., private partner) is not necessarily optimal. Under certain conditions, government ownership is optimal (i.e., the government partner should hold all control rights). Concerning ownership of the residual value of the project once a project has concluded, it is not optimal for these rights to automatically revert to the public partner because in that case, *ex ante* investment incentives are reduced. Instead, residual ownership should be allotted to the private partner, and the public partner should have the option to negotiate a mutually beneficial transfer of ownership.

Contractual commitments on sharing the value of a project require an assessment of trade-offs between cash flows and private benefits and how such tradeoffs are affected by the allocation of control rights. Aghion and Bolton (1992) consider a project that yields a cash flow as well as private benefits. Each partner in the project cares about different benefits; the investor in the project cares only about cash flow, while the entrepreneur receiving the investor's funding is interested in maximizing both cash flow and private benefits. Thus, the partners' interests conflict. In this context, control rights specify who makes decisions affecting the tradeoff between cash flow and private benefits. Aghion and Bolton find that the partner who controls the decisions once the project is underway will then divert resources, or make other decisions, in order to serve his or her own interests. Thus, control rights should be assigned for particular events based on which partner will make the least inefficient decision at that point. Jensen and Meckling's (1976) work on incentives in corporate finance is related. These authors consider the decisions of an investor who cares only about the value of the project, and a manager who cares about both the value of the project and the non-pecuniary benefits. The value of a firm or project is not fixed; rather, it depends on the actions taken by management and management's consumption of non-pecuniary benefits. Hart (2001) argues that the Aghion-Bolton model, with its emphasis on the independence of control rights from cash flow rights as well as the association of these rights with future contingencies, is supported by empirical work (Kaplan and Stromberg 2001).

6.3 PPP for infrastructure and provision of public services: empirical analysis

Empirical analyses relating to PPPs and incomplete contracting theory are few. More often, researchers turn to survey-based methods and case-study approaches to assess current and past PPP relationships and to extract lessons for future partnerships. In this section, we discuss the recent empirical, survey-based and case-study research addressing contracting issues for PPPs generating impure public goods in the form of infrastructure and provision of public services.

Infrastructure development projects involve significant risks given the large capital investments and long project time periods needed to negotiate contracts and construct, operate, and maintain assets. Traditionally, these projects (e.g., bridges, roads, telecommunications, railroads, energy) were funded, constructed and managed by the public sector because these projects produced impure goods. Increasingly, however, public agencies have looked to improve efficiency by using private-sector expertise and financing through PPP mechanisms. When an infrastructure PPP is formed, the private partner usually manages the finance, planning, and construction of the asset base upon which services will be generated. Once constructed, ownership or operating rights for public utilities can revert to the public partner or may be assigned to private firms.

Using PPPs for development and maintenance of infrastructure allows the government to avoid levying distortionary taxes by using private-sector funding repaid through project user fees. More important, these PPPs can transfer many of the risks associated with long-term capital projects (e.g., construction risk, operating risk, revenue risk due to demand shortfall, financial risk, regulatory risk, and environmental risk) to the private sector. Infrastructure financed by PPPs holds particular promise for developing countries, as it allows governments that do not have sufficient financial resources, risk-bearing capability or intellectual capital to build their country's infrastructure (Irwin *et al.* 1997; Alonso-Condo *et al.* 2007).

Economic theory predicts that given a full set of control rights, a private partner will exercise market power by setting prices above the optimal level and producing quantity below the optimal level. By forming PPPs, the government can retain some control over production and pricing decisions and can limit the private firm's use of market power (Limi 2008). Of particular importance is the structuring of the renegotiation process so as not to distort each partner's incentives (Gausch 2004). In practice, designing contracts for construction and operations of infrastructure that result in appropriate risk sharing and balance control rights is a challenge.

6.3.1 Empirical findings of bundling

A primary finding from the theoretical research, that bundling of construction and operating processes through PPPs may increase efficiency (Hart 1997; Hart 2003; Bennett and Iossa 2006), has been the focus of some empirical research. Bundling transfers control rights over assets to the private partner, thus providing incentives for relation-specific investments. If the quality of the service can be specified, theory predicts that a PPP could provide optimal investment incentives for the private partner (Hart 2003).

Chong *et al.* (2006) evaluate organizational choice and performance of PPPs using regression analysis and a database of information relating to 5,000 French local public water authorities. The analysis finds that consumer prices are higher for water supplied under any of the four forms of PPPs accounted for in the analysis rather than water supplied under direct public management. Moreover, the form of PPP that represents the greatest allocation of control rights to the private partner, build-to-operate-and-own concessions, results in the highest consumer prices. The authors point to several factors that may contribute to these results, including inadequate *ex ante* competition between private partners and nontransparent partnership selection procedures. Although these PPP relationships in France are considered to be 'administrative contracts' and as such, give the public-sector authority the right to unilaterally change the contract after signing, thus addressing concerns about *ex post* opportunistic behaviour by the private partner, it is not clear how often this provision is invoked and thus, how credible is this threat.

Blanc-Brude *et al.* (2009) also evaluate PPP efficiency in contrast to traditional procurement for road construction projects. Using a database of 227 road projects, of which 65 are PPPs, financed by the European Investment Bank between 1990 and 2005 in all EU–15 countries and Norway, the authors evaluate *ex ante* costs in the form of bidder's construction prices. They find that a PPP road project, which can be viewed as allocating greater control rights to the private partner, is 24 per cent more expensive, *ex ante*, than roads built through traditional procurement with more limited private control rights. The authors note that *ex post* cost overruns for traditionally procured roads are reported to be close to this estimate. While the authors argue that this finding may undercut the increased efficiency argument for bundling projects (i.e., transferring control rights over assets to the private partner), this finding seems to point to the need to compare *ex ante* contract costs to the full range of *ex post* costs including construction cost overruns, renegotiation costs and operating costs, in order for a determination of efficiency to be made.

Cabral and Saussier (2007) evaluate both quality and cost in PPPs and differences in control-rights allocations across countries. They use a case-study approach to evaluate PPP provision of prisons in three countries: Brazil, France and the United States.[2] From previous research, they find that in Brazil, PPP prisons resulted in certain cost reductions and an increase in the quality of services provided; in France, PPPs led to an increase in both cost and quality; and in the United States, researchers observed reductions in both cost and quality. Cabral and Saussier attribute these differences across countries to differences in the assignment of decision rights (control rights). The authors assert that in the USA, all decision rights are assigned to the private partner, while in France and Brazil, decision rights are split between the private and public partners. The private ownership of control rights in the USA means that the private partner controls not only the building of the facility but also the operation, and it is difficult for the government to monitor the behaviour of the private operator. The authors suggest that the split of decision rights in France and Brazil makes it more likely that civil servants will be present inside the prison and able to verify the quality of services. If prisons can be viewed as goods with large impurity, as defined by Francesconi and Muthoo (2006) (i.e., public goods with strong private-goods attributes), then the better outcome – given sharing of control rights by the public and private partner – supports the theoretical formulation of Francesconi and Muthco that is presented in Table 6.1. Cabral and Saussier (2007) attribute the higher costs in France to the relatively lower allocation of control rights to the private partner versus the allocation in Brazil. The greater freedom given to private partners in Brazil allows the greater adoption of managerial innovations. These findings highlight the importance of carefully allocating control rights between partners on a detailed risk-by-risk level.

6.3.2 Empirical findings of PPP governance

A second focus of quantitative and case-study research is the evaluation of PPP governance mechanisms, contract flexibility and partner attributes. Zheng *et al.* (2008) use a case-study approach to evaluate how contractual and relational governance mechanisms are used in management of two long-term, complex PPP supply arrangements. While contractual governance implies well-defined control rights, relational governance relies on informal arrangements based on trust and experience rather than formal contracts for managing relationships. Relational governance also implies more fluid control rights. Some researchers argue that relational governance promotes flexibility, solidarity and information exchange, while others argue that developing these arrangements consumes resources and may restrict new opportunities (Zheng *et al.* 2008). Zheng *et al.* (2008) find that relational and contractual mechanisms are complementary and, moreover, that relational assumptions frame the contracting process as one of either distrust or commitment. Contractual governance mechanisms, once set up, offer less flexibility but stabilize partnership, whereas relational governance mechanisms are more fragile and can erode quickly.

Desrieux *et al.* (2010) also analyse the role of relational contracts in the form of repeated or multiple relationships between a local government and a private partner. After developing a theoretical model showing how multiple or bundled relationships can improve performance and reduce costs (due to the government's option to continue a relationship or end it, i.e., threat strategy), the authors formally test the model using a database of the contractual choices made by 5,000 French local public water authorities.[3] The regression analysis shows that the use of the same private partner for both the distribution and the sanitation of water is associated with a significant price reduction for consumers. While the authors point to the importance of relational contracts in generating their findings, the model results could also be interpreted as stemming from the retention of important control rights by the local government that give them flexibility to respond to partnership outcomes.

Athias and Saussier (2007) evaluate the tradeoff between rigid and flexible contracts using a database of 71 concession contracts for toll roads across eight countries. They find that several factors are related to increased flexibility in contracts, as defined by price renegotiation terms, including higher traffic uncertainty (i.e., revenue uncertainty), increased reputation as measured by number of previous contracts between the partners, and stronger country-specific institutional frameworks for contract enforcement. This increased flexibility essentially gives the private partner more control rights over future contingencies. The analysis indicates that the characteristics of the partners affect contract design and thus control rights designations.

Araujo and Sutherland (2010) provide a broad evaluation of PPPs in OECD countries based on an ad hoc OECD questionnaire on infrastructure investment and on data on nearly 2,000 PPPs. The paper gives quantitative characterization of PPPs in OECD countries, generates an indicator to assess how well suited country-specific policy frameworks are to benefitting from PPPs, and provides guidelines for contract structure. The authors conclude that the heterogeneity of this indicator across countries suggests there would be gains from improved policy frameworks for some countries.

Relational governance, which can involve high levels of flexibility and thus private control, may complement contractual governance or strong institutional frameworks. This research highlights the importance of governance and, specifically, the balance of contractual versus relational governance for PPPs.

6.4 Operational framework

The theoretical literature on incomplete PPP contracts has been developed with a focus on analytical tractability. As many of the authors acknowledge, many important aspects of PPP contracts are ignored. For example, the theoretical work typically assumes symmetric bargaining power, though this is rarely the case. Empirical research on PPPs and incomplete contracts is also limited.

Using the theoretical literature and limited empirical research as a guide, we have developed a three-stage framework to evaluate PPP contracts and the embedded control rights. This three-stage framework can be used to analyse failures in already existing PPPs and help prevent pitfalls in future PPPs. Prior to entering Stage 1 of negotiations with a specific partner, it is vital for the public partner, in particular, to engage in 'pre-contract' preparations of self-assessment and partner selection. In Stage 1, the private and public partners negotiate an incomplete contract that assigns front-end control rights over decision making and back-end property rights (i.e., control rights) over the partnership's assets and the goods produced by the PPP. Once these rights are assigned, the partners make investments. In Stage 2, the partners make management decisions through bargaining. This bargaining will lead either to the non-cooperative bargaining solution or to the cooperative bargaining solution, the latter of which maximizes the joint benefit to both partners. In Stage 3, the partners respond to an unanticipated shock by either concluding their partnership or beginning the process again at Stage 1 by renegotiating the allocation of control rights and property rights. If the partners choose to renegotiate, the control rights will generally be distributed differently.

6.4.1 Pre-contract stage: defining the bargaining space

The PPP is based on a contractual commitment that involves more than public-sector regulations being imposed on a private party. Public institutions, in particular, would benefit from beginning this process with a self-assessment to identify their primary objectives in seeking out private partners, their strengths and assets, and the desired complementarities with potential private partners.[4] Given the insights from incomplete contracting theoretical literature, this self-assessment and the evaluation of potential partners should be performed through a lens focused on the likely nature of any partnership output (i.e., the degree of public versus private output), the likely relative contribution of potential partners' assets, the relative valuation of output likely to be generated by a partnership, and the degree of control that is likely to be demanded or forfeited by a potential partner. The objective is to choose the potential partner that maximizes the expected relationship outcome, given the results of the assessments of self and potential partners. As such, these assessments are essential to selecting a partner who will form an effective partnership.

Though the order in which partnership negotiations proceed is of little consequence, it is vital for the public partner to be deliberate early in the process to avoid seemingly innocuous *ex ante* decisions that can severely limit the options for control rights. At each point in a PPP, the public institution must consider the long-term consequences of all relationship decisions. Private firms often actively seek government contracts and make restricted partnership offers, leaving public institutions in a passive role. The public institution can instead take proactive steps to seek out well-matched partners that complement their strengths. Moreover, by actively evaluating and approaching potential private partners, a public institution can form a consortium with a group of specialized partners, rather than responding to offers from single partners. Although self-assessment and actively seeking out partners require a higher initial investment of effort, they provide the public partner with the greatest degree of control over the selection of partners, and thus implicitly define the degree of control over the remainder of the partnership process. In other words, a proactive approach can significantly broaden the public institutions' choice set. Similarly, a proactive approach by the private firm can significantly increase its control in the negotiating process.

The pre-contract effort on the part of both partners will lay the foundation not only for developing the formal contract but also for setting the stage for the relational contract. As discussed by Zheng *et al.* (2008) and Desrieux *et al.* (2010), the informal trust and information-exchange environment of the relational contract act as a complement to a formal PPP contract. In cases where PPPs are likely to be repeated, the relational contract and the informal control rights allocation within take on even greater importance.

6.4.2 Stage 1: negotiating the contract

Once a partner has been selected, the public and private partners negotiate a contract that allocates a share of the front-end control rights and back-end property rights to each of the partners. The front-end control rights specify the resources committed by both partners (i.e., investments) and designate control rights (decision-making power) over the partnership's investments and production processes. The back-end property rights assign ownership of partnership outputs and detail the distribution of these outputs. As discussed in the theoretical and empirical literature, this allocation of control and property rights implicitly assigns the risks associated with the partnership. These risks include planning risk, misspecification of output requirements risk, design risk, construction and time schedule risk, operation risk, demand risk, risk of changes in public needs, legislative/regulatory risk, financial risk and residual risk (Iossa *et al.* 2007).

In the first stage, if control rights over investments are not given completely to either partner (i.e., control rights are ill specified), each partner makes decisions that minimize their respective input while making sure the combined investments are sufficient for a successful joint venture. Given the diversity in the nature of partnership investments, it is difficult for partners to balance their respective asset contributions. These asset contributions can be tangible, such as equipment, buildings or funding, or intangible 'knowledge' assets (Rausser *et al.* 2000). Unlike tangible assets, the value of intangible assets is difficult to determine and relies on many factors, such as the nature of the asset and the degree of complementarity. Knowledge assets may be tacit (e.g., know-how) or codifiable. Tacit knowledge draws on skills and techniques and is transferred by demonstration, apprenticeships, personal instruction and provision of expert services. Codifiable knowledge can be reduced to messages and is easily transferred. Knowledge assets can assume the form of a non-rivalled or inexhaustible good. In other words, sharing this information will not reduce the amount available to others. Although non-rivalled, these assets are not necessarily public goods in that it may be possible to exclude access by others.

Fully characterizing a partner's assets or investments (i.e., control and/or property rights) is vital for capitalizing on complementarities among the different assets held by the public and private partners and for negotiating over the respective contributions made by each partner. Private institutions are likely to have access to funding, state-of-the-art equipment and tools, market expertise and marketing resources. In return, public institutions can offer preferential access to public resources such as seed banks or university researchers, assistance in meeting government and agency requirements and obtaining contracts, and positive public image. While some of these assets are easy to accommodate contractually (e.g., funding, equipment), others are more challenging to capture (e.g., positive public image).

The investment of resources on the front end is fairly transparent. The implications of choosing governance structures for the partnership, however, are not. The governance structure of a partnership assigns control on the front end and ownership at the back end, thus determining how the partners will interact, make decisions, resolve conflicts and terminate the partnership (if necessary). Several researchers find that the flexibility of governance structures, presence of relational contracts, and even country-specific policy frameworks play a key role in PPPs (Athias and Saussier 2007; Zheng *et al.* 2008; Araujo and Sutherland 2010; Desrieux *et al.* 2010). Of primary importance in setting up a governance structure is specifying how the project will be evaluated and under what conditions the scope will be changed. At the conclusion of the partnership, the governance structure determines how back-end property rights are invoked and, thus, realized outputs and benefits are distributed.

As discussed, PPPs often require numerous types of input from each partner and produce numerous products, each falling somewhere on the spectrum from private to public good.[5] Thus, partners are negotiating over a set of investments and a set of expected outputs that do not have a one-to-one mapping (i.e., one partnership input is likely to contribute to the production of several outputs). Efficient allocation of control rights in PPPs will then likely depend on assessing the nature of all partnership outputs. In practice, this suggests that control rights should be defined for each output of the partnership. While PPP contracts can accommodate this complexity, accurate *ex ante* assessment of expected outputs, in order to maximize efficiency, is a challenge. While the valuation of each partner for each of these outputs may be determined, the relative contribution of each partner's investments to each output is murky and difficult to define.

6.4.3 Stage 2: decision making through bargaining

In Stage 2, the partners jointly manage the partnership by making decisions based on a two-person, two-phase bargaining game (see Rausser *et al.* (2011) for an extension of this analysis to an *n*-person bargaining game). In the first phase, the partners decide what threats to invoke if no agreement is reached. These threat strategies, chosen to maximize their payoff while minimizing effort based on control-rights and property-rights assignments in Stage 1, determine the disagreement payoffs. These strategies may not be carried out and may not be explicit. All that is required is the potential of a threat. In other words, the boundaries for a Pareto move to a cooperative solution will be set by the equilibrium determination in the first stage of the game of the disagreement payoff.

In this stage, the partners will achieve an efficient outcome in which the partners exercise their rights and share the benefits. The partner holding the relevant control right is aware of the non-controlling partner's influence and selects an action that maximizes the controlling partner's payoff given the non-controlling partner's threats (Rausser *et al.* 2008). The outcome of this stage is a cooperative solution on the efficiency frontier, constrained by the disagreement payoffs.

6.4.4 Stage 3: a shock to the partnership

In Stage 3 of the agreement, the partners respond to unanticipated shocks. Here we consider a shock to be an event for which there is no explicit contingency that affects the partnership once it is underway. The partners have two options in response to a shock: 1) they can conclude the partnership and exercise their back-end property rights over the assets and goods produced by the partnership; or 2) they can renegotiate the control rights and property rights designated in Stage 1. If the partners choose renegotiation, the balance of bargaining power may be different than during initial negotiations. A partner may find himself or herself in either a more vulnerable or a stronger position depending on the nature of the shock and the outcome of the partnership to this point.

If terminal conditions of the partnership have been reached, the partners assess outcomes and consider whether to renew the agreement. Public institutions, lacking until recently any formal method for review of partnerships with private institutions (see 'Value for Money Assessment Guidance' (Treasury 2006)), have developed a variety of evaluation policies. These methods rely mainly on anecdotal feedback to evaluate how the partnership proceeded. The informal review and general impression of both partners are coupled with evaluations of tangible outcomes and success in meeting project deadlines to generate an overall assessment of PPP performance.

6.5 Implementation of operational framework

6.5.1 R&D PPP

Research and development processes once were thought to follow a straight path from publicly provided basic research to privately conducted applied research. The route to innovation is now recognized to follow a more indirect path, in a form that cannot be codified (David 1997). In the USA, in particular, research relationships between academics and industry that have successfully allowed for the transfer of people and ideas have led to 'MIT envy' in other countries. The new paradigm for research and development is one of public–private partnerships for research through which universities, government research institutes, think-tanks, consultancies, campus-based companies and private firms can coordinate and collaborate on a range of research activities from formal, multi-year, multi-project partnerships to informal arrangements. A multitude of examples of these research relationships now exist across many disciplines, including biomedical, pharmaceutical, agricultural and technological science.

The task of forming these relationships, however, is complex and delicate. Many lessons have been learned as public criticism and scrutiny of PPPs in research has become increasingly intense (Press and Washburn 2000). Several issues, such as conflict between public and private interests, setting research priorities (Rausser et al. 2008), ownership of and access to intellectual property (e.g., issues of hold-up and blocking patents), and publication delays fuel the current debate and very often present insurmountable obstacles to forming research partnerships. Some observers claim that basic research since the 1990s has declined due to an increased focus on short-term commercial targets (Slywotsky 2009). Others suggest that such partnerships have been hindered by an inability to successfully turn basic research findings into commercially viable technologies (Wadhwa and Litan 2009).

A host of external forces is pushing public researchers to actively engage with private researchers. Among these forces are diminishing federal and State funds for public-goods research and increased State funding for private–public research. In addition, legislation (e.g., the Bayh-Dole Act), the restructuring of many large life-sciences firms, and an alignment of private and public research incentives have contributed to this trend. Moreover, the traditional research paradigm (under which there is a one-way flow from basic science conducted in public institutions to applied research and commercialization undertaken largely by private industry) has shifted to one of chaotic research and development (R&D). Increasingly, public and private researchers are engaging in interactive research relationships with exchange and collaboration in all stages of research.

Complementarities between scientific and practical knowledge have the capacity to generate rapid and far-reaching innovation. Public and private agents seek attributes and assets in prospective partners that complement their own abilities and resources. Although the potential benefits of research partnerships are clear, the potential risks to both parties are complex. These risks pose serious obstacles to the successful formation of research PPPs.

The goal in forming comprehensive research partnerships is to balance the set of complex tradeoffs – to maximize research opportunities while controlling related risks. For public institutions, which have diverse, complicated and sometimes conflicting objectives, having well-conceived core principles, *ex ante*, before entering research partnerships, is a prerequisite for forming successful relationships. If adhered to, these principles translate into a set of constraints on how much control may be relinquished (or must be retained) by the public partner in a research agreement or contract in order to serve its mission.

At the initiation of a research agreement, it is impossible to predict and plan for all events that will occur as the research moves forward. What can be considered, however, are the control rights. In the context of research agreements, control rights specify the degree to which a partner retains control over the research process as it unfolds. These options are embedded within the agreement negotiated by the involved parties, and therefore are considered *ex ante*, before committing to a particular contracting party.

Previous theoretical literature on PPPs has focused on the optimal allocation of control rights when producing either a private or public good and so does not provide a complete framework to evaluate research relationships that produce impure goods. PPPs can, however, be structured to accommodate impure goods (Spielman *et al.* 2007; Rausser *et al.* 2008; Rausser and Stevens 2009). Francesconi and Muthoo (2006) find that given equal investment by both partners, and given that the impurity of partnership output can be characterized as neither large (private goods) nor small (public goods) but a mix of private and public goods outputs, the partner who has a lower valuation of the partnership outputs should receive all control rights (see Table 6.1). This research suggests that for research outputs, which can be characterized as having both private- and public-goods aspects, control rights should be allocated to the public partner if research outputs are more valued by the private partner (as with marketable innovations), or, alternatively, to the private partner if the relationship generates outputs that are more highly valued by the public partner (such as publications of research findings). Furthermore, because partnerships involve a broad set of investments as well as a varied set of expected outputs, it may be efficient for control rights to be defined for each output of the partnership.

The fundamental practical issue in forming research and development partnerships, however, is assessing the value of the suite of options that are defined *ex ante*, when the partners enter a contractual agreement, before the research takes place. Whether to accept certain contractual provisions is essentially an investment decision that takes place under uncertainty. In the case of research, not only are the probabilities of particular events (i.e., the chance of developing a commercial innovation) difficult to determine, but the stream of benefits, given that specific events occur, is unknown. As a result, the primary institutional failure in structuring research and development agreements is the absence of a mechanism for securitization. Put and call options inherent in a research agreement, options to forfeit (sell) or obtain (buy) the benefits of the research, are ill-defined. In essence, there is no system for valuing the key aspects of the partnership, such as time to expiration for licensing options. Given the difficulty in determining the respective value of each partner's investments and in specifying respective valuations of partnership outputs, the theoretical findings on impure goods can provide only general guidance in specifying control rights for research partnerships.

6.5.1.1 Operational framework for research PPPs

PPPs for research come in many forms, ranging from large, multi-project, multi-year 'strategic alliances' to single, targeted clinical trials. Collaborations may cover a single research project or, alternatively, involve 'mega-agreements' that cover a large range of interactions. Research projects may have short or long time horizons. Public institutions may enter agreements with a single private company or, instead, with groups of firms sharing a common interest (industry consortia). No matter the exact form of a particular arrangement, these relationships can be characterized using the Operational Framework (Rausser and Ameden 2003; Rausser and Stevens 2009). At the heart of this three-stage structure are the control rights that stem from the inherent contingencies in the research process and are embedded in any research agreement.

During the 'pre-contract stage', each potential research collaborator lays the groundwork for a research partnership by conducting a self-assessment to identify its primary objectives, its research strengths and assets, and the desired complementarities (Rausser and Ameden 2003). The next step is to find and select a partner. While private firms often seek government contracts and approach university researchers, leaving public institutions to take a passive role, public institutions can instead actively seek out well-matched partners, providing public partners with the greatest degree of control and substantially broadening the public institution's choice set.

Given the results of the self-assessment, the university can seek out well-matched partners who complement their strengths (Rausser and Ameden 2003). A university should then consider with whom to partner and the best mechanism for doing so given the associated tradeoffs concerning the private partners' type, size, objectives, assets, the type of relationship, and the value of previous experience. For example, larger private institutions may have greater financial and scientific resources, while smaller institutions may be more flexible. A university may prefer to collaborate with a national company and access its proprietary research tools. Alternatively, it may choose to focus on serving the local business community by partnering with a local startup. The nature and objectives of the partners will dictate certain collaborating mechanisms – perhaps a 'strategic alliance' for a larger university and company when all research takes place on campus, or a short-term, targeted research project between a medium-sized university and a small start-up when research takes place both off and on campus.

In Stage 1, partners negotiate the 'front-end' control rights and 'back-end' property rights (Rausser and Ameden 2003). Front-end control rights enumerate the resources committed by each partner and give the partners decision-making power over the partnership's investment and production processes. The potential partners seek complementarities among the different assets held by each. Private institutions are likely to hold such assets as funding; specific, state-of-the-art scientific research tools (e.g., EST sequences, enabling technologies) and associated tacit knowledge about how to work with these technologies; proprietary databases; and commercialization and marketing expertise. In return, public institutions offer scientific expertise, basic science, and leads on new research. The ultimate objective is to combine the different attributes of the partners' respective assets in the most productive combinations for the research partnership. The back-end property rights assign ownership of assets (i.e., research results) and determine how this information is disseminated, the process for establishing ownership (patent rights), and how the innovation will be licensed. Each of these issues is crucial in determining how both the pecuniary and non-pecuniary benefits of the research are shared by the partners and by the public.

In Stage 1, the partners also negotiate the governance structure that will guide actions in Stage 2 (Rausser and Ameden 2003). The governance structure of the research agreement defines how the partners will interact, make decisions, resolve conflicts and terminate the agreement (if necessary). It specifies the structure of any oversight committee, how the research agenda is selected, and the scope of the agreement. These three factors, in turn, determine the embedded optionality. The composition (i.e., university or industry majority) and operating rules for the oversight group are vitally important for the balance of control in the research partnership. The most important consequence of the governance structure is the selection of the research agenda and intellectual leads for the projects. Given that selection of a project and researcher implicitly defines results, the power to define the research agenda translates into the power to influence the research outcomes. In addition to identifying how the research proposals will be evaluated, the governance structure specifies how the agreement will be administered and if the scope will be changed (i.e., the agreement extended or terminated).

In Stage 2, the partners jointly manage the partnership by making decisions based on a two-person, two-phase bargaining game (Rausser and Stevens 2009), given the specifications of the governance structure. This bargaining will lead either to a non-cooperative bargaining solution or to a cooperative bargaining solution that maximizes the joint benefit to both partners. In Stage 3, the partners respond to an unanticipated shock by either concluding their partnership or renegotiating the allocation of control rights and property rights. After Stage 3, the partners assess the outcome of their partnership and consider whether to renew the agreement.

There is little consequence to the order in which different aspects of a partnership are negotiated. It is vital, however, for a public institution to be deliberate early in the process, when seemingly innocuous decisions *ex ante* may severely limit its control or flexibility at crucial junctures *ex post* (Rausser and Ameden 2003). For example, a university that decides to enter negotiations with a single large company for a first round of research may find that the company's competitors are not interested in entering negotiations for the second round due to the perceived 'closeness' of the first firm to the university. At each point in a research relationship, it is important for the university to consider the long-term consequences of all relationship-related decisions.

6.5.2 Transportation infrastructure

In this subsection, we apply our operational framework to transportation infrastructure PPPs. Specifically, we examine the outcome of specific road construction PPPs in Australia, Mexico and Chile. PPPs in each of these countries have long-term project horizons and have completed all three stages of our operational framework.

Australia offers a leading example of infrastructure PPPs for several reasons. Australia has had extensive experience with these arrangements, dating back to 1985, and now all territorial and State governments turn to the private sector for design, financing, construction and management of transportation projects (Czerwinski and Geddes 2010). Australia is a primary infrastructure investor abroad and the large road and rail systems there play an important role in the country's economy (Czerwinski and Geddes 2010). The Australian government has been successful in using PPPs to increase the provision of an impure good (roads) by designing contracts that directly address the private sector's concerns about risk sharing (Brown 2005).

New South Wales (NSW), the largest state in Australia by population, has facilitated the growth of PPPs by setting up two government entities that handle PPP administration.

NSW's first PPP came as the result of an unsolicited proposition in 1985 from a partnership of two transportation facility construction and operation companies (Czerwinski and Geddes 2010). The Sydney Harbour Tunnel project, a build-own-operate-transfer (BOOT) partnership, arose in order to address congestion that had developed around the Sydney Harbour Bridge. In typical BOOT partnerships, the private partners construct, own, operate and capture revenues in Stage 2 and, after a fixed period of time, transfer ownership to the government in Stage 3. In this partnership, the public partner's 'pre-contract stage' before entering contract negotiations was limited. In Stage 1, the government undertook substantial revenue risk by guaranteeing a minimum revenue level, while the private partners assumed primarily construction risk. The government gave the private partner control rights over construction processes, factors that affected revenue risk, while assuming the revenue risk. The imbalance of financial risk in this project was most likely due to the passive pre-contract posture of the NSW government and its inexperience with negotiating such projects.

Over time, risk allocation in NSW PPPs has changed, shifting from initial agreements driven by contractors unwilling to bear much financial risk to consortium structures with third-party backing that accept the brunt of the revenue risk (Czerwinski and Geddes 2010; Brown et al. 2009). This is illustrated by the Hills M2 Motorway PPP in NSW, a 21-km motorway that opened in 1997. In Stage 1 of this BOOT PPP, the negotiated contract specified that the private partner bore the traffic risk with no direct payments or guarantees from the public partner. The private partner agreed to pay the public partner for the right to levy a toll, contingent on the private partner earning a pre-determined minimum rate of return. In another NSW PPP, the Cross City Tunnel, the contract specified that the private partner bore all of the traffic volume revenue risk, along with the design and construction risks. The favourable risk-sharing arrangement of this PPP from the public partner's perspective was likely due to the competitive bidding process that required bidders to specify the size of their payment to the public partner for the right to levy a toll. The private agent who made the highest bid was chosen to be the private partner for this project. In this case, the proactive pre-contract effort on the part of the public partner yielded favourable contract terms and control-rights delegations.

As for the general trend concerning price-setting mechanisms in these Australian PPPs, the government found that potential private partners would enter into a contract only if the contract included price-setting mechanisms that correctly reflected their financial and operating risks (Rausser and Stevens 2009). The Australian government addressed these concerns in Stage 1 negotiations by sharing price-setting control rights with the private partners. The public and private partners would jointly set prices in Stage 2 to reflect the private partner's risks and to allow price flexibility in response to unanticipated shocks in Stage 3. By keeping contracts flexible and allocating some price-setting control rights to the private partner, and setting prices according to the private partner's risks, these contracts align partners' expectations for pricing and reduce the need for renegotiation. This allocation of control rights has decreased unanticipated shocks (the latter are addressed, when necessary, in Stage 3) and allowed the Australian government to form successful PPPs to finance infrastructure.

Governance risks, and associated allocation of control rights over governance structures, can be an issue for PPPs. CityLink, a BOOT PPP road project in Australia's State of Victoria that connected three existing highways in Melbourne, opened in 1999. During Stage 1, the partners negotiated to share risk between the private partner, public partner, and users of the link, with the private sector bearing the risk of all events except those that the State was able to manage (Hodge 2004). Based on observations of risk associated with CityLink, Hodge (2004) argues that while commercial risks were transferred to the private partner and managed well, governance risks were not successfully handled by the State. Governance issues associated with City Link include the absence of a publicly available economic or financial evaluation prior to project initiation, the exclusion of the consumers' interests (no allowance for due process), and allowing an extended project timeline of up to 54 years (Hodge 2004). These issues could perhaps have been avoided through a more effective self-assessment in the pre-contract effort leading up to Stage 1.

A further issue associated with infrastructure PPPs is that of network risk, an area where public and private partners have diverging incentives (Chung et al. 2009). As with incentives involved with repeating partnerships, network risk involves competing projects or activities that fall outside of a particular PPP but affect the demand for the PPP output. These competing projects constitute a Stage 3 unanticipated shock to the PPP. While governments are interested in offering many options for road travel to reduce congestion, private partners depending on toll revenues are interested in reducing competing road options for consumers so that profitability is assured. These risks can be addressed by Stage 1 negotiations concerning non-compete clauses, which prohibit a public partner from developing unplanned competing transportation projects, or less restrictive compensation clauses, which, in Australia, are part of a broader 'Material Compensation Clause' requiring specific allocation of potential adverse effects risks (Czerwinski and Geddes 2010). A PPP in the United States, 91 Express Lanes, was controversial because of its non-compete clause. Litigation ensued over the widening of a competing highway, causing the nature of non-compete clauses to change in successive PPP contracts. Under a compensation clause that was part of the CityLink PPP contract, a compensation claim was made by the private partner because roads near the project were redeveloped and represented competition for CityLink. Currently, the trend in Australia is away from compensation clauses, which give the private partner significant control rights, toward greater assumption of competing-facility risk by the private sector. It is now the practice in Australia to include standard clauses that designate specific network risk allocations that potential private bidders must take as given during the bidding process. This trend may represent a move toward the allocation of a greater share of control rights to the partner with the lower valuation, as is suggested by Francesconi and Muthoo (2006) for PPP outputs that have significant private-goods aspects. In this case, that was the government partner.

The recently completed EastLink, Victoria's second fully electronic toll way, provides a snapshot of the current state of PPP procurement processes, contract structures, and lessons learned in Australia. In this case, the public partner engaged in a full pre-contract assessment of the project, self and potential partner. Prior to issuing a request for proposals (RFP), Victoria completed a business case analysis of the project, formed a separate entity to oversee the procurement and negotiating process, and asked for expressions of interest, allowing interested private partners to sketch out their proposal (Brown et al. 2009). The RFP was directed at two private-partner consortia. As part of the RFP, the government included tolling rate and structure as a bid variable and required sharing of revenues in excess of forecast level. The RFP also specified evaluation criteria and allowed the operation time period to be a bid variable. Thus, the public partner actively set the PPP bargaining space by defining minimum control-rights designations at the outset of the partnership in the pre-contract stage. In Stage 1, the government set an opening date for the project and specified that the State was under no restrictions concerning other transportation projects but that the private partner was entitled to compensation if net adverse impacts occurred. Moreover, the governance structure (which would come into play in Stage 2) required independent experts to verify and oversee design and construction and two years of operation. And finally, in Stage 1, key performance indicators to be used in Stage 2 and upon project assessment were agreed to. The project opened five months ahead of schedule and encountered few claims or issues along the way. The success of the EastLink PPP was likely due to active positioning by the government and the careful, experienced allocation of control rights early in the RFP.

An earlier, less successful example of transportation PPPs is the build-operate-transfer (BOT) partnerships formed between the Mexican government and private partners as part of the national Highway Program (1989–1990) (Ruster 1997). In Stage 1, the PPP contract used the private partner's construction cost and revenue projections to estimate operation time (Rausser and Stevens 2009). The government chose the private partners based solely on projected cost and, thus, the private partners had incentives to underestimate costs and underbid competing firms. As a result, in Stage 3, the shock of high construction and management costs unanticipated by the government would bring about renegotiation of the time period for operation prior to transfer and of the associated control rights, so that the private partners could recover their costs. Rather than terminate these agreements in Stage 3, the government chose to renegotiate but did not share decision-making authority or provide incentives for efficient use of control rights. Moreover, as the government's willingness to be flexible and renegotiate became clear, the private partners were given the incentive to over-capitalize costs because larger investments by the private partners invariably led to longer operation time periods. The Mexican BOT partnerships were not successful because the misallocation of control rights in Stage 1 led to Stage 3 renegotiations that distorted the private partners' incentives.

The Chilean government undertook a similar BOT partnership to improve the country's roads (Gómez-Lobo and Hinojosa 1999). To avoid the difficulties the Mexican government encountered with renegotiations, the partners shared decision-making authority, leading to a more efficient outcome given that these infrastructure PPPs generated impure goods (see Table 6.1 and Francesconi and Muthoo 2006). Anticipating renegotiation, the contracts allocated some price-setting control rights to the government in Stage 1. All contracts fixed the operations time period and gave the government decision-making authority over minimum toll levels. The contracts set a ceiling on toll revenues during the operations time period, requiring the private partner to forfeit any revenues over this ceiling to the government. To allow for the private partner's revenue risk, the government agreed to pay fixed subsidies if the revenue from operating the toll did not cover costs. The Chilean government was able to avoid losing bargaining power due to Stage 3 shocks by using a shared authority to establish in the contract a clearly defined range for private-partner earnings and by establishing a framework for earnings outside of that range.

6.6 Concluding remarks

PPPs are on the rise. The theoretical research on incomplete contracts and PPPs indicates that the conceptual and operational framework for structuring PPP contracts, and for evaluating performance, should take into account the type of good the partnership produces. We present a three-stage operational framework that focuses on the allocation of front-end control rights and back-end property rights. During the 'pre-contract stage', the partners define the bargaining space by evaluating themselves and potential partners. In Stage 1, the partners form a contract that assigns control and property rights. Once these rights are assigned, in Stage 2, the partners bargain over whether management decisions will be made cooperatively or non-cooperatively. In Stage 3, the partnership may experience an unanticipated shock. In response to this shock, the partners may return to Stage 1, by renegotiating the assignment of control and property rights, or they may conclude the partnership.

Though partnerships have been efficiently applied in Europe and some developing countries, PPPs in the United States and Canada have not been as successful. For example, surveys of infrastructure PPPs have found governments were unable to reduce their budgets, while the private partners have had trouble generating a profit (Swimmer 2001; Boardman *et al.* 2006). In these projects, the partners generally failed because their incentives were misaligned as a result of the assignment of control and property rights. Using our operational framework to assign control and property rights that align incentives, PPPs could well become more successful.

While much of the theoretical and empirical literature on PPPs focuses on developing efficiency-achieving incentives within an individual agreement, little consideration has been given to incentives that fall outside a specific agreement. Many PPP agreements are up for renewal once completed, giving the public institution an incentive to ensure that the private partner is satisfied with the results of the partnership. Given the increasing financial pressure on public institutions, this may affect conduct within a current project. In other words, these agreements are not necessarily one-shot games; instead, they may be better characterized as a single round of a repeated game. Thus, the possibility of partnership renewal may create incentives for public institutions to develop a reputation for yielding to a private partner's interests. This highlights one of the primary concerns with PPPs: that public institutions will fail to look for funding from sources other than their current partners and will become dependent on renewing these partnerships. As a result, public institutions face diminished bargaining power as they lose the ability to walk away from negotiations with one partner and enter negotiations with a new partner. If recognized, these issues may be addressed by choosing a partner with strong incentive alignment and by placing safeguards within the partnership contract. On the other hand, having an opportunity to repeat a partnership may create positive performance incentives for the private partner wishing to extend previous partnership benefits. In any case, having clear measures of PPP productivity is vital, not only in order to assess PPPs that have been completed, but also in order to successfully allocate control rights in contracts for PPPs yet to occur or ongoing.

Notes

1 There is no consistent definition of control rights and property rights in the literature. In this chapter, we use control rights to refer to the authority to make decisions during the production process (the front end) and property rights to refer to ownership of either the partnership's assets or the goods produced by the partnership (the back end).

2 Cabral and Saussier (2007) base their case studies on earlier empirical studies of prison performance.

3 The database is made up of observations from 1998, 2001 and 2004.

4 From a practical perspective, Ahadzi and Bowles (2004) surveyed individuals associated with concluded PPP projects in the UK, including projects funded by the Private Finance Initiative launched in the UK in 1992. They also evaluated initial negotiations of PPPs and associated delays and bidding costs, and identified the attributes of private and public partners who influenced successful negotiation of PPP contracts. Ahadzi and Bowles find that key attributes for the private-sector partner include the strength and nature of their consortium, the quality of their technical proposal, and the quality of their financial proposal. For the public-sector partner, organizational and technical capabilities are important. In addition, their results reveal differences between private and public partners in their valuation of risk, previous experience and the impact of public opinion.

5 For example, Aghion and Bolton (1992) address this issue, separating cash flow from private benefits and control rights on each.

References

Aghion, P. and Bolton, P., 1992. An Incomplete Contracts Approach to Financial Contracting, *Rev. Econ. Stud.* 59(3), pp. 473–94.

Aghion, P. and Tirole, J., 1997. Formal and Real Authority in Organizations, *J. Polit. Econ.* 105(1), pp. 1–29.

Aghion, P., Dewatripont, M. and Rey, P., 1994. Renegotiation Design with Unverifiable Information, *Econometrica* 62(2), pp. 257–82.

Ahadzi, M. and Bowles, G., 2004. Public–Private Partnerships and Contract Negotiations: an empirical study, *Construction Management and Econ.* 22, pp. 967–78.

Araújo, S. and Sutherland, D., 2010. *Public–Private Partnerships and Investment in Infrastructure.* [OECD Economics Department Working Papers No. 803] OECD Publishing.

Athias, L. and Saussier, S., 2007. *Contractual Flexibility or Rigidity for Public Private Partnerships? Theory and evidence from infrastructure concession contracts.* [MPRA Paper 10541] University Library of Munich, Germany.

Bennett, C. and Iossa, E., 2006. Delegation of Contracting in the Private Provision of Public Services, *Rev. Ind. Organ.* 29(1), pp. 75–92.

Besley, T. and Ghatak, M., 2001. Government Versus Private Ownership of Public Goods, *Q. J. Econ.* 116(4), pp. 1343–72.

Blanc-Brude, F., Goldsmith, H. and Välilä, T., 2009. A Comparison of Construction Contract Prices for Traditionally Procured Roads and Public–Private Partnerships, *Rev. Ind. Organ.* 35, pp. 19–40.

Boardman, A., Poschmann, F. and Vining, A., 2006. Public–Private Partnerships in the U.S. and Canada: there are no free lunches, *J. Comp. Policy Analysis* 7(3), pp. 1–22.

Brown, C., 2005. Financing Transport Infrastructure: for whom the road tolls, *Australian Economic Review* 38(4), pp. 431–8.

Brown, J., Pieplow, R., Driskell, R., Gaj, S., Garvin, M., Holcombe, D., Saunders, M., Seiders, J. and Smith, A., 2009. *Public–Private Partnerships for Highway Infrastructure: capitalizing on international experience.* [Report No. PL-09-010] FHWA.

Cabral, S. and Saussier, S., 2007. *Organizing Prisons Through Public–Private Partnerships: evidence from Brazil, France and the United States.* [Working Paper 2007-21] ADIS.

Chong, E., Huet, F., Saussier, S. and Steiner, F., 2006. Public–Private Partnerships and Prices: evidence from water distribution in France, *Review of Industrial Organization* 29, pp. 149–69.

Chung, D., Hensher, D. and Rose, J., 2009. An Empirical Study of Risk Perception in PPP Tollroad Projects. In: Thirteenth IRSPM conference, April 6–8, 2009, Copenhagen Business School, Denmark.

Czerwinski, D. and Geddes, R., 2010. *Policy Issues in U. S. Transportation Public–Private Partnerships: lessons from Australia.* [Report 09-15] MTI, San José State University, California.

David, P., 1997. The Knowledge Factory, *The Economist*, October 4, 1997 (Survey, pp. 1–22).

Desrieux, C., Chong, E. and Saussier, S., 2010. *Putting All One's Eggs in One Basket: Relational Contracts and the Provision of Local Public Services.* [Online] Available at http://papers.ssrn.com/sol3/Delivery.cfm/SSRN_ID1468401_code329326.pdf?abstractid=1258482andmirid=1 [Accessed 24 October 2010].

Dewatripont, M. and Maskin, E., 1995. Contractual Contingencies and Renegotiation, *Rand J. Econ.* 26(4), pp. 704–19.

Engel, E., Fischer, R. and Galetovic, A., 2007. *The Basic Public Finance of Public–Private Partnerships.* [Working Paper 13284] NBER.

France3coni, M. and Muthoo, A., 2006. *Control Rights in Public–Private Partnerships.* [Discussion Paper 2143] Institute for the Study of Labor (IZA).

Gómez-Lobo, A. and Hinojosa, S. 2000. *Broad Roads in a Thin Country: infrastructure concessions in Chile.* [Policy Research Working Paper 2279] The World Bank.

Grossman, S. and Hart, O., 1986. The Costs and Benefits of Ownership: a theory of vertical and lateral integration, *J. Polit. Econ.* 94(4), pp. 691–719.

Hart, O., 1995. *Firms, Contracts, and Financial Structure.* Oxford, UK: Clarendon Press.

Hart, O., 2001. *Financial Contracting.* [Working Paper 8285] NBER.

Hart, O., 2003. Incomplete Contracts and Public Ownership: remarks, and an application to public-private partnerships, *Econ. J.* 113(486), pp. C69–C76.

Hart, O. and Moore, J., 1988. Incomplete Contracts and Renegotiation, *Econometrica* 56(4), pp. 755–85.

Hart, O. and Moore, J., 1990. Property Rights and the Nature of the Firm, *J. Polit. Econ.* 98(6), pp. 1119–58.

Hart, O. and Moore, J., 1999. Foundations of Incomplete Contracts, *Rev. Econ. Stud.* 66(1), pp. 115–38.

Hart, O., Shleifer, A. and Vishny, R., 1997. The Proper Scope of Government: theory and an application to prisons, *Q. J. Econ.* 112(4), pp. 1126–61.

Hodge, G., 2004. The Risky Business of Public–Private Partnerships, *Australian Journal of Public Administration* 63(4), pp. 37–49.

Iossa, E., Spagnolo, G. and Vellez, M., 2007. *Contractual Issues in Public–Private Partnerships.* [Report] World Bank.

Jensen, M. and Meckling, W., 1976. Theory of the Firm: managerial behavior, agency costs and ownership structure, *J. Financial Econ.* 3, pp. 305–60.

Kaplan, S. and Stromberg, P., 2001. *Venture Capitalists As Principals: contracting, screening, and monitoring.* [Working Paper 8202] NBER.

Press, E. and Washburn, J., 2000. The Kept University, *Atlantic Monthly*, March, 39–54.

Rausser, G., and Ameden, H. 2003. *Structuring Public–Private Research Agreements*, UC Berkeley Working Paper.

Rausser, G. and Stevens, R., 2009. Public–Private Partnerships: goods and the structure of contracts, *Annual Review of Resource Economics* 1, pp. 75–98.

Rausser, G., Ameden, H. and Simon, L., 2000. Public–Private Alliances in Biotechnology: can they narrow the knowledge gaps between rich and poor?, *Food Policy* 25(4), pp. 499–513.

Rausser, G., Simon, L. and Stevens, R., 2008. Public vs. Private Good Research at Land-Grant Universities, *J. Agric. Food Ind. Organ.* 6(2), art. 4.

Rausser, G., Swinnen, J. and Zusman, P., 2011. *Political Power and Economic Policy: Theory, Analysis, and Empirical Applications.* New York: Cambridge University Press.

Ruster, J., 1997. *A Retrospective on the Mexican Toll Road Program (1989–94).* [Public Policy for the Private Sector Note No. 125] The World Bank Group.

Sadka, E., 2006. *Public–Private Partnerships: a public economics perspective.* [Working Paper 06/77] IMF.

Slywotzky, A., 2009. Where Have You Gone, Bell Labs? How basic research can repair the broken U.S. business model, *BusinessWeek*, available online at http://www.businessweek.com/magazine/content/09_36/b4145036681619.htm.

Spielman, D., Hartwich, F. and von Grebmer, K., 2007. *Sharing Science, Building Bridges, and Enhancing Impact: public–private partnerships in the CGIAR.* [Discussion Paper No. 00708] IFPRI.

Swimmer, D., 2001. The Current State of Canadian Infrastructure. In: A. Vining and J. Richards, eds. *Building the Future: issues in public infrastructure in Canada.* Toronto: C.D. Howe Institute, pp. 18–33.

Tirole, J., 1999. Incomplete Contracts: where do we stand?, *Econometrica* 67, pp. 741–81.

Treasury, HM. 2006. Value for Money Assessment Guidance. London: Scottish Futures Trust.

Wadhwa, V. and Litan, R.E., 2009. Turning Research into Inventions and Jobs, *BusinessWeek*, available online at http://www.businessweek.com/technology/content/sep2009/tc20090918_628309.htm.

Wang, C., 2007. *Public Investment Policy and Industry Incentives in Life Science Research.* Ph.D. thesis, Oregon State University.

Zheng, J., Roehrich, J. and Lewis, M., 2008. The Dynamics of Contractual and Relational Governance: evidence from long-term public–private procurement arrangements, *J. Purchasing and Supply Management* 14, pp. 43–54.

Is public–private partnership obsolete?
Assessing the obstacles and shortcomings of PPP

Claude Ménard[1]

7.1 Introduction

Public–Private Partnership, or Private Sector Participation as it is also known in a politically more sensitive terminology, has been high on the agenda of public decision makers, think-tanks, and consulting firms since the late 1990s. The World Bank Group has, for example, created a specific entity – the Public-Private Infrastructure Advisory Facility (PPIAF) – in charge of following up the development of these arrangements. The European Commission long ago delivered a Green Paper on the issue (European Union, 2004a). The OECD has produced several reports related to it, and the topic continues to feed the agenda and publications of numerous think-tanks (e.g. the French *Institut de la Gestion Déléguée*), as well as those of renowned private actors (e.g. PricewaterhouseCoopers). Such examples can easily be extended. And the number of conferences and publications on PPP is impressive. This raises questions: Why all the buzz? To what extent does it correspond to what is going on in the 'real' world? Is PPP a myth, a panacea, or an irreversible movement?

PPP is primarily a contractual approach to the delivery of infrastructures, goods and services traditionally provided by the public sector or by private operators subject to tight 'command-and-control' regulation, such as public utilities. However, as rightly emphasized by New Institutional economists, PPP is a very special contractual practice as it seeks to introduce market-type relationships in a context in which non-market forces play a major role. Indeed, PPP refers to arrangements in which the allocation of property rights, as well as decision rights between public authorities and private operators, overlaps, with blurred boundaries when it comes to the delineation of some substantial rights and the distribution of risks. For example, a network can be built and operated by a private operator although public authorities remain the leading (if not the exclusive) investor, and may hold some important decision rights, as often happens in the water and sanitation sector. Another good illustration of overlapping rights is when a government transfers the construction, maintenance and operation of prisons to a private operator while wardens remain under its control. The extension of overlapping rights in the delivery of goods and services considered of 'general interest' in the now received terminology determines the specific form of a contract and the resulting governance problems.

One way to explore in more depth the problems at stake is to restrict the analysis of PPP to those contracts associated with the delivery of 'critical services', understood as services essential to avoiding economic or social disruptions. These mainly include the provision of network infrastructures, such as water and sanitation, energy, transportation, or communications (Moteff *et al.*, 2003; European Union, 2004b).[2] Such sectors are of particular significance because of their strategic impact on the economy (and the population) and because they actually involve a majority of investments under PPP arrangements. In this chapter, I mainly examine the role and difficulties of PPP relating to these network infrastructures. However, notwithstanding specificities such as the duration or the amplitude of investments involved, these arrangements share difficulties found in all other PPPs, which follow on from the partial and often ambiguous transfer of risks and responsibilities across public–private boundaries. These differentiate PPP from alternative solutions (full privatization or full integration in publicly owned entities).

Indeed, the specificity of PPP and related contracts results from the identity and role of the parties involved, which has an impact through at least three intertwined dimensions: 1) a legal dimension, since one party to the arrangement (the public authorities) also defines the rules of the game and has a say in the implementation and respect of the clauses and requirements of the agreement; 2) an economic one, since the player who is initially responsible for assessing the costs and benefits of 'going PPP' operates as subrogate for stakeholders – in the last resort all citizens – who are not residual claimants;[3] and 3) a political dimension, since the goods and services provided concern users who also act as citizens-voters, at least in democratic regimes, thus exposing decision makers to the risk of third-party opportunism. Taking into account these three dimensions means that institutional endowments, as well as institutional design, are key factors in the decision to endorse a PPP and to choose the form it will take, with their impact on the solution selected deeply affecting its performance.

In what follows, I mainly focus on the economic dimension, although it is important to keep in mind the two other dimensions when it comes to the design (*ex ante*) and the implementation (*ex post*) of these arrangements. Actually, most arguments developed by the proponents of PPP relate to economic factors. The virtues expected from the participation of private interest in the provision of goods and services long considered as the 'prerogative' of government are now well-known and have been widely publicized, particularly by international organizations and lobbyists. They are deeply embedded in the shift of values regarding the economic role of government. The economic advantages of PPP are essentially seen to be gains in efficiency, thanks to incentives associated with private investments and their identifiable residual claimants. PPP should be particularly suitable when full privatization is not possible or very hard to implement, because of strategic issues (as in the defence sector), risks associated with major, long run sunk-costs (as in water and sanitation), or public resistance to the loss of control over critical resources (as with energy). A positive impact of PPP should show up in terms of:

1 lower prices, since private partners have an incentive to reduce costs if the contract is properly designed;
2 increased productivity, as the allocation of labour will be less politicized;
3 increased output, given that revenues depend more directly on the rate of connection;
4 self-sustainability, since private participation requires revenues superior to costs, at least if risks are properly transferred;

5   superior delivery of infrastructure and public services at a time of strongly depleted public finance; and last but not least
6   a reduction of political interference, thus reducing risks of corruption.

Of course, each of these presumed advantages has been challenged, with data often showing unpredicted increases in prices, lower investment than expected, increased corruption due to the small number of competitors involved, and short-term budgetary relief opening the door to long-term instalments that burden public finances. Thus, from its beginnings, the development of PPP has been accompanied by strong controversy, even when we put aside ideological conviction, which is not an easy task when it comes to the positions endorsed by its proponents and opponents. Facts and figures about the actual performance of PPP, and its shortcomings when compared to the high expectations often generated, feed the debate.

The goal of this chapter is not to add one more brick to these ongoing controversies. It is rather to show that the potential advantages and possible failures of PPP are rooted in the very nature of its organizational arrangements and the actual design of contracts for which it provides an umbrella, as well as in the institutions in which it is embedded and that define the capacity to implement and monitor these arrangements properly. The resulting problem of adequacy between PPP as an organizational solution and the institutional framework in which it has developed help to explain many of the difficulties PPP faces, which are rooted in the intertwined allocation of rights, generating continuous tensions among parties. Notwithstanding considerable efforts to circumvent these problems, for example through more detailed contracts with more complex clauses regarding the transfer of risks and the responsibilities of parties, tensions remain that are apparently inherent to PPP and that partially explain its cyclical development, with significant ups and downs.

In what follows, I capture these difficulties in what I identify as a double alignment problem. On the organizational side, which is embedded in the contractual agreement, there is a problem of adequacy between the intertwined allocation of rights and the setting up of appropriate governance. This problem is particularly acute for network infrastructures that involve monopolistic segments remaining in the hands of 'public utilities' (e.g. transmission in the electricity sector, or rail tracks in the railroad industry).[4] On the institutional side, which refers to institutional endowments and the capacities of enforcement they determine, the special status of one party to the agreement, namely public authorities, comes out of its capacity to alter the rules of the game while the contract is ongoing. This raises a problem of adequacy between the contractual nature of the approach, which requires the transfer of substantial rights to a private operator, and the legitimate control that public authorities intend to keep over the delivery of goods and services considered as essential for and by citizens. In a sense, this double alignment problem reflects difficulties that are inherent to hybrid arrangements (Ménard, 2012), but that are amplified by the institutional asymmetry between the parties involved, which introduces a societal dimension to the problem.

The chapter is organized as follows. The next section comes back to the double alignment problem more explicitly, with particular attention to PPP in the provision and management of network infrastructures. Section 7.3 summarizes some evidence illustrating the difficulties at stake. Section 7.4 looks more systematically at the 'alignment' problem rooted in the peculiarities and flaws of the contractual arrangements that shape PPPs and of the institutions in which they are embedded. Section 7.5 concludes with some remarks about the future of PPP.

7.2 The double alignment problem

One important contribution of New Institutional Economics (NIE) has been to disentangle issues regarding organizational choices and those relating to institutional rules in which they are embedded, while simultaneously referring to a common set of concepts, mainly: property rights; modes of governance allocating and transferring these rights (with particular attention to contracts); and the related transaction costs. Indeed, along the organizational dimension (often identified as 'Williamsonian') as well as the institutional one (classified as 'Northian'), a key issue has to do with the adequacy of organizational and institutional solutions with the transactions at stake.[5] The interactions of these two dimensions when it comes to the provision of network infrastructures, which is the main focus of this chapter, help to explain the difficulties that the diffusion and implementation of PPP face.

7.2.1 The 'critical' nature of network infrastructures

PPP has raised particularly high expectations in the four sectors in which most investments are concentrated: telecommunications, energy, transportation, and water and sanitation. These sectors capture a substantial part of network infrastructures often described as 'critical'. Critical infrastructure involves assets and services crucial to: 1) supporting economic development and growth, for example road systems or energy; 2) maintaining socio-economic cohesion, which includes the provision of services guaranteeing property rights or safety of access to strategic facilities such as airports or ports; 3) promoting social goals inherent to developed economies, for example providing basic access to communication means or to safe water and sanitation (Moteff *et al.*, 2003: 8 ff.; Künneke *et al.*, 2010: 496 ff.).

It is also in these sectors that PPP faces its most substantial problems. For infrastructure to meet the requirements above, it must satisfy conditions that make its development and maintenance particularly complex:

1 The *scope* of transactions over which control must be exercised encompasses a wide set of parameters. Defining rights of access to transmission lines in the provision of electricity illustrates the difficulty.
2 Appropriate *control* mechanisms need to be implemented for guaranteeing the exactitude of goods or services delivered. Air traffic control provides an example.
3 Essential functions must be satisfied when needed, making *reliability* a key factor. Delivering safe drinking water or building and maintaining sewerage systems that prevent epidemics illustrate the importance of this criterion.
4 The provision of infrastructure must be conceived so as to guarantee *sustainability* in the long run, making the system economically and environmentally viable. The development of adequate public transportation illustrates the point.

This qualification of what is expected from critical infrastructure substantiates the double alignment problem (organizational and institutional) that PPP faces.

To begin with, complex transactions are involved that require coordination between parties with distinct or even diverging preference functions. This is so within a specific infrastructure: for example, the production, transmission and distribution of electricity need tight coordination among partners, whether they rely on public or private operators. For the latter, it also means arrangements based on sophisticated contracts, at least as soon as there is not a single firm in a monopoly position. Moreover, when the provision of the relevant critical infrastructure depends on partnerships involving private operators, parties are submitted to the monitoring of one of them, which inevitably creates asymmetric positions. Indeed, public authorities keep control over some strategic decisions, either directly, such as through a 'department of public works', or indirectly, when a publicly appointed regulator supervises the implementation of the contract and disciplines the operator(s).

Second, coordination is also required for infrastructures that are apparently independent from each other; for example, the efficiency of urban transportation requires complementarities among different means (bus, tramway, subway, etc.) but also with other infrastructures; for example, an adequate road system and the related sources of energy. The responsibilities for such coordination are never entirely in the hands of private operators. The intensity of public intervention may vary. Nevertheless, public decision makers necessarily interfere with operators on such issues. The result is a blurred area of decisions, which raises acute problems for PPP since parties have goals that differ substantially. Hence the importance and difficulty of allocating rights and risks in PPP, and the key role of the institutions framing the decision process of public authorities.

Third, the delivery of critical infrastructure imposes significant investment with a life cycle of its own, usually a long time span. An immediate consequence is that the corresponding organizational solution rarely fits with the political cycle, particularly in democracies: periodic elections mean that the strategy of the public authorities may change, challenging the viability of long term investments required from the operator(s). Indeed, as infrastructure concerns users who are also citizens, political interference is almost inevitable. This situation raises the question of the appropriate institutions needed to provide adequate incentives for the operator(s), such as securing property rights, guaranteeing autonomy in the exercise of decision rights, etc. However, there is a flip-side to the coin. Public authorities are also tied up by the arrangement: once PPP has been chosen to deliver critical infrastructure, political decision makers become vulnerable to the failures of their private partner(s). Many of the projects concerned and the commitments that accompany them are just 'too important to fail': in case of threatening flaws, public authorities have strong incentives to compromise to keep the ball rolling!

Consequently, the critical nature of much infrastructure for which PPP is considered imposes specific constraints that differ from usual business-to-business contracts. It raises complex problems with respect to the adequacy of PPP, as an organizational solution, as well as with the capacity of existing institutions to support and monitor this solution properly. Moreover, as the characteristics above suggest, the two dimensions deeply interact.

7.2.2 Organizational alignment

From an organizational point of view, relying on PPP for the production and delivery of critical infrastructure faces specific difficulties rooted in the constraints identified above, and shapes the nature of transactions at stake. First, network infrastructures involve heavy sunk investment, with a rate of return spread over the long term, so that risks of opportunistic behaviour among parties are high. Second, they usually benefit from large economies of scale, which create important barriers to entry (and to exit as well!). Third, they benefit from what has been called a 'club effect': the larger the number of agents connected to the infrastructure or using it, the more beneficial it tends to be for the provider(s) and the more satisfying it is for users. Fourth, users benefit, or suffer, from these infrastructures over a long period of time. Fifth, because of these characteristics and because there is a tight connection between the role of users as consumers and as citizens, conditions under which services are delivered remain highly politicized, either through direct intervention, as when public authorities are in charge, or through different forms of regulation. In the terminology of transaction cost economics, these properties have a strong impact on the attributes of the transaction at stake (the contract in the case of PPP): the frequency of these transactions is likely to be low, with contracts mostly medium or long term; investments required are highly specific, meaning that once they are made they can hardly be redeployed to other activities; and uncertainty may be high, particularly if rights are not properly and clearly allocated.[6]

Indeed, although PPP may correspond to a variable transfers of rights, depending on the agreement, 'partnership' means that public authorities keep control over key property rights in the last resort, whatever the form partnership takes, which makes it different from full privatization. However, private operators also hold property rights, for example over facilities or the technology they may use: leases or concession contracts in the energy sector or rail transportation illustrate this well. Similarly, although substantial decision rights might be transferred to private operator(s), public authorities usually keep control over key ones, for example determining tariffs or indexation formulas, or imposing constraints that make a contract subject to adaptation, as when local authorities own buses and determine the core characteristics of services to be offered while transferring the operation and maintenance of the system to a private operator.

Two important consequences result from this intertwined allocation of rights. First, the design of an adequate governance mechanism to reach joint decisions remains arduous, whether it has to be defined in the contract or whether it depends on interactions with regulatory authorities, or both. From a transaction cost perspective, PPP neither operates through pure market forms, nor is it a hierarchy. It is a hybrid arrangement, which poses specific problems of coordination, as we shall see later. Second, a controversial issue has to do with the ambiguous status of the residual claimant. Because rights are split between public authorities and the private operator(s), with zones in which they overlap, and because users are payers in-last-resort, as consumers or taxpayers or both, defining rights of the operator(s) as the residual claimant is a continuing source of tension and controversy.

In other words, PPP faces classical transaction cost problems, deriving from adequacy/ inadequacy between the form of PPP chosen and the frequency of transactions under consideration, the significance of specific investments required, and the uncertainty regarding the status of the residual claimant. The status of PPP as hybrid arrangements, neither operating in a pure 'market' regime nor benefiting from the properties of an integrated organization (a 'hierarchy'), makes the governance issue particularly difficult to solve.

7.2.3 Institutional alignment

As already mentioned, the role of public authorities as party to the agreement and as decision maker with respect to the rules framing the agreement makes political interference almost inevitable. Even in one of the most radical experiences – the movement towards full privatization of network infrastructures in the UK – boundaries delineating rights changed repeatedly: for example, the rail network was renationalized following safety and financial problems and terms determining the price of water were redefined in the face of public pressure.

Contrasting public–private partnership with privatization on the one hand (the 'market' solution) and public provision of network infrastructures on the other hand (the 'hierarchical' solution) helps to explain its institutional specificity. With *full divestiture*, the key issue concerns the institutions required to secure property rights, including the role of agencies or courts in charge of guaranteeing the respect of commitments by the parties. A major difficulty with this solution lies in having institutions powerful enough to constrain deviant governments without being so powerful that they facilitate predatory practices. With *full public control* over network infrastructures, as with state-owned 'public utilities', the main problems stem from the lack of adequate incentives and the political interference that go with direct public monitoring.

In this respect, PPP clearly falls in-between these polar cases. As such, it shares the characteristics of hybrid arrangements linking private partners in business-to-business agreements, such as strategic alliances, franchising and so forth (Ménard, 2012). Indeed, PPP involves joint investments between autonomous partners. It requires specific coordination devices to monitor shared resources. And it confronts problems of allocating risks and defining rent sharing rules since contributions and responsibilities are often hard to disentangle. At the same time, PPP differs from standard hybrid agreements among private partners because of the type of asymmetry involved, since public authorities operate simultaneously as a partner and as the instance defining and implementing the rules of the game, at least in last resort. Indeed, it must be remembered that even 'independent' regulators or judges are appointed by governments. The institutional matrix is therefore central as a support to PPP, but can also be a major source of misalignment when it generates high uncertainty and/or casts doubts on the securing of rights over sunk investments for the private operator(s).

Hence, deciding to choose PPP for providing and/or monitoring network infrastructures requires assessing the adequacy of existing institutions in at least three areas. First, are there political checks and balances that will limit the propensity of public authorities to reap the political as well as financial benefits of PPP, once specific investments have been made? Second, and symmetrically, are there enough administrative capabilities to monitor the agreement properly while avoiding the risk of capture by the private operator(s)? Third, and last but not least, is there a judiciary that has the competence and the authority to constrain parties when they stray from the agreement?

To sum up, finding whether the 'right' institutions are in place or can be easily implemented, and finding the right mode of governance embedded in these institutions and fitting it to the properties of the transaction at stake remain major challenges and might be a source of conflict, inefficiency, as well as costly adjustments (Ménard, 2009). This double alignment problem might also explain many of the difficulties in the acceptance, development and monitoring of public–private partnerships.

7.3 The slow and uneven spread of PPP

Indeed, notwithstanding high expectancies of PPP and the militancy of its promoters – particularly donors and international organizations, and private operators of course – the choice of this mode of organization in the provision of key network infrastructures remains relatively limited, and has evolved cyclically, with ups and downs since the initial boom of the mid-1990s. The sector and geographical distribution of PPP also provides valuable indications on the difficulties at stake.

7.3.1 From water and sanitation . . .

Water and sanitation systems have been high on the list of priorities of decision makers over the last two decades, because of their importance for the survival of human beings and the challenges they face with the massive migration of populations to major cities. This is particularly so in developing and emerging economies.[7] At the same time, the important sunk investment these systems require, in a context of tight public budget constraints, has made PPP an attractive solution, particularly when associated with financial commitments from private operators.

However, the results are far from meeting the expectations of intense private commitments. A study by Gassner *et al.* (2009) examined reforms implemented over the period 1992–2004 in all developing countries. Out of a sample of 977 cases in the water and sanitation sector, they identified 141 cases of private participation, 10 per cent of which were total or partial divestitures, while the remaining 90 per cent adopted various forms of PPP ; mainly concessions or lease and management contracts. State-owned entities thus remained the prevailing mode of organization throughout these reforms. The database developed by the World Bank on Public–Private Infrastructure (the PPIAF project) provides slightly more optimistic data. For the period 1990–2006 and for the same sector worldwide, 526 projects involving private participation were identified. However, when it comes to the significance of private commitments, they remain modest if a handful of major projects are excluded, projects that have not always been successful, as demonstrated by the case of Buenos Aires where the concession contract has been breached. Figure 7.1 illustrates these trends, making a distinction between 'large private investment commitments' and 'other commitments'. It clearly indicates how much PPP peaks depend on specific projects.

It is also interesting to look at the forms private participation has taken. Full or partial divestiture, which are variances of privatization, represent a very small portion of the projects, while contractual agreements with relatively low financial risks for the private operators involved have largely dominated, as Figure 7.2 from the same database confirms.

7.3.2 . . . to other infrastructure

Notwithstanding their importance for human beings and the high expectations that PPP could help in meeting ambitious targets such as those defined in the 'Millennium Project' (UN, 2005), water and sanitation *de facto* represent only a small part of PPP. According to the World Bank, for the period 1990–2000 this sector accounted for 6 per cent of the total investment commitments to infrastructure projects with private participation and less than 3 per cent in

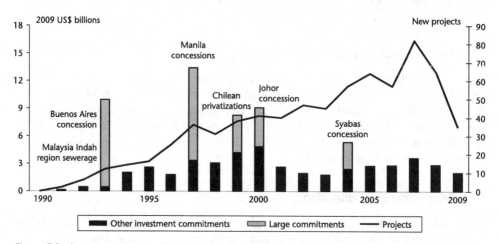

Figure 7.1 Investment commitments to water projects with private participation

Source: World Bank and PPIAF, PPI Database

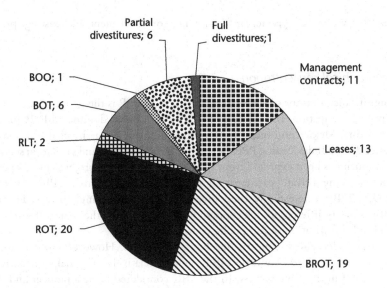

Figure 7.2 Water utility projects with private participation

Source: World Bank and PPIAF, PPI Database, 12-2010

the years 2001–8. At the same time, electricity represented 29 per cent and 23 per cent respectively, while telecoms took the lion's share of PPP, rising from 42 per cent to 54 per cent of the total. An OECD study of all forms of private participation in the MENA region confirms these trends[8]: over 84 per cent of private investments in the network infrastructures of this region were concentrated in the energy and telecommunication sectors (Kauffmann and Wegner, 2007: 13–17). More generally, it is in these sectors that full or partial privatization was the most significant. Out of the top ten companies involved in private participation for the period 1990–2006, nine were in the telecom business.[9] In other words, whatever form it took, private participation concentrated on the two most profitable sectors, namely telecommunications and to a lesser degree energy. Figure 7.3 summarizes this uneven distribution of participation

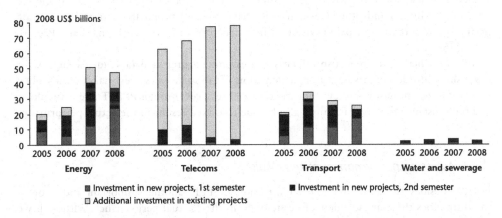

Figure 7.3 Investment commitments in infrastructure projects with private participation in developing countries, by sector and implementation status, 2005–08

Source: World Bank and PPIAF, PPI Database, 12-2010

among sectors, with the spectacular dominance of investment in existing projects in telecoms.

7.3.3 Geographical concentration

Another significant indicator of the uneven diffusion of PPP is the geographical concentration of private participation. For the period 1990–2006, Brazil dominated PPP, followed by China, Argentina, Mexico and India. In the late 2000s, this hierarchy changed, with China and to a lesser degree India leading PPP. For example, in the water and sanitation sector alone, in which so much has been expected from PPP, 89 per cent of the projects and 85 per cent of investment involving private participation in 2008 were in China. (PPI Database, last consulted Dec. 2010). Interestingly, these investments also increasingly involved local entrepreneurs (the story is different for telecoms and energy, in which the trade-off is more polarized around full privatization or full public control).

The data provided above concern developing countries. However, similar conclusions can be reached for developed countries: PPP remains relatively marginal, concentrated in a few countries and in the same sectors. In the UK, considered to be a pioneer and the most advanced country in the development of private sector participation through its 'Private Finance Initiative' (PFI) programme, a report by Her Majesty's Treasury (Britain's Finance Ministry) in 2003 noted that over 85 per cent of public investment was still delivered through conventional procurement, which is definitely distinct from PPP. A worldwide investigation on PPP by PricewaterhouseCoopers (2005) identified 206 projects in developed countries for the years 2004–5, of which 50 per cent were in Europe (including Turkey), mostly in the UK (all sectors), to a lesser degree in France and Portugal (roads and water) and Spain (ports, roads, water and wastewater). Australia, Canada and Japan were the main countries concerned outside Europe.[10] In some countries, there might even be a 'privatization reversal', with the reintroduction into the public sector of services previously delivered through PPP. Data collected by Warner and Hefetz (2007: 563 ff.) on local government service delivery in the USA for the period 1992–2002 showed a progress of direct public delivery (from 54 per cent to 59 per cent), while complete contracting out went down, from 28 per cent to 18 per cent. At a more anecdotal level, Paris and Grenoble in France have abandoned their water concessions, switching back to a public 'régie', while the citizens of Munich and other German cities have rejected proposals to introduce private participation in the municipal provision of infrastructure and services (Ménard and Peeroo, 2011: 315–16).

In sum, whether we look at specific cases or examine aggregate data, evidence suggests at best a slow diffusion of private sector participation and in some cases a reversal of trends when it comes to the provision of key infrastructure and services through PPP. These difficulties, and the resistance they reveal, might also be due to mixed results in the actual performance of PPP.

7.3.4 Assessing performance: mixed results

Indeed, besides the slow and uneven diffusion of PPP, another important indicator of the difficulties these arrangements face stems from their actual performance. Although we already have over 15 years of cumulated experiences and increasing datasets, assessing the performance of PPPs in order to determine whether the mixed results observed are due to organizational and/or institutional misfits is not an easy task.

One way to capture the misalignment between the choice of PPP as an organizational solution and the existing institutions is to develop cost/benefit analysis. However, this is not a simple exercise when it comes to assessing whether PPP was the right choice or not. First, finding the adequate data is not that obvious: for example, private companies operating in a competitive environment are legitimately reluctant to deliver information about their costs or their investments in specific projects. Second, changes in public policies (for example, in environmental or fiscal rules) might alter the significance of the data available. Third, and even more important to our approach, these costs and benefits require comparative evaluation: What are they? And what would they have been in an alternative organizational solution?[11]

However, numerous empirical studies have shown discrepancies between expected performance (including those specified in the contract) and observed results. Although most of them have emphasized failures in contractual design, several contributions have also exhibited the misalignment of the form of PPP chosen with the existing institutions. It is beyond the scope of this chapter to review these studies, but some lessons deserve consideration.

Two pioneering examinations of several reforms of water and sanitation systems involving private operators (Savedoff and Spiller, 1999; Shirley *et al.*, 2002) have shown how much the success or failure of PPP depends on the design of the contract and the governance it frames. But even more important are institutional endowments, particularly the capacity of the political system and the judiciary to monitor properly the relationship between public authorities and private operators. In many cases, the need for adaptation *ex post*, once the contract has been agreed upon, involves many jurisdictions and institutions, thus generating heavy economic and political transaction costs (see Ménard and Clarke (2002) on Conakry, Guinea; or Xun and Malaluan (2008) on Manila, the Philippines).

This is confirmed by several more quantitatively oriented analyses. In a pioneering econometric study, focusing on the French urban water sector, which has a long tradition of private sector participation, Ménard and Saussier (2002) revealed the mixed results in the performance of concessions and lease contracts, compared to public *régies* operating within the same institutional environment. Their explanation focused mainly on organizational misfit. Wallsten and Kosec (2008) reached similar conclusions about the urban water supply in the USA, referring rather to the conditions of implementing the rules of the game. In another study, Wallsten (2001) extensively examined reforms adopted in 31 countries in the telecom sector, which might be particularly favourable to the introduction of PPP or even full privatization, given the technological developments which have facilitated the opening of the systems, while the profitability of the sector made it very attractive to private operators. He had already shown that there was no significant effect of the reallocation of ownership alone on service coverage and labour efficiency. The key issue is rather whether competition has been introduced or not, as this points to the embeddedness of organizational solutions into their institutional environment. This is particularly significant, since in many cases concerning network infrastructures, PPP is introduced in a context of some competition for the market (often an opening limited to a few competitors), without competition in the market (once the contract has been allocated, the winner is in a monopoly position).

Last, the extensive study by Gassner *et al.* (2009) mentioned above goes beyond the water and sanitation sector, and also includes the electricity sector. It reviews over 1,200 reformed utilities, with 301 of them involving private sector participation, and the authors were somewhat more optimistic about the positive impact of PPP.[12] However, they also expressed serious concerns, particularly with respect to investment (p. 4 in general, p. 39 for electricity, p. 45

for water). Increased investment per worker could indeed be largely due to reduction in staff numbers, with little actual new investment. Another interesting lesson from this study is that the form of private participation matters. In the words of the authors, 'greater degrees of private participation [are] associated with stronger gains in productivity and service quality' (Gassner *et al.*, 2009: 47).

These mixed results need to be explained. In line with my initial hypothesis regarding the double alignment problem, I shall argue that it is the organization structuring the allocation of rights and, in the last resort, the institutional capacities to implement and monitor the related transfer of risks that play a crucial role in the difficulties that PPPs face. It is this combination that determines the attractiveness of PPP to private operators and frames the possibility for the new arrangements to meet expectations that might well have been too high from the very beginning, partially due to the ideological considerations of proponents of PPP.

7.4 Why is PPP so difficult?

From a standard economic perspective, the slow diffusion and difficult implementation of PPP are quite challenging. Notwithstanding strong support from international organizations and public donors, as well as the favourable bias of governments viewing PPP as a way to develop infrastructure in a context of tight financial constraints, the slow adoption of PPP and the contrasted results of existing experiences cast doubt on the relevance of this organizational solution for the delivery of critical infrastructure.

In an extensive review of PPP in urban water utilities in developing countries, Marin (2009) summarized well the problems at stake:

> It is clear from the many experiences of the past 15 years that public–private partnership is not a magic formula to address all the multiple issues of failing public water utilities in the developing world. For many governments in developing and transition countries, PPP projects have proved to be complex undertakings that carry strong political risks and large uncertainties as to the magnitude and timing of the expected benefits. Contractual targets are difficult to set and baseline data are seldom reliable; they generate many opportunities for conflict. Private operators do not always deliver and have a tendency to seek renegotiations to their advantage. Reforms can become easily subverted by vested interests. Many obstacles can lead to conflicts and costly early termination.
>
> *(Marin 2009: 10)*

These difficulties go far beyond the urban water sector or developing countries. For example, in France only 430 projects were recorded from 2004 to 2010. And this despite France's long tradition of private participation in key sectors such as water, sanitation and multi-services, and notwithstanding the strong impulse the government intended to provide to PPP, with a favourable regulation adopted in 2004, followed by a supportive law in 2008. About one-third of the projects concerned the renovation or construction of buildings, 25 per cent the improvement of existing facilities (mostly public lighting), and 15 per cent the delivery of sports and cultural facilities.[13] In other words, the development of PPP remained modest, with most projects being relatively minor ones and/or concerning a segment in the delivery of public goods or services that is not particularly complex.

Slow penetration might be temporary, due to the newness of the arrangement (although some forms of PPP go back to the nineteenth century!). Disappointing outcomes and the retreat from PPP to public provision are more challenging for conventional wisdom, which has strongly emphasized the potential gains of private participation. In addition, they challenge the view of economists aware of organizational issues, but who focused on the *ex ante* ambiguities in the allocation of property rights with little concern for their actual implementation and monitoring (Hart, 2003). They also challenge the view of economists aware of the institutional factors involved, who emphasized political opportunism of rent-seeking governments or political stubbornness fed by ideological motivations as preventing the adoption of solutions that would otherwise allow a 'high level equilibrium' to be reached (Savedoff and Spiller 1999: 13 ff.).

I do not deny the relevance of these factors. However, taken individually, they provide at best partial explanations: weak or badly defined property rights do not explain the failure of well-designed contracts (at least from a theoretical standpoint) or the slow diffusion of PPP in countries with well-defined rights and adequate institutions to implement them; and political opportunism or ideological motivations can hardly explain some puzzling facts, for example, why PPP has developed so far mostly in Brazil or China. My point is that we should look at the overlapping of organizational and institutional dimensions that are at the very core of PPP, with a broader view of the resulting adequacy/misfit given the transaction at stake. It might be that difficulties lie in the combination of the *economic transaction costs* of coordinating partners and monitoring contracts with the appropriate allocation of rights, and the *political transaction costs* of establishing/adapting institutions and building a stable coalition in line with the choice of PPP for developing and/or upgrading network infrastructures.

7.4.1 The allocation of rights and the related problems of governance

Overlapping rights among parties to a PPP make transaction costs particularly significant. These costs follow from the complexities of defining responsibilities among partners, writing a contract that sets them out (the infamous 'ink costs'), determining and implementing procedures to attract and select private operators, and monitoring the relationship established under the type of PPP selected. This last aspect, the *ex post* implementation of a contract, is particularly significant because of the many problems and adjustments not anticipated at the time a contract is established. Coordination and adaptation problems resulting from the blurred areas of decision rights generate conflicts and repeated renegotiations. There is no simple governance solution to deal with these difficulties: finding the organizational arrangement that fits the transactions at stake is a major challenge. It is so because the property rights in which decision rights are embedded are unevenly distributed, with overlapping zones. These are issues that the term 'partnership' elegantly conceals. The development of regulation and regulatory agencies to monitor these problems, a solution that is quite universal since almost everywhere the provision of infrastructure involving private operators remains highly regulated, is a complementary source of complexity, and carries associated transaction costs.

The distinction between property rights and decision rights, partially inspired by the theory of incomplete contracts (Hart, 2003; Baker *et al.*, 2008), is helpful for understanding the issue of the appropriate allocation of responsibilities in PPP and the organizational misfits it possibly produces. Property rights refer to the control over the choice, implementation, and discard of assets, while decision rights concern the usage of these assets.[14] Of course, the allocation of these rights is also an issue in the polar cases of full public control (typically, state-owned enterprises) or full privatization. In the former, decision rights can be spread across different departments or ministries, handicapping the management of public utilities and the delivery of adequate infrastructure and services. In the latter, regulation and actions of regulators monitoring competition and guaranteeing the minimum coordination required by network infrastructures, for example in defining rights of access, can severely restrict the domain of choice for private operators and generate inefficiencies. Hence, failing governance due to poorly allocated rights is not the privilege of PPP.

However, the problem is particularly acute with PPP, because the rights of 'partners', which in principle should be distinct and well defined by the contract linking the parties, overlap *ex ante*, at the time the contract is designed, as well as *ex post*, at the time it is implemented. Moreover, sources of misfit coming out of the blurred allocation of rights differ according to the type of contract. The closer a contract is to public monitoring, as with management or service contracts, the more likely will conflicts relate to the allocation of decision rights, since private operators have no or very little control over property rights. Symmetrically, the closer PPP gets to full privatization, as with concessions, the more likely tensions will relate to the long run allocation of property rights, since risks of opportunistic behaviour from governments increase once major sunk investments have been made by private operators. Unfortunately, we lack systematic data that would substantiate these differences.

7.4.2 Turbulence in contractual relations

Nevertheless, some problems and consequences can already be pointed out from information collected in numerous case studies. First, the allocation of rights is closely interconnected with the allocation of risk among partners, a continuing source of tensions in PPP (and a much less consequential problem with State-owned enterprises or with full privatization),[15] because ambiguities in the delineation of rights and risks are almost inevitable. There are different types of risks at stake: technical, operational, financial, regulatory, political and social. Although each type may require specific solutions, they all end up challenging the stability of PPP. Case studies and econometric tests converge on the significance of these sources of tension. In an extensive review of the introduction of PPP in the reform of the urban water system in Conakry (Guinea), Ménard and Clarke (2002: 273 ff.) identified inefficiencies resulting from the overlapping of risks and responsibilities, notwithstanding a relatively well-designed set of contracts. These linked the public operator in charge of developing the primary network (SONEG – *Société Nationale des Eaux de Guinée*) and a mixed public-private operator (SEEG – *Société d'Exploitation des Eaux de Guinée*) responsible for the secondary network and users' connections. Although the arrangement (the core of which was a lease contract between SONEG and SEEG) resulted in a significant improvement compared to the disastrous performance of the public provision of water before reform, repeated conflicts due to organizational misfits embedded in overlapping rights among entities with different goals and different preference functions ended up in continuing political interference. Risks and responsibilities were frequently arbitrated at the government level or even through international arbitration.

More generally, in an extensive survey of public–private partnerships in Latin America, with a dataset of over 1,000 contracts granted from 1985 to 2000 and covering key critical sectors (water and sanitation, electricity, transportation and telecommunications), Guasch (2004) has shown that overlapping rights and needs to adjust to changing risks ended up in systematic renegotiations. On average, renegotiation took place just 2.2 years after contracts were awarded, with a lower rate in the electricity and telecommunications sectors. In these industries, full privatization and/or more intense competition had led to defined rights and responsibilities. Conversely, the renegotiation rate was much higher in transportation and in water and sanitation, notwithstanding contracts intended to be long term and the presence of automatic adjustment clauses, for example indexed prices. Figure 7.4 summarizes the data.

This dataset suggests that ambiguous risk-sharing, stemming from overlapping investments and overlapping responsibilities in dealing with exogenous shocks, results in few tractable claims from public as well as private partners. What the data also reveal, through the contrast between water and other sectors, is that tensions and conflicts are particularly severe in contracts involving major sunk investments, with private operators facing financial risks related to exchange rates, and/or restrictions imposed on profit transfers, and/or political interference, problems often amplified when foreign companies are involved.[16] Renegotiations have direct consequences on costs as well as on coordination capabilities, which may explain the increasing reluctance of private operators to assume major risks in PPP, which translates into a shift from concessions to less risky lease or management contracts. Moreover, higher financial costs for private operators born out of higher risk premiums might partially cancel out advantages expected from their participation. Institutional stability is a key element here, and it may help to explain some successes of authoritarian regimes in implementing PPP.[17]

Second, even with contracts of relatively limited impact, for example when key rights remain controlled by public authorities as with management or service contracts, monitoring arrangements might face serious difficulties, with both sides confronting problems of expertise that can hamper their relationship. Private operators might not have all the competences and resources required, for example because the size of the project or the technological knowledge needed exceed their capacities and this may push local authorities to address multinational firms. However, the latter might be reluctant to carry financial risks if political interference is a potential threat; they might require *ex ante* guarantees (for example, hostage clauses) that are difficult to implement *ex post*; and they have competences that might make access to information and monitoring the contract difficult for public authorities. Symmetrically, the public partner might lack skills to deal with complex contracts and to monitor them properly, often a major problem for small- and medium-sized cities and/or for developing countries with limited human assets. Ambiguities in the allocation of decision rights might also impede coordination, generating costly externalities: for example, reduced

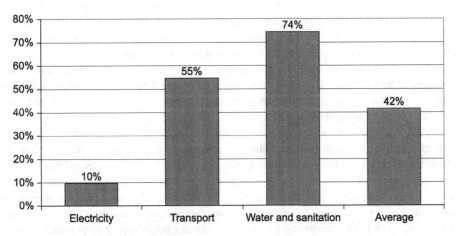

Figure 7.4 Concessions' renegotiations in Latin America (1985–2000)

Source: based on data provided in Guasch, 2004: Ch. 1, p. 13

public managerial control when strategic decision rights are transferred to private operators might reduce the expertise of public authorities, leading to important monitoring difficulties. This issue of organizational alignment between competences of parties to the arrangement is well illustrated by problems of coordination of public transportation in several large cities worldwide, which might speak in favour of increased public control or 'pro-active' planning of private interventions (Barter, 2008: Section 3).[18]

These difficulties in assigning and implementing rights and responsibilities translate into transaction costs. *Ex ante*, bureaucratic costs for parties to PPP might be significantly higher than expected. In a lecture on the potential role of PPP in the development of infrastructure in Africa, the then European Commissioner Louis Michel emphasized the resources the establishment of such partnerships requires from public bureaucracies, donors, local authorities, and private operators.[19] The problem is that we do not know much about these costs, and what they represent comparatively to the administrative costs of organizing the provision of the same goods or services by public entities. Yet, there are indicators suggesting they are not negligible, for example the small number of private bidders in so many cases because costs of bidding are too high.[20]

Ex post, conditions of implementation may also be taxing. For example, the frequent re-negotiations pointed out above involve direct administrative costs for both sides. They also involve indirect costs, particularly those related to the weakened credibility in commitments, which is partially reflected by the evolution of risk premiums. Moreover, assessing the advantages and costs of PPPs should also take into account the costs of those projects never achieved at the very stage of their initial design, or adopted but never implemented, or initiated but abandoned *en route*. According to the PPIAF database, 267 projects involving private sector participation were cancelled or distressed over the period 1990–2008, representing a mere 6 per cent of the total number of projects, but 8 per cent of investment and over 37 per cent in the water and sewerage sector.[21] This might suggest that PPP, as an organizational solution, does better in sectors with low sunk investments and might be much less adapted to sectors with highly dedicated assets, for which the adequacy of institutions matters greatly, since it mitigates or amplifies risks.

Once again, the lack of adequate data to substantiate the significance of these costs is unfortunate. However, indications suggest that difficulties in delineating and implementing rights through contracts translate into lengthy and costly procedures, often amplified by detailed guidelines that seek to prevent, *ex ante*, risks of opportunism or corruption, as well as by devices created to control the *ex post* implementation of such agreements. For example, on average over two years and often up to five years were taken up from preliminary studies to the beginning of actual investment in PPPs, among the 15 members of the European Union, for the period 2000–2005.[22] It must be emphasized that these delays are particularly significant because they are averages, including a majority of relatively simple projects developed under particularly favourable conditions with respect to institutions and human capacities.

Last, there is also a drawback to these complex procedures, which is often ignored or underestimated. This concerns the rigidities they introduce in contracts. Indeed, there is a tradeoff between establishing constraining rules to prevent opportunism on both sides of partnerships, and thus introducing rigidities that generate costly adjustments and potential conflicts on the one hand, and choosing more flexible rules that facilitate adjustments but might cancel out the advantages expected from competitive pressure on the other hand (Andres *et al.*, 2009). This tradeoff is particularly acute for projects with important long-term sunk investments.

7.4.3 The nature of contracts involved: what it means to have a 'relational' contract with the public sector

Similar problems exist in business-to-business agreements. However, they take particular forms when it comes to PPP. Indeed, by definition, PPP encompasses key requirements imposed by public authorities upon private operators. Of course, requirements also exist in business-to-business contracts. However, there are specificities to PPP.

First, notwithstanding the possibility of negotiating, these are contracts in which, in the last resort, one party imposes the rules of the game and can unilaterally alter them while the contract is being carried out. Second, the long-term properties embedded in the delivery of infrastructure and/or in the goods and services expected from them make these contracts almost inevitably incomplete; the transaction costs of establishing detailed contracts with well defined adjustable clauses to adapt to changing circumstances in the long run are far too high most of the time. It also means that changes and adaptation must be expected and will have to be monitored. Part of the adaptation is relatively 'formalizable', as with the periodic adjustments to variations in the price of energy in contracts for public transportation. But many adjustments are also based on 'informal' agreements, in that their properties and even the procedures for determining them are not made explicit in the contract. Typically, risk sharing in long-term projects obeys this logic of quite informal rules and procedures, as illustrated by PPP in the defence industry (Oudot and Ménard, 2010: 199 ff.).

Actually, 'informal' is not the right term. As suggested by Goldberg (1976) and Macneil (1978) and developed by Baker et al. (2002) among others, such adaptation is better captured by the concept of 'relational contract', in which substantial clauses are more concerned with procedures than with specific content. Now, relational contracts raise specific problems when it comes to partnership between public authorities and private operators: how 'relational' can a long-term contract with the public sector be? The standard approach has emphasized the risk of capture of public authorities or their regulatory bodies by private operators, for example, corrupting civil servants to get a contract or to modify an existing one (Martimort and Straub 2009: 69 ff.). This is surely a concern, but there is more to the story. As emphasized by several contributions in line with New Institutional Economics, there is also the risk of government opportunism, with public authorities changing the rules of the game while the contract is underway, or changing the interpretation of existing rules (Levy and Spiller, 1994: 202 ff.; Shirley and Ménard, 2002: 17–25; Guasch, 2004: 60 ff.; Spiller, 2010). Notwithstanding similarities with risks that characterize private contracts, this opportunistic behaviour differs because political power can impose changes in the rules of the game, given States' general monopoly of force (North et al., 2009: 13 ff.).

There is another, long-ignored aspect that makes relational contracts particularly risky when it comes to PPP: the risk of opportunistic behaviour by third parties. The continuous pressure which interest groups can put on public authorities goes far beyond traditional lobbying by private operators. For example, lobbying by environmentalists, user associations, etc., leads democratic governments towards the implementation of rigid contracts with private operators (Spiller 2009: 45 ff.). In order to avoid criticism by such third parties, which have strategic interests of their own, or to avoid the risk of being accused of biases due to the influence of these groups, governments tend to negotiate and write contracts that are much more procedural than those among private parties.[23] This makes adaptation almost inevitable, and particularly costly. This is true *ex ante*, for example because it imposes particularly stringent conditions at the time bids are opened, thus reducing the scope of potential competition. And it is also the case *ex post*, with conditions of implementation that might seriously infringe on the managerial capacity of operators.

Claude Ménard

7.4.4 Institutional misfits: political transaction costs

The resulting rigidities, as well-intentioned as they might be, translate into high economic transaction costs, as well as what North (1990) identified as political transaction costs. Indeed, one important component of these costs comes out of the institutional alignment or misfit in the rules of the game framing the implementation of PPP. Institutions provide an essential support in making commitments credible and facilitating implementation, but they also impose constraints that translate into costs for both parties to partnerships.

Legislation, which delineates the space within which contracts are designed and implemented, is particularly relevant here. To secure transactions and provide adequate incentives, relatively comprehensive legislation is needed, with private operators looking for guarantees while public authorities need to legitimize their choice of PPP. Establishing an appropriate legal framework is not that obvious, as illustrated by its slow progress in the EU: laws regarding PPP were only recently adopted in Spain, Ireland, and France (as late as 2008) while drafts are still being discussed in most other EU members, as well as at the level of the European Commission. The existence of a well-defined legal system and of a powerful judiciary can also carry ambiguous effects. On the one hand, it makes commitments credible: parties are aware that in case of diverging interpretation or conflicts, they can go to arbitration and, in the last resort, address courts. On the other hand, legal support might turn into legal impediment, since it introduces rigidities in the negotiation, costly procedural obligations *ex ante* as well as *ex post*, and as it is rooted in diverging national traditions, making the task of international operators complex and costly. The success of PPP therefore depends on a delicate equilibrium between the need for legal support and a judiciary that make commitments credible; and the risks of a system that is either incompetent, imposing arbitrariness on parties, or powerful enough to engage parties in highly procedural and costly relationships.

Then, of course, there is the issue of political institutions. By definition, PPP involves government/public authorities. Therefore, rules delineating the political decision process, for example the presence or absence of checks-and-balances to restrain the risk of capture by political parties, or the existence of political institutions that reduces the duration of negotiations or that facilitates the resolution of disputes, are important factors to take into account.[24] Another dimension is the existence of a competent and uncorrupted bureaucracy to support the political decision process and the implementation of the contract once it has been approved. The adequacy of such institutions is a strategic factor in the success or failure of PPP.

To sum up, complex institutions are needed to secure PPP. However, the implementation of appropriate institutions is path dependent, may have a pace that by far exceeds that of PPP, and can result in high political transaction costs, up to the point of paralyzing the adoption of otherwise advantageous arrangements between public authorities and the private sector. For example, the costs of establishing a consensus among policy makers to avoid future challenges and accusations of favouritism may result in rigidities that translate into slowness in negotiations and costly renegotiations, generating misfits between expectations and delivery of public goods and services. These critical difficulties of adaptation often provoke negative reactions of users who are also taxpayers . . . and voters.

7.4.5 From misfits to users' dissatisfaction

The resulting tension between the rigidities introduced in PPP to avoid risks of capture and the need for adaptation has an important impact on how this organizational solution is perceived by citizens. Risk of dissatisfaction is a major concern for the development of PPP and may have dramatic consequences when it comes to the point of challenging existing agreements or even pushing towards the breach of existing contracts, as illustrated by the now well-known case of the termination of the contract for the provision of water between Buenos Aires and a private consortium led by Suez.[25]

The creation of user committees, often at the initiative of one of the two parties, is a clear signal of this concern.[26] Yet there are few studies on the perception of PPP by citizens. Bonnet *et al.* (2006: 7–16) have extensively reviewed polls on different forms of private sector partici-pation (including full privatization) in Latin America, from 1998 to 2005. After initial, highly positive expectations of these arrangements, dissatisfaction rates increased systematically, pushing governments to slow down or abandon strategies favouring private sector participa-tion, or even reneging on existing contracts. Casual evidence pointing in the same direction is found in user reactions to the privatization of water in England and Wales, which pressured the regulator (OFWAT, the Water Services Regulation Authority) to revise the rules of the game before the date agreed upon initially. Most of the time, dissatisfaction crystallizes around clauses of contracts perceived as penalizing important categories of the popula-tion (typically prices or rates and/or costs of connection), pinpointing what is viewed as bad organizational design. Dissatisfaction may also relate to the conditions of implementing and monitoring the agreements by public authorities (typically problems of insufficient control or corruption). These relate to the inadequate institutional rules and flaws in authorities' capacities to enforce a contract.

One important underlying question is whether this dissatisfaction is durable or 'transitory': i.e. whether the difficulties in switching from public provision to private participation are due to a slow learning process, particularly on the public side, or if it stems from the inadequacy of PPP, when it comes to the delivery of network infrastructures. One source of tension in PPP is that public authorities often address private operators to solve problems they cannot monitor anymore, or that could have a negative impact on the political career of policy makers: for example, financing the renovation or expansion of existing infrastructure through taxes, increasing revenues of the operator so as to satisfy the needs for new investments, improving productivity by firing surplus employees, reducing opportunistic behaviour among users such as illicit connections through tighter control and penalties, etc. Under these conditions, reforms involving private participation translate into price rises; layoffs so that employment in the utilities concerned falls; metering households to control their actual consumption better and thus pushing up bills, etc. These measures feed opposition from vested interests, but also skepticism among larger segments of the population. Empirical evidence, such as periodic polls about the perception of PPP in France by the *Institut de la Gestion Déléguée*, or the rejection of private participation in the provision of public services in several German cities illustrate the significance of these negative reactions and the fact that they are not confined to developing countries (Ménard and Peeroo, 2011: 322 ff.).

It is not easy, and can be quite costly, to monitor this dissatisfaction in order to contain or reverse this perception, through better information about the long-term effects of private participation, compensation for laid-off employees, protection against disruption of services for the poorest households etc. This is not only a matter of communication or public relations: it might impose a different approach to contracting with private operators, for example with the more active participation of users which may also translate into reduced efficiency and higher costs for the operator, or with changes in institutional rules that may challenge the legitimacy of policy makers or significantly reduce their capacity to monitor the development of infrastructures continued to be considered as 'public services'. Resistance from citizens who do not perceive value for their money in the changes involved, or from policy makers facing the perspective such dissatisfaction could feed, and often does, signals the end of PPP.

7.5 Is 'no future for PPP' the verdict?

In this chapter, I have attempted to point out some major difficulties that PPP is facing. I have argued that it has to deal with a double alignment problem. On the organizational side, a key issue is the allocation of rights. With PPP, the distinction between property rights and decision rights is particularly relevant since they are often partially dissociated from each other in the different types of contracts, while at the same time they correspond to an allocation of risks and responsibilities between public and private partners that often overlap. The resulting imbrications of rights lead to economic transaction costs that might be high or even intractable, either because of the complex issues to be solved *ex ante* in establishing the contract, or because of the costs of disentangling responsibilities and risks in the *ex post* implementation of the contract.

But there is more to the story. On the institutional side, PPP requires credible commitments among parties in an asymmetry of positions of a very special type. Indeed, one party (the public authorities) also makes the rules of the game, which opens room for significant arbitrariness. This is not to say that private operators are left without defences: they may capture the rule maker, for example through corruption; they may influence the decision making process, for example through lobbying; or they may even rely on institutions that partially prevail on local ones, as with multinationals going to international arbitration. Of course, all of the above are particularly significant when it comes to partnerships that involve important sunk investments, which is often the case for network infrastructures, which have attracted the largest volume investment under PPP as an organizational solution. The difficulties in finding an adequate institutional environment lead to political transaction costs.

All of these difficulties are embedded in the relational nature of contracts at stake, with 'relational' having a special meaning here, precisely because of this interaction between the properties of the organizational solution (and the blurred allocation of rights that often goes with it), and the characteristics of the institutions involved (with high risks of opportunism that they may facilitate). Ongoing financial uncertainties have amplified these difficulties. Even in institutionally stable countries, PPP has slowed down. According to the pro-PPP *Financial Times*, Britain's long celebrated PFI (PPP) programme has seen the number of deals and their value fall to their lowest levels for a decade, and the causes of this might go beyond short-term problems. Indeed, a recent paper in this newspaper concluded: 'The bigger question is whether the balance of risk and rigidity truly benefits the public sector. Too often, projects have turned out to require additional public sector support when the private sector has run into difficulties.' (*Financial Times*, January 15, 2010). Actually, the number and value of projects worldwide has had ups and downs repeatedly, since PPP bloomed in the discourse of international organizations and donors, as well as governments in the 1990s. All in all, private sector participation remains modest. For example, the pioneering PFI program, often cited as remarkable, remained the tip of the iceberg of British investment in infrastructure. According to a report by Britain's Finance Minister (the Chancellor of the Exchequer), dated 2010: 'The Private Finance Initiative (PFI) is a small but important part of the Government's strategy for delivering high quality public services.'[27]

Nevertheless, PPP is likely to remain relatively high on the agenda of policy makers and to develop, although slowly. There are several reasons why it should be so. First, financial constraints on public authorities, which have been amplified by the financial crisis, are not going to diminish anytime soon. Second, the need for major investments in infrastructure is going to put increasing pressure on politicians, particularly with the rapid expansion of large urban agglomerations almost everywhere in the world, and the rapid development of inter-regional and international trade. Third, incentive issues and related dissatisfaction with the public provision of goods and services requiring major sunk investments and tight coordination will feed expectations of better management, which creates pressures to raise private sector involvement. Fourth, ideological motivations, which feed suspicions about the role of government, will also support the idea that PPP is a solution, if not the solution to public investment!

However, progress should remain slow and relatively modest, and might be accompanied by a switch in the type of PPP, for reasons explored in this chapter. On the organizational side, these include: the significance of investments at stake, at least when it comes to network infrastructures; the risks of governmental opportunism, since the political cycles differ so much from investment cycles; and the pressures from third parties, which tend to make contracts between public authorities and private operators increasingly rigid. These trends result in a paradox when it comes to the choice of contract: on the one hand, data suggest that more rights transferred to private operators tend to make contracts more efficient; on the other hand, risks facing private operators push them to favour management or lease contracts so as to avoid the high risks associated with substantial sunk investments. Hence, we can expect the development of mild forms of PPP in the future, mainly in management and services contracts.

This tendency should be amplified by institutional factors. Making public commitments credible in order to secure private investment and guarantee adequate rates of return, rather than systematically allocating risks to public authorities or donors, are issues that have been explored quite extensively by New Institutional Economists. They have exhibited the role of checks-and-balances in the political system; of a strong and independent judiciary; and of autonomous and competent regulators, as key institutional actors (Spiller and Levy, 1994; Spiller and Tommasi, 2005, Ch. 20). However, changing institutions to attain these goals is hard. It is a long-term process with a lot of 'trial-and-error' and no guarantee of success (North et al., 2009: 32–55 and 112–22). One major difficulty is the implementation of institutions that are strong enough to limit political arbitrariness and third party opportunism, but flexible enough to allow adaptation. The lack of such an institutional environment in so many of the countries that most need private sector participation will push in the same direction as organizational issues, in other words towards the development of quite mild forms of PPP.

To sum up, public–private partnership in building network infrastructures and contributing to the delivery of public goods and services is going to stay with us and to progress. But one may also quite safely predict that: 1) this participation will remain limited when it comes to major investment and will rather contribute by providing adequate managerial capacities, so that management and lease contracts should prevail; 2) building institutions that fit the needs of secured private participation will remain high on the agenda of policy makers and international donors, but will also challenge our poor understanding of what adequate institutions are and how they impact on the interaction between public authorities and private operators. These issues are of great concern to decision makers, but also define an important research agenda.

Notes

1 Previous versions of this paper were presented at conferences and seminars in Delft (TU), Lausanne (EPFL), Singapore (NUS), Paris (Sorbonne). I am indebted to participants for their comments and

to the co-editors (Piet de Vries and Etienne Yehoue) for their help and supportive suggestions. Nicholas Sowels helped polish the paper. The usual disclaimer fully applies.

2 The PPIAF (World Bank group) database focuses on these sectors.

3 Hence, the often-observed public outcry and the resulting tensions between parties to the contract when the private operator, which is the residual claimant in a PPP, makes large *ex post* profits.

4 'Public utilities' is a misleading name in these cases since these monopolistic segments can as well be under private control (but usually tightly regulated).

5 For a general overview of NIE contributions, see Menard and Shirley, 2005/2008.

6 Problems are partially different when it comes to the delivery of goods or services without network properties, such as building and operating a hospital or a prison and charging users, for example local or regional authorities, accordingly. However, even in these cases, the allocation of rights often remains a problem. Whether wardens in a prison operated through PPP should be under the control of public authorities or the private operator illustrates the difficulty well.

7 The problem is also important in developed countries because of aging water and sanitation infrastructures, and the massive investment their upgrading requires.

8 The MENA (Middle East and North Africa) region comprises Algeria, Egypt, Israel, Jordan, Lebanon, Malta, Morocco, Syria, Tunisia and Turkey.

9 In the PPI database, private participation includes all forms of private investments. In the case of telecoms in developing countries, it represents almost all investments since there has been only negligible public investment in this sector. As a result of the definition of PPP in this database, which includes full privatization, the data may underestimate the role of PPP in water and sanitation and overestimate its role in telecoms.

10 Data may even overestimate the significance of private participation. For example, a public corporation contractually involved in participation in another public entity might be classified as PPP (this seems to be the case for the water sector in Portugal, for example, or for public corporations investing in developing countries).

11 For a good assessment of methodological issues at stake, see Gassner *et al.*, 2009, pp. 13–32. See also the pioneering paper by Masten *et al.* (1991) on assessing organizational solutions comparatively. Clarke *et al.* (2002) have proposed a methodology, applied to water reform in Guinea, to assess alternative solutions.

12 Strangely, in the initial version published as a working paper by the World Bank, the authors expressed a much more nuanced evaluation, concluding that '*the true impact of PSP may have been overstated in previous research*'. (Gassner *et al.*, 2007: 27–9. My emphasis, CM.)

13 Source: *Mission d'Appui aux Partenariats Public-Privé*, http://www.ppp.bercy.gouv.fr/liste_projets_extract_boamp.pdf. Last consulted: April 2011. See also Ménard *et al.* (2009).

14 In legal parlance, property rights refer to rules concerning 'usus', 'usus fructus' and 'abusus', so that decision rights are included within that concept. Therefore the legal definition only partially corresponds to the economic concept.

15 However, there may be tensions between regulators and private operators about risks to be supported by the latter in the case of full privatization.

16 This is well illustrated by the impact of the Asian financial crisis of 1998 on PPPs in Manila, or the role of the Argentinean crisis of 2001–2 in the breach of contract between Buenos Aires and the consortium led by Suez.

17 According to the PPIAF dataset, China has recently become the leading country for the implementation of PPPs, particularly in the water and sanitation sector.

18 More dramatic consequences of the ambiguous allocation of decision rights were illustrated by the initial problems of coordination, resulting in serious accidents in the British railway system after its privatization (Yvrande and Menard, 2005: 676 ff.).

19 'Panafrican Public–Private Partnerships,' Brussels, 30 November 2007.

20 Of course, this is also true in developed countries, in which PPP tends to be extremely procedural in order to prevent capture, corruption, etc., with high costs for bidders, thus dramatically reducing their number.

21 Last consulted: 10 December 2010.

22 My calculation (CM), based mainly on PricewaterhouseCoopers (2005, particularly pages 29, 31 and 64). See also for France, Ménard *et al.* (2009).

23 See Bajari and Tadelis (2001), although their paper is not specifically about PPP but more generally about contracts between public authorities and private operators.

24 For a pioneering econometric analysis of the impact of political and other institutional factors in choosing PPP as an organizational solution, see Hammami *et al.* (2006).
25 Such cases are particularly significant because they challenge the reputation of parties involved and, above all, the very image of PPP as an adequate solution.
26 Examples are the French *Commission Consultative sur les Services Publics Locaux*, created by law; and many users' committees initiated by operators such as Suez or Veolia to facilitate the acceptance and monitoring of their contracts in developing and emerging countries.
27 http://webarchive.nationalarchives.gov.uk/20100407010852/http://www.hm-treasury.gov.uk/ppp_index.htm, National Archives. According to this data set (last consulted 29 November 2010), 667 projects were signed from 1996 to 2010, many of them of relatively limited size.

References

Andres, Luis A., Jose Luis Guasch and Sebastian Lopez Azumendi (2009) 'Regulatory Governance and Sector Performance: Methodology and Evaluation for Electricity Distribution in Latin America'. In: C. Ménard and M. Ghertman (eds), *Regulation, De-Regulation and Re-Regulation*. Cheltenham: Edward Elgar Pub., Ch. 6, pp.111–50.
Bajari, Patrick and Steve Tadelis (2001) 'Incentives versus Transaction Costs: A Theory of Procurement Contracts', *Rand Journal of Economics*, 32 (3): 387–407.
Baker, George, Robert Gibbons and Kevin Murphy (2002) 'Relational Contracts and the Theory of the Firm', *Quarterly Journal of Economics*, 117 (1), 39–84.
Baker, George (2008) 'Strategic Alliances: Bridges Between Islands of Conscious Power', *Journal of the Japanese and International Economies* 22 (2): 14663
Barter, Paul A. (2008) 'Public Planning with Business Delivery of Excellent Urban Public Transport', *Policy and Society*, 27 (2): 103–14.
Bonnet, Celine, Pierre Dubois, David Martimort and Stephane Straub (2006) 'Empirical evidence on satisfaction with privatization in Latin America: welfare effects and beliefs', Toulouse: IDEI, Working paper, October 2006. 60 pp.
Clarke, George and Claude Ménard (2002) 'A Transitory Regime: Water Supply in Conakry, Guinea'. In M. Shirley (ed.), Ch. 8: 273–316.
European Union (2004a) *Green Paper on Public–Private Partnerships and Community Law on Public Contract and Concession*. Presented by the Commission, Brussels, 30/04/2004.
European Union (2004b) *White Paper on Services of General Interest*. Communication from the Commission to the European Parliament, the Council, the European Economic and Social Committee and the Committee of the Regions. Brussels, 12.05.2004.
Financial Times, 'PFI feels the pinch. UK Government must treat private financing with care', January 15, 2010.
Gassner, Katharina, Alexander Popov and Natalyia Pushak (2009) *Does Private Sector Participation Improve Performance in Electricity and Water Distribution?* Washington: The World Bank, Public-Private Infrastructure Advisory Facility.
Goldberg, Victor (1976) 'Regulation and Administered Contracts', *Bell Journal of Economics*, 7: 527–43.
Guasch, Jose Luis (2004) *Granting and Renegotiating Infrastructure Concessions: Doing it Right*. Washington: The World Bank.
Hammami, Mona, Jean-Francois Ruhashyankiko and Etienne B. Yehoue (2006) 'Determinants of Public–Private Partnerships in Infrastructure.' Working Paper 06/99, IMF.
Hart, Oliver (2003) 'Incomplete Contracts and Public Ownership: Remarks, and an Application to Public-Private Partnerships', *The Economic Journal*, 113 (March): C69–C76.
Kauffmann, Cécile and Lucia Wegner (2007), 'Privatisation in the MEDA region: where do we stand?' OECD, Development Center, Working Paper # 261, July 2007.
Künneke, Rolf, John Groenewegen and Claude Ménard (2010) 'Aligning modes of organization with technology: Critical transactions in the reform of infrastructures', *Journal of Economic Behavior and Organization*, 75 (3): 494–505.
Levy, Brian and Pablo Spiller (1994) 'The Institutional Foundations of Regulatory Commitment', *Journal of Law, Economics and Organization*, 9 (Fall): 201–46.
Macneil, Ian R. (1978) 'Contracts: Adjustments of a Long Term Economic Relation under Classical, Neoclassical, and Relational Contract Law', *Northwestern University Law Review*, 72: 854–906.

Claude Ménard

Marin, Philippe (2009) *Public–Private Partnership for Urban Water Utilities. A Review of Experiences in Developing Countries*, Washington: The World Bank, Public–Private Infrastructure Advisory Facility.

Martimort, David and Stéphane Straub (2009), 'Infrastructure Privatization and Changes in Corruption Pattern: The Roots of Public Discontent', *Journal of Development Economics*, 90 (1): 69–84

Masten, Scott E., James W. Meehan and Edward E. Snyder (1991) 'The Costs of Organization', *The Journal of Law, Economics and Organization*, 7 (1): 1–25

Ménard, Claude (2009) 'Why to reform infrastructure and with what institutional arrangements? The case of public private partnerships in water supply'. In: R. Kunneke, J. Groenewegen and J.F. Auger (eds), *The Governance of Network Industries*, Cheltenham: Edward Elgar Publisher, Ch. 2: 25–45.

Ménard, Claude (2012) 'Hybrid Modes of Organization. Alliances, Joint Ventures, Networks, and Other "Strange" Animals'. In: R. Gibbons and J. Roberts, *The Handbook of Organizational Economics*, Princeton: Princeton University Press: 1066–1108.

Ménard, Claude and George Clarke (2002) 'A Transitory Regime: Water Supply in Conakry, Guinea.' In: M. Shirley (ed.) *Thirsting for Efficiency: The Economics and Politics of Urban Water Reforms*. Amsterdam: Elsevier-Pergamon: 273–316.

Ménard, Claude and Stéphane Saussier (2002) 'Contractual Choice and Performance.' In: Eric Brousseau and Jean-Michel Glachant (eds) *The Economics of Contracts. Theory and Applications*. Cambridge (UK): Cambridge University Press. pp. 440–62.

Ménard, Claude and Mary Shirley (eds) (2005/2008) *Handbook of New Institutional Economics*. Berlin-Boston-Dordrecht: Springer Verlag.

Ménard, Claude and Aleksandra Peeroo (2011) 'Liberalization in the Water Sector: Three Leading Models.' In: M. Finger and R. Kunneke (eds) *International Handbook of Network Industries. The Liberalization of Infrastructure*. Cheltenham: Edward Elgar, Ch. 18: 310–27.

Ménard, Claude, Jean-Michel Oudot, Laurent Garcin, Julie de Brux and Marie-Joelle Kodjovi (2009) *L'évaluation préalable dans les contrats de partenariat*. Institut de la Gestion Déléguée – CEF-O-PPP, April. 62 pp.

Moteff, J., Copeland, C., Fischer, J. (2003) *Critical infrastructure: What makes an infrastructure critical?* Report to the Congress. Congressional Research Service.

North, Douglass C. (1990) 'A Transaction Cost Theory of Politics', *Journal of Theoretical Politics*, 2 (4): 355–67

North, Douglass C., John J. Wallis and Barry R. Weingast (2009) *Violence and Social Orders. A Conceptual Framework for Interpreting Recorded Human History*. Cambridge (UK): Cambridge University Press.

Oudot, Jean-Michel and Claude Ménard (2010) 'Opportunisme ou équité? Le cas des contrats d'approvisionnement de défense', *Revue Française d'Economie*, 24 (3): 196–226.

PricewaterhouseCoopers (2005) *Delivering the PPP Promise: A review of PPP issues and activities*. PricewaterhouseCoopers.

Savedoff, William and Pablo Spiller (ed.) (1999) *Spilled Water. Institutional Commitment in the Provision of Water Services in Latin America*, Washington: Inter-American Development Bank.

Shirley, Mary (ed.) (2002) *Thirsting for Efficiency: The Economics and Politics of Urban Water Reforms*, Amsterdam: Elsevier-Pergamon.

Spiller, Pablo T. (2009) 'An institutional theory of public contracts: regulatory implications.' In: Claude Ménard and Michel Ghertman, (eds) *Regulation, De-Regulation and Re-Regulation*, Cheltenham. Edward Elgar Pub. Chap. 3: 45–66.

Spiller, Pablo T. (2010) 'Regulation: A Transaction Cost Perspective'. *California Management Review*, 52 (2): 147–58.

Spiller, Pablo and Mario Tommasi (2005) 'The Institutions of Regulation: An Application to Public Utilities.' In: Ménard and Shirley (eds) 2005/2008, Ch. 20: 515–44.

UN Millennium Project (2005) *Health, Dignity, and Development: What Will It Take?* New York: United Nations Millennium Project.

Wallsten, Scott (2001) 'An Econometric Analysis of Telecommunication Competition, Privatization, and Regulation in Africa and Latin America', *Journal of Industrial Economics*, 40 (1): 1–19.

Wallsten, Scott and Katrina Kosec (2008) 'The effects of ownership and benchmark competition: an empirical analysis of US water systems,' *International Journal of Industrial Organization*, 26: 186–205.

Warner, Mildred E. and Amir Hefetz (2007) 'Beyond the Market versus Planning Dichotomy: understanding privatisation and its reverse in US cities', *Local Government Studies*, 33 (4): 555–72.

Xun, Wu and Nepomuceno A. Malaluan (2008) 'A tale of two concessionaires: a natural experiment of water privatization in Metro Manila'. *Urban Studies* 45 (1): 207–29.

Yvrande, Anne and Claude Ménard (2005) 'Institutional Constraints and Organizational Change. The Case of the British Rail Reform', *Journal of Economic Behavior and Organization*, 56 (4): 675–99.

Websites

Her Majesty's Treasurer: http://webarchive.nationalarchives.gov.uk/20100407010852/http://www.hm-treasury.gov.uk/ppp_index.htm

Institut de la Gestion Déléguée : http://www.fondation-igd.org

Mission d'Appui aux Partenariats Public-Privé : http://www.ppp.bercy.gouv.fr/liste_projets_extract_boamp.pdf

Public-Private Infrastructure Advisory Facility: http://www.ppiaf.org/ppiaf/page/private-participation-infrastructure-database. Last consulted: December 2010.

Game theory and PPP[1]

S. Ping Ho

8.1 Introduction

Game theory can be defined as 'the study of mathematical models of conflict and cooperation between intelligent rational decision-makers' (Myerson, 1991). It can also be called 'conflict analysis' or 'interactive decision theory', which can more accurately express the essence of the theory. Still, game theory is the most popular and accepted name. In PPPs, conflicts and strategic interactions between promoters and governments are very common and play a crucial role in the performance of PPP projects. Many difficult issues such as opportunisms, negotiations, competitive biddings, and partnerships have been challenging the wisdom of the PPP participants. Therefore, game theory is very appealing as an analytical framework to study the interaction and dynamics between the PPP participants and to suggest proper strategies for both governments and promoters.

Game theory modelling method will be used throughout this chapter to analyse and build theories on some of the above challenging issues in PPPs. Through the game theory modelling, a specific problem of concern is abstracted to a level that can be analysed without losing the critical components of the problem. Moreover, new insights or theories for the problem concerned are developed when the game models are solved. Whereas game theory modelling method has been broadly applied to study problems in economics and other disciplines, it is only recently that, this method has been applied to study problems in engineering management problems, including PPPs (see Ho, 2001, 2005; 2006; Ho and Tsui, 2009; Ho and Tsui, 2010). It is our contention that, in PPP research, there will be great potential in gaining important new insights and building new theories by applying this method. These new theories will help practitioners, including governments, developers and bankers, to better cooperate, with higher efficiency and effectiveness.

This chapter has two major objectives. First, the concept of game theory and the application of game theory modelling in PPPs will be introduced. Second, new insights and theories concerning PPPs from the game theory modelling will be presented and discussed; particularly, focusing on the opportunism problems and the contingency view of PPPs as a governance structure. The organization of this chapter is as follows. Section 8.2 introduces the basic concepts of game theory and game theory modelling. Section 8.3 discusses the problems of unbalanced profit structure in PPP projects, crucial to the game theory modelling in PPPs. In section 8.4, a model concerning another opportunism issue, renegotiation/hold-up problem, will be discussed. In terms of game theory modelling, this model demonstrates how to abstract a problem and develop theories. In terms of PPPs, this model provides important policy implications concerning the renegotiation/hold-up problem. Sections 8.5 and 8.6 deal with asymmetric information problems in PPPs. Section 8.6 focuses on the signalling games and examines some popular signals sent by developers. Section 8.7 emphasizes governments' screening strategies for differentiating the types of the promoters/bidders. Section 8.8 proposes a contingency theory for PPPs as a governance structure that combines the models in sections 8.4 to 8.6. Section 8.9 presents a case study of Taiwan High Speed Rail, one of the largest PPP projects in the world, and illustrates the opportunism problems and their transaction costs, caused by wrongly adopting PPPs as a governance structure for this project. Section 8.10 concludes this chapter.

8.2 Basic concepts of game theory and game theory modelling

The following introduction of the fundamentals of game theory basically follows Gibbons (1992) and Binmore (1992). Here games will be categorized by whether or not players move sequentially and whether or not the information is complete. In terms of a moving sequence of players, there are two basic types of games: static games and dynamic games. Complicated by the information held by players, the games can be further categorized into: static games with complete information, dynamic games with complete information, static games with incomplete information and dynamic games with incomplete information. Fudenberg and Tirole (1991), Mas-Collel *et al.* (1995) and Myerson (1991) have excellent in-depth discussions on game theory. Readers who already have knowledge of game theory may skip this section; otherwise, they are advised to read this section so as to better understand the game theory modelling applications presented in the chapter.

8.2.1 Static game of complete information

Some essential concepts and definitions in game theory are illustrated by examples of a two-player game. General cases of n-players definitions are omitted for convenience. The first example is the prisoners' dilemma, as shown in Fig. 8.1. Two suspects are arrested and held in

| | | **Player 2** | |
		Confess	Not confess
	Confess	(–6, –6)	(0, –9)
Player 1			
	Not confess	(–9, 0)	(–1, –1)

Figure 8.1 Static game: prisoners' dilemma

Reproduced with permission from ASCE

separate cells. If both of them confess, they will be sentenced to jail for six years. If neither of them confesses, they will be sentenced for only one year. However, if one confesses and the other does not, the honest one will be rewarded by being released (in jail for zero years) and the other will be punished with nine years in jail. In Fig. 8.1, the first number in each cell represents player 1's payoff and the second number is for player 2. We use the left side of the table to represent player 1 and use the top of the table to represent player 2.

Figure 8.1 is a 'normal form representation' of a game that specifies the players in the game, the strategies available to the players, and the payoff of each player for his strategy. The normal form representation is usually used in representing a static game in which they act simultaneously, or more generally, each player does not know the other player's decision before he makes his own decision. If the payoff matrix as shown in Fig. 8.1 is known to all players, then the payoff matrix is 'common knowledge' to all players in a game. In addition, the players of a game are assumed to be rational; i.e. it is assumed that the players will always try to maximize their payoffs. This is one of the most important assumptions in any economic analysis. If the players' rationality and the game structure, including payoffs, are common knowledge, the game is called a game of 'complete information'. Conversely, if each player's possible payoff is privately known by himself only, it is a game with incomplete information or asymmetric information.

To answer how each prisoner will play/behave in this game, the *Nash equilibrium*, one of the most important solution concepts in game theory, will be introduced. If game theory makes a unique prediction about each player's choice, then it has to be that each player is willing to play the strategy as predicted. Logically, this prediction should be the player's *best response* to the other player's predicted strategy. No single player will want to deviate from the predicted strategy, that is, the strategy is *strategically stable* or *self-enforcing* (Gibbons, 1992). This prediction following the above solution concept is called a '*Nash equilibrium*' (NE). In the prisoners' dilemma, although the (Not confess, Not confess) may seem better for both players, it is unstable since every player wants to deviate from this solution to get extra benefit or avoid the other's betrayal. Any suspect who deviates from (Confess, Confess) will be hurt and any suspect who deviates from (Not confess, Not confess) will be rewarded. Therefore, the only predicted strategy that no player wants to deviate from is (Confess, Confess) and this is the Nash equilibrium in the prisoners' dilemma.

In some games there will be multiple Nash equilibriums; fortunately the existence of multiple equilibriums will not be a problem. Much of the game theory is an effort to identify a compelling equilibrium in different classes of games to make the prediction appealing (Gibbons, 1992). For example, the concepts of mixed strategy Nash equilibrium or focal point can resolve the problem of multiple Nash equilibriums. Detailed treatment of this issue will not be introduced here.

8.2.2 Dynamic games of complete information

Most of the analysis in this research will use the dynamic game with complete or incomplete information. However, the previous introduction of static game is essential because those concepts will be used repeatedly in other classes of games and in this chapter. In contrast to static games, players in a dynamic game move *sequentially* instead of simultaneously. Since the moves are sequential, it will be easier and more intuitive to represent a dynamic game by a tree-like structure, called an '*extensive form*' representation. In a dynamic game, suppose that the player who moves at a later stage can fully observe previous players' moves and know his own location in the game tree. This assumption is called the 'perfect information' assumption. In dealing with games of incomplete information, the games will be transformed into games of 'imperfect information', where the player who moves at a later stage cannot fully observe previous players' moves.

We will use the following simplified Market Entry example to demonstrate the concepts of game analysis. A new firm, New Inc., wants to enter a market to compete with a monopoly firm, Old Inc. The monopoly firm does not want the new firm to enter the market, because new entry will reduce the incumbent firm's profits. Therefore, Old Inc. threatens New Inc. with a price war if New Inc. enters the market. Figure 8.2 shows the extensive form of the market entry game. If the payoffs shown in Fig. 8.2 are known to all players, the payoffs are 'common knowledge' to all players. If the game structure, including payoffs, is common knowledge, the game is called a game of 'complete information'. The game tree shows 1) New Inc. chooses to enter the market or not, and then Old Inc. chooses to start a price war or not, and 2) the payoff of each decision combination.

A possible game prediction is that Old Inc. can use the strategy: to play 'start a price war' if New Inc. plays 'enter', so that Old Inc. can threaten New Inc. not to enter the market. As a result, it may seem that 'stay out' and 'start a price war if enter' is a solution satisfying the Nash equilibrium concept. Nevertheless, as shown in Fig. 8.2, the threat to start a price war is *not credible* because Old Inc. will not start a price war if New Inc. does enter; instead, Old Inc. will maximize the payoff by playing 'no price war' after New Inc. enters the market unless Old Inc. is behaving *irrationally*. New Inc. knows the threat's incredibility and therefore will maximize the payoff by playing 'enter'. Thus, the Nash equilibrium of the Price War game is (Enter, No price war), an equilibrium that does not rely on the player to carry out an incredible threat. In a dynamic game, the equilibrium solution is a subgame perfect Nash equilibrium, which satisfies the sequential rationality by maximizing each player's payoffs in the subgames backward recursively (Gibbons, 1992).

8.2.3 Static games of incomplete information

Games of incomplete information or asymmetric information are also called 'Bayesian games', because they involve the use of Bayes' rules in solving the equilibrium. Therefore, static games of incomplete information are also called static Bayesian games. The core issue of incomplete information is the existence of '*private information*' that is known only to specific

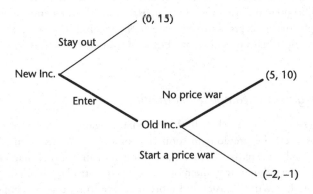

Figure 8.2 Simplified market entry game

players instead of to all players. This private information usually refers to the payoff functions of the players. The players with private information are called informed players. Similarly the players who are uncertain of the other players' payoff functions are uninformed players. The equilibrium of a Bayesian game is called '*Bayesian Nash equilibrium*'. We won't be using this type of game in the models presented in the chapter.

8.2.4 Dynamic games of incomplete information

After the introduction of static games of incomplete information, no extra explanation is required on what a dynamic game of incomplete information is. However, the possible equilibriums of this class of games are much more complicated than other classes of games, yet still closely related. In this class of games, asymmetric information on payoff functions will be converted to asymmetric information on players' 'types', where a different type of player has a different payoff function. The central concern of the equilibrium for this class of game is to resolve the asymmetric information problem by differentiating the 'type' of a player. Since many games in the PPPs fall into this category, it is critical to fully understand their characteristics and the games' equilibrium concept: *perfect Bayesian equilibrium*.

In dynamic games of complete information, the subgame-perfect Nash equilibrium has to rule out incredible threats and time-inconsistent promises. However, in contrast to subgame-perfect Nash equilibriums, the perfect Bayesian equilibriums for dynamic games of incomplete information cannot be obtained through backwards induction because they need to be checked back and forth circularly. The primary steps to solve for perfect Bayesian equilibriums are to:

- find possible candidates for perfect Bayesian equilibriums; and
- check each candidate or each class of candidates for the satisfaction of perfect Bayesian equilibriums' sufficient conditions.

Two basic kinds of equilibrium are often checked for possible solutions. The first is the 'pooling equilibrium', under which different types of informed players act indifferently and the uninformed player cannot differentiate the players' types according to their decisions. The second kind is the 'separating equilibrium', under which different types of informed players act differently and, thus, the uninformed player can differentiate the types of informed players. For detailed explanations of why these conditions should be satisfied, one may refer to Gibbons (1992) and Fudenberg and Tirole (1991).

Spence (1973) was the first to show how 'signalling' could be a solution to the asymmetric information problem. He modelled that, first, nature determines the types of worker's productivity ability: high (H) or low (L), with probability p of being type H. Here we name the high-ability worker as 'worker H' and low-ability worker as 'worker L'. Second, the worker learns his ability and chooses his education level as a signal: high education or low education. Third, the firm observes the worker's education level and offers the appropriate wage level, choosing from high wage or low wage.

The two basic possible equilibriums to be checked are:

8.2.4.1 Pooling equilibrium

Intuitively, if the low-ability worker can obtain a high level of education as easily as the high-ability worker, the low-ability worker would want to obtain a high education level to

S. Ping Ho

convince the firm that he is a high-ability worker. In this case, the firm cannot believe the signal sent by the workers, and therefore, will not offer a high wage level to the worker with a high education level.

8.2.4.2 Separating equilibrium

The conditions for the signal to be effective or for the solution to be a separating equilibrium must be that it is not in the low-ability worker's interest to imitate the high-ability worker. In this case, the firm will believe the signal regarding productivity ability and offer wages accordingly. These conditions can be expressed mathematically. Cho and Krep (1987) further showed that the separating equilibrium will be the only possible equilibrium. Detailed discussion regarding the job market signalling game can be found in Spence (1973, 1974) and Cho and Kreps (1987).

8.2.5 Theory building through game theory modelling

To build theories through game theory modelling, first, a game theory model will be developed to properly abstract the problem of concern. In this step, appropriate assumptions have to be made for simplifying the problem so as to focus on a few critical components. In addition to the knowledge of game theory, this model setup process needs sufficient domain knowledge for the problem. A thorough literature review or case studies generally will provide better and more precise understandings of the relevent problem and associated issues.

The second step is to solve for the conditions of all possible or specific equilibriums of the game model. The number of possible equilibriums and the complexity of the equilibrium solutions depend on the complexity of the game model and the number of variables associated with payoff functions.

The last step is to link the equilibrium conditions to the issues of the problem. If the equilibrium solutions are complicated, identifying possible contextual or contingency variables will narrow the possible solution space and provide more insights for the problem. Once the logic between different variable configurations and possible equilibriums is established, theories concerning the problem can be developed.

8.3 Problems of unbalanced profit structures in PPPs

8.3.1 Profit structure and profit pool of a PPP project

In PPPs, the sources of the promoters' investment returns will come not only from the returns on equity investments in the concessionaire, but also from the construction and operation contracts since the promoters would often act as the *major* contractors for construction and operation. Therefore, the promoters, being the controlling shareholders, will aim to maximize the overall value of the combined pool of profit components. In other words, the profit structure of promoters is inconsistent with that of the passive shareholders of concession firms.

The profit structure of a PPP investment can be better explained by the PPP business model illustrated in Figure 8.3, which shows that the returns on PPP investment include equity returns, construction contract returns and operation contract returns. We will call the three profit components together the PPP 'profit pool'. From the promoter's

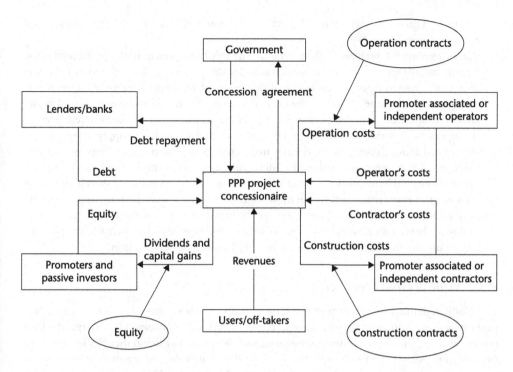

Figure 8.3 Promoters' profit structure and profit pool in PPP projects

perspective, the profits from a PPP investment are the overall returns from the profit pool. Moreover, how these components are pooled in terms of their relative proportion will have major influences in determining the returns from the profit pool, the promoters' investment and potential opportunism, and the interactions between the government and promoters.

- *First Component: Equity Returns.* The first component in the profit pool is the equity return in a PPP firm, defined as equity value minus equity investment. In PPPs, following the project finance practice, the promoters will become one of the major shareholders of the PPP firm, and will be called 'controlling shareholders' in this chapter. The equity invested by non-promoters will be considered as the 'passive equity', owned by 'passive shareholders'. Unlike the passive shareholders, such as insurance companies, who mainly focus on the returns from equity investment, the promoters, being the controlling shareholders, will aim to maximize the *overall* value of the combined pool of profit components. In other words, the equity returns are not the only profits sought by the promoters in a PPP project.
- *Second Component: Construction Contract Returns.* The construction contract returns refer to the profits from promoters being the construction contractors of a PPP project. As Walker and Smith (1995) observed, since most construction firms are thinly capitalized and rely heavily on short-term debt financing for their capital needs, they are usually reluctant to invest their limited and expensive capital in PPP equity and largely focus on construction

contracts. This is especially true when the concession period is long and the returns from equity are slow.

- *Third Component: Operation Contract Returns.* The third component in the profit pool is the returns from operation contracts undertaken by the promoter. The operation contracts refer to the contracts for the daily operation and regular maintenance after the project is completed or the operation commences. For example, the insurance policies for the facility properties, firm employees or operation liability can be considered part of the operation contracts. Other operation contracts may include supply contracts for operational inputs, contracts for regular maintenance and contracts for outsourcing services, etc. Those who are capable of undertaking operation contracts and consider these contracts profitable may invest in the project as one of the controlling shareholders. An important characteristic of the operation contract returns is that the returns are possible only when the project is completed and the PPP firm continues with the operation. This difference between construction contract returns and operation contract returns plays an important role in the governance design of PPPs as we shall discuss later.

8.3.2 Value of Profit Pool (VoPP)

The VoPP is defined by the sum of the returns from the above three components of a PPP profit structure. VoPP, thus, can be considered the net value to a promoter from a specific PPP investment; i.e., the overall profits to the promoter. Whereas traditional theories in corporate finance emphasize that a firm's objective is to maximize its value, or, equivalently, to maximize equity value, we argue that the objective of a PPP firm should be assumed to maximize the promoter's VoPP, because the VoPP is the returns of the major shareholder of the PPP firm, also the promoter. Note that, for passive or minority shareholders, equity returns are still their sole returns from the project and, therefore, the maximization of equity value is the objective of their investment. We argue that the deviation of the PPP promoter's objective from traditional objective in a non-PPP firm creates serious problems, especially opportunisms, when the profit structure is unbalanced.

8.3.3 Problems of unbalanced profit structure

An unbalanced profit structure in PPPs develops when the PPP profit structure is skewed to focus on the short-term profits, particularly, the construction contract returns. The unbalanced profit structure underlying PPPs gives the controlling shareholders the incentives of opportunism. The ownership structure of PPPs further gives the controlling shareholders the capability to exploit private information in seeking appropriable rents from passive investors. The controlling shareholder may benefit from manipulating the construction contract prices and clauses and, as a result, the minority shareholders, subject to severe information asymmetry, will suffer from losses in equity returns. As such, controlling shareholder–passive shareholder conflicts may seriously impair the financial situation and performance of the project and lead to significant transaction costs in PPPs.

In the cases where equity is allowed to be raised publicly before project completion, the passive shareholders will be in an even weaker position because of the serious information asymmetry in unfinished projects and the reduced equity investments from the controlling shareholders. Moreover, since the use of project finance in PPPs allows a low equity ratio, the danger of early public equity raisings due to the unbalanced project structure problem is further aggravated.

8.4 Problems of financial renegotiations/hold-up in PPPs: dynamic games of complete information

Financial renegotiation and the associated hold-up problems may happen when project cost, market demand or other market conditions become significantly unfavourable and cause the promoter to renegotiate with the government for subsidies or rescue. The dilemma faced by the government is that although financial renegotiation is not legitimate, the government is often tempted to accept the renegotiation because of the gigantic costs of project failure. Such inconsistency creates serious opportunism problems and associated transaction costs. A game theory model developed by Ho (2006) analysed the strategic interactions concerning renegotiation/hold-up and proposed related procurement and management policies from the perspective of renegotiation/hold-up. We shall present the model and discuss how the problem is modelled and what the major policy implications are.

[Subsections 8.4.1 and 8.4.2 are excerpted from Ho's (2006) work with permission from ASCE.]

8.4.1 Inefficiency due to financial renegotiation/hold-up

8.4.1.1 Ex-ante inefficiency: aggressive investment and bidding

Expectation of government for renegotiation under project distress may cause opportunistic bidding, typically seen in construction practice. In opportunistic bidding, bidders, in their proposals, intentionally understate the possible risks involved or overstate the project profitability to outperform other bidders. In their pilot study on opportunistic bidding, Ho and Liu (2004) show that, if a builder can make an effective construction claim, the builder will have an incentive to bid opportunistically. Similarly, if a request for renegotiation is always granted, promoters would have an incentive to bid optimistically or aggressively to win the project. An overly optimistic proposal can have a higher chance of winning given the fact that much crucial and promoter-specific project information in the bid proposal can be very difficult to verify and the government tends to favour those proposals with optimistic financial forecasts. Therefore, if the bidders have an *ex ante* expectation of *ex post* renegotiation, they will have an incentive to bid opportunistically. Since this logic between governments' rescuing subsidies due to renegotiation and the project's early failure due to opportunism is not straightforward, the importance of the financial renegotiation problem is underemphasized.

8.4.1.2 Ex-post inefficiency during the concession period

In his repossession game example, Rasmusen (2001) shows that if renegotiation is expected, the agent may choose inefficient actions that will reduce overall or social efficiency but increases the agent's payoff. In PPPs, after signing the concession, moral hazard problems may also occur if renegotiation is expected. As promoters are frequently the major contractors of PPP projects, they may not be concerned about cost overruns because they may benefit from such overspending. Moreover, promoters may not be concerned about the operation efficiency either during the operation period.

8.4.2 Modelling of financial renegotiation/hold-up and the equilibriums

The behavioural dynamics of the renegotiation, or government rescue, play a central role in PPP administration given that information asymmetry generally exists. Here, game theory is applied to analyse how the government will respond to the promoter's request for renegotiation and the impact of such renegotiation on PPPs.

8.4.2.1 Model setup

The game theory framework shown in Fig. 8.4 is a dynamic game expressed in an extensive form. Suppose a PPP contract does not specify any government rescue or subsidy in the face of financial crisis. Neither does the law prohibit the government from bailing out the PPP project by providing a debt guarantee or extending the concession period. Suppose also that government is not encouraged to rescue a project without compelling and justifiable reasons. Cost overrun or operation losses caused by inefficient management or normal business risk are not considered just reasons for government rescue, whereas adverse events caused by unexpected or unusual equipment/material price escalation may be justified more easily. It should be reasonable to assume that if the government grants a subsidy to a project on the basis of unjustifiable reasons, the government may suffer the loss of public trust or suspicion of corruption.

The dynamic game, shown in Fig. 8.4, starts from adverse situations where it is in the promoter's (denoted by D in the game tree) or lending bank's best interests to bankrupt the project if the government (denoted by G) does not rescue the project. Alternatively, the promoter can also request government rescue and subsidize for the amount of U, even though the contract clause does not specify any possible future rescue from the government. Here U is defined as the present value of the net financial viability change, and is considered as the maximum possible requested subsidy. Note that U is not the actual subsidy amount. The actual subsidy is determined in the renegotiation process discussed later.

On the other hand, if a PPP project is bankrupted, the payoff of government is $-b(G + \tau)$, the *political cost due to project retendering*, where G is the least required government funds for financially restructuring a project when a project is bankrupted and retendered, and τ is the opportunity cost for replacing promoters, which may include the retendering cost and the cost of interruption due to the bankruptcy and retendering process. Suppose that for a PPP

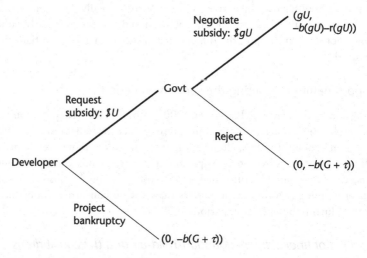

Figure 8.4 Renegotiation game's equilibrium path

project to proceed beyond procurement stage, the project must have been shown to provide facilities or services that can be justified economically. In this game, it is assumed that retendering is desired by government as often observed in practice if a project is going bankrupt.

Alternatively, as shown in Fig. 8.4, the promoter can negotiate a subsidy starting with the maximum amount U, where the subsidy can be in various forms such as debt guarantee or concession period extension. Typically the bank will not provide extra capital without a government debt guarantee or other subsidies. Because the debt guarantee is a liability to the government, but an asset to the promoter, a debt guarantee is equivalent to a subsidy from government. Other forms of subsidy may include the extension of the concession period, more tax exemption for a certain number of years, or an extra loan or equity investment directly from government.

After the promoter's request for subsidy, the game proceeds, as shown in Fig. 8.4, to its sub game: 'negotiate subsidy' or 'reject'. If the government rejects the promoter's request, the project will be bankrupted and retendered and the payoff for both parties will be $(0, -b(G + \tau))$. If the government decides to negotiate a subsidy, expressed by the *rescuing subsidy ratio g*, a ratio between 0 and 1, the payoff to the promoter and the government will be $(gU, -b(gU) - r(gU))$, respectively, where $-b(gU) - r(gU)$ is the *political cost due to the rescuing subsidy to a private party*, including two functions b and r, as we shall explain later. To rescue a PPP project and provide rescuing subsidy to the original PPP firm could bring serious criticism toward government. If the government lacks compelling reasons for the subsidy, the criticism will cause significant *political* cost depending on the magnitude of the subsidy. The differences between the two functions will be discussed in detail later. Here 'g' is not a constant and is used to model the process of 'offer' and 'counter-offer'. More details on negotiation modelling using g can be found in Ho and Liu (2004).

8.4.2.2 Modelling of political costs

• Political cost of bailing out

If government negotiates the subsidy with the existing promoter and rescues the project, the function of the political cost to government is modelled here as $b(gU) + r(gU)$, where $b(\bullet)$ is the function of political cost of budget overspending, and $r(\bullet)$ is the political cost of over subsidization. The mathematical modelling of the political cost of bailing out is based on the fundamental concept that resources are scarce. If the government has unlimited funds to spend there would be no political cost for bailing out a project. Since the government only has limited budget there will be a political cost should the additional funds be needed for the project. The more the government funds are needed, the higher the political cost is. Here $b(gU)$ measures the political cost caused by budget burden from subsidies and is considered the 'basic' political cost. As shown in Fig. 8.5, the political cost of bailing out should be an *increasing* function of the amount of subsidy, gU.

In addition to the basic political cost, it is assumed that for the subsidy exceeding a justifiable amount, further political costs, $r(gU)$, would be incurred to reflect a serious resource misallocation. To define the function $r(\bullet)$, we shall first define J, the amount of the subsidy that can be justified without criticism of over subsidization, In the model 'J' is termed the 'justifiable subsidy', which is considered by the public an eligible claim for subsidy. 'J' can be measured by imagining the amount of 'claim' that could be granted to the promoter had the case gone to court. For example, the damages due to force majeure might be considered justifiable. If the subsidy is less than the justifiable claim, the government will not be blamed for over subsidization. Therefore, as illustrated in Fig. 8.5, $r(\bullet)$ can be defined so that $r(gU)$ is zero

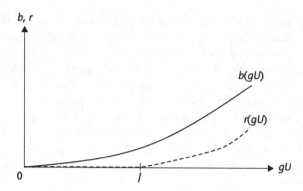

Figure 8.5   Political costs of bailing out

when $gU \leq J$ and that $r(gU)$ becomes an increasing function when the subsidy is greater than J, meaning that the government will be criticized for over subsidization or suspected of corruption, and will suffer further political cost in addition to the basic political cost. The overall political cost of bailing out, $b(gU) + r(gU)$, as shown by the kinked curve in Fig. 8.6, is obtained by adding the two components in Fig. 8.5.

- Political cost of project bankruptcy

Assuming the lending bank can effectively monitor the project's financial status, it may be inferred at the time of bankruptcy that the overall value of the project is less than or close to the estimated total outstanding debt. As a result, under near bankruptcy conditions, it is unwise for the bank to continue providing additional capital and, thus, the lending bank will deny further capital requests, even when such capital is still within the project's original loan contract.

When a project is bankrupted, it will be considered 'sold' to government and retendered to another private promoter given the assumption that the project is still worth completing. The government may want to regain control of the project for retendering because a PPP contract is usually related to public services and cannot be transferred directly to a new promoter without a new concession. From this point of view, to government, bankruptcy is equivalent to a costly replacement of the promoter. Because of the use of project finance in PPPs, the project to be retendered by the government will still be mainly financed by debt. As a result, when a project is bankrupted, the amount of budgeting burden can be modelled as $G + \tau$. Following the definition of function $b(\bullet)$, the political cost of project bankruptcy can be modelled by $b(G + \tau)$, as shown in Fig. 8.6.

8.4.2.3 'Rescue' or 'no rescue': Nash equilibriums of the rescue game

As mentioned previously, the financial renegotiation game tree derived above will be solved backward recursively and its Nash equilibrium solutions will be obtained. Since the values for the variables in the game's payoff matrix are undetermined, the payoff comparison and maximization cannot be solved for a unique solution. However, the conditions for possible Nash equilibriums of the game can be analysed. There are three candidates for the Nash equilibriums: 1) the promoter will 'request a subsidy' and the government will 'negotiate a subsidy'; 2) the promoter will 'request a subsidy' and the government will 'reject'; and 3) the promoter will choose 'project bankruptcy'. The first equilibrium will be called 'rescue equilibrium' and the second and third equilibriums will be 'no rescue equilibriums'.

Ho (2006) solved for the conditions for 'rescue equilibrium' and showed that it is impossible to rule out the 'no rescue equilibriums'. As shown in Fig. 8.6, when G is less than S, the intersection of the curves $b(gU) + r(gU)$ and $b(G + \tau)$, the rescue equilibrium will be obtained. Furthermore, this condition for rescue equilibrium will be expected by the promoters and will induce the opportunistic behaviours from the promoters. The most important policy implication from the analysis by Ho (2006) is that government policies on PPPs should try to reduce the magnitude of S so as to decrease the possibility of opportunism from the promoters. For example, as shown in Fig. 8.7, when the slope of function $r(\bullet)$ becomes steeper due to certain policies, the magnitude of S will be reduced significantly. Similarly, S can also be effectively reduced when J or τ is reduced.

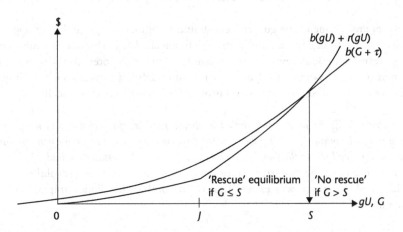

Figure 8.6 Conditions for 'rescue' equilibrium and 'no rescue' equilibrium

With permission from ASCE

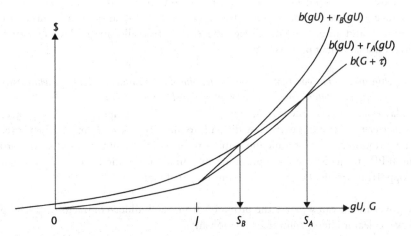

Figure 8.7 Impacts of the change of $r(\bullet)$ on the equilibriums

With permission from ASCE

8.5 Governing principles and policy implications for project procurement and management

Governing principles and administration policy implications can be obtained from the game theory analyses. While the proposed model does not provide the approaches to quantifying the game parameters, this pilot study focuses on the characteristics of the game parameters/functions and the relationship between these parameters. The focus will be on which strategies can reduce the renegotiation problem and enhance the administration in PPPs. Suggested governing principles and administration policies for PPP projects are given as follows.

Governing Principle 1: Be well prepared for renegotiation problems, as it is impossible to rule out the possibility of renegotiation and the 'rescue' equilibrium.

Since it is impossible to rule out the 'rescue' equilibrium, the government should be well prepared for the opportunism problems induced by the *ex ante* expectation of renegotiation as discussed previously. Policy implications from this principle include:

- In project procurement, the government should recognize the possibility of opportunism problems and cannot consider the promoter's financial plan as a binding, credible contract.
- The government could devise a mechanism to induce promoters to reveal more private information. For example, the government can establish a formal policy to disqualify a promoter if they are shown to have a history of behaving opportunistically.

Governing Principle 2: Although renegotiation is always possible, the probability of reaching 'rescue' equilibrium should be minimized and could be reduced by strategies that increase the political cost of over subsidization, $r(\bullet)$, and reduce the promoter replacing cost, τ, and the justifiable subsidy, J.

One way to reduce the opportunism problems is to minimize the probability of 'rescue' equilibrium and the promoter's expectation of the probability. Policy implications of this principle may include:

- Laws may regulate the renegotiation and negotiated subsidy, and such laws will increase $r(\bullet)$, when the subsidy is not justifiable.
- A good monitoring or 'early warning' system can give the government enough lead time to prepare for replacing a promoter with minimal impact, and hence, reduce τ.
- To reduce J, the government should pay attention to the quality of the contract in terms of content and implementation, e.g. the scope, risk allocation, documentation, and contract management process.

Governing Principle 3: The government should determine a fair justifiable subsidy, J, which corresponds to the promoter's responsibilities and allocated risks specified in the contract.

Holliday *et al.* (1991) argue that because of the scale and complexity of PPP projects they are *often promoter-led*, and it is extremely difficult to identify a clear client–contractor relationship. The 'promoter-led' phenomenon implies information asymmetry and an opportunism problem in PPP projects where the promoter may hide information and have an incentive to behave opportunistically. Policy implications may include:

- The government can separate the promoter from the builder/contractor in a PPP project to have a clearer client–contractor relationship.
- The government can assign third-party experts to serve on the Board of the project company to ensure proper monitoring and the collection of accurate information.

- Risk assignment between the concessionaire and government should be made explicitly in the agreement. This could help to determine a fair J in the future.
- The government should carefully consider and specify when they may intercede and what they should do. By temporarily taking over a project, the government should focus on having more information regarding J and G, and on reducing τ through gaining longer lead time to prepare for the retendering.

8.6 Promoters' PPP strategies for signalling: dynamic games of incomplete information

8.6.1 Signalling games in PPPs

Signalling games are the most widely applied class of dynamic games of incomplete information. The first move of such a game is initiated by the player often called 'Sender'. The Sender has private information regarding his type; e.g. low productivity-ability or high productivity-ability. In the PPP signalling game, the promoter is the sender of signals and the government is the receiver. The main idea is that effective communication can occur if one type of player is willing to send a signal that would be too expensive for the other type of player to send (Gibbons, 1992). Thus, it is important to know which signals under which conditions will reach the separating equilibrium in the PPP signalling game. The signalling game analysis is expected to provide both the promoters and government with deeper insights toward their strategies in PPPs.

In a PPP project, the promoter will send signals to the government in order to convince the government regarding the promoter's type. From the perspective of the unbalanced profit structure problem, the promoter's types can be categorized into 'long-term profit oriented' (LT type) or 'short-term profit oriented' (ST type), which can be determined by the relative magnitudes of different components in the profit structure. Examples of signals may include the equity level of the project cost, the financial projections and the self-exclusion of being a construction contractor, etc. One can also view *the proposal* itself *a collection of signals*. The actions of the government after receiving the 'signals' or proposals would be the proposal evaluation scores that lead to the decision of project awarding.

8.6.2 Separating equilibriums of the PPP signalling game and equity ratio as a signal

The following analysis will be on the conceptual level so that the readers will not be distracted by the technical difficulties. In a PPP project, the promoter's payoffs are the VoPP, as discussed earlier. The VoPP and the relative magnitudes of its three components depend on the type of the promoter, which is unknown to the government. For the government, it is natural to favour a type LT promoter over a type ST promoter. In a signalling game, the LT promoter may try to send *costly signals* to signify the promoter's type. The costs of the signals are mostly reflected on the impacts, mostly negative, on the VoPP. For the signal to be effective so as to reach the separating equilibrium, the costs of the LT promoter's signal must be significantly lower than the ST promoter's costs for sending the same signal. If the costs of a signal must render the VoPP negative, the promoter will not send such signal.

As argued previously, it is assumed that the government's major concern is the project's financial viability, reflected by the returns to the shareholders, the first component of the

VoPP. However, the government's concern for the financial viability is inconsistent with the promoter's concern for the VoPP. As argued previously, with a highly unbalanced PPP profit structure, it is possible that the promoter may have a loss on equity investment but still enjoy a high overall VoPP due to the significantly higher construction contract profits. Therefore, in a signalling game where the government is unsure about the promoter's type, the *LT* promoter's goal is to send the signals that convince the government that they have positive and reasonably good returns on equity investments. For example, some PPP promoters use 'high equity ratio' as a signal for positive equity investment returns, because, if the project is not financially viable, the high equity ratio will yield tremendous losses in equity. However, the costs of using high equity ratio also raise the costs of the PPP investment since the required return rate/capital costs for equity is much higher than that of debts or bank loans. Here the high equity ratio may constitute a separating equilibrium because the *ST* promoter usually cannot send the same signals. The use of high equity ratio is too costly for the *ST* promoter because without the compensation from the construction contract returns, the promoter may have a negative VoPP due to the losses from equity investment.

Note that a signal may be effective only under the game equilibrium; that is, the government can differentiate the quality or costs of the signal. If the government does not recognize the cost difference of the signal, then the *LT* promoter may not be willing to convey such costly signal. We shall come back to this off-equilibrium situation and its strategy implications in section 8.7.

8.6.3 Other possible signals and their effectiveness

Previously, it was concluded that the promoter's high equity ratio can be an effective signal. Further analysis on the effectiveness of other potential signals sent by promoters can be evaluated. Here, we will discuss the effectiveness of some other popular signals sent by promoters. Note that the conclusions on the signal effectiveness can be different under different contexts.

8.6.3.1 Low project costs

It is reasonable that the government prefers those proposals that suggest lower project costs. However, since PPP projects are not procurement by traditional design-bid-build or design-build scheme, the proposed project costs are not paid by the government and not binding, there are virtually no subsequent costs/losses to the promoter for proposing understated, untruthful project costs. As a result, low project costs should not be an effective signal for separating equilibrium. In the off-equilibrium situation where the government does not realize the ineffectiveness of such signal, if the low project costs are one of the government's important evaluation criteria, the *ST* promoter may have incentives to imitate the low-cost promoters in order to enhance the proposal's winning probability. Consequently, if the government takes low project costs as a good signal, the cost information disclosed in the bid proposals will be distorted.

8.6.3.2 High future operating cash flows

The proposal's future operating cash flow or toll revenue projection is also one of the project's most critical financial figures because the project's financial viability mainly depends on such cash inflows. However, they may be also the most unreliable figures in the project proposal. Similar to the project cost signal, since the projection of project cash inflows is not binding and the costs reporting the overly optimistic projection are minimal, this signal should be ineffective, let alone the difficulty of estimating the revenues for the long concession period. Unfortunately, inexperienced governments often take these cash inflow projections as one of the critical signals without evaluating their credibility or quality. When wrong signals are taken, the information will be distorted and the government will choose the wrong promoter.

8.6.3.3 Concession period proposed and profit/risk sharing scheme

The concession period and profit/risk sharing scheme shown in the proposal are almost *binding provisions* although the concession contract has not been signed. Therefore, the concession period and profit/risk sharing scheme will have material impact on the promoter's VoPP for different types of promoters. These two signals may be more effective in general.

8.6.3.4 Requesting no government subsidies

The subsidies from the government may be in the form of government debt guarantee, operating revenue guarantee, or direct subsidies for construction costs. These guarantees typically are provided only when the project's future revenue is not high enough or too uncertain such that the project cannot be financially viable without the government guarantee. In this case, some proposals may require certain government guarantees. However, the government usually prefers that the promoter does not require any subsidies or guarantees from the government. But, it is difficult to enforce such promise appeared in a proposal, especially when the government cannot tolerate project failures and does not have clear policies regarding post-awarding negotiation or financial renegotiation. In other words, if governments are subject to be easily held up, requesting no subsidies in the proposal should not be taken as a good signal.

Alternatively, we argue that the government should thoroughly analyse the PPP project's financial feasibility from both the promoter's and shareholder's perspectives and decide whether subsidies are necessary before requesting proposals. If it is decided that the subsidies may be necessary, the government should form and announce the subsidy policies upon the invitations for proposals. At the same time, the government should do its best to prohibit or discourage any post-awarding requests for the subsidies if the promoter did not ask for the subsidies in the proposal. Under such context, requesting no subsidies may become an effective, credible signal.

8.6.3.5 Self-restriction of not becoming a construction contractor

By definition, the *LT* promoter's major profits are mainly from equity returns, E-I, and/or operating related contract returns, P_O, instead of construction contract returns, P_C; thus, it may be less costly for the LT promoter to exclude himself from becoming the future construction contractor. This signal should be very effective. However, the signal may cause additional costs to the PPP firm/project, instead of the promoter, because of the sacrifice of the benefits of better design integration through contractor's actively participating in the early stage. The additional costs may render the proposal in an unfavourable situation in competitive bidding. Moreover, even for the LT promoter, many PPPs projects cannot be financially feasible without the extra returns from partially undertaking the construction contracts.

8.7 Government PPP strategies for screening: dynamic games of incomplete information

8.7.1 Screening games and PPPs

Alternatively, governments can play screening games by becoming the first mover and setting criteria for screening out unwanted promoters. 'Screening' was used to refer to the market process studied in Rothchild and Stiglitz (1976), in which the information problem in the insurance model was similar to that in Spence's (1973) job market model as discussed previously in the introduction to game theory. In the screening game, the Receiver initiates the move and the Sender responds. An effective screening scheme design can induce the Sender to reveal private information or types. For example, in the job market analysis, the firm may make the first move by specifying a menu of contracts regarding the education levels and wage offers. The workers will then respond by selecting their preferred contracts. In the job market, an effective screening menu of contracts would induce the worker H to select the contract with a high education level and a high wage, and the worker L to select a low education level and a low wage contract. On the other hand, an ineffective screening scheme cannot induce the workers to reveal their types. For instance, if the difference in the wage level is too large, it may be optimal for worker L to imitate worker H by investing more in education and obtaining the high wage. If the difference in the wage level is too small, it may be optimal for worker H to select low education, thus eliminating the need to incur high education cost.

The use of screening criteria can be regarded as governments' strategies for the implementation of PPPs. The central issues and the game equilibrium concepts are very similar to those in signalling games. An effective screening criterion must be that only those who are of the desired type can satisfy the requirement with reasonable costs. We argue that since PPP projects are usually initiated by governments, who often have specific goals to achieve, playing screening games seems to be more sensible and effective for governments than waiting for the promoter or bidders to guess what the government wants and to send out ineffective signals.

8.7.2 Government roles, strategies and promoter's decisions

As argued previously, the promoter's maximization rationale should be applied to the investment's VoPP, instead of the equity value of the PPP firm. As a result, the promoter will make decisions according to the VoPP maximization rationale. However, if the government imposes certain PPP criteria or a policy for screening, the promoter's optimal decision will be affected by the policy. For example, if the government is constrained by the law or policy that forbids any forms of subsidy toward rescuing distressed projects, 'no rescue' will be the equilibrium of the financial renegotiation game, expecting that it will be more difficult to hold up the government, and the promoter will then be less likely to bid aggressively.

8.7.2.1 Government roles and strategies

Smith (1999) maintained that 'by the beginning of the twentieth century, the relationship between the private sector and government in infrastructure procurement had begun to reach some kind of maturity.' He summarized that the relationship had forced the government to take on more possible roles today than before, including regulator, customer, facilitator, investor, planner, protector of the public interest, defender of the realm, guarantor, an agent of economic change and supporter of export trade, etc. Depending on differences in countries and economic and political environments, the emphases on the government's roles are different. As a result, different roles expected of the government by the public will result in different policies, and different policies will have critical impacts on the government's attitudes or strategies toward PPPs. For example, governments in emerging countries that mainly act as a planner and an agent of economic change may not have the policies against subsidizing a distressed PPP project, since the government's major role is to provide the infrastructure and boost the economy. In this case, the fairness concern may not be as important as that in developed countries. On the contrary, a government that mainly acts as a protector of public interest may have tighter regulations on the PPP project's tendering and contract management in order to prevent corruption, over-subsidization of the project, or project's unreasonably high returns.

8.7.2.2 Government's PPP strategies

The awarding of a PPP project under a competitive scheme will usually be given to the proposal wining the highest overall evaluation scores. Thus, the evaluation criteria for assigning scores to a proposal will be crucial to the promoter's developing and bidding strategies. In PPPs, government screening strategies may be transformed into the evaluation criteria. From separating equilibrium perspective, effective evaluation criteria will have the promoters self-select into different levels of the criteria according to their characteristics so that only the desired promoters will be selected or stand out.

8.7.3 Effectiveness of government PPP screening strategies

In this section, the effectiveness of some popular or possible government screening strategies or promoter evaluation criteria will be discussed. In fact, since the screening games are almost the same as the signalling games except for the moving sequence, the effectiveness of the signals discussed previously can be applied to the PPP screening when these signals are used as screening criteria.

8.7.3.1 Financial package as an evaluation criterion

According to Tiong (1996), among those factors critical for success in winning a PPP project, 'financial viability' was recognized as one of the most important critical for success. Tiong (1996) listed some typical government evaluation criteria in a PPP project's financial package, including high equity level, low construction cost, acceptable tolls/tariff levels, and short concession period. In practice, governments typically will weight the project's financial viability heavily in evaluating a proposal. The weighting of financial feasibility can range from 20 per cent to 50 per cent. As discussed in signalling games, the problem of focusing on the financial package is that the promoter's 'true' estimated figures are often unknown to the government and that the figures in the promoter's proposal may be manipulated toward winning the project. Therefore, overly emphasizing the financial plan will encourage the bidders to use optimistic estimations and will favour aggressive bidders.

8.7.3.2 High equity level evaluation criterion

According to Tiong (1995), an equity level or equity ratio requirement is commonly specified in Request for Proposals (RFPs). In addition to minimum equity ratio required, some RFPs may further state that a higher equity level is preferred. Tiong (1995) argued that the rationales behind this criterion are: 1) a high equity level will reduce the project's debt burden; 2) it signifies the promoter's faith in the project's viability; and 3) it may motivate the promoter to complete the project on time and on budget. From the perspective of game theory, these rationales mean that a high equity level may either be a valid *signal* to signify the promoter's private information, such as project viability, or be able to *screen out* unqualified promoters. We may infer that a high equity level ratio is generally an effective strategy because, for promoters with a profit structure skewed to construction contract returns, it may be more difficult to counterbalance the loss due to equity investment when the equity ratio is high. Therefore, in screening rationale, the requirement of a high equity level may screen out those promoters who do not have a financially viable project.

Nevertheless, a high equity ratio as a criterion should be used with caution because the effectiveness is not guaranteed and the costs of this criterion to the promoters or society are very high. First, if the profit structure is highly unbalanced and skewed to the construction contract returns, it is possible that the loss due to a certain level of higher equity ratio can still be compensated. Second, the equity ratio for screening purposes should exclude the equity from passive shareholders because the equity from passive shareholders is not related to the promoter's VoPP. In other words, the high equity ratio should be directly contributed by the promoter. Third, the use of a high equity ratio will deviate from the spirit of project financing arrangement in PPPs and will significantly increase the cost of capital and eventually be reimposed on the project users. In fact, it is very difficult in practice for promoters to finance a large-scale project with a high equity ratio. As a result, the high equity ratio criterion may discourage the participation of private parties.

8.7.3.3 Having explicit government subsidy policy

As discussed earlier in the renegotiation model, under the 'no rescue' equilibrium, the government will not provide subsidies should critical adverse events occur. With an explicit policy on limiting government's rescuing subsidy, subsidies for rescuing concession firms will be difficult to justify. Because of the difficulty in holding up the government for renegotiation, the VoPP of the *ST* promoter will be reduced significantly and the ST promoter will eventually be screened out by, before, or during the tendering process.

Note that the *non-confusion* of the PPP policy is no less important than the policy itself. If the government does not specify the policy regarding the post-awarding renegotiation, there will be two consequences. First, prudent and responsible promoters may assume that there will be no post-awarding subsidy and evaluate the investment accordingly. Second, aggressive promoters will be in a better position in bid competition by factoring in the fact that the PPP project will have a 'rescue' equilibrium through renegotiation. Then, in the proposal selection, the government may favour the aggressive promoter's proposal since the proposal's figures based on the 'rescue' equilibrium will outperform others' proposals. In this case, the government will fail in selecting a responsible promoter. On the contrary, if the government clearly specifies the conditions of post-awarding subsidies, all promoters will explicitly evaluate the value of the subsidy on the same ground. In this case, the government will have a better chance in awarding the project to a better promoter.

8.8 A contingency view of PPPs as a governance structure: When and why?

While PPPs provide a new alternative for providing infrastructures, many failures in PPPs have shown us that PPPs, under certain situations, can be a wrong governance structure for providing infrastructures. However, few theories offer a systematic view on when PPPs are or are not a good governance structure and, perhaps more importantly, why. Here we try to answer these questions by integrating the transaction cost economics and game theory view of PPPs.

8.8.1 Transaction costs as a criterion for evaluating PPPs as a governance structure

While the higher efficiency due to better pooling of resources and high-powered incentives is largely emphasized in PPPs, the impact of transaction costs embedded in PPPs is often understated. In fact, as we have observed in practice, the high transaction costs could render PPPs an inferior alternative for providing infrastructure. The definition of transaction costs here focuses on the costs due to opportunistic behaviours or the prevention of opportunistic behaviours. Different governance mechanisms present different trade-offs between benefits and transaction costs and, therefore, choosing from the alternative schemes of infrastructure deliveries entails careful evaluation of the comparative tradeoffs between transaction costs and benefits.

From the transaction cost economics (TCE) perspective, there might be distinctive and substantial transaction costs embedded in PPPs because of the potential opportunism. These transaction costs include those that can be observably identified and measured, and those that are hidden, not easily assessed. The hidden transaction costs may significantly undermine the expected benefits and sometimes cause disastrous impacts on the society or project success. Specifically, we argue that there are two major sources of transaction costs in PPPs, namely, the unbalanced profit structure problem and the hold-up induced renegotiation problem, which have been discussed in detail in previous sections. The magnitude of the transaction costs thus depends on many factors associated with the two problems. Different types of projects in different environments or institutions will have very different transaction costs; therefore, a contingency theory of PPPs as a governance structure is desired.

8.8.2 Transaction costs and the dynamics between governments and promoters

Ho and Tsui (2009) proposed a process model, as depicted in Figure 8.8, for the strategic interactions between governments and promoters in PPPs. This model integrates the signalling view and the screening view of PPPs. For government, it is essential to establish screening policies that may reduce the incentives for and capability of opportunism. Similarly, the promoters will make their investment decisions, such as concession negotiation, equity investment, and management efforts, etc., either in response to the government strategies, or as signals of their types. All decisions made by the players are jointly determined by each player's objective and the interaction dynamics/game being played. Particularly, we assume that the government's objective is to maximize the overall social welfare (through which the government also maximizes the political benefits) and the promoter's objective is to maximize the overall returns from the PPP profit pool, i.e. VoPP. The degree of goal incongruence influences the interactions between the government and promoters.

In equilibrium, project characteristics and institutional environments that are related to information asymmetry, renegotiation and other opportunism problems will affect the parties' interaction dynamics and decisions. We shall identify these project and institutional factors later in order to determine whether PPPs are a good governance structure.

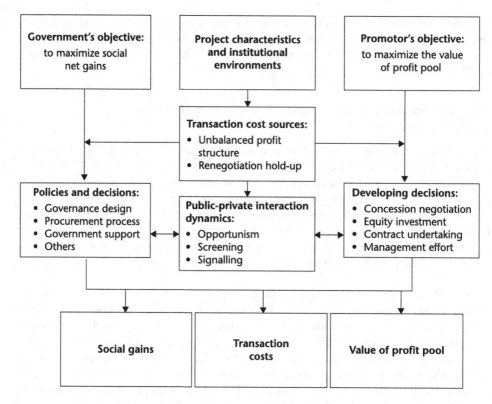

Figure 8.8   The process framework of PPP interaction dynamics

8.8.3 The difficulties of screening and signalling: problems and causes of off-equilibrium

8.8.3.1 Difficulties of screening

In PPPs, the government can freely specify any combination of evaluation criteria and their weights. If the government clearly specifies the criteria and weights in the project's RFPs, the RFPs will become the menu of contracts in a screening game. An effective screening scheme may induce each promoter to *self-select* into the contract or evaluation scheme so that the best promoter will earn highest evaluation points.

Nevertheless, building an effective evaluation/screening scheme for PPP projects is a difficult task. One major reason is that there are many evaluation criteria and there is no framework that can assess the impacts of each criterion on the promoter's profit structures. Therefore, the government must understand and be able to quantify or assess the impacts of each evaluation criterion on the promoter's profit structures. Although Ho (2001) proposed a real option framework for quantitatively assessing the VoPP, governments often lack the professional capability to apply such complicated models. Fortunately, with the concept of 'unbalanced profit structure' discussed previously, governments can at least qualitatively assess the possibility of opportunism and the magnitude of induced transaction costs.

8.8.3.2 Difficulties of signalling

Following the preceding discussion, it may appear that some signals are very effective. For example, self-exclusion from undertaking construction contracts while the promoter's equity ratio is high can be a very effective signal. However, if the government has very limited knowledge on how to judge a signal, as we have often observed in practice, the use of effective signals may be too costly to the promoter and may even place the promoter in an unfavourable position in bid competition. If the promoter wants to adopt a certain signal, the promoter should make sure that the government understands why the signals are effective that only a 'good' promoter can send. Sometimes, the promoter who adopts and sends out effective signals should take the responsibility to educate the public and government as to why the signals are effective. Unfortunately, this is a very difficult task due to the conflict of interest and the government's lack of professional ability and slow learning.

8.8.3.3 Off-equilibrium and transaction costs

To complicate the problems, if the government is too naive or too inexperienced in PPPs, the transaction costs caused by opportunism will be high, much higher than the costs of preventing the opportunism through signalling and screening. PPPs will become an inappropriate governance structure if the transaction costs are too high. For instance, given certain institutional environments and project characteristics, it is very likely that the screening strategies by the government will be either too stringent or too easily satisfied and that the signals sent by the promoters/bidders will not be recognized by the government as an indication of promoter's types. In this case, the results will be 'off-equilibrium' and the probabilities of project failure will be high. When the failure of the project is unendurable by and unacceptable to the government, the government would be easily held up by the concessionaire after the concession has been granted. There are few choices for the government but to bail out the project or provide *ex post* subsidies in the event of distress. Having foreseen the government's actions, the promoter would submit opportunistic bids *ex ante* in order to win the concession, and, then, appropriate excess profits *ex post* from the government, at a costs to the public. Consequently, the economic efficiency cannot be achieved in equilibrium due to the incorrect adoption of PPPs as a governance structure for the particular project.

8.8.3.4 Governments' slow learning curve

One may argue that governments and promoters will gradually learn from experiences and eventually reach the desired equilibrium. However, governments often show a very slow learning curve in PPPs. Because of the slow learning curve, the transaction costs in PPPs will be much larger due to the off-equilibrium impacts. We argue that there are three major reasons contributing to the slow learning curve. First, governments suffer from the rigidness of bureaucracy and have limited incentives and flexibilities in adjusting their practices or standard procedures. Sometimes, even when it may appear that a particular bidder is the best one for the project, governments cannot do much in favouring this bidder but can only follow the standard procedure and use standard bid evaluation criteria and weights for procurement. Second, each PPP project is unique, considering the possible different situations, such as project types, locations, local governments involved, financing agencies, bidders, political environment, and the economy, etc. Therefore, it is very hard for governments or even academics to accurately and objectively determine what the major causes are for project failures and to learn lessons. As a result, governments often learn little from past experiences in PPPs. Third, PPPs are often misused as a tool by governments for boosting the economy for governments' re-election purposes. They may be too soft on promoters in *ex ante* negotiation or *ex post* renegotiation so that more infrastructures can be provided in a short period of time. If a project succeeds, the government takes the credit and, if the project fails, it is likely that the consequences will be borne by the new government in the next term. Therefore, as we have observed, PPPs have often been applied to those projects that can be easily procured by traditional delivery methods or to those that are not in great need. Thus, governments seldom admit these mistakes they have made and hence will not be able to learn. While governments have a slow learning curve, promoters learn rapidly due to market competition and their profit maximization objective. When the two distinctive learning speeds combine, it will be optimal for promoters to engage in opportunism, instead of sending signals that will not be correctly taken.

8.8.4 A contingency view of PPPs as a governance structure

As shown in Fig. 8.8, the interaction dynamics between the public and private sectors affect each party's evaluation of the outcomes of a PPP project, namely, social gains, transaction costs and the VoPP. More specifically, from the game theoretic perspective, whether PPPs are a good governance structure for a particular project depends on many factors, primarily centering on the potential transaction costs due to unbalanced profit structures and renegotiation/hold-up problems. These factors can be categorized into project factors and institutional factors, as summarized in Table 8.1. More detailed discussions are given below.

8.8.4.1 Factors causing high transaction costs due to unbalanced profit structures

Project factors that may cause high transaction costs due to an unbalanced profit structure may include the following:

- The profit structure tends to severely skew to large construction contract returns. For example, this may happen when the project scale is very large, the equity ratio is very low, and the major promoter is the future contractor.
- The profession of the major promoter is not related to the future operation. This is usually a sign of potential unbalanced profit structure. On the other hand, when the profession of the major promoter is directly related to future operation, as is the case in most power plant PPPs, there will be much less concern for unbalanced profit structure.
- The uncertainty of future tolls/revenues is too high to make a reasonable forecast. For example, revenue forecast on rail/high-speed rail projects or on those unfamiliar, first-time projects is usually very imprecise. For this reason, promoters will heavily discount their long-term equity and operation returns and then inevitably focus on other short-term returns.

The institutional factors associated with unbalanced profit structure may include:

- An inexperienced government does not have professional capability in PPPs. In this case, the government may not realize the problem and associated costs of opportunism due to unbalanced profit structure.
- The legitimacy of government's subsidy for capital needs is high. In this case, the equity investment may be much lower than usual and, thus, will cause unbalanced profit structure.

Table 8.1 Negative factors for PPPs as a governance structure

Project factors	Institutional factors
• Project scale: too large to fail [R] • Project importance: too important to fail [R] • Project complexity: too difficult to replace the incumbent firm [R] • Profit structure: skewed to large construction contract returns [U] • Profession of the promoter: not related to future operation [U] • Uncertainty of future tolls/revenues: too high to have a reasonable forecast [U]	• Government's professional capability in PPPs: inexperienced [U, R] • Financial market: immature [R] • Government's tolerance for project failure: low [R] • Legal system: immature [R] • Legitimacy of government subsidies: high [U, R]

[U]: factors contributing to unbalanced profit structure;
[R]: factors contributing to renegotiation/hold-up

8.8.4.2 Factors causing high transaction costs due to renegotiation/hold-up

Project factors that may cause high transaction costs due to renegotiation/hold-up may include the following:

- The scale of the project is too large to fail. In this case, the government will be more likely to be held up for rescue if the project fails. In practice, few governments will allow mega-PPP projects to fail.
- The project is too important to fail. Specifically, when the project is politically important or has certain symbolic meaning to the government's performance, the project is usually not allowed to fail.
- The project is too complicated such that it is too costly to replace the incumbent promoter. In projects with very complicated know-how in construction or in operation it is often very difficult to replace the incumbent promoter; thus, the government can be easily held-up for renegotiation.

The institutional factors associated with the renegotiation problem may include:

- The inexperienced government without professional capability in PPPs can also cause the hold-up for renegotiation. For example, inexperienced governments may tend to use PPPs for large projects or important projects.
- When the financial market is immature, there will be few alternatives to handle a distressed project except the subsidy from government. In developed countries with mature financial markets, problems of project distress are often resolved through market mechanism; e.g. the two rounds of financial restructuring in the Channel Tunnel.
- When the government has low tolerance for project failure, the promoter may sense the government's attitude and the opportunity of hold-up.
- Similar to an immature financial market, an immature legal system can provide few alternatives other than government subsidies in resolving project distress.
- Last, legitimacy of government subsidies will form the promoter's *ex ante* expectation on the opportunity for renegotiation/hold-up.

8.9 Case study of Taiwan High Speed Rail

Ho and Tsui (2010) conducted a case study of the Taiwan High Speed Rail (THSR) project in studying the opportunism problems in PPPs. Here we shall discuss this case from the perspective of PPPs as a governance structure.

8.9.1 General background

The THSR project is the largest transportation infrastructure in Taiwan and also one of the largest PPP projects in the world. The concession period is 35 years. The high speed rail connects Taiwan's major cities from north to south by running trains at up to 300 km/hour through the 345 km route. The capital structure of the THSRC was originally targeted at 30 per cent equity and 70 per cent debt ratio, and was later revised to 25 per cent:75 per cent equity and debt ratios. Taking almost seven years, Taiwan High Speed Rail was completed in January 2007, with a 14-month delay. The actual total costs of the project upon completion were about $17.3 billion, including $3.2 billion costs committed by government and $14.1 billion invested by private parties, taking account of $1.7 billion cost overruns.

8.9.2 The tendering and construction of the project and the crises encountered

There were only two alliance teams competing for the project, Taiwan High Speed Rail Alliance (THSRA) and China High Speed Rail Alliance (CHSRA). Since the technical concerns were limited due to the technology maturity, the competition was focused on the financial issues. In their financial proposal, CHSRA requested government to invest $4.6 billion to make the project financially viable. On the other hand, THSRA requested zero additional government investment, and further promised that the government may receive at least $3.2 billion royalty-like payback from the project operation revenue. Finally, the project was awarded to THSRA in September 1997. The financial projection of THSRA immediately received criticism for being overly optimistic.

The first crisis faced by the Taiwan High Speed Rail Corporation (THSRC), the concession firm, was the inability to obtain the debt financing of $10 billion after winning the concession. In this project, the private promoters did not utilize the international debt markets for financing partly because the Taiwan government subsidized the loan interest by a rate far below the market. However, since the THSR was the first PPP mega-project in Taiwan, the banks had no faith in financing the project at a below market fair rate without government's 'full' debt guarantees. At last, a trilateral agreement was negotiated among the government, the THSRC, and the syndicate bank, which provided that the government shall assume the outstanding debt in the event that the concession agreement is terminated for any reason. Among the $10 billion of debt financing, $8.6 billion came from government owned/controlled banking systems and only $1.4 billion belonged to private commercial banks. Note that in this event the Prime Minister Mr. Hsiao explicitly expressed his attitude toward the project that 'the project is not allowed to fail' and 'government will do everything to support the project'.

The second crisis concerned the raising of equity. According to the concession contract, the total amount of equity to be raised was $4 billion and the timetable for equity raising was specified in the debt financing contract. The fulfilment of the timetable was a prerequisite for withdrawing funds from the loan credit facility. For the following seven years before project completion, the THSR constantly had difficulties fulfilling the equity requirement. The inability to raise sufficient equity had caused the crisis of the THSRC's breach of the concession contract. The major reason for the crisis was that the market had substantial doubt about the project's profitability and considered the THSRC's financial proposal too optimistic. Note that the doubt on the project profitability could also be seen from the initial shareholders' reluctance and their refusal to invest more equity later on, although they had the capacity to do so. As a result, a couple of rounds of renegotiation took place and finally the banks had to accept the THSRC's proposal to reduce the total equity amount to $3.3 billion.

The Taiwan government played a crucial role in bailing out the THSRC from the equity raising crisis. The government was criticized for having the government owned/controlled enterprises (GOEs) make substantial equity investment in the THSRC. However, the last equity investment of $0.23 billion by the government-controlled non-profit organizations in September 2005 caused one of the most serious criticisms of the government's unjustifiable aid and failure in monitoring the project. During this equity raising crisis, the government announced again that 'government is determined to ensure the completion of the high speed rail'. As discussed previously, for projects that are too important or too big to fail, government will often suffer from the soft budget constraints. In fact, the government's 'September 2005 equity investment' was later criticized by the court which judged it illegal for this non-profit organization to make the equity investment. Until then, the total passive equity investment by GOEs, government controlled non-profit organizations, and government owned banks was about 37.4 per cent of total equity, while initial equity invested by the promoters was only about 28.5 per cent of total shares.

The third crisis was the cost overrun. Around one year before project completion, only three months after the government's 'September 2005 equity investment', the THSRC announced that the total cost overrun was estimated to be $1.7 billion or so due to the estimated one year schedule delay and construction cost overrun. Due to the serious political impact of previous government illegal equity investment, the government had ruled out the possibility of providing any equity investment or liability guarantees. For the first time, the government formally announced that it would make plans to take over the project if the THSRC could not raise either equity or debt to finance the additional capital needs. After the government took the 'hard' position on the budget constraint, the THSRC could no longer hold up to renegotiate and, thus, decided to supplement the capital gap through debt financing, even though it was a daunting task for the THSRC to obtain another $2 billion debt at this stage to supplement the capital needs for cost overruns.

8.9.3 Financial distress

THSRC has been facing financial difficulties since the commencement of operations in 2007, due to the overly optimistic forecast of market demands. The actual operational revenues met less than half of the forecast. As a result, the revenue could not cover the operating costs and expenses. In 2008, THSRC generated $0.7 billion in revenue, while the total costs and expenses amounted to about $1.47 billion, including depreciation and amortized expenses $0.58 billion and interest expenses $0.53 billion. Until the end of 2008, THSRC had suffered from an accumulative loss of equity in the amount of $2.05 billion, more than 60 per cent of the total equity amount. According to the concession contract, THSRC shall maintain its equity/debt ratio above 25 per cent at the end of each fiscal year. In fact, THSRC could not have complied with such requirement since the year 2003. By the end of the year 2008, the equity/debt ratio had dropped to 6.96 per cent and THSRC had no capability to fill the financial gap, which had obviously constituted the material breach of the concession contract.

Notwithstanding, the government continued to tolerate the breach of contract. As of January 2010, the government was still determined to bail out the project and kept lending a hand to the concessionaire. The government's current plan is to help THSRC obtain a new loan to repay the old one.

8.9.4 Remarks

8.9.4.1 Problems due to unbalanced profit structures

From the perspective of PPP profit structure, the original promoters/shareholders controlled the whole procurement of the construction in the amount of $14.1 billion while only $0.89 billion was injected by the original investors in the equity of THSRC. Therefore, given such unbalanced profit structure, the controlling investors/promoters naturally had the incentives to over estimate the traffic demands to win the concession, recoup their investment, and let the passive stakeholders suffer the losses during the operation period. In fact, the promoters were seriously criticized that they had recovered most of their investments from the undertaking of the construction contracts of the project.

The THSR project demonstrated how transaction costs were incurred due to unbalanced profit structures. When the promoters identified rent-seeking opportunities due to the project's unbalanced profit structure, they would bid very aggressively using overly optimistic financial projection so as to win the project. The actual traffic demands of THSR during operation were only half of the original estimates in their bids and the projects were both delayed by a year or so. Since the project was awarded to the firms with the most unrealistic forecasts, they soon faced financial difficulties either during the construction phase or in the early stage of operation. The promoter of the THSR has made excess profits during the courses of government rescues and/or undertaking the project's major contracts. The failure of the project and the inefficient project execution created substantial transaction costs to the government.

Moreover, we found that this project exhibited project and institutional characteristics discussed earlier in section 8.7 that had led to unbalanced profit structure in PPPs. The THSR project was unique and the first of its kind in the country. Consequently, the information asymmetry between government/public and constructors was considerable and created excess construction profits and the incentives for the constructors to become the controlling promoters. In addition, since the project scale was so big that investments from passive shareholders were needed, the constructor-promoters could limit their equity investments to smaller proportions. As a result, the THSR project was prone to a highly unbalanced profit structure, which then led to subsequent project failures and transaction costs. From the governance structure perspective, this case study showed that there were many substantial disadvantages in adopting PPPs as the governance structure for projects exhibiting the characteristics in Table 8.1.

8.9.4.2 Problems due to renegotiation/hold-up

From the perspective of renegotiation/hold-up, a government takeover of the project involved substantial costs because of the original debt guarantee provided by the government for the first syndicate loan. If the concession contract was terminated early, the government must assume the outstanding amount of the first syndicate loan, around $8.45 billion according to THSRC's annual report of 2008. As a result, the government was subject to hold-up and intended to grant subsidies to THSRC in expectation of turning the situation around and delaying the project's insolvency.

We also found that this project exhibited some characteristics that might cause governments to be held up. For example, since this project was one of the largest PPP projects in the world, the political and economic impacts of failure were extremely high and the government was held up for renegotiation. Contrarily, in the more mature institutional environments such as the UK and France, the inefficiency caused by being held-up was well recognized and the public had very limited tolerance toward renegotiation. For example, in the Channel Tunnel project, the two governments made it explicit that no subsidies could be granted in any cases. Again, this case showed that there were many substantial disadvantages in adopting PPPs as the governance structure for projects exhibited characteristics shown in Table 8.1.

8.10 Conclusions

In PPPs, conflicts and strategic interactions between PPP promoters and governments are very common and play a crucial role. Many complicated issues such as opportunism, negotiations, competitive bidding, and partnerships challenge the wisdom of both governments and promoters. Thus, game theory, focusing on the strategic interactions and economic behaviours, is very appealing as an analytical framework to study the interaction and dynamics between the PPP participants and to form proper strategies for both governments and promoters. In this chapter, game theory modelling is used for analysis. In particular, we focus on the opportunism problems and the determinants of PPPs as a governance structure. Through the game theory modelling, problems concerned are abstracted to a level that can be analysed. Moreover, new insights or theories for the problems involved are developed using these models. These new theories can help practitioners, including governments, developers and bankers, to better coordinate together with higher efficiency and effectiveness.

In this chapter, first, we identify two major opportunism problems commonly seen in PPPs, namely, the unbalanced profit structure problem and renegotiation/hold-up problem. These two problems contribute to the major transaction costs in PPPs, related to transactional hazards and inefficiency. The magnitude of these transaction costs has a critical impact on whether PPPs are a suitable governance structure for a specific project. Second, we present two approaches that aim to restore the efficiency due to the opportunism in PPPs. In the first approach, the promoters try to send signals to the government to signify that they are the long-term profit oriented type promoters. In the second approach, the government tries to use screening strategies to discourage opportunistic, short-term-profit oriented promoters from participating in PPP projects. The effectiveness of some popular or potential signalling and screening strategies is also discussed. Third, the contingency view of PPPs as a governance structure is presented. We argue that the slow learning curve of governments and the fast learning curve of promoters tend to render imbalance in the equilibrium and, thus, limit the effectiveness of signalling and screening strategies. Thus, the focus of whether PPPs can be a good governance structure for a particular project turns to those factors that affect the propensity of opportunisms in unbalanced profit structure and renegotiation/hold-up. Last, the case study of the Taiwan High Speed Rail project shows how those unfavourable factors for PPPs as a governance structure proposed by the contingency theory actually contribute to the high transaction costs in the project.

We believe that governments can benefit from the proposed contingency framework by avoiding the use of PPPs when project and/or institutional factors predict possible significant transaction costs caused by opportunisms. By doing so, higher efficiency will be achieved and the project success rate will increase. At the same time, when PPPs are used in the right projects, the long-term profit oriented promoters will benefit from the reducing pressure from the opportunistic promoters and, thus, slow higher willingness to participate and have better performance.

Acknowledgement

Support for this article from National Science Council of TAIWAN (Grant number: NSC 99-2628-E-002-023) and the Shimizu Visiting Associate Professorship at Stanford University is greatly appreciated. Particularly, I would like to express my gratitude to Professor Ray Levitt at Stanford, the Director of Collaboratory Research for Global Projects (CRGP), for his vision in the potentials of game theory modelling in engineering management and for his kind invitation to visit Stanford from 2010 to 2011. At Stanford, I had the honour to offer a graduate course: 'Game Theory Modelling in Engineering', sharing my research experience in the science and art of game theory modelling, and to collaborate with scholars in CRGP on several research projects. Last but not least, I would like to thank Dr Reinoud Joosten, Dr Etienne Yehoue and Dr Piet de Vries for their valuable comments and suggestions.

Note

1   This article is supported by the Shimizu Visiting Associate Professorship at Stanford University and the National Science Council of TAIWAN (Grant number: NSC 99-2628-E-002-023).

References

Binmore, K. (1992). *Fun and Games: A Text on Game Theory*. D.C. Heath, Lexington, MA.
Cho, I. and Kreps, D. (1987). 'Signaling games and stable equilibria.' *Quarterly Journal of Economics*, 102, 179–221.
Fudenberg, D. and Tirole, J. (1991). *Game Theory*. The MIT Press, Cambridge, MA.
Gibbons, R. (1992). *Game Theory for Applied Economists*. Princeton University Press, Princeton, NJ.
Ho, S. P. (2001). *Real Options and Game Theoretic Valuation, Financing and Tendering for Investments on Build-Operate-Transfer Projects*. Ph.D. Thesis, Department of Civil and Environmental Engineering, University of Illinois at Urbana-Champaign, Urbana, IL.
Ho, S. P. (2005). 'Bid compensation decision model for projects with costly bid preparation.' *Journal of Construction Engineering & Management*, 131(2), 151–9.
Ho, S. P. (2006). 'Model for financial renegotiation in public–private partnership projects and its policy implications: game theoretic view.' *Journal of Construction Engineering & Management*, 132(7), 678–88.
Ho, S. P. and Liu, L. Y. (2004). 'Analytical model for analyzing construction claims and opportunistic bidding.' *Journal of Construction Engineering & Management*, 130(1), 94–104.
Ho, S. P. and Tsui, C. (2009) 'The Transaction Costs of Public–Private Partnerships: Implications on PPP Governance Design.' Lead 2009 Specialty Conference: Global Governance in Project Organizations, South Lake Tahoe, CA.
Ho, S. P. and Tsui, C. (2010). 'When are Public–Private Partnerships not an Appropriate Governance Structure? Case Study Evidence.' *Proceedings of Construction Research Congress 2010*, Banff, Canada.
Holliday, I., Marcou, G. and Vickerman, R. (1991). *The Channel Tunnel: public policy, regional development and European integration*. Belhaven Press, New York.
Mas-Colell, A., Winston, M. and Green, J. R. (1995). *Microeconomic Theory*, Oxford University Press, New York.
Myerson, R. B. (1991). *Game Theory: Analysis of Conflict*. Harvard University Press, Cambridge, MA.
Rasmusen, E. (2001). *Games and information*. Blackwell Publisher Inc., Malden, MA.
Rothchild, M. and Stiglitz, J. (1976). 'Equilibrium in competitive insurance markets: an essay on the economics of imperfect information.' *Quarterly Journal of Economics*, 90, 629–49.
Spence, A. M. (1973). 'Job market signaling.' *Quarterly Journal of Economics*, 87, 355–74.

Spence, A. M. (1974). *Market Signaling: Informational Transfer in Hiring and Related Screening Processes.* Harvard University Press, Cambridge, MA.

Tiong, R. L. K. (1995). 'Competitive advantage of equity in BOT tender.' *Journal of Construction Engineering & Management*, ASCE, 121, 282–8.

Tiong, R. L. K. (1996). 'CSFs in competitive tendering and negotiation model for BOT projects.' *Journal of Construction Engineering & Management*, ASCE, 122(3), 205–11.

Walker, C. and Smith, A. J. (1995). *Privatized infrastructure – the BOT approach.* Thomas Telford Inc., New York.

9

Corruption in public–private partnerships[1]

Elisabetta Iossa[2] and David Martimort[3]

9.1 Introduction

Fighting corruption in public procurement is essential to ensure the good functioning of public services. Corruption increases the cost of public services and hampers the efficiency of their provision. It undermines citizens' confidence in public institutions and 'hurts everyone whose life, livelihood or happiness depends on the integrity of people in a position of authority' (Transparency International, 2006).

Corruption does not typically involve just a redistribution of the surplus from one economic agent to another. It leads instead to an inefficient allocation of resources and thus to the destruction of surplus. Under corruption, the firm bribes the public official to secure a benefit to which it is not entitled. It may, for example, ensure a higher price for the service or it may unduly improve its position in the tender relative to those of its competitors. If the most efficient firm still wins the tender with the project design and execution unaffected, then corruption only leads to a reallocation of the surplus. But an inefficient allocation arises if instead an inefficient firm secures the contract thanks to the bribe, or an inefficient project is approved. Here, the cost of the service provision will be higher than necessary and/or its quality will be lower, at the expense of users and taxpayers.

The economics literature has shown that the efficiency loss due to corruption depends on a number of factors, including the type of procurement mechanism, the award criterion and the contract design. In this chapter we take the insights from the literature to discuss the potential scope and cost of corruption in a particular type of concession contract: a public–private partnership (PPP).

PPPs are long-term procurement contracts where the supplier takes responsibility for both financing and building the infrastructure and for its managing and maintenance. The DBFO model ('Design', 'Build' 'Finance' and 'Operate'), the BOT model ('Build', 'Operate' and 'Transfer') or the BOO ('Build', 'Own' and 'Operate') are all common contractual modes that feature bundling of building and operation in a single contract with a single contractor (or consortium of contractors). PPPs are used across Europe, Canada, the USA and a number of developing countries for the provision of public infrastructures and services in sectors such as transport, energy, water, IT, prisons, waste management, schools, hospitals and others.[4]

Corruption in PPP projects is relevant in all the three stages of the project: at decision stage, at tender stage and during contract execution. Due to the bundling of project phases into a single long-term contract, PPPs contracts typically require long procurement time to be allocated, complex contract negotiations and careful supervision during contract implementation. Over the 20 or 30 years of the contract many contingencies may arise that need to be regulated by the contract. Both at tender stage and at contract negotiation stage, there is then scope for corrupt deals that benefit a contractor at the expense of final users. Further, during contract execution, the quality of the service needs to be monitored and contingencies may arise that call for a change in pricing or service conditions. Corruption at contract execution stage may then compromise a rigorous application of the contract. To illustrate, Cheng and Wang (2009) report that, according to the Chinese Audit Office (2008), 64 out of 106 leased PPP projects that were audited in China showed signs of corruption.

In this chapter, we shall discuss how PPPs may perform in the presence of corruption at each of the three stages of the procurement process, and derive implications for the choice of PPPs. The chapter is organized as follows. Section 9.2 discusses the scope for corruption at decision stage. Section 9.3 analyses corruption at tender stage. Section 9.4 studies corruption during contract execution. Section 9.5 focuses on anti-corruption policy, while Section 9.6 briefly concludes.

9.2 Corruption at decision stage

The parties involved in project identification may include the public officials responsible for approving the project and potential project owners, funders and contractors. Corruption at decision stage occurs where one or more of these individuals seek to choose a project primarily for their own illicit profit or benefit. For example, incumbent politicians seeking re-election may pressure a public official into building new projects, the 'white elephants', that are of little use and seldom completed but will secure electoral benefits. Government ministers responsible for approving the project may be bribed by the contractor to commission an airport project as a concession, although the PPP option is not the most desirable one.

Filtering 'white elephants'. As clearly pointed out by Engel (2011) in his review of PPPs, PPP agreements may help filtering white elephants more than other traditional forms of procurement.[5]

Under a PPP, the contractor provides the initial funds to design the project and build the infrastructure. It then recoups this initial investment through user charges or availability payments made by the government. User charges are typically used for transport projects, leisure centres, energy and waste projects. Here, the contractor bears (some or all of) the demand risk and thus relies on future demand to make its investment profitable. When instead users do not pay, as is the case of prisons, often also of schools and hospitals, the contractor receives a payment from the government for making the service available to users but it does not bear demand risk. The project returns are therefore largely independent of the future demand for the service.

With the first type of projects, contractors will typically be unwilling to invest their own finances in projects that have little or negative value and that are unable to secure a positive future stream of profits. The private finance component of PPP projects may then help filtering 'white elephants' and reduce the scope for corruption at decision stage. However, as pointed out by Engel (2011), this filtering of 'white elephants' will not take place if the projects are financed with subsidies or if there is an implicit guarantee that the government will bail out troubled concessionaires.

Allocating rents. PPP contracts are characterized by the transfer of a high degree of construction and operational risk to the private sector, in order to provide incentives for investing in cost reduction and quality improvements during construction and operation. Also, demand risk, legislative risk and availability risk may be transferred. Risk transfer may result in high-powered incentives and excessive informational rents to the contractor in adverse selection contexts. These rents may then provide the contractor with an incentive to capture the decision-maker in order to manipulate his decision so that PPP is always the preferred procurement option. What are the consequences for efficiency and contract design of this form of corruption at decision stage?

As we have seen, the main distinguishing feature of PPP, compared to traditional procurement methods, is the bundling of project design, building, finance and operation into a single contract with a firm or a consortium of private firms, generally including a construction company and a facility-management company. In traditional procurement these project phases are instead separated and regulated by different contracts with different firms (or done in house by the Authority). A problem with traditional procurement therefore is that the firm in charge of the construction or design phase of the project has no incentives to take into account the effect of its choices on the cost of operating the infrastructure and thus providing the service or on the social benefit/demand for the service. The consequence of this is that five or ten years after the infrastructure is built, its low quality will lead to higher maintenance and operating costs and to expenses that could have been avoided had the construction been done to higher standards. Furthermore, social benefits/demand will be lower.

Following Iossa and Martimort (2011a), suppose for example that social benefits from the service are stochastic (due to unexpected changes in user needs or macroeconomic conditions) and influenced both by the innate quality of the infrastructure, denoted by a, and the operating effort, denoted by e, so that one unit of service yields a benefit to users worth

$$B = b_0 + ba + e + \eta,$$

where η is a random shock, and b is a positive parameter capturing the effect of a on B (for services where users pay, B can be interpreted as the number of units consumers are willing to buy).

The operating cost of providing one unit of service is also stochastic (due to maintenance and operational risks) and depends on the quality of the infrastructure a and operating effort e. This externality is positive when improving the quality of the infrastructure reduces operational costs. For example, a better prison design may improve security (i.e. social benefit) and reduce the number of guards necessary to meet security standards. In other cases, improving the quality of infrastructure increases operational costs. An innovative design of a school may lead to improved lighting and air quality, and therefore better educational outcomes, but may also increase maintenance costs. The externality is then negative. These features are captured by considering the following cost function

$$C = \theta_0 - \gamma e - \delta a + \varepsilon,$$

where ε is a random variable capturing operational risk, and where $\delta > 0$ (resp. $\delta < 0$) when the externality is positive (resp. negative). γ is a positive parameter capturing the effect of e on C.

In this context, social welfare maximization requires the choice of infrastructure quality a to take into account both the effect of a on B (given by ba) and the effect of a on C (given by $-\delta a$). However, when the firm in charge of designing and building the infrastructure is not also in charge of operations, it will not take into account the effect of a on C or on B. When there is a positive externality ($\delta > 0$), this firm will therefore underinvest.

The idea behind PPP agreements is, then, to try to prevent this underinvestment by bundling all stages of the project, from building to operation, into one contract, and then transferring operational risk to the consortium of firms. At the time of designing the project or of building the facility, the consortium has incentives to take into account how its choices will impact on the costs of maintaining and operating the infrastructure, C, for the whole duration of the contract. The positive externality (δa) from construction to operation is then internalized and better infrastructures are built in order to reduce operational costs. This insight is common to the literature on public procurement and PPPs (see also Hart, 2003; Bennett and Iossa, 2006; Martimort and Pouyet, 2008).

When instead a better infrastructure raises operational costs ($\delta < 0$), perhaps because it is more costly to maintain, unbundling may be preferred since internalizing the externality through bundling would reduce the incentives of the consortium to invest in quality infrastructure. This may exacerbate the underinvestment problem that arises under traditional procurement where low quality infrastructure (low a) is built since the firm does not fully take into account the impact of its investment a on social benefits B.

Martimort and Pouyet (2008) then consider how the possibility of corruption may alter the choice of procurement mechanism, PPP vs traditional procurement. By hiding evidence on a negative externality that would optimally call for unbundling, the decision-maker may let the firm enjoy some extra information rent associated with an inefficient choice of bundling.

To reduce the scope and gain from such form of corruption deal, the authors suggest that the contract design during operations needs to be altered so as to reduce the degree of risk transfer to the private sector. With less transfer of operational risk (so that the firm's payoff is less responsive to changes in C) or less transfer of demand risk (so when users pay, the firm's payoff is less responsive to changes in B), the informative rent of the firm will decrease, thus reducing the scope for corruption. But this brings an efficiency loss in terms of reduced incentive benefits from bundling design, construction and operation in a single contract. Corruption at decision making stage therefore reduces the scope for PPP agreements.

9.3 Corruption at tender stage

Corruption at tender stage may take a variety of forms. The needs of the public authority may be altered so as to favour a specific contractor; the call for tender may not be given adequate advertisement; the output specifications may be modified so as to exclude undesired competitors; the time to reply to the tender call may be shortened so as to make it difficult to submit an offer to firms that had inadequate information earlier; restricted tender procedures may be chosen so as to invite only 'friendly' firms; the award criteria may be designed so as to increase discretion and scope for corruption, and so on.

Evidence suggests that, whatever the procedure or the award criteria, a corrupted public official can find the way to favour the corrupted firm. However, some procurement methods and award criteria may lend themselves better to corrupted deals. In this section we consider the implications for PPPs of different factors that may ease corruption at tender stage.

Auction vs negotiation. To get the best deal, how should the PPP contract be procured? A first issue is whether the contract should be negotiated with a contractor or instead be auctioned off.

With an auction, the public authority may get a better deal through the lower prices or higher quality that the firms' competition on price and quality dimensions may generate. Also, transparency of the procurement process may be enhanced rendering corruption deals more difficult to sustain.

But competition may also fail to generate its potential benefits. First, it may take too much time: the call for tender needs to be prepared, time needs to be given to bidders to prepare their offer and the committee needs time to evaluate and compare the offers. All this can make tendering cost high and tendering time extremely long, creating an additional cost for society in terms of delayed provision of the public service. Also, the long tendering time with the high bidding costs may limit the participation of firms and result in little competition. Furthermore, auctions may perform poorly for complex projects where it is difficult to anticipate all the contingencies that may arise during the contract life. Contractual design can be so incomplete that extensive renegotiations during the contract execution are inevitable, rendering the price competition at tender stage less meaningful. Auctions may also stifle communication between buyers and sellers, preventing the buyer from using the contractor's expertise when designing the project (see Bajari and Tadelis, 2010).

How do these considerations apply to PPP projects? Most PPP projects are complex. They are long-term projects that comprise all stages of the provision of a public service, from the design of the project to the construction of the infrastructure and then the provision of the service. This contributes to requiring high tendering costs, long tendering times and high bidding costs, discouraging participation. Albeit with differences between sectors, it has been estimated that in the U.K., PPP tendering periods last an average of 34 months (NAO, 2007) and that procurement costs can reach 5–10 per cent of the capital cost of a project (Yescombe, 2007).

Furthermore, the project design dimension in PPPs plays a critical role. The contract is often incomplete due to the complexity of the project, and communication between bidders and the public authority is critical since it is often the case that the latter knows its needs but not the best way to meet them. Communication may take place through procurement mechanisms, such as the Competitive Dialogue, that allow a pre-bidding phase where the public authority evaluates the ideas and proposals of all bidders and gives feedback before a final offer is submitted. But these procurement methods are very costly and time consuming.

Because of these features, absent corruption, competitive tendering is valuable mainly for high value contracts where the potential cost saving from competition may be significant. Indeed, most countries provide rules compelling public officials to award the public contract via competitive tendering when the value of the contract is high.

For small contracts, or when the potential competition is limited, negotiation may be preferred to the tendering process. Granting discretion to public officials to use the information available to select the procurement method may therefore bring the benefit of saving on tendering costs and shortening procurement times.

But discretion may be abused. To the extent that corruption is easier with direct negotiation than with a competitive tender procedure, corrupted officials may frequently choose to negotiate the contract also when an auction would be preferred.

Auriol (2006) considers the possible distortions that may arise when the public official has private information on whether it is better to procure the good via direct negotiation with the supplier rather than to auction it. Firms may bribe the official to be chosen as contractor rather than to call an auction. This causes a distortion in the choice of the procurement form, which raises the cost of procurement.

Stricter procurement rules providing for the use of competitive tendering will then have to be implemented to reduce the scope for corruption. Even when the potential benefits from

Elisabetta Iossa and David Martimort

competitive tendering are small (say because potential competition is small), competitive tendering will be required by law. Thus, corruption at tendering stage increases tendering costs and lengthens tendering times.[6]

Similar considerations apply as to the choice of the auction mechanism. In Italy, for example, public authorities tendering for a PPP contract can choose among three different mechanisms: a one-stage auction with a scoring rule, a two-stage auction, where bidders first submit proposals and then compete in prices, and the Competitive Dialogue Procedure. Discretion allows the authority to choose the procedure that is most suitable to the specific project characteristics or market circumstances but this may leave scope for corruption. Reducing the opportunities for corrupt deals then calls for a reduction in the discretion granted to the public authorities. This in turn may prevent the public authority from taking into account specific circumstances or project characteristics. The cost of corruption is then the efficiency loss that an increased level of rigidity in the procurement process, and a reduction in discretion, may bring.

The award criterion. In practice, procuring the public service through competitive tendering is not sufficient to protect the public authority from the risk that its public officials will accept a bribe in exchange for some kind of favouritism. The public official may alter the demand needs of the public administration so as to make the success of a specific contractor inevitable; the call for tender may not be advertised adequately so as to avoid competition from other contractors; the time elapsing between the call for tender and the request for proposal may be made so short as to make it impossible to prepare the bids adequately; the tender specifications may be so contractor-specific as to identify the winner already; the tender design and the bids or the award criterion may be manipulated so as to favour a specific contractor, and so on.

However, some auction formats or award criteria lend themselves to corruption more readily than others. This is the case, for example, with the 'most economic advantageous tender' (MEAT) criterion, widely used in PPP to provide incentives for firms to submit offers with innovative project designs that may benefit final users.

Under MEAT, the scoring rule rewards not just a low price but also a high-quality offer, according to weights that are specified in advance by the public authority. The higher the weight attached to the quality dimension, the greater will be the incentives of firms to innovate on this dimension and submit offers with valuable project design. But a higher weight attached to the quality dimension also leads to a higher scope for manipulation by corrupted officials. To the extent that quality is non-measurable, there is indeed an element of discretion in the assignment of points to the quality offer, which leaves scope for manipulation.

For example, consider Burguet and Che (2005) who study whether corruption undermines price competition and the efficiency of the allocation in a model with bribery competition where the award criterion comprises both quality and price dimensions.

The buyer procures a good and is alert to both quality and price, contractors submit multidimensional (price and quality) offers and simultaneously compete in bribes. The public official (or committee) manipulates the quality offers to favour the contractor that wins the bribing competition.[7]

So for example suppose two firms, firm 1 and firm 2, simultaneously submit quality/price bids (q_i, p_i) and bribe offers, where q_i denotes the quality offer, p_i the price offer and b_i the bribe. The public official compares b_1 with b_2. If $b_1 > b_2$, the public official favours firm 1 by exaggerating its quality offer q_1 by an amount m (the manipulation power) as long as firm 1 wins with the manipulation. With a scoring rule reflecting the public authority's preferences and assigning value $V_i = q_i - p_i$ to an offer (q_i, p_i), firm 1 wins if the following condition is satisfied:

$$q_1 - p_1 + m > q_2 - p_2.$$

If the agent can significantly manipulate the quality offers to favour the contractor (that is, if m is high), corruption in procurement softens price competition and inflates the cost of procurement. If the efficient firm (the one that would win the auction absent corruption) bribes the public official to obtain a higher score on the quality offer, it will now win the auction with a less aggressive price offer (that is, with a higher p_i). If a competitor makes a bribe offer that secures the favour of the corrupted official, this inefficient firm will win the auction despite a high price offer.

If, instead, the public official has little manipulation power (m low), but this can still be effective in influencing price competition, then corruption in procurement hardens price competition and lowers the cost of procurement. Intuitively, if the efficient firm anticipates that the public official may manipulate the quality offer of the competitor, it will submit a more aggressive price offer (that is, a lower p_i) to compensate for the quality manipulation of the rival and thus secure the win. The winner of the auction remains the most efficient firm.

These results suggest that providing for a scoring rule that assigns weights to PPP project quality so as to incentivize innovation may lead to much higher prices and to an inefficient allocation. In fact, corruption may also prevent innovation altogether, as firms anticipate the possibility to win the auction through corruption and thus quality manipulation. Estache and Imi (2009) report, indeed, that setting the optimal scoring rule remains problematic in PPP, as the complexity of the selection process is likely to increase the susceptibility to rent-seeking activities.

How should the award criterion for PPP projects then be selected? Burguet and Che (2004) also address the question of how the buyer should design his award criterion to limit the adverse effect of corruption. In particular, they investigate what should be the relative weight in the scoring rule that is assigned to the price and the quality offer.

A greater weight on the price offer generates two conflicting effects. On the one hand, it distorts quality choices, thus lowering the surplus that the buyer can obtain from the provision of the service. On the other hand, it reduces the capacity of the public official to manipulate the offers, which in turn helps to intensify price competition. Thus, instead of using a scoring rule assigning value $V_i = q_i - p_i$ to an offer (q_i, p_i), the buyer may gain by raising the weight on p_i and lowering that on q_i by modifying the scoring rule to $V_i = \alpha q_i - (1 - \alpha)p_i$ with $\alpha < 1/2$. So for example, with $V_i = q_i - p_i$, at $q_1 = q_2$ and $p_1 > p_2$, the high price offer p_1 wins if the manipulation power satisfies:

$$m > p_1 - p_2.$$

With the scoring rule $V_i = \alpha q_i - (1 - \alpha)p_i$, instead, the threshold level of m is higher. To ensure that the corrupted firm wins the tender, the level of manipulation needs to satisfy:

$$V_1 = \alpha(q_1 + m) - (1 - \alpha)p_1 > V_2 = \alpha q_2 - (1 - \alpha)p_2,$$

i.e.

$$m > \frac{1 - \alpha}{\alpha}(p_1 - p_2)$$

which is a more stringent condition.

The effect of corruption on the efficiency of the procurement process. The above discussion highlights how corruption may bring different consequences. First, the most efficient firm may still manage to secure the contract, but at a higher price. Here corruption does not lead to allocative efficiency but to a transfer of resources from the procurement authority (which pays a higher contract price) to the public official (who enjoys the bribe) and the firm (which enjoys a higher contract price). Second, the efficient firm may bid more aggressively to prevent its rivals from unduly securing the contract through bribing. Here, corruption benefits the buyer by leading to a reduction of the cost of procurement for the public authority. Third, an inefficient firm may win the tender in exchange for a bribe to the public official. With the most efficient firm failing to win the tender, the cost of corruption is a loss in efficiency and an increase in procurement cost for the public authority.

In Burguet and Che (2004), which case arises mainly depends on the extent of the manipulation power, which we reinterpreted as the weight attached to the quality dimension in the scoring rule. In practice a number of other factors also contribute to determine the scope and consequences of corruption.

For example, considering the urban land market in China in 2003–7, Cai et al. (2009) highlighted a link between the characteristics of the product sold in the auction, which defines the stake of corruption, and the auction format chosen by corrupted officials. When the stake from corruption is higher, officials select the auction format that lends itself better to corruption. There are two main types of auction: a regular English auction and an unusual type of auction that they call a two-stage auction. They find that the use of the two-stage auction is more widespread for properties that exhibit characteristics compatible with a higher stake from corruption, and sales prices are lower.

The form of corruption used also affects the consequences of corruption. In Compte et al. (2005), corruption occurs through bid adjustment rather than quality manipulation. The corrupted firm is allowed to secretly review its offer once all other firms have submitted theirs so as to submit a new price offer which secures the contract. This form of bid readjustment may soften price competition to such an extent as to make price collusion among firms easier to sustain. If a firm defects from a price agreement, that firm's deviation can be detected by the corrupted firm, which can then punish the deviation by readjusting its offer and winning the auction. Here corruption leads to collusion and surplus destruction.

Corruption may facilitate collusion also in another way. Through bribing, the illegal cartel may secure the protection from investigation of public officials or anti-trust authorities, reduce controls and ensure the rules and procedures are not changed to make it more difficult to sustain the agreement (Della Porta and Vannucci 2007).

9.4 Corruption at post-tender stage

Ensuring appropriate planning of infrastructure and public service projects and a fair tendering process does not suffice to protect procurement contracts from corruption. Corruption may take place during contract drafting and execution. Considering roads projects founded by the Bank between 1999 and 2009, the World Bank (2011) found that fraud in the implementation of a contract was one of the most common forms of misconduct.

Corruption during contract execution may take a variety of forms. Corrupted public officials may secure better conditions to the firm during the renegotiation of the contract for some required adaptations of the service. Second, public officials may also manipulate circumstances to apply contingent clauses embedded in the contract, justifying price revisions or contract lengthening. Furthermore, the quality standard agreed at tender stage may not be delivered without the authority being compensated by the contractor. As reported by Søreide (2002), and references therein, the contractor may use substandard materials and construction shortcuts without this being reported by a dishonest public official. Corrupted officials may protect the contractor when the materials invoicing is falsified. The technical expertise of the procurement department can be bribed to ignore part of the contract or to waive penalties for underperformance.[8] Albano and Zampino (2011) show that in a sample of 800 inspections for Italian procurement contracts between September 2006 and April 2007, 437 were not at the required contractual level. But in only 16 cases (3,66 per cent) were penalties enforced, although whether this was due to corruption could not be ascertained.

Contract enforcement. As argued by Piga (2011), post-tender corruption is a more serious problem than corruption at tender stage. The award procedure receives the highest level of attention from various stakeholders. This makes it easy to spot changes in tender documents provided by contractors. For instance, IT-secure technologies make it difficult to change prices by modifying tender documents received. Awarding the tender at a higher price than the market price could be risky as stakeholders can easily benchmark the outcome with the price available in the market. Changing the required good or service to be purchased, or abusing discretion in the award criterion, can also be risky due to the ease of spotting deviations from standard documents used by other procuring entities.

Instead, post-tender corruption is out of the public eye and more difficult to spot. Contract execution is monitored less effectively by judges, authorities and media than corruption at tendering stage since contract execution involves long and expensive periods of monitoring and often greater expertise than what is needed for making price comparisons or unveiling blatant favouritism in the tender documents. Post-tender corruption is also monitored less by rival suppliers who cannot properly see the nature of the services delivered.

Contract incompleteness and renegotiation. Post-tender corruption is an issue particularly relevant for PPP contracts whose long-term nature and complexity makes *ex-post* adjustments likely to occur. When user needs change over the long length of the project, or when legislative changes introduce new standards, the service characteristics must be renegotiated. About 30 per cent of PPP contracts were indeed renegotiated within two years after being awarded, as reported by Guasch (2004).

At this stage, corruption may occur. The contractor may pay the public official so as to be favoured in the renegotiation over price and contract terms, leading to excessive prices, undue lengthening of the contract, substandard quality and so on. The greater the contract incompleteness, the higher the scope for corruption at contract renegotiation stage. Further, the anticipation that the contract will be renegotiated often affects the bidding at tendering stage (Bajari *et al.*, 2006). The contract is secured not so much by the firm that is the most efficient one but by the firm that is more able to anticipate the future renegotiations and extract gains from corrupt deals. This firm could therefore bid a very low price at tender stage, certain of a future rent at renegotiation stage .

Contingent clauses. PPP contracts typically provide for 'Specific Circumstances' clauses, which list a number of 'supervening events' for which the authority provides some sort of relief for the contractor. The Standardized UK contract gives an example of these clauses (see HM Treasury, 2006). 'Compensation Events' require the authority to provide monetary compensations to the contractor following the occurrence of events beyond the contractor's control and that result in a delay to service commencement and/or increased costs to the contractor. Specific changes in law that affect the contract, say by modifying standards of service in a given sector, for example, fall within this category.

Another form of contingent clause widely used in PPPs is constituted by 'Relief Events' clauses. These refer to events preventing the contractor from meeting its obligations, in respect of which the contractor bears the financial risk in terms of increased costs and reduced revenue, but for which it is given relief from the application of penalties or from contract termination. The events include fire, explosion, lightning, storm, tempest, flood, bursting or overflowing of water tanks, apparatus or pipes, ionizing radiation, earthquakes, riot and civil commotion.

Furthermore, PPP contracts typically provide for revenue guarantees. These are guarantees by the public authority that in states in which revenues from user fees are lower than some pre-specified amount, the contractor will receive monetary compensation from the public authority. Revenue guarantees shift risk from the contractor to the authority, and like specific-circumstances clauses, they are contingent on the realization of some external event.[9]

These contingent clauses create scope for corruption at post-tender stage. Complacent public officials may report states of the world that justify a contingent subsidy or a change in contractual conditions that unduly improves the financial position of the firm. When self-reporting is used, complacent public officials may fail to control reports or to denounce misreporting.

Hemming (2006) reports that many countries have poor records of the guarantees they have provided to the contractors and that little transparency exists on their extent and application. Engel et al. (2011) report that in Chile there is evidence that the authority relies solely on traffic data provided by the contractor, having neglected to set up independent procedures to collect this information. Government guarantees are triggered by low traffic flows, so firms have incentives to underreport traffic.

To analyse how post-tender corruption affects the design and performance of PPP contracts, Iossa and Martimort (2011b) consider a public procurement context where project net revenues (hereafter 'revenues' for brevity) increase with the contractor's operating effort and are affected by shocks reflecting market conditions. The revenue function thus takes the following form:

$$R = \theta + e + \zeta.$$

where e is the operating effort, capturing for example the higher demand from users of transport services when service reliability, on-the-train services, or the efficiency of the ticketing system are higher. The operating effort e improves revenues but its provision is costly for the operator and difficult to observe for the public authority.

θ represents a demand or productivity shock that occurs before the operational stage, because, for example, of changes in legal standards of service or innovations in the procedure. In transport concessions, building excavation may reveal archaeological sites delaying construction, macroeconomic conditions may change affecting future demand, and so on. θ is unknown to all parties at the time a PPP contract is signed. But as events unfold, there arises an informational advantage of the operator on the productivity shocks that affect the building stage, the operator being able to observe the realized level of θ. θ also embeds an element of verifiability. A public official can gather information to bridge the information gap with the firm. The public officials may verify the realized state and be corrupted to make false reports. In the absence of such information, self reporting by the firm may be used.

The random variable ζ represents a demand or productivity shock that occurs during the operational stage and that cannot be verified. In transport concessions, demand can be affected unpredictably by competition from other modes or facilities, by the conditions affecting the wider network, such as economic activity levels or tourism demand, and by the price of inputs (e.g. fuels), and it is difficult to disentangle the effect of each of these factors.

In this setting, with perfect monitoring – that is when the country's institutions comprise reliable and independent procedures to collect information on contract performance –

optimal risk sharing calls for the set up of contingent clauses where the contractor is compensated for the occurrence of events beyond its control that negatively affect its revenues. This risk sharing is obtained by setting up a payment mechanism with the following structure:

$$t = \alpha + \beta R,$$

where t, the payment received by the firm, comprises a fixed component α and a variable component βR. The fixed component can be thought of as an availability payment due to the firm for making the infrastructure available to final users. The variable component is given by the percentage β of revenues R retained by the firm; $1 - \beta$ being instead paid to the government. When β is higher, the firm retains more revenue risk.

To maximize efficiency, the contract includes a contingent clause providing for the fixed payment α to change when external conditions change. For example, suppose that input prices increase so that the revenues decrease by $(\bar{\theta} - \underline{\theta})$ and the share of revenues kept by the firm decrease by $\beta(\bar{\theta} - \underline{\theta})$. Denote by $\alpha(\underline{\theta})$ the fixed payment received by the firm when a low productivity shock $\underline{\theta}$ is observed and by $\alpha(\bar{\theta})$ the fixed payment when a high productivity shock $\bar{\theta}$ is observed. Then it follows that by setting

$$\alpha(\underline{\theta}) - \alpha(\bar{\theta}) = \beta(\bar{\theta} - \underline{\theta})$$

when the firm's revenue share decreases by $\beta(\bar{\theta} - \underline{\theta})$, the firm receives an increase in the fixed payment, $\alpha(\underline{\theta}) - \alpha(\bar{\theta})$, that perfectly compensates the loss in revenues. The firm is fully insured against changes in exogenous conditions. As the revenue shock θ is exogenous and thus outside the firm's control, this contingency clause reduces the risk premium, without weakening incentives.

Such contingent clause is equivalent to a *revenue guarantee* ensuring that the firm enjoys total revenues of

$$\alpha(\bar{\theta}) + \beta(\bar{\theta} + e + E_\xi \zeta)$$

in each state of the world ($E_\xi \zeta$ denotes the expected value of ζ), since in state $\underline{\theta}$ it will obtain:

$$\alpha(\underline{\theta}) + \beta(\underline{\theta} + e + E_\xi \zeta) = \alpha(\bar{\theta}) + \beta(\bar{\theta} - \underline{\theta}) + \beta(\underline{\theta} + e + E_\xi \zeta)$$
$$= \alpha(\bar{\theta}) + \beta(\bar{\theta} + e + E_\xi \zeta).$$

The size of β captures the transfer of the residual revenue risk to the operator. Although the contractor is fully ensured against θ, he bears revenue risk at operational stage because of the shock ζ which cannot be verified. While it would be optimal for insurance purposes to also insure the contractor against revenue risk ζ, this would require allowing the firm's payment to be independent of R. That is, β would have to be zero. But with the firm's payment only given by the availability component α, the firm would have no incentive to increase revenues by exerting operating effort e as it would get no benefits from higher effort. For this reason, the optimal level of β is positive and it trades off incentives with risk premium. A higher risk transfer (higher β) raises the operator's incentives (raises e), but at the cost of a higher risk premium to compensate the firm for the operational risk he bears.

How does corruption affect the optimal payment structure? When monitoring can be ineffective, because of corruption and weak monitoring technologies, using contingent contracts leaves scope for public officials to manipulate relevant information to favour the contractors. Iossa and Martimort (2011b) then show that the contract should make less use of contingent clauses and leave more exogenous risk to the contractor. This is done by reducing the extent of the revenue guarantee by setting

$$\alpha(\underline{\theta}) - \alpha(\bar{\theta}) < \beta(\bar{\theta} - \underline{\theta}).$$

In the extreme case where monitoring technologies are so unreliable, or public officials so corrupted, that no revenue guarantees should be used, the payment structure should exhibit:

$$\alpha(\underline{\theta}) - \alpha(\bar{\theta}).$$

These changes in the payment structure compared to the benchmark of strong institutions create inefficiencies. Since the firm is less insured against revenue shocks beyond its control, the risk premium increases. This raises the cost of the project and calls for a reduction in the use of revenue sharing as a mechanism to provide incentives. That is, as $\alpha(\underline{\theta})$ gets closer to $\alpha(\bar{\theta})$ the level of β decreases, which in turn weakens the incentives of the firm to exert operational effort e. The cost of corruption at contract execution stage is the increase in *ex post* risk faced by the contractor, which in turn calls for weaker incentives at operational stage. Since the main advantage of PPPs is related to the incentives provided via bundling and risk transfer, the scope for PPPs is reduced when corruption and weak monitoring make risk transfer more costly, that is under weak institutions.

This result provides the basis for recommending against the use of PPP in countries with weak institutions for complex projects such as complex IT and transport projects, where demand risk is high and revenue shocks are difficult to forecast or verify. When uncertainty is high ($\bar{\theta} - \underline{\theta}$ is high), for example because demand risk is high, state-contingent clauses that reduce the risk exposure of the contractor are most valuable. In these instances, weak institutions with little transparency at contract execution stage have more to lose from the use of rigid contracts to fight corruption. Overall the scope for PPPs is lower when project risks are higher.

9.5 Anti-corruption policy

To fight corruption in PPP procurement, typically three main measures have been undertaken around the world [10]

Decision stage. In this phase, the critical issue is how to make sure that the goods and services to be purchased or the investment to be made is socially and economically justified and that the best of the various alternatives is chosen to meet the assessed need. Transparency International views as key at this stage the transparency of the evaluation process. In line with this view, in the UK, for example, to ensure that the PPP option is chosen when it is efficient, regulations have been introduced to require local public administrations to compile the public sector comparator (PSC). The PSC is a costing of a conventionally financed project delivering the same outputs as those of the PPP deal under examination. It provides a benchmark against which both relative functionality and value for money of the proposed PPP solution can be assessed.

The value of the PSC is twofold. First, it requires the public administration to think carefully as to the cost of the project. Second, it increases transparency and accountability. When the PPP option is approved because found more convenient than the PSC, there is a reputational loss that is suffered by the administration if later renegotiations and contract changes cause the PPP option to become worse than the PSC.

However, the use of PSC has been the subject of considerable debate about its reliability, accuracy and relevance. In the UK many cases have been recorded where the PSC was incorrectly used as a pass or fail test. In these cases the desire to show that the PPP deal was 'cheaper' than the PSC has led to manipulation of the underlying calculations and erroneous interpretation of the results.[11]

Other anti-corruption measures can be undertaken at decision-making stage. Transparency International (2006) for example also considers it important to enable the civil society to participate in the decision-making process. This makes it possible to: check the needs of society; enable accountability; and identify necessary/unnecessary elements of the goods, services or investment to be acquired. Public consultations can be implemented, for example, by asking stakeholders to express their views on an infrastructure proposal in a questionnaire. Public hearings may also be useful to help assure that public concerns are fully invited and reflected.

Tendering stage. To reduce the scope for corruption at tendering stage, in many countries, rules have been introduced to require the use of competitive tendering to procure public services via PPPs, with transparency and adequate advertising of tender calls or sufficient time to prepare bids. Some countries have also chosen to allow for the MEAT criterion, while others have shown a preference for the lowest price offer. Further, best practices have been designed so as to help the public authority reduce the scope for corruption by their public officials (see e.g. the procurement guidelines of the World Bank, 2011; and Lengwiler and Wolfstetter, 2006) or increase the scrutiny of auditing offices. Centralized PPP Units have been created so as to support local authorities in their tendering process and contract design. Further, as highlighted by Compte et al. (2005), if the firms participating in a procurement process are subject to careful scrutiny by the public authority, they will not have an incentive to bribe but to compete on price and quality dimensions in order to secure the contract. Auditing can then help to re-establish the benefit of competition and ensure that the most efficient firm will win the auction.

Additional safeguards against corruption that governments consider are provided by the application of the Integrity Pact concept to the bidding process. As it has been demonstrated quite successfully in a number of countries, Integrity Pacts (IP) can be implemented in less competitive situations (markets) by introducing transparency measures and even fostering participation and accountability. This is the case, for example, of the IP implemented in Argentina in 2003 for the textbook supply for the Ministry of Science and Education (see Transparency International 2006). IPs commit bidders and authority to refrain from bribery. Also, IPs provide for bidders to disclose all commissions and similar expenses paid by them to anybody in connection with the contract; sanctions will apply when violations occur. These sanctions range from loss or denial of contract, forfeiture of the bid or performance bond and liability for damages, to debarment for future contracts on the side of the bidders, and criminal or disciplinary action against employees of the government. Koessler and Lambert-Mogiliansky (2010) analyse the incentives of firms to voluntarily commit to a transparent behaviour in a competitive procedure. They show that under certain conditions such commitment can eliminate corruption when it is pure extortion. However, in other circumstances, it may be useful to make commitment conditional (the commitment of one firm is valid only if the other firms also commit) and to explicitly reward with a selection advantage the firms who choose to commit.

Contract execution stage. Third, some rules and procedures have also been designed so as to reduce the incidence of corruption at contract execution stage. They provide, for example, for the compulsory use of standardized contracts to prevent bribes being offered in exchange for favourable contract terms. Standardized contracts are widely used for example in the UK (see HM Treasury, 2007).

However, making it compulsory to use a standardized contract comes at the cost of reducing the extent to which valuable local or specific information can feed into the contractual agreement. It may therefore be advisable to use an 'intermediate' approach towards contract standardization where the public-sector party is given the option to introduce changes into the standardized contract but these changes must be motivated and recorded. The benefit of this increased flexibility would then have to be weighed against the cost of a higher risk of corruption and favouritism (see Iossa et al., 2007, for a more in-depth discussion).

It is quite well recognized that salaries may play an important role in anti-corruption programmes. The low salaries of public officials were, for example, seen as one of the main explanations of the high level of corruption in Singapore during the colonial period. In 1972, when public finances allowed it, Singapore raised significantly the salaries of ministers and senior civil servants to the level of the top earners in the private professions to ensure competitive pay and avoid the brain drain that had characterized the past years of government. The effectiveness of Singapore's Anti-corruption Policy is reflected in the consistently low CPI index from 1995 to the present and Singapore's high ranking in the World Bank Good Governance Index.

But incentivizing the public officials to behave honestly is not just a matter of raising the overall salary. One way to increase incentives is to link more explicitly the budget of the government agency in charge of monitoring, or even the salary of the individual public official, to the effectiveness of its monitoring and thus the monitoring outcome.

To understand the rationale for this policy, consider again Iossa and Martimort (2011b). The incentive of the firm to bribe the public official stems from the size of the contingency payment (the revenue guarantee) that is provided for in the procurement contract. The firm has incentives to report that a negative revenue shock $\theta = \underline{\theta}$ has hit operations and the public official, corrupted by the firm, has an incentive to support this claim.

To fight corruption the public authority can offer a wage schedule for the public official that provides incentives not to make false claims. This incentive payment must be designed to make the public official prefer to take it rather than be corrupted.[12] There is then a good reason to pay an extra wage to the public official when he provides informative and verifiable reports that revenues are not low. Fighting corruption then requires reaching a balance between two forces. The first is the cost of anti-corruption policies that is incurred to create accountability. This is given for example by the cost of improving the auditing technology or by the extra wage of the public official. The second force has a more indirect impact. It captures the efficiency gain of using contingency clauses to allocate risks effectively and avoid transferring too much risk to the contractor. A better risk allocation results in a lower cost of capital for privately financed PPP projects and/or in greater participation of private firms in the PPP tender.

Contract Transparency. Disclosure of contractual terms and performance information can improve monitoring and help authorities to provide the right incentives to public officials involved. In practice many public authorities argue that contract clauses must be confidential since their disclosure could damage the contractor by revealing strategic information to its competitors. This may be true for information about the production processes and strategic choices, but confidentiality is more difficult to justify for contractual terms such as payment schemes, quality standards, deductions, prices, etc. or for other output-related measures (revenues).

Ex post analyses such as Gosling (2004), however, have revealed that even in a country such as the UK, with a good general level of accountability and a lively public debate, non-binding 'best practice recommendations to disclose information were seldom followed by public administrations, even when directly asked for the information'. It is clear, therefore, that in countries with weaker general accountability and public debates, non-binding disclosure requirements are likely to have little or no impact.

Perceived corruption vs actual corruption. Transparency International, a non-profit anti-corruption organization, launched in 1995 the Corruption Perceptions Index (CPI). The CPI ranks almost 200 countries by their perceived levels of corruption, as determined by expert assessments and opinion surveys. This is potentially a very useful tool, since actual corruption is difficult to measure. Corruption deals cannot be observed and the number of corruption convictions in a country does not necessarily mean that the level of corruption is higher; it may suggest that anti-corruption prosecutions are more effective.

But is perceived corruption correlated with actual corruption? What is it that should be tackled: actual corruption or perceived corruption? Holken (2009) examines the accuracy of corruption perceptions by comparing the reported perceptions about corruption of inhabitants of an Indonesian village with a more objective measure of 'missing expenditures' in a road-building project. He finds that villagers' perceptions are correlated with actual corruption but only to a limited extent; this is in part because officials hide corruption where it is hardest for villagers to detect. He also finds that there are biases in reported perceptions. For example, the greater the ethnic heterogeneity in the population or the less homogeneous the religious belief, the greater the perceived perception but not the actual one. Further, more participation in the social decision making in the village reduces perceived corruption but not necessarily actual corruption.

The findings illustrate the limitations of relying solely on corruption perceptions, whether in designing anti-corruption policies or in conducting empirical research on corruption, although the value of the CPI index in bringing the corruption issue to the fore and in stimulating discussions is unquestionable.

Other interesting insights were obtained by Martimort and Straub (2009), who explain the empirical evidence showing that perceived corruption increases with privatization. Under State ownership, managers may bribe public officials to secure higher subsidies, at the expense of taxpayers. Under private ownership, they may bribe public officials to secure higher prices or less stringent regulation, at the expense of consumers. With privatization, the cost of corruption thus shifts from taxpayers to consumers and perceived corruption may then increase as a result. How does perceived corruption change with the use of PPP agreements rather than traditional procurement? PPPs are likely to result in higher prices for the service. In this respect, the choice of PPPs can lead to an increase in the corruption perception precisely as privatization does in Martimort and Straub (2009).

9.6 Conclusions

In this chapter, we have discussed the scope for corruption in PPPs at each of the three stages of the procurement process: the decision stage; the tender stage; and the contract execution stage. We have seen how the level of complexity of these procurement mechanisms leaves great scope for manipulation by corrupted officials and firms at each of these three stages of the procurement process. Before delegating to local governments the task of procuring public services through PPPs, central governments should therefore ensure that procedures are in place to ensure transparency of the decision process, accountability of public officials involved in the process, access to contractual information by stakeholders and media, widespread use of standardized contracts and limited use of revenue guarantees or monetary compensation.

Notes

1 We would like to thank Piet de Vries and Etienne Yehoue for having invited us to contribute to this *Routledge Companion to Public–Private Partnerships*. For useful suggestions we wish to thank Leo Dieben, Ariane Lambert-Mogiliansky and Etienne B. Yehoue.
2 DEF, University of Rome Tor Vergata, CEPR CMPO and EIEF. Email: Elisabetta.Iossa@uniroma2.it. This author wishes to acknowledge financial support from the Italian Ministry of Education, University and Research (MIUR).
3 Paris School of Economics-EHESS. Email: david.martimort@parisschoolofeconomics.eu.
4 For a discussion on the optimality of bundling in PPPs, see e.g. Bennett and Iossa (2006); Martimort and Pouyet (2008); and Iossa and Martimort (2011a).
5 Political corruption is widespread in procurement. Using a dataset of all the public procurement tenders administered by Italian municipal governments between 2000 and 2005, Coviello and Gagliarducci (2010) investigate the relationship between the time politicians remain in power and the functioning of public procurement. They find that political longevity reduces the efficiency of public spending, decreasing the number of bidders participating in tenders and the winning rebate. They also find that having the same mayor in power for an additional term increases the probability that the contract is awarded to a local firm or to the same firm repeatedly. They interpret these figures as evidence that repeated interactions between politicians and contractors increase the chances of collusion at the local level. Without this effect political longevity should result in an increase in the efficiency of public spending, as mayors acquire experience and learn over time to better administer the procurement process. These findings are compatible with the predictions of Burguet and Perry (2009) who find that time reduces the asymmetric information between mayors and bidders, making corruption easier to sustain.
6 Delegating the choice of the tendering mechanism to a centralized procurement authority may help to reduce the scope for corruption at local level and secure savings in the public sector. Bandiera *et al.* (2009) study the introduction in Italy of a centralized purchasing authority (Consip) and find that there are sizable cost reductions in centralizing the purchase of standardized goods because of the higher competition among contractors. However, procurement costs are not minimized. A waste of public funds was recorded although the data showed that this was mainly due to red tape rather than bribes.
7 The first theoretical contribution to consider quality manipulation is Laffont and Tirole (1991). They assume that the auctioneer has some leeway in assessing complex multidimensional bids, and is predisposed to favour a given bidder.
8 In Iossa and Spagnolo (2011), contractual penalties for underperformance may make a corrupt agreement more stable, facilitating corruption.
9 Engel et al. (2007) derived the price duration and revenue guarantees in a typical concession contract where users pay. The optimal contract involves both a State-dependent subsidy in low-demand States and a State-dependent revenue cap above which the government collects all revenues.
10 For a wider discussion on anti-corruption policies in public procurement, see Transparency International (2006).
11 See House of Commons' reports at: http://www.publications.parliament.uk/pa/cm200203/cmselect/cmpubacc/764/76404.htm.
12 On the endogenously determined degree of corruption in regulatory hiearchies, see Tirole (1992); Kofman and Lawarée (1996); Auriol (2006); Lambert-Mogilianski (1998); and Martimort and Straub (2009).

References

Albano, G.L. and R. Zampino, (2011), 'The Integrity of Centralized Procurement Processes in Italy: What Do Data about the Management of National Frame Contracts Tell Us?' Consip Working Paper, Rome, Italy.

Auriol, E., (2006), 'Corruption in Procurement and Public Purchase,' *International Journal of Industrial Organization*, 24: 867–85.

Bajari, P. and S. Tadelis, (2010), 'Auctions Versus Negotiations in Procurement: An Empirical Analysis,' *Journal of Law, Economics and Organization*, 25: 372–99.

Bajari, P., Houghton, S. and S. Tadelis, (2010), 'Bidding for Incomplete Contracts: An Empirical Analysis of Adaptation Costs,' mimeo.

Bandiera, O., Prat, A. and T. Valletti, (2009), 'Active and Passive Waste in Government Spending: Evidence from a Policy Experiment,' *American Economic Review*, 99: 1278–308.

Bennett, J. and E. Iossa, (2006), 'Building and Managing Facilities for Public Services,' *Journal of Public Economics*, 90: 2143–60.

Burguet, R. and Y.K. Che, (2004), 'Competitive Procurement with Corruption,' *The RAND Journal of Economics*, 35: 50–68.

Burguet, R. and M.K. Perry, (2009), 'Preferred Suppliers in Auction Markets,' *The RAND Journal of Economics*, 40: 283–95.

Cai, H., V. Henderson and Q. Zhang, (2009), 'China's Land Market Auctions: Evidence of Corruption,' National Bureau of Economic Research, 15067, USA.

Celentani, M. and J. Ganuza, (2002), 'Corruption and Competition in Procurement,' *European Economic Review*, 46: 1273–303.

Compte, O., Lambert-Mogiliansky, A. and T. Verdier, (2005), 'Corruption and Competition in Procurement Auctions,' *The RAND Journal of Economics*, 36: 1–15.

Coviello, D. and S. Gagliarducci, (2010), 'Building Political Collusion: Evidence from Procurement Auctions,' *IZA Discussion Papers* no. 4939, Institute for the Study of Labor (IZA).

Della Porta, D. and A. Vannucci, (2007), 'Mani Impunite. Vecchia e Nuova Corruzione in Italia', VII-257 Editore Laterza.

Engel, E., R. Fisher and A. Galetovic, (2007), 'The Basic Public Finance of Public–Private Partnerships,' *Journal of the European Economic Association*, 5: 18.

Engel, E., R. Fisher and A. Galetovic, (2011), 'Infrastructure PPPs: When and How,' mimeo, Yale University.

Estache, A. and A. Iimi, (2011), 'The Economics of Public Infrastructure Procurement in Developing Countries: Theory and Evidence,' CEPR, London.

Guasch, L., (2004), *Granting and Renegotiating Infrastructure Concessions: Doing it Right*, World Bank, Washington, DC.

Hemming, R., (2006), Public–Private Partnerships, Government Guarantees and Fiscal Risk, Technical Report, International Monetary Fund (IMF), Washington, DC.

Holken, B. A. (2009), 'Corruption Perceptions vs Corruption Reality,' *Journal of Public Economics*, 93: 950–964.

HM Treasury, (2006), *PFI: Strengthening Long-Term Partnerships*, Crown, London.

Iossa, E. and D. Martimort, (2011a), 'The Simple Micro-Economics of Public Private Partnerships,' SSRN Discussion Papers, CEIS.

Iossa, E. and D. Martimort, (2011b), 'Post-Tender Corruption and Risk Allocation: Implications for Public–Private Partnerships,' mimeo.

Iossa, E. and G. Spagnolo, (2009), 'Contracts as Threats: on a Rationale for Rewarding A while Hoping for B', CEIS Working Paper no. 147, Rome.

Iossa, E., G. Spagnolo and M. Vellez, (2007), 'Contract Design in Public–Private Partnerships', Report prepared for the World Bank, Washington, DC.

Klein, M., (1998), 'Bidding for Concessions,' Policy research Working Paper Series 1957, The World Bank, Washington, DC.

Koessler, F. and A. Lambert-Modigliansky, (2010), 'Committing to Transparency to Resist Corruption,' mimeo, Paris School of Economics.

Kofman, F. and J. Lawaree, (1996), 'On the Optimality of Allowing Collusion,' *Journal of Public Economics*, 61: 384–407.

Laffont, J.J. and J. Tirole, (1991), 'Auction Design and Favoritism', *International Journal of Industrial Organization*, 9: 9–42.

Lambert-Mogilianski, A., (1998), 'On the Optimality of Collusion in Contracts,' *Review of Economic Design*, 4: 131–84.

Lengwiler, Y. and E. Wolfstetter, (2006), 'Corruption in Procurement Auctions', in *Handbook of Procurement*, G. Piga and G. Spagnolo eds, 412–32. Cambridge University Press, Cambridge.

Martimort, D. and J. Pouyet, (2008), 'Build It Not: Normative and Positive Theories of Public–Private Partnerships,' *International Journal of Industrial Organization*, Special Issue on PPPs, 26: 393–411.

Martimort, D. and S. Straub, (2009), 'Infrastructure Privatization and Changes in Corruption Patterns: the Roots of Public Discontent,' *Journal of Development Economics*, 90: 69–84.

NAO, National Audit Office, (2007), *Improving the PFI Tendering Process*. National Audit Office, HC149, London.

Piga, G., (2011), 'A Fighting Chance against Corruption in Public Procurement?' in *International Handbook on the Economics of Corruption*, vol. 2, T. Søreide and S. Rose-Ackerman, eds, Edward Elgar, Cheltenham.

Rose-Ackerman, S., (1999), *Corruption and Government: Causes, Consequences, and Reform*, Cambridge University Press, Cambridge.

Søreide, T., (2005), Grey Zones and Corruption in Public Procurement: Issues for Consideration, in *Fighting Corruption and Promoting Integrity in Public Procurement*, OECD, Paris.

Tirole, J., (1992), 'Collusion and the Theory of Organizations,' in *Advances in Economic Theory: Proceedings of the Sixth World Congress of the Econometric Society*, J.-J. Laffont ed., Cambridge University Press, Cambridge.

Transparency International, (2006), *Handbook for Curbing Corruption in Public Procurement*, Transparency International.

Yescombe, E., (2007), *Public Private Partnerships: Principles of Policy and Finance*, Butterworth-Heinemann, Oxford.

World Bank (2011a), *Guidelines: Procurement of Goods, Works, and Non-Consulting Services under IBRD Loans and IDA Credits & Grants*, The International Bank for Reconstruction and Development, World Bank, Washington.

World Bank (2011b), Curbing Fraud, Corruption, and Collusion in the Roads Sector, Integrity Vice Presidency, World Bank, Washington.

Part IV

Financing of public–private partnerships

10

PPPs and project finance

*E. R. Yescombe**

10.1 Introduction

The US National Council for PPPs describes a PPP as:

> a contractual agreement between a public party (federal, state or local) and a private
> sector entity. Through this agreement, the skills and assets of each sector (public and
> private) are shared in delivering a service or facility for the use of the general public. In
> addition to the sharing of resources, each party shares in the risks and rewards potential
> in the delivery of the service and/or facility.[1]

This broad definition does not imply that the use of private finance is an essential element of
PPPs. For example, it would include design and build contracts, in which the private-sector
contractor takes on the risks of cost overruns and on-time completion (as compared to typical
public-sector design-bid-build procurement where these risks largely remain with the public
sector), but with financing of construction mainly by the public-sector party making stage
payments as construction milestones are reached. However, the transfer of risk from the
public to the private sector is a common theme.

Private finance may be considered a key element of PPP structures if we use a narrower
definition – describing a PPP as a contract between a public- and private-sector party under
which the latter will design, build, finance, operate and maintain a public-sector asset, being
reimbursed by user payments (e.g. road tolls) or payments by the public party,[2] or a combination
of the two. This narrower definition will be used for the purposes of this chapter, which
reviews the interaction between private finance and PPPs, in particular as used in the specialized lending technique known as 'project finance'.

Private finance provides additional support for the transfer of risk by a PPP to the private
sector, because there is 'capital at risk', on which losses will be made if the project goes wrong
(rather than just the limited losses which apply if the private party is being paid fees and has
no investment), and so the private party (or its lenders, as will be seen) is incentivized to sort
out the problems rather than lose this capital.

PPPs involving private finance do place an additional burden on public officials compared
to other types of public procurement. First, instead of just procuring the construction of the

facility concerned, they have to consider the contractual requirements for both construction and operation over a long period of time. But on the other hand, the long-term thinking required for PPPs is clearly better than a public procurement approach, which considers mainly the capital cost and ignores long-term operating costs and risks. Second, public officials also need to understand the requirements of private finance, i.e. what is required to make a deal 'bankable', both to make an initial assessment whether a project is basically likely to be viable as a PPP taking the requirements of private finance into account, and in due course to assess the reality of bidders' financing plans.

Of course there are arguments about whether the higher cost of private versus public finance can be justified by the 'value' of the risks being transferred to the private sector. These issues are considered elsewhere in this book – but it is probably worth remarking that clearly proving the case either way *ex ante* for any particular project is virtually impossible since such a proof depends on unprovable assumptions on risks and costs stretching forward for many years (not just construction but also operation, maintenance and lifecycle/renewal costs), and equally *ex-post* proof is also impossible since a PPP project that did happen cannot be compared with a public procurement that did not.

10.2 Project finance

Project finance is a lending technique that involves lending against the cash flow of particular projects. Its modern use for infrastructure projects dates back to power-generation projects in the US in the 1980s. However, the concept has a much longer history than this in other fields such as natural resources.[3] Similarly, private finance for public infrastructure long pre-dates the recent growth of the PPP market, for example the renewal of the British road system from the mid-eighteenth to mid-nineteenth centuries (before the arrival of railways) by turnpike trusts, which raised private loans to pay for road improvements, repaid by collecting tolls.

Since project-finance lenders lend against cash flow, a project suitable for project finance has to be able to 'stand alone', with a separately identifiable cash flow. This also means that the project should be undertaken by a company whose sole business is the project (the 'project company', often also called a 'special-purpose vehicle' (SPV)), so that the cash flow is not diverted to other businesses, and the lenders' security is not diluted. The lenders' security is primarily the project's contracts, and the cash flow derived from these, rather than the value of any physical assets. In the case of a PPP the project assets are generally public assets, which cannot serve as security – it is self-evident that lenders financing, say, a hospital PPP cannot foreclose on the hospital and sell off the building.

The overlap between what is required for project finance and the structure of a PPP is therefore obvious, but although project finance is widely used for PPPs, it is not found in all cases. Small projects (say up to US$25 million of capital costs, although this is not a precise boundary line) are usually financed directly by companies using their own resources, i.e. through corporate finance. Some larger projects are also financed in this way, especially during the construction phase (but may be refinanced using project finance thereafter). In general, such corporate-finance debt can normally only be raised by an established business, not a new project, and depends on the past record and current financial position of the borrower, rather than relying on projections of future cash flow from its new project.

10.3 Project finance in the PPP context

To look in more detail at how project finance fits into the PPP structure, Figure 10.1 shows the key 'building blocks' for one typical model of PPP project, in this case a toll road. A PPP of this type, where users pay for a service, is often called a concession.

It will be seen that the finance for the project has two elements: equity provided by investors; and project-finance debt, provided by lenders (as discussed below these may be banks or bond investors). The finance is provided to the project company, which uses it to build the project. The finance is repaid using the cash flow from tolls, which the project is entitled to charge under its concession contract with the public party. The project's operating and maintenance costs also have to be paid from these tolls.

Another key aspect of the structure is that the project company sub-contracts the construction of the road, and (sometimes but not always) its operation and maintenance, to external sub-contractors. This means that some of the risks involved in the project are passed down from the project company to the sub-contractors, thus reducing the risks in providing equity and debt funding to the project company itself.

Figure 10.2 shows the other common PPP model, based on the British Private Finance Initiative (PFI) structure, where the contract payments are derived from the public party

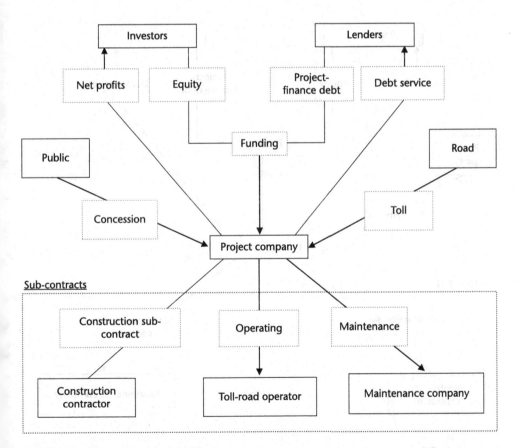

Figure 10.1 Concession-model PPP

Adapted from Yescombe (2007), Figure 1.2

229

rather than users – this is typically used for social infrastructure projects such as schools and hospitals, but also in other sectors such as roads where tolls are not payable to the project company. In such cases the project company is usually paid for making the project 'available' to the public party, and penalized if the availability is reduced, or the service standards are not maintained.

It will be seen that the financing structure for both types of PPP is the same, the difference being that in a concession the cash flow comes from the general public as users of the road, whereas in the PFI model the cash flow derives from payments by the public party. These different sources of cash flow have risk implications, but do not affect the fundamental financial structure.

As Figures 10.1 and 10.2 illustrate, PPPs provide *finance* for public-sector infrastructure, but do not provide *funding*, taking the latter to mean payments that cover the cost of the infrastructure. When infrastructure is procured by the public sector, funding is provided by tax revenues or government borrowing. In a PPP the need for funding is shifted in time, but does not disappear. So in the case of user-paid PPP the funding is provided by the users of the service, and in the case of the PFI model the funding is provided by the public party.

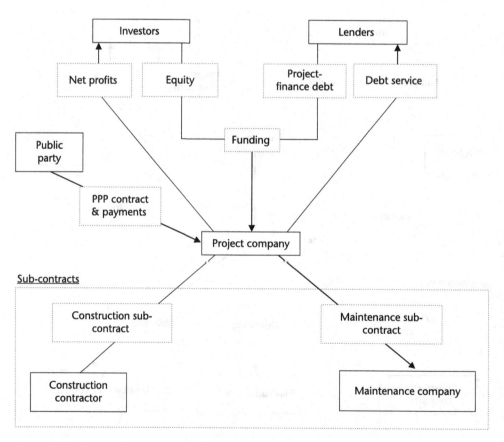

Figure 10.2 PFI-model PPP contract

Adapted from Yescombe (2007), Figure 1.3

10.4 Why use project finance?

As the more detailed discussion below will make clear, project finance is complex, slow and expensive, in addition to the already complex process of undertaking a PPP. What are the advantages that balance these problems and make it worthwhile pursuing?

The main benefit of project finance is that it enables a project to raise a high ratio of debt to equity ('leverage' or 'gearing'): a typical toll-road project may cover 70–80 per cent of its capital expenditure through project-finance debt, while a lower risk project in the social infrastructure field, e.g. a school or hospital, may raise 80–90 per cent. Debt is cheaper than equity, and so the higher the leverage, the lower the financing costs of the project, and hence its cost to the user or the public party.

Project finance also enables an investor to borrow more against a project investment than it would be able to raise based on its corporate balance sheet, and provides long-term finance which would probably not otherwise be available to the investor, so increasing investment capacity and hence competition in bidding for PPPs, which should result in better value for money.

Project finance also improves the transparency of the project for the public party: because the project company is financed on a stand-alone basis, the financial effect of any changes to the project which the public party requires can be easily measured.

Furthermore, the extra due diligence provided by lenders, discussed below, helps to validate and monitor the project, to the benefit of the public sector.

However, as already mentioned, the higher cost of project finance compared to public-sector financing is a disadvantage that has to be balanced against the other advantages of private-sector finance.

10.5 Sources of finance

There are two sources of financing in a project-finance structure – equity and debt.

Equity is provided by investors in the project, who own the project company. Depending on the nature of the PPP and the risks involved, equity investment provides about 10–30 per cent of the total capital financing. If all goes well with the project, equity investors receive a relatively high rate of return on their investment but if things do not go as expected they are the first to lose.

Third-party debt for the 70–90 per cent balance of the capital cost can either be provided by banks or by bond finance. A bond is a tradable instrument through which non-bank investors can provide a loan to the project company. The financing terms and risks assumed by lenders or bond investors are substantially similar whether financing is through a bank loan or a bond.

10.5.1 Equity investment

Equity investors are often sub-contractors, e.g. for construction of the facility – for such parties the equity investment is a way of securing work. The problem with such investment, however, may be that contractors only have a short-term interest in the project, and will concentrate on getting their profit out during construction rather than consider longer-term risks and returns.

But there is also a large pool of international investment funds that invest in PPP project equity because of the relatively safe long-term revenues which this provides: pension funds and life-insurance companies are especially interested in this type of cash flow. These investors may serve as a counterbalance to the short-termism of contractors, but here too there can be short-termism, as one class of such investors may also concentrate on short-term returns, aiming to sell their investment after completion of construction, with the project operating normally. This will provide a high rate of return to investors as the value of the project will automatically increase once it has passed the initial high-risk construction phase successfully – the new investors who come in at that stage will normally be investing for a long-term, reasonably secure equity cash flow, and thus be willing to accept a lower rate of return, so creating an opportunity for the original investors to sell at a significant profit.

A large part of the equity investment may be provided in the form of subordinated loans rather than share capital. This is usually because in most countries debt interest is tax-deductible whereas dividends on shares are not.

10.5.2 Bank debt

Project finance for PPPs is part of a large international project-finance market, and, to a certain extent, PPPs have to compete for debt finance with other project-finance sectors. An indication of the scale of the market can be seen from Table 10.1, which provides figures on global commercial bank project-finance debt in the last few years. (It should be noted that these figures include refinancings as well as debt for new projects, and are probably incomplete because they largely depend on individual banks providing the data.)

While bank project-finance lending in 2011 had not recovered to the peak in 2008, before the full effect of the 'credit crunch' (discussed in more detail below) had been felt, it has remained comparatively strong, reflecting the good performance of the project-finance sector during the economic downturn, which itself reflects the high level of care taken with this type of lending compared to some other areas of banking. In particular, infrastructure lending, which includes PPPs, had largely recovered by 2011.

It must be said that banks are not natural providers of the long-term debt required for project financing PPPs (up to around 25 years, depending on the country and market sector), as they do not have long-term financing to match this long-term lending. Indeed in some markets – the USA and Spain are examples – the domestic banks typically do not provide such long-term lending. In these cases the gap is filled by banks providing shorter term loans (5–7 years) in the expectation that the loan will be refinanced either by new bank debt on maturity or a bond issue. Alternatively foreign banks may provide the long-term lending in lieu of domestic banks – this happens in the US PPP market.

Table 10.1 Commercial banks – project-finance loans by sector

US$ millions	2006	2007	2008	2009	2010	2011
Power	57,106	76,518	89,858	56,289	73,300	80,499
Infrastructure	48,737	51,197	58,272	38,817	55,160	45,329
Natural resources	49,938	47,332	63,292	32,508	46,115	54,272
Telecommunications	3,137	5,556	6,260	8,118	13,383	5,314
Other	21,691	39,384	32,876	3,454	20,217	28,073
	180,609	219,986	250,557	139,186	208,174	213,487

Source: based on *Project Finance International,* annual market surveys

10.5.3 *Bond market*

Bond financing is generally far less important than bank finance in the PPP market. Bond financing is usually about 10 per cent of the international project finance loan market as a whole (the balance being provided by banks as discussed above). However, for PPPs bond financing has been concentrated in particular markets such as the UK, USA, Canada and Australia and thus has played a much larger proportional share in these markets.

Bond investment usually takes place through funds rather than direct purchase of the bonds. This is because for typical bond investors – insurance companies and pension funds, who are looking for a long-term cash flow to meet their liabilities – project finance lending is more complex than their ordinary bond business and it is not economic to retain the staff to undertake the necessary risk assessment and monitoring. However, there are conspicuous exceptions to this approach, where the bond investor considers that the business has enough 'critical mass' for it to be worthwhile setting up a project-finance department, Canada being the main recent example.

Another party was generally involved in the process of raising funds for a project through a bond – bond 'monoline' insurers. These are insurance companies that cover bondholders against a loss due to default by the bond issuer, i.e. they take on the credit risk. They developed this business from their involvement in the US municipal bond market, which includes project-finance bonds that rely on the revenues from particular projects.[4] Monoline insurance improved the credit rating of the bond, making the finance cheaper (even after allowing for fees payable to the insurer). It also made it easier to raise funds for very large projects. In the UK in particular the PPP bond market was dependent on this insurance cover. Most monoline insurers incurred heavy losses in the 'credit crunch' from insurance of bonds that securitized US sub-prime home loans, although their project-finance business remained sound, and as a result largely disappeared from the PPP bond market. So the alternatives now are either for the bond investors to develop their own PPP/project finance expertise as discussed above and invest directly, or 'credit enhancement' may be provided to a bond issue by a bank letter of credit, which guarantees repayment.

Credit-rating agencies also usually play a role in bond financing, as their rating provides assurance to investors that the credit risks have been reviewed by an independent party. The rating agency issues a credit rating for the bonds which determines their pricing, and how easily they can be placed in the market by the bond lead manager, usually an investment bank. A typical PPP bond would carry a BBB/Baa credit rating from Standard & Poor's or Moody's, placing it on the lowest rung of 'investment grade' credits, which may be below the grade required by many funds, hence the need for credit enhancement as discussed above.

Financing may also be provided by a combination of bank loan and bond finance: the bank finance is used during the (higher risk) construction period, with a bank providing a relatively short-term loan maturing two to three years after completion of construction. Then the bank loan is refinanced with a bond. This structure makes sense because bank loans are more flexible than bonds (e.g. they can be drawn as and when needed to pay for construction, rather than in one amount all at once as is required for a bond), whereas bond investors are more natural long-term providers of finance.

The term 'lender' is used below to refer to both banks and bondholders.

10.6 Lenders and risk

A lender to a PPP project has 'downside but no upside'; i.e. if the project goes seriously wrong the lender may lose some or all of its money, but if the project goes better than expected the lender is not paid any more than the fixed rate for its debt. A lender is thus earning a relatively limited and fixed rate of return, and is not prepared to take on excessive risks to earn this return.[5] It is the equity investor who gets the benefit of upside on the project, but who also takes the greater risk and so suffers the first loss if the project goes wrong. Therefore the equity investor expects a much higher return for its risk than the lender does.

If a risk is allocated to the project company, and not passed to other parties – for example sub-contractors, or mitigated, e.g. by insurance – what this really means is that the risk is being taken by the lenders, since if the risk does crystallize the project company has to pay for the consequences – but it will have little cash to do so because its past cash flow will have been disbursed to fund the debt service and provide a return to investors. Equity investors may not want to throw good money after bad by reinvesting in a failing project, nor do they normally give the lenders any guarantees, which means that the problem is likely to fall on the lenders, who have the most money at risk. So it follows that lenders take a conservative view on any risks to be left with the project company, and to a considerable extent this governs the risk allocation between the public and private parties for any PPP project in which project finance is being raised. It is also worth noting in this context that low-probability, high-impact risks, on which an equity investor might be willing to take a commercial view, are generally unacceptable to lenders.

Risk analysis is thus at the heart of the credit procedure for the lenders, as well as the basis for measuring whether a PPP project is value for money for the public party. The general principle is that risks should be allocated to the party best able to deal with them, and manage their financial consequences, but in reality this principle may be affected by detailed negotiating power on each side. Reviewing project risks is a key aspect of the 'due diligence' process, which aims to assure lenders that the facility can be built for the projected cost, perform as expected, operate within projected budgets and so on. (In fact the same process needs to be carried out by the public party and the equity investors, but it is very much governed by lender requirements.)

This risk analysis begins with drawing up a 'risk matrix', setting out all conceivable risks that might arise in the project. Some of the broad categories within such a matrix are set out below, but these, and the examples of specific risks, are only illustrative, and do not purport to be a complete list of all the risks a project may face, which may run into several hundred when analysed in detail.

10.6.1 Credit risk

Before even considering the risks inherent in the project itself, the lenders will want to be sure that the parties involved are of suitable credit standing.

In a PFI-model PPP, the public party should have both the legal power and the budget to enter into the PPP contract. The lenders will also want to ensure that they have appropriate legal rights if the public party does not pay on time.

Even though a project financing is not guaranteed by the equity investors, the lenders will want to assure themselves: first, that the investors have the experience and technical know-how to enter into the PPP contract; and second, that if it does get into temporary problems, the investors will have the sources to protect their investment by increasing their investment, if this makes commercial sense for them.

The lenders also review the credit standing of the key sub-contractors, especially the construction contractor. Problems may arise, for example, where the contractor has been bidding aggressively for work in a large PPP programme, relying on its equity investment to subsidize these costs instead of treating the two at arm's length, or because the project is too large in relation to the contractor's balance sheet, so that small cost overruns or delays have a disproportionate effect on its financial stability. This could result in the project having to find a new contractor, probably at a higher price. In such cases the equity investors may write off their investment, and the lenders then have to step in to save the project and protect their investment. This type of private-sector credit problem may cause a delay in delivery of the project, for which the project company should be appropriately penalized, but in most cases should not involve extra cost for the public party – this is the purpose of risk transfer in PPP projects.

10.6.2 Site risks

The risks that the project site may not be acquired or obtain planning or other permits are risks which are generally taken on by the public party, since the PPP project is performing a public function. Other site-related risks such as ground conditions, pollution from prior activities on the site and delays due to the discovery of antiquities may be split between the public party and the project company; insofar as these are allocated to the project company they are usually passed down to its construction sub-contractor. Lenders generally will not allow the project company to retain such site risks.

10.6.3 Construction-phase risks

The risks that the project can be built on time, to specification and on budget are of course allocated to the project company by the public party, since this is one of the key aspects of risk transfer to the private sector in PPPs. The project company then usually signs a 'turnkey' contract with its construction sub-contractor (who as mentioned above may be one of its shareholders, but lenders will insist that such contracts are signed on an arm's-length basis). Under the type of contract the construction company quotes a fixed price and hands over the project on completion in full working order (so the client just has to 'turn the key' and enter), and will suffer penalties if it is not completed on time or to specification. Penalties for late completion will reflect the project company's loss of income, since payments under the PPP contract are not usually made until the project is properly completed.

A turnkey contract also passes the design risk to the construction company, as compared to the typical public procurement where the public party designs the project and then calls for bids to build it: a common consequence of the latter is cost overruns, as the contractor will do its best to find flaws in the design and then claim that these cause extra construction costs.

It should be noted that the construction sub-contractor will charge more for a turnkey contract than would be charged for a standard contract where the same types of risk and penalty do not apply – risk assumption is never without cost, which brings us back again to the general value-for-money in PPPs of balancing risk transfer against increased cost.

10.6.4 Operation-phase risks

Risks in the operation phase revolve around whether the long-term costs of the project turn out higher than originally projected. It should be borne in mind that over a contract for 25 years or more, the operation-phase costs will normally be a multiple of the project's original capital cost.

These long-term costs can be divided into three categories: operating costs – i.e. the regular costs which the project company incurs year-by-year such as staff, premises, utilities and other regular supplies; maintenance costs for the project – which become difficult to predict the further ahead the prediction; and lifecycle or renewal costs – i.e. for replacement of equipment, such as heating boilers, or e.g. for major renewal of the surface of a road. Again these are difficult to predict over a long term, and the transfer of these risks to the private sector is another key value-for-money argument in favour of PPPs.

Once more the project company may seek to pass these risks to sub-contractors but this is more difficult because of their uncertainty, and residual risks may well remain with the project company. Thus operation-phase risks may become a key aspect of the project risks for the lenders.

10.6.5 Usage risk

In the case of a concession, this is the risk that usage of the project may be less than expected, and hence that revenues are below projections. In a toll-road project, for example, this risk will crystallize if fewer drivers than expected make use of the road, either because traffic levels in general are less than projected, or because drivers are not willing to pay the tolls charged. Long-term traffic projections for a particular road are notoriously unrealizable because they are affected by so many external factors – general growth in traffic is a function of the general growth in the economy, fuel prices and government action such as changes in fuel taxes, but traffic on a particular road may also be affected by a change elsewhere in the transport network such as building a new road nearby, or an improvement in public transport which takes drivers off the road. Lenders therefore take a highly conservative view of traffic projections and similar usage risks.

These uncertainties mean that it is not uncommon for the public party to take part of the usage risk of a concession project, e.g. by providing minimum usage or revenue guarantees, sufficient to cover the lenders' requirements, but below the level which the equity investors would require to achieve their required rate of return, thus leaving the latter with some usage risk.

For availability-style or service contracts under the PFI model the usage risk is generally taken by the public party. What this means in practice is that if, say, a PFI school is no longer required (perhaps because of population movements within a city) the payments under the PPP contract are still due even if no-one uses the school. As discussed below, such contracts can be cancelled, but there are significant costs involved. But it must be borne in mind that any public building could become a 'white elephant' in such circumstances, whether financed by the public sector or through a PPP.

And even where the usage risk is taken by the public sector, this does not mean that there are no risks related to usage left with the project company. For example, the more a building or road is used, the greater its maintenance and lifecycle costs are likely to be – and as discussed above this is a risk that is always left with the project company.

The most common example of usage risk being taken by the project company under the PFI model is that of 'shadow toll' roads: here the project company is paid according to usage of the road by drivers, but the drivers themselves do not pay tolls – in effect the public party pays the tolls on their behalf.

10.6.6 Macro-economic risks

These are risks related to the wider economy, over which no party has control – interest rates, inflation and (in some cases) exchange rates.

10.6.6.1 Interest rates

As discussed above, banks generally use short-term deposits to finance long-term project-finance loans. Their pricing is based on the short-term cost of funding (e.g. for six-month deposits) plus a profit margin. This means that the interest rates on bank project-finance loans are constantly changing, which poses a high risk to the stability of the project company's cash flow. During the construction phase of the project interest payments are capitalized and added to the overall cost of the project to be financed, so if interest rates are higher than projected the project will suffer a cost overrun and hence have insufficient financing. During the operating phase of the project the cash flow available to repay the debt and provide a return to the equity investors, will be eroded by higher interest rates, so reducing the lenders' cash-flow cover (discussed below) and the return to the equity investors.

The risk of the project company having to pay higher interest rates than originally projected is generally not acceptable to lenders (or indeed the other parties to a PPP project), and therefore the project company enters into interest-rate hedging arrangements, usually with the banks providing the loan finance. The most common form of hedging is an interest-rate swap, whereby the project company swaps its 'floating rate' interest liability for a fixed rate. The bank interest-rate swap market is part of the complex market for financial derivatives, and is quite separate from the loan market. Bonds almost always carry a fixed rate, so the issue of interest-rate risk does not arise with them.

10.6.6.2 Cost inflation

Inflation is a long-term risk for all projects: this is normally dealt with by allowing increases in payments by the public party or users in line with an agreed inflation index. However, there is no reason to increase the whole amount of these payments for inflation: a large part of the project company's cost will be the fixed costs of repaying its debt, which are unaffected by inflation. If payments are fully indexed against inflation this will make them apparently more attractive to begin with since they will be lower than if only partially indexed: however, this leaves the public party or the user with a much higher long-term risk that inflation will increase payments excessively. This mismatch is also generally unacceptable to lenders for the reverse reason: if inflation rates are lower than the assumptions made in the financial model this will leave the project company with insufficient cash flow. The latter problem can be dealt with by the project company raising an inflation-indexed bond issue, or entering into an inflation swap (which works in a similar way to an interest-rate swap) with its banks, but this is patching over a problem that need not be created in the first place. Unfortunately, short-term cost considerations for the public party may still induce it to accept 100 per cent inflation indexation of its payments.

10.6.6.3 Currency risk

Exchange-rate risks may arise, for example, if the project involves the import of capital equipment which is priced in a foreign currency: again if the home currency depreciates, the project's capital costs will go up. And again hedging through the well-established currency markets should deal with this problem.

A greater issue arises – generally in developing countries – where the debt is in a foreign currency. This can lead to catastrophe for the project company if a sharp depreciation of the home currency takes place, and this risk is generally unacceptable to lenders. Long-term currency hedging, for the term of the project debt, will generally not be available. This means that debt finance for PPPs in countries that do not have a long-debt debt market in the local currency may prove very difficult, although development-finance institutions may be able to play a role in such cases.

10.6.7 Political risks

A major long-term risk for many PPPs is a future change in the law that imposes extra costs on the project. For example, new safety legislation or environmental requirements may require extra investment. This could impose an unpredictable extra cost on the project company, which has not been allowed for in its financial projections. No government can or will bind its successors not to change the law in a way which adversely affects the PPP project, and the best that can be done here is for the PPP contract to require the public party to compensate (at least partially) the project company (as discussed below) if this happens. However, compensation is usually limited to changes in law that particularly relate to the PPP project, or the sector in which it operates. Changes such as increases in general tax rates are a business risk which any project company has to face.

But a PPP project may also be subject to wider political risks, an issue on which lenders are very sensitive. If a PPP loses political support – e.g. because of a change in government – this can easily lead to difficulties for the project company. Lenders are therefore reluctant to enter into projects that have been or are likely to be the subject of political controversy.

When making loans to PPPs in developing countries, external lenders may require political-risk insurance – provided by export-credit agencies, development-finance institutions and the private insurance market – to cover the project against political interference, as well as risks such as war or civil unrest.

10.6.8 Insurance

Insurance plays a significant role in the financing of PPP projects, as it provides a way of dealing with risks which no party wishes to assume. Apart from the normal business insurances, including those for physical damage of the project facility, and general public liability, the lenders will also require the project company to take out delay in start up ('DSU') and business interruption ('BI') insurances. The purposes of these (which add considerably to the normal insurance costs) are to compensate the project company for loss of revenue if, say, due to a fire, construction of the project is delayed (DSU), or the project has to be rebuilt (BI), hence ensuring that fixed operating costs can be covered and the lenders can be paid on time.

10.6.9 Third-party revenue

A risk issue that mainly crops up in some types of PFI-model projects is that of third-party revenues. For example, in a waste-incineration project, the public party will pay the project company a 'gate fee' for processing each tonne of waste, but the project company may subsidize the gate fee by also taking in private-sector waste, and generating electricity for sale into the grid system. Lenders do not normally lend against the private-sector contracts, which are typically short-term and with parties whose credit risk may not be strong, and take a conservative view of the revenues that may be obtained by power generation. So although a larger waste incinerator creates economies of scale, a waste company bidding for a new PPP contract has to balance this against the lenders' unwillingness to lend the same proportion of debt against an incinerator which is larger than that required for the PPP contract.

10.6.10 Relief events/compensation events

The PPP contract reflects the risk analysis set out above, and normally places these risks in four categories:

10.6.10.1 Project risks

These are risks assumed by the project company, which may be mitigated by passing the risk to sub-contractors (discussed further below) – typical examples would be completion of the project on time and on budget, most operating costs, or interest-rate movements.

10.6.10.2 Relief events (also known as temporary *force majeure*)

These are risks which are assumed by the project, but if the risks occur the project company is given time to sort out the problem – a typical example would be a fire at the project facility. The project company's revenues from the public party or users will stop if the facility can no longer provide the required service, but the PPP contract will not be terminated for this failure. The event may be covered by insurance (discussed above).

10.6.10.3 Compensation events

These are events for whose effect the public party assumes liability. If they occur the project company must be compensated, usually on the basis of 'financial equilibrium' i.e. the project company and its lenders must be put in the same position they would have been in had the event not occurred. This will typically mean preserving the equity investors' rate of return and the lenders' cover ratios (discussed below). A typical example would be construction of a new free road that competes with a concession-based toll road.

10.6.11 *Force majeure* (also known as act of God)

These are risks that no party is willing to assume, and whose occurrence is likely to mean that the project cannot continue. The list of such risks is likely to be quite narrow, because most risks should come into one of the three categories above. A *force majeure* event usually results in the termination of the project.

From the lenders' point of view this categorization of risks is at the heart of their credit analysis.

10.7 Lenders' security

As discussed above, in a PPP project financing the lenders cannot normally take security over the physical assets of the project because these are public assets – a road, a school, a hospital and so on. Furthermore, the assets may have a highly specific use, and hence little value if sold off to recover a debt

To make up for this, the lenders have several other layers of security – it is the combination of all these which makes project financing a PPP project a basically sound and safe type of lending.

First, the due diligence that the lenders carry out is far more detailed than is typically found in other types of lending. The lenders take no aspect of a project on trust, but investigate it in detail, using professional advisers as necessary. These advisers normally include lawyers, to review the project contracts and sub-contracts, technical advisers, to review the project's technical feasibility and costs, advisers such as traffic consultants where there is usage risk in the project, accountants to review the project's accounting and tax projections, and insurance advisers. The lenders also either construct their own financial model of the project, or review in detail the model provided by the investors' financial adviser. The result of this can be seen in the loss experience of lenders to the PPP sector: typically losses are very low, and compare very favourably with other types of lending.

Then there are further layers of security, each discussed in more detail below:

- contract assignments and direct agreements;
- control and monitoring of cash flows;
- cover ratios;
- contract termination provisions.

10.7.1 Contract assignment and direct agreements

The first layer of security is an assignment of all the major project contracts (i.e. both the PPP contract and the project company's sub-contracts). This will include assignment of the security held to support these contracts, e.g. bonding for the construction sub-contractor's completion liabilities. The lenders also enter into separate 'direct agreements' with these parties enabling them to step in and take over the contracts if necessary to protect their interests. Lenders also take security over the project insurances.

The most important of the direct agreements is that between the lenders and the public party: the latter might wonder why such an agreement is necessary, since finance is the private party's responsibility but in fact this agreement is for the benefit of the public-sector side of the table as well. If the project loan goes into default the lenders – who will assume control of the project at that point – need time to organize themselves to step in and work out a way of dealing with the problem. It is in the interests of the public party to give them some extra time (usually about six months after the PPP contract itself would otherwise have been in default), since if the lenders cannot sort out the problem – which they have an incentive to do as otherwise they will have to write off their loan – it will be thrown into the public-sector's lap.

The lenders also take a pledge of the shares of the project company, which gives them another way to step in and take management control of the project.

In reality, it is unusual for the lenders to have to take action using any of this security. The fact that it exists is enough to ensure that the project company's equity shareholders will do as the lenders require once the loan is in default.

10.7.2 Cash-flow controls and reserve accounts

Cash-flow control by the lenders has two phases – the construction and operation phases of the project. During construction the lenders control the disbursement of funds and, e.g., only allow payments to the construction sub-contractor when the lenders' technical adviser has certified that the works have been carried out in accordance with the construction contract. The construction budget is continuously monitored against actual expenditure to ensure that there are enough committed equity and debt funds left to complete the facility. If this is not the case the lenders will intervene to take control of the project and consider how best to move forward.

Table 10.2 Cash flow 'cascade'

Cash In:	+ Operating revenues
Cash Out:	– Operating costs (incl. taxes)
	– Maintenance/lifecycle costs
	– Other capital expenditure
	– Interest and other finance costs
	– Debt principal repayments
	– Transfers to reserve accounts
	– Mandatory prepayments ('cash sweep')
	= Payments to equity investors (shareholder debt service and dividends)

During the operation phase the lenders apply a strict cash-flow 'cascade', which determines the order in which cash flow from the facility is to be applied. Typically this operates as in Table 10.2.

The project company's operating revenues from the PPP contract are thus applied, first to pay its operating costs, second to pay maintenance and lifecycle (equipment renewal) costs, third for any necessary additional capital expenditure (e.g. because a change in safety legislation makes a modification to the facility necessary), then to pay interest on the debt and other finance costs (e.g. lender fees), and then to repay debt principal instalments. Then the project company will probably be required to set funds aside in 'reserve accounts' (escrow accounts), to provide extra security for the lenders; the two most common types of reserve account are:

- *debt-service reserve account* (DSRA): this is usually required to hold enough to cover the next six months' payment of interest and repayment: it normally has to be in place on completion of construction, when debt payments begin, which means that it actually has to be funded as part of the project's capital costs;
- *maintenance reserve account* (MRA): this is very specific to the facility's maintenance cycle, but in general the aim of the MRA is to build up cash reserves to cover anticipated 'spikes' in maintenance or lifecycle (replacement) costs, e.g. a major overhaul, road resurfacing, or replacement of capital plant.

There may also be other specific reserve accounts, such as a change in law reserve, to ensure that the project company has funds available if money has to be spent, e.g. to meet new safety regulations.

Then a 'cash sweep' may be applied. This is intended to cover a facility where the cash flow may be quite variable, and so surplus cash is used in the good years to pay debt down early. Finally the cash left at the bottom of the cascade is available to be paid out to equity investors, but before this can happen the project company also has to demonstrate that it is meeting the minimum required cover ratios, which are discussed next.

10.7.3 Cover ratios

As project finance is all about cash flow, it is not surprising to find that lenders rely heavily on cash flow-based financial ratios to assess their lending. These are known as 'cover ratios', and two main types of cover ratio are applied in project finance:

- *annual debt-service cover ratio* (ADSCR): this is the ratio of net operating cash flow before debt service (and any transfers to reserve accounts) divided by the debt service for the annual

period concerned. It is usually calculated on an annual rolling basis every six months. This
shows the ability of the facility to meet its debt-service payments as and when they fall due.
- *loan-life cover ratio* (LLCR): this is the ratio of the net operating cash flow before debt
  service for the remaining life of the loan, divided by the loan outstanding. This shows that
  even if there is a temporary problem in any one year, the facility can pay off its debt during
  the remaining loan life.

These ratios are used in two ways. During the due-diligence process the lenders (or the rating
agency in the case of a bond) will determine the minimum levels of ADSCR and LLCR they
wish to see in the financial projections for the model. This will largely determine how much
debt the project company can borrow, as illustrated in Table 10.3.

The level of cash flow cover required by lenders is a function of the perceived risk of the
project. A low-risk project will require lower cash flow cover, say a minimum ADSCR of
1.25:1, and hence can borrow more money, whereas a high-risk project may require 1.75:1
and hence can borrow less money.

Second, once the project is complete and operating, the lenders continue to monitor these
ratios every six months – both the historic ratios for the last year and the projected ratios for
the remaining project term. Projections are usually based on advice from the lenders' technical adviser. If any of these calculations show, say, an ADSCR of 1.15 when the original
required minimum was 1.25, this may trigger a cash flow 'lock-up' by the lenders. This means
that the cash flow cascade is turned off at the point when surplus cash was due to be paid out
to equity investors, and the cash retained in the project company as extra security for the
lenders until the ADSCR has gone back above the lock-up level. Moreover, if the ADSCR
goes down further, say to 1.05, this triggers a default by the project company, and the lenders
will then be in charge of the situation.

10.7.4 Contract termination provisions

One aspect of a PPP contract that lenders and their legal advisers examine closely is the provisions for early termination. Lenders will want to ensure that their interests are protected in
such situations. Early termination may typically arise for one of three reasons:

- default under the PPP contract by the project company;
- default by the public party, or decision by the public party to terminate the contract early,
  e.g. because it no longer fits public policy in some way;
- *force majeure.*

Table 10.3 Cover ratio – effect on loan amount

		25 years	25 years
	Debt term	25 years	25 years
	Interest rate	6%	6%
[a]	Project cash flow (pre-debt service) p.a.	1,000	1,000
[b]	Annual debt service cover ratio	1.30	1.15
	Maximum annual debt service ([a] ÷ [b])	769	870
	Amount of debt which can be raised (annuity repayment)	9,833	11,116

Source: Yescombe (2002), Table 10.2

242

It might be thought that if the project company defaults the contract should be torn up and its investors and lenders should be paid nothing. However, in most cases the project company will have done something which has some value – it may have failed to build a road, for example, but the road may still be half-built. Therefore the project has some value, which has to be taken into account. This may be done by independent arbitration to establish the current value of the project, taking into account what needs to be done to set it right, with the public party paying this sum in return for taking the project over. Alternatively the value can be established through an auction process, whereby other private-sector parties may bid to take over the contract, and whatever is raised from this auction is paid to the project company. The lenders obviously have first call on this money – there is therefore a trade-off for lenders between letting the project company default, and probably losing some of their loan, and putting more money into the project to keep it going, and so recover their loan that way.

Default by the public party should be a relatively rare event, but it is not unlikely, in the course of a long-term PPP contract, that the public party may need to terminate the contract – either case is treated in the same way. The public party will want an option to terminate if the project no longer meets public-policy requirements. For example, population changes may mean that a school is no longer required in a particular location. The public party must have the long-term flexibility to decide that the PPP contract is no longer needed, but again fair compensation is expected, both by equity investors and lenders. Obviously the lenders expect to be fully repaid in this situation, and equity investors expect to get their investment back, with compensation for loss of future profits. This clearly makes terminating a PPP contract expensive, but it must be borne in mind that if the public sector procures, say, a school which turns out not to be needed in 10 years' time, knocking the school down is not without cost, because this means that the public-sector investment in this building has also been lost. Therefore criticism of long-term PPP contracts as being inflexible somewhat misses the mark, although it is true to say that termination of a PPP does incurs costs compared to a publicly-procured facility, primarily because of the need to compensate the equity investors for loss of profits.

As already said, termination for *force majeure* is a rare event. The most likely scenario may be that the facility is damaged by an insured event such as a fire, but the lenders form the view that even allowing for the insurance proceeds, restoration of the facility is not economically viable. In such circumstances the lenders will want to use the insurance proceeds to pay off their loan (which the insurance company may or may not allow), and the damaged facility is handed back to the public party. Some PFI-model contracts, such as those used in the UK, may required the debt to be paid off in full in this termination scenario, although the argument for doing so is quite weak since the public party would probably be paying more than the project is worth in this situation.

10.8 Public party's security

It should be remembered that the lenders do not have security over the public infrastructure facility itself: this remains in public ownership, or reverts to it automatically at the end of the PPP contract (whether by early termination for default or on its final expiry). Since the facility provides a public service, the lenders cannot be allowed to put this service in jeopardy by foreclosing over the facility. In fact in many cases this would be of little value to the lenders: they cannot foreclose on a road and sell it off – all they need to do is foreclose on the contract to operate the road (i.e. the PPP contract) and sell this off.

The corollary of this is that the public party always has the physical assets as its security, so that if the project company defaults, it will get the assets back under its control, as discussed above. Of course in the last analysis, the public party has the responsibility of continuing to ensure provision of the public service that the PPP contract is intended to provide. So if the PPP project does go wrong and no private party can be found to take it over and sort out its problems, the problems fall back onto the public party.

A public party, used to requiring performance bonding for works or services being procured directly, may feel uneasy about the lack of such security. But the project company cannot provide any form of bonding: it has no free assets to back such bonding, as all its assets are pledged to the lenders. And if the project company's investors were asked to provide bonding, this would negate the non-recourse nature of the funding structure, which is an essential element of project finance.

10.9 Changing the deal – the effect of project finance

PPP contracts normally have provisions for making changes to the contract during its life, to provide some operational flexibility for the public party. The cost of changes is dealt with in the way described above for compensation events – the financial equilibrium of the PPP contract has to be maintained (and while the change is being implemented the public party cannot normally make payment deductions because this work affects the service in some way – this is know as an 'excusing cause'). Such changes are of interest to lenders as they may alter the balance of risk in a way that upsets the assumptions on which their loan was originally made, and therefore significant contract changes require lender consent.

But the involvement of lenders in contract changes is likely to go beyond just giving consent: any change which requires new capital expenditure has to be financed in some way – ideally using a similar proportion of debt as in the original financing to keep down the cost of the change to the public party. Lenders will not normally commit in advance to finance changes and are in a monopoly position with respect to new finance because they already hold the security, which a new lender would also want. It is possible to prepay the lenders and refinance the whole debt but this is obviously likely to be an expensive solution. If the lenders are not prepared to provide the new finance on reasonable terms, then the only alternative is likely to be for the public party to finance the change itself.

10.10 Effects of the 'credit crunch'

International project-finance lending, both in PPPs and other sectors, survived very well the severe worldwide recession that begin in 2008: the level of losses incurred by banks and other lenders in project finance was low compared to other areas of lending such as personal, housing and corporate finance. There can be little doubt that the case for project finance as a low credit-risk type of lending – contrary perhaps to first impressions – stood up well under testing conditions. The reasons for the low loss rates clearly relate to the extensive due diligence and careful controls which banks use in project finance.

However, project finance did not stand up so well in another respect – that of liquidity. First, like all types of lending, and as the figures in Table 10.1 show, the 'credit crunch' resulted in a sharp cut-back of new lending. The cut-back was greatest in the regions that suffered most from the recession, as Table 10.4 shows.

As can be seen, lending in the Americas and Western Europe had yet to recover by 2011. This reduction in lending led to some governments taking measures to fill the financing gap for PPP projects: the British government set up the Treasury Infrastructure Finance Unit (TIFU) which offered banking-style debt finance if sufficient debt could not be raised from

Table 10.4 Commercial bank project-finance loans by region

(US$ millions)	2006	2007	2008	2009	2010	2011
Americas	44,012	44,476	42,086	20,058	25,535	38,383
Asia-Pacific	39,214	44,842	70,741	56,614	98,708	91,764
Western Europe	58,778	68,374	86,638	35,736	59,457	50,597
E. Europe/FSU	3,385	8,609	15,717	5,951	4,023	13,128
Middle East and Africa	35,220	53,685	35,376	20,829	20,452	19,615
	180,609	219,986	250,557	139,186	208,174	213,487

Source: based on *Project Finance International,* annual market surveys

the market. The need for its services proved to be very limited – it only participated in lending for one large PPP contract – but it may have also served to prevent banks exploiting the lack of competition.

But lack of liquidity also led to a result that has raised long-term questions about the current models for project finance, and hence financing of PPPs. As already said, banks are not natural long-term lenders – certainly not for the type of long-term of finance required for PPPs – and there had always been an implicit assumption that project-finance loans were liquid, i.e. they could be syndicated (sold off) to other lenders if the original bank required more liquidity. This proved not to be the case in and after 2008, and of course lack of liquidity was also one major reason for problems in other financial markets at that time.

This is likely to mean that as new capital requirements for banks are developed, a greater emphasis will be based on reducing maturity mismatches, e.g. funding long-term project-finance loans with short-term deposits. At the very least this will make project finance more expensive (although it would be fair to say that excess liquidity in the years before 2008 led to banks pricing project finance too cheaply). But the longer term result may well be that banks find project finance increasingly unattractive, and withdraw from the market entirely, as some major banks had already done even before 2008.

The only way to fill this gap is to turn to the non-bank sector, i.e. the bond market. But as has already been seen the project-finance bond market is much smaller than the bank market, and it would require some major changes in approach for the bond market to step into the gap, in particular willingness of bond investors to take the risks on PPP projects without credit insurance, and to build up their staffing to assess and monitor the risks of such projects. However, there are some promising signs as far as PPP projects are concerned – in Canada, for example, pension funds and life-insurance companies have largely filled the banking gap on PPP projects, reflecting the fact that, like their US counterparts, Canadian banks generally avoid long-term lending. The British government is also taking steps to encourage participation by pension funds and life-insurance companies in such lending.

10.11 Conclusion and prospects for project finance

In any case project finance is likely to remain more expensive than was the case in the boom years before 2008, and naturally this raises questions whether the extra cost for PPPs can be justified on a value-for-money basis compared to public finance. But lenders are not making excessively large margins on project finance – the higher cost is inevitable given the high level of supervision and control required compared to most other debt finance. In fact reductions in underlying long-term interest rates since 2008 have meant that the total cost of bank finance – their profit margin plus their underlying cost of funds – has not really increased.

There is every indication that governments around the world will continue to use private finance as one practical method of dealing with the 'infrastructure gap' from which most countries suffer. Project finance provides the only realistic way of mobilizing this private finance on the scale required.

Notes

* YCL Consulting Ltd., London – www.yescombe.com
1 See their website – www.ncppp.org (visited 4 October 2011).
2 The public party may be a central government ministry, department or agency (MDA), a regional or state government MDA, or a country or municipality.
3 For example, in the 1880s the French bank Crédit Lyonnais provided finance in this way for the development of the Baku oil fields (Yergin 1991: 60).
4 These are not PPPs where the projects concerned are public-sector owned, but 'private activity bonds' can also be raised through the US municiple bond market for certain types of private-sector infrastructure projects, which may be PPPs, and which would then benefit from the same tax exemptions as other municipal bonds. Bonds of this type are not included in the international statistics quoted above.
5 Hence the aphorism attributed to Mark Twain, 'A banker is a man who lends you an umbrella when it's not raining.'

Further reading

This chapter is based primarily on the author's experience working in the PPP/project-finance market. There is a considerable literature on project finance: the books below provide a general introduction to this topic.

Esty, B.C., (2003) *Modern Project Finance: A Casebook*, Hoboken, NJ: Wiley.
Finnerty, J.D., (2007) *Project Financing: Asset-based Financial Engineering*, 2nd edn, Hoboken, NJ: Wiley.
Perrot, J.-Y. and Chatelis, G. (eds), (2000) *Financing of Major Infrastructure and Public Service Projects: Public–Private Partnership – Lessons from French Experience Throughout the World*, Paris: École Nationale des Ponts et Chaussées.
South Africa National Treasury, (2001) *Project Finance: Introductory Manual on Project Finance for Managers of PPP Projects*, Johannesburg: National Treasury.
Yergin, D., (1991) *The Prize*, New York: Simon & Schuster.
Yescombe, E.R., (2002) *Principles of Project Finance*, San Diego, CA: Academic Press.
Yescombe, E.R., (2007) *Public–Private Partnerships: Principles of Policy and Finance*, Oxford: Butterworth-Heinemann.

Journals covering project finance and PPPs include:
Infrastructure Investor, PEI: London
Partnerships Bulletin, Rockcliffe: London
Public Works Financing, Westfield: NJ
Project Finance International, Thompson Reuters: London
Project Finance, Euromoney: London
Toll Roads News: Frederick, MD

See www.yescombe.com for an online bibliography of PPP-related studies and other material.

Part V

Public sector economics and public–private partnerships

11

Risk allocation model (RA model)

The critical success factor for public–private partnerships

Gerhard Girmscheid

11.1 Introduction

Public–Private Partnership (PPP) has established itself internationally as a popular and successful alternative for the fulfilment of public responsibilities. The objective of a PPP is to create synergetic effects through risk transfer, the provision of specific expertise and economic competence by the private sector in combination with the public sector. Those synergies develop through optimal risk allocation that reflects the partners' capacity.

According to Jacob and Kochendörfer (2002) 'optimal' risk allocation is the crucial success factor for the long-term profitability of a PPP (Figure 11.1).

A standardized and systematic risk allocation approach is, however, not recognizable in practice. An empirical study conducted by ETH Zurich [Girmscheid and Pohle (2010)] with the participation of established, partly internationally active PPP consultant companies in

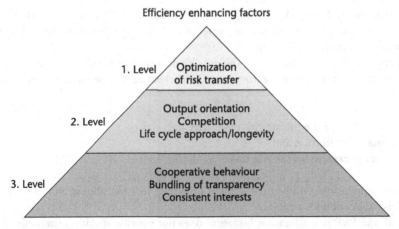

Figure 11.1 Efficiency pyramid – efficiency-enhancing factors in PPP

Source: Jacob and Kochendörfer (2002)

Germany and Switzerland confirmed those assumptions. The study showed that the risks with no legal restrictions are allocated mostly according to intuitive, habitual and opportunistic aspects that are influenced by the negotiating strength of the players. There is generally an absence of explicit decision criteria and methods for achieving a cost minimal allocation of risk and thus optimal risk allocation for the public sector considering the risk coverage capacity of the private partner.

This chapter presents a risk allocation model for PPP, which relies on an earlier study [Girmscheid and Pohle (2010)]. The model aims to enable the parties in a PPP to identify, assess and evaluate the long-term risk of this partnership and to process a systematic and optimal allocation of risk with the help of explicit decision criteria.

11.2 Related literature

Besides the relevant standard literature about corporate risk management [Girmscheid (2007a)], and project and corporate risk management [Girmscheid and Busch (2008a); Girmscheid and Busch (2008b); Schierenbeck (2003)], an increasing literature addresses the subject of risk management specifically for PPP. This literature includes: Akintoye *et al.* (2003); BMVBW (2003); Boll (2007); Boussabaine (2007); Elbing (2006); Grimsey and Lewis (2002); HM Treasury (2004); Merna and Lamb (2003); Partnerships Victoria (2001); Racky (2009).

Although most of these studies refer to the importance of risk analysis and allocation at the early stage of project preparation to increase the economic success of the project [Akintoye *et al.* (2003); BMVBW (2003); European Commission (2002); Grimsey and Lewis (2002)], they do not provide the instruments for putting risk allocation into practice.

According to the general understanding of practice and research, 'optimal' risk allocation will be achieved only if none of the players is taking risks that could be influenced more efficiently through the other player [PPP Task Force NRW (2007)]. This matches the common risk allocation principle whereby a risk should be assigned to whoever is able to manage it more cost effectively [Akintoye *et al.* (2003); Boussabaine (2007); European Commission (2002)].

As such, it appears that there are no concrete criteria according to which the risks could be allocated. The only clue for optimal risk allocation is the competence of the players, which according to research and practice should form the basis for risk allocation [Akintoye *et al.* (2003); Boussabaine (2007); European Commission (2002); PPP Task Force NRW (2007)]. Explicit criteria for determining the competence and consequently using it as an allocation criterion are, however, also missing.

Boussabaine (2007) mentions only the possibly insufficient financial capacity to take the transferred risk as a threat to project success. Girmscheid (2006) postulates three dimensions of risk allocation:

- means to influence the probability of occurrence;
- minimization of impact; and
- risk coverage capacity of the risk taker.

These three dimensions will be used as input principles to a risk allocation model to achieve optimal risk allocation for a project.

Overall, the PPP risk allocation literature does not provide specific criteria for ensuring the cost-minimized allocation of risks and, therefore, a successful partnership for both players. Only the basics of a risk management process are displayed as well as the standard tools for identification and assessment of PPP project risks. The process of risk allocation and the financial consequences of such allocation are not, however, addressed.

As part of the research project 'PPP – State of Practice – Risk identification and risk allocation in PPP for the maintenance of municipal road networks,' ETH Zurich conducted an empirical study [Girmscheid and Pohle (2010)] to identify the state of the art in PPP risk allocation and the evaluation criteria employed by banks when assessing companies and approving investment loans in Germany and Switzerland.

Building on these findings, this chapter develops the concept for a risk allocation model (RA model) that allocates risk according to the three dimensions of risk allocation.

The tridimensional RA model gives public authorities an instrument for cost-minimized risk allocation according to specific allocation criteria and, in doing so, ensures optimal risk allocation among the players under consideration of the risk load capacity.

11.3 PPP – risk allocation model (RA model)

The generic RA model is organized in seven modules, as shown in Figure 11.2.

In module 1, the risk categories are organized by system structures that determine the task fulfilment of a PPP. This provides a generic-hierarchical structure among risk fields and their risk groups along with their risk types/individual risks. Furthermore, the risks are analysed and assessed regarding their impact and probability of occurrence and classified according to importance [Girmscheid and Busch (2008b)].

In module 2 the risks identified in module 1 will be structured in terms of optimizability to achieve the optimal risk load distribution which is assessed and determined by considering the probability of occurrence as well as the impact of single risks.

Module 3 deals with the time dependence and consequent development of risks identified in module 1 and the structuring of these risks according to their time-related occurrence into one-off, non-periodic, and periodic risks.

Module 4 shows the aggregation of risk load with Monte Carlo simulation.

In module 5 the asset/profit risk model is developed. The risk load is classified in normal, stress and crash risk loads. The exposure of profit and equity capital is measured by the value of risk parameters.

In module 6 the risk coverage dimensions of a PPP project or the the related Special Purpose Company (SPC) are established according to the basic concept developed by Girmscheid (2007a) by analyzing the cash flow and equity dimensions of the SPC.

In module 7 the risk load resistance capacity is tested. The RA model enables the decision maker to determine the necessary risk coverage at each stage of the PPP project according to the risk escalation to normal, stress and crash level. The RA model consisting of the seven modules presented above is to be used by the PPP contract party that wants to support the RA decision insofar as to assess whether sufficient risk coverage is available for the risk load resulting from the RA chosen or calculated according to the risk minimum principle. If the risk coverage is not assured, the allocation of critical risks must be checked. This means that procurement may have to be terminated if a risk allocation solution, which prioritizes PPP during the process of cost efficiency analysis, cannot be found.

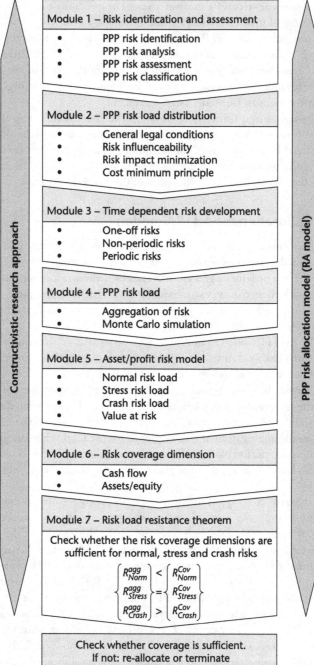

Figure 11.2 Risk allocation model (RA model)

11.3.1 Module 1 – PPP risk identification and assessment

The risk associated with a specific project or a specific area of responsibility is generally identified on the basis of a generic-logical structure in which the risk is organized and structured according to categories.

For system-theoretical reasons, risk categorization is structured on the basis of generic-hierarchical structures that determine the assignment of public tasks (Figure 11.3). Girmscheid and Busch (2008b) developed the hierarchical-horizontal classification of risks. The classification structures risks in risk fields and their risk groups with their risk types and single risks. The vertical risk structure divides into risk cause levels in the risk fields of politics, contracts, design, construction and operations.

This risk categorization must be performed for the specific project or task, and needs to contain the specific risk clusters to enable systematic and structured risk analysis.

An empirical study was conducted to identify the typical risk clusters for task fulfilment, e.g. in municipal street maintenance [Girmscheid and Pohle (2010)], in which they were categorized into a two-dimensional risk matrix that was structured horizontally into risk fields, risk groups and risk types, and vertically into politics, contracts, design, construction and operations (Table 11.1).

This risk categorization matrix can be used to systematically evaluate the specific municipal and situational risks associated with procurement and task fulfilment.

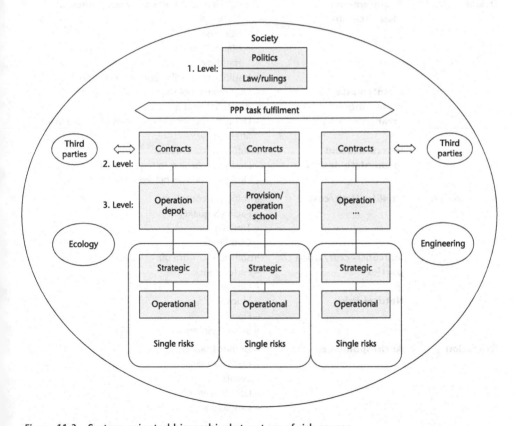

Figure 11.3 System-oriented hierarchical structure of risk causes

Gerhard Girmscheid

Table 11.1 Risk categorization of PPP risks subdivided into risk fields, risk groups and risk types (according to Girmscheid and Pohle (2010))

Risk fields (causes of risk)	Risk group	Risk type/individual risks
Politics	**Amendments to law**	– Political/legislative changes – Changes in government – Changes in taxation
	Budget modifications	– Planning changes – Budget coverage changes
	Standard modifications	– Changes in technical standards – Changes in operational standards
Contracts	**Contractual amendments**	– Changes in general project conditions – Contract misinterpretation – Unspecified technical problems or environmental influences
	Partner	– Bankruptcy – Failure to perform/insufficient performance of contract by partner
	Change of requirements	– Changes in user demands – Demographic/social changes

Design	**Requirement identification**	– Insufficient identification of requirements:
		  – Technical
		  – Utilization
		  – Maintenance
		  – Hand-over
		– Insufficient specification of requirements

	Maintenance and replacement arrangements	– Cost overrun of maintenance and replacement due to difficult access – Unprofitable recycling options of replacements after life cycle
	Inaccurate and incomplete design	Insufficient control of: – Design according to requirements – Design interfaces between trades
Construction	**Quality/time/cost**	Insufficient control of: – Facility's quality – Time limits – Cost limits
	Subcontractor/third parties	Insufficient control of: – Performance – Quality
	Natural risks	– Storms – Floods – Severe winters
Operation	**Anthropological risks**	– Demonstrations – Festivals/parades – Events – User behavior – Vandalism

Performance/ quality risks	– Restrictions on usability:
	  – Availability
	  – Inspection
	  – Maintenance
	  – Replacement
	– Time variance of component replacements
	– Cost variance of component replacements
	– Inappropriate SLA
	– Infrastructure condition at the end of the concession

Management	– Poor planning – Contract misinterpretation – Insufficient control – Restrictions

The risks are structured according to check lists (Table 11.1), and subsequently analyzed and evaluated. The risk evaluation represents a prognosis of the probability of occurrence (P) and impact (I) of identified risks [Girmscheid and Busch (2008b)]. Thus, the expected risk costs of risk type *i* can be expressed as:

$$R_{E,i} = P_{E,i} \times I_{E,i} \qquad (1)$$

where

$P_{E,i}$ expected probability of occurrence of risk type i
$I_{E,i}$ expected impact (amount of loss) of risk of risk type i

The subsequent risk classification serves to sort the risks according to the urgency with which they must be addressed. Based on their assessed impact and likelihood of occurrence and on the anticipated risk costs, the relevance of the risks for the project can differ. Different methods are applied when classifying risks. The portfolio method (Figure 11.4, both panels) and ABC

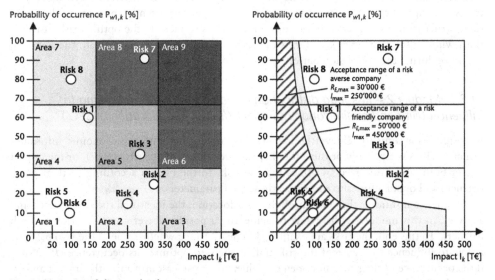

Figure 11.4   Portfolio method

Gerhard Girmscheid

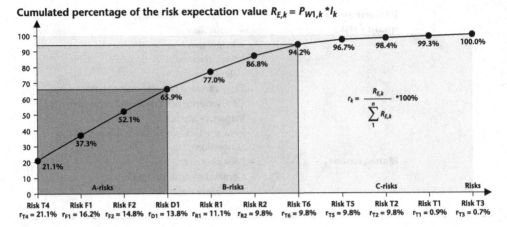

Cumulated percentage of the risk expectation value $R_{E,k} = P_{W1,k}*I_k$

$$r_k = \frac{R_{E,k}}{\sum_1^n R_{E,k}}*100\%$$

Figure 11.5 ABC analysis

analysis (Figure 11.5) [Girmscheid and Busch (2008b)] are very appropriate and widely used for this purpose. The portfolio method, with the dimensions of impact and probability of occurrence, indicates the relevance of these dimensions. Furthermore, a hyperbola can be defined to limit the single risks (Figure 11.4, right panel).

The ABC analysis identifies risk categories (A risks, B risks, C risks) and is usually subjected to more detailed risk evaluation.

The risk categories can be interpreted as follows:

• A: major risks, therefore strong need for risk monitoring and treatment.
• B: medium risks, therefore need for risk monitoring and treatment.
• C: minor risks; therefore little need for risk monitoring and treatment.

Generally the risks according to Table 11.1 can be structured in different ways, namely in terms of temporal or optimizability aspects depending on the intended purpose of the structure. Structuring risk in terms of optimizability serves to identify the optimal risk distributions whereas structuring risk in terms of temporal aspects serves to evaluate the risk load exposure during the concession period.

11.3.2 Module 2 – Risk load distribution – evaluation of risks according to influenceability and minimization of impact ('initial risk allocation of SPC')

Risk allocation aims to achieve the lowest risk costs in line with the economic minimum principle. This is especially possible if either the probability of occurrence (P_i), or the impact (I_i), or both, are minimized by allocating the risks to the players according to their competences and opportunities to minimize those two parameters.

In order to minimize the costs through risk allocation, the identified risks are studied and analysed in this module with a view to achieving a possible lower cost allocation to both partners. To this end, the risks are examined in detail to see whether one of the two partners is able to influence the cause of the risk and, as such, to optimize its occurrence ($P_{i,opt}$) or – if the occurrence of the risk is not open to influence – to at least minimize the impact and, as such, the consequences of the risk ($I_{i,opt}$) (Figure 11.6). If neither of the partners is able to

256

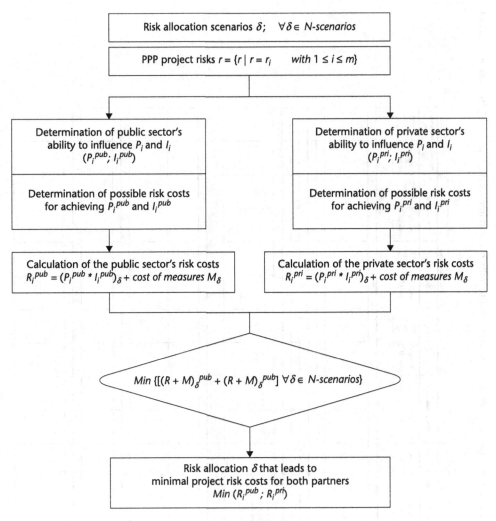

Figure 11.6 Flow chart for the minimization of risk costs R_i

influence the probability of occurrence nor the impact of the risk, the risk can be shifted to either party. The cost of associated measures M_i to reduce the probability of risk occurrence and/or the impact of risks as well as the risk costs R_i must be included in the overall risk handling cost evaluation (Table 11.2).

With the support of a simulation algorithm the different scenarios δ (Table 11.2) of risk allocation and associated chosen measures to reduce the probability of occurrence, or the impact, of risks will be checked with reference to the minimal risk cost and finally with reference to the risk coverage capacity of the public and private partners.

For demonstration reasons three examples are given in Table 11.2. The risk field 'change in technical requirements' is always clearly assigned to the private sector. Therefore the risk will be 100 per cent of the responsibility of the private partner in all possible scenarios. The same applies to the risk field 'festival/parades' for the public sector respectively. In the case of

Table 11.2a Extract from the risk allocation matrix – Scenario δ of risk cost minimization according to influence and impact minimization (The table is filled out partially for demonstration reasons)

| Risk fields: | | | Risk costs (per year) | | | Ability to influence the individual risk cost parameters | | | | Cost of measures | | Risk distribution scenario | | | | | | Risk costs per risk taker (R^{Pri}_i bzw. R^{Pub}_i) | |
| | | | | | | Ability to influence the probability of occurrence | | Ability to influence the impact | | | | Scenario δ-1 | | Scenario δ | | Scenario δ+1 | | | |
No.	Risk groups / Risk types		P_i	I_i	R_i	Measures (How?)	Party (Who?)	Measures (How?)	Party (Who?)	Private sector (Pri)	Public sector (Pub)	Private sector (R^{Pri}_i)	Public sector (R^{Pub}_i)	Private sector (R^{Pri}_i)	Public sector (R^{Pub}_i)	Private sector (R^{Pri}_i)	Public sector (R^{Pub}_i)	Private sector (R^{Pri})	Public sector (R^{Pub})
I	**Politics**																		
A	*Amendments to law*																		
1	Political / legislative changes: *New requirements for use due to legislative changes:* - *building safety standard* - *building energy standard* - *size of rooms for special use*																		
2	Changes in government																		
B	*Budget Modifications*																		
1	Planning changes																		
2	Budget coverage changes																		
C	*Standard Modifications*																		
1	Changes in technical standards							Analysis of trends and developments in construction; ongoing training	Pri			100%	0%	100%	0%	100%	0%		
2	Changes in operational standards																		
II	**Contracts**																		
A	*Contractual amendments*																		
1	Changes in general project conditions: *e.g. modification of requirements during contract period*																		
2	Contract misinterpretation																		
3	Unspecified technical problems or environmental influences: *e.g. existing contamination on the building site*																		
B	*Partner*																		
1	Bankruptcy / insolvency																		
2	Failure to perform / insufficient performance of contract by partner: *e.g. SLA - default of partner*																		
C	*Change of requirements*																		
1	Changes in user demands																		
2	Demographic / social changes: *Demographical changes of community in reference to facility requirements:* - *number of users* - *quality of users* - *change of social groups*																		

Table 11.2b Extract from the risk allocation matrix – Scenario δ of risk cost minimization according to influence and impact minimization (The table is filled out partially for demonstration reasons)

No.	Risk fields / Risk groups / Risk types	Risk costs (per year) P_i	I_i	R_i	Ability to influence the probability of occurrence — Measures (How?)	Party (Who?)	Ability to influence the impact I_i — Measures (How?)	Party (Who?)	Cost of measures — Private sector (Pri)	Public sector (Pub)	Scenario δ-1 Private sector (R^{Pri})	Scenario δ-1 Public sector (R^{Pub})	Scenario δ Private sector (R^{Pri})	Scenario δ Public sector (R^{Pub})	Scenario δ+1 Private sector (R^{Pri})	Scenario δ+1 Public sector (R^{Pub})	Risk costs per risk taker (R^{Pri} bzw. R^{Pub}) Private sector (R^{Pri})	Public sector (R^{Pub})
III	**Design**																	
A	*Requirement identification*																	
1	Insufficient identification of requirements: -technical -utilization -maintenance -hand-over																	
2	Insufficient specification of requirements: -technical -utilization -maintenance -hand-over				Quality control / involvement of experts	Pub					100%	0%	80%	20%	70%	30%		
B	*Maintenance and replacement arrangements*																	
1	Cost overrun of maintenance and replacement due to difficult access																	
2	Unprofitable recycling options of replacements after life cycle																	
C	*Inaccurate and incomplete design*																	
1	Insufficient control of design according to requirements																	
2	Insufficient control of design interfaces between trades																	
IV	**Construction**																	
A	*Quality / time / cost*																	
1	Insufficient control of quality																	
2	Insufficient control of time limits																	
3	Insufficient control of cost limits																	
B	*Subcontractor / third parties*																	
1	Insufficient control of performance: eg noise and dust																	
2	Insufficient control of quality																	
C	*Natural risks*																	
1	Storms																	
2	Floods																	
3	Severe winters																	

Table 11.2c Extract from the risk allocation matrix – Scenario δ of risk cost minimization according to influence and impact minimization (The table is filled out partially for demonstration reasons)

No.	Risk fields: Risk groups / Risk types	Risk costs (per year) P_i	I_i	R_i	Ability to influence the probability of occurrence: Measures (How?)	Party (Who?)	Ability to influence the impact I_i: Measures (How?)	Party (Who?)	Cost of measures: Private sector (Pri)	Public sector (Pub)	Scenario δ-1: Private sector (R^{Pri})	Public sector (R^{Pub})	Scenario δ: Private sector (R^{Pri})	Public sector (R^{Pub})	Scenario δ+1: Private sector (R^{Pri})	Public sector (R^{Pub})	Risk costs per risk taker (R^{Pri} bzw. R^{Pub}): Private sector (R^{Pri})	Public sector (R^{Pub})
V	**Operation**																	
A	*Natural risks*																	
1	Storms																	
2	Floods																	
3	Severe winters																	
B	*Man-made risks*																	
1	Demonstrations																	
2	Festivals / parades				Approval / ban by the public sector	Pub	Specifications of scope and location	Pub			0%	100%	0%	100%	0%	100%		
3	Events																	
4	User behaviour																	
5	Vandalism: – during opening hours – outside opening hours																	
C	*Performance / quality risks*																	
1	Restrictions on usability regarding: – availability – inspection – maintenance – replacement																	
2	Time variance of component replacements: – durability – service – quality – utilization																	
3	Cost variance of component replacements: – future price development – new technologies																	
4	Inappropriate SLA: – cleanliness – intervention procedures in event of malfunction – replacement interruption for operation equipment – appearance quality of interior and exterior																	
5	Infrastructure condition at the end of the concession																	
D	*Management*																	
1	Poor planning																	
2	Contract misinterpretation																	
3	Insufficient control																	
4	Restrictions																	

The table is filled out only partially for demonstration reasons!

Legend:
P: Probability of occurrence
I: Impact
R: Risk cost

Pub: Public partner
Pri: Private partner

the risk field 'insufficient specification of requirements' different risk distribution scenarios are possible as shown in Table 11.2.

The following questions can be asked to assess who is able to shoulder the risk at lower cost:

* Who is able to influence the occurrence of the risk (probability of occurrence)?
* Who is able to influence the consequences of the risks by minimizing the impact?
* Which measures must be taken, and at what cost, to minimize the occurrence and/or impact of the risks (cost of measures)?

Non-allocable risks (e.g. stipulated by law) must be assigned to only one partner (e.g. sovereign risks) and fixed in terms of their assignment. Risks that have no clear allocation criteria can be allocated to either partner.

Table 11.2 clearly shows the existence of various subjective distribution options, especially in respect of risks that can be influenced by both partners, irrespective of any assessment with regard to the probability of occurrence and/or impact. This produces various risk allocation scenarios δ.

Risks that cannot be clearly assigned to any of the partners – because they cannot be allocated on grounds of statutory requirements nor based on their occurrence or impact influenceability, for example – should be assigned to the partner who does not have to take any extreme speculative costs into consideration.

Risks where the probability of occurrence and/or impact is clearly influenceable generally result in minimum risk costs.

The quality of the distribution should be checked by several experts, bearing in mind the project conditions and the specific circumstances, based on a modified Delphi method [Franke (1991)]. The original Delphi method is an anonymous written survey of experts. In the case of the modified Delphi method the experts are gathered for a joint structured debate.

The various risk distribution scenarios according to the above stipulated requirements can be derived from Table 11.2. The costs of measures M_i for reducing the risk must be taken into account alongside the risk costs themselves in order to determine the risk handling costs in each scenario δ.

Several allocation scenarios δ can be simulated for the purpose of determining the minimum risk cost.

For each scenario δ the risk cost for the private and public partner will be determined as follows:

* The risks will be broken down in terms of optimizability to determine the optimal risk allocation.
  $R_i \rightarrow R_\varepsilon$ where $\varepsilon \in \{i;j;k;l\}$ and refers to risk types depending on optimizability.
* The scenario δ produces the following risk costs for the private partner:

$$R_\delta^{Pri} = \left\{ \begin{array}{l} \sum_i (P_{i,opt}^{Pri} \star I_i) + \sum_j (P_j^{Pri} \star I_{j,opt}^{Pri}) \\ + \sum_k (P_{k,opt}^{Pri} \star I_{k,opt}^{Pri}) + \sum_l (P_l^{Pri} \star I_l^{Pri}) + \sum_{i,j,k,l} M_{i,j,k,l} \end{array} \right\}_\delta \qquad (2)$$

The residual costs for the public sector amount to:

Gerhard Girmscheid

$$R_{\delta}^{Pub} = \left\{ \begin{array}{l} \sum_i (P_{i,opt}^{Pub} \star I_i) + \sum_j (P_j^{Pub} \star I_{j,opt}^{Pub}) \\ + \sum_k (P_{k,opt}^{Pub} \star I_{k,opt}^{Pub}) + \sum_l (P_l^{Pub} \star I_l^{Pub}) + \sum_{i,j,k,l} M_{i,j,k,l} \end{array} \right\}_{\delta} \qquad (3)$$

where

i	Risks whose probability of occurrence can be optimized but not the impact
j	Risks whose impact can be optimized but not the probability
k	Risks whose probability of occurrence and impact can be optimized
l	Risks whose probability of occurrence and impact cannot be optimized (non-influenceability of risks)
Pub	Public partner
Pri	Private partner
R_{δ}	Sum of risk costs (of the private partner and/or public sector) in scenario δ
$P_{i,opt}$	Optimized probability of occurrence of risk r_i
$I_{j,opt}$	Optimized impact (amount of damage) of risk r_i
P_j	Non-optimizable probability of occurrence
I_i	Non-optimizable impact
P_l	Non-influenceable probability of occurrence
I_l	Non-influenceable impact
$M_{i/j/k/l}$	Cost of measures to reduce the probability of occurrence or the impact of risk $\varepsilon \in \{i;j;k;l\}$
δ	different scenarios of risk allocation

- The total risk costs for the PPP project in risk allocation scenarios δ are the sum of the total risks costs of both partners, as follows:

$$R_{\delta}^{PPP} = R_{\delta}^{Pri} + R_{\delta}^{Pub} \quad where \ \delta \in \mathbb{N} \qquad (4)$$

where

R_{δ}^{PPP} total risk costs of the PPP project in scenario δ
R_{δ}^{Pri} risk costs of the private partner in scenario δ
R_{δ}^{Pub} risk costs of the public sector in scenario δ

- The cost-minimized risk allocation scenario out of $1 \leq \delta \leq n$ scenarios of risk allocation is determined as follows:

$$R_{min}^{PPP} = \min_{1 \leq \delta \leq n} \left\{ R^{PPP} \mid R_{\delta}^{PPP} = (R_{\delta}^{Pri} + R_{\delta}^{Pub}) \right\} \qquad (5)$$

11.3.3 Module 3: – Time-dependent development of risks in PPP projects

Unlike temporary construction projects, the risks of a PPP extend over the planning, construction and operation phases with a target horizon of between 20 and 30 years. The temporal risk exposure is not constant; it changes dynamically over the course of the project (Figure 11.7).

Accordingly, the general types of risk are broken down in terms of temporal aspects below. This delineates the breakdown in terms of optimizability aspects discussed in module 2.

$$R_i \rightarrow R_h \quad where \ h \in \{j;k;r\}$$

All risks still exist at the start of the concession period $t = 0$ and the risk load is therefore at its highest level. As the concession period progresses, the risks occur ($R_h = I_h \times P_h(W = 1)$) or

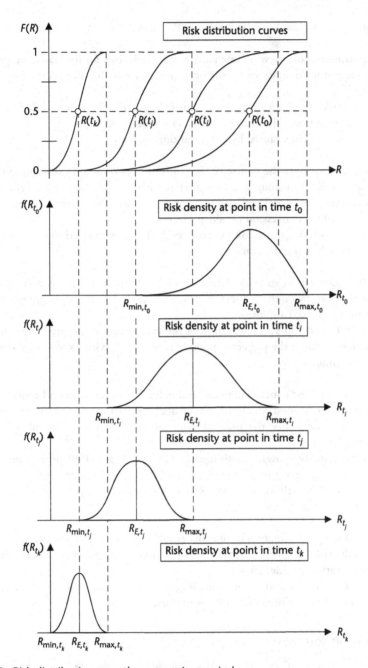

Figure 11.7 Risk distribution over the concession period

they do not occur ($R_h = I_h \times P_h(W = 0) = 0$) or their impact lessens over the residual concession period, where W is a random variable taking the value 1 if risks occur and value 0 if they do not. As such, the remaining risk loads decline over the residual period.

This lessening of the risk loads over the concession period is clearly shown, above all, by one of the crash risks – the bankruptcy of the Special Purpose Company as follows:

Gerhard Girmscheid

The highest aggregated risk costs occur at point in time $t = 0$ as a result of:

- the commissioning of a new private partner with risk costs for the transition phase;
- the new request for quotations for the operating phase with assumption of the guarantee risks;
- the PPP fee risk for substitute partners (this may prove to be much higher on an annual basis (accumulated over the entire concession period)); and
- technical risks and risks caused by users and third parties.

The risk loads decline over the course of the concession period up to the end of the period. The risk costs for commissioning a substitute partner in the case of bankruptcy decline consistently and proportionally relative to the project since a new partner must be commissioned at the end of the concession period anyway.

The impact of such declining risk over the residual concession period can alternatively be derived from the following illustrations:

- Figure 11.8: Derivation and calculation of the loss/impact if the private partner prematurely withdraws from the project at point of time $t_i^I = t_0^{II}$, with progressive annual amortization and fixed annuities.
- Figure 11.9: Derivation and calculation of the loss/impact if the private partner prematurely withdraws from the project at point of time $t_i^I = t_0^{II}$, with fixed annual amortization and variable annuities.

Index I stands for the 'first concession phase' and index II stands for 'second concession phase'. In the cases above the 'second concession phase' does not start at point of time t_{end} but at point of time t_i^I. As a consequence the residual value of the 'first concession phase' cannot be amortized completely.

This example clearly shows that time-dependent risks of a PPP project are subject to dynamic change, relative to variable point t_i as a result of the long duration.

For purposes of this analysis, the risks are classified by their temporal periodicity irrespective of the type of risk as follows:

- One-off risks, e.g. termination of the concession.
- Non-periodic risks: risks that occur only at certain, longer intervals, e.g. repairs/renewal of systems (heating, façade, etc.).
- Periodic risks: risks that can occur at ongoing intervals, such as maintenance and servicing costs, e.g. excessive maintenance costs or inefficient processes.

11.3.3.1 One-off cost risks

As an example, the risk of termination of a concession is considered here. The loss and/or impact associated with this risk is the product of the integration of the remaining annuities from point in time t_i^I of the departure (bankruptcy) of the private partner up to the end of the concession period t_{end}^I. This analysis and procedure are identical for all costs that are scheduled for amortization over the entire concession period and which cannot be amortized by terminating the concession or by other conditions.

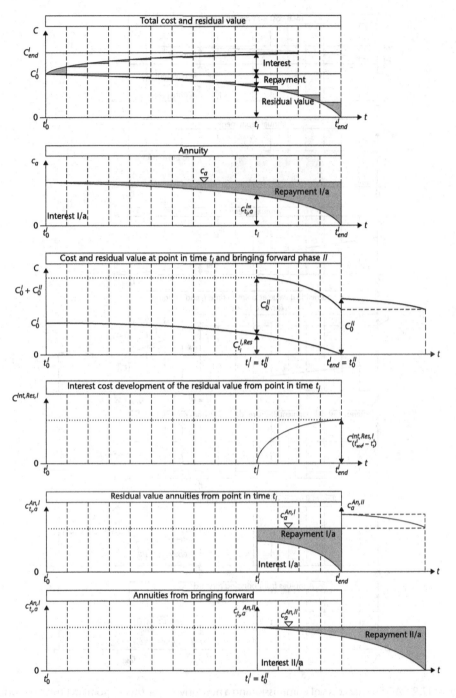

Figure 11.8 Additional costs of commissioning a new private partner at point in time t_i following bankruptcy or dismissal, with fixed annuities

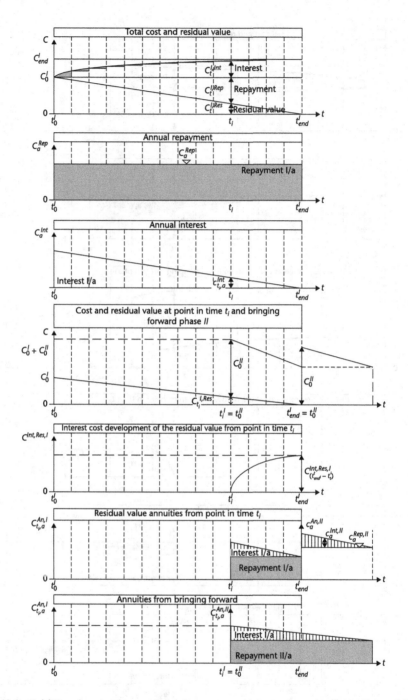

Figure 11.9 Additional costs of commissioning a new private partner at point in time t_i following bankruptcy or dismissal, with fixed annual amortization and variable annuities

The impact of the one-off risks is as follows:

$$I_{j,t_i}^{One} = C_{j,(t_i^I - t_{end}^I)}^{Int} + C_{j,t_i}^{Res}$$

$$I_{j,t_i}^{One} = \int_{t_i^I}^{t_{end}^I} c_{j,a}^{An}(t)dt = \int_{t_i^I}^{t_{end}^I} c_{j,a}^{Int}(t)dt + \int_{t_i^I}^{t_{end}^I} c_{j,a}^{Rep}(t)dt$$

(6)

where

I_{j,t_i}^{One}	Impact of the one-off risk j at point in time t_i
$C_{j,(t_i^I - t_{end}^I)}^{Int}$	Residual interest costs when the one-off risk j occurs at point in time t_i
C_{j,t_i}^{Res}	Residual value when the one-off risk j occurs at point in time t_i
$c_{j,a}^{An}(t)$	Annual annuity
$c_{j,a}^{Int}(t)$	Annual interest
$c_{j,a}^{Rep}(t)$	Annual repayments
t_i^I	Termination of the concession
t_{end}^I	End of the concession period

The one-off risk costs are evaluated in terms of their probability of occurrence and their impact:

$$R_{j,t_i}^{One} = I_{j,t_i}^{One} \times P_j(W_j)$$

(7)

Generally there is not just one deterministic value for the impact. The expected value $I_{j,t,E}$ usually lies within an interval $[I_{j,t_i,min}^{One}; I_{j,t_i,max}^{One}]$ with a normal, beta, rectangular or triangular density function.

The significance of the probability of occurrence $P_j(W_j)$ used to compute the expected risk costs is as follows:

$P_j(W_j)$ should, for example, amount to 60 per cent = 0.6. This means that in a random area with 1,000 incidents, the incident $W = 1$ will occur 600 times and, with it, the risk with its full impact. The incident $W = 0$ would, however, occur in 400 cases and, as such, the risk would not exert any impact.

The risk costs for one-off risks are finally expressed as follows:

$$R_{j,t_i}^{One} = I_{j,t_i}^{One}(p_{j,t_i}) \times P_j(W_j) = \begin{cases} 0 & if \quad P_j(W = 0) = 1 - \alpha \\ I_{j,t_i}^{One} & if \quad P_j(W = 1) = \alpha \end{cases}$$

(8)

This also forms the basis for a Monte Carlo simulation. The following applies to the practitioner's method which assumes only deterministic mean values and/or expected values:

$$R_{j,E,t_i}^{One} = I_{j,E,t_i}^{One} \times P_{j,t_i}$$

where

R_{j,t_i}^{One}	Risk costs of one-off risks j at point in time t_i, e.g. bankruptcy of the PPP Special Purpose Company

I_{j,t_i}^{One} Impacts of one–off risks j at point in time t_i

$P_j(W_j)$ Probability of occurrence of one–off risks j where $P_j(W_j) \in [0;1]$ and $W_j \in \{0;1\}$

$I_{j,t_i,\min,5\%}^{One}$ 5 per cent fractile of the impact interval with density distribution

I_{j,E,t_i}^{One} Expected value of the impact with density distribution

$I_{j,t_i,\max,95\%}^{One}$ 95 per cent fractile of the impact interval with density distribution

11.3.3.2 Non-periodic cost risks

Temporal change also affects the non-periodic risks. Consider for example Figure 11.10. If the heating system must be renewed at point in time t_i the cost or timing risk of its breaking down no longer exists at point in time t_j because it has already happened. The only continuing risk is that of maintenance costs.

At point in time t_i, therefore, both the cost risk and the time risk (Figure 11.10) exist (for all renewal and repair measures) for the example of the heating system and façade.

The cost and time deviation risk for renewing systems and sub-systems, such as the façade of a building, can be formulated as follows:

$$R_{k,t_i}^{N-Perio} = R_{k,t_i,Sys}^{Ren} = (C_{k,t_i,Sys}^{Ren} - C_{k,t_i,Sys,E}^{Ren}) \times P_{k,t_i}^{Cost}(W_{k,t_i}^{Cost}) + C_{k,t_i,Sys}^{Ren}(1+q)^{(t_k^{+-}-t_{k,E})*P_{j,t_i}^{Time}(W_{j,t_i}^{Time})}$$

$$with \ t_k^{+-} \in \left[t_{k,t_i,5\%}^{+-};t_{k,t_i,95\%}^{+-} \right] \ and \ C_{k,t_i,Sys}^{Ren} \in \left[C_{k,t_i,\min5\%}^{Ren};C_{k,t_i,\max95\%}^{Ren} \right] \tag{9}$$

where

$R_{k,t_i,Sys}^{Ren}$ Risk costs of non-periodic risks k at point in time t_i (e.g., renewal of systems or components)

$C_{k,t_i,Sys}^{Ren}$ Real costs of non-periodic risks k at point in time t_i in one interval with distribution density

$C_{k,t_i,Sys,E}^{Ren}$ Expected value of the real costs of non-periodic risks k at point in time t_i

$C_{k,t_i,\min5\%}^{Ren}$ 5 per cent fractile of the real costs of non-periodic costs k at point in time t_i

$C_{k,t_i,\max95\%}^{Ren}$ 95 per cent fractile of the real costs of non-periodic costs k at point in time t_i

$P_{k,t_i}^{Cost}(W_{k,t_i}^{Cost})$ Probability of occurrence of cost deviation from the expected value of the real costs where $P_j(W_j) \in [0;1]$ and $W_j \in \{0;1\}$

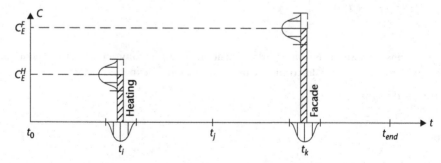

Figure 11.10   Non-periodic technical cost and time risks associated with the repair and renewal of systems and components

t_k^{+-}	Incident before (−) or after (+) expected point of time
$t_{k,E}$	Expected point in time of the renewal
$t_{k,J_i,5\%}^{+-}$	5 per cent fractile of the deviation from the expected point in time
$t_{k,J_i,95\%}^{+-}$	95 per cent fractile of the deviation from the expected point in time
$P_{k,J_i}^{Time}(W_{k,J_i}^{Time})$	Probability of occurrence of postponement from the expected point in time
k	$k \in \{Heating; Roof; Facade; . . .\}$
$\Delta t_k = (t_k^{+-} - t_{k,E})$	Captures the postponement of the renewal from expected point in time

11.3.3.3 Periodic cost risks

The periodic cost risks include mainly the ongoing costs for:

*   administration;
*   cleaning;
*   servicing;
*   maintenance.

These costs can be defined within a relatively narrow bandwidth at point in time $t = 0$. The price index must be taken into account when determining the development of these costs in the future. At point in time t_0, however, these costs may fluctuate as a result of uncertainties surrounding the market prices or scope of work. Moreover, the price index is usually extrapolated into the future based on retrospective data and, as such, is only definable within a bandwidth.

This clearly shows that the costs and the inflation index vary around an expected value in one interval. This uncertainty can prove to be an opportunity or a threat and is therefore a typical risk.

The various cost and inflation indices can be related to different goods and services:

$$\mu I = \begin{bmatrix} WI \\ MI \\ SI \\ CI \\ PI \end{bmatrix} \tag{10}$$

where

WI	Wage index
MI	Materials index
SI	Systems index
CI	Construction index
PI	Price index

The uncertain development of these goods and services indices will be expressed in an interval, that is:

$$\mu I \in [\mu I_{min}; \mu I_{max}]$$

Gerhard Girmscheid

The risk costs of the periodic risks are composed on the one hand of the variance of the expected annual cost at the start of the concession and on the other hand of the variance of the expected price increase over the concession period, as follows:

$$R_{r,t_i}^{Perio} = \sum_{t=0}^{t_i} \Delta c_{r,t_0} \times (1+\mu I)^t + \sum_{t=0}^{t_i} c_{r,t_0,E} \times [(1+\mu I + \Delta \mu I)^t + (1+\mu I)^t]$$

$$\text{with } \Delta c_{r,t_0} = c_{r,t_0} - c_{r,t_0,E} \tag{11}$$

$$c_{r,t_0} \in [c_{r,t_0,\min}; c_{r,t_0,\max}]$$

where:

$c_{r,t_0,}E$ Annual expected costs at point of time $t = 0$ for corresponding periodic services
c_{r,t_0} Potential annual actual costs at point of time $t = 0$ for corresponding periodic services
$\Delta \mu I$ Potential variance of the price increase $(+/-)$

11.3.4 Module 4 Risk load analysis at equidistant intervals

The respective risks of each respective project time horizon must be aggregated to produce the total risk load for the respective period of analysis.

The expected value of the risk costs of a PPP project is determined as follows:

$$R_{E,(t_i-t_{end})} = \sum_{t=t_i}^{t_{end}} (\sum_{j=1}^{n} R_{j,E,t_i}^{One} + \sum_{k=1}^{m} R_{k,E,t_i}^{N-Perio} + \sum_{r=1}^{s} R_{r,E,t_i}^{Perio}) \tag{12}$$

where

$R_{E,(t_i-t_{end})}$ Expected value of the total risks in interval $(t_i - t_{end})$
R_{j,E,t_i}^{One} Expected value of the one-off risks j at point in time t_i
$R_{k,E,t_i}^{N-Perio}$ Expected value of the non-periodic risks k at point in time t_i
R_{r,E,t_i}^{Perio} Expected value of the periodic risks r at point in time t_i

The risk analysis commences at point in time t_0 and is prospectively 'renewed' over the course of the project, e.g. at five-year intervals. The risk analysis should also be tracked on a yearly basis. The decision analysis for allocating the risks is, however, performed at point in time $t_i = t_0 = 0$. The risk load in the time interval $(t_i - t_{end})$ can be represented in terms of its impact and probability of occurrence as follows:

$$R_{E,(t_i-t_{end})} = (\sum_{j=1}^{n} I_{j,E,(t_i-t_{end})}^{One}(p_j) \times P_j(W_j)$$

$$+ \sum_{k=1}^{m} I_{k,E,(t_i-t_{end})}^{N-Perio}(p_k) \times P_k(W_k) \tag{13}$$

$$+ \sum_{r=1}^{s} I_{r,E,(t_i-t_{end})}^{Perio}(p_r) \times P_r(W_r))$$

where

$I_{j,E,(t_i-t_{end})}^{One}(p_j)$ Expected value of the impact of one-off risks j in time interval $(t_i - t_{end})$
$P_j(W_j)$ Probability of occurrence of one-off risks j

$I^{N-Perio}_{k,E,(t_i-t_{end})}(p_k)$ Expected value of the impact of non-periodic risks k in time interval $(t_i - t_{end})$

$P_k(W_k)$ Probability of occurrence of non-periodic risks k

$I^{Perio}_{r,E,(t_i-t_{end})}(p_r)$ Expected value of the impact of periodic risks r in time interval $(t_i - t_{end})$

$P_r(W_r)$ Probability of occurrence of periodic risks r

$p_{j/k/r}$ Density function of the respective impact of j / k / r

$W_{j/k/r}$ Digital number $W_j \in \{0;1\}$ relating to incident occurrence

The density function of the risk impacts lies in the intervals of the types:

$$I^x_{j/k/r,(t_i-t_{end})}(p_{j/k/r}) \in [I^x_{\min j/k/r,(t_i-t_{end})}; I^x_{\max j/k/r,(t_i-t_{end})}] \in \mathbb{R} \tag{14}$$

where

$$x = \{One-off;\ N\text{-}Periodic;\ Periodic\}$$
$$f(I^x_{j/k/r}) = p_{j/k/r}$$

Based on the density function for the impacts of the individual risks, the expected value $P_{j/k/r,E}$ can be formulated as follows using the static principle of linear momentum (Figure 11.11):

$$I^x_{j/k/r,E} \cdot 1 = \int_{I^x_{\min j/k/r}}^{I^x_{\max j/k/r}} I^x_{j/k/r}(p) \times p^x_{j/k/r}\, dI^x_{j/k/r}(p) \tag{15}$$

Monte Carlo simulation is used to determine the probabilistic aggregation of the risk load to enable an assessment not just of the expected value but also of the entire risk interval and its density function. The density function of such a Monte Carlo simulation (MCS) will be achieved by simulating different scenarios l to accumulate individual risks based on a random generator to produce the total project risks density function of the PPP Special Purpose Company. The random generator (e.g. Latin Hypercube) is used to generate random risk incidents in each scenario l. MCS uses two random numbers.

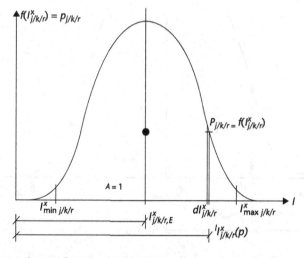

Figure 11.11   Impact density function – calculation of the expected value

The first random number $Z(W)_{j/k/r,t_i} \in \{0;1\}$ determines the occurrence and/or non-occurrence of a risk $j / k / r$. When the probability of occurrence is $P(W)_{j/k/r,t_i} = \alpha_{j/k/r,t_i}$ the occurrence of the random number will materialize as $Z(W)_{j/k/r,t_i} = 1$ in $\alpha_{j/k/r,t_i}$ cases and will materialize as $Z(W)_{j/k/r,t_i} = 0$ in $1 - \alpha_{j/k/r,t_i}$ cases for all simulation runs $l = n_1 < \infty$. The second random number $Z(I_{j/k/r,t_i}) = \{Z(I_{j/k/r,t_i}) \in \mathbb{R} \mid (\leq Z(I_{j/k/r,t_i}) \leq 1)\}$ serves to determine the characteristics of the impact, which are derived from the cumulative distribution function of the risk cost impact $F(I_{j/k/r,ti})$ of each individual risk $j / k / r$ in the specific simulation run l.

MCS is used to perform the following calculations in the $l > n_1 \sim 10{,}000$ scenarios and/or simulations: Determination of the risks costs of risk $j / k / r$ in the interval of impact $[I_{\min j / k / r,t_i}; I_{\max j/k/r,t_i}]$ in scenario l:

$$
{}^{l}R_{j/k/r,(t_i-t_{end})} = {}^{l}I_{j/k/r,(t_i-t_{end})}(P_{j/k/r,(t_i-t_{end})}) \times P_{j/k/r,(t_i-t_{end})}(W_{j/k/r})
$$

$$
= \begin{cases} 0 & \text{if } {}^{l}P_{j/k/r,(t_i-t_{end})}(W_j=0)=1-\alpha \\ {}^{l}I_{j/k/r,(t_i-t_{end})} & \text{if } {}^{l}P_{j/k/r,(t_i-t_{end})}(W_j=0)=\alpha \end{cases} \tag{16}
$$

The total risk costs for the analyzed period $(t_i - t_{end})$ in scenario l are derived as follows:

$$
{}^{l}R_{(t_i-t_{end})} = \sum_{j/k/r=1}^{n/m/s} {}^{l}R_{j/k/r,(t_i-t_{end})} \tag{17}
$$

The total risk cost distribution in the density function (Figure 12) is produced as follows, after completion of $l >$ e.g. 10,000 scenarios:

$$
R_{(t_i-t_{end})}(p) = \{R_{(t_i-t_{end})}(p) \in (R_{\min(t_i-t_{end})} \leq R_{E,(t_i-t_{end})} \leq R_{\max(t_i-t_{end})}) \subset \mathbb{R}\} \tag{18}
$$

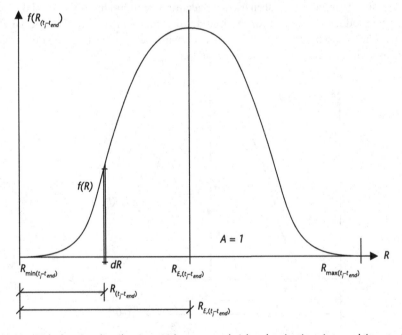

Figure 11.12   Risk density distribution with expected risk value in time interval $(t_i - t_{end})$

The expected risk costs of the residual project period $(t_i - t_{end})$ can be derived from the density function developed through MCS as follows:

$$R_{E,(t_i - t_{end})} = \int_{R_{min}}^{R_{max}} R_{(t_i - t_{end})}(f(R))dR \tag{19}$$

Alternatively the expected risk costs can be determined as follows after $l = n_1$ scenarios:

$$\begin{aligned}
R_{E,(t_i - t_{end})} = \sum_{l=1}^{n_1} (\sum_{j=1}^{n} ({}^l I_{j,(t_i - t_{end})}^{One}(p_j) \times {}^l p_j) \times P_j(W_j) \\
+ \sum_{k=1}^{m} ({}^l I_{k,(t_i - t_{end})}^{N-Perio}(p_k) \times {}^l p_k) \times P_k(W_k) \\
+ \sum_{r=1}^{s} ({}^l I_{r,(t_i - t_{end})}^{Perio}(p_r) \times {}^l p_r) \times P_r(W_r))
\end{aligned} \tag{20}$$

11.3.4.1 Use of Monte Carlo simulation to determine the density and distribution function of risk costs

Monte Carlo simulation requires a large number of simulation runs, whereby each run corresponds to a possible risk scenario with a combination of different random risk incidents within the analysed project. The simulation of possible risk scenarios, e.g. for a PPP project, is performed with the help of random numbers and the original data, such as shown in Figure 11.13 as an example.

Simulation of the occurrence $W_{j/k/r}$ of individual risk j/k/r in simulation run l
Since a risk might, but does not absolutely have to, occur, a probability $P_{W1;j/k/r}$ of its occurrence has to be estimated. This can then be used to map the probability density $f(W)$ and the distribution function $F(W)$ for the discreet random variable $W_{j/k/r}$ 'risk occurrence' in the form of a digital function that can adopt the characteristics $W_{j/k/r} = \{0;1\}$ for purposes of activating the risk occurrence.

City-Areal superstructure, Zurich	Initial data for calculating the PPP risk costs for the quotation no. 59/2003								
		Modelling the risk occurrence		Modelling the impact					
No.	Designation	Probability of occurrence $P_{W1;j/k/r}$ [%]	Probability density $f(W)$	Minimum loss I_{min} [€]	Expected loss I_E [€]	Maximum loss I_{max} [€]	Density function $f(I_{j/k/r})$	Mean value $I_{E;j/k/r}$	Standard deviation $\sigma_{I;j/k/r}$
1	Incomplete scope of work	60%	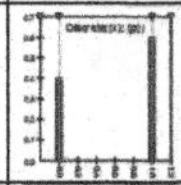	100'000	150'000	300'000	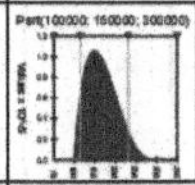	166'667	35'635
2.	Extreme architectural quality requirements	80%	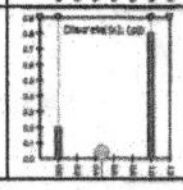	60'000	85'000	110'000	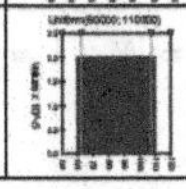	85'000	14'434

Figure 11.13 Original data for calculating the residual risk (selection)

$$f(W) = \begin{cases} P_{W_1;j/k/r} & \text{if } W = W_1 = 1 \\ 1 - P_{W_1;j/k/r} & \text{if } W = W_0 = 0 \end{cases} \quad \text{with } W \in [0;1] \text{ and } 0 \le P_{W_1;j/k/r} \le 1 \qquad (21)$$

where

$f(W_{j/k/r})$ Probability density of random variable $W_{j/k/r}$
$P_{W_1;j/k/r}$ Probability of occurrence of individual risk $j/k/r$
W_1 Characteristics of random variable $W_{j/k/r}$ for 'risk occurrence'
W_0 Characteristics of random variable $W_{j/k/r}$ for 'risk non-occurrence'

The incident 'risk occurrence' is given the value $W_{j/k/r} = W_1 = 1$, whereas the incident 'risk non-occurrence' is given the value $W_{j/k/r} = W_0 = 0$. The values $W_{j/k/r} = 0$ and $W_{j/k/r} = 1$ act as multipliers for the impact to determine the risk costs in the respective project simulation. The probability density and the distribution function for a probability of occurrence $P_{W_1;j/k/r}$ of individual risk $j/k/r$ of 60 per cent are shown in Figure 11.14.

With the help of random number $Z_{W;j/k/r}$, the inverse function $G(F(W_{j/k/r}))$ is used to calculate the value of $W_{j/k/r}$ for simulation run l and the individual risk $j/k/r$ and to determine whether the risk will occur ($W_1 = 1$) or not ($W_0 = 0$) in simulation run l.

$$G\left(F(W)_{j/k/r}\right) = G\left(^l Z_{W,j/k/r}\right) = {^l W_{j/k/r}} \quad \text{with } 0 \le Z_{W,j/k/r} \le 1 \qquad (22)$$

where

$G(F(W)_{j/k/r})$ Inverse function of $F(W)_{j/k/r}$
$^l W_{j/k/r}$ (0∨1); characteristics of random variable $W_{j/k/r}$ of individual risk $j/k/r$ in simulation run l

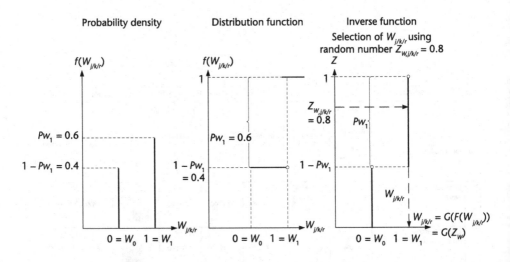

Figure 11.14   Probability density, distribution function and inverse function for the occurrence of risk $j/k/r$

$^lZ_{W,j/k/r}$ Random number for determining $W_{j/k/r}$ of individual risk $j/k/r$ in simulation run l

Since the Latin Hypercube Sampling method possesses an 'internal memory' and intervals that have already been selected cannot be used again, the individual risk $j/k/r$ occurs exactly 600 times with a probability of occurrence $P(W = 1) = 0.6$ in, e.g. 1,000 iteration runs; the value for W equals one. Since it does not occur in the other 400 cases, the value for W is zero.

Simulation of the impact $I_{j/k/r}$ of individual risk $j/k/r$ in simulation run l
A loss will be suffered if individual risk $j/k/r$ occurs. The exact amount of this loss is, however, virtually impossible to predict in most cases. The safer approach is to define a range, e.g. an interval, for this risk loss, within which the impact will lie. In the absence of accurate data, triangular, normal and BetaPERT distribution have proven to be suitable for roughly modelling the impact. The density function $f(I_{j/k/r})$ of these distributions is defined by the three values I_{min} 'minimum loss', I_E 'expected loss' and I_{max} 'maximum loss'. A distribution function $F(I_{j/k/r})$ of impact $I_{j/k/r}$ is derived from the density function of the impact $f(I_{j/k/r})$. This produces the following formulae for a BetaPERT distribution:

$$f(I_{j/k/r}) = Beta\,PERT(I_{min}, I_E, I_{max}) \quad where\, I_{min} \leq I_{j/k/r} \leq I_{max}$$

$$F(I_{j/k/r}) = \int_{I_{min}}^{I_{j/k/r}} f(I_{j/k/r})\,dI_{j/k/r}$$

(23)

where

$f(I_{j/k/r})$ Density function of the random variable of impact $I_{j/k/r}$

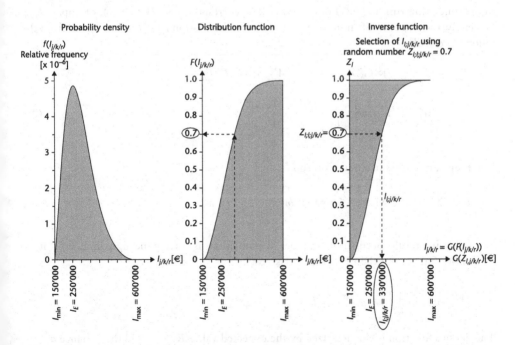

Figure 11.15   Possible density, distribution and inverse function for impact $I_{j/k/r}$ of risk $j/k/r$

I_{min} Minimum impact of individual risk $j/k/r$
I_E Expected impact of individual risk $j/k/r$
I_{max} Maximum impact of individual risk $j/k/r$
$F(I_{j/k/r})$ Distribution function of the random variable of impact $I_{j/k/r}$

Figure 11.15 shows the BetaPERT distribution for impact $I_{j/k/r}$ of an individual risk $j/k/r$ with the values $I_{min} = 150{,}000$ €, $I_E = 250{,}000$ € and $I_{max} = 600{,}000$ € in the shape of its density, distribution and inverse functions.

With the help of random number $Z_{Ij/k/r}$ that corresponds to the function value $F(I_{j/k/r})$, the inverse function $G(F(I))$ is used to determine the value of impact $I_{j/k/r}$ in the current scenario l for risk $j/k/r$.

$$G(^{l}F(I_{j/k/r})) = G(^{l}Z_{Ij/k/r}) = {}^{l}I_{j/k/r} \quad \text{where } 0 \le Z_{Ij/k/r} \le 1 \tag{24}$$

where

$G\left({}^{l}F(I_{j/k/r})\right)$ Inverse function of $F(I_{j/k/r})$

${}^{l}Z_{Ij/k/r}$ Random number for determining the impact $I_{j/k/r}$ of individual risk $j/k/r$
                 in simulation run l

${}^{l}I_{j/k/r}$ Characteristics of random variable $I_{Ij/k/r}$ of individual risk $j/k/r$ in simula-
                 tion run l

Risk costs $R_{j/k/r}$ of individual risk $j/k/r$ in simulation run l
The level of risk costs of individual risk $j/k/r$ in simulation run l are derived from the product of the random variable $W_{j/k/r}$ and the associated impact $I_{j/k/r}$. In the event that the risk occurs in the simulation run, the level of risk costs $R_{j/k/r}$ corresponds to ($W_{j/k/r} = 1$), of impact $I_{j/k/r}$. Generally, the risk costs of an individual risk $j/k/r$ in simulation run l can be derived from the following calculation:

$$
{}^{l}R_{j/k/r} = G({}^{l}Z_{Wj/k/r}) \times G({}^{l}Z_{Ij/k/r}) = G(F({}^{l}W_{j/k/r})) \times G(F({}^{l}I_{j/k/r}))
$$

$$
= {}^{l}W_{j/k/r} \times {}^{l}I_{j/k/r} = \begin{cases} 0 & \text{if} \quad {}^{l}W_{j/k/r} = 0 \\ {}^{l}I_{j/k/r} & \text{if} \quad {}^{l}W_{j/k/r} = 1 \end{cases} \tag{25}
$$

PPP project risk costs in simulation run l:

$$
{}^{l}R = \sum_{j/k/r=0}^{m/n/s} {}^{l}R_{j/k/r} \quad \text{where } 1 \le j/k/r \le n/m/s \tag{26}
$$

The following results occur if the number of simulations is correspondingly high at $l = n_1$.
  Density function of the PPP project risk costs:

$$
f\left(R_{(t_i - t_{end})}\right) = f\left({}^{l}R_{E,(t_i - t_{end})}; \sigma^2_{(t_i - t_{end})}\right) \tag{27}
$$

The density function is characterized by the expected value ${}^{l}R_{E,(t_i - t_{end})}$ and the variance $\sigma^2_{(t_i - t_{end})}$.

Distribution function of the PPP project risk costs:

$$F\left({}^{l}R_{(t_i-t_{end})}\right)=\int f\left({}^{l}R_{E,(t_i-t_{end})};\sigma^2_{(t_i-t_{end})}\right)dR \tag{28}$$

where:

$$0 \leq Z_{xj/k/r} \leq 1 \text{ and } Z_{xj/k/r} \in \mathbb{R} \text{ with } x \in \{W_{j/k/r}; I_{j/k/r}\}$$

and

${}^{l}R_{j/k/r}$	Random variable of the risk costs of individual risks $j/k/r$ in simulation run l
${}^{l}R$	Total risk costs of simulation run l
$G(F({}^{l}W_{j/k/r}))$	Inverse function of $F({}^{l}W_{j/k/r})$ in simulation run l
$G(F({}^{l}I_{j/k/r}))$	Inverse function of $F({}^{l}I_{j/k/r})$ in simulation run l
${}^{l}I_{j/k/r}$	Characteristics of random variable $I_{j/k/r}$ of individual risk $j/k/r$ in simulation run l
${}^{l}W_{j/k/r}$	Characteristics of random variable $W_{j/k/r}$ of individual risk $j/k/r$ in simulation run l
$n/m/s$	Number of individual risks
n_1	Total number of simulation runs
${}^{l}R_E$	Expected value of the risk costs of the PPP project
${}^{l}R_{min}$	Minimum risk costs of the PPP project
${}^{l}R_{max}$	Maximum risk costs of the PPP project
${}^{l}R_{95}$	95 per cent fractile of the risk costs of the PPP project
${}^{l}R_5$	5 per cent fractile of the risk costs of the PPP project
σ	Standard deviation of the risk costs of the PPP project
${}^{l}Z_{Wj/k/r}$	Random number for selecting whether individual risk $j/k/r$ occurs in simulation run l
${}^{l}Z_{Ij/k/r}$	Random number for selecting the impact characteristics $I_{j/k/r}$ of individual risk $j/k/r$ in simulation run l

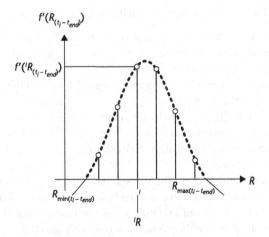

Figure 11.16 Density function of the risk costs of the PPP project based on the MC simulation

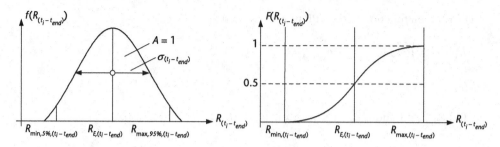

Figure 11.17 Probability density function and cumulative distribution function of the risk costs of the PPP project during period $(t_i - t_{end})$

The MCS density function f' of the PPP project risk costs is assumed normal with measure 1 ($A = 1$) to simplify the following calculations (Figure 11.16):

$$f(R_{(t_i-t_{end})}) = f \frac{f'(R_{(t_i-t_{end})})}{\int_{R_{min}}^{R_{max}} f'(R_{(t_i-t_{end})}) dR} \qquad (29)$$

Expected value of the risk costs of the PPP project during period $(t_i - t_{end})$ (Figure 17):

$$R_{E,(t_i-t_{end})} = \int_{R_{min}}^{R_{max}} R_{(t_i-t_{end})} \times f(R_{(t_i-t_{end})}) dR \qquad (30)$$

Variance of the risk costs of the project during period $(t_i - t_{end})$:

$$\sigma^2_{(t_i-t_{end})} = \int_{R_{min}}^{R_{max}} (R_{(t_i-t_{end})} - R_{E,(t_i-t_{end})})^2 \times f(R_{(t_i-t_{end})}) dR \qquad (31)$$

$$f(R_{(t_i-t_{end})}) = f(R_{E,(t_i-t_{end})}; \sigma^2_{(t_i-t_{end})})$$

11.3.4.2 Example of a case for performing Monte Carlo simulation

In this example, the project risk $R_{(t_i-t_{end})}$ is comprised of 15 individual risks. Table 11.3 shows the spreadsheet that is required for the Monte Carlo simulation based on Latin Hypercube sampling. It contains the results from only one simulation run *l*. If $n_1 = 10'000$ simulations runs are needed, the software program evaluates the spreadsheet 10'000 times and collates the results for $R_{(t_i-t_{end})}$. Due to the normalization ($A = 1$), the evaluation of the simulation results produces a density function $f(R_{(t_i-t_{end})})$ and a distribution function $F(R_{(t_i-t_{end})})$.

For our case study, 10'000 simulation runs produce the graphs shown in Figure 11.18. The simulation produces an expected value of the risk costs $R_{E,(t_i-t_{end})}$ of 818'908 € and a standard deviation $\sigma_{(t_i-t_{end})}$ of 326'444 €.

In the event of interdependencies in the shape of correlation coefficients between two or more risks, they can be taken into account relatively simply in the simulation with the aid of a correlation matrix. For specialized literature on information about the various means of incorporating correlations into sampling processes, refer to Vose (1996).

Based on the results graphs, a specific deterministic risk premium $R_{Est;\alpha}$ can be selected for the identified risks of the PPP project, with a statistical safety level α.

Table 11.3 Monte Carlo simulation spreadsheet for one simulation run I, based on MS-Excel©

City Areal superstructure, Zürich
Monte Carlo simulation of the risk costs $R_{Project}$ to determine the risk premium for quotation no. 59/2003

Designation of individual risks		Modelling the risk occurrence		Modelling the impact					Risk costs
No.	Designation	Probability of occurrence $P_{wtijk/r}$ [%]	Random variable of the risk occurrence $W_{tijk/r}$ [-]	Density function $f(I_{ijk/r})$	Minimum loss I_{min} [€]	Expected loss I_{E} [€]	Maximum loss I_{max} [€]	Random variable of the impact $I_{ijk/r}$ [€]	Cost of the individual risks (in simulation run I) $R_{ijk/r}$ [€]
1.	Incomplete scope of work	60%	1	BetaPERT	100'000	150'000	300'000	166'667	166'667
2.	Extreme architectural quality requirements	80%	1	Normal	60'000	85'000	110'000	85'000	85'000
3.	Execution deadline: contract penalty	90%	1	Triangular	45'000	150'000	175'000	123'333	123'333
4.	Property developer's credit rating / payment behavior	40%	0	Triangular	200'000	266'000	340'000	268'667	0
5.	Foundation soil: poorer than expected	25%	0	BetaPERT	150'000	250'000	500'000	275'000	0
6.	Soil contamination: Excavation	15%	0	BetaPERT	35'000	70'000	120'000	72'500	0
7.	Soil contamination disposal charge	15%	0	BetaPERT	70'000	140'000	200'000	138'333	0
8.	Tightness of the horizontal sealing blanket	25%	0	BetaPERT	80'000	150'000	250'000	155'000	0
9.	Functional warranty Ventilation – Facade	20%	0	Dreieck	150'000	300'000	450'000	300'000	0
10.	Quality deficiencies of the slotted wall	10%	0	BetaPERT	75'000	120'000	250'000	134'167	0
11.	Calculation of external services provision: building technology	30%	0	BetaPERT	100'000	200'000	350'000	208'333	0

(Continued overleaf)

Table 11.3 Continued

City Areal superstructure, Zürich

Monte Carlo simulation of the risk costs $R_{Project}$ to determine the risk premium for quotation no. 59/2003

No.	Designation	Modelling the risk occurrence		Modelling the impact					Risk costs
		Probability of occurrence $P_{Wtij,k,r}$ [%]	Random variable of the risk occurrence $W_{tij,k,r}$ [-]	Density function $f(I_{ij,k,r})$	Minimum loss I_{min} [€]	Expected loss I_E [€]	Maximum loss I_{max} [€]	Random variable of the impact $I_{tij,k,r}$ [€]	Cost of the individual risks (in simulation run I) $R_{tij,k,r}$ [€]
12.	Calculation of external services provision: facade	25%	0	BetaPERT	200'000	320'000	450'000	321'667	0
13.	Building physics: room acoustics	25%	0	Normal	25'000	35'000	45'000	35'000	0
14.	Bankruptcy of the SC for construction supervision works	35%	0	BetaPERT	50'000	120'000	180'000	118'333	0
15.	10 year warranty on the roof seal	35%	0	Triangular	30'000	75'000	125'000	76'667	0
					ΣI_{min}: 1'370'000	ΣI_E: 2'431'000	ΣI_{max}: 3'845'000	$\Sigma I_{tij,k,r}$: 2'478'667	$R_{Project,I}$: **375'000**

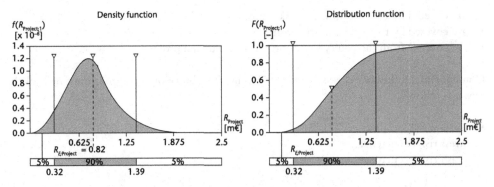

Figure 11.18 Graphs of the results of the Monte Carlo simulation in the form of a density function $f(R_{(t_i - t_{end})})$ and a distribution function $F(R_{(t_i - t_{end})})$ for the risk costs

The use of Monte Carlo simulation is subject to various requirements with regard to the risk analysis:

- A total risk is frequently composed of various influencing variables (partial risks). In this case the correlation has to be taken into account.
- Empirical data are often not available for the risk forecast. They must be estimated with the aid of expert assessments in a reasonable range.
- The range of the risk costs' probability of occurrence and their impact is weighted through a density function.

Unlike other techniques, Monte Carlo simulation offers further advantages:

- Correlation matrices can be used to easily model interdependencies among partial risks.
- Increasing the iteration steps is an easy means of increasing the accuracy of the analysis.
- Complex mathematical functions (e.g. logarithmic or exponential functions and if/then instructions) can be integrated into the model.
- Since MCS is an acknowledged method of simulation, the level of acceptance for the results is higher.
- The model behaviour can be examined fairly easily.
- Changes to the model can be quickly incorporated and compared with earlier results.

11.3.5 Module 5 – Asset/profit risk model (APR model)

The following issues now need to be assessed, based on the developed analysis of the PPP project with its risk distribution function $F(R)$:

- Which risk costs are covered by the deterministic risk premium?
- How much risk coverage capacity can the profit cover?
- Which risks must be covered by equity?

Sufficient risk coverage capacity must be available at all times, in light of the risk distribution of the PPP project. Clarification is also required as to whether risks with a certain probability of occurrence:

- are covered by the deterministic risk premiums;
- are covered by the deterministic profit;
- are covered from the equity share and the accumulated profit.

Consequently, following Girmscheid (2007a), the probability of occurrence must be broken down as follows

- normal risk occurrence;
- stress risk occurrence;
- crash risk occurrence.

This leads to the APR model based on the risk model for project-oriented companies as developed by Girmscheid (2007a). The Asset/Profit Risk Model aims to clarify how the PPP risks change over the long-term duration of the PPP project, and how they impact:

- deterministic risk premiums;
- deterministic profit;
- equity.

Equally, the risk coverage capacity needed for the forecasted prospective risks can be derived from the Asset/Profit Risk Model. This aspect of the APR Model, in particular, is an excellent support tool for:

- determining the cash flow capacity;
- defining the share of equity;
- defining the contractual agreement to secure the financial and the asset-creating capacity over the entire concession period.

The APR model for PPP builds on the cash flow risk model and asset profit risk model developed by Girmscheid at the Massachusetts Institute of Technology [Girmscheid (2007a), (2007b), (2007c)]. Further detailed information can also be found in Girmscheid and Busch (2008a).

The risk development in a PPP project is shown in Figure 11.19. The full range of the risks over the entire term $(t_0 - t_{end})$ still exists at point in time t_0. The residual risks decline in the subsequent intervals over the residual term. These residual risks decline as a result of:

- Potential occurrence ($W = 1$) or non-occurrence ($W = 0$) of risks in the previous intervals.
- Reduction of the impact of the risks depending on the remaining duration of the project.

Figure 11.19 shows a qualitative example of the risk progressions in the intervals $(t_0 - t_{end}) > (t_i - t_{end}) > (t_j - t_{end}) > (t_k - t_{end})$.

An APR model (Figure 11.20) must be established for each changing risk development over the term of the PPP project $(t_i - t_{end})$ (Figure 11.19).

The APR model is obtained by transforming (creating a mirror image of) the respective risk distribution function at point in time $t_0 \leq t_i \leq t_{end}$ (see also Girmscheid (2007a), (2007b), (2007c); and Girmscheid and Busch (2008a)).

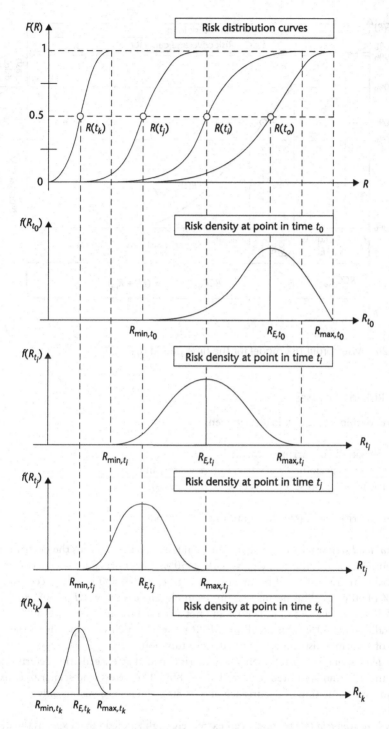

Figure 11.19 Risk development during the concession period in a PPP project

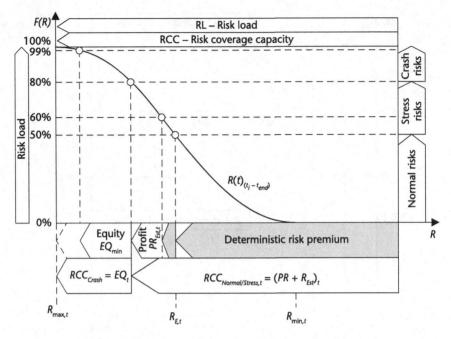

Figure 11.20 Asset/profit risk model for the time period ($t_i - t_{end}$)

11.3.5.1 Risk load classes

For differentiation of the risk loads between:

- lesser, repeatedly occurring/annual;
- moderate, non-periodic (every two to five years); and
- rarer, usually one-off severe (every five to 30 years).

The following risk load categories and limits are introduced for the risks:

- *Normal load scenario (N)* represents a normal risk load that exceeds the deterministic risk premium R_{Est} and is limited, e.g. by $VaR_\alpha = 50\%$. The 'normal load scenario' constitutes a probabilistic limitation of occurrence of, e.g. $\alpha_N = 50\%$ and is only exceeded in $(1 - \alpha) = 50\%$ of all cases. This means that, for example, the cash flow $CF_\alpha = 50\%$ and the profit $PR_\alpha = 50\%$ are achieved in $\alpha_N = 50\%$ and not achieved in only $(1 - \alpha) = 50\%$ of all cases. Generally, $\alpha_N = 50\%$ is assumed for a PPP project, which corresponds to the expected value of a normal distribution of the density function.
- *Stress load scenario (S)* represents a high risk load that exceeds the deterministic risk premium R_{Est} and is limited, e.g. by $VaR_\alpha = 80\%$ The 'stress load scenario' constitutes a probabilistic limitation of occurrence of $\alpha_S = 80\%$ and is exceeded in only $(1 - \alpha) = 20\%$ of all cases.
- *Crash load scenario (C)* represents an extremely high risk load that exceeds the deterministic risk premium R_{Est} and is limited, e.g. by $VaR_\alpha = 99\%$. The 'crash load scenario' constitutes a probabilistic limitation of occurrence of $\alpha_C = 99\%$ and is exceeded in only $(1 - \alpha) = 1\%$ of all cases.

The public and private partners are responsible for defining the boundaries of the interval ranges for normal, stress and crash risk loads; these can be defined during the bidding process based on the new EU award models:

- competitive dialogue;
- negotiation proceedings.

Both award models are based on the selective choice of bidders and negotiations between the client and the contractor in the award process. The two methods differ only in terms of the content of the negotiations.

The necessary risk coverage capacity can then be allocated, based on the risk load profile (Figure 11.20) for the respective residual duration of the concession $(t_i - t_{end})$ and the definition of the normal, stress and crash risk load intervals. This allocation of risk coverage capacity to the respective risk profile (risk load) at the respective point in time t_i up until the end point in time t_{end} of the concession enables the seamless configuration of the necessary risk coverage capacities at each and every point in time during the concession. The APR Model not only enables the definition of how much risk coverage is needed at any one point in time; it also shows whether the risk coverage is possible at all and, as such, whether the PPP Special Purpose Company has the capacity to sustain a mutually successful, long-term partnership.

A temporary shortage of risk coverage can, by all means, be tolerable and may even be necessary. Over the entire duration of the project, however, care must be taken to secure the availability of sufficient risk coverage capacity and to ensure that the anticipated profit and recovery of equity after fulfilment of all contractual obligations are guaranteed. The opportunities and threats associated with the generation of profit and recovery of equity therefore need to be evaluated.

11.3.5.2 Risk load theorem – Value at Risk

The APR model shows that neither the profit nor the equity of the private partner are affected as long as the risks occurring over the duration of the PPP are equal to or smaller than the deterministic risk premium. The profit and/or equity of the private partner are only jeopardized at the risk of the public partner if the risk occurrences cause higher risk costs. To this end an opportunities–threats calculus has been developed for financial application, known as the 'return on risk adjusted capital' (*RoRaC*).

$$RoRaC = \frac{Net\ result}{Risk\ capital} \tag{32}$$

This evaluation parameter can assess the opportunities and threats in order to secure the anticipated profit and the recovery of the equity. Value at Risk is, moreover, used for the risk capital that corresponds to the risk coverage capacity. Since the deterministic risk premium is already earmarked for covering the expected risks, the risk capital is reflected only by the profit and equity.

$$RoRaC = \frac{Net\ result}{Risk\ coverage\ capacity\ (RCC)} \tag{33}$$

The following must apply:

$$VaR \leq RCC \tag{34}$$

Then the $RoRaC$ can be expressed as follows:

$$RoRaC \leq \frac{Net\,result}{Value\,at\,Risk} \tag{35}$$

The 'net result' equals the 'net income' of the SPC, which corresponds to revenues consolidated with:

- operating expenses and income;
- financial expenses and income;
- extraordinary expenses and income;
- as well as taxes.

The same time horizon in numerator and denominator should be applied when calculating the $RoRaC$.

According to the APR Model (Figure 11.20), the VaR is the amount of risk costs that exceeds the deterministic risk premium and reduces the profit or even the equity. As such, the following must apply for the Value at Risk in this APR Model:

$$VaR_t = R_{a,(t_i - t_{end})} - R_{Est,a,(t_i - t_{end})} \tag{36}$$

Pursuant to the definition of the risk classes, the following VaR results for each risk load level:

- Normal load scenario ($\alpha_{N,min} \cdot 50\%$; $\alpha_{N,max} = 60\%$)

$$VaR_{N,a,t_i} = R_{N,\alpha \leq 50-60\%,(t_i - t_{end})} - R_{Est,a,(t_i - t_{end})} \text{ where } VaR_N \geq 0$$

- Stress load scenario ($\alpha_{S,min} = 60\%$; $\alpha_{S,max} = 80\%$)

$$VaR_{S,a,t_i} = R_{N,\alpha \leq 80\%,(t_i - t_{end})} - R_{Est,a,(t_i - t_{end})} \text{ where } VaR_S \geq 0$$

- Crash load scenario ($\alpha_{C,min} = 80\%$; $\alpha_{C,max} = 99\%$)

$$VaR_{C,a,t_i} = R_{C,\alpha \leq 99\%,(t_i - t_{end})} - R_{Est,a,(t_i - t_{end})} \text{ where } VaR_C \geq 0$$

The following limit analysis applies for the profit and/or loss range of a PPP project (see Figure 11.21):

$$PR_{Est,t_i} \text{ const.}$$

For the development of the scenarios $RoRaC = \dfrac{Net\,result}{Value\,at\,Risk}$ is assumed initially for the sake of simplicity.

Profit range:

$$VaR_{t_i} \leq 0$$

$$VaR_{t_i} = R_{a,(t_i - t_{end})} - R_{Est,a,(t_i - t_{end})} \leq 0$$

$$RoRaC_{t_i} = \frac{PR_{Est,t_i}}{VaR_{t_i}} \leq 0$$

$$PR_{\alpha,t_i} = PR_{Est,t_i} - \underbrace{(R_{\alpha,(t_i-t_{end})} - R_{Est,\alpha,(t_i-t_{end})})}_{\leq 0} \geq PR_{Est,t_i}$$

$$VaR_{t_i} = 0$$

$$VaR_{t_i} = R_{\alpha,(t_i-t_{end})} - R_{Est,\alpha,(t_i-t_{end})} = 0$$

$$RoRaC_{t_i} = \frac{PR_{Est,t_i}}{\lim VaR_{t_i} \to 0} = +\infty$$

$$PR_{\alpha,t_i} = PR_{Est,t_i} - VaR_{t_i} = PR_{Est,t_i}$$

$$VaR_{t_i} = PR_{Est,t_i}$$

$$VaR_{t_i} = R_{\alpha,(t_i-t_{end})} - R_{Est,\alpha,(t_i-t_{end})} = PR_{Est,t_i}$$

$$RoRaC_{t_i} = \frac{PR_{Est,t_i}}{PR_{Est,t_i}} = 1$$

$$PR_{\alpha,t_i} = PR_{Est,t_i} - VaR_{t_i} = 0$$

<u>Loss range:</u>

$$VaR \geq PR_{Est,t_i}$$

$$VaR_{t_i} = R_{\alpha,(t_i-t_{end})} - R_{Est,\alpha,(t_i-t_{end})} \geq PR_{Est,t_i} < EQ_{t_i}$$

$$RoRaC_{t_i} = \frac{PR_{Est,t_i}}{VaR_{t_i}} \leq 1$$

$$PR_{\alpha,t_i} = PR_{Est,t_i} - VaR_{t_i} < 0$$

Parts of the equity EQ_{t_i} are required for coverage now!

$$VaR \to EQ_{t_i}$$

$$VaR_{t_i} = R_{\alpha,(t_i-t_{end})} - R_{Est,\alpha,(t_i-t_{end})} >> PR_{Est,t_i}$$

$$RoRaC_{t_i} = \frac{PR_{Est,t_i}}{\lim VaR_{t_i} \to \infty} = 0$$

In this case the remaining equity EQ_{t_i} of the SPC is needed.

$$RoRaC_{t_i} = \frac{PR_{Est,t_i} + EQ_{t_i}}{VaR_{t_i}} \geq 1$$

$$VaR \rightarrow +\infty \Rightarrow RoRaC \rightarrow 0$$

This produces the following profit/loss ranges for the PPP project, respectively a PPP Special Purpose Company:

<u>Profit range:</u> $1 \leq RoRaC < +\infty$

<u>Loss range:</u> $0 \leq RoRaC < 1$

The $RoRaC_n$ is non-dimensional as a result of the relation indicated above. The higher the value, the better the use made of the resources used to cover the risks relative to the target profit of the PPP Special Purpose Company. If the value for the VaR approaches zero, e.g. no resources are used to cover risks, the $RoRaC_n$ is *infinitely large* (Figure 11.21). The PPP project

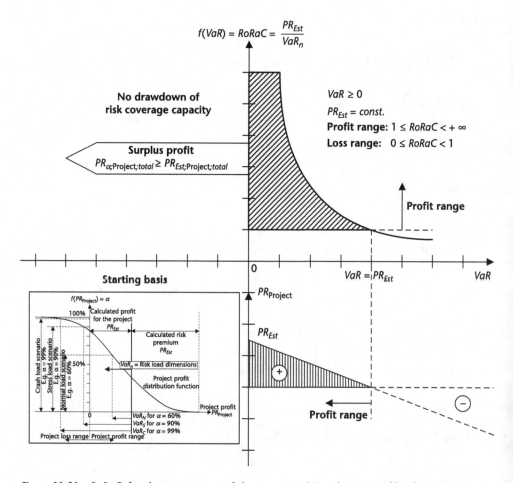

Figure 11.21 $\quad RoRaC_n$ for the assessment of the opportunities–threats profile of a PPP project

in the analysed scenario is profitable as long as the VaR is less than the estimated deterministic profit of the PPP project $PR_{Est,(t_i - t_{end})}$. The project in the analysed scenario will break-even if the VaR is equal to the estimated deterministic profit of the project $PR_{Est,(t_i - t_{end})}$. In this case, the $RoRaC_n$ equals 1.

If the $RoRaC_n$ is less than 1, the VaR is larger than the estimated deterministic profit of the project $PR_{Est,(t_i - t_{end})}$. In this load scenario, the project is therefore in the loss range. The same considerations apply to the equity that is used for the project. The target net result then contains the estimated deterministic profit PR_{Est,t_i} and the respective residual equity EQ_{t_i}.

11.3.6 Module 6 – Risk coverage dimension – evaluation of the risk coverage capacity of the Special Purpose Company

Module 6 serves to analyse the risk coverage capacity of the PPP project and/or the private partner's Special Purpose Company to cover the risk exposure levels of normal, stress and crash risk loads. The risk coverage capacity of the PPP project and/or Special Purpose Company is evaluated on the basis of the risk coverage concept for companies [Girmscheid (2007a); Girmscheid (2006)].

This risk coverage concept for Special Purpose Companies is derived from Basle II/III requirements. According to Gleissner and Füser (2003), company credit ratings must focus on two different areas: an evaluation of the financial capacity (quantitative evaluation criteria) and an evaluation of the sustainability (qualitative evaluation criteria) of a company, together with an evaluation of the risks and depreciation associated with the investment [Gleissner and Füser (2003); Standard & Poor's (2006)].

This work addresses only PPPs that are organized as Special Purpose Companies with equity paid in by the private partner. From an accounting perspective, these SPCs are 'stand-alone' organizations with limited equity and can therefore be viewed as separate enterprises. Hence, the same risk coverage dimensions as designed by Girmscheid and Busch (2008a) for companies can also be applied to PPP projects:

- financial dimension of PPP cash flow;
- asset dimension of PPP equity.

Accordingly, the creditworthiness of a PPP project or SPC (the risk coverage capacity of the private partner) can be evaluated at two different levels. Asset capacity is evaluated on the basis of the private partner's equity capital share in the PPP project, while the financial capacity of the SPC is assessed in terms of its ability to generate positive cash flow over the long term. The financial capacity and sustainability of the SPC are assessed at two levels in line with the different risks to be borne.

11.3.6.1 Normal and stress coverage capacity

Financial capacity and sustainability are measured in terms of the potential to generate cash flow surpluses. Normal coverage capacity is derived from the annual cash flow surplus and serves to cover the (minor) normal-load risks that occur constantly.

$$RCC^{Cov}_{Normal,t} = CF^{PPP}_{a,surp,t} = PR_{Est,surp,t} + R_{Est,t} \qquad (37)$$

Gerhard Girmscheid

where

$RCC^{Cov}_{Normal,t}$ Normal coverage capacity

$CF^{PPP}_{a,surp,t}$ Annual cash flow surplus generated by the PPP project

$PR_{Est,surp,t}$ Estimated surplus profit in year t

$R_{Est,t}$ Estimated risk premium in year t

a annual

Stress coverage capacity is derived from the cash flow surplus that has accumulated over several years and serves to cover stress-load risks (medium risks).

$$RCC^{Cov}_{Stress,(t_0-t_i)} = \sum_{t=t_0}^{t_i} \widetilde{CF}^{PPP}_{a,SP,t} = \sum_{t=t_0}^{t_i} (PR_{Est,surp,t} + R_{Est,t}) \tag{38}$$

where

$RCC^{Cov}_{Stress,(t_0-t_i)}$ Stress coverage capacity;

$\sum_{t=t_0}^{t_i} \widetilde{CF}^{PPP}_{a,SP,t}$ Cash flow surplus accumulated by the PPP project from t_0 to t_i

11.3.6.2 Crash coverage capacity

Asset stability is assessed on the basis of the equity capital capacity of the Special Purpose Company. This share in equity is used to financially hedge against risks that cannot be covered from the accumulated cash flow surplus. The cash flow surplus increases consistently from year 1 to year n. Major risks are not assumed to occur to any great extent until the contract is well under way, for example as a result of an aging infrastructure.

Crash coverage capacity is derived from the SPC's equity capital in the project and from the accumulated surplus cash flow, and serves to cover crash-load risks (major risks).

$$RCC^{Cov}_{Crash,(t_0-t_i)} = \widetilde{EQ}^{SPC}_{t_i} + \sum_{t-t_i}^{t_{end}} \widetilde{CF}^{PPP}_{a,SP,t} \tag{39}$$

where

$RCC^{Cov}_{Crash,(t_0-t_i)}$ Crash coverage capacity

$\widetilde{EQ}^{SPC}_{t_i}$ Equity capital of the SPC

Generally, the liquidation of equity capital is possible to a limited extent only. This can be utilized, e.g. when the private partner ceases to act as operator and withdraws from the project.

In order to secure the instrument of risk coverage for the various scenarios, care must be taken to ensure contractual agreement that the private partner's equity capital, the risk premium and the profit surplus may not be withdrawn prematurely and unmonitored from the project. Thus, parts of the annual cash flow surplus should be accumulated on a shared blocked account to enable coverage of risk costs, especially at stress level (larger operational risks). The remaining blocked cash flow earns interest and will be available for the SPC at the end of the concession period.

11.3.6.3 Estimation of the risk coverage capacity

The risk coverage capacity in a PPP project is composed of the following components:

- Deterministic risk coverage that is reflected in the price $R_{Est,\alpha}$
- Surplus profit $PR_{Est,surp,t}$ (possibly also minimum profit)
- Equity brought into the project by the private partner EQ_t.

The risk coverage capacity changes dynamically in line with the risk load over the term.

The necessary structural elements for arriving at this concept for the formation of risk coverage capacity are as follows:

- The estimation of the annual costs of a PPP and the total cost over the concession period are developed, together with the chosen estimated deterministic risk and profit premiums. The estimation summary produces the life cycle-oriented price.
- The development of risk coverage capacity is then broken down into financial elements of cash flow and those of the equity shares.

Financial elements that impact cash flow
The financial risk coverage capacity consisting of cash flow is derived from the estimated prospective cost of the PPP. The financial risk coverage is related to the following annual cost shown in Figure 11.22:

- annuity evolution of borrowed capital and equity;
- annual operating costs for cleaning, heating, etc.;
- annual costs for inspection, maintenance and minor repairs;
- non-periodic repair and renewal of systems and components.

together with their total evolution (Figure 11.23).

Based on these cost estimations the profit premium is deterministically chosen, as well as the risk premium, which is, however, related to risks associated with the contract obligations.

The deterministic risk premiums for the risks (Figure 11.24) are determined and considered once for the construction of the system and continually (linearly) for the operation, together with the costs of future repair and renewal (non-periodic individual risks). In addition, the chosen estimated deterministic profit premiums (Figure 11.24) are determined as a premium margin related to all estimated costs and are considered for the construction, operation and repairs over the concession period. The estimated cumulative total of the deterministic risk and profit premiums provides the base potential of the financial risk coverage capacity of cash flow (Figure 11.24; bottom). The pricing for the concession over its duration is shown in Figure 11.25. The price is comprised of the estimated cost elements as already discussed and the chosen estimated deterministic risk and profit premium. The deterministic risk premium generally only considers the expected risk value with a probability of occurrence of $\alpha = 50 - 60\%$.

Financial elements that affect assets
Generally, 20 to 50 per cent equity must be provided for a PPP project in order to debt finance the remaining investment requirement (50 to 80 per cent). The sustainability analysis developed here shows very clearly that the share of equity provided by the private partner to such a long-term PPP project acts as a stabilizing element. This stabilizing partnership element

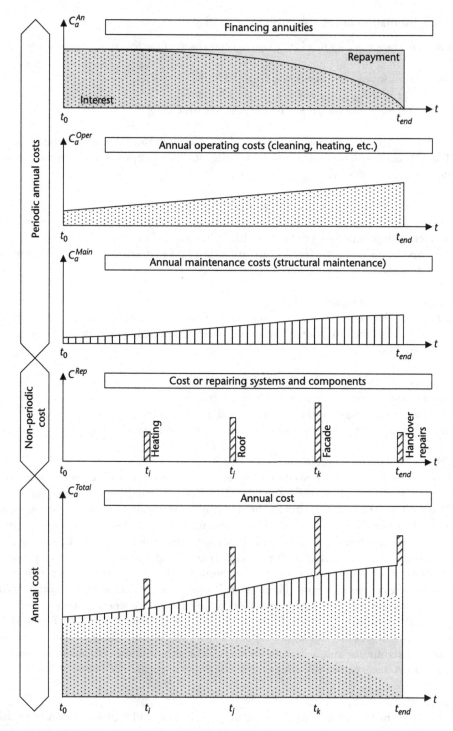

Figure 11.22 Estimation of the annual costs of a PPP

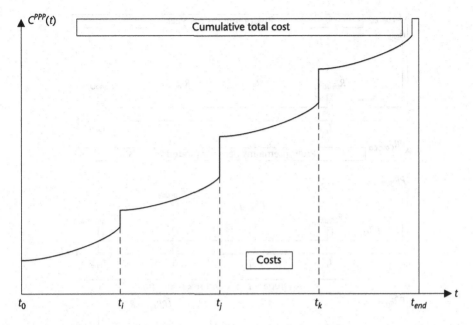

Figure 11.23 Estimation of the PPP project costs – cumulative total cost

secures the long-term entrepreneurial interest of the private partner while at the same time serving as a crucial means of protecting the public partner against crash risks.

All PPP concepts that allow the early withdrawal of equity and debt financing by the private partner, e.g. forfaiting, enable opportunistic behaviour on the part of the private partner in the absence of a strategic element of security. These PPP concepts, which are rewarded by seemingly lower risk premiums levied for the debt financing, provide scope for opportunistic behaviour on the part of the private partner through:

- earning over-weighted profits during the construction at the expense of the operating phase;
- withdrawal of the private partner during the operating phase with no possibility of restrictions through public authorities to hinder such an exit.

If forfaiting loans are agreed for a PPP project, the public partner must insist that the private partner invests equity that can only be redeemed annually as an annuity through the PPP fee. Figure 11.26 shows the evolution of the substantial real estate and asset values. A market value analysis has not been performed, given that the utilization is usually specific.

Operation of a property or system results in wearout of the same which causes the asset to depreciate in value. System components, systems (e.g. HVAC) or structural modules, such as roofs or façades, have to be repaired or renewed at certain intervals (Figure 11.26). Figure 11.26 also shows the evolution of the private partner's equity that is tied up in the project. The borrowed capital is not shown.

Two alternative amortization approaches are shown in Figure 11.26 in respect of the evolution of the tied-up equity:

- Amortization with annual fixed annuities and progressive repayment (declining curve, see Figure 11.8).

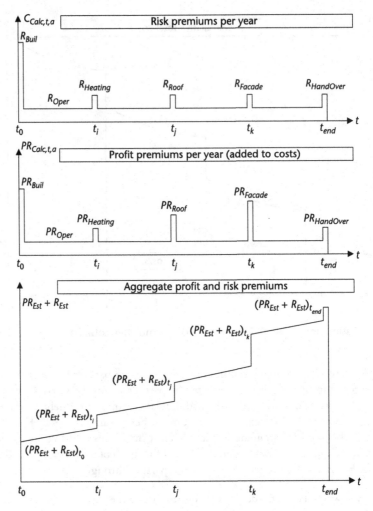

Figure 11.24 Estimation of the PPP project cost supplements – profit and risk premium as potential normal and stress risk coverage

- Amortization with annual variable annuities and fixed annual repayment (linear curve, see Figure 11.9).

Tying up this capital over the duration of a PPP project serves as protection against crash risks, e.g. withdrawal or bankruptcy of the private partner during the concession period to protect the public partner.

Risk coverage capacity
The risk coverage capacity can be identified on the basis of the analysis of cash flow and equity development during the concession period. The risk coverage capacity (RCC) can therefore be summarized (Figure 11.27) as:

- Short-term RCC: Estimated deterministic profit and risk premium.
- Long-term RCC: Tied-up equity of the private partner.

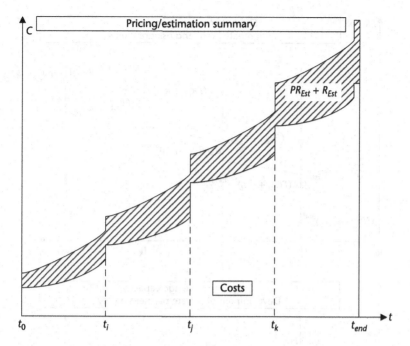

Figure 11.25 Pricing/PPP estimation summary

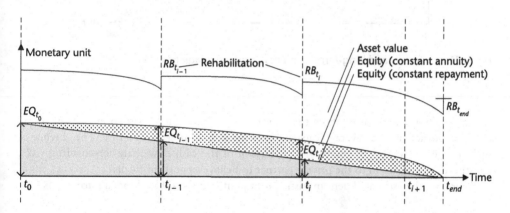

Figure 11.26 Asset value and equity development as potential risk coverage

The total risk coverage capacity comprising the short-term and long-term elements is shown in Figure 11.28. The overall analysis shows that the equity is tied up and can only be withdrawn by the private partner through ongoing annuity payments.

By contrast, the private partner can withdraw the short-term risk coverage from the PPP Special Purpose Company on an ongoing basis since it is included in the cash flow of the PPP fee. This would possibly result in insufficient risk reserves over the short term to cover minor and moderate risks. In the absence of any contractual hurdles, the private partner could even withdraw the unutilized and/or accumulated deterministic risk premium for covering risks that occur at a later date as profit from the company.

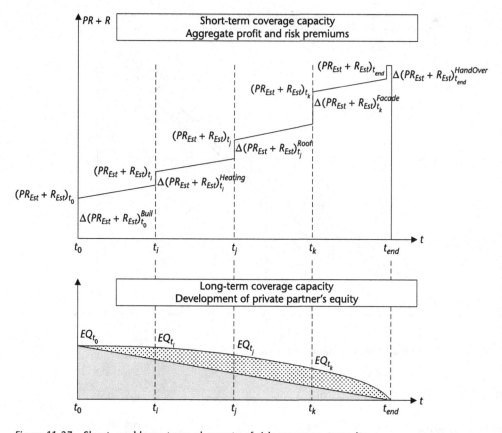

Figure 11.27 Short- and long-term elements of risk coverage capacity

These potential scenarios show that contractual hurdles must exist to ensure the availability of sufficient risk coverage capacity over the entire duration of a PPP. The absence of such hurdles in respect of equity and protection of the cash flow share for covering risks, constitutes an invitation to the private partner to behave opportunistically.

Therefore the estimated deterministic profit premium should be divided into:

- Minimum profit – earned directly.
- Surplus profit – secured for normal and stress risk coverage.

The estimated deterministic profit premium can consequently be expressed as follows:

$$PR_{Est,t} = PR_{Est,min,t} + PR_{Est,surp,t} \tag{40}$$

As such, the following hurdles (Figure 11.28) should be established to protect the financial and asset stability against the potentially occurring risks in a PPP:

- Contractually define a minimum share of equity with successive repayment in annuity form.

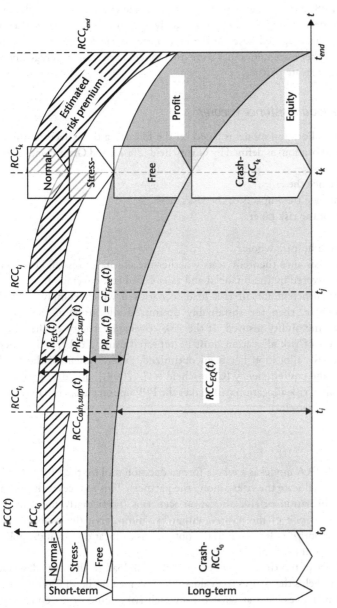

Legend:

$RCC_{EQ}(t)$ = Private partner's equity in the project
$PR_{Est,min}(t) = CF_{Free}(t)$ = Minimum profit that the private partner can utilize freely
$RCC_{Cash,surp}(t)$ = Surplus profit and estimated risk premium is securely booked to a joint account $(PR_{Est,surp}(t) + R_{Est}(t))$
$R_{Est}(t)$ = Surplus profit
$PR_{Est,surp}(t)$ = Estimated risk premium

Figure 11.28 Total risk coverage capacity

- Form cash flow reserves from the unutilized deterministic risk premium $R_{Est,t}$ and any surplus profit $PR_{Est,surp,t}$ (Figure 11.28). These reserves should be paid into a separate account of the PPP Special Purpose Company. Withdrawal of the reserves must adhere to contractually agreed conditions and must be signed by both partners.

This safety net (Figure 11.28) ensures that sufficient risk coverage capacity is available up to the end of the concession period, and for the contractually agreed return of the real estate and/or system in a contractually agreed state. At the end of the concession period, all of the accumulated financial and other asset values that were used to secure the risk coverage but not utilized are returned to the private partner.

11.3.7 Module 7 – Risk load resistance theorem

The multi-dimensional risk allocation model is based on the following three decision dimensions (base variables of risk allocation) as defined by Girmscheid (2007a) and Girmscheid (2006):

- players' ability to influence the risks;
- players' ability to minimize the impacts of the risks; and
- risk coverage capacity of the risk taker.

which combines them into a holistic whole.

This module 'risk load resistance theorem' tests whether the normal, stress and crash risk loads are capable of being covered by the financial and asset-based risk coverage funds.

If the risk coverage is sufficient for all risk load scenarios δ which comply with the economic minimum principle, then the sustainably optimized allocation of the risks is complete and the risk-bearing ability assured. If the risk coverage capacity of the SPC is lower, however, the process of risk allocation must be repeated using a cybernetic process (Figure 11.29). Once the risk allocation has been optimized, an assessment of the Public Sector Comparator (PSC) and cost efficiency [Girmscheid et al. (2008)] should be performed to assess whether the 'possible' risk allocation still makes the PPP option cheaper than the task fulfilment by the public sector itself.

11.4 Conclusion

The first two modules of the RA model as a whole form a decision tool for the PPP parties to systematically and rationally allocate the risks among the partners. This reduces intuitive and habitual behaviour. The formation of risk allocation scenarios (particularly for risks that cannot be assigned clearly to one of the parties, either by minimizing the probability of occurrence or the impact or both) leads to an initially optimal risk allocation through application of the economic minimum principle.

Module 3 adds the aspect of the time dependency of the risk load to the steps described above. The time assessment helps the parties to evaluate the risk load of the PPP project over the concession period. This makes clear at what time which risks could occur considering likewise the amount of risk load and the corresponding probabilistic distribution at that point of time. Module 4 shows the aggregation of risk load with Monte Carlo Simulation.

On the one hand, modules 5 and 6 allow the private partner to calculate its risk and profit premium to ensure a real minimum coverage of the risk loads. On the other hand, the public authorities are able to check what part of the profit and what part of the risk premium

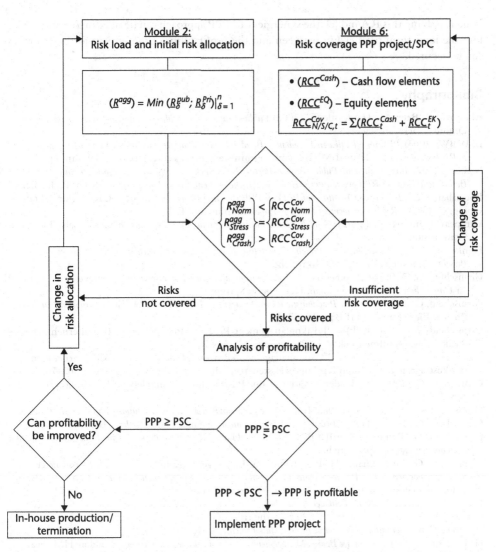

Figure 11.29 Risk load resistance theorem – testing the risk-bearing capacity of the SPC

needs to be secured on a blocked account over the concession period. This ensures that the appropriate real reserves are available to cover probabilistic risks that materialize over the concession period. Furthermore a blocked reserve fund needs to be established for repairs and renewal.

Module 7, last, reviews the initial optimal risk allocation by checking whether the available risk coverage (consisting of the estimated risk premium, the cash flow surplus and the time dependent equity share) exceeds the risk loads over the time of the concession period.

By using this RA model, the PPP parties are able to identify and assess the risks, as well as to process a systematic optimal allocation of those risks. The parties are supported objectively:

- to assess a target risk allocation;
- to formulate proposals for the other parties based on a transparent optimization process; and
- to assess the SPC regarding its risk coverage capacity.

When applying this RA model, the synergies of a PPP approach can be maximized and therefore the long-term partnership between and the profitability of the project for both parties can be secured.

Bibliography

Akintoye, A., Beck, M., Hardcastle, C. (2003) *Public–Private Partnerships – Managing risks and opportunities*, Oxford: Blackwell Science.

BMVBW (2003) *PPP im öffentlichen Hochbau – Band III: Wirtschaftlichkeitsuntersuchung, Arbeitspapier Nr. 5: Risikomanagement*, Berlin: BMVBW (Bundesministerium für Verkehr, Bau- und Wohnungswesen).

Boll, P. (2007) *Investitionen in Public–Private-Partnership-Projekte im öffentlichen Hochbau unter besonderer Berücksichtigung der Risikoverteilung – Eine theoretische und empirische Untersuchung*, Köln: R. Müller.

Boussabaine, A. (2007) *Cost Planning of PFI and PPP Building Projects*, Abingdon, UK: Taylor & Francis.

Elbing, C. (2006) *Risikomanagement für PPP-Projekte*, Lohmann: Eul.

European-Commission (2002) *Guidelines for successful Public–Private-Partnerships*, Brussels: European Commission.

Franke, A. (1991) *Risikobewusstes Projekt-Controlling Risikoanalyse und Risikobewertung als Aufgaben des Projekt-Controllings*, Bremen, 5 Mikrofiches.

Girmscheid, G. (2006) *Strategisches Bauunternehmensmanagement – Prozessorientiertes integriertes Management für Unternehmen in der Bauwirtschaft*, Heidelberg: Springer.

Girmscheid, G. (2007a) *Holistic Probabilistic Risk Management Process Model for Project-Oriented Enterprises*, Zürich: Eigenverlag des IBB an der ETH.

Girmscheid, G. (2007b) 'Risikomanagement-Prozess-Modell für Bauunternehmen – Risikobelastungsdimensionen', in *Bauingenieur*, 82, 53–61.

Girmscheid, G. (2007c) 'Risikomanagement-Prozess-Modell für Bauunternehmen – Risikostragfähigkeits – und Risikoprozesssteuerungsdimension', in *Bauingenieur*, 82, 62–70.

Girmscheid, G. (2009) 'Risikoidentifikations – und Risikoallokationsmodell', in *Bauingenieur*, 12-2009, p. 505–12.

Girmscheid, G., Busch, T. A. (2008a) *Unternehmensrisikomanagement in der Bauwirtschaft*, Berlin: Bauwerk.

Girmscheid, G., Busch, T. A. (2008b) *Projektrisikomanagement in der Bauwirtschaft*, Berlin: Bauwerk.

Girmscheid, G., Pohle, T. (2010) *PPP – Stand der Praxis: Risikoidentifizierung im Strassenunterhalt und Risikoverteilungskonzept*, Zurich,

Girmscheid, G., Lindenmann, H.-P., Schiffmann, F., Dreyer, J. (2008) *Kommunale Strassennetze in der Schweiz: Formen neuer Public Private Partnership (PPP) – Kooperationen für den Unterhalt*, [Bern]: Eidgenössisches Departement für Umwelt, Verkehr, Energie und Kommunikation UVEK.

Gleissner, W., Füser, K. (2003) *Leitfaden Rating Basel II: Rating-Strategien für den Mittelstand*, München: Vahlen.

Grimsey, D., Lewis, M.K. (2002) 'Evaluating the risks of public private partnerships for infrastructure projects', in *International Journal of Project Management*, 20, 107–18.

HM Treasury (2004) *The Orange Book – Management of Risk – Principles and Concepts*, London: HM Treasury.

Jacob, D., Kochendörfer, B. (2002) *Effizienzgewinne bei privatwirtschaftlicher Realisierung von Infrastrukturvorhaben*, Köln: Bundesanzeiger

Merna, A., Lamb, D. (2003) *Project Finance: The Guide to Value and Risk Management in PPP Projects*, Oxford: Euromoney Books.

Partnerships Victoria (2001) *Partnerships Victoria Guidance Material: Risk Allocation and Contractual Issues: A Guide*, Victoria, Australia: DTF.

PPP Task Force NRW (2007) *Public Private Partnership im Hochbau – Anleitung zur Prüfung der Wirtschaftlichkeitsuntersuchung von PPP-Projekten im öffentlichen Hochbau*, Public Private Partnership-Inititative NRW (Federführung: Finanzministerium des Landes Nordrhein-Westfalen).

Racky, P.S.P. (2009) 'Empfehlungen für die vertragliche Allokation betriebsphasenspezifischer Risiken bei PPP-Projekten im Schulbau', in *Bauingenieur*, 12-2009, p. 513–21.

Schierenbeck, H. (2003) *Risiko-Controlling und integrierte Rendite-/Risikosteuerung*, Wiesbaden: Gabler.

Standard & Poor's (2006) *Corporate Ratings Criteria (2006)*, New York: The McGraw-Hill Companies.

Vose, D. (1996) *Quantitative risk analysis a guide to Monte Carlo simulation modelling*, Chichester: Wiley.

12

Public budget norms and PPP

An anomaly

Piet de Vries[*]

12.1 Introduction

Politicians have a good *prima facie* case for PPP. First, private involvement in public provision may bring in a drive for efficiency the public sector is not famous for; PPPs may produce value-for-money. Second, PPP entailing private finance may relieve public-budget stress. Obviously, the potential efficiency merit of PPPs is a conditional promise, requiring well-deliberated choices, e.g. concerning contractual design. It is in particular the private-finance opportunity of PPPs that immediately may reward politicians. In an investment-and-service-PPP project, private finance may replace public-budget investments. The very first candidates for PPPs are infrastructure projects requiring huge capital expenditures. PPP infrastructure projects enable politicians cutting the public budget to save substantial amounts of money, while simultaneously holding on to provisions the public sector is considered to be responsible for. Together with the potential value-for-money, PPPs seem to bring together the best of two worlds.

That sounds too good to be true. In particular the private-financing route may raise some doubt. Frequently, State guarantees accompany private finance arrangements in PPP enticing financiers to invest. Or, the public partner guarantees the services charges of a privately financed project. In many cases, the private-financing element in PPP might or definitely will bring about future public budget consequences. It has repercussions on the transparency of public sector's future budget position. Finally, the private-financing route of a PPP may impact a nation's fiscal sustainability.

Governments are well aware of the fiscal-sustainability risk PPPs may entail, and promote transparency of government activities and financial involvement. In particular, accounting rules and statistical rules for national accounts aim to safeguard the public-budget transparency. For instance the EU and the USA apply comparable classification standards to deal with private financing in a PPP context. Besides these PPP-tailored standards governments apply overall budget norms to safeguard fiscal sustainability, i.e. deficit and public-debt norms. The European Union serves as an example showing up an anomaly between specific PPP national accounting rules and general public-budget norms. The specific norms do not subsume under the general public-budget norms. It will be identified

301

that a basic difference in the demarcation of public-versus private produces the anomaly. This chapter will demonstrate that this norm irregularity may harm the transparency that a sound public finance practice so barely requires. A proposal to remedy the issue follows.

The chapter is organized as follows. Section 12.2 defines PPP and private financing. Transfer of risks features a PPP. In this respect, it is instructive to define the concept of funding and financing. Section 12.3 deals in some details with the risks investment-and-service projects entail. It gives a sample sheet of the budget risks of private financing the public partner might be exposed to. This risk excursion is required to see the potential public-budget implications of PPP. Section 12.4 presents the classification standards for private financing in a PPP context as developed by the United Nations System of National Accounts, and discusses national and international applications for statistical purposes. Section 12.5 presents the general public-budget norms as a concern with a nation's fiscal sustainability. Section 12.6 discusses the anomaly that the preceding sections highlight. It shows that the specific norms are detrimental to the transparency concerning fiscal sustainability. Finally this section presents a proposal to remedy the anomaly. Some conclusions follow.

12.2 Definition of PPP and private financing

Broadly defined, a PPP involves a contractual cooperation between public and private partners to realize jointly formulated goals for an investment-and-service project, with a well-specified risk division, to create value-for-money as added value to the taxpayer. The investment-and-service feature of a PPP sets it apart from outsourcing public services to the private sector. The private partner takes care of items such as design, build, finance, and operate. A PPP project is based on a long-term contract that requires specific private sector investment in assets straightforwardly related to the PPP. The contract specifies the investment-related services the public partner may expect. The lion's share of the investment-and-service projects involves infrastructure that the public sector traditionally assumes responsibility for. The assignment of this responsibility to the private sector results in a (partial) transfer of risks to the private partner. These risks may involve:

- design risks;
- construction risks;
- finance risks;
- demand or usage risks;
- availability risks;
- operation and maintenance risks.

The transfer of risks is seen as a central feature of PPPs. It fuels the private-sector drive for efficiency. 'Adequate transfer of risks from the government to the private sector is a key requirement if PPPs are to deliver high-quality and cost-effective services to consumers and the government' (IMF 2004: 3).

Regarding the transfer of risks, it is relevant to mention a frequently used infrastructure distinction:

- Economic infrastructure, i.e. the hard infrastructure that facilitates the daily economic activities. It involves power stations, sea- and airports, roads, waterways, railways, and

other networks for services such as telecommunication, water, electricity, and public transport.
- Social infrastructure, i.e. assets such as school buildings, public sector offices, prisons.

The project types correspond in their focus on final-output performance. It is the final output that counts for the public, for which the PPP makes the private partner assume responsibility. At the same time, the type distinction results in a difference in the relevance of the risks transfer. Demand risks profile the economic-infrastructure-PPP projects. Will the demand volume be sufficient to safeguard the profitability of the investment? The usage risk is the dominant economic-infrastructure risk issue. PPPs for social-infrastructure projects predominantly concern the availability of accommodation. For these accommodation-based PPPs the risks transfer is related in particular to this availability, and the accommodation-related service levels. Availability and service performance must guarantee the investment profitability, though it might be that the private partner is exposed to the demand risk; government paying per inmate, per day.

The public sector may involve a central government department, a regional or local government, or a public agency; in short a public authority. Usually, the private sector will found a special purpose vehicle, to set up a project company. The public authority and the project company form the contracting parties in a PPP.

Two basic arrangements dominate the PPP field:

- Concessions: the concession gives the project company (concessionaire) a licence to build and exploit the (infrastructure) facility, and (predominantly) users pay the project company for the services. Subsumed in this category is the franchise model in which the project company pays a lump sum for the right to exploit an infrastructure asset and to be reimbursed by toll payments.
- Project Agreements: the public authority pays the project company for availability, maintenance, cleaning, etc. or takes care of shadow-toll payments for the use of the service by the public. The British Private Finance Initiative (PFI) is an example of the Project Agreement arrangement.

Clearly, private financing is a main feature of both arrangement types. In this respect, it is fruitful to distinguish between financing and funding:

- Financing refers to the acquisition of loans, equity and hybrid capital titles to pay for a certain investment. It involves the liabilities side for all assets invested in at a certain point in time. The balance sheet reflects that position; it is a 'snapshot'.
- Funding involves the recovery of all costs incurred to provide a product during a certain period. It is reflected in the income statement. The user charges paid for the services constitute (part of) the funding. The income statement is a 'moving picture'.

The concession is represented by cell V, and the contract arrangement by cell IV in Table 12.1. These arrangements are in line with the basic PPP concept as a private-investment-and-service project. However, the PPP practice is too unruly to fit into these two cells. Besides the private versus public option of financing and funding, it frequently occurs that the financial features of the PPP result from a mixture of public and private involvement. Therefore, the 3-by-3-matrix of Table 12.1 gives a broad illustration of the PPP practice.

Table 12.1 Matrix of financing/funding possibilities

	Public funding	Private funding	Public/private funding
Public financing	I	II	III
Private financing	IV	V	VI
Public/private financing	VII	VIII	IX

The risk transfer discussion in section 12.3 will demonstrate the relevance of the financing-funding scheme.

To recap: PPP is an investment-and-service project undertaken by a (private) project company to provide services on behalf of the public authority. Private financing means private loans, equity and hybrid capital titles that serve as investment payment.

12.3 Transfer of risks

Usually the private sector will fund a special purpose vehicle (SPV) to set up a PPP-project company. The financing complement of the SPV is project finance, featuring SPV's risk management. Subsection 12.3.1 briefly presents the SPV and project finance. Subsection 12.3.2 discusses the risk issues of project finance, and the allocation of risks in the PPP context. Insight into the allocation of these risks precedes a good grasp of the public-budget implications of project finance. Subsection 12.3.3 gives an overview of State guarantee practices in PPPs, summarizing public finance's vulnerability to private financing in a PPP context.

12.3.1 Special purpose vehicle and project finance

The SPV is a financial ring fence around the investment-and-services project to separate it from any other business activities of the private partner(s). It forestalls financial contamination. Consequently, project finance is the natural answer to address the financing issue of a SPV. Asset-specificity features the capital expenditures in the investment-and-service PPPs. Investment projects in infrastructure, such as in energy, and natural resources require vast up-front capital expenditures that are useless if the project fails; the upfront investment concerns sunk cost, bygones. The sunk-cost feature of the assets renders these unfit for debt security. Accordingly, the leverage ratio is not suitable to assess lenders' safety in project finance. Therefore, the cash flow is lender's pledge in financing a SPV. The project's cash flow is the collateral for the lender. In project finance 'CADS' is the basic ratio, i.e. cash flow available for debt service. Financing and funding welded together are a main feature of project finance.

Another main and highly relevant feature of project finance is the high debt/equity ratio; debt financing varies from 70 up to 95 per cent of the capital expenditure (Yescombe 2002: 8). At the same time, the investors' financing is on a non-recourse base, no more than strictly limited guarantees for the project-finance debt. In a PPP-context the high leverage may limit the cost to the public authority; it will incentivize the project control of the debt lenders.

12.3.2 Risks and project finance

Project finance is beneficial to the investors. Its usually high leverage (debt/equity ratio) may offer the investors a superior return on equity, at the same time limiting their risk to the amount of the equity investment. Consequently, the debt lenders in a project-finance undertaking find themselves in a vulnerable position. There is no, or strictly limited, recourse to the financial potential of the investors. The project's cash flow must guarantee the debt service. However, risk and uncertainty surround cash flows. Since, at the financial close cash flow is a future item.

It is debt-lenders' dependency on the cash flow of the project that directs their attention to the project contracts. The project contracts consist of those between the project company (SPV) and the subcontractors for construction, operation, and maintenance of the facility. It is these contracts that originate the cash flow. They are the pivotal documents in a PPP as they arrange the risk transfers, e.g. in back-to-back agreements passing through potential claims to the subcontractors. Actually, these risks-transferring contracts form the security package for the debt lenders; key factors in project finance. The lenders demand an empty risk box; all risks allocated elsewhere. This bias in project-finance-risk allocation entails uncertain effects on the future budget of public authorities, violating public-budget transparency as shown below.

The SPV disposes of four general options for risk-allocation guarantees for debt lenders:

- risk retained by the public authority is relatively best guarantee;
- risk retained by the project company is relatively worst guarantee;
- reallocation to subcontractors requires additional checks-and-balances devices;
- risk transfer to end users depends on the relevant price elasticity of demand.

Discussing the risk allocation in an SPV, it is relevant to distinguish non-market from market risks.

- The non-market risks may be passed down to subcontractors. They comprise the techno-logical and environmental risks of construction and completion, operating and mainten-ance. The debt lenders will demand additional guarantees concerning the quality of these risk-passing-over devices. Mismatch of contracts between the project company and the subcontractors, and the incompetence of the subcontractors, will directly harm debtors' interests. Accordingly, it is relevant to assess the risks the construction subcontractor itself entails; their competence to undertake the work, their credit standing, and possible conflicts of interests. Concerning the fixed-price clause, a large-scale project is, in spite of the fixed-price condition, never 100 per cent fixed. Changes in project schedule, unfore-seen events and latent defects in 'brownfield' projects may unavoidably require price adjustments. These issues also may result in later completion. The completion risks may entail additional financial costs and deferred revenues, for which incomplete contracting offers opportunities to put in claims. Moreover, shared responsibility (between main- and subcontractors) frequently results in non-responsibility. The risks passed down to subcon-tractors, making the contractual relations intractably complex, may entail unforeseen outlays for the public authorities, violating the public-budget transparency.
- The concession model is exposed to market risks, i.e. demand risk. Long-term contracts that guarantee the future cash flow may convince debt lenders, e.g. future-debt securitiza-tions. In this respect, a secondary market of project loans may emerge, diversifying the risks of project financing. At the same time, public authorities' responsibility for a facility may result in public coverage against default risk, or a minimum-demand guarantee.
- In a project agreement in the PPP context, such as the British Private Finance Initiative (PFI), the public authority will retain the market risk. In particular, large infrastructure:

projects are exposed to such enormous demand risk that these can barely be borne by the project company or its subcontractors. Shadow-toll payments or revenue guarantees leave the public authority exposed to the market risks of usage.

The SPV and the inherent project finance involve instruments to limit private partners' risk exposure, and in particular to forestall default-risk contamination. The cash-flow is the basic collateral. As a future item this collateral requires additional security, i.e. from public authorities' side. The frequently used SPV in a PPP context has uncertain effects on future public budget.

12.3.3 State guarantees in PPPs

The European PPP Expertise Group (EPEC) distinguishes three types of State guarantee used in PPPs; i.e. finance guarantees, PPP contract provisions, and sub-sovereign creditworthiness guarantees (EPEC 2011: 13–17).

The finance guarantees may involve loan guarantees 'under which the Government guarantees the lenders' the debt service 'if the PPP company fails to do so' (EPEC 2011: 13). Another instrument in this respect involves the refinancing guarantee given by the government. The government repays the lenders if the PPP company fails in refinancing close to maturity.

The PPP contract provisions perform a wide variety of State guarantees, some already discussed in the preceding subsection. These guarantees are often granted through the PPP contract between the public and the private partners. Revenue or usage guarantees, and guaranteed minimum service charges limit the PPP-company's exposure to demand risk 'irrespective of the performance of the PPP company' (EPEC 2011: 15), the EPEC report adds. Here, public authorities' responsibility reemerges. Termination- and residual-value payments protect the PPP company against premature termination of the PPP contract. Standard arrangements provide government payments that 'reflect the value of the terminated contract or of assets handed back to the government' (EPEC 2011: 15).

Finally, the sub-sovereign creditworthiness guarantee makes the payment obligation of a sub-sovereign entity as secure as a central government obligation. ' "Letters of intent" or formal contractual commitments' of the central government back up sub-sovereign's obligations (EPEC 2011: 17).

It goes without saying that the value of all these State guarantees to entice potential private partners taking a financial stake in a PPP, finally depends on the creditworthiness of the State itself. At the same time, a lack of transparency concerning these guarantees is detrimental to this very same creditworthiness. Concerns about the public-finance transparency are at stake. For instance, Velloso (2008) reports that in a sample of 30 countries, only 60 per cent 'note their contingent liabilities in budget documentation presented to the Legislature' (Velloso 2008: 11). In this respect, it is important to realize that implicit contingent liabilities such as the contractual provisions discussed further complicate the transparency. In general it is the notion 'too important to fail', applicable to many of the PPP projects, that may cause unexpected public-budget outlays, i.e. implicit contingent liabilities. Accurate reporting is required to guarantee public-finance transparency.

12.4 National accounting and PPP

PPP mixes the public interest with private interests, bringing uncertainty about each partner's financial involvement in it. Does a privately financed road with free, public access belong to the private or to the public sector? Therefore, public-finance transparency about PPP begins with delineating the difference between the public and the private sector. Subsection 12.4.1 delineates private and public sector in a specific manner. In forms the basis for the statistical treatment and national accounting issues of PPP in subsequent subsections. Subsection 12.4.2 deals with the overall framework of the UN System of National Accounts. Subsection 12.4.3 presents the statistical treatment of PPP assets in the European Union context. Subsection 12.4.4 presents the IMF summary of the statistical treatment of PPP assets and liabilities.

12.4.1 What delineates the public sector?

Originally, consumption features governments. They levy taxes to pay for distributing goods and services free of charge, and redistribute income. The Sovereign and the Chancellor keep the books of receipts and expenses. Therefore, cash-based accounting is the natural public-accounting system, assisting the annual decision process of the government as an income-spending entity. At the same time, governments are producers of public provisions and utilities. In this respect, the government may be seen as a wealth-creating entity, a look-alike of the private enterprise. However, cash accounting is not equipped to address the investment peculiarities of government's production side. It sees the acquisition of investment goods as consumption, disregarding their long-term fruitful returns that may justify a long-term debt. Therefore, it is argued that accrual-based accounting is more appropriate than cash-based, offering the decision makers management information about assets and liabilities, and charges for cost of capital, depreciation and maintenance costs. Governments face a dilemma: cash or accrual accounting.

The widespread application of PPPs and the creation of public agencies since the 1980s deepened the cash-versus-accrual dilemma in two interrelated respects. First, the cash system treats private financing of public investments just as a partitioning of a non-recurrent expense over a row of fiscal years to come. It offers politicians the inviting avenue to present an austerity programme without decreasing provisions level. Consequently, this cosmetic fiscal advantage for politicians endorses the case for accrual-based accounting in the public sector. Sound public-finance reporting concerning the private financing element in PPP inevitably enforces government embracing accrual accounting or a kind of hybrid accounting disclosing information about assets and liabilities. For that matter, it is an international trend that governments adopt an accrual-based or a hybrid system (EPEC 2010: 5). Second, besides the application of PPPs, it is in particular the creation of autonomous public agencies since the 1980s that requires accrual-accounting as a control device for supervisory bodies and legislators (EPEC 2010: 6). It all reflects the impact of New Public Management that has profiled public management during past decades (Boston et al. 1996).

It is the basic perspective on government as a wealth-creating entity and its application in practice that result in assimilating public accounting to private-sector accounting, with assets and liabilities as pivotal constituents of wealth. Therefore, the inherent delineation route is ownership. Who owns which assets and/or liabilities in the PPP the reporting is about? In this perspective, there is no further basic difference between the public and the private partners. Consequently, it is ownership as substance, *economic* ownership that counts, not its legal counterpart. Two types of accounting criteria have been used to determine on whose balance sheet the assets and liabilities should be recognized.

- *Risks-and-rewards* criteria: 'The economic owner of an entity such as goods and services, natural resources, financial assets and liabilities is the institutional unit which is entitled to claim the benefits associated with the use of entity in the course of an economic activity by virtue of accepting the associated risks' (Harrison 2006: 2). The risks-and-rewards criteria stem from accounting standards for lease practices distinguishing operational from financial lease. A financial lease is 'one in which the lessee has substantially all the risks and rewards associated with the ownership of the asset, other than the legal title'. 'The transfer of risks and rewards are in substance acquisitions or sales' and therefore should as such be reflected in the balance sheet (Heald and Georgiou 2011: 222).

- *Control* as criterion originates from financial accounting issues concerning consolidated statements. What should be the percentage of investee's shares in a company to be included in the consolidated balance sheet (Heald and Georgiou 2011: 222)?

For that matter, the ownership criteria are interrelated. For instance, without control the risks-and-rewards criteria have no substance. Both approaches find application as laid out below.

The PPP-accounting issue may refer to two types of accounting purposes. First, PPP as an issue for financial accounting based on international, generally accepted accounting principles (GAAP) measuring financial performance of individual entities. It involves reporting at a micro level, e.g. classifying the PPP-project assets as public or private. Second, the PPP-accounting issue refers to national accounting, i.e. the statistical treatment of PPP activities profiled by macroeconomic considerations concerning fiscal sustainability, frequently used in an international perspective for comparative analysis. For instance, should a PPP liability be classified as private, or added to public-budget debt? At issue is the transparency of public-finance effects of PPP, directing the attention to the national-accounts perspective on PPP that will be elaborated here.

12.4.2 UN System of National Accounts (SNA)

The overall statistical framework for national accounts is the UN System of National Accounts, 2008 (SNA 2008). It is applicable worldwide, released under the auspices of the United Nations, the European Commission, the Organisation for Economic Co-operation and Development, the International Monetary Fund and the World Bank Group. The SNA 2008 represents an update of the System of National Accounts 1993. One update concerns PPP. SNA 2008 mentions: 'The *1993 SNA* did not give guidance on the treatment of public-private partnerships' (SNA 2008: 653).

Unchanged in the SNA 2008 version is the application of the risks-and-rewards criteria. SNA 1993 treatment of financial lease shows adherence to classifying by risks and rewards.

> Financial leases may be distinguished by the fact that all the risks and rewards of ownership are, de facto, transferred from the legal owner of the good, the lessor, to the user of the good, the lessee. In order to capture the economic reality of such arrangements, a change of ownership from the lessor to the lessee is deemed to take place, even though legally the leased good remains the property of the lessor, at least until the termination of the lease when the legal ownership is usually transferred to the lessee.
>
> (SNA 1993: 171)

For that matter, financial lease is the counterpart of operational lease. In operational lease the legal owner retains the risks and rewards of the asset. It is comparable to rent.

The SNA 2008 guideline for PPP assets is founded on the considerations applied earlier to financial lease; risks-and-rewards criteria classify the PPP assets.

> As with leases, the economic owner of the assets related to a PPP is determined by assessing which unit bears the majority of the risks and which unit is expected to receive a majority of the rewards of the assets. The factors that need to be considered in making this assessment can be broadly divided into two groups, those associated with acquiring the asset and those associated with using it in production.
>
> Some of the risks associated with acquiring the asset are:
>
> a The degree to which the government controls the design, quality, size and maintenance of the assets;
> b Construction risk, which includes the possibility of additional costs resulting from late delivery, not meeting specifications or building codes and environmental and other risks requiring payments to third parties.
>
> Some of the risks associated with using the asset in production are:
>
> a Supply risk, which covers the degree to which the government is able to control the services produced, the units to which the services are provided and the prices of the services produced;
> b Demand risk, which includes the possibility that the demand for the services, either from government or from the public at large in the case of a paying service is higher or lower than expected;
> c Residual value and obsolescence risk, which includes the risk that the value of the asset will differ from any price agreed for the transfer of the asset to government at the end of the contract period;
> d Availability risk, which includes the possibility of additional costs or the incurrence of penalties because the volume and/or quality of the services do not meet the standards specified in the contract.
>
> (SNA 2008: 452–3)

The detailed enumeration of the potential risks does not forestall some arbitrariness in a classification. The long-term nature of the PPP transaction(s) entails that only in the long run do the PPP provisions reveal their true economic character. The SNA 2008 gives an example:

> the assets typically have service lives much longer than the contract period so that the government will control the assets, bear the risks and receive the rewards for a major portion of the assets' service lives. Thus, it is frequently not obvious whether the private enterprise or the government controls the assets over their service lives or will bear the majority of the risks and reap the majority of the rewards.
>
> SNA 2008: 452)

Moreover, implicit government guarantees, e.g. for infrastructure facilities 'too important to fail', raise further vagueness about the risk allocation, as presented above.

Obviously, the risks-and-rewards criteria allow several interpretations, underlining that the classification of the assets and liabilities inevitably is a partly arbitrary affair.

Piet de Vries

12.4.3 National accounting in EU and PPP assets

As mentioned, the European Commission is one of the participating organizations in the SNA project. SNA constitutes the framework for the 'European system of national and regional accounts' (ESA95). ESA95 'collects comparable, up-to-date and reliable information on the structure and developments of the economy of the Member States of the European Union', required for comparative analysis of the national accounts of the EU-member states (Eurostat 2010a). ESA safeguards within the EU the uniform statistical treatment of macro-economic figures.[1]

Understandably, the European statistical treatment of PPP accounting is the risks-and-rewards approach, in line with the SNA framework. At the same time, its application is restricted, in sharp contrast with the elaborated SNA 2008 treatment quoted. The decision tree opposite presents the treatment of PPP in national accounting by the Statistical Office of the European Communities, Eurostat.

A Eurostat news release summarizes its classification policy concerning PPP assets as follows:

> Eurostat recommends that the assets involved in a public–private partnership should be classified as non-government assets, and therefore recorded off balance sheet for government, if both of the following conditions are met:
>
> 1 the private partner bears the construction risk, and
> 2 the private partner bears at least one of either availability or demand risk.
>
> (Eurostat 2004a: 1)

'In some cases', Eurostat adds in the news release:

> the risk analysis, as mentioned above, might not give clear conclusions (for instance if at least for two categories the share in risk may be estimated as balanced or based on very fragile hypotheses). In these cases, some additional elements in a partnership contract should also be taken into consideration. Apart from an analysis of the nature of the partners (notably in specific cases where the partner is a public corporation), the importance of government financing, the effect of government guarantees or provisions relating to the final allocation of the assets could be in some cases appropriate supplementary criteria.
>
> (Eurostat 2004a: 2)

The Eurostat 'Manual on Government Deficit and Debt' justifies the restrictive application of the risks-and-rewards criteria as follows. The PPP reality learned is that the partners share risks. Normally some risks, such as for very exceptional events, are taken by the government. Therefore, according to the Manual, the classification issue concern the analysis of the risk allocation between the contractual parties; transfer of "all risks" is an inappropriate test (Eurostat 2010: 257). The Manual underlines that this risk analysis is a rather complicated affair. It is quite normal that within a risk category the parties are sharing the risk. *Therefore, the analysis of the risks borne by each party must assess which party is bearing the majority of the risk in each of the categories mentioned above* (Eurostat 2010: 257).

It may be inferred from these Eurostat quotes that risk criteria to classify the PPP assets offer various interpretation options. It induces Akitoby *et al.* to conclude that 'the Eurostat decision [classifying PPP assets] creates moral hazard, making it more likely that PPPs will be designed to meet a minimum standard of risk transfer than an optimal level' (Akitoby *et al.* 2007: 14). Support to this conclusion is given by the complicated risk-(re)allocation practices

310

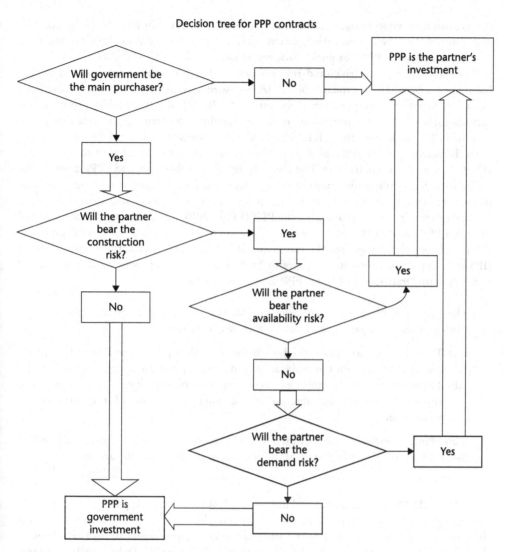

Figure 12.1 Eurostat decision tree

Source: European Commission (EC 2004: 26)

of an SPV. Main contractors may pass on risks to a number of subcontractors, as discussed in subsection 3.2, causing an opaque web of responsibilities and diffusely reallocated risks. Furthermore, explicit and implicit State guarantees will obscure the perspective on the risk allocation. In reality the risk analysis Eurostat proposes will change the asset classification in a *tour de force* with inevitably arbitrary outcome. Finally, it is plausible that the option to leave out demand risk will cause a bias in the risk allocation. The private sector is the right partner to bear the construction and availability risks, well-equipped to control these. For that matter, the transfer of construction and availability risks of technologically finalized projects, such as roads, hardly involves a risks exposure for the private partner. On the contrary, the demand risks in particular of infrastructure facilities (deter) private investors. In many cases it would be irresponsible for the private partner to accept the demand risks, unless the government grants guarantees concerning, e.g., minimum revenue level (Akitoby *et al.* 2007: 14). Akitoby *et al.* conclude that the Eurostat classification criteria may 'disguise the medium-to-long-term implications of many PPPs for public finances' (Akitoby *et al.* 2007: 14).

The alternative to the risks-and-rewards criteria is the control criterion. In 2006 the International Accounting Standards Board (IASB) issued 'Interpretation 12' of its International Financial Reporting Interpretation Committee (IFRIC 12). IFRIC provides private-sector entities guidance on the reporting of assets and liabilities concerning a service concession agreement (SCA). In part, the IFRIC 12 refers to the classification issue of PPP assets; i.e. as far as the private partner in the SCA does not directly charge the public as third party users. IFRIC 12 applies the control test. The test is straightforwardly relevant to PPPs in which the public partner controls or determines: 1) the asset-related services that the non-government partner provides, to whom it must provide them, and at what price; and 2) any significant residual interest in the assets at end of the PPP (EPEC 2010: 22). A private partner involved in such a PPP contract should not recognize the assets on its balance sheet. As a result, the IFRIC 12 control test triggered the International Public Sector Accounting Standard Board (IPSASB) to publish a consultation paper in 2008. The most recent application of the control test, Exposure Draft 43 (ED 43), for PPP assets is worded as follows:

> The grantor shall recognize an asset provided by the operator and an upgrade to an existing asset of the grantor as a service concession asset if:
>
> 9(a) The grantor controls or regulates what services the operator must provide with the asset, to whom it must provide them, and at what price; and
>
> (b) The grantor controls—through ownership, beneficial entitlement or otherwise— any significant residual interest in the asset at the end of the term of the arrangement.
>
> This Standard applies to an asset used in a service concession arrangement for its entire useful life (a 'whole-of-life' asset) if the conditions in paragraph 9(a) are met.
>
> (IPSAS 32: 2011: 7)

The IPSAS ED 43 accounting standard mirrors the IFRIC 12 rules. Application of the ED 43 makes PPP considerably more restrictive as an off-public-budget practice than the Eurostat risks-and-rewards criteria. The British Office of Budget Responsibility (OBR) calculates for the UK an increase of 2.5 per cent (of GDP) of the Public Sector Net Debt (PSND) in March 2011 due to the transition from risks-and-rewards to control classification test (OBR 2011: 42). For the EU, EPEC rightly expects that the control approach would generate substantial 'over-reporting' for Eurostat purposes (EPEC 2010: 25). In this respect, since 2009 the UK has applied a double reporting; IPSAS ED 43 (control) principles for public sector accounting purposes, and a risks-and-rewards test for statistical purposes based on ESA 95 (Heald and Georgiou 2011: 242).

12.4.4 The IMF summary

The 'IMF Monetary and Financial Statistics; A Compilation Guide 2008' words the statistical-treatment issue of PPP assets and liabilities as 'the proper sectorization of the deposit accounts held by SPEs (Special Purpose Entities), public–private partnerships, or BOT (Build, Operate, Transfer) schemes in the financial sector, and of the loans extended to these entities' (IMF 2008: 63). The substance of economic ownership is decisive in the statistical, national accounts, treatment. At the same time, the IMF Guide admits that identification of the economic owner of fixed assets is a complex affair due to complex sharing risks of returns of the assets.

The 'IMF Guide for Public Sector Debt Statistics 2011' is based on the SNA 2008. Box 4.14 in that Guide summarizes the risks identified by SNA, presented in subsection 12.4.2, as relevant for classifying the PPP assets. On the other hand, the IMF Guide mentions that:

> Further developments in the treatment of PPPs in the SNA await the adoption of standards under development by the International Public Sector Accounting Standards Board (IPSASB).
>
> (IMF 2011: 81)

The criteria that operationalize the economic ownership may vary, as shown above. The recent Eurostat 'Manual on Government Deficit and Debt' adds classification criteria to the restricted Eurostat approach of the three main risks formulated in 2004. For instance, Eurostat considers that the residual-value risk of the PPP assets may give 'strong additional arguments for recording the assets as government assets' (Eurostat 2010: 259). A pre-determined price indicates public-sector exposure to the residual-value risk, and hence an argument for classifying the PPP assets as public. Another reason for classifying them as public is majority financing by the grantor of capital cost during the construction phase (Eurostat 2010: 260).

Some countries are following accounting standards (for example, IPSAS) applicable to financial leases. According to IPSAS, a financial lease actually results in acquiring an asset by the lessee. The lessee finances the asset by borrowing from the lessor who is paid by lease installments. In short, financial lease is an off-budget route, recognized as such by several public authorities responsible for the budget norms, such as the US Congressional Budget Office (CBO) (US CBO 2003). The upfront investment of the financial lease is recorded in the government's balance sheet, as asset and liability, increasing public debt.

IPSAS treat a lease as a financial lease to the extent that the following criteria are met:

(i)   the contract period covers most of the useful life of the asset;
(ii) the asset is transferred to the lessee (the public sector unit in the case of a PPP) at the end of the contract;
(iii) the lessee can purchase the asset at a bargain price at the end of the contract;
(iv) the present value of payments prescribed in the contract is close to the fair market value of the asset; and
(v)   the asset is useful mainly to the lessee. (IMF 2011: 83)

This IMF summary presents that the classification criteria are growing towards one another. The criteria quoted show the interrelatedness between economic ownership identified by risks-and-rewards criteria, versus economic ownership as control. The five criteria for financial lease imply that the lessee is exposed to the risks the assets entail. On the other hand, these criteria may be rephrased in terms of the control criteria as formulated in the IPSASB Exposure Draft 43. In a paraphrase, the control criteria imply that the economic owner disposes of the assets during its whole-life time. The risk criteria (i) to (v) are tantamount to whole-life-time control of the PPP asset. Therefore, the additional Eurostat criterion concerning residual-value risk indicates a congruence tendency. Nevertheless, the actual classification practices result in substantial public-budget differences. Firmly formulated, the risks-and-rewards criteria form an avenue to off-balance sheet budgeting, whereas the control approach blocks this road. For the time being, for many politicians the avenue seems to be too inviting to block the control approach.

12.5 National accounting of PPP, fiscal sustainability and an anomaly

This section establishes that the national-accounts treatment of PPP assets and liabilities is not in line with the transparency terms fiscal sustainability requires. This is an anomaly that stems from a difference in defining the public vis-à-vis the private sector. Subsection 12.5.1 briefly presents the national accounts definition of the public sector. Subsection 12.5.2 deals with the concept of fiscal sustainability and the public-sector definition that applies to this concept. Subsection 12.5.3 discusses the anomaly. The final subsection suggests a basic approach to remove the anomaly.

12.5.1 National-accounts definition of government

Accounting standards apply ownership as the criterion to distinguish the public and private spheres. Internationally, this is the dominant demarcation strategy. The IMF, the UN System of National Accounts (SNA), the US Congressional Budget Office (CBO), and EU Eurostat apply the ownership route. It is not the legal notion of ownership, but economic ownership that is decisive in determining what belongs to the public and what to the private sector. According to the IMF, control defines economic ownership. 'Control depends on the nature of the relationship between two entities', elaborated in a power and a benefit element (IMF 2009: 8). Control is fuelled by the power to govern the financial and operating policies of another entity, by the ability to benefit from the activities of that other entity. The IMF quotes emphasize the control criterion as defining economic ownership. As shown in section 12.4, the UN SNA and Eurostat apply the risks-and-rewards criteria.

Within the difinition chosen a bipolar public sector may be distinguished, as represented in the IMF figure below (Figure 12.2). On the one hand, there is the general government, which is assumed to bear responsibility for:

- providing goods and services to the community as a whole or to individual households on a non-market basis;
- making transfer payments to redistribute income and wealth; and
- financing their activities, directly or indirectly, mainly by means of taxes and other compulsory transfers from units in other sectors. (IMF 2009: 13–14)

On the other, there is the Public Corporation part, which involves enterprises owned and/or controlled by government units. A corporation may be a source of profit or other financial gain to its owners (IMF 2009: 11).

It is straightforwardly related to the economic ownership definition of the public sector to consider, for national accounting purposes, government as a corporation, just a public counterpart, which wealth is reflected in a balance of assets and liabilities. Consequently, this business perspective dictates the classification to the specific boundary issues raised by joint ventures of private companies and public entities, public sector leasing from private firms, social security schemes, and PPPs.

As shown, the leading classification method is the risks-and-rewards approach, as applied by SNA and Eurostat. An alternative is the control criterion to decide on economic ownership. In the national account context, the classification criteria bring statistical transparency and consistency, facilitating international, macroeconomic comparisons. The final aim of these classification procedures is 'to ensure the correct accounting of the impact on the government deficit' and public debt of boundary issues such as PPPs (Eurostat 2004: 2). The

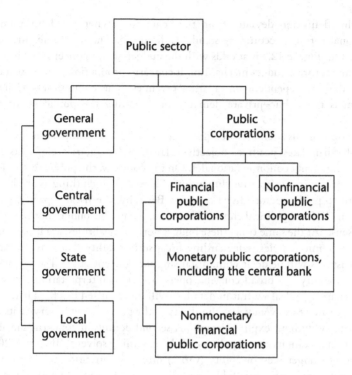

Figure 12.2 Public sector
Source: IMF (2007: 19)

classification of the PPP assets and liabilities straightforwardly impacts the public-finance figures of deficit and debt.

12.5.2 Another definition of the public sector and fiscal sustainability

The Economic and Monetary Union of the European Union(EMU) and the fiscal convergence criteria of the Maastricht Treaty offer an excellent opportunity to explain the significance of national-accounts rules for fiscal policies; i.e. for deficit–GDP and debt–GDP ratio. This explanation starts with a definition of the public sector that deviates from the economic ownership definition, as discussed in Section 12.4.

Governments levy taxes. It is the fiscal capacity of the public sector that sets it apart from the private. Taxation consists in compulsory payments without directly identifiable reciprocal rewards. A variety of taxes and social premiums form the budget of the public sector. The public sector is the counterpart of the private. In the private sector prices are paid for (market) products. Tit-for-tat transactions and the price mechanism allocating resources characterize the private sector. The public-sector counterpart of the price mechanism is the budget mechanism. Governments produce goods and services on a *non-market* basis paid by compulsory payments, i.e. taxes and social premiums. It results in the following definition of the public sector.

> The public sector is the budget sector, and requires a budget mechanism to allocate the taxation revenues that lack the identifiable reciprocals.

Obviously, this definition deviates from the economic ownership delineation applied in the international national accounting standards discussed. The bipolar feature of the public sector as shown in Figure 12.1 is at odds with the budget-sector concept. Public corporations basically do not require a budget mechanism. It concerns production entities that entail transactions; basically not dependent on taxation revenues. The compulsory-versus-voluntary-payment item is the public–private demarcation, defining the public sector by its fiscal capacity.

This definition entails a remarkable difference from the ownership definition. The ownership approach formulates positive, objective classification criteria; e.g. risks-and-rewards criteria have immanent economic rationales. On the contrary, the public sector defined by its fiscal capacity brings in a normative dimension. There is no such thing as an absolute, objectively set limit to public sector's fiscal capacity. Basically, the fiscal capacity, public-budget sector's share in GDP is a political choice. Therefore, the public-budget norms concern norms in the literal sense. At the same time, these budget norms, fiscal rules, are linked in economies with sound economic policies, safeguarding fiscal sustainability that may prompt a nation's wealth. Both aspects will be dealt with, discussing the concept of fiscal sustainability.

Fiscal sustainability is a broad concept, open to various interpretations. It is beyond the scope of this chapter to deal with it in detail. It will be discussed briefly. First, sustainability may be seen as related to solvency, i.e. 'the ability of the government to service its debt obligations in perpetuity without explicit default'. A second definition concerns the ability of the government 'to maintain its *current* policies while remaining solvent' (Burnside 2004: 1). The British Office of Budget Responsibility (OBR) directs its attention to this second sustainability definition, applying a twofold approach to the question 'whether the UK public finances are sustainable over the long term. First, we look at the fiscal impact of past government activity; second we look at the potential fiscal impact of future government activity'. Consequently, the OBR confronts these projections with the ageing population and the additional public spending that 'age-related items such as health care and pensions' will entail (OBR 2011: 3). Clearly, the concept of fiscal sustainability is highly dynamic, and the analysis should take account of this (Burnside 2004: 1).

The basic concept in the fiscal sustainability analysis is the *'government budget constraint'*, which is an equation:

net issuance of debt = interest payments – primary balance – seigniorage.

(Burnside 2005: 12)

Clearly, for the lifetime version of the budget constraint it is required to take account of inflation, interest rate, and exchange rates for foreign debt. The lifetime budget constraint states that the initial debt obligations equal the present value of seigniorage revenue and primary surpluses (Burnside 2005: 14).

The primary balance is the pivotal term in complying with the constraint. In particular, the primary balance of annual public revenues and expenditures is the outcome of political processes: the normative element in fiscal sustainability. However, in the equation the normative element is hidden by the relative value of the primary balance. From a normative point of view, it is the level of revenues (taxes) and expenditures in relation to GDP that is relevant for the affordability to comply with the constraint. A collective-taxation burden above a certain percentage of GDP might make it increasingly difficult to raise primary surpluses. Non-compliance with the budget constraint, the equation demonstrates, inevitably results in ever increasing taxes or government insolvency, i.e., in non–normative effects.

Immanent economic rationales behind the rules for fiscal sustainability may well be observed in the EMU case. The preparatory study of the Delors Commission 'Report on Economic and Monetary Union' foresaw the difficulties that 'a monetary union would require a single monetary policy and responsibility for the formulation of this policy vested in one decision-making body'. National authorities' decision may impact on the overall domestic and external economic situation of the Community. Therefore, the 'Community as a whole, should place binding constraints on the size and the financing of budget deficits' of the member states (EC 1989: 14). Subsequently, The Maastricht Treaty Article 104c mentions the establishment of reference values for deficit and public debt to avoid excessive government deficit and debt (EC 1992: 14). The Stability and Growth Pact (SGP) fixes these values:

- a sustainable public deficit of max. 3% of GDP;
- a sustainable public debt level of max. 60% of GDP.

At a nominal growth rate of GDP of 5 per cent, and 2 per cent inflation, these norms result in a steady-state relationship between deficit and debt. Externalities will announce themselves if a member state does not comply with these fiscal rules. Unsustainable public debt of an individual member country of the monetary union will result in interest rate differentials on public debt between the member states due to differential national default risk, by definition excluding interest differentials due to expected exchange rate depreciation and exchange rate risk premium. The interest effect further impacts the sustainability, and speedily results in an impossible situation, forcing other member states to bail out the insolvent government, in spite of their non-liability according to Maastricht Treaty, Article 104b. Furthermore, as Buiter *et al.* (1993) very early predicted, failure to bail out the problematic government in a situation of financial interdependence might spread a financial crisis to other member states (Buiter *et al.* 1993: 62).

Norms for public deficit and debt also have immanent rationales. Within a monetary union of sovereign states non-compliance with these may bring the union into peril. Without a union, negligence will impact citizens' wealth by inflation, interest rate, and exchange rate effects. Finally, it is citizens' vulnerability to the public sector's fiscal capacity that is at stake in compliance or non-compliance with the fiscal rules concerning deficit and debt.

12.5.3 An anomaly in classifying public sector involvement in PPP

Economic ownership criteria featuring the public sector versus the fiscal capacity feature of the public sector lead to an anomaly in the statistical treatment of the public-deficit and debt figures. Neither the risks-and-rewards criteria nor the control criterion offer a watertight guarantee that a classification of PPP assets and corresponding liabilities also results in an accurate reproduction in fiscal-sustainability terms. On the contrary, in many PPP cases the risks-and-rewards approach will classify the assets and corresponding liabilities as private sector items, whereas simultaneously the public partner is obliged to pay the annual instalments for years to come. Cell IV in Figure 12.1 reflects this example in a pure form: 100 per cent private financing of the assets combined with 100 per cent public funding. The ownership approach concludes off-public budget financing, though, in effect, public debt and deficit increase. The control criterion too may cause adverse conclusions regarding fiscal sustainability. De facto public control of the PPP assets by regulations and contractual provisions will classify the assets and liabilities as public, and relevant for public debt and deficit. However, this criterion does not account for situations of private funding of the investment, e.g. by tollage. The control version of ownership classification is potentially too strict from the fiscal point of view.

This irregularity stems from the basic difference in perspective on government. In the ownership approach government is seen as a wealth-creating entity whose conduct is reflected in risks and rewards, and via the income statement finally reported in the balance sheet: a natural applicant of accrual accounting. In this perspective private versus public funding is a non-issue.

However, in the fiscal-sustainability perspective private versus public funding is precisely the issue. Public funding of privately financed investments entails long-term taxation obligations that harm public-finance transparency and impact fiscal sustainability. As discussed, finally it is taxpayers' vulnerability that gives the fiscal sustainability and the transparency about it its significance. Payments without the immanent check of identifiable reciprocals, i.e. taxes, require an external limitation: the government budget constraint: basic concept in the fiscal sustainability analysis.

The irregularity of the ownership vis-à-vis the fiscal approach uncovers a *statistical* anomaly. The European System of Integrated Economic Accounts (ESA 95) may serve as an excellent example. ESA 95 applies the restrictive version of the risks-and-rewards criteria, which easily and very frequently result in an underestimation of the long-term fiscal consequences of a PPP. At the same time, it is the very *raison d'être* of ESA 95 to constitute the common statistical format to produce public-finance data in particular as 'a legal requirement for Member States under regulation, in particular the Excessive Deficit Procedure (EDP)' (EPEC 2010: 8). ESA 95 should offer transparency about the fiscal implications of PPP in terms of deficit–GDP and debt–GDP ratio. This is the statistical anomaly.

In the Eurostat context, the classification as private-balance items without recognizing an item as a part of public debt will very often happen. The restrictive Eurostat application of the risk criteria offers amply opportunity for choosing the off-public budgeting of upfront investment expenditures (Eurostat 2004a). For instance, the Eurostat treatment of the British PFI arrangements, with annual public funding of services, classifies the PPP assets and its financial liabilities as private. As mentioned, the British Office of Budget Responsibility (OBR) calculated for the UK an increase of 2.5 per cent (of GDP) of the Public Sector Net Debt (PSND) in March 2011 due to the transition from risks-and-rewards to control classification test (OBR 2011: 42). This might be a slight overestimate due to the adverse statistical consequences of the control criterion, discussed above. Moreover, for years the UK has been a front runner in PPP practices with the criticized mix of private financing and public funding. So, on average for the whole EU the underestimation of the ESA 95 treatment of PPP assets and corresponding liabilities might be less than the UK figure, but nevertheless substantial.

ESA 95 complies with the UN SNA. In this respect, the anomaly issue also refers to non-Eurostat countries, though as a weaker version, considering the relatively extensive application of risks criteria the SNA classification claims. At the same time, it is the basic difference in perspective on government that precludes claiming an adequate classification from a fiscal sustainability perspective.

12.5.4 An approach to remove the anomaly

The statistical anomaly identified may hit taxpayers' vulnerability, obstructing the transparency as a *conditio-sine-qua-non* for the fiscal sustainability the taxpayer should be informed about. Moreover, the off-balance sheet opportunities the anomaly offers to politicians justify considering the anomaly issue as a real threat to that fiscal sustainability. In particular, in the

Eurostat classification practice the issue may have topical relevance. It is beyond the scope of this chapter to design the classification standards that comply with the fiscal sustainability norms. However, it is obvious to formulate the basic rule removing the anomaly:

> A private-financing component of a PPP that potentially or definitely results in prospective taxation amounts to public debt and is relevant to the calculation of any public-sector deficit, and should be reflected in the government-budget constraint.

In this respect, the financing–funding matrix (Table 12.1) is instructive. Cell V reflects the genuine concession, the real off-balance sheet financing and funding, a withdrawal of the government, a reduced appeal to the taxpayer. Cells II and VIII represent situations in which the upfront public financing does not impact the fiscal sustainability. In all other cases the PPP practices impact the fiscal sustainability to varying degrees. A classification as a format for consistent fiscal sustainability statistics should follow these lines. In other words, the classification should address this question: What will, or might be, the incremental fiscal consequence of PPP?

12.6 Conclusions

The private-finance opportunity of PPP appeals to politicians. It offers the better of two worlds: a maintained level of 'public' provisions, while reducing public expenditures. Accounting standards aim to forestall the optical illusion the private-finance avenue might cause. National-account standards specifically developed to classify PPP assets and liabilities apply the economic ownership criteria. The ownership approach matches with the public management perspective adopted in many Western countries since the 1980s. Governments are like firms, should be managed as such, and may benefit from the management information accrual-based accounting offers. In this context, it is appropriate to apply the ownership criterion as decisive in classifying assets and liabilities as public or private. More specifically, it is the UN SNA approach of the risks-and-rewards criteria that finds worldwide application. The risk approach fits with the very PPP feature as a risk-transferring device. At the same time, the risk allocation is an awkward issue to dispel, in particular given the almost always incomplete nature of the PPP contracts; implicit guarantees and risk reallocation practices highly complicate the classification. For that matter, the control criterion as an alternative approach to economic ownership runs in comparable issues to make it operational.

However, the main objection that may be raised against the economic ownership approach is that it neglects the basic feature of government: its fiscal capacity. It is the fiscal capacity that is foremost in the national accounts standards for macroeconomic purposes. National accounts serve as a format to report on public finance in a consistent manner. The concept of fiscal sustainability with its key indicators debt–GDP and deficit–GDP ratio is basic. In this perspective, the public sector's involvement in PPP raises just one question: does it cause increasing fiscal consequences impacting the government budget constraint?

Consequently, an anomaly emerges in national accounting. The PPP tailored accounting standards may classify PPP assets and liabilities as private, while these impact the fiscal sustainability by, e.g., public funding obligations for years to come. It is a statistical anomaly that, in particular in the EU, raises doubts about the public-debt and deficit-ratios of member states. Removing the anomaly, it is highly relevant to distinguish between financing and funding. A basic classification rule obeying the government budget constraint is to consider the increasing fiscal effects of public-funding involvement in PPP.

Notes

* I am indebted to Peter B. Boorsma, Hans de Groot, Ger Vergeer and Etienne B. Yehoue for their useful comments on the draft version of this chapter.
1 For that matter, in Europe the revised ESA of 2008, based on the updated SNA 1993, will be implemented in 2014 (Eurostat 2009).

References

Akitoby B., R. Hemming and G. Schwartz (2007) Public Investment and Public-Private Partnerships, *Economic Issues 40*, Washington DC: International Monetary Fund.

Boston, J., J. Martin, J. Pallot and P. Walsh (1996) *Public Management: The New Zealand Model.* Auckland: Oxford University Press.

Buiter, W.H., G. Corsetti and N. Roubini (1993) Excessive Deficits: Sense and Nonsense in the Maastricht Treaty, *Economic Policy 8, 16.* 58–100.

Burnside, C. (2004) Assessing New Approaches to Fiscal Sustainability Analysis, in: *World Bank Latin America and Caribbean Department's report on Debt Sustainability Analysis.* http://www.google.nl/search?hl=nl&source=hp&q=Burnside+C.+%282004%29+Assessing+New+Approaches+to+Fiscal+Sustainability+Analysis+&gbv=2&oq=Burnside+C.+%282004%29+Assessing+New+Approaches+to+Fiscal+Sustainability+Analysis+&aq=f&aqi=&aql=&gs_sm=s&gs_upl=3978139781015054111110101010121812181211110 (accessed 22 January 2012).

Burnside, C. (ed.) (2005) *Fiscal Sustainability in Theory and Practice,* Washington DC: The World Bank.

European Commission (EC) (1989) *Report on Economic and Monetary Union* (Delors Report). http://aei.pitt.edu/1007/1/monetary_delors.pdf (accessed 22 January 2012).

EC (1992) *The Maastricht Treaty.* http://www.eurotreaties.com/maastrichtec.pdf (accessed 23 January 2012).

European Commission (Eurostat) (2004) *Long Term Contracts between government units and Non-government Partners (Public–Private Partnerships),* Luxembourg: Office of Official Publications of the European Communities.http://epp.eurostat.ec.europa.eu/cache/ITY_OFFPUB/KS-BE-04-004/EN/KS-BE-04-004-EN.PDF (accessed 20 March 2012).

Eurostat (2004a) News release 18/2004-11 February 2004. http://epp.eurostat.ec.europa.eu/cache/ITY_PUBLIC/2-11022004-AP/EN/2-11022004-AP-EN.HTML (accessed 13 January 2012).

Eurostat (2009) *Update of the SNA 1993 and Revision of ESA95.* http://epp.eurostat.ec.europa.eu/statistics_explained/index.php/Update_of_the_SNA_1993_and_revision_of_ESA95 (accessed 13 January 2012).

Eurostat (2010) *Manual on Government Deficit and Debt,* Luxembourg: Publications Office of the European Communities.

Eurostat (2010a) *Glossary ESA95.* http://epp.eurostat.ec.europa.eu/statistics_explained/index.php/Glossary:ESA95 (accessed 17 January 2012).

European PPP Expertise Group (EPEC) 2010, *Eurostat Treatment of Public-Private Partnership* Luxembourg: EPEC. http://www.eib.org/epec/resources/epec-eurostat-statistical-treatment-of-ppps.pdf (accessed 4 January 2012).

EPEC (2011) *State Guarantees in PPPs,* Luxembourg: EPEC. http://www.eib.org/epec/resources/epec-state-guarantees-in-ppps-public.pdf (Accessed 3 January 2012).

Harrison, A. (2006) *Definition of Economic Assets,* SNA/M1.06/14, Fourth meeting of the Advisory Expert Group on National Accounts, 30 January–8 February 2006, Frankfurt http://unstats.un.org/unsd/nationalaccount/AEG/papers/m4EconAssets.pdf (accessed 3 January 2012).

Heald, D. and G. Georgiou (2011) The Substance of Accounting for Public–Private Partnerships, *Financial Accountability & Management, 27(2),* 217–47.

International Monetary Fund (IMF) (2004) *Public–Private Partnerships,* (Teresa Ter-Minassian), 12 March 2004, Washington DC: IMF.

IMF (2007) *Manual on Fiscal Transparency,* Washington DC. http://www.imf.org/external/np/pp/2007/eng/051507m.pdf (accessed 20 March 2012).

IMF (2008) *Monetary and Financial Statistics; A compilation Guide 2008,* Washington DC: IMF. http://www.imf.org/external/pubs/ft/cgmfs/eng/pdf/cgmfs.pdf (accessed 17 January 2012).

IMF (2009) Ian Lienert, *Where Does the Public Sector End and the Private Sector Begin?* WP/09/122, Washington DC: IMF.

IMF (2011) *Public Sector Debt Guide*, Washington DC: IMF. http://www.tffs.org/pdf/method/ PSDS11fulltext.pdf (accessed 18 January 2012).

International Public Sector Accounting Standard (IPSAS) (2011) *Service Concession Arrangements: Grantor (October 2011)*, New York: International Public Sector Accounting Standard Board. http:// www.ifac.org/sites/default/files/publications/files/IPSAS%2032%20final%20v2%20(3).pdf (accessed 18 January 2012).

Office of Budget Responsibility (OBR) (2011) *Fiscal Sustainability Report*, London: The Stationery Office Limited. http://budgetresponsibility.independent.gov.uk/wordpress/docs/FSR2011.pdf (accessed 17 January 2012).

System of National Accounts (SNA) (1993) http://unstats.un.org/unsd/nationalaccount/docs/1993sna. pdf (accessed 9 January 2012).

System of National Accounts (SNA) (2008) http://unstats.un.org/unsd/nationalaccount/docs/ SNA2008.pdf (accessed 9 January 2012).

United States Congressional Budget Office (US CBO) (2003) *The Budgetary Treatment of Leases and Public/Private Ventures*, Washington DC: CBO Paper.

Velloso, R. (2008) *Good Practices in Fiscal Risks Disclosure; International Experiences*, 28–29 October 2008. http://www.imf.org/external/np/seminars/eng/2008/fiscrisk/pdf/velloso.pdf (accessed 16 December 2011).

Yescombe, E.R. (2002) *Principles of Project Finance*, London: Academic Press.

Part VI

Recent financial crises and public–private partnerships

13

Weathering the financial crisis

Public–private partnerships and the government response

Philippe Burger, Justin Tyson, Izabela Karpowicz
and Maria Coelho[1]

13.1 Introduction

The recent global economic and financial crisis has generated challenges at all levels of economic policy decisions. Governments in advanced countries and emerging markets faced an urgent need to act concurrently on different fronts: systemically or politically sensitive economic sectors were bailed out; the general downfall in economic activity was counteracted; and vulnerable groups were protected from declining incomes. These costly actions were taken in a context of falling government revenues and shrinking domestic and foreign financing, with medium- to long-term consequences for budgets and debt.

In a number of countries, anti-crisis packages included higher public investment, at times implemented through public–private partnerships (PPPs). The potential role of these arrangements as counter-cyclical fiscal policy tools is sizeable given that they can be used to support private sector recovery and generate employment. Yet, the growing number of PPPs in recent years[2] and their contractual structures may entail fiscal risks for governments that can be exacerbated by the financial crisis.

PPPs showed themselves to be vulnerable to both the financial and the real impact of the crisis. Although the final consequences and duration of the crisis are not yet known, the likely effects on PPPs can already be identified. Both existing and planned (hereafter pipeline) PPP programmes were affected through various channels, such as the availability and cost of credit, lower growth, and unforeseen exchange rate movements. Depending on the contractual arrangement between the parties, the changed distribution of risks can shift the cost-burden between the parties, weakening the attractiveness of PPPs. Parties were forced to reevaluate risk.

The challenge facing PPPs lies in securing their economic benefits while at the same time containing fiscal risks. Whenever possible, the value-for-money (VfM) of existing projects should be maintained by aligning government interventions in selected projects/contracts with broader fiscal policy objectives, and ensuring interventions are temporary, transparent, costed and budgeted.

This chapter studies the impact of the global financial crisis on PPPs based on a theoretical framework and country evidence. Section 13.2 briefly describes PPPs; Section 13.3 identifies

325

the channels through which the crisis affected PPPs and assesses country and programme-specific vulnerabilities; Section 13.4 presents evidence on the impact of the crisis based on answers to a questionnaire sent to select countries; Section 13.5 discusses country responses and proposes measures to enhance the attractiveness of PPPs and principles for preserving VfM and protecting the budget. These fall under the general rubric of how governments cope with infrequent, catastrophic events.

13.2 Public–private partnerships

The underlying rationale for choosing PPP over traditional procurement or private-sector provision is improved VfM. VfM is maximized when the project maximizes the net present value of social benefits – benefits less costs – of a project over its entire life cycle.[3] VfM tests can vary, but typically involve a risk-adjusted comparison of the PPP and public procurement alternatives. In practice, PPPs have also been used to circumvent government accounting rules by moving borrowing off the public sector balance sheets, under the misconception that doing so creates fiscal space for other activities.[4]

The impact of the financial crisis and ensuing economic downturn on PPPs varies depending on the phase of development:

- **Operational phase**: The PPP is negotiated, the construction phase is completed (if applicable), and services are being provided by the private partner(s).
- **Construction phase**: The PPP is negotiated, but the construction of physical assets is still under way and service provision has not commenced.
- **Pipeline phase**: The PPP is planned, and may even be tendered. However, the public and private partners have not reached financial closure and physical works have not started.

Box 13.1 Definition of PPPs

A PPP is an arrangement in which the private sector participates in the supply of assets and services traditionally provided by the government. However, the literature on PPPs has not reached consensus on a precise definition (cf. Hemming 2006; IMF 2004; OECD 2008; European Commission, 2004; Standard and Poor's 2005; EIB 2004). For the purposes of this chapter, the term PPP covers arrangements usually characterized by the following:

1 An agreement between a government and one or more private partners whereby the private partner(s) undertakes to deliver an agreed upon quantity and quality of service.
2 In return for the delivery of the agreed upon quantity and quality the private partner(s) receives either a unitary charge paid by government or a user charge (e.g. a toll) levied by the private partner on the direct recipients of the service.
3 An emphasis on a whole-of-life approach. The private partner(s) is usually responsible for both the construction and operational phases of the project.
4 Some degree of risk sharing between the public and private sector that in theory should be determined on the basis of which party is best able to manage each risk, thus ensuring that the PPP optimizes VfM.

13.3 Transmission mechanisms: threats, vulnerabilities and risk

To assess the impact of the global financial crisis on PPPs, the realization of risk can be broken down into a function of threat and vulnerability:

Risk realization = f(threat, vulnerability)

where *threat* is defined as the probability that some negative event occurs in the future, e.g. through one of the channels identified below, and *vulnerability* is linked to PPP-specific or country-specific factors that capture the 'preparedness' of the involved parties to either prevent a threat from materializing or cope with its adverse impact.[5] Vulnerability can be considered as lack of capacity and/or desire of the parties to ensure that, through proper risk and project management, the actual outcome conforms as closely as possible to the expected outcome. The outcome, or *risk realization*, is the potential impact on the PPP stemming from the interaction of threats and vulnerabilities. For instance, a drop in traffic volumes is a *threat* to toll-road PPPs. However, in this example *risk* is present only if there is a corresponding *vulnerability*, such as the lack of a minimum revenue or traffic guarantee that allows the private partner to cope with the impact.

13.3.1 Crisis transmission mechanisms: threats

Several channels can be identified through which the financial crisis, the associated increase in risk aversion and the ensuing recession affected PPP programmes. The channels include:

- **Upward pressure on interest rates**. Although policy rates in many developed economies decreased to historically low levels following the advent of the crisis, emerging markets saw an increase in both corporate and sovereign bond rates. In most economies, developed or emerging, spreads between corporate and sovereign rates spiked starting mid-2008 to levels not seen since the Asian crisis, the dotcom bubble or the Argentine crisis, indicating an increase in risk premiums (Figure 13.1), before moderating during 2009.

  - The resulting increase in the cost of borrowing affected projects in the pipeline phase and existing projects with refinancing needs (most likely those in the construction phase) and/or variable interest payments.

- **Decrease in the availability of credit**. Liquidity constraints affected not only the price of credit, but also the quantity available as financial institutions rationed credit regardless of price and banks were wary of extending loans. The downgrading of monoline insurance companies (which guaranteed the repayment of infrastructure bonds at a fee) also shrank the bond market for infrastructure projects. In those cases where banks might have been interested in extending loans, they were constrained by the size of their capital (Abadie 2008). Figure 13.2 presents data on project finance syndicated loans by region (including PPP projects). After a peak late in 2008, project finance loans declined sharply in the first quarter of 2009, before recovering somewhat in the latter part of 2009. The effect is most pronounced in Western Europe and Africa. The Asia Pacific region is a notable exception where the advent of the crisis barely halted the rise in project finance, probably due to the dominant role of the State in the banking sectors of the large economies.

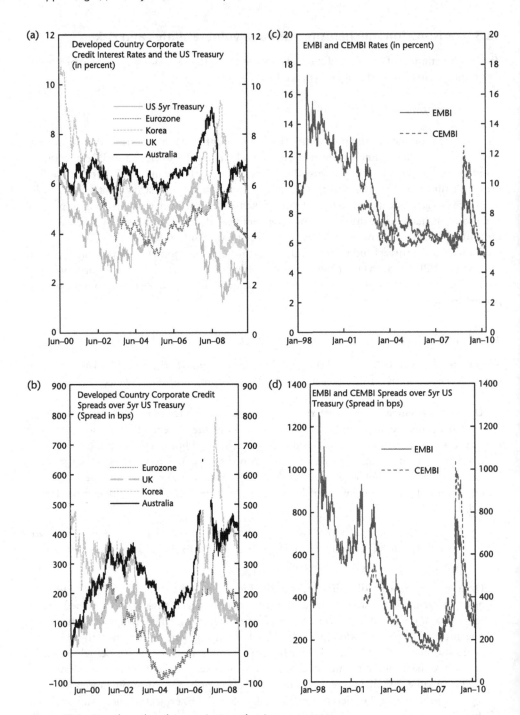

Figure 13.1   Developed and emerging market interest rates

Source: Bloomberg Financial Markets L.P. *Eurozone Corp Composite A index from 03/29/02-03/26/2010, Korean Industrial A index from 06/19/00-03/26/2010, Australian Corp A index from 06/19/00-03/26/2010, UK Swap index from 06/19/00-03/26/2010, 5yr US Treasury from 06/19/00-03/26/2010, EMBI graph from 01/02/98 to 03/25/2010, and CEMBI graph from 01/02/02 to 03/25/2010.* Retrieved from Bloomberg terminal.

EMBI = Emerging Market Bond Index; CEMBI = Corporate Emerging Market Bond Index

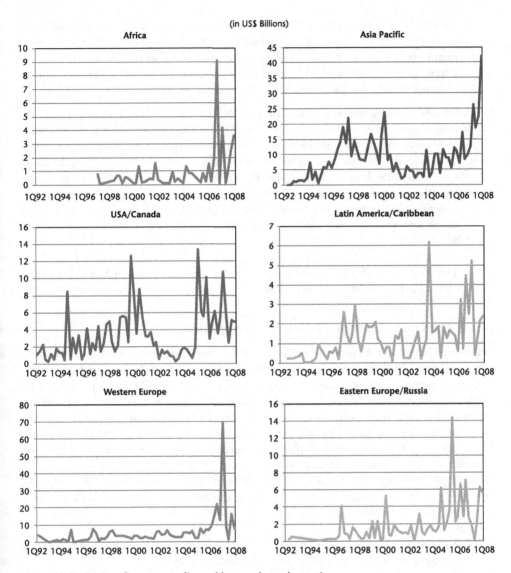

Figure 13.2 Project finance syndicated loan volume by region

Source: Thomson Reuters. *Global syndicated project finance loans from 1992 Q1 to 2009 Q1*. Retrieved April 17 2009. http://www.thomsonreuters.com

   – The most affected PPPs were those in the pipeline phase. Existing PPPs (both those in the construction and those in the operational phase) would already have secured credit through signed agreements with financial institutions, although possibly with residual refinancing needs.

• **The real effects of the economic slowdown on revenue cash flows**. The impact of lower demand for services on the revenue cash flows had, and will still have, knock-on effects for debt servicing capacity and overall profitability. Examples include lower revenues from landing fees in airports and lower toll-road revenues.

- This threat mainly affects PPPs in the operational and pipeline phases. Those in the operational phase suffer from the reduced cash flow – especially where the private partner is reliant on direct user charges (as opposed to service payments from the government). For PPPs in the pipeline phase, the downturn could affect the estimates of future profitability and hence the viability of the project.

- **Unforeseen exchange rate movements**. Where the private partner had sizeable, unhedged, external debt, these movements could have had an impact on the balance sheet and debt servicing capacity of PPP projects. In some emerging market countries hedging is impossible due to the absence of forward markets for their currencies. In other cases, partners may have underestimated the exchange rate risk involved. Projects may also be affected by the increased cost of imported capital goods (if the PPP is still under construction) and imported operational inputs. Figure 13.3 shows the spike in implied exchange rate volatility for selected currencies over the end of 2008 and beginning of 2009 period.

  - The PPPs most affected would have been those in the operational or construction phase that have unhedged external debt.

13.3.2 Crisis transmission mechanisms: vulnerabilities

PPP vulnerabilities to the crisis can be project-specific or extend more widely to the partnership framework. Project-specific vulnerabilities are those that can be managed within the project's structure, such as a high, unhedged level of external debt or projects based on overly optimistic project revenue forecasts without a corresponding guarantee. Partnership vulnerabilities are more complicated and involve the interaction of project specific vulnerabilities, contract structure, and the institutional framework for PPPs. For instance, authorities could be vulnerable to explicit contingent liabilities, such as a higher likelihood of guarantees being called (exchange rate, minimum traffic, revenue). This could pose a fiscal risk if insufficient provisions have been made in the budget to cover the obligations. Similarly, partnerships (public and private sectors) can be vulnerable to implicit contingent liabilities, like contractor failure and/or contract renegotiation, even if guarantees do not exist.

The institutional context is key to managing PPPs to secure their benefits while containing risks. Key elements to reducing partnership vulnerability include:

- **Robust public investment planning**. Crucial components include a systematic approach to investment planning, project selection and prioritization, and a framework to consider future implications of projects for the budget. International experience can help identify *a priori* which sectors and types of projects are most suited to PPPs.
- **Adequate distribution of risks between the government and the private sector**. Better VfM is realized if the party that has better control over a feature of the project that drives VfM also bears the risk associated with it. Risk can be endogenous to both parties.
- **A sound legal framework**. A strong and reasonably detailed legal framework can set the parameters for handling PPPs and also provide assurance to the private sector that contracts will be honoured. The more transparent and credible the enabling environment, the less risk premium is charged by private investors in PPPs.[6]

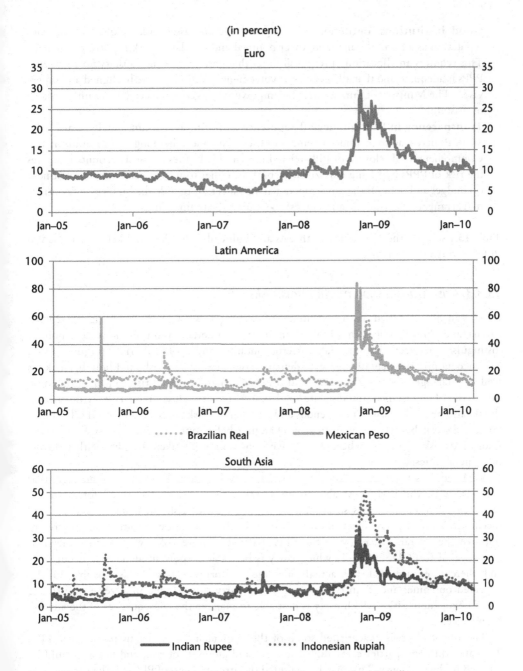

Figure 13.3 Annualized implied exchange rate volatility versus the US dollar

Source: Bloomberg Financial Markets L.P. *Implied foreign exchange volatility indices (EURUSDV1M, USDINRV1M, USDBRLV1M, USDIDRV1M, USDMXNV1M) from 01/04/2005 to 03/25/2010.* Retrieved from Bloomberg terminal.

- **Regulations limiting aggregate government exposure**. These might include: 1) flow limits on annual total PPP-related payments and contingent commitments; and 2) stock limits on the overall size of the PPP programme or total project liabilities, as part of a wider debt management strategy. Any rule should be consistent with the wider fiscal framework.

- **Good institutions**. Institutions can help manage and assess risks, build government's reputation as a good partner, and lower political and regulatory risk for private partners. This requires an allocation of responsibilities that ensures that the capacity for managing PPPs is adequate and that all agencies' involvement in PPPs is properly aligned and supervised. The Ministry of Finance may be empowered to veto projects that are unaffordable or wasteful.
- **Transparency in PPP finances**. The absence of specific accounting and disclosure rules for PPPs may lead to an understatement of fiscal risks and other long-term commitments. Comprehensive disclosure of PPP-related risks and liabilities in fiscal accounts mitigates the risk of PPPs bypassing expenditure controls, either to move costly public investment off budget and debt off the government balance sheet, or to hide the high cost of contractual arrangements (such as guarantees) to secure private financing.

Table 13.1 sets out the interaction of threats and vulnerabilities that are likely to have led to PPP risk during the crisis.

13.3.3 Crisis transmission mechanisms: risks

Risks can be classified in a multitude of ways (cf. OECD 2008; Li *et al.* 2005a; Merna and Smith 1996). In PPPs, as in most commercial ventures, it is common to distinguish between commercial, macroeconomic and political risk (Figure 13.4). Macroeconomic risks entail aggregate demand risk, interest rate risk, and liquidity risk, as well as exchange rate risk. The materialization of macroeconomic risk can, in turn, cause other risks. For instance, interest rate or demand risk can cause credit risk. A distinction should also be made between exogenous and endogenous risk (Li *et al.* 2005b; OECD 2008). Some risks can be actively managed by changing behaviour; these are endogenous risks. Exogenous risks are those where such active steps cannot be taken to reduce either threats or vulnerabilities.

VfM requires that risk be allocated to the party best suited to carry, or manage, that risk – that is, the party best able to ensure that the actual outcome conforms to the expected outcome and does so at least cost. This type of risk allocation should provide incentives for each party to act in order to manage the risk allocated to them and therefore improve the overall efficiency of the PPP. To best allocate risk, two questions need to be answered (OECD, 2008): 1) which party is best able to prevent an adverse occurrence and thereby ensure that the actual outcome conforms as closely as possible to the expected outcome; and 2) in the case where no party can prevent an adverse occurrence (i.e. an exogenous risk), which party is best able to manage the consequences of the adverse occurrence.

The financial crisis exacerbated some of the risks facing the various parties of a PPP. Typically, different parties carry different types and amounts of risk, and not all would be affected in the same way. This may have altered the attractiveness of PPPs for the parties most affected and reduced their interest in participating in PPPs without adequate compensation. As such they would not want to enter into new PPP agreements, refinance debt in existing PPPs or continue operating under an existing agreement.

Risk can be managed in several ways (OECD 2008), including through:

- **Risk avoidance** – the risky activity is not undertaken as, for example, when a public body opts for public procurement.

Table 13.1 Channels of transmission of the financial crisis

	Risk threat and vulnerability		Risk realization	
	Threat	Vulnerability	Effect on private partners	Effect on the government
Financial	Interest rates hike	Large borrowing or refinancing need; variable interest rates	Higher debt service=increasing costs; liquidity problems; questionable feasibility of some projects given lower returns.	Timing of investments (postponing): tradeoff between PPPs and traditional concessions altered. Possible cash flow support to corporates.
	Unavailability of credit	Underfinanced project or new project	Lowered capacity to refinance; shorter loans; shift to bonds and equity vs. bank loans.	Termination of existing projects, failure to achieve financial close of new projects; capital injections.
		Revenues from the project and/or assets securitized; securities indexed, and insured.	Losses from downgrade of bonds; lowered capacity to refinance given lack of insurers; shorter loans and shift to bonds and equity vs. bank loans.	
	Decline in stock market prices	Companies do not hold sufficient levels of their capital in cash	Reduced capital of banks. Reduced lending; solvency problems and recapitalization.	Reduced investment for new and existing PPPs and recapitalization costs.
Real	Exchange rate depreciation	Sizeable external debt, currency mismatches, dollarization	Corporate balance sheets if borrowing externally. Counterbalancing: increase in demand if service is export oriented (including highway). Higher input costs if inputs are imported.	Increased external debt service (financing constraints) and lower attractiveness for new investments relying on external borrowing; private sector defaults if widespread dollarization; call of guarantees. Counterbalancing force: switch from foreign consumption to domestic investment.
	Slump in domestic demand	Commercial projects depending on user fees and explicit contractual guarantees	Corporate balance sheets and pricing of credit by financial partners; liquidity problem; contractor failure and pressure to renegotiate.	Lower domestic revenue (financing constraints) leading to lower investment affecting new and old PPPs; commercial projects risk; call of guarantees due to decline in fees/tolls; pressure to bail out failing contractors and renegotiate.

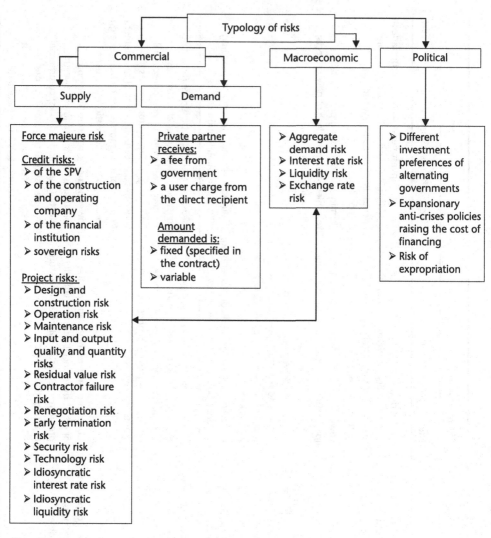

Figure 13.4 Typology of risks affecting PPPs

- **Risk prevention** – action is taken to reduce vulnerabilities, for example, when a PPP consortium borrows in domestic currency to avoid exchange rate risk.
- **Risk transfer** – risk is transferred to another party through a contractual arrangement, such as minimum traffic guarantees, but can remain within the partnership.
- **Risk retention** – risk is retained by a specific party who, in theory, should have the incentive to reduce its cost implications. For example, a construction company can manage effectively to reduce the probability of design risks, while a government can reduce the likelihood of policy/regulatory changes.[7]
- **Risk insurance** – financial coverage for the loss from a negative outcome.

Box 13.2 Effect of a crisis on PPP partners

A large financial and economic crisis may affect the balance sheets of all the parties to the PPP. These are:

- the relevant government department or agency;
- the private partner(s) responsible for the construction of the asset;
- the private partner(s) responsible for operating the asset and delivering the service;
- the private partner(s) responsible for financing the project;
- the special purpose vehicle, usually owned by one or more of the private partner(s).

In theory, allocating exogenous risks to the private partner(s) cannot increase VfM as there is nothing that the private partner(s) can do to manage the risk responsibly. However, this does not mean that the private partner should not carry any exogenous risk – the private partner would normally be expected to carry some macroeconomic risk such as weathering normal business cycle movements. While some risks are either endogenous or exogenous to all parties, there are also risks that might be exogenous to the private partner, but endogenous to the government (e.g. the risk of expropriation). Where a risk is exogenous to both the private partner and the government, the private partner will only carry the risk if the expected cost can be recuperated through the contractual arrangements.

Risks that under normal circumstances are endogenous (and are transferred to the private partner) might become unmanageable (almost exogenous) in a global crisis. For example, in a credit crunch where liquidity dries up and long-term risk premiums increase significantly, private partners may become unable to manage credit risk. A global recession may have an impact on demand, beyond what could be adequately managed by a private partner within normal operations, and consequently extend beyond the project to the partnership.[8] It is the transmission of risk to the partnership that is most likely to entail fiscal costs.

13.4 Impact of the crisis: evidence

The impact of the financial crisis on PPP programmes can be seen by exploring different data sources and country survey responses. Evidence of difficulties in accessing finance in the 2008/9 crisis is found in the shifting preferences of financial institutions. In a survey of more than 20 of the leading banks in the UK PPP market, PricewaterhouseCoopers (PwC) found that a significant effect of the financial crisis was a marked shift in the preference of financial institutions away from long-term loans and towards loans with a much shorter term to maturity (Davies 2009). Willingness to lend for long maturities depends, according to the PwC survey, on strong client relationships and strong refinancing incentives. However, there were also banks that, due to limited capital, were unable to enter contracts with a relatively long maturity. Longer term PPPs (concluded for, say, 20 years and over), could potentially only secure loans for shorter periods. This exposed the private operators to more refinancing risk in the form of credit availability and future interest rate volatility.

Data from the World Bank Public–Private Infrastructure Advisory Facility (PPIAF) also show that the financial crisis affected, and continues to affect, new projects in emerging market countries.[9] The data provide two distinct snapshots, one in March 2009 and another in September 2009. The first cut-off date provides a perspective on PPP prospects in the

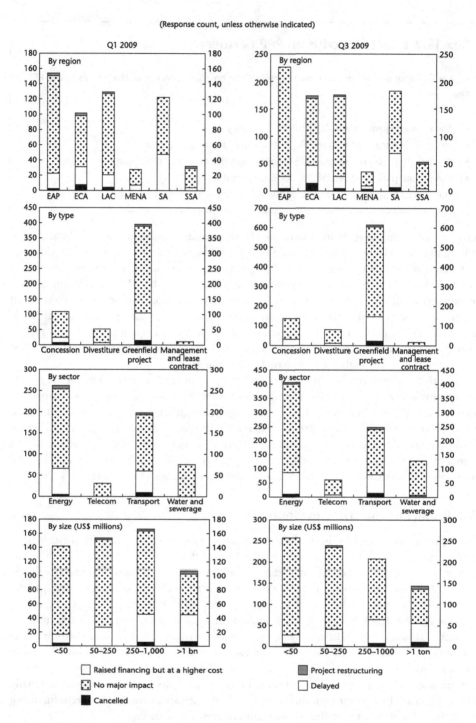

(Response count, unless otherwise indicated)

Figure 13.5 Effect of financial crisis on PPP projects in emerging markets, 2009

Source: World Bank and Sustainable Development Network, PPI Project Database

EAP: East Asia and Pacific; ECA: Europe and Central Asia; LAC: Latin America and Caribbean; MENA: Middle East North Africa; SA: South Asia; SSA: Sub-Saharan Africa

midst of the crisis; the later cut-off provides a view on changes that occurred as the outlook improved. Of the 564 projects surveyed between July 2008 and March 2009, many were affected by the financial crisis (Figure 13.5). Several points stand out:

- **Uncertainty regarding future demand, access to finance and the cost of financing caused most delays**. In total 116 projects, or 21 per cent, reported delays, 16 projects were cancelled, while 6 projects that did obtain finance were only able to do so at a higher cost.
- **South Asia (predominantly India) and transitional economies in Europe and Central Asia accounted for most delays**. Eastern Europe and Central Asia also contained most projects that were cancelled. Asia Pacific had the highest number of unaffected projects.
- **The largest delays were in the energy and transport sectors**. New projects and projects in excess of $250 million were also more likely to register delays.

The picture appears to improve slightly as growth prospects pick up and financial constraints ease. By September 2009, the percentage of projects reporting delays is down to 18 per cent from 21 per cent; 77 per cent of projects report no major impact compared with 74 per cent earlier. The general pattern by sector and project type is consistent with the earlier data. The data are not strictly comparable due to the changing sample size. Nonetheless, if one follows the evolution of 498 projects that can be individually tracked between the first and third quarter of 2009, a similar story of improvement emerges (Figure 13.6). Of the projects

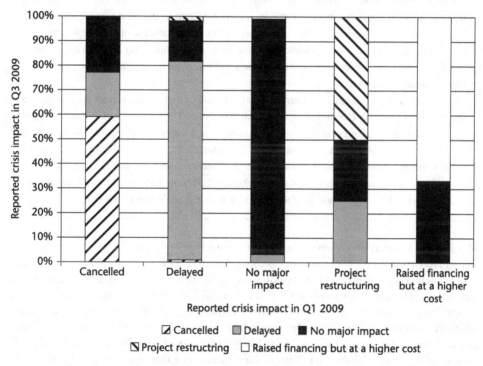

Figure 13.6   Change of PPP project status between first and third quarters of 2009 (in percent)

Source: World Bank and Sustainable Development Network, PPI Project Database

Note: Evolution assessed over a constant sample of 498 projects; cancelled projects include terminated projects and those with a high probability of being cancelled

Philippe Burger, Justin Tyson, Izabela Karpowicz and Maria Coelho

delayed, or concerned about delays, in the first quarter, 15 per cent report no major impact six months later; 30 per cent of those that could only access credit at higher rates earlier, similarly recorded no major impact at the end of the third quarter; and projects needing restructuring in the first period also showed signs of improvement.

A separate survey of selected countries conducted during the crisis confirms the transmission mechanisms from the financial crisis to PPP programmes.[10] In response to a questionnaire sent to a selected group of countries about the impact of the financial crisis on their PPPs and the fiscal accounts, most of the respondents identified the cost of borrowing and access to finance as the main crisis transmission mechanisms. These channels were affecting the project pipeline. Some countries indicated that reduced demand would also act as a channel, while other respondents felt exposed to the risk of contractor failure and/or project renegotiation. Few were worried about exchange rate risk, perhaps reflecting adaptation to past crises (Box 13.3). Most respondents confirmed the presence of linkages between PPP projects and the fiscal budget, either in the form of payments to the private partners or receipts from them.

Box 13.3 The crisis, emerging markets, foreign investment and exchange rates

Ettinger *et al.* (2005) show that in the aftermath of the Asian crisis and the dotcom bubble burst, private participation in PPP projects in emerging markets declined and only started to increase again in 2004/5. They also show that the largest contribution to the drop came from reduced investments by advanced countries in emerging market PPPs. Consequently, emerging markets became more reliant on the mobilization of domestic sources of financing. This can be problematic if local financial markets are underdeveloped and too small to generate enough savings to finance large-scale projects.

Developed country financiers often form part of consortia that include private operators, who bring with them skills and technical expertise that may not exist in the local market. Thus, reduced participation by advanced country investors may result in a lower rate of technological transfer. However, reliance on domestic investors also has advantages. Domestic investors very often understand the local investment climate better than foreign investors, and can exercise better control over their investments (Angelides and Xenidis 2009). In addition, domestic investment usually also implies a significant reduction, if not elimination, of exchange rate risk.

The surveyed countries present a variety of institutional frameworks to deal with crisis-related risks (Box 13.4). Most respondents said that their PPP programmes were integrated within a wider, medium-term investment planning framework. More than half the respondents had formal guidelines in place for risk allocation and for accounting – both important components for transparency. More than half also made some effort to quantify the risks to which the government was exposed and include the costs in the budget. However, no country had undertaken updated estimates of the likely fiscal cost of any risks materializing in the context of the crisis. While some countries felt there was a risk of contractor failure and/or renegotiation, their legal frameworks had provisions to deal with this eventuality.

At the time of the survey (Spring 2009), the crisis had already begun to affect PPP programmes, especially the pipeline of new projects. Half of respondents saw the key VfM criteria for new projects changing – specifically, private partners in PPPs were less willing to retain certain risks, such as interest rate risk and financial closure risk and were seeking greater contributions or guarantees from the government. Some countries thought it was probable that previously planned PPPs would proceed instead as publicly procured projects. A minority of countries responded that they thought it was more likely that guarantees would be called on existing PPPs.

Box 13.4 Country evidence: effects of the crisis on PPPs

Canada

PPP Canada, which reports to the Minister of Finance, met with several developers to assess the potential impact of the financial crisis on the P3 programme. A key challenge was access to financing stemming from the lower risk tolerance of lenders (with respect to project and refinancing risks) and higher costs for international project finance institutions, particularly European banks, due to cost of raising Canadian dollars. Private sector analysts noted that credit market capacity had become a concern especially for larger projects over $500 million. In addition, long term loans for P3 were now more difficult to secure as many foreign banks formerly active in this niche had withdrawn from the market. Obstacles to reaching an agreement during the negotiations phase in one province resulted in choosing to procure the project using a design-build, fixed-price contract, although the preferred bidder had already arranged committed debt and equity. Notwithstanding these difficulties, the projects carried out at the federal level were not considered more likely to proceed as public investment.

Korea

Although private investment had steadily increased since the introduction of PPPs, the pipeline of new PPP projects declined mainly due to aggravating financial conditions. The contract-signing volume fell sharply in 2008, increasing the likelihood that the amount of private investment actually executed would shrink in the future. The contracts signed were less than 70 per cent of the initial projection. Interest rates and access to financing were identified as the main channels through which the financial crisis has affected or is expected to affect existing PPP projects and the pipeline. However, the real effects of the economic slowdown on the profitability of existing PPPs also materialized with a 10 per cent decrease in annual port traffic recorded in February 2009. Timely project implementation was impaired by an extended preparation period necessary for feasibility and VFM studies, and for the coordination of different interests during negotiations. In line with the surge in financing costs for private proposals, the government's risk aversion increased while risk allocation to the private partner was changing: reportedly, private partners were less willing to take on interest rate risk.

South Africa

The government identified a number of risks from PPPs to which the budget was exposed through contractual structures and guarantees, as well as through the institutional framework. These are: demand risk, residual value risk, exchange rate risk, renegotiation risk, early termination risk and inflation risk. The budget included provisions for the expected annual cost of these risks, which were treated as contingent liabilities. The financial crisis was reported to have affected new PPPs, their profitability, and the risk aversion of the government. While financing

---

for existing private partners in the PPP project pipeline was not affected by the crisis, new potential private partners were hit by higher interest rates and lower access to financing. Although the real effects of the economic slowdown on the profitability of existing PPP projects could not be quantified, lower demand was identified as the main channel of transmission of the crisis. The government reported that the higher borrowing costs and lower expected returns on equity influenced VfM choices for the PPP project pipeline and the allocation of risks between the private partner and the government.

Source: questionnaire responses.

13.5 Managing crisis risks for PPPs

Private partners' interest in PPPs may fade during crises because of an unfavourable risk–return trade-off. Prior to the 2008/9 crisis, the 'great moderation' and the perceived ability of monetary authorities to smooth fluctuations created perceptions of a less risky economy. The recent crisis has magnified macroeconomic risks, affecting also the perceptions about risks by the various PPP parties and the private sector risk–return trade-off. Moreover, the ability of private partners to cope with higher costs by passing them on to service users may be limited by the regulatory environment.

Governments can act to enhance the attractiveness of PPPs and shift the risk–return balance. As the crisis progressed, governments extended support to PPPs through various modalities. Examples are the sharing of interest rate risk in Korea (Box 13.5), loan guarantees in France, and direct loans in France and the UK.[11] Some of these approaches were included as integral components of stimulus packages and involved:

- **Relying on strong institutional and regulatory frameworks** – for example, in Chile the bidding mechanism for PPPs is based on a Least Present Value of Revenues approach, in which contracts always have a variable term date, depending on demand realizations (Irwin and Mokdad 2010) and in Mexico, the Program to Promote Public Private Partnerships in Mexican States intended to strengthen the legal and institutional capacity of state governments, so they can apply harmonized PPP models (IADB 2007).
- **Facilitating access to credit through guarantees** – for example, in Australia, the State governments have offered syndication guarantees to achieve financial closure (Irwin and Mokdad 2010). Project specific guarantees were also provided in France (Zatezalo-Falatar 2010), Portugal and Spain. In Kazakhstan, the government extended guarantees for bonds and loans to concession projects; co-funding was included in the fiscal budget as subsidies or state investment (Chemonics International Inc. 2008).
- **Facilitating access to credit through public funding** – for example, in France, co-funding was provided from Caisse des Depots as part of the stimulus package (Zatezalo-Falatar 2010) and the UK established a public lender-of-last-resort facility for PPPs under its Private Finance Initiative (Farquharson and Encinas 2010).
- **Facilitating access to credit through state–owned banks** – countries with dominant state-banking sectors used these institutions to offset the drop in private financing, e.g. Brazil and India sourced additional funding mainly from state-owned banks (PPIAF 2009). This is consistent with a wider trend of using state involvement in the banking sector to promote counter-cyclical policy responses.

Box 13.5 Government measures to reinvigorate PPPs

Canada

Canada did not have a formal PPP programme until recently. Previously, the government part-nered with the private sector to leverage private financing and expertise and improve federal infrastructure, but in an ad hoc manner. Through infrastructure programmes, the government has also made commitments and contributions to provincial and municipal PPPs, including the Canada Line and the Kicking Horse Canyon projects in British Columbia; Highway 30 in Québec; and the Edmonton ring road in Alberta. Established in 2008, PPP Canada administers a $1.2 billion P3 Fund to further develop the PPP market. The Corporation has not begun financing projects and is expected to issue an initial call for applications to the P3 Fund in 2009–10. A number of Canadian provinces have taken concrete steps towards the use of PPPs and the devel-opment of their respective markets. The provinces of British Columbia, Ontario and Quebec have each created institutions and developed programmes focused on using P3s or similar arrangements, which are active in health and hospitals, roads, schools, and other sectors. The Government of Alberta's 2008 Budget Plan included approximately $6 million for the Alternative Capital Financing office to explore alternative financing options for capital projects, including PPPs. Similar steps have been taken by Canadian municipalities, such as the City of Ottawa, which has officially endorsed the concept of PPPs and established a PPP office.

Korea

The government announced a fiscal stimulus package in response to the financial crisis with more than 15 per cent of the envisaged investment to be carried out through PPPs. The package is accompanied by measures to reduce financial burdens on PPPs, smooth interest rate changes, and shorten project implementation. The measures introduce: 1) lower equity capital require-ments on concessionaires (5–10 per cent); 2) for large-scale projects, higher ceilings on guaran-tees provided by the Infrastructure Credit Guarantee Fund (50 per cent); 3) help in changing equity investors for some projects; 4) compensation for the preparation of proposals to encourage more vigorous competition during bidding; 5) sharing of interest rate risks with concessionaires; 6) compensation for the excess changes in base interest rates through grading of risks at the time of the concession agreement; and 7) shorter periods for readjusting bench-mark bond yields.

Source: questionnaire responses.

Based on country policy responses during the crisis and the PPP literature, some potential government interventions can be identified; many steps are variations of provisions that already exist in contracts and can be adapted to deal specifically with a crisis. These steps can be taken to support PPPs at various stages:

- **for PPP pipeline projects**, where contracts are still to be signed, some of the proposals below could be used to encourage participation.
- **for existing projects** (construction and operational phase), where contracts are already signed and the private partners want to renegotiate the terms of the contract, governments

may choose to provide financial support. Renegotiation may also provide governments with the opportunity to establish greater VfM where it was previously lacking.

13.5.1 Intervention measures

The literature suggests a number of measures to help a country tackle the impact of the crisis or improve the attractiveness of PPPs for private partners by facilitating access to finance and improving the risk–return balance.[12] The list below is presented to illustrate the range of alternatives, with the risk exposure of the government increasing as one goes down the list.

- **Concession extension**: extends the tenure of the agreement to allow the private partner to generate the return needed to ensure the viability of the project.
- **Subsidy**: output-based cash subsidies are the measure most transparently linked to the ultimate objective of the PPP. Alternatively, tax breaks or subsidies could be paid either to the private partners or to direct users of the service (possibly in the form of vouchers).
- **Grant**: extended to improve the attractiveness of the project and reduce the overall exposure of the private partner to risk – these should be subject to conditions.
- **Minimum revenue guarantee**: the guarantee ensures that the private partners can cover the repayment and servicing of their debt liabilities. The provision of a minimum revenue guarantee obviates a debt guarantee.
- **Exchange rate guarantee**: provides protection to a private partner in the case where the domestic currency depreciates significantly thereby protecting the foreign currency earnings of the private partner when the private partner is a foreign company.
- **Debt guarantee**: guarantees the repayment of all or part of the debt.
- **Subordinated loan**: the government provides a standing loan facility on which the private partner can draw if necessary – this may reduce the cash-flow risks that the servicing of senior debt may cause.
- **Equity measures**: guarantees for all or part of the equity values (the private partner can sell its equity stake to the government at an agreed price).
- **Step-in rights**: in the case of contractor failure, governments may be able to step in and re-tender the PPP or may have to take over the operation, if there is fiscal space.

However, as these options ultimately entail greater risk and cost for the taxpayer, they should be considered only under certain conditions. For example, when there are extreme circumstances beyond the control of the private partner(s), when the intervention yields positive – and maximum, conditional on the crisis conditions – VfM, and when the government is compensated for accepting additional risk (i.e. the support comes at a price for the private partner). The following section outlines some key principles to guide intervention.

13.5.2 Intervention principles

A government's actions to enhance the attractiveness of PPPs may also increase its own exposure to risk. Given that risks not allocated to the private partner are retained by the government, the latter might be left with undesirably high exposure that could persist over time. To avoid this situation, while maintaining VfM, some principles should be followed[13]:

- **Intervention should be justified on economic grounds**. This may be the case if the service in question is a public good or a good with a positive externality, the delivery of which is usually not (entirely) left to the private sector, but rather requires some form of government intervention. For such goods, the government may have an interest in ensuring delivery is not disrupted, e.g. through contractor failure.

- **Interventions should support the wider fiscal policy stance**. Supporting PPPs is just one way for fiscal policy to stimulate the real economy. Ensuring a smooth stream of PPP projects and reducing their vulnerability could support a countercyclical stance. This support should be weighed against other options for countercyclical policy.
- **The measures should be quantified and included in the budget framework**. To mitigate the government's exposure to future fiscal risk, any measures should be included within the annual budget process and their medium-term impact assessed, including future government liabilities. A robust budgeting and accounting framework is critical for reducing public decision makers' incentives to move support measures off the balance sheet, especially during crisis when public borrowing may be constrained.
- **Public support should not endanger fiscal sustainability**. When negotiating possible interventions, governments should be mindful that a crisis might create financial difficulty not only for the private party, but also for the government. Investor concerns over fiscal sustainability could drive up public sector borrowing costs and thus limit the potential, and desirability, of public support for PPPs.
- **Government measures should be contingent on circumstances**. Once the crisis subsides, perceptions regarding the risk–return trade-off, as well as information on borrowers, might improve. This could lead to an easing of credit constraints.
- **Access to the public purse should come at a price**. To mitigate moral hazard and ensure that the private partner continues to effectively manage the risk assigned in the contract, any government support that acts as insurance should be priced accordingly. This may involve charging fees for the guarantees, contingent loans or other financing options. In addition, should the public sector reduce the private partner's exposure to downside risk, they should also share in the upside.[14]
- **Intervention should seek to maintain VfM**. The risk borne by the private partner should still be sufficient to ensure the desired VfM. In the case of exogenous risk, the manner and scale at which the risk is mitigated should not undermine efficiency incentives by guaranteeing a certain rate of return for the private partner.
- **The policy should be publicly disclosed**. Measures to counter the crisis run the risk of being seen as changes to the 'rules' and could potentially engender moral hazard in the future. Clearly articulated and transparent policies could mitigate this risk.

13.5.3 'Trip switch' clauses

To ensure measures are temporary, government intervention could include contingency clauses (or 'trip switches'). Once the economy exits the crisis and the risk–return trade-off for private partners improves, the measures should become obsolete. Trip switch clauses should state the mitigating steps to be implemented, as well as indicators, such as interest rate spreads and output measures, that activate the clauses. Furthermore, in the interest of sound public finance, the clauses should also specify indicators that will 'deactivate' government intervention – the recent easing of credit constraints and apparent recovery in the project pipeline reinforce the importance of a 'built-in' exit strategy for government involvement.

Following negotiations or renegotiations, these clauses can be included in both new and existing contracts. To the extent that existing contracts are affected by the crisis and private partners request renegotiation of the contractual terms, the government could choose to limit renegotiations to the type of measures discussed below. This will strengthen the hand of government and limit the pressure on government to renegotiate the terms of the contract *de novo*.

The following types of trip switches can be considered for associated intervention measures:

- **Contract extensions**: If revenue (or operational profit) temporarily falls below a predetermined level, the contract could automatically be extended by a pre-negotiated period to allow the private operator to generate the required rate of return. To prevent moral hazard, the fall in profit should be correlated with general economic conditions, as measured by pre-agreed-upon indicators that register severe downturns (e.g. a decrease in activity that exceeds two standard deviations, calculated, for example, with a moving window of 20 or 40 quarters).

- **Output-based subsidy and guarantees**: If revenue (or operational profit) temporarily falls below a predetermined level, government would pay an output-based subsidy that ensures that the private partner can cover its interest costs. As with a contract extension, the contingency (or 'trip switch') clause is only activated if the drop in demand that the private partner experiences is correlated with an indicator of severe economic contraction, rather than endogenous risks (e.g. a drop in relative demand for the output as a result of quality or service characteristics that fall short of expectations).

- **Revenue enhancement (shadow tolls)**: Related to the output-based subsidy is the temporary substitution of a partial shadow toll (i.e. a toll per user paid by government and not the direct recipient), financed with debt. Once the recession is over, the shadow toll is scrapped, and the toll increases to repay the debt incurred during the recession. During the recession demand is supported by the reduced toll and thus improves the earnings of the PPP, while during the boom, the higher toll reduces demand.

- **Subsidy for interest rate increase**: Instead of providing temporary finance to the PPP, government could aid the PPP by paying a grant that covers the excess over what is considered a normal upper range for interest rate movements (where 'normal' depends, in part, on the creditworthiness of the borrower). This subsidy should only be paid in the case of variable interest rate loans (of any maturity) where the interest rate is expected to return to normal levels, or short-term fixed-interest rate loans. The increase in the interest rate should not be due to idiosyncratic risky behaviour by the private partner. A normal upper range for interest rate movements should be defined in the contract.[15]

- **Government finance**: The government could finance some or all of the debt to address the short-run difficulty experienced by the private operator. A trip switch clause would provide the government with the option to sell its debt stake in the project after two or three years, or, preferably, if market indicators specified in the clause reach pre-crisis levels. The debt stake can then be sold in an open tender process. In this manner government addresses a short- to medium-term problem with a short- to medium-term solution and does not commit itself to the long-term provisioning of finance. This measure, though, should be used very sparingly since it increases the exposure of government significantly, leaving only the equity stake of the private partner at risk.

- **Debt–equity switch**: The contract could include a contingency clause that requires some of the bond-financed debt to be turned into equity if revenue falls below a level that enables the servicing of debt. An improved debt/equity ratio would de-leverage the balance sheet and alleviate the pressure on interest payments. However, it would also dilute the shareholding and hence the control of existing shareholders. This operation could be thrown into reverse once revenue improves again.

Governments should ensure they have sufficient skilled personnel to both negotiate and manage the implementation of the clauses.[16] Should a government wish to implement contingency clauses but face a shortage of skilled personnel, it should opt for clauses based on uncomplicated, straightforward indicators. Thus indicators should be relatively easy to assess with data that are accessible and verifiable by all parties. The indicator and the data used should also not be open to manipulation by any party to the contract. Examples would include interest rate spreads, total revenue earnings and total production figures. Uncomplicated, straightforward indicators are also easier to negotiate, thereby reducing contract negotiation time and cost.

13.6 Conclusion

The financial crisis affected PPPs around the world, suspending or delaying the implementation of projects – primarily those under preparation – through financial as well as real channels. The principal channels of crisis transmission have been the cost and the availability of project funding.

Governments have chosen to support PPPs – sometimes as part of a wider fiscal stimulus package – by changing the risk sharing arrangements and facilitating access to credit via guarantees and direct loans, mainly extended by State-owned banks or other public institutions.

These and other suggested measures may increase governments' exposure to PPPs and alter the balance of risks, thus affecting the VfM of PPPs. Intervention measures must be coherent with the overall direction of the macroeconomic policy and thus fiscally sustainable. Private partners' incentives should be preserved to the best extent possible, while at the same time ruling out moral hazard and protecting the public purse. Intervention measures should be employed only under extreme, unforeseen circumstances, and be contingent upon the manifestation of such circumstances.

'Trip switch' clauses suggested in this study offer some possibilities for limiting the intervention measures in time by providing an automatic exit strategy that ensures the temporary nature of government's support. These should be supported by sound budgeting, legal, and accounting frameworks.

Notes

1 We would like to thank Robert Gillingham, Sanjeev Gupta, Rolando Ossowski and the participants of the FAD seminar for useful comments, Ada Karina Izaguirre for sharing the PPIAF database with us, Jukka-Pekka Strand and Vickram Cuttaree for valuable inputs, and the country officials for their responses to the questionnaire. This chapter was written while Philippe Burger was a visiting scholar at the IMF's Fiscal Affairs Department.

2 The national PPP programmes have grown over time and, in some countries, constitute a large share of investment. For instance, the total capital value of PPP in Korea equalled 6.7 per cent of GDP at the end of 2008, while in Portugal it equalled 5.6 per cent at the end of 2007. For South Africa, Peru and Canada the figures for 2008 are smaller: respectively 1.7 per cent, 2.6 per cent and 1.4 per cent of GDP.

3 While some VfM tests also minimize the net present value of cost, the optimal option selected on a VfM basis is not necessarily the least expensive option available as adjustments are made for quality and risk.

4 Fiscal space is only apparent, since a PPP merely replaces the debt incurred through traditional procurement with the present value of future service charges, which usually include a component to service the PPP debt.

5 Positive surprises or upside risk can also materialize, but are not analysed in this chapter.

6 See Part 3 of IMF (2008) for a more complete discussion.

7 By nature, PPPs are more vulnerable to policy and regulatory changes than many other private activities because they imply construction and/or service provision of public goods.

8 The tails of the risk distribution may have been impossible or too costly to manage for the private partner.

9 The survey includes projects that reached financial closure, were awarded to a winning bidder, or reached the final stage of the tender/negotiation phase in July 2008 and onwards. It also includes projects awarded before July 2008, but still trying to reach financial closure and projects that were operational before July 2008, but were trying to raise additional financing.

10 The questionnaire was sent to 20 countries. The results reported in the chpater are based on the answers of Canada, Colombia, Korea, Mozambique, Peru, Portugal, U.K., and South Africa.

11 Source: Fiscal Risk Questionnaires, IMF Fiscal Affairs Department.

12 The measures are summarized from Angelides and Xenidis (2009), Estache et al. (2007) and Irwin (2003).

13 It is not yet clear to what extent government interventions did abide by these principles; the apparent reliance on State-owned banks to support PPPs means that the eventual costs to the fiscal budget may remain hidden.

14 A good example is that of the Chilean exchange rate guarantee, outlined in Hemming (2006).

15 For instance, suppose that the average interest rate equals 8 per cent, while under normal conditions interest rates have a two standard deviation variation equal to three percentage points. A contract may then state that government will pay a subsidy to cover the cost related to all basis points in excess of the 300 bps (i.e. when the interest rate exceeds 11 per cent).

16 Negotiating the initial inclusion of the clauses is often not the most difficult part, since this can be handled by external technical advisors employed by government during the negotiation phase. However, once the contract is in place, managing the implementation (as well as possible pressure to renegotiate) in the absence of skilled personnel might become problematic.

References

Abadie, Richard, 2008, 'Infrastructure finance: surviving the credit crunch,' *Talking Points*, August (London: Public Sector Research Centre–PricewaterhouseCoopers).

Angelides, Demos and Yannis Xenidis, 2009, 'PPP Infrastructure Investments: Critical Aspects and Prospects,' in *Policy, Finance and Management for Public–Private Partnerships*, ed. by A. Akintola and M. Beck (London: Wiley-Blackwell).

Chemonics International Inc., 2008, 'Kazakhstan: PPP Opportunities in a Young Country,' June (Washington: Report prepared for USAID).

Correia da Silva, Luis, Antonio Estache and Sakari Järvelä, 2004, 'Is Debt Replacing Equity in Regulated Privatized Infrastructure in Developing Countries?' World Bank Policy Research Working Paper 3374, August (Washington: World Bank).

Davies, Paul, 2009, 'A Review of Lending Appetite for Public Private Partnership Financings,' *Talking Points*, January (London: Public Sector Research Centre–PricewaterhouseCoopers).

Estache, Antonio and Tomás Serebrisky, 2004, 'Where Do We Stand on Transport Infrastructure Deregulation and Public-Private Partnership?' World Bank Policy Research Working Paper 3356, July (Washington: World Bank).

Estache, Antonio, Ellis Juan and Lourdes Trujillo, 2007, 'Public–Private Partnerships in Transport,' Policy Research Working Paper 4436 (Washington: World Bank).

Ettinger, Stephen, Michael Schur, Stephan von Klaudy, Georgina Dellacha and Shelly Hahn, 2005, 'Developing Country Investors and Operators in Infrastructure,' Trends and Policy Options No. 3, May (Washington: Public–Private Infrastructure Advisory Facility).

European Commission, 2004, *Green Paper on Public–Private Partnerships and Community Law on Public Contracts and Concessions*, COM (2004) 327 def. (Brussels: European Commission).

European Investment Bank, 2004, 'The EIB's Role in Public–Private Partnerships (PPPs),' July 15 <www.eib.org/Attachments/thematic/eib_ppp_en.pdf>.

Farquharson, Ed and Javier Encinas, 2010, 'The U.K. Treasury Infrastructure Finance Unit: Supporting PPP Financing During the Global Liquidity Crisis,' PPP Solutions, March (Washington: International Bank for Reconstruction and Development).

Hemming, Richard, 2006, *Public–Private Partnerships, Government Guarantees, and Fiscal Risk*, Special Issues Paper, Fiscal Affairs Department (Washington: International Monetary Fund).

Inter-American Development Bank (IADB), 2007, 'Program to Promote Public Private Partnerships in Mexican States,' Donors Memorandum (Washington: Inter-American Development Bank/ Multilateral Investment Fund).

International Monetary Fund, 2004, 'Public–Private Partnerships,' Fiscal Affairs Department, <www.imf.org/external/np/fad/2004/pifp/eng/031204.pdf>.

International Monetary Fund, 2008, 'Public Investment and Public–Private Partnerships: Addressing Infrastructure Challenges and Managing Fiscal Risks,' Fiscal Affairs Department (Washington: International Monetary Fund).

Irwin, Timothy, 2003, *Public Money for Private Infrastructure: Deciding When to Offer Guarantees, Output-Based Subsidies, and Other Forms of Fiscal Support for Privately Provided Infrastructure Services*, World Bank Working Paper No. 10, July (Washington: World Bank).

Irwin, Timothy and Tanya Mokdad, 2010, *Managing Contingent Liabilities in Public Private Partnerships Practice in Australia, Chile, and South Africa*, World Bank Report, PPIAF (Washington: World Bank).

Li, Bing, Akintola Akintoye, Peter Edwards and Cliff Hardcastle, 2005a, 'Critical Success Factors for PPP/PFI Projects in the UK Construction Industry,' *Construction Management and Economics*, Vol. 23, No. 5, June, pp. 459–71.

Li, Bing, Akintola Akintoye, Peter Edwards and Cliff Hardcastle, 2005b, 'The Allocation of Risk in PPP/PFI Construction Projects in the UK,' *International Journal of Project Management*, Vol. 23, pp. 25–35.

Merna, Tony and Nigel J. Smith, 1996, *Projects Procured by Privately Financed Concession Contracts*, Vol. 1 and 2 (Hong Kong: Asia Law and Practice, 2nd edn).

OECD, 2008, *Public–Private Partnerships: In Pursuit of Risk Sharing and Value for Money*, (Paris: Organisation for Economic Co-operation and Development Publishing).

Public–Private Infrastructure Advisory Facility (PPIAF), 2009, *Assessment of the Impact of the Crisis on New PPI Projects*, PPIAF (Washington: World Bank).

Standard and Poor's, 2005, 'Public Private Partnerships: Global Credit Survey 2005,' April 25 (New York: Standard and Poor's).

Ye, Sudong, 2009, 'Patterns of Financing PPP Projects,' in *Policy, Management and Finance of Public–Private Partnerships*, ed. by A. Akintola and M. Beck (London: Wiley-Blackwell).

Zatezalo-Falatar, Milica, 2010, 'Public Private Partnerships in France – State Guarantee Supports the Congested Pipeline,' *The Columbia Journal of European Law Online*, Vol. 16, pp. 71–5.

14

Financial and sovereign debt crises and PPP market structure[1]

Etienne B. Yehoue[2]

14.1 Introduction

What originated in the world's most advanced financial system in 2007 as the Sub-Prime Mortgage crisis quickly transformed itself into one of the most severe financial crises since the Great Depression. A number of the largest and oldest financial institutions became subjects of bankruptcy, takeover, reorganization or government intervention, leading to one of the most significant transformations of the financial services landscape in history. As the financial services sector found itself in a full-scale crisis, funding availability and cost were severely impacted (Fengate 2008).

This, combined with the subsequent economic meltdown along with the reduced demand that follows, is a critical development for the strength and viability of PPP markets. PPPs are arrangements between the public and private sectors in which risks are appropriately shared between the two entities and financing is diversified to involve private sources. The prosperity of PPP markets requires strong demand and availability of financing at reasonable costs. Any crisis affecting demand, the cost of financing and its availability has the potential of challenging the viability of PPP arrangements. The financial crisis was so severe that some important market segment financing PPPs, the monoline bond market for example, had to close to new transactions. Thus, analysing the implications of the crisis for PPPs appears vital.

Some studies have offered some anecdotal and country evidences based on case studies (e.g. Desilets 2009; Liyanage 2011) and others have examined the transmission channels of the crisis and emphasized the fiscal risks for government responses (e.g. Burger *et al.*) in Chapter 13 of this volume.

This chapter, using a more comprehensive database and covering a longer time horizon (1990–2011), addresses three fundamental issues. First, it analyses the impacts of the 2007–9 financial crisis on PPPs using not only a trend analysis, but most importantly newly compiled data on systemic liquidity easing measures undertaken by emerging and developing countries during the crisis. The trend analysis is based on assessing the evolution of PPPs before, during, and after the crisis. The use of systemic liquidity easing measures is to capture the severity of the crisis in order to assess its impacts on PPPs. These measures were undertaken by central banks primarily to ease liquidity conditions and are defined below. They were developed and

349

compiled by Ishi *et al.* (2009). The measures are not linked to PPP market structure; they are used as a proxy for the financial crisis. The intuition is that the higher the number of measures undertaken, the tighter were the liquidity conditions and the more severe was the crisis. In other words, the number of these measures is used as a proxy to capture the severity of the crisis. The chapter uses these measures only in the context of assessing the impacts of the crisis on PPPs. These impacts are found to be short term and somewhat weak, especially given the severity of the crisis.

Second, the chapter examines the driving factors of the weak and short-term nature of the impacts of the most severe crisis since the Great Depression. In other words, the factors underpinning the resilience of PPP markets are analysed. The chapter argues and finds evidence that PPP market structure has been readjusted in the course of the crisis. The re-adjustments have mainly occurred along two broad dimensions: PPP financing structure (including the sources) and PPP schemes. The readjustments have not only increased some types of risks for the private sector and allowed a better screening of PPP promoters' long term commitment, but have also called for an enhanced role of public entities. The chapter argues that such readjustments were at the core of the resilience of PPP markets.

Third, the longer time horizon including 2011 allows the opportunity to also assess the impact of the ongoing sovereign debt crisis in the Euro area on PPPs. In light of the enhanced role for governments in the new PPP market structure, it is found that the sovereign debt crisis in the Euro area that began in 2011 and is still ongoing has had a much bigger impact on PPPs in 2011 than the 2007–9 financial crisis.

The chapter is organized as follows. The next section analyses the PPP trends before the crisis. Section 14.3 briefly summarizes the crisis and introduces the systemic liquidity easing measures. Section 14.4 develops the conceptual framework for analysing the crisis impacts and offers an assessment of the impacts of the crisis on PPPs. Section 14.5 offers evidence supporting the contention that the financial crisis has effectively induced the PPP market structure to change. Section 14.6 examines the impacts of the sovereign debt crisis in the Euro area on PPP. Section 14.7 concludes.

14.2 PPP trends before the crisis

For the emerging and developing countries, the trends of PPPs are analysed using the *World Bank's Private Participation in Infrastructure (PPI)* database.[3] The database is comprehensive and available over 1990–2011, but covers only emerging and developing countries. For the advanced countries, the chapter relies on data compiled by *Public Work Financing* (PWF), obtained from the Organization for Economic Cooperation and Development (OECD) for the cumulative data over 1985–2010, and from PWF 2011 survey for the cumulative data over 1985–2011. These data are available only on a cumulative basis for total planned (including funded) PPP projects over 1985–2010 and over 1985–2011. Data are also available on a cumulative basis for effectively funded projects over 1985 to October 2009 and 1985 to October 2010.[4] Use is also made of data from OPP Deutschland AG reported by Muller (2009).

Over the course of 1990–2007 public–private partnerships grew significantly for both advanced and developing countries, but with marked variation over time, regions, and depending on the type of private participation (Figures 14.1, 14.2, 14.3, 14.4 and 14.5). Both advanced and developing countries witnessed this significant increase but to varying degrees.

For the emerging and developing countries, the annual average growth rate for PPP project count over 1990–2007 was 77.6 per cent in the energy sector, 28.6 per cent in the telecom sector, 18.3 per cent in the transport sector, and 32.8 per cent in the water and

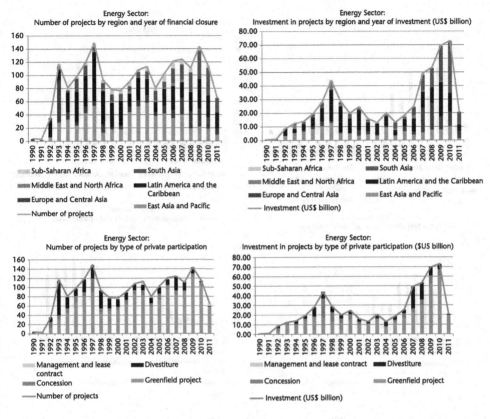

Figure 14.1 Energy sector: PPP count, investment, and type of private participation (developing countries and emerging markets)

Source: Based on World Bank's Private Participation in Infrastructure Database

sewerage sector. In terms of investment, the annual average growth was 67 per cent in the energy sector, 23.4 per cent in the telecom sector, 24 per cent in the transport sector, and 207.6 per cent in the water and sewerage sector.

Despite the overall increase of PPPs both in terms of project count and investment over 1990–2007, there were some variations across sectors within the period. For example, by and large, PPP count and investment steadily increased from 1990 to 1997 regardless of the sector. However, the energy and telecom sectors exhibited a very sharp increase in 1993 before moderating to an increase that followed the overall trend. In addition, while the telecom sector exhibited more fluctuations with a declining trend in terms of project count, there was a marked increase over 2006–7. Also the pattern of investment in the sector has shown a steady increase since 2003, suggesting that even though it might have fewer projects, they require higher investment, which is growing (Figure 14.2). On the other hand, despite the high and growing number of projects in water and sewerage sector, the related investment is more modest (Figure 14.4).

All the regions of the world experienced the marked and steady increase in PPPs over the period 1990–7 (Figures 14.1, 14.2, 14.3 and 14.4). However, following the 1997 Asian crisis,

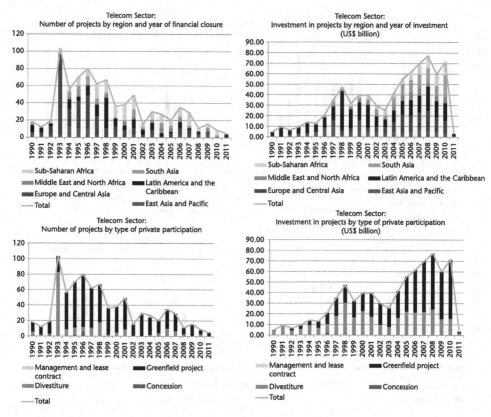

Figure 14.2 Telecom sector: PPP count, investment, and type of private participation (developing countries and emerging markets)

Source: Based on World Bank's Private Participation in Infrastructure Database

the trend reversed starting for most sectors in 1998, when PPPs experienced a sharp decline both in terms of project count and investment and which lasted for about three years for the energy and transport sectors. The trend reversal was more prolonged for the telecom sector, but was shorter (one year) for the water sector. Across sectors it is apparent that Asia, especially East Asia and Pacific, was at the core of the decline (Figures 14.1, 14.2 and 14.3). The water and sewerage sector appears to be the least affected by the 1997 crisis as authorities may have managed to save projects providing basic services. PPPs recovered overall in 2002–3 to various degrees across sectors and the recovery was led by Asia. With some fluctuations, this momentum was, by and large, maintained until 2007.

Overall, over 1990–2007, the average annual growth of PPP investment in the energy sector was 109.5 per cent in East Asia and Pacific, 163.6 per cent in Europe and Central Asia, 11 per cent in Latin America and the Caribbean, 199.6 per cent in Middle East and North Africa, 375 per cent in South Asia, and 204 per cent in Sub-Saharan Africa. In the telecom sector, on average, PPP investment annual growth was 51.4 per cent in East Asia and Pacific, 82 per cent in Europe and Central Asia, 25 per cent in Latin America and the Caribbean, 179.4 per cent in Middle East and North Africa, 102 per cent in South Asia, and 20.5 per cent in Sub-Saharan Africa. In the transport sector the annual average growth rate stood at 107 per cent in East Asia and Pacific, 103.6

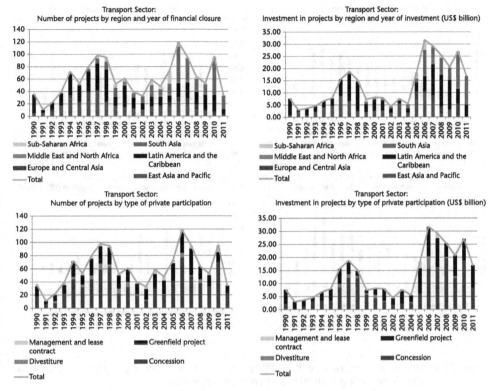

Figure 14.3 Transport sector: PPP count, investment, and type of private participation (developing countries and emerging markets)

Source: Based on World Bank's Private Participation in Infrastructure Database

per cent in Europe and Central Asia, 63.7 per cent in Latin America and the Caribbean, 91.3 per cent in Middle East and North Africa, 151 per cent in South Asia, and 12.4 per cent in Sub-Saharan Africa. In the water and sewerage sector, these average growth figures stood at 495.4 per cent in East Asia and Pacific, 469.7 per cent in Europe and Central Asia, 90 per cent in Latin America and the Caribbean, but PPP investment fell by 100 percent in Middle East and North Africa, by 100 per cent in South Asia, and by 90.5 per cent in Sub-Saharan Africa.

Despite the decline in investment for the water and sewerage sector in Middle East and North Africa, in South Asia, and in Sub-Saharan Africa, overall investment in PPPs has increased in these regions as the increases in other sectors outweigh the water and sewerage sector decline. The high percentages observed above need to be put in context of low initial levels of PPP investments (Figures 14.1, 14.2, 14.3 and 14.4).

For advanced countries, no cross-country consolidated database similar to the *World Bank* PPI database is available that I am aware of, so the analysis relies on *Public Works Financing – International Major Projects Survey* (PWF 2010 and 2011) data and other anecdotal evidence. The survey data include projects that represent various combinations of public and private sector risk-taking and cumulative data since 1985. The data do not allow comprises PPP trends over 1990–2007 to be isolated for analysis, so for advanced countries, the chapter simply offers broad analysis based on cumulative data over 1985–2010 and over 1985–2011.

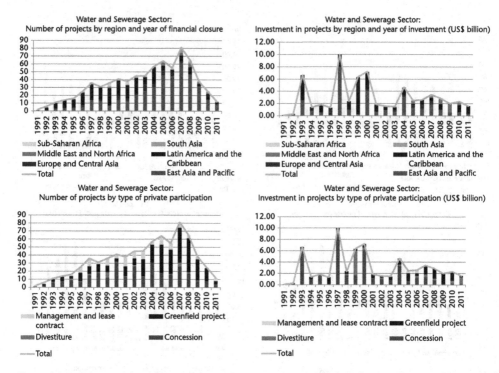

Figure 14.4 Water and sewerage sector: PPP count, investment, and type of private participation (developing countries and emerging markets)

Source: Based on World Bank's Private Participation in Infrastructure Database

According to the database, the USA accumulated a total of 495 planned (including funded) PPP projects worth about US$ 213 billion over 1985–2011. The number of projects effectively funded over 1985 to October 2009 amounts to 356 with US dollar value exceeding 52 billion. Those funded over 1985 to October 2010 stand at 377 with US dollar value of more than 68 billion. Though time series data would be a preferable source, these observations nonetheless suggest that in the USA PPP projects are likely to have been increasing over time, in particular after 2009. More precisely, in the USA, the data indicate that the growth rate between the cumulative funded projects over 1985 to October 2009 and the cumulative funded projects over 1985 to October 2010 is about 6 per cent for project count and 31 per cent for the corresponding dollar investment. According to the database, from October 2009 to October 2010, PPP count increased by 21 new projects and investment increased by US$16 billion in the USA.

For Europe, projects accumulated over 1985–2011 amount to 1,048 and cost more than US$ 635 billion. Out of these, those effectively funded over 1985 to October 2009 stand at 642 with a total investment of about US$ 303 billion. Those funded over 1985 to October 2010 amount to 699 with total dollar investment of about US$ 353 billion. According to the database, the growth rate between the cumulative funded projects over 1985 to October 2009 and the cumulative funded projects over 1985 to October 2010 is about 9 per cent for project count and 17 per cent for the corresponding dollar investment. These growth rates stand respectively at 51 per cent and 96 per cent for Canada. From October 2009 to October 2010,

PPP count increased by 57 projects, and investment increased by US$ 50 billion in Europe. Over the same period in Canada, PPP count increased by 43 projects, while investment increased by US$ 22 billion.

Figure 14.5 displays the cumulative PPP count and investment for total planned (including funded) projects and those effectively funded over 1985 to October 2009 and 1985 to October 2010 for the USA, Canada, Europe, and the world. The growth rates for these cumulative statistics are also displayed.

According to the 2011 survey data, for the entire sample, among funded projects over 1985–2010, road PPPs represent almost half of all PPPs in value (US$ 361 billion out of US$ 744 billion for the entire sample) and a third in number (651 out of 1,969). Rail appears in the second position with dollar value (US$ 176 billion) followed by buildings (US$ 125 billion), suggesting that the transport sector has the lion's share with total value US$ 538 billion out of US $744 spread over 821 projects out of 1,969. The database also indicates that Europe represents about half of total PPP investment value (US$ 353 billion out of US$ 744) and more than a third of total project number (699 out of 1,969) (Figure 14.5).[5]

For additional evidence on the rising trend of PPPs before 2007, data from OPP Deutschland AG for Germany reported by Muller (2009), but only for the building and road construction sector, are used. PPPs in the sector present a clear increasing trend from 2002/03 to 2007 in terms of both number and investment (Figure 14.6).

Overall, before the 2007–9 financial crisis, PPPs display rising trends across regions and sectors, both in terms of project count and investment. For emerging and developing countries for which detailed data are available, greenfield projects appear to be the key driver regardless of sector. The telecom and energy sectors appear to be the ones receiving most investment, followed by the transport sector. The water sector receives significantly less investment even though the number of projects is important. For advanced countries the transport sector, in particular road construction, appears to be the dominant sector.

Before analysing the dynamics of PPP markets over 2008–9, especially for emerging and developing countries, the analysis addresses the crisis that hit the world in 2007. It introduces the systemic liquidity easing measures, whose number will be used as a proxy of the severity of the crisis.

14.3 The financial crisis

In the summer of 2007, the world witnessed the first manifestations of a severe financial crisis that originated in its most advanced financial system. In August 2007, the Federal Reserve and the European Central Bank started implementing unprecedented systemic liquidity easing (SLE) measures that increased in number, magnitude, and novelty and as such they are non-traditional (Ishi et al. 2009).

Following the collapse of Lehman Brothers in September 2008, liquidity conditions sharply worsened. The resulting severe tightening of bank dollar funding, along with doubts about bank asset quality, contributed to an increase in perceived counterparty risk, and interbank rates rose and became more volatile. Banks' reluctance to lend to each other also increased demand for central bank funds (liquidity). Figure 14.7 shows the three-month LIBOR-OIS spread, an indicator of global dollar liquidity tightness, which significantly widened from mid-September to mid-October. The drying up of the global bank dollar funding markets also reflects the inability to roll over debt (Yehoue 2009).

As the crisis expanded and global financial conditions took a turn for the worse in September 2008, emerging markets, too, began to experience liquidity strains and a number of them

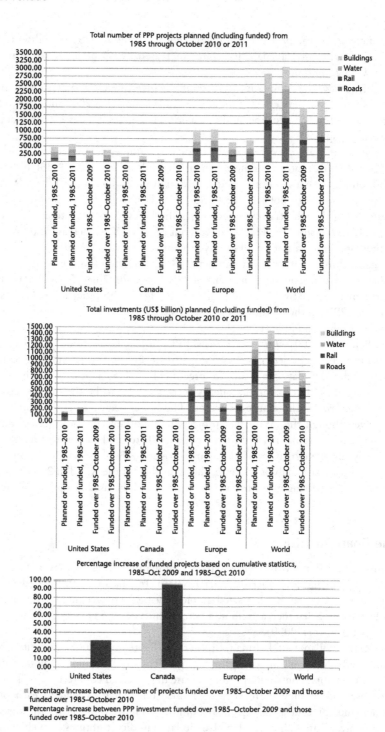

Figure 14.5 PPPs in advanced countries on a cumulative basis

Source: Based on *Public Work Financing Newsletter* vols. 242 and 264, October 2010 and 2011, www. PWFinance.net

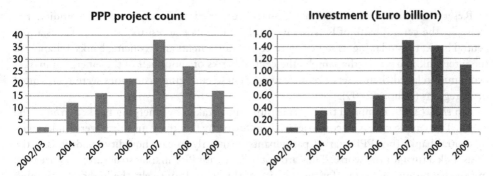

Figure 14.6 Germany – development in PPP projects in building and road construction
Source: Based on OPP Deutschland AG

began taking the SLE measures. The measures include: foreign exchange liquidity support, cross-country foreign exchange swap arrangements, domestic liquidity support facilities, and relaxation of reserve requirements. Their description below is based on Yehoue (2009).

Measures relative to foreign exchange liquidity support include provisions of dollar liquidity to local markets, easing of foreign exchange liquidity requirements, relaxation of existing foreign exchange facility terms, and the introduction of new foreign exchange facilities. A number of emerging economies eased conditions on foreign exchange credit instruments and introduced new ones. For example, policymakers in Korea abolished regulatory restrictions on dollar financing from the offshore forward market, introduced a competitive auction swap facility, and took steps to facilitate foreign exchange financing to exporters. The central bank of Russia set aside $50 billion in foreign exchange reserves for use by banks and corporations to meet foreign liability obligations. The central bank of Brazil stepped up foreign exchange swaps, eased collateral requirements, and extended direct financing to private companies for debt repayment and capital investments (Yehoue 2009).

Measures relative to cross-country foreign exchange liquidity require the involvement of at least two central banks whereby the liquidity providing central bank offers its currency to the domestic central bank through a foreign exchange swap, and the domestic central bank distributes the foreign exchange to local counterparties in need. Nine of the economies covered were involved in such arrangements. The Fed, European Central Bank (ECB), the Swiss National Bank (SNB), as well as the Nordic central banks were the main liquidity providers. For example, the Fed set up liquidity arrangements with Brazil, Korea, Mexico, and Singapore. The ECB, the SNB, and the Nordic central banks established arrangements for emerging market economies in Europe. These measures were undertaken when foreign exchange liquidity conditions became very tight during the crisis (Yehoue 2009).

The aim of domestic liquidity support measures is to ease domestic liquidity shortages by targeting key credit markets such as commercial paper, corporate bonds, and equity markets. In the sample, about seventeen emerging market economies undertook such measures to alleviate domestic liquidity conditions. For example, the central bank of Russia expanded eligible collateral. The central bank also introduced uncollateralized lending to banks due to acute difficulties in the interbank market. The Bank of Korea stepped up repossession operations by broadening eligible collateral, expanding the number of counterparties, and it also contributed to a bond stabilization fund (Yehoue 2009).

Reserve requirement relaxation measures are aimed at freeing up bank liquidity. For example, the central bank of Russia gave banks immediate access to their own funds at the central bank, thus relaxing its stance on reserve requirements and reducing banks' reliance on the interbank market. In the sample, the central banks of about half of the emerging market economies relaxed their reserve requirements. These emerging economies were represented in all regions (Yehoue 2009).

Ishi *et al.* (2009) compiled the SLE measures undertaken by emerging markets around the world. The sample covers 39 countries.[6] It is noteworthy that these measures were undertaken by central banks (not PPP market participants) primarily to ease liquidity conditions as the crisis took a turn for the worse. They are not linked with PPP market structure; they are used in this chapter just as a proxy for the severity of the crisis. Intuitively, the higher the number of the measures undertaken at a given date, the tighter are the liquidity conditions, justifying the need for the undertaking of these measures. In other words, a higher number of the SLE measures at a given date is an indication of a severe phase of the crisis. A higher total number of SLE measures in a given country is an indication that the liquidity impact of the crisis on the country was very severe, suggesting the country was hit harder relative to others with a lower total number of SLE measures.

Figure 14.7 displays total number of measures undertaken per date. As can be seen from the figure, the number of measures reached their peak in October 2008 following the collapse

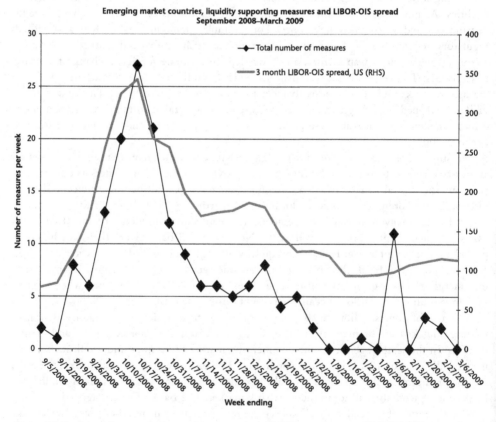

Figure 14.7 Emerging market countries: number of SLE measures and LIBOR-OIS spread

of Lehman Brothers in September, which was a very severe phase of the crisis. Figure 14.7 also shows the high correlation between the number of these measures and the three-month LIBOR–OIS spread, an indicator of global dollar liquidity tightness. The very high correlation between the number of these measures and the global dollar liquidity tightness confirms that it can be used as a good proxy for the severity of the crisis. The number of these measures is used below to analyse the significance of the impacts of the crisis on PPPs.

14.4 The financial crisis and PPPs

In this section the financial crisis and PPP market are put together to analyse potential impacts from the crisis and also to uncover whether there are any crisis-induced changes in PPP market structure. First, a conceptual framework is laid out, and second, evidence is analysed in light of the conceptual framework.

14.4.1 Potential impacts of the crisis on PPPs: the conceptual framework

An obvious channel through which the crisis would affect PPPs is cost and access to finance.[7] The severity of the crisis led to the closure of the monoline bond market, which, over the past 10 years, has been the financing structure of choice for major PPP projects. One consequence was the increased reliance on the banking sector market. However, capital requirements for banks along with liquidity tightness induced high funding costs and made private bank financing very difficult. Even though PPP risk profile has not changed and is perceived as such by banks, limited funding availability and higher credit margins make their financing more challenging. These observations suggest that the crisis would have significant negative impacts on PPPs.

On the other hand, markets or PPP stakeholders could also be smart, readjust and counter the negative impacts, thereby lowering the net impacts of the crisis. This could be achieved through readjusting the market structure of PPPs. The readjustment could occur along two broad dimensions; the financing structure and PPP schemes.

The financing structure readjustment could be done through altering the debt/equity ratio of PPPs. For example, some years before the crisis, 90/10 was the standard debt/equity ratio for projects, suggesting high levels of leverage, more risk for lenders, and raising a moral hazard issue as the low level of equity could lead to high risk taking during the implementation phase. In the crisis environment characterized by tight liquidity conditions and high counterparty risks, lenders might justifiably be reluctant to finance high leverage projects. Altering the financing structure by lowering debt/equity ratios could make projects more attractive to investors. A low debt/equity ratio also signals project viability and the long term commitment of the private sector or PPP promoters. Ho's chapter in this volume argues that the long-term commitment signal by PPP promoters or the screening by governments of promoters' long term commitment is most effective when the equity is mainly provided by PPP promoters and not non-promoters or passive shareholders. He adds that some PPP promoters use low debt/equity ratio, that is, high equity ratio as a signal for positive equity investment returns, because if the project is not financially viable, the high equity ratio will yield tremendous losses in equity. Clearly, an adjustment in debt/equity ratios could be a response to the crisis.

The financing structure readjustment could also be made by increasing government financing through State-owned development banks, bilateral or multilateral financial agencies. As the monoline bond market—which has been an important financing structure for major PPP projects over the past ten years—has closed to new transactions and the capital adequacy ratio requirements, combined with tight liquidity conditions and higher funding costs, have increased the strain on the project finance banking model, additional government or multilateral agency financing would be crucial to sustain PPP markets.

The involvement of development banks and multilateral agencies in PPPs is not new. For example, the World Bank Group—through its private sector operation arm, the International Finance Corporation (IFC), and its insurance operation arm, the Multilateral Investment Guarantee Agency (MIGA)—supports individual infrastructure projects through direct lending and guarantees to private sponsors in addition to providing transaction advisory services to governments for preparing, structuring, and tendering projects for bid.

It has been recognized that the involvement of multilateral institutions or regional development banks such as the World Bank, the Asian Development Bank (ADB), the African Development Bank (AfDB), and the Inter-American Development Bank (IDB), has improved the standards of transparency and accountability in the PPP development process. International experience has shown that their participation has not only provided comfort to the private partners and commercial lenders, particularly with respect to governance issues and the feasibility of the venture, but is also seen as reducing the risk for key stakeholders such as the private sector and governments (ADB 2006). Clearly, multilateral agencies have been involved one way or another in PPPs. The key issue is about increasing their engagement and the ability of the PPP markets to capitalize on their participation.

With regard to PPP schemes, the readjustment could be made through a mechanism where some types of market risk transfer to the private sector are relatively moderate compared to the pre-crisis era without jeopardizing the basic principle of risk-reward that is at the core of PPP arrangements.[8] After all, the concept of PPP is built on the principle of risk sharing between the public and private sectors with the qualification that each specific risk should be transferred to the entity best suited to manage it.

For example, in time of financial distress followed by economic meltdown, demand is generally lower. According to the International Monetary Fund, in 2008 world trade volume grew at a slow rate of about 3 per cent and declined by about 11 per cent in 2009.[9] A consequence of such development is low traffic volumes as less merchandize transported from production sites to sea ports for export. High unemployment rate from the economic meltdown could also translate into low traffic volumes. In these circumstances the private sector appears less suited to bear the demand risk in tolled road PPP projects for example. In such cases, PPP projects could be structured based on an availability payment scheme rather than on traffic volume or use. A PPP based on an availability payment scheme is one where the private entity receives payment based on ensuring that the service or capacity in infrastructure is made available regardless of actual traffic or use. For a volume based PPP, payment is linked to traffic volume or use. In the pre-crisis world, the volume based PPP was the standard. But addressing the challenges of the crisis may have required adjusting PPP arrangements to availability payment schemes.

These readjustments certainly call for an increased role for governments. At the same time, they increase not only the burden of risk on the private investors or PPP promoters, but also the likelihood of the viability of the projects through the low debt/equity ratios or the high equity ratios. Thus, the basic risk-reward principle that characterizes PPP is not challenged.

While the crisis was severe and could affect the number and investment size of PPPs, proper adjustments in PPP market structure could alleviate the impacts of the crisis and even make PPPs safe investment opportunities for investors. Asset classes matter in time of financial distress. For example, during the crisis, equity price went down, but sovereign yields,

CDS spreads and corporate bond spreads all went up with high volatility (Figures 14.8 and 14.9). Many investors avoided these types of assets, and may have shown interest in the asset profile that infrastructure investments offer.

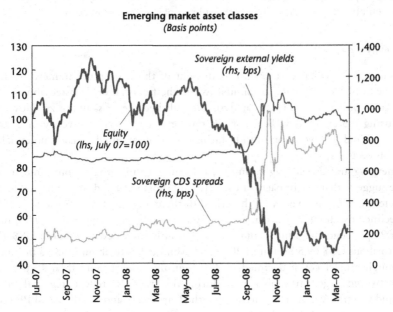

Figure 14.8 Emerging market asset classes

Source: Based on Bloomberg, DataStream, Morgan Stanley and Yehoue (2009)

Figure 14.9 Emerging market external bond spreads

Source: Based on Bloomberg, DataStream, Morgan Stanley and Yehoue (2009)

This conceptual framework shows that the crisis could affect PPPs through funding cost and its availability. It also shows that there are mechanisms through which markets could adjust. As such, the impacts of the crisis on PPPs may not be as trivial as one might think at first glance, depending on what force dominates. Assessing the impacts of the crisis on PPPs is then an empirical question, which is the subject of the next subsection.

14.4.2 Evidence

In this subsection evidence is examined in light of the conceptual framework developed above. The available PPP data are annual, while the financial crisis lasted about two years. This makes a proper econometric analysis difficult because of sample size. However, PPP trends during the crisis, as well as correlations between the crisis severity indicator highlighted above and the evolution of PPP during the crisis, are used to assess potential impacts of the crisis on PPPs.

In emerging and developing countries, in terms of PPP project count and investment, evidence suggests that the impacts of the crisis are short term and somewhat weak as might be expected, given the severity of the crisis. In the energy sector for example PPP project count declined by about 10 per cent in 2008 but immediately recovered in 2009, increasing by about 29 per cent. Investments in the sector steadily increased from about US$ 49 billion in 2007 to about US$ 69.5 billion in 2009 and even further to about US$ 73 billion in 2010 (even though project count declined in 2010), an increase of more than 48 per cent over 2007–10. By and large, this global trend during the crisis also reflects regional patterns. In Europe and Central Asia, Latin America and the Caribbean, and South Asia, PPP projects in the sector expanded both in terms of number and of investments during the crisis. In East Asia and Pacific, while project count declined during the crisis, investments expanded at least until 2010. In Middle East and North Africa and Sub-Saharan Africa where PPP projects were not significant in the past, only a marginal decline in PPP occurred during the crisis. Greenfield projects remain dominant despite the crisis (Figure 14.1).

In the telecom sector, PPP project count had an overall declining trend and investment a rising trend well before the crisis. Any impacts from the crisis appear fairly mixed. PPP project count declined by about 62 per cent in 2008, but investment increased by about 10 per cent from about US $ 70 billion to more than US $ 77 billion that year. In 2009, project count recovered (at least partially), increasing by about 45 per cent, while investment declined by about 22 per cent from more than US$ 77 billion to about US$ 60 billion. In 2010, project count declined by about 44 per cent, while investment increased by 19 per cent from about US$ 60 billion to more than US$ 71 billion. Overall, the regional pre-crisis pattern was not altered during the crisis. In terms of the type of private participation, greenfield projects remain dominant as was the case in the pre-crisis era (Figure 14.2).

In the transport sector, the impacts of the crisis were noticeable but short term. PPP project count declined by about 43 per cent in 2008, and further by about 16 per cent in 2009, before bouncing back in 2010, increasing by more than 81 per cent. Investments in the sector declined by about 13 per cent in 2008 from more than US$ 29 billion to more than US$ 25 billion, and further by about 18 per cent in 2009 from more than US$ 25 billion to more than US$ 21 billion, before recovering in 2010, increasing by about 31 per cent from more than US$ 21 billion to more than US$ 27 billion. The declines in project count and investments in the sector were mainly brought about by East Asia and Pacific and South Asia. Europe and Central Asia also contributed but to a lesser extent. In terms of type of private participation, concession appears to be the dominant type, contrary to the first two sectors (Figure 14.3). The relatively significant impact of the crisis in this sector dominated by concession seems to suggest that some specific characteristics of the concession type PPPs may have made them less resilient, but markets seem to have adjusted quickly as evidenced by the recovery in 2010.

In the water and sewerage sector, signs of the crisis impacts were also noticeable but short term. PPP project count declined by about 20 per cent in 2008, by more than 41 per cent in 2009, and further by about 34 per cent in 2010. Investment declined by more than 16 per cent in 2008 from US$ 3.4 billion to about US$ 3 billion, and further in 2009 by about 30 per cent from about US$ 3 billion to US $ 2 billion. Investment recovered in 2010, increasing by about 17 per cent from US$ 2 billion to US$ 2.3 billion. The overall decline in the sector is mainly due to the decline in East Asia and Pacific, which was leading the pre-crisis increasing trend of project count. In terms of type of private sector participation, greenfield projects and concession appear to be evenly distributed in the pre-crisis era, but greenfield projects took over after the crisis for project count. For investment, on the other hand, while concession was dominant in the pre-crisis era, greenfield projects took over after the crisis (Figure 14.4).

For advanced countries, despite the decline observed in 2008 and 2009 for Germany in the building and road construction sector (Figure 14.6), overall, PPP count in Europe increased by 57 projects and investment increased by US$ 50 billion from October 2009 to October 2010 (Figure 14.10). More precisely, in the UK for example, Rose (2008) and Thadeen (2009) report that despite the setbacks from the financial crisis, PPP markets have remained quite healthy. Rose (2008) and Liyanage (2011) point to more than 640 signed Private Finance Initiative projects including 540 that are operational in 2007. They note that in 2008, 25 more projects have closed with an investment value of more than £4 billion. Liyanage (2011) reports that 32 projects have reached financial closure within the first nine months of 2009 for a total investment value of about £5 billion. Thus, evidence suggests that any impacts of the crisis were likely to be short term and perhaps not substantial.

The resilience of PPP markets in advanced countries was not confined to Europe. As highlighted above, from October 2009 to October 2010, PPP count increased by 21 projects and investment by US$ 16 billion in the USA. In Canada, these increases stood respectively at 43 new projects and US$ 22 billion.

From the analysis above, overall, some decline was observed in some sectors during the crisis, but this was short term, especially given the severity of the crisis. In other words, the evidence for the decline of PPPs during the crisis appears somewhat mixed or weak. But to what extent can these declines be attributable to the crisis per se?

This issue is addressed by setting the systemic liquidity easing (SLE) measures highlighted earlier in this chapter as an indicator of the severity of the crisis against the number of PPP projects reaching financial closure during the crisis.[10] This is done by considering the total consolidated number of PPP projects for each country as well as by sector, and the total number of SLE measures per country. The higher the number of SLE measures for a given country, the tighter were the liquidity conditions for the country during the crisis, suggesting that the country was hit hard by the crisis. If the crisis were to have any significant impacts on PPP markets, one would expect a strong negative correlation between the number of the SLE measures and PPP projects counts.[11]

Figure 14.10 shows the correlations of the number of SLE measures with the total consolidated PPP project number during 2008–9, and with the project number in various sectors. Except for the water and sewerage sector where the correlation is negative but very low at

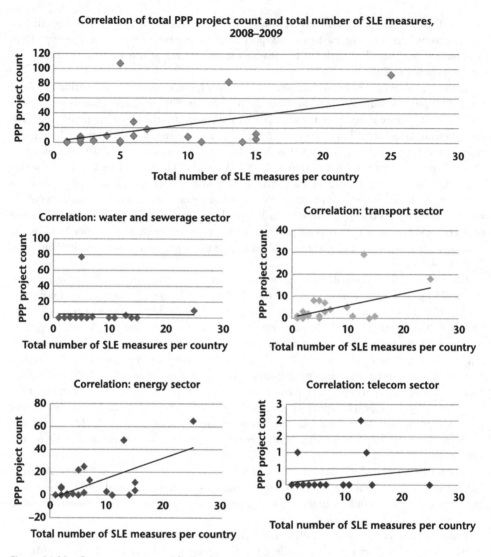

Figure 14.10 Cross-country correlation between SLE measures and PPPs during the crisis

Source: Based on Word Bank PPI database and Ishi, Stone, and Yehoue (2009)

−1 per cent, none of the other correlations is negative. The correlation stands at 48 per cent for the transport sector, and 21 per cent for the telecom sector. Only for the energy sector is the correlation above 50 per cent, standing at about 65 per cent. In aggregate, the correlation stands at about 45 per cent. Generally, these correlations appear weak and do not show any significant negative impacts of the crisis on PPP markets. If anything, they are by and large positive. Of course, no structural inferences (such as that PPP count increased during the crisis) can be drawn because these correlations are not strong and there are other factors that affect PPPs; without controlling for them, one cannot draws such a conclusion. If there were any significant impacts of the crisis on PPPs, they would have however transpired in strong negative correlations. This suggests there are no significant negative impacts of the crisis on PPPs.

These correlations combined with the evolutions of PPPs during the crisis highlighted above suggest that the crisis may have had some impacts on PPPs, but these impacts were somewhat not substantial and of short term. In light of the severity of the crisis, this suggests that PPP markets have been resilient and have adjusted quickly.

Across the board, by 2010, PPP markets had already recovered from the 2007–9 financial crisis. However, a simple observation of the 2011 data shows a drastic decline in PPP in every sector both in terms of number of projects and investment. It is hard to link this severe and drastic reversal directly to the 2007-09 crisis *per se*. Instead, this is analysed below in the context of spillovers from the ongoing European sovereign debt crisis.

Before tackling this question, the issue of why the 2007–9 crisis impacts were short term and not substantial on PPPs is first addressed. This is done by assessing whether there is evidence that PPP market structure has been readjusted.

14.5 The financial crisis-induced new PPP market structure

In light of the conceptual framework developed earlier, evidence is analysed to uncover any shifts in PPP market structure. The conceptual framework offers two broad dimensions along which market structure readjustments could occur: the financing structure and PPP schemes.

Before the crisis 90/10 debt equity ratio was the standard as highlighted earlier. Figure 14.11 displays debt/equity ratios for emerging and developing countries for PPP project finance over 2008–10. The shift from high debt/equity ratios in the pre-crisis era to low debt/equity ratios during the crisis is drastic, and shows that the proportion of PPP investment with a financing arrangement exhibiting lower debt/equity ratio increased after the crisis hit (Figure 14.11). In particular, loan volume signed with debt/equity ratios of 80s/20s or higher was 34 per cent in 2007 and 37 per cent in 2008. That proportion dropped to 13 per cent in 2009 and even further in 2010 to 9 per cent, suggesting that fewer projects closed with high debt/equity ratios. Izaguirre (2010) reports that surveyed greenfield electricity projects

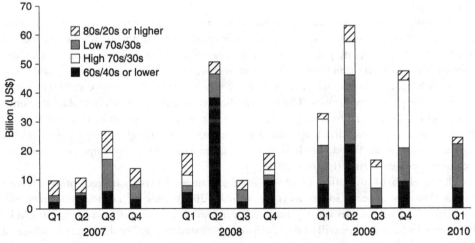

Figure 14.11   PPP investment financed by project finance in emerging and developing countries by debt/equity ratio and quarterly, 2008–10

Source: Based on Izaguirre (2010) and Projectware, Dealogic

reaching financial closure in the first quarter of 2010 indicated debt /equity ratios in the low to mid 70s/30s and even in the 60s/40s. It is clear that markets shifted from the high leverage ratios in the pre-crisis era to moderate leverage ratios, lending support to the conjecture put forward in the conceptual framework.

Analysing the PPP projects reaching financial closure during the crisis, based on three case studies, Desilets (2009) highlights the increased role of bilateral or multilateral financial agencies in reaching financial closure. For example, analysing the phase II of the A1 motorway[12] in Poland, which reached financial closure in December 2008, Desilets (2009) points out that the financing came from the European Investment Bank (€575 million or 54 per cent of the total of €1.07 billion), the Nordic Investment Bank (€150 million or 14 per cent), and the Swedish Export Credit Corporation (€345 million or 32 per cent). Even though the project was structured as a PPP, the financing does not include any private sources, just bilateral and multilateral financial institutions.

A similar pattern is observed in another project he studied, Kenya's Lake Turkana Wind Power Project (LTWP). While AfDB has initially committed to provide only 30 per cent of the financing, the crisis has forced AfDB to agree to act as Mandated Lead Arranger for the financing of US$ 405 million (70 per cent of the total cost), whereby the Bank will provide US$ 135 million in direct loan and seek additional financing from other development or private financial agencies. The remaining 30 per cent will be provided by the LTWP consortium in the form of equity. This highlights both the increased role of multilateral agencies and the shift to lower debt/equity ratios.

In Asia, ADB has reengineered new ways of doing business, by modifying its policies and procedures, making them more flexible and compatible with the needs and priorities of its PPP clientele. The reengineering also includes adoption of new financing instruments such as multi-client financing facility and local currency loans as well as extension of the range of goods and services eligible for ADB financing such as land, recurrent costs, severance payment and leased assets. The Bank also stands ready to consider, if need be, extending multi-tranche financing facility and local currency loans to qualified PPP projects in various forms including: private sector loans or equity investments—by ADB's private sector operation arm—to project companies, and provision of guarantee to commercial lenders (ADB 2006).

The World Bank has now made 30-year loans available to governments of middle-income countries and allows the borrowers to tailor their repayment schedule to address the specific needs of projects. Properly put together with private finance, these loans can greatly reduce debt service or amortization costs and the need to shore up tariffs to make projects viable. The use of such hybrid schemes has increased, especially in an effort to reduce the total cost of financing for poor communities. The Bank is also stepping up its efforts in mobilizing long-term and local currency financing to minimize currency risk exposure. In particular, the Bank stands ready to mobilize long-term domestic financing through a currency swap facility for financing projects that do not have the capacity to earn foreign exchange and as such are exposed to currency risks (Hofman 2010).

The World Bank also offers a wide range of guarantee and risk management instruments to stimulate private-sector investments. As Hofman (2010) notes, for a concession agreement, a partial risk guarantee can assure private sector investors that the concession terms would be honoured. Otherwise they will be financially compensated by the World Bank, an AAA-rated guarantor.

In addition to multilateral institutions, national development banks have also been very active. Izaguirre (2008) points out that in the case of Brazil and India, governments have been the most active in facilitating financing. In particular, the government of Brazil secured US$ 42.6 billion in additional funding for the national development bank, BNDES, to finance infrastructure projects as well as other sectors. The Indian government has allowed the public infrastructure finance company, IIFCL, to facilitate long term funding for infrastructure by providing subordinate debt. Since the crisis, the main sources of project financing in Brazil and India, both countries which account for a significant share of total PPP projects, have been public sector banks (Izaguirre 2008).

With regard to PPP schemes, Desilets (2009)—in another case study, Florida I-595, a 35-year concession highway in the USA, which reached financial closure on March 3, 2009—points out that for the first time in the USA an availability payment was used. This is a key testament that the PPP market structure has effectively changed as a result of the crisis. He reports that even though the road will be tolled, the bidders were not comfortable assuming market risk given the financial and economic climate induced by the crisis. He refers to the shift as a major one for the US market in which toll roads are the standard and usually provide the revenue for concessionaires on highway projects.

Another indication justifying why investors may have more appetite for PPPs based on an availability payment scheme may be found in cost of financing. Ernst & Young's PPP team in the UK reports that the average margin for availability payment-based PPPs increased from 82 basis points to 94 basis points between May and August 2008. In that month of August 2008 volume-based payment PPPs had an average margin of 155 basis points, more than 60 basis points higher than in May.[13]

Multilateral agencies can also help governments to meet their obligations in availability-based PPPs. For example the World Bank has put in place a 'Viability Gap' facility to help projects needing public subsidy support. The aim is to ensure that government's financing support to a project is available in a timely manner acceptable to the private sector (Hofman 2010).

The evidence presented in this section indicates that the PPP market structure has changed due to the crisis. PPP markets appear to have adjusted quickly to the new crisis-induced environment. This seems to explain the short-term nature of the impacts of the crisis on PPPs. Notice that in the discussion of the readjustment of PPP market structure, no use is made of the SLE measures. The reason is that, as explained earlier, the SLE measures are simply used as a proxy to capture the severity of the crisis in order to assess the crisis' impacts on PPPs. On the other hand, the readjustment of PPP market structure is a response to the crisis.

In the new PPP market structure, the role of the public sector has been enhanced either by increased financing through development banks or other public banks, bilateral and multilateral agencies, or through the public sector assuming some types of market risks such as the ones assumed in availability payment schemes for example. The enhanced public sector role could potentially have fiscal sustainability implications for governments, so this has to be done appropriately to preserve fiscal sustainability. Issues related to fiscal sustainability have been addressed at length in Chapter 13 in this volume. Instead, this chapter focuses on the resilience of PPPs from the market structure perspective.

14.6 The ongoing Euro area sovereign debt crisis and PPPs

As highlighted above, by 2010 PPP markets had broadly recovered from the 2007–9 financial crisis. However, in emerging and developing countries, from 2010 to 2011, PPP project count declined by about 43 per cent in the energy sector, more than 44 per cent in the telecom sector, about 65 per cent in transport, and 52 per cent in water and sewerage. From 2010 to 2011, investment declined from about US$ 73 billion to about US$ 21 billion (a fall of 71 per cent) in energy sector, from US$ 71.3 billion to US$ 3.5 billion (95 per cent) in telecom sector, from US$ 27 billion to US$ 17 billion (37 per cent) in transport, and from US$ 2.3 billion to US$ 1.6 billion (32 per cent) in water and sewerage. Such drastic declines across the board were not seen even at the height of the 2007–9 crisis. It is hard to directly link this drastic reversal to the 2007–9 crisis. Instead, it is analysed in the context of spillovers from the ongoing European sovereign debt crisis.

In the new PPP market structure that emerged from the 2007–9 crisis and is set out above, the role of the public sector has been enhanced. This, implicitly, assumes that the public sector is healthy enough to fully assume its new enhanced role to facilitate good functioning of the new PPP market structure. However, the sovereign debt crisis that began in 2011 in the Euro area and is still ongoing has challenged the fiscal sustainability across Europe, with sovereign ratings downgraded in many Euro area countries including some big ones. Private banks are now being called on to share the sacrifices by accepting some forms of restructuring of some countries' sovereign debts. Europe is not unique on the fiscal sustainability issue, as the USA also faces its own fiscal challenges, with its rating downgraded in 2011.

These developments have implications for the smooth functioning of the new PPP market structure. They affect the financing ability of bilateral or multilateral agencies, which are expected to play a more prominent role in the new PPP market structure. They also affect the public sector ability to accept some market risks as required in the new market structure.

The consequences will not be localized just to Europe or the USA. These developments have implications for the entire world. The USA and Europe are major shareholders in many of the bilateral or multilateral financial agencies around the world called upon to play a bigger role in the new PPP market structure. This has implications for a number of emerging and developing country PPP projects whose viability is linked to the remittances and export demand from Europe as these affect the vibrancy of the economies of these countries. These developments also create global anxiety and affect the risk taking behaviour of those same private investors called upon to increase the equity ratios in PPP arrangements.

In a recent study, Bayoumi and Vitek (2012) use a macroeconomic model to analyse spillovers from an intensification of the Euro area sovereign debt crisis on a set of economies. The study suggests: 1) shocks originating in the Euro area have output shocks in a broader subset of economies than shocks originating in the USA; 2) financial shocks have larger output spillover effects than real, monetary or fiscal policy shocks; 3) financial shocks are truly global: only emerging market economies with closed capital accounts would be spared, but advanced economies and emerging market economies with open capital accounts would not be spared. To the extent that the vibrancy of these economies is affected by the spillovers, demand will be damaged and as a result, the PPP markets of these economies will be impacted.

Clearly, in this financially integrated world, the Euro-area debt crisis has severe consequences for the rest of the world and may have been affecting the post 2007–9 financial crisis PPP markets through both the public and private sectors. This might be the cause of the drastic decline observed across sectors on PPPs in 2011. The debt crisis, by affecting both the public and private sectors, seems to make the negative impacts on PPPs more severe. The 2007–9 crisis originated in the private sector and governments across countries have been coming to the rescue through various forms of stimulus, which help temper the impacts of the crisis. The sovereign debt crisis, on the contrary, originated in the public sector, which is expected to play a bigger role in the new PPP market structure, but also affects the private sector, which has claims on governments. Thus the sovereign debt crisis seems to have the potential to be more harmful.

14.7 Concluding remarks

PPP arrangements, by allowing risk sharing with private entities and funding diversification to involve private sector financing, have became increasingly widespread over the past two decades. The arrangements have become a key component of governments' attempts to revive infrastructure investment in advanced as well as developing and emerging market economies. However, the recent financial crisis has severely decreased the availability of credit in the markets and created a lack of confidence in financial institutions. This development, combined with the subsequent reduced demand resulting from the economic meltdown that follows, has made the viability of the existent PPP market structure a challenge.

The chapter first assesses the impacts of the 2007–9 financial crisis on PPPs. Combining trend analysis with the use of systemic liquidity easing (SLE) measures as a proxy for the severity of the crisis, it is found that the impacts of the crisis on PPPs are short term and somewhat weak, especially given the severity of the crisis.

Second, examining the factors underpinning the resilience of PPP markets, the chapter argues that readjustments of the market structure of PPPs were at the core of the resilience. The readjustments have affected not only the financing structure of PPPs but also the schemes of the arrangements. In the new market structure, debt/equity ratios have shifted from the standard 90/10 to the range of 70s/30s or even lower, suggesting an increased risk burden for private investors or PPP promoters, and the role of bilateral and multilateral financial institutions has increased. The public sector is also called upon to assume more market risks through for example availability payment schemes.

Third (and final), the impacts of the ongoing sovereign debt crisis in the Euro area are assessed, especially in light of the enhanced role for the public sector in the new PPP market structure. The chapter finds that the Euro area sovereign debt crisis that began in 2011 and is still ongoing has had a much bigger impact on PPPs in 2011 than the 2007–9 financial crisis.

Notes

1 PPP stands for Public–Private Partnerships.
2 I would like to thank Piet de Vries for useful suggestions.
3 The database is under the umbrella of the *World Bank's Public–Private Infrastructure Advisory Facility (PPIAF)*.
4 The database comprises data collected by PWF's International Major Projects Survey. It includes projects in 131 countries that are being planned, built or are operated. According to PWF (2010), the survey aims to describe projects where governments are seeking to contract the delivery of public infrastructure services to the private sector. Notice that the survey covers only 131 countries, it is not exhaustive in the sense that it does not cover all the PPP projects around the world.
5 *Public Works Financing* – International Major Projects Survey and OECD (2009).
6 The economies covered are: Argentina, Brazil, Bulgaria, Chile, China (P.R.), Hong Kong (SAR), Colombia, Costa Rica, Croatia, Czech Republic, Egypt, Estonia, Hungary, Iceland, India, Indonesia, Israel, Kazakhstan, Korea, Latvia, Lithuania, Malaysia, Mexico, Nigeria, Pakistan, Peru, Philippines, Poland, Romania, Russia, Saudi Arabia, Serbia (Republic of), Singapore, South Africa, Thailand, Turkey, Ukraine, Uruguay, Vietnam.
7 This is also highlighted in Burger *et al.* (2013).
8 Desilets (2009) alludes to this in one of his case studies.
9 International Monetary Fund, *World Economic Outlook*, April 2011. The world trade volume growth was 8.7 per cent in 2006 and 7.5 per cent in 2007.

10 The analysis using investments or project costs yields similar results.
11 Notice that there is no time lag for the SLE measures, their undertaking at time t simply reflects the liquidity conditions at that time and the correlation is loosely computed with the PPP count of the same period.
12 The A1 motorway is a PPP project that will run from the port city of Gdansk on the Baltic Sea to the Polish-Czech border.
13 Ernst & Young's United Kingdom Infrastructure Report, 2008.

References

Asian Development Bank, 2006, *Facilitating Public–Private Partnership for Accelerated Infrastructure Development in India*, Workshop Report, December.
Bayoumi, Tamim and Francis Vitek, 2012, 'Spillovers from an Intensification of the Euro Area Sovereign Debt Crisis: A Macroeconomic Model Based Analysis,' Mimeograph, International Monetary Fund.
Burger, Philippe, Justin Tyson, Izabela Karpowicz and Maria Delgado Coelho, 2013, 'Weathering the Financial Crisis: Public–Private Partnerships and the Government Response,' in this volume.
Desilets, Brien, 2009, 'PPPs Projects and Financial Crisis: Short-Term Impacts and Medium-Term Trends,' Institute for Public-Private Partnerships, Inc.
Fengate Capital Management Ltd, 2008, 'The 2008 Financial Crisis and its Impact on Public Private Partnerships,' Ontario, Canada.
Ho, S. Ping, 2013, 'Game Theory and PPP,' in this volume.
Hofman, Bert, 2010, 'Multilateral and Bilateral Roles in Infrastructure Development in the Philippines,' Speech delivered at the Conference 'Infrastructure Philippines 2010: Investing and Financing in Public-Private Partnership Projects,' November 17–19, Pasay City, Philippines.
International Monetary Fund, 2011, *World Economic Outlook*, April.
Ishi, Kotaro, Mark Stone and Etienne B. Yehoue, 2009, 'Unconventional Central Bank Measures for Emerging Economies,' IMF Working Paper No. 09/226.
Izaguirre, Ada Karina, 2008, 'New Private Infrastructure Projects in Developing Countries Have Started Being Affected by the Financial Crisis,' *World Bank's Private Participation in Infrastructure Data Update Note* No 20.
Izaguirre, Ada Karina, 2010, 'Investment in new Private Infrastructure Projects in Developing Countries Slowed Down in the First Quarter of 2010,' *World Bank's Private Participation in Infrastructure Data Update Note* No 38.
Liyanage, Champika, 2011, 'Impact of Global Financial Crisis on PPPs,' Symposium: Public Private Partnerships in Transport: Trends & Theory – Research Roadmap.
Muller, Berhard, 2009, 'Impacts of the Credit Crisis on the German PPP Market?' ASEM Conference Public Private Partnerships in Infrastructure, 15–16 October, Seoul, Korea.
Organization for Economic Cooperation and Development, 2010, 'From Lessons to Principles for the use of Public–Private Partnerships,' 32nd Annual meeting of Working Party of Senior Budget Officials 6–7 June, Luxembourg.
Public Work Financing, 2010, *International Major Projects Survey*, No. 242, October.
Public Work Financing, 2011, *International Major Projects Survey*, No. 263, October.
Rose, Andrew, 2008, 'The Impact of the Credit Crisis on the PPP Market,' The PPP Financing Conference, November 27.
von Thadden, Goetz, 2009, 'The Financial Crisis and the PPP Market,' Regional Conference on Concessions and Public Private Partnerships, 3–4 December, European PPP Expertise Centre (EPEC).
Yehoue, Etienne B., 2009, 'Emerging Economy Responses to the Global Financial Crisis of 2007–09: An Empirical Analysis of the Liquidity Easing Measures,' IMF Working Paper WP/09/265.

Part VII

Governance of public–private partnerships

15

Partnership arrangements in public–private partnerships

Insights from Irish road public–private partnerships

Istemi S. Demirag and Richard Burke

15.1 Introduction

This chapter evaluates the existing literature on the different partnership arrangements that develop in public–private partnerships (PPPs). An overview of PPPs and the key stakeholders that come together to create these partnerships is provided. This is then followed by a discussion of the Irish PPP structure with particular emphasis on Ireland's PPP roads sector. An overview of some of the key stakeholders and their relationships in Irish road PPPs is examined. The role that PPPs have played in improving Ireland's road network is then highlighted. Within the PPP structure three types of partnerships are discussed: the relationship between the public sector bodies responsible for PPPs; the relationship between the procuring authorities and the Special Purpose Vehicle (SPV); and finally the relationship between the SPV members. We draw on examples from the international literature on the extent to which these partnerships have developed worldwide. A number of factors from the literature, such as flexibility, cooperation, trust and risk transfer, that may contribute towards successful partnerships in PPP are described.

While a lot of the previous PPP literature concentrates primarily on the relationship between the public and private sector (see for example, Edwards and Shaoul 2003; Dutz 2003; and Demirag *et al.* 2005), we suggest that it is not just partnership between the public and private sector that is needed for a successful PPP, but partnership across the three different levels identified above in the PPP structure is required. The paucity of research on the different types of partnerships that develop in PPP is an important omission, hence it was decided to focus on a number of different partnerships in PPP. More recently, the literature has highlighted the importance of other stakeholders and the relationships or partnerships they form in the PPP process. The relationship between public sector bodies in PPP is investigated by Koch and Buser (2006) and Van Marrewijk *et al.* (2008), while the relationship among SPV members is explored by Koch and Buser (2006). Asenova and Beck (2010) and Demirag *et al.* (2011 and 2012) examine the significance of the financiers in the PPP process, while the importance of peripheral stakeholders in PPP is examined by Klijn and Teisman (2003). This chapter aims to contribute to this body of literature by studying a wide range of stakeholders and the various partnerships that develop, in general, and in particular from the Irish PPP roads sector. Partnerships and relationships between the public and private sector are important to examine because unless these key stakeholders interact, collaborate, function and communicate effectively, the PPP will ultimately result in sub-optimal behaviour among the stakeholders, which in turn will consequently lead to the failure of the PPP.

15.2 Overview of Irish roads public–private partnerships

The Irish government used the UK's Private Finance Initiative (PFI) model as a blueprint when implementing PPPs into the Republic of Ireland. In June 1999 the first pilot projects on PPPs in the Republic of Ireland were announced. These projects involved a number of sectors including education and roads. A detailed analysis of PPPs in procurement and operation in Ireland can be found on the Irish government's PPP website (http://ppp.gov.ie) and more extensive detail on the roads sector can be found at www.nra.ie.

In the Republic of Ireland a significant number of foreign firms with experience and international expertise have invested in PPPs. These foreign firms also include Irish contractors and investors within the SPV, increasing the onus on partnership and close collaboration with each other. A report published by the Irish Business and Employers Confederation (IBEC) (2009: 5) found that 83 per cent of businesses perceived Irish infrastructure to be of poor standard, thus placing an emphasis on the acute need for increased spending on infrastructure. The Irish government is anxious to try and upgrade Irish roads to European levels. A recent joint report by IBEC and KPMG (2011) entitled 'What Next for Infrastructure, Infrastructure Insights for Ireland' highlights the importance of Ireland using PPPs to improve its infrastructural standards. The first PPP programme in roads resulted in €2.1 billion in private sector investment, nonetheless Ireland is ranked 29th out of 139 countries in terms of competitiveness in the 2010–11 Global Competitiveness Report, which highlights the need for Ireland to improve its infrastructure and encourage more private sector investment. Ireland's fiscal problems also highlight the importance of encouraging more private investment. Ireland is also placed as low as 25th among 28 countries in terms of infrastructure quality, and the European Competitiveness Report 2009 and National Competitiveness Council's 2010 Report have outlined how Ireland has fallen behind other European countries in terms of infrastructure investment (IBEC and KPMG 2011).

Figure 15.1 below shows the Irish government's organization for the transport sector and a number of initiatives implemented for its development.

15.3 Overview of the key PPP stakeholders

SPV members have different synergies and competencies that are critical for the PPP to come to fruition and be successful (see Figure 15.2 for a complete list of the stakeholders in Irish road PPPs). PPPs can lead to a lot of contention among the different stakeholders and by their very actions, stakeholders have the power to 'make or break' a PPP project (El-Gohary et al. 2006: 604).

There is a plethora of stakeholders involved in PPP projects. Some stakeholders, such as the SPV and the procuring authorities, are more heavily involved in the PPP process than others. Klijn and Teisman (2003: 141) refer to the importance of peripheral stakeholders in the PPP process. Peripheral stakeholders have an interest in the PPP but are not directly related to it. Various bodies, such as unions and interest groups, will be concerned with the PPP. The partnerships and relationships between the multiple stakeholders are crucial to the

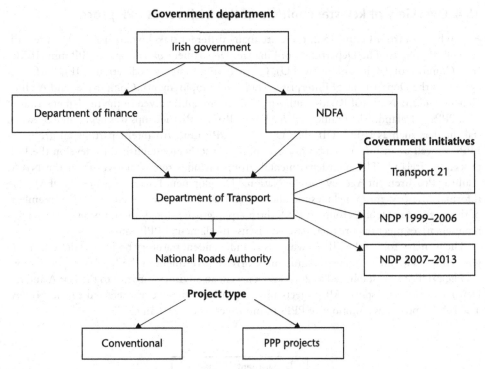

Figure 15.1 Government initiatives to secure Ireland's road development

NDFA – National Development Finance Agency; NDP – National Development Plan

PPP's ultimate success. It can be very difficult to manage multiple expectations but if the government has appropriate mechanisms in place this can help to stimulate effective partnership. A potential mechanism is through risk transfer and, in particular, demand risk transfer from the public to the private sector, as discussed later on in the chapter. PPP provides an opportunity for stakeholders with different strengths and competencies to come together to provide a service typically provided by the public sector. It represents an opportunity for synergistic relationships to be created where responsibilities and risks can be shared. Different stakeholders will become more prominent in their influence throughout the PPP process (Broadbent and Laughlin 2004: 95), with stakeholders relying on each other in the PPP process and possessing resources that will be useful to each other (Klijn and Teisman 2003: 137–138).

The importance of the SPV relationship is exacerbated by the large number of stakeholders that make up the concessionaire companies, which in many cases comprise both domestic and international firms. These domestic and international firms have cultural differences and individual norms that pose challenges for concessionaire managers and can also be difficult to integrate. The SPV also seeks to transfer a considerable amount of risk to subcontractors in PPP (Demirag et al. 2011, 2012) creating even more relationships, partnerships and interaction.

15.4 Overview of key stakeholders in the Irish roads PPP process

As can be seen from Figure 15.2, there are many different stakeholders involved in the Irish roads PPP process. The Department of Finance, Department of Transport, PPP unit, IBEC, Irish Congress of Trade Unions (ICTU), Construction Industry Federation (CIF), Forfás (an agency of the Department of Enterprise, Trade and Employment), Comptroller and Auditor General and the National Roads Authority (NRA) are all involved in the implementation of road PPPs in Ireland. The Framework for Public Private Partnerships was negotiated between stakeholders such as IBEC, CIF, ICTU and the PPP unit. An interdepartmental group on PPPs, as well as an informal advisory group, have also been established to develop the PPP process in Ireland. The interdepartmental group includes representatives from the NRA, Railway Procurement Agency and the National Development Finance Agency (NDFA). The informal advisory group includes members of ICTU, IBEC, and the CIF as well as members of the interdepartmental group on PPPs (http://ppp.gov.ie). In addition, unions and business representatives meet on a regular basis to discuss fundamental PPP issues.

The primary role of the NRA, which is an independent statutory body, is to deliver on the government's mandate of encouraging more private investment in the Irish transport sector.

The NDFA was established in 2003 and it acts in an advisory capacity to the NRA and the Department of Transport. All projects utilizing private finance are referred to the NDFA. The NDFA procures a number of PPPs in most sectors other than roads.

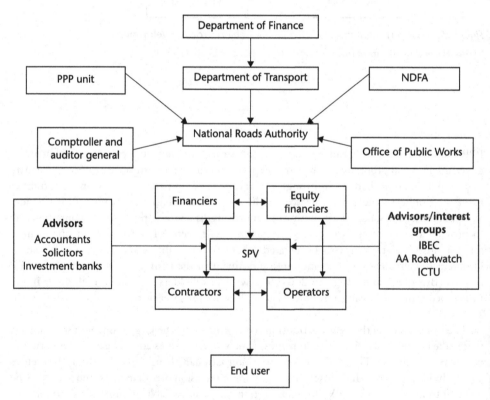

Figure 15.2 Overview of key stakeholders in the Irish road PPP process

AA – Automobile Association

Table 15.1 PPP investment in National Development Plan 2007–13

Sector	Value €m
Transport	7,035
Environmental services	271
Government infrastructure	191
Tourism	180
Schools	540
Second and third level education	595
Social housing	255
Health service	415
Justice	795
Recreation and heritage	288
Total	10,565

(Adapted from National Development Plan 2007–2013, obtained from http://ppp.gov.ie)

In a joint report IBEC and KPMG (2011) have called for the establishment of a 'National Infrastructure Authority' in order to speed up the improvement of Irish infrastructure. This Authority would report directly to the government. Furthermore, IBEC and KPMG (2011) believe that this Authority should utilize the vast experience of the NRA and share knowledge across all departments.

The extent of Irish PPP investment across a number of sectors is illustrated in Table 15.1. In terms of Irish PPP expenditure, the transport sector accounts for the majority of the outlay. Although some problems have manifested themselves in other sectors, such as prisons, social housing and education, the first tranche of Irish road PPPs has been successful to date and all projects have been completed on time and within budget. The government has also not been required to bail out the SPV in any Irish toll road PPPs to date. It is, however, too early to draw any firm conclusions on the success or otherwise of the Irish PPP roads sector as it will be another 25 to 30 years before their completion. Nonetheless IBEC and KPMG (2011) are adamant that PPP represents the best way of securing Irish infrastructural investment given the current global financial crisis and Ireland's fiscal problems. These problems have constrained the ability of the Irish government to finance infrastructural projects, and hence private sector investment through PPP can reduce the burden on exchequer finances.

15.5 Partnerships in Irish roads PPPs

PPP involves a number of different stakeholders from different networks coming together. The Central PPP unit in Ireland, a centre of expertise, was established in 1999 and plays an important role in the PPP process. It shares its expertise across all Irish PPPs and consists of a number of technical experts and advisors. The partnerships that develop in the PPP structure are illustrated in Figure 15.3 within the context of the Irish PPP roads sector. Three types of partnerships are identified from the literature: first, agency; second, club partnerships (Smith *et al.* 2006); and third, public–public partnerships (Hodges and Grubnic 2010). We apply these partnerships specifically to PPP. For the purposes of this chapter we view agency partnerships in the context of PPP, which effectively involves the private sector delivering the PPP on behalf of the government. In PPPs the SPV represents club partnerships as

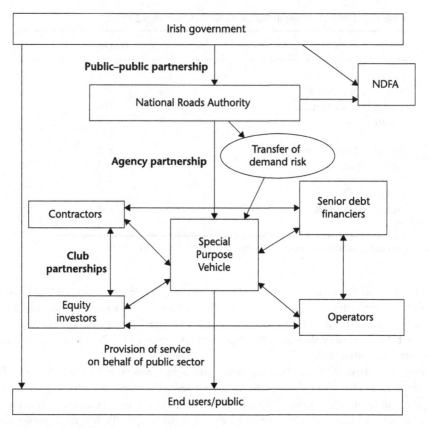

Figure 15.3   Partnerships in Irish roads PPPs

(Adapted from Smith et al. 2006; Baker et al. 2009; Dunn Cavelty and Suter 2009; Hodges and Grubnic 2010)

members club resources together and collaborate for the mutual benefit of the project. Partnerships between public sector organizations involved in PPP represent the public–public partnerships.

Figure 15.3 describes the different types of partnership that develop within the PPP framework. The Irish PPP roads sector is used to illustrate and describe these partnerships. The Irish government, NRA and NDFA form the public–public partnership among the public sector bodies responsible for implementing and overseeing the PPP. The agency partnership refers to the public–private partnership between the NRA and the SPV, and the club partnership refers to the relationship between the SPV members. In Irish roads PPPs, the SPV consortia tend to consist of both domestic and international companies. This diagram shows the complexity of PPP arrangements and the vast array of stakeholders involved in the PPP process. It also shows how demand risk as an incentive contributes towards partnership in PPP. Both the public and private sectors will benefit through revenue share when demand exceeds expected levels on toll based schemes. The different members of the SPV are encouraged to manage demand risk collectively and encourage as many vehicles as possible onto the toll road PPP. The other factors we identify in Table 15.2 from the literature also contribute towards partnership in PPP.

Table 15.2 Factors contributing towards partnerships in PPP

Factors contributing towards partnership	Empirical work
Collaboration – This refers to the different parties in PPP working in unison together on key PPP tasks.	Skelcher *et al.* (2005), Agranoff (2006), Smyth and Edkins (2007), Koppenjan and Enserink (2009)
Autonomy – This refers to the parties in PPP being provided with freedom and left to their own devices to make key decisions in PPP.	Baker *et al.* (2009)
Goal congruence – This refers to parties having similar goals within the PPP process and working together to attain the same goals/objectives.	Koppenjan (2005), Runde *et al.* (2010)
Flexibility in contracts – This refers to the extent to which contracts are flexible in PPP, with flexibility allowed rather than a contractual rigid inflexible approach.	Edwards and Shaoul (2003), Smith *et al.* (2006), Baker *et al.* (2009), Norton and Blanco (2009), Runde *et al.* (2010), Athias and Sausier (2010), English and Baxter (2010)
Incentives – These refer to rewards which incentivise parties to work towards the project's objectives.	Asenova and Beck (2003), Koppenjan and Enserink (2009), Dunn-Cavelty and Suter (2009), English and Baxter (2010)
Payment mechanisms – This refers to the form of payment mechanism used to incentivise the private sector party in PPP. Availability/unitary payments and 'user pays' fees are two forms of payment mechanisms in PPP.	English and Baxter (2010)
Trust – This refers to the extent to which the parties rely on and believe in each other in PPP.	Koppenjan (2005), Koch and Buser (2006), El-Gohary *et al.* (2006), Klijn and Skelcher (2007), English and Baxter (2010)
Goodwill – This refers to the way in which parties will show a sense of camaraderie and willingness to help the other party in the agreement.	English and Baxter (2010)
Relational management – This is meant in the sense that the parties form a real relationship rather than a strictly contractual relationship in the PPP.	Smyth and Edkins (2007)
Knowledge and resource sharing – This refers to the willingness of the parties in PPP to share ideas, good practices as well as financial resources in the PPP process.	Asenova and Beck (2003), Klijn and Teisman (2003), Agranoff (2006), Hodges and Grubnic (2010)
Governance schemes – The rules and regulation under which a particular system works.	Teisman and Klijn (2002), Agranoff (2006), Hodges and Grubnic (2010)
Risk transfer – Risks are transferred from the public sector to the private sector in PPP in order to ensure Value For Money.	Van Ham and Koppenjan (2001), Edwards and Shaoul (2003), Dunn-Cavelty and Suter (2009), Runde *et al.* (2010)

We now explore three types of partnership in PPP and refer to the role of incentives in creating and complementing these partnerships. Examples of these partnerships from the literature worldwide are provided. Stakeholders from the public sector, private sector and advisors, among others, come together to instigate and ensure the success of the PPP process. These stakeholders will have made a number of decisions within their own networks. PPPs thus represent a more expanded enlarged network, which can be inherently more complex and challenging. The fact that the SPV members monitor each other also improves the possibility of PPP success. Smith *et al.* (2006) identified such horizontal monitoring between club members as crucial to the club partnership's success and this is clearly the case also with PPP.

15.6 Relationship between public sector entities

Although PPPs involve an important relationship between the public and private sectors, the relationship between the public sector bodies responsible for implementing PPPs is also crucial. Usually a number of public sector bodies will be involved in implementing PPPs, such as finance and transport departments, and procuring as well as local authorities. In Ireland the NDFA works in close conjunction with the NRA. Public sector organizations operate on behalf of the government. However, they often have their own individual agendas (Koppenjan 2005). The government will want PPP projects to be successful as it will garner increased support from the electorate (Dutz 2003: 4), hence there can be a considerable political cost if these projects fail. Although one of the biggest challenges of PPP is to reconcile differences between the public and private sectors, another major concern is to deal with the differing preferences of these different levels of government (Koppenjan 2005: 140–1), especially as local authorities will often be involved in implementing PPPs. Koppenjan (2005), in examining transport PPPs in the Netherlands, found that a lack of trust and failure by PPP stakeholders to interact initially caused difficulties in the formation of the PPP. Using the A4 and Valburg PPPs as examples, he found conflict was evident between ministers and the local authorities as differing goals and objectives inhibited the effective coordination of the public authorities (Koppenjan 2005).

Van Marrewijk *et al.* (2008) found considerable problems in the Environ PPP in the Netherlands as conflict was evident between the public sector organizations involved in the PPP. Cultural differences between the two offices of public works organizations affected the project. One particular organization was used as it had the expertise in infrastructure construction. Due to having a lack of control it quit the project at one stage. A government investigation was necessary due to the difficulties with the Environ project. Such was the extent of the difficulties that the Transport Authority also had to intervene when project difficulties emerged (Van Marrewijk *et al.* 2008). In contrast to some of the difficulties in Dutch PPPs, Hodges and Grubnic (2010) provide evidence of successful partnerships among ten local government authorities (LGAs) involved in e-government partnerships in the UK. They outline that long-term successful partnerships are possible where an effective organizational structure that facilitates the organization's goals in a fair, transparent and accountable fashion is implemented. The partners worked collaboratively towards achieving their performance targets (Hodges and Grubnic 2010). Political and financial stability at governmental level is also crucial to ensuring the PPP's success, and restructuring at a local government level may undermine the functioning of the partnership (Hodges and Grubnic 2010). Moreover, it is essential that governmental agencies act in the best interests of government as this ensures accountability to the government and the taxpayer (Fourie and Burger 2000).

Within this section the significance of the relationships between the public sector bodies in PPP was discussed. The literature highlights the importance of all levels of government including the local authorities in implementing PPPs successfully. The local authorities need to fully understand the PPP process given their role in its implementation. Trust, collaboration and communication across all government departments will improve the PPP process. Our review of the literature exemplifies the difficulties that were encountered in the Netherlands in fostering partnership, due to a number of factors including cultural differences and differing goals between public sector organizations. This was in contrast to the UK where a stronger relationship between public sector bodies in e-government partnerships was evident with a strong organizational culture and a collaborative relationship contributing towards this.

15.7 Relationship between the procuring authority and SPV

A strong relationship between the public and private sectors is the very essence of a successful PPP and balancing their objectives is a huge challenge. In particular we look at the impact of risk transfer on the relationship between the public sector and the SPV. Geddes (2005) suggests that in order for the PPP to prosper the public and private sectors must have a strong relationship. Geddes (2005: 22) explains that 'A partnership where the public sector involvement is primarily for public policy reasons but the private sector involvement is primarily for commercial reasons will not flourish unless the representatives of the two sectors appreciate (and respect) the other's motivation.' Incentives and revenue sharing through excess demand in PPPs are one potential way in which this may occur. It becomes crucial therefore to explore why the various partners want to be involved in the PPP where they often have conflicting objectives. The government's aim will be to ensure that the service provided to society is not diminished in any way and that 'checks and balances' are in place to protect societal interests. These checks and balances are in terms of rules and guidelines to ensure that the contract is being carried out as expected (Dutz 2003: 2–3). On one hand, the public may become increasingly cynical when they see the huge returns that accrue to the private sector in successful PPPs. On the other, the public also become increasingly sceptical of PPP as a policy tool if more PPPs continue to fail (Asenova and Hood 2006), hence an effective, functioning PPP that meets societal and private sector goals is desirable.

A study in the USA conducted by Runde *et al.* (2010) provides examples of a marine terminal project in Maryland and a toll road in Florida and recommends that they be used as best practice for future PPPs, because in them the public sector and private sector coordinated excellently as a team to deliver the PPPs. Furthermore Runde *et al.* (2010: 69–70) argue that the landscape has changed in PPP:

> The redefining of PPPs ultimately is a re-emphasis on 'partnership'. Instead of maximising leverage and upfront proceeds, investors and municipalities are increasingly partnering to construct processes and transactions that are collectively beneficial, financially secure and adequately flexible to meet the more dynamic, economic, social and political conditions.

Runde *et al.* (2010: 73) use the example of revenue-sharing contracts in the Port of Oakland and Port of Baltimore as helping to instil more partnership between the public and private sector. The government and the private sector benefit if the PPP is successful (Dong and Chiara 2010: 89). In the Republic of Ireland since the initiation of hard toll PPPs, the government has ensured that revenue sharing stipulations are prevalent and this has arguably helped stimulate stronger partnerships in PPPs.

Rigid inflexible contracts can prevent such strong relationships developing. When contracts are standardized it only leads to more rigidity (Iossa *et al.* 2007). On the other hand, it could be argued that projects with large investments are often best to be more rigid, but the long term nature of the service may require more flexibility (Iossa *et al.* 2007: 59). Runde *et al.* (2010: 73) propose that more flexible concession agreements will help more 'true partnerships' to develop. Flexible contracts are referred to as contracts where the wording of the contract is not taken literally to the letter of the law, and when some difficulties or uncertainties emerge in projects the contract can be made more flexible for the greater good and long term viability of the project. Rigid contracts, on the other hand, are firm and fixed with no scope for change. This is substantiated by Koppenjan and Enserink (2009) and Athias and Saussier (2010) who identify rigid contracts as an impediment to the PPP's success. Importantly the tradeoff between flexibility and incomplete contracts should be considered. Clearly defined contracts with some degree of flexibility should lead to better PPP outcomes. Some degree of flexibility allows the parties to resolve any grievances or problems that may emerge in the PPP, but such flexibility may incur significant transaction costs. Indeed, achieving an adequate degree of flexibility in a PPP contract can be very difficult (Athias and Saussier 2010). In their work Athias and Saussier (2010) analyse the extent of renegotiation evident in both flexible and rigid contracts. They find that contracts which exhibit considerable uncertainties, such as toll road PPPs, are less rigid. If the country has a strong institutional environment, contracts are less likely to be rigid (Athias and Saussier 2010).

In general, due to the unforeseen risks involved, PPPs tend to result in incomplete contracts. Large infrastructure projects by their very nature involve considerable uncertainty (Dong and Chiara 2010). Where such uncertainties are evident some degree of flexibility is crucial (Dong and Chiara 2010) as behavioural attitudes and user attitudes can alter over the contract (Iossa et al. 2007: 57). For example, in terms of road PPPs, it is very difficult to predict the number of vehicles that will use a road over a period of 25–30 years, as the SPV cannot control a lot of the variables that impinge on traffic levels such as Gross Domestic Product and fuel prices (OECD 2008).

Excessive risk transfer can significantly reduce incentives in PPP and create a poor relationship with the SPV. Penalties for poor performance need to be stringent in the contracts (Iossa *et al.* 2007: 25). Service quality and expected performance levels need to be clearly articulated in the contract specification and met in order to ensure the PPP's success.

Within toll road PPP contracts, demand risk in particular can be very difficult to manage. It could be argued that the use of demand risk as an incentive encourages congruent goals between the public and private sectors. In hard toll PPPs, the SPV are highly incentivized to keep the road open and to provide a quality service. Nonetheless the SPV assume significant demand risk.

Risk is transferred from the public to the private sector only where it incentivizes the SPV and the government recognize that demand risk transfer to the private sector may make the PPP less attractive to financiers and will most likely increase the company's cost of capital (Iossa *et al.* 2007: 41–2).

Risk transfer also emerged as a significant issue in the formation of partnerships in a study conducted by English and Baxter (2010) who, utilizing a longitudinal study encompassing five case studies, examined the changing relationship between the SPV and public sector in the provision of PPP prisons in Australia. They found evidence of incomplete contracts in the prison sector in Victoria State. Approaches to risk transfer and performance measurement altered over their study. Incentive and payment mechanisms have also changed and there is now a far greater emphasis on partnership, flexibility, trust and collaboration between the different stakeholders responsible for operating the prisons. Goodwill, trust and relational contracting are now evident between the SPV and the procuring authority and this has improved the process considerably. Risk transfer is far more appropriate and the government are now responsible for correctional and core services, thus limiting project risk considerably for the contractors.

According to Norton and Blanco (2009), the public sector in Spain is more pragmatic in its view of risk and tries not to excessively transfer risk. This results in more flexible, less complicated contracts whereby the public sector and SPV work together to solve any problems. They argue that UK local authorities are more constrained in terms of the level of autonomy they are allowed. A competitive process and 'hard bargaining' between the public and private partners is more evident in the UK. Norton and Blanco (2009) conclude that the UK approach is far more standardized, and argue that the Spanish network-based approach allows more genuine partnerships in PPP to develop.

The empirical work of Smyth and Edkins (2007) who conducted an electronic survey in the UK indicated that the SPV perceived the public sector very negatively. Risk transfer was not the fundamental issue in developing partnership and they outline how partnerships require collaboration despite the level of risk transferred. They call for the increased management of relationships in order to ensure the PPP's success. The authors argue that the SPV should be more proactive in fostering collaboration, which would infer a movement from relational contracting to relational management. Findings from this study also show that the SPV perceived the public sector as failing to build up a collaborative relationship with the private sector. This illustrates the importance of the public sector trying to forge and foster a closer relationship with the SPV for the PPP's success.

Edwards and Shaoul (2003), examining two UK PFI information technology projects, reveal that the disparity in power between smaller public sector agencies and large providers of the service mitigates the extent to which they can enforce the contract. These contracts were not flexible and affected the relationship between the partners. The lack of flexibility in the contracts was noted from the public sector's perspective. Although effective risk transfer and VFM were not attained, the public sector found that enforcing the contract or ending the partnership was difficult. In effect the public sector was tied into the project or partnership 'for better for worse' (Edwards and Shaoul 2003: 397).

Expertise is also crucial within procuring authorities. Often the public and private sectors will hire consultants to assist them on PPP deals. Sometimes a conflict of interest may occur as the consultant may have assisted the public sector on one deal and the private sector on another (Iossa et al. 2007: 10). This illustrates that although PPPs involve a large network, the network can also be a very small world in terms of the available experience. This has been clearly evident in an Irish context. Traffic forecasters work for the SPV on some deals and for the public sector on other deals in Ireland. An added problem is that the SPV may headhunt the expertise in the public sector.

Asenova and Beck (2003: 201), who conducted a survey on PFI projects in the UK from the perspective of financial providers, also stress the importance of the public and private sectors becoming more collaborative in the PPP approach rather than acting in their own self- interest. They express their desire for the public sector and financiers to form a more solid partnership whereby the financier's expertise in risk management is shared with the public sector. This collaborative approach involves stakeholders working together to achieve goals, and trust can develop when the different stakeholders become familiar with each other and are content that the stakeholder will not do anything harmful.

In summary, the literature review covered here indicates that the importance of balancing the different objectives of the private and public sectors is fundamental. Revenue sharing is identified in the USA as helping to improve the partnership between the government and SPV, and this is also evident in Irish toll road PPPs as the Irish government have ensured revenue share provisions are in place in these contracts. Risk transfer has important implications for the partnership between the SPV and public sector. Collaboration, trust and goodwill were also acknowledged as factors in improving the relationship between the SPV and the public sector. Our review of the international literature revealed that PPP contracts were more flexible in the USA, Spain and Australia in contrast to more standardized contracts evident in the UK. Such flexibility is noted as improving the partnership between the SPV and public sector, nonetheless the incidence of incomplete contracts and transaction costs must be considered by the public sector. The general public will become more sceptical of the use of PPP as a policy tool if the private sector try to renegotiate PPP contracts to their advantage on a regular basis.

15.8 Relationship between SPV members

Within the SPV there will be a number of different financiers and private sector companies who must work together. These financiers will have invested a considerable amount of debt and equity into these projects. It is essential to examine the relationship between SPV members as failure for these members to interact will lead to the demise of the PPP. Koch and Buser (2006) recognize the importance of partnership between private sector partners and acknowledge that within Denmark there are only a few significant contractors in the PPP sector. Strong partnerships are evident throughout Irish tollroad PPPs among the SPV members. A contributory factor towards developing these partnerships is the provision of incentives such as the income that can be generated from tolls. Such incentives foster an even stronger partnership. Horizontal accountability and monitoring between SPV members arguably help the PPP process. The different members of the SPV may also have conflicting goals in PPP, with the senior debt financiers being more risk averse (Demirag et al. 2010 and 2011, 2012) while the equity investors have a far greater appetite for risk. The composition of partnerships can alter over time. SPV members may leave the SPV or sell their stake to another entity. PPP failure can be minimized by encouraging SPV members to invest more equity in PPP projects (Fourie and Burger, 2000: 719), which helps foster increased goal congruence in the PPP. The more equity they have in the projects the more they are incentivized to ensure that it performs well.

The evidence in Ireland suggests that SPV members are in it for the long haul; however, in some Irish hard toll PPPs investors have sold on some of their stake. The strength of the relationship between Irish PPP concessionaire members is evidenced by the fact that they have bid within the same consortia for subsequent PPP schemes in the Republic of Ireland. The foreign private sector companies have also stayed in Ireland for subsequent schemes, suggesting their appreciation for the synergies provided by their Irish counterparts.

Irish toll road PPPs involve a number of members within the SPV. In one particular scheme there were four different contractors, two of which were international. An international toll operator was also used to operate the toll plaza. Irish companies are very much in their infancy in managing toll road PPPs; hence they have integrated many foreign companies with the expertise into their consortia, thus expanding the number of partners in the SPV. Within Irish hard toll PPPs the SPV members have all invested equity in the projects, which may encourage goal congruence and stimulate effective partnership as all the parties will want to ensure that the project is financially robust. Demand risk as an incentive in hard toll PPPs helps to tie all the partners into the PPP. Transferring demand risk thus helps to align the interests of parties within the SPV. Although the SPV is penalized in availability based PPPs if they fail to adhere to certain performance criteria the ramifications are far more significant in hard toll PPPs, because if the road is closed or maintenance problems exist it will seriously impinge on the number of cars on the road, which affects profitability, and ultimately may lead to the demise of the company and PPP.

In this section we have indicated that the SPV will often consist of both international and domestic companies as observed in many Irish toll road PPPs. Demand risk transfer in toll based PPPs creates an incentive for the SPV, because the actual level of traffic will affect how profitable the PPP is for the private sector as they receive the toll fees from the user. If SPV members invest more equity in PPP projects they will be more incentivized for it to perform well as they will also benefit considerably, the more profitable the PPP becomes. This creates a big incentive for the SPV to increase the number of road users to generate more toll income. The success of the relationship between the members in Irish toll road SPVs may be the reason why these companies are bidding together for subsequent PPP projects.

15.9 Concluding remarks

This chapter examined three types of partnership: the relationship between the public sector bodies responsible for PPPs; the relationship between the procuring authorities and the SPV; and finally the relationship between the SPV members. An emphasis was put on the Irish toll road PPP sector, its structure and the key stakeholders involved. PPPs have helped to reduce Ireland's infrastructural deficit, particularly in the roads sector. The international evidence on the level of partnership in PPP is finely balanced where some partnerships have worked and some failed.

We argued that it is not just public and private coordination that is needed for a successful PPP, but public authorities also need to work effectively together. Often more than one public sector authority will be involved in implementing the PPP, amplifying the importance of developing partnerships within the public sector. The literature highlighted the importance of all levels of government including local authorities in implementing PPPs. Trust and collaboration across these departments can improve the relationship between public sector bodies. The relationship between the public sector and the SPV is also crucial in the PPP process. The literature identified collaboration, goodwill and flexibility as factors that can affect this relationship. We also considered the potential impact of risk transfer on the relationship between the public sector and SPV. Demand risk may provide an incentive for the private sector to ensure that the road is in the best possible condition for motorists. This helps to create a strong relationship between the procuring authority and the SPV. Notwithstanding this, establishing a good relationship between the SPV and procuring authority can be difficult due to their contrasting objectives. The use of revenue share agreements in road PPPs is one potential way of aligning the goals of the public and private sector.

Partnership between SPV members is also crucial in the PPP process. The number of private sector companies and financiers in the SPV can make it difficult to develop partnership. Creating incentives for the SPV through mechanisms such as the transfer of demand risk can contribute towards an effectively functioning PPP. Arguably it encourages greater interaction and horizontal accountability between the SPV members. They need to work together and monitor each other throughout the tendering and operational phase to ensure the financial robustness of the PPP. The strength of the relationship between the members in Irish toll road SPVs may be observed by virtue of these companies bidding together for subsequent PPP projects.

We also identified a number of factors that may contribute towards better partnerships: mutual trust, collaboration, transparency, incentives and flexible contracts may help foster partnerships in PPPs. These variables might be helpful in supporting the success of a PPP. The literature is delicately balanced on whether flexible or rigid contracts work best in PPP. In Spain, Australia and the USA more flexible agreements are advocated. The degree of flexibility in PPP contracts will have implications for the relationship between the public and private sectors. Contracts need to be firm but fair, allowing some flexibility or scope should difficulties or conflicts arise between the public and private sectors. However, if projects are too flexible, then significant transaction costs may result so it is very much a delicate balancing act and can change on a contract by contract basis.

Future research exploring the extent of these partnership arrangements empirically in the Irish and other international contexts would be useful in order to see whether, and if so why, there are differences both between sectors and among countries.

References

Agranoff, R. (2006) Inside Collaborative Networks: Ten Lessons For Public Managers. *Public Administration Review*, 66 (S1): 56–65.

Asenova, D. and Beck, M. (2003) The UK Financial Sector and Risk Management in PFI Projects: A Survey. *Public Money and Management*, 23 (3): 195–203.

Asenova, D. and Beck, M. (2010) Crucial Silences: When Accountability met PFI and Finance Capital. *Critical Perspectives on Accounting*, 21 (1): 1–13.

Asenova, D. and Hood, J. (2006) PFI and the Implications of Introducing New Long-Term Actors into Public-Service Delivery. *Public Policy and Administration*, 21 (4): 23–41.

Athias, L. and Saussier, S. (2010) *Contractual Flexibility or Rigidity for Public Private Partnerships? Theory and evidence from infrastructure concession contracts*, Discussion Paper Series, EPPP DP NO.2010-3 Online, available from http://www.webssa.net/files/images/Athias–Saussier–2010.pdf (Accessed 7 May 2010).

Baker, K., Justice, J.B. and Skelcher, C. (2009) The Institutional Design of Self Governance: Insights from Public–Private Partnerships, in *The Politics of Self Governance*, edited by Sørensen, E. and Triantafillou, P. pp 77–94, Ashgate Publishing Limited, Aldershot, England.

Broadbent, J. and Laughlin, R. (2004) Striving for Excellence in Public Service Delivery: Experiences from an Analysis of the Private Finance Initiative. *Public Policy and Administration*, 19 (4): 82–99.

Demirag, I., Dubnick, M. and Khadaroo, I. (2005) A Framework for Examining Accountability and Value for Money in the UK's Private Finance Initiative, in *Corporate Social Responsibility, Accountability and Governance: Global Perspective*, edited by Demirag, I., Greenleaf Publishing, Sheffield, England.

Demirag, I., Khadaroo, I. Stapleton, P. and Stevenson, C. (2010) *Public Private Partnership Financiers' Perceptions of Risks*. Institute of Chartered Accountants, Scotland.

Demirag, I., Khadaroo, I. Stapleton, P. and Stevenson, C. (2011) 'Risks and the financing of PPP: Perspectives from the financiers', *The British Accounting Review*, 43 (4): 294–310.

Demirag, I., Khadaroo, I. Stapleton, P. and Stevenson, C. (2012) 'The Diffusion of Risks in Public Private Partnership Contracts', *Accounting, Auditing and Accountability Journal*, 25(8), 1317–39.

Dong, F. and Chiara, N. (2010) Improving Economic Efficiency of Public Private Partnerships for Infrastructure Development by Contractual Flexibility Analysis in a Highly Uncertain Context, *The Journal of Structured Finance*, 16 (1): 87–99.

Dunn-Cavelty, M. and Suter, M. (2009) Public–Private Partnerships are no Silver Bullet: An Expanded Governance Model for Critical Infrastructure Protection. *International Journal of Critical Infrastructure Protection*, 2(4): 179–87.

Dutz, M. (2003) *PPP Systems for Good Governance of Public Service Provision: A menu of support options for contract, design, bidding and monitoring*. Draft discussion document, World Bank, December 2003: 1–23.

Edwards, P. and Shaoul, J. (2003) Partnerships for Better for Worse, *Accounting, Auditing and Accountability Journal*, 16 (3): 397–421.

El-Gohary, N.M., Osman, H. and El-Diraby, T.E. (2006) Stakeholder Management for Public Private Partnerships. *International Journal of Project Management*, 24 (7): 595–604.

English, L. and Baxter, J. (2010) The Changing Nature of Contracting and Trust in Public Private Partnerships: The Case of Victorian PPP prisons, *ABACUS*, 46 (3): 289–319.

Fourie, F.C.v.N. and Burger, P. (2000) An Economic Analysis and Assessment of Public Private Partnerships. *The South African Journal of Economics*, 68 (4): 693–725.

Geddes, M. (2005) *Making Public Private Partnerships Work, Building Relationships and Understanding Cultures*, Gower Publishing Limited, Aldershot,, England.

Hodge, G. and Greve, C. (2010) Public–Private Partnerships: Governance Scheme or Language Game. *Australian Journal of Public Administration* 69 (S1): S8–S22.

Hodges, R. and Grubnic, S. (2010) Local Authority e-government Partnerships in England: A Case Study. *Financial Accountability and Management*, 26 (1): 42–64.

IBEC (2009) Public–Private Partnerships Delivering During Recession. *IBEC PPP Council Report*, IBEC, January 2009, Online, available from http://www.ibec.ie (Accessed 9 June 2010).

IBEC, KPMG. (2011) What next for Infrastructure, Infrastructure Insights for Ireland. Online, available from http://www.ibec.ie/ (Accessed 10 June 2011).

Iossa, E., Spagnolo, G. and Velez, M. (2007) Contract Design in Public Private Partnerships, *Report Prepared for the World Bank*, Online, available from http://www.gianca.org/PapersHomepage/Best%20Practices%20on%20Contract%20Design.pdf (Accessed 1 April 2010).

Klijn, E.-H. and Skelcher, C. (2007) Democracy and Governance Networks: Compatible or Not? *Public Administration*, 85 (3): 587–608.

Klijn, E.-H. and Teisman, G.R. (2003) Institutional and Strategic Barriers to Public Private Partnership: An Analysis of Dutch Cases. *Public Money and Management*, 23 (3): 137–46.

Koch, C. and Buser, M. (2006) Emerging Metagovernance as an Institutional Framework for Public Private Partnership Networks in Denmark. *International Journal of Project Management*, 24 (7): 548–56.

Koppenjan, J.F.M. (2005) The Formation of Public Private Partnerships: Lessons From Nine Transport Infrastructure Projects in the Netherlands, *Public Administration*, 83 (1): 135–57.

Koppenjan, J.F.M. and Enserink, B. (2009) Public Private Partnerships in Urban Infrastructures: Reconciling Private Sector Participation and Sustainability. *Public Administration Review*, 69 (2): 284–96.

Norton, S.D. and Blanco, L. (2009) Public Private Partnerships: A Comparative Study of New Public Management and Stakeholder Participation in the UK and Spain, *International Journal of Public Policy*, 4, (3–4): 214–31.

OECD (2008) 'Transport Infrastructure Investment: Options for Efficiency', *International Transport Forum*. Online, available from http://www.internationaltransportfoum.org (Accessed March 2010).

Runde, J., Offutt, J.P., Selinger, S.D. and Bolton, J.S. (2010) Infrastructure Public Private Partnerships Re-defined: An Increased Emphasis on 'partnerships', *Journal of Applied Corporate Finance*, 22 (2): 69–73.

Skelcher, C., Mathur, N. and Smith, M. (2005) The Public Governance of Collaborative Spaces: Discourse, Design and Democracy, *Public Administration*, 83 (3): 573–96.

Smith, M., Mathur, N. and Skelcher, C. (2006) Corporate Governance in a Collaborative Environment: What Happens When Government, Business and Civil Society Work Together, *Corporate Governance: An International Review*, 14 (3): 159–71.

Smyth, H. and Edkins, A. (2007) Relationship Management in the Management of PFI/PPP projects in the UK. *International Journal of Project Management*, 25 (3): 232–40.

Teisman, G.R. and Klijn, E.-H. (2002) Partnership Arrangements: Governmental Rhetoric or Governance Scheme, *Public Administration Review*, 62 (2): 197–205.

Van Ham, H. and Koppenjan, J.F.M. (2001) Building Public–Private Partnerships: Assessing and Managing Risks in Port Development, *Public Management Review*, 3 (4): 593–616.

Van Marrewijk, A., Clegg, S.R., Pitsis, T.S. and Veenswijk, M. (2008) Managing Public–Private Megaprojects: Paradoxes, Complexity, and Project Design, *International Journal of Project Management*, 26 (6): 591–600.

Websites used

National Roads Authority website, available from http://www.nra.ie/ (accessed March 2009)

Department of Finance PPP website, available from http://ppp.gov.ie/ (accessed March 2009)

On the perception and management of legal risks in public–private partnerships for infrastructure

Yiannis Xenidis

16.1 Introduction

Public–Private Partnerships have been extensively applied since the early 1990s both for upgrading existing and developing new infrastructure. Funding shortages from national governments, increasing demands for qualitative and in time infrastructure services and a policy for stronger involvement of the private sector in the infrastructure market led to the adoption of this project delivery scheme both in developing and developed countries, worldwide, and for all types of infrastructure. PPPs have taken several forms ranging from pure privatization to well-structured partnerships with various levels of commitment between the public and the private sector (Carmona, 2010; PPIAF and ICA, 2008; Estache *et al.*, 2007; Levinson *et al.*, 2006; Thomsen, 2005 and others). As PPPs were expanding their application to various infrastructure sectors, they evolved to respond to different requirements that were defined by: a) the various stakeholders; b) the different types of infrastructure; and c) the various contexts of infrastructure delivery in different countries. Beyond these fundamental factors, others such as the economic environment, the growing research on several aspects of PPPs, and the lessons learned from previous applications of PPPs have also contributed to the elaboration and improvement of the partnership framework between the public and the private sector in delivering, operating and maintaining infrastructure. Therefore, the current state-of-the-art is considerably advanced compared to that of the previous decade. This conclusion is further supported by a simple overview of the rate of failure of PPP projects developed worldwide, as presented in Figure 16.1.

Based on the types of project status as described in the Private Participation in Infrastructure Projects Database (2011) failure was considered in the cases of: a) cancelled projects, i.e. projects where the private sector has exited from the partnership either by *'selling or transferring its economic interest back to the government before fulfilling the contract terms'*, or by *'removing all management and personnel from the concern'*, or by *'ceasing operation, service provision, or construction for 15 per cent or more of the license or concession period, following the revocation of the license or repudiation of the contract'*; b) distressed projects, i.e. projects *'where the government or the operator has either requested contract termination or are in international arbitration'*; and c) merged projects, i.e. projects *'that have been acquired by other projects in the database and consolidated in one project'*.

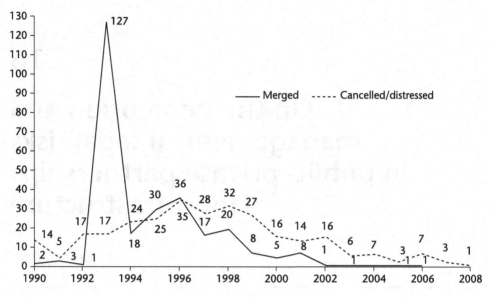

Figure 16.1 PPP projects cancelled/distressed or merged in the period 1990–2008

Data Source: Private Participation in Infrastructure Projects Database (2011)

Figure 16.1 clearly demonstrates a significant reduction of the number of PPP projects that reached financial closure (i.e. agreement between the partners concerning the partnership's funding scheme) in the period 2000–8 and eventually failed compared to the corresponding number for the period 1990–9. This reduction refers to the low- and middle-income countries at the world level and is independent of the economy sector where the projects were developed (Private Participation in Infrastructure Projects Database, 2011). Therefore, it can be inferred that the reason for the reduction of failures in PPPs can be attributed not to specific regional or sector characteristics but rather to the experience and knowledge gained with regard to the PPP framework in theory and practice. Moreover, Table 16.1 indicates that current practice in implementing PPPs is proved to be sufficient, at least, in terms of achieving viable partnerships in the long run. Based, again, on the data of the Private Participation in Infrastructure Projects Database (2011), it is clear that PPPs in low- and middle-income countries have low rates of failure (cancelled/under distress) both in terms of number of projects and amounts of investment.

However, despite the experience gained and the progress achieved in forming PPPs, it is evident that the very same fundamental issues that drew the attention of researchers and practitioners from the beginning are still topics of research and investigation, and generate lively discussions between the stakeholders, as well as in societies. The review by Tang *et al.* (2009) of 85 studies published from 1998 to 2007 on PPP projects in the construction industry has provided an interesting insight on the critical topics on PPPs; their conclusions are presented in Table 16.2.

Table 16.2 evidently shows that PPPs financing and risks management are highlighted as important issues both by the study of experience (empirical studies) and the study of the specific project delivery scheme (i.e. the PPP) at a more theoretical level (non-empirical studies). Apart from these critical topics and the issue of the concession period, which is also raised, the rest are related to the framework of PPPs, which can be decomposed into the

Table 16.1 Analysis of infrastructure projects developed with private participation in low- and middle-income countries worldwide, 1990–2010

Data highlights	Sector			
	Energy	*Telecom*	*Transport*	*Water and sewerage*
Number of countries with private participation	106	133	84	62
Number of projects	1,952	798	1,291	731
Investment (US$ million)	548,279	761,394	275,597	62,543
Cancelled/under distress projects (% of total projects)	108 (5%)	49(6%)	77 (6%)	63 (9%)
Cancelled/under distress investment in US$ million (% of total investment)	32,598 (6%)	24,633 (3%)	19,383 (7%)	20,632 (33%)

Data Source: Private Participation in Infrastructure Projects Database (2011)

Table 16.2 Current and future research topics on PPPs

Empirical studies	Non-empirical studies	Future research
Financing	Financing	Financing
Risks	Risks	Risks
Relationships	Project success factors	Strategies in choosing the right type of PPP
	Concession periods	Concession periods Development of PPP models Contractual agreements

specific issues of stakeholders' relationships and the partnership's type (model). Therefore, it becomes clear that, while a PPP is now far from being considered as a new project delivery scheme, the knowledge required to successfully apply it is still incomplete. The questions raised are inevitable: why, despite the significant amount of research and experience on PPPs, do their fundamentals still require a rigorous investigation? Should the issues of financing and risk allocation continue to constitute the main body of research on PPPs or should the focus be moved elsewhere?

The answers to these questions are evident: there is still a lot of improvement to achieve concerning the implementation of PPPs and this improvement is expected through better understanding and modeling of the PPP framework. While the focus on traditional and well studied topics such as those of financing and risks allocation has been proven supportive towards the achievement of more successful PPPs, it is the less explored field of the legal-contractual framework that needs to be further investigated to advance understanding on PPPs. This is the aim and potential contribution of this chapter: to highlight the necessity of a systematic research and stimulate interest for further investigation on the legal–contractual framework of PPPs. This will be achieved by arguing that the most common risks, as well as critical success factors of PPPs are inherent, rather than case-based, to this project delivery scheme; furthermore, they can be successfully managed through the legal-contractual framework provided that this is considered in a new context, which is broader in terms of definition and content compared to the current perception. For the sake of completeness in presenting a framework for PPPs legal risk management, it will be, also, argued that short-term contracts could constitute an alternative for successful PPPs compared to incomplete or other forms of contracts currently used. This chapter aims at contributing to the goal of achieving more successful PPPs by highlighting the perceptions and tools for managing legal risks in PPPs.

16.2 The dynamics of PPPs

PPPs are characterized by two significant and unique properties: a) the dual or multiple roles of the key stakeholders, namely the public authority, the lenders, the concessionaire, and the contractor; and b) the strong dependence on the economic and social environment in which they are developed. Both properties, as shown in the following three subsections, constitute the main risks sources and are strongly related to the critical success factors of this project delivery scheme. The identification and the analysis of the dynamic nature of PPPs, which is due to these properties, will result in: a) the understanding of the context in which many significant risks and critical success factors should be considered to avoid misinterpretations and confusion both in risk allocation and risk analysis; and b) the identification of the requirements for managing these risks. The results of this analysis, consequently, lead to the suggestion of the appropriate risk management tool for infrastructure projects delivered through PPPs.

16.2.1 The impact of the key stakeholders' roles on the risk profile of PPPs

PPPs, as repeatedly identified in many studies (Shan *et al.*, 2011; Pangeran and Wirahadikusumah, 2010; Thomson and Goodwin, 2005 and others), present high complexity due to the relationships between the involved stakeholders. Related research and experience gained on PPPs have provided best practices and models that facilitated a high-level identification of the expectations and the motivation for the stakeholders to establish such relationships. This has been mainly achieved by focusing on performance appraisal of the PPP project delivery scheme and identification of key performance indicators for the success of PPP projects (Alinaitwe, 2011; Zhao and Wang, 2007; Levinson *et al.*, 2006; Jamali, 2004; Jefferies *et al.*, 2002 and others). However, the – per case – implementation of risk management mechanisms and financial structures due to the particularities of each project retain the complexity (Thomson and Goodwin, 2005), which is evident in the different contractual agreements established between the stakeholders in various PPP projects (Cunha Marques and Berg, 2011).

PPPs are the only procurement system where the key stakeholders, namely the public authority, the lenders, the concessionaire and the contractor, have dual or multiple roles. In traditional procurement systems the roles of the client, the funder and the contractor are either distinct, or the client can, also, act as a funder. In PPPs the various relationships, which are formed between the key stakeholders and presented in Table 16.3, result in a multiplicity of roles for them in the partnership.

The multiplicity of the roles of the key stakeholders results in the necessity of compromising conflicting interests and clarifying relationships that after seem paradoxical. Table 16.3 indicates several cases that justify this argument:

1 The lender in the bidding phase often provides consulting services for the development of the financial tenders to several competing bidders, while, at the same time, he acts as a consultant to the public authority that seeks advice on the development of the proper financial structure and strategy for the PPP (Thomson and Goodwin, 2005). Considering that financing is ensured both from the loans and the contribution of the partners in equity, it is questionable whether the lender seeks the optimum financial structure for the partners or the best alternative for its own interests.

2 The concessionaire develops the project upon the public authority's invitation and with the obligation to meet the specifications set by the public authority. At the same time, in almost all cases, the public authority guarantees a minimum revenue for the concessionaire both in remunerative (e.g. highways, water supply, etc.) and non-remunerative (e.g. schools, hospitals, etc.) projects. Considering the profit-making mindset of the private sector, it is questionable how the interests of the public authority are secured.

3 The contractor, i.e. the entity that actually constructs the project, is most often an entity very closely related to the concessionaire; it is either a company directly participating in the Special Purpose Vehicle (SPV) that is formed as the legal entity of the concessionaire or a legal entity that is actually strongly affiliated to the main partner of the SPV. Considering that the contractor's profits from the project are gained until the end of the construction phase, it is questionable whether the concessionaire acts as a client and supervisor or as a partner of the contractor.

Successful PPPs prove that the management of the complexity generated from the multiple roles of the key stakeholders is feasible; however, it is a daunting task (Thomson and Goodwin, 2005), because it contradicts a basic requirement in project management, which is the clear distinction and delineation of the project stakeholders' roles (Bryde, 2008).

16.2.2 The impact of the economic and social environment on the risk profile of PPPs

Galilea and Medda (2010) present a statistical analysis where they conclude that success of PPPs in transportation infrastructure is influenced by the political, social and economic context of development. Although their study focuses on the empirical data of a specific sector (transportation) it is conceivable that their results can be considered as equally applicable to all PPPs. This is because PPPs share inherent characteristics that are irrespective of any specific sector's particularities. These characteristics, which are discussed in this subsection, constitute sources of risks, which are significantly affected by the socioeconomic environment.

PPPs are, inherently, exposed to more financial and economic risks compared to any other type of infrastructure procurement system. This is due to the financial structure of a PPP

Table 16.3 Relationships between key stakeholders in PPPs

Key stakeholder	Concessionaire	Contractor	Lender	Public authority
Concessionaire	–	Funder	Client	Client
Contractor	Client	–		
Lender	Client/Funder	–	–	Client
Public authority	Client/Guarantor	–	Client	

project and the long concession period, which is identical to the project's completion period. Considering the first factor, the usual and basic financial structure of a PPP involves: a) loans granted from credit institutions; b) equity raised by the private and the public sectors; c) income generated during the operation of the project; and d) grants provided from the public sector. This structure is, evidently, vulnerable to the whole spectrum of potential economic problems, i.e. from public economy deficiencies (e.g. debt, deficit) to private economy deficiencies (e.g. insolvency, liquidity shortfalls). The adverse impact on PPPs of a problematic economic environment is shown in Figure 16.2.

Figure 16.2 explicitly shows that after 1997 and 2007–8 a significant reduction of PPPs followed, which in the second case has become very critical with a record of 64 per cent less projects initiating in 2011 compared to the respective number of projects for 2007. The observed pattern in the initiation of PPPs should not be attributed to any other cause than the global economy, since the pattern is observed irrespectively of region or sector (Private Participation in Infrastructure Projects Database, 2011). Considering that infrastructure funds, which are used in PPPs are mostly available by large international funding organizations, it can be reasonably assumed that turbulence in the global economic environment has an adverse impact on new PPPs. Therefore, appropriate models such as those suggested by Moszoro and Gasiorowski (2008), Zhang (2005) and other researchers, which introduce the parameters of capital structure, financial viability, inflows during operation, debt service and loan coverage ratios, etc. are required to optimize the financial structure of a PPP and determine the financing mechanism that will ensure the unhindered provision of services from the PPP project during potential default periods.

Other very critical issues are the social and political environment in which PPPs are developed. Considering that the concession period usually lasts between 25–40 years, it is easy to assume that, despite the capacity of the models used, the experience of the participating entities and the level of commitment to the concession contract clauses, the security of such an agreement against future conditions remains low. This is because the factors that primarily

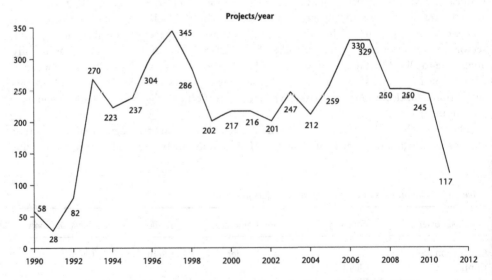

Figure 16.2 Number of PPP projects initiated per year in the period 1990–2011

Data Source: Private Participation in Infrastructure Projects Database (2011)

contribute to the initiation and success of PPPs are hardly foreseeable for such a long period. Examples of these factors are the demand for the PPP project's services, the customers' purchasing power, the stability of the prices, political considerations such as corruption and law-abiding tradition, social impact assessment (Zhao and Wang, 2007) and social considerations such as ethics, culture, and tradition (Hammami et al., 2006; Barbas, 2010). All the above factors play an equally significant role for the success of a PPP. Public opposition, in many cases, originates not from real facts, but from perceptions or strong beliefs that are inherent in long traditions and cultural mindsets, which are difficult to overcome. For example, the involvement of the private sector in the delivery of services for education, health or imprisonment is accepted, in most of the cases, when confined to supportive work; if extended to the offer of the main services (e.g. courses, medical care and detention respectively), it causes strong opposition, because these services are considered the public sector's responsibility (El-Gohary et al., 2006; Renda and Schrefler, 2006). Another example is that of the perception of public property; in many cases, resources such as water are considered public assets that should retain their 'open-access' status and should not be exploited for profit by the private sector (Tecco, 2008). However, the social factor should not be considered only in the macro-analysis perspective (i.e. as a generic feature in the investment's environment). In fact, many failures of PPPs have been reported, both in developing and developed countries, due to well-identified, yet poorly-treated causes, such as: a) lack of basic education in PPPs; b) insufficient raising of public awareness in PPP projects; and c) lack of transparency in processes and contract details (El-Gohary et al., 2006). Therefore, public opposition that may jeopardize a PPP project during its whole life cycle can be the outcome of both social mentality and case-based deficiencies.

16.2.3 Risks and critical success factors of PPPs

The literature as successfully reviewed in Tang et al. (2009) presents a significant amount of studies on risks in PPPs, rendering them one of the most exploited yet, still, attractive topics in the field. Table 16.4 presents only a fraction of identified risks in PPPs, classified in specific risk categories. It emerges from the table that although several risks originate in the same inherent property of a PPP, they are considered as being of different nature and, consequently, they are classified in different risk categories. For example, 'Joint venture risks' are identified and classified by Choi et al. (2010) as creditworthiness risks, while the relationship risks identified by Bing et al. (2005) could be easily considered as a detailed analysis of the joint venture risks. Another example is the case of 'Anthropogenic man made risks' and 'Level of public opposition to project' risk. Demonstration or vandalism are attributes of both risks; however, despite the practically identical definition, 'anthropogenic man made risks' are classified as operating risks, while the 'Level of public opposition' risk is classified as a social risk; thus two very similar risks are classified into two completely different contexts.

This observation leads to the conclusion that the context of definition of several critical risks in PPPs is rather vague and that indicates a potential source of the discrepancies between researchers. Considering that most of the studies in the literature that identify PPPs risks are based on empirical data or questionnaire surveys, it is inferred that a similar variability in the classification of PPP risks is also encountered among the stakeholders in PPPs; hence this variability's impact on the risk allocation process is conceivable.

The same conclusion, as with risks, can be reached by reviewing the literature on the issue of Critical Success Factors (CSFs) in PPPs. CSFs constitute a discrete and systematically studied issue, which can be considered as a complement to the risk management issue, since

Yiannis Xenidis

Table 16.4 Review of classification of risks relevant to PPPs' inherent properties of PPPs

PPPs' inherent properties for risks triggering	Risks identified in the literature	Risk category as identified in the literature	Source
Key stakeholders' roles	Insolvency/default of sub-contractors or suppliers	Construction risks	Bing et al. (2005)
	Governmental breach of contract	Creditworthiness risks	Choi et al. (2010)
	Joint venture risks		
	Lack of commitment from either partner	Relationship risks	Bing et al. (2005)
	Inadequate distribution of authority in partnership		
	Organization and co-ordination risk		
Social environment	Changes of requirements (Changes in user needs, Demographic/Social changes)	Contractual risks	Pohle and Girmscheid (2009)
	Anthropogenic man made (demonstration, opportunistic behavior, vandalism)	Operating risks	
	Level of public opposition to project	Social risks	
	Lack of tradition of private provision of public services		
	Strong political opposition/ hostility	Political and government policy risks	Bing et al. (2005)
	Level of demand for project	Project selection risks	
	Operational revenues below expectation	Operation risks	
	Low level of service prices	Market risks	Choi et al. (2010)
Economic environment	Competition	Market and revenue risks	Zheng and Tiong (2010)
	Foreign exchange	Financial risks	
	Failure to raise funds		
	Financial attraction of project to investors	Project finance risks	Bing et al. (2005)
	Poor financial market	Macroeconomic risks	
	Influential economic events		

achieving the required level of maintenance of CSFs in a project is actually an output of successful risk management and, simultaneously, a cause of project risks reduction. Table 16.5 presents the relation to the inherent properties of PPPs of a fraction of those identified in the CSF literature. A key observation from this table is that there is substantial convergence in the literature concerning the CSFs for PPPs, which is evident from the repetitive identification of the same factors, in terms of content, despite the different wording (e.g. 'Projects that are socially and environmentally feasible' and 'Society acceptance' identified, respectively, by Qiao et al., 2001 as cited in Alinaitwe 2011 and Levinson et al., 2006). The identified CSFs

Table 16.5 Review of critical success factors of PPPs and their relevance to PPPs' inherent properties

PPPs' inherent properties	CSF identified in the literature	Source
Key stakeholders' roles	Trust	Jefferies *et al.* (2002) and Spackman (2002) as cited in Jamali (2004)
	Compatibility/complementary skills	Jefferies *et al.* (2002) and Hagen (2002) as cited in Jamali (2004)
	Consortium structure	Jefferies *et al.* (2002)
	Existing JVs/strategic alliances	
	Government's continuous involvement	Spackman (2002) as cited in Jamali (2004)
	Commitment symmetry	Samii *et al.* (2002) and Hagen (2002) both as cited in Jamali (2004)
	Resource dependency	Samii *et al.* (2002) as cited in Jamali (2004)
	Common goal symmetry	
	Alignment of cooperation working capability	
	Converging working cultures	
	Appropriate risk allocation and risk sharing in doing business	Qiao *et al.* (2001) and Grant (1996) as cited in Alinaitwe (2011)
	Government involvement by providing support	Stonehouse *et al.* (1996) as cited in Alinaitwe (2011)
	Well organized local partners/public agencies	Salzmann and Mohamed (1999) as cited in Alinaitwe (2011)
	Shared authority between public and private sectors	Kanter (1999) and Stonehouse *et al.* (1996) as cited in Alinaitwe (2011)
	Commitment/responsibility of public-private sectors	Hardcastle *et al.* (2006) as cited in Alinaitwe (2011)
	Strong private consortium	
Key stakeholders' roles/ Social environment	Social support and developed culture of partnership	Duffield (2005) as cited in Alinaitwe (2011)
Social environment	Projects that are socially and environmentally feasible	Qiao *et al.* (2001) as cited in Alinaitwe (2011)
	Society acceptance	Levinson *et al.* (2006)
	Community support	
Economic environment	Developed legal/economic framework	Jefferies *et al.* (2002)
	Financial capability	
	Stable macro-economic environment including low inflation, stable exchange and interest rates	Qiao *et al.* (2001); Tiong (1996) as cited in Alinaitwe (2011)
	Available financial market	Qiao *et al.* (2001) as cited in Alinaitwe (2011)

are also in accordance with the identified risks that have been summarized in Table 16.4 (e.g. the risk of 'Lack of commitment from either partner' is in full accordance with the 'Commitment symmetry' critical success factor). Therefore, the observation of the same phenomenon for CSFs as with risks above leads to the assertion that the key stakeholders' roles and the economic and social environment affect PPPs in specific modes, which albeit clearly identified either as risks or CSFs, are, in many cases, perceived in different ways.

This variability in perception results in different categorizations of the critical parameters (i.e. risks and CSFs) for successful PPPs and, consequently, in different methodological tools and techniques for proper management of these parameters. Then, the undoubted progress in achieving successful PPPs, which is independent of geographic or industry features as demonstrated in Figures 16.1 and 16.2 and Table 16.1, has to be the result of the application of tools that deal directly and uniformly with the inherent properties of PPPs. The only tools that can integrate the economic and social aspects and define the relationships between the stakeholders in PPPs in such a way that, successfully, transforms experience and gained knowledge to best practices in PPPs development, are the legal and regulatory provisions of both the legal framework and the contract. An example that substantiates this conclusion is the United Kingdom's legal and regulatory model for PPPs. As will be shown in the following section, this model, which is considered to be a very successful one, is applied, worldwide, with more or fewer modifications, and constitutes an important similarity for the newer generations of PPPs. Therefore, it can be assumed that there is a relation between the progress, globally, in achieving successful PPPs, regardless of sector or regional limitations and the wide application of a specific legal and contractual model.

Once the importance of the legal and regulatory provisions in treating the sources of risks and the risks, which are inherent in PPPs, is acknowledged, then the next issues to discuss concern the structure and the orientation of the legal framework and the contract, in order to achieve successful PPPs. These issues are discussed in the following section.

16.3 Managing the dynamics of PPPs

Risks and CSFs are not exclusively related to the three factors identified in the previous section, namely the key stakeholder's roles, the social, and the economic environment. Several other risks exist that are classified in other categories such as, for example, technical risks (Levinson et al., 2006; Samii et al., 2002 as cited in Jamali, 2004; Jefferies et al., 2002; Qiao et al., 2001 and Keong et al., 1997 as cited in Alinaitwe, 2011). For these types of risk, several tools and techniques have been developed that primarily facilitate the assessment of the impact and, consequently, indicate the risk response measures required from the entity that bears the risks. It is, however, a methodologically easy task to assess the impact of risks such as 'Schedule overrun' or 'Cost overrun'. This is not the case with a great number of risks that are frequent in PPPs and are normally classified under the terms 'Legal' (Bing et al., 2005) or 'Legal and regulatory' (Choi et al., 2010) or 'Contractual' or 'Political' (Pohle and Girmscheid, 2009) risks. Such risks and CSFs are presented in Tables 16.6 and 16.7 respectively.

The risks and CSFs identified in Tables 16.6 and 16.7 are evidently difficult even to classify, let alone to quantify. For example, Pohle and Girmscheid (2009) classify 'Changes in law' (i.e. changes in legislation, changes in government policy and changes in taxation) as political risk, while Bing et al. (2005), and Zheng and Tiong (2010) classify the very same risk as legal. Pohle and Girmscheid (2009) move a step forward in their classification and they consider under the term 'Political' some risks that normally are considered as financial or legal (e.g. 'Changes of budgets', 'Changes in standards'), while they name as contractual risk,

Table 16.6 Review of political and legal risks of PPPs

Class	Risks identified in the literature	Source
Legal	Legislation change Change in tax regulation Industrial regulatory change	Bing *et al.* (2005), Zheng and Tiong (2010) Bing *et al.* (2005)
Legal and regulatory risks	Disallowance of long-term financing Legal effectiveness of governmental guarantee Ban on guaranteed rates of return Right to select Engineering, Procurement and Construction contractor Prohibition of cross-border design and construction Uncertainty of selecting method of concessionaire	Choi *et al.* (2010)
Contractual risks	Contractual changes (Changes to the general project conditions, Contract formulation, Unforeseen technical problems or environmental impacts) Partner related (Bankruptcy, Failure of the partner to perform/provide the requisite quality) Changes of requirements (Changes in user needs, Demographic/Social changes)	Pohle and Girmscheid (2009)
Political risks	Changes in law (Changes in legislation, Changes in government policy, Changes in taxation) Changes of budgets (Rescheduling, Coverage of budgets) Changes in standards (Construction standard, Operating standard, Technical standard)	
Political and government policy	Unstable government Expropriation or nationalization of assets Poor public decision-making process	Bing *et al.* (2005)

some that could easily be classified as economic or social (e.g. 'Changes in user needs', 'Demographic/Social changes'). Pohle and Girmscheid (2009) seem to attribute a significant number of PPP risks to the legal (contractual)–political context; however, they are not the only ones: in a previous research, Xenidis and Angelides (2005) present a classification of legal risks that encompass political, social and organizational risks. The argument for such a classification is simple, yet strong: All these risks depend on the statutory and regulatory boundaries of the legal and contractual framework that governs a PPP. Xenidis and Angelides (2005) graphically represent this dependency in Figure 16.3.

What Figure 16.3 actually illustrates is that any social needs and expectations at a specific time-period depend on the prevailing social standards and can be satisfied by a formal social organization, which is governed by the legal and regulatory framework developed by the

Table 16.7 Review of political and legal critical success factors of PPPs

Class	CSF identified in the literature	Source
Political	Political stability-opposed/support	Jefferies *et al.* (2002) and Qiao *et al.* (2001) as cited in Alinaitwe (2011)
	Good governance	Quio *et al.* (2001) and Keong *et al.* (1997) as cited in Alinaitwe (2011)
	Government acceptance	Levinson *et al.* (2006)
Legal	Transparency and competition in procurement	Alinaitwe (2011)
	Approval process-efficiency/complicated negotiations	Jefferies *et al.* (2002)
	Transparent and sound regulatory framework	Pongsiri (2002), as cited in Jamali (2004)
	Favorable legal framework	Tiong (1996) as cited in Alinaitwe (2011)

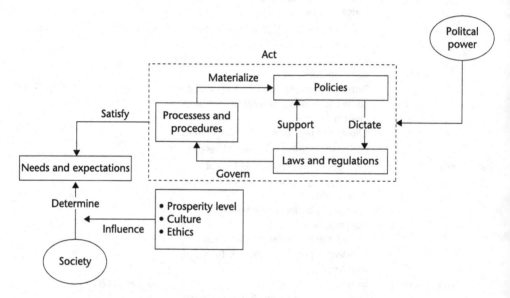

Figure 16.3 The use of laws and regulations as an interface for social, political and organizational aspects

Source: The Legal Risks in Build-Operate-Transfer projects, Xenidis, Y. and Angelides D.C., *Journal of Construction Research*, 6(2), © 2005 World Scientific Journals

political power that implements policies in favour of the society. In this context, all the risks that are generally classified as 'political', 'legal' or 'contractual', regardless of their specific nature, are actually mapped in the contract and, thereafter, constitute well-defined contract clauses; hence, the only risk that remains is that of the misinterpretation of the contract or the negligence on its enforcement (Xenidis and Angelides, 2005) and this should be the definition of legal risk.

The critical issues under discussion, namely the management of the dynamics of PPPs and the reasoning of the increasing success in achieving viable PPPs are, in this context, fully explicable. Instead of applying a loose stakeholders' management tool such those proposed in the literature (Walker *et al.*, 2008), emphasis should be given to perceiving the legal–contractual context of PPPs in a broader sense, because this is the key to confront both quantifiable and non-quantifiable risks. The legal framework and the governing contracts of PPPs, i.e. the legal context in which PPPs are developed, is the dominant critical factor that by integration of all other issues can lead to a successful or failed PPP. In other words, it is the topic of 'contractual agreements' that Tang *et al.* (2009) highlight as a discrete topic of research that should be primarily investigated among any other specific topic with regard to PPPs. Having identified, in an academic approach, the capacities and significance of the legal context for PPPs, focusing, especially, on those dimensions that encompass social, political and organizational (inside the partnership) issues, it becomes important to investigate the evolution of legal frameworks that allowed for more successful PPPs globally.

16.3.1 Evolution of the legal framework for PPPs

The implementation of PPPs in the modern era begins, according to almost all historic approaches on the subject, in the UK, which is considered as the pioneer country in applying PPPs and a best practice example for the rest of the world (Abdel Aziz, 2007). In fact, most of the countries globally, either because of the use of common law (La Porta *et al.*, 1998) or because of late implementation of the PPP project delivery scheme that allowed for previous study of the UK's example are applying a model very similar to the UK's for PPPs.

The early experience with PPPs in the UK, as well as in Canada and the USA, which also implemented this project delivery scheme very early compared to the rest of the world, reveals, not unreasonably, a very project-specific regulatory framework; considering the lack of past experience in this infrastructure delivery scheme, both with regard to the partnership's requirements and the level of readiness of the public sector to support such a process, a project-specific approach should be anticipated (Abdel Aziz, 2007). However, in due time, in all the above-mentioned countries, a case-based development of guidelines and policies resulted in the standardization of contracts and institutionalization of PPPs (Abdel Aziz, 2007). Standardization is considered as a policy that promotes transparency and trust between partners, facilitates timely understanding of the terms of the partnership, and increases the confidence of the entities and personnel involved on the rightness of decisions and actions in setting up and operating a PPP (Mahalingam, 2010).

In the UK the first edition of Standardization of PFI Contracts ('SoPC') was published in 1999, followed by three more editions in 2002, 2004 and 2007 (HM Treasury 2007); the last edition has been updated, on a yearly basis, until 2010. The objectives of the standardization are quoted from the previous edition:

> The three main objectives of the guidance remain unchanged. First, to promote a common understanding of the main risks which are encountered in a standard PFI project; secondly, to allow consistency of approach and pricing across a range of similar projects; and thirdly, to reduce the time and costs of negotiation by enabling all parties concerned to agree a range of areas that can follow a standard approach without extended negotiations.
>
> (*HM Treasury 2007*)

From this quote, it is evident that standard PPPs present a certain high level of similarity that allows for a uniform approach in risks management irrespective of project particularities such as geography or sector. That became evident, progressively and upon gaining of experience that allowed the identification of certain inherent characteristics of this project delivery scheme by those involved actively in the subject. In some cases, as for example, in British Columbia (BC), Canada, the same conclusion allowed for a more advanced standardization: the procurement process for PPPs is identical to the Capital Asset Management Framework (CAMF), which applies to publicly funded capital assets (e.g. schools, hospitals, etc.) (Abdel Aziz, 2007). Therefore, the implementation of PPPs in BC follows a well-known and widely accepted pattern, which is also applied in other forms of infrastructure development.

The experience gained and the drive for greater efficiency resulted in a progressive shift of concern from the issue of raising funds to other critical issues related to social and political risks such as transparency, public accountability and quality of services; all these, as already identified in the previous sections, are issues strongly connected to the viability of a PPP.

Concerning disclosure, the practice in BC, Canada, is among the most advanced, since it is applied at the maximum acceptable level by integrating several practices: a) full disclosure of tender documents; b) disclosure of responses to tender documents; c) disclosure, under specific requirements, of the final concession agreement; d) disclosure of the opinions of auditors on the evaluation and selection process of contractors; and e) justification of the selection of the PPP project delivery scheme based on value-for-money for the project (Abdel Aziz, 2007). In Switzerland, a country with strong foundations in democratic processes, PPPs are not excluded with regard to transparency requirements from what is applied in every aspect of public life; they are subjected to citizens' approval through referenda, since the legal system reflects a tradition of public consent and exercise of control for any issue that involves specific legal and financial requirements (Lienhard, 2006). Accountability of the PPPs' partners to the whole spectrum of the public law, the public's opinion and the steering processes during operation of the project ensure transparency and safeguard public interest in PPPs (Lienhard, 2006).

Quality of services, as mentioned above, is another issue that progressively drew attention, in practice. The incorporation of quality requirements for a PPP project is set either as a prequalification criterion in the bidding stage or as an award criterion in the operation phase (Rui Cunha and Sanford, 2010). In the second case, an evolution in the type of contracting resulted in the so-called performance-based these do not force the private entity to achieve quality standards agreed in the project's design, but oblige the contractor to achieve a certain performance level for the provided services for which it is compensated (service-based approach) (Abdel Aziz, 2007). Since in performance-based contracts compensation is tied to the supply of quality services, the private entity is forced to fulfil all quality requirements throughout the lifecycle of the project (Garvin, 2010).

A critical issue of utmost importance, identified already from the early periods of PPPs implementation, is that of renegotiation. The provision for renegotiations of contract clauses, in certain circumstances that obviously jeopardize the viability of the partnership, is mandated to incomplete contracts. However, practice has shown that this option in most cases turns in favour of the private entity, because it is in a better position to impose its will (Rui Cunha and Sanford, 2010; de Brux, 2009); unfortunately, in many cases the option for renegotiations is, even, abused by the private partner (de Los Angeles Baeza and Vassallo, 2010; Gómez-Lobo and Hinojosa, 2000).

The conclusion that derives from the previous analysis is that, in time, the theoretical and empirical frameworks of PPPs have evolved to address more effectively: a) the expectations and the incentives of the partners; and b) the means to achieve successful partnerships.

Therefore, the question raised is with regard to the potential of proposing even more effective legal tools that could integrate all the aspects discussed so far and constitute a risk-response tool, primarily, against risks of political, social and organizational nature. Such an effort is attempted in the following section.

16.4 A proposal for an effective legal context for PPPs

The main objective of a successful legal context for PPPs should be achieving or satisfying the expectations of all parties involved. To accomplish that, several critical parameters in the form of risks and critical success factors should be considered and addressed properly. Considering previous experience and progress for over 20 years and having in mind the existence of a vast body of knowledge with regard to PPPs, it is correct decisions that are crucial to establish an effective legal context for PPPs.

The first constituent for such a context is the existence of a distinct law that sets out the framework for developing PPPs. The absence of specific regulatory frameworks has led to infrastructure projects through specific contracts that primarily satisfied the requirements of the private sector, namely the security of the investment, in terms of viability and profitability, at the expense of the public sector. Whenever problems arose the results were either cancellations or significant increases of transaction costs and hefty penalties for contract changes (Farlam, 2005). Lienhard (2006), having studied the Swiss example that lacks such a law, proposes its institutionalization, but only after careful considerations, which are also applicable in all similar cases. Lienhard (2006) proposes the following two basic considerations: 1) the existence of a common ground between the two legal systems for PPPs, i.e. the original and adapted from another country. This is because, generally, it is not always feasible for a country to apply the best practices of other countries due to differences in the political and legal cultures; 2) the existence of substantial experience in PPPs prior to the passing of any law, in order to efficiently determine the required provisions. Abdel Aziz (2007) proposes also the introduction of a specific legal framework to institutionalize the implementation of PPPs instead of implementing them through specific, case-based acts. Furthermore, he is in favour of a more generic and broad-content law that: a) allows the selection of the best option among the several procurement systems, which are applicable for infrastructure, and; b) enables public authorities at different administration levels to decide on critical issues with regard to PPPs. In this way, several of the usual reasons for a project's distress or even cancellation can be eliminated by administrative acts instead of the time-consuming and more rigid process of law amendments. A law with such characteristics seems also appropriate in other cases where PPPs are implemented with little confidence about their effectiveness as, for example, the case in Spain (Allard and Trabant, 2008) or where they face barriers at the institutional, organizational and political levels as in the case of India's state level PPPs (Mahalingam, 2010). Garvin (2010) refers to Guash (2004) and the result of his research wherein a positive association was found between the frequency of renegotiations and the absence of a regulatory framework embedded in a law. For the sake of completeness, reference should be made to successful practices in PPPs in the absence of a specific law (e.g. the case of Germany), but under a robust legal system in terms of structure and enforcement (Essig and Batran, 2006).

The law should anticipate the use of contracts between partners with regulators. While Grout and Stevens (2003) in Garvin (2010) characterize the public's role in PPPs as that of a regulator via contract, Stern (2009) suggests that the regulators should be external and independent and should operate under specific and transparent procedures. The need for external regulators is justified, according to Stern (2009), considering the following requirements for

PPPs: a) definition of effective business and accounting standards; b) creation and restoration of trust between the partnership's internal and external stakeholders; and c) protection of the public interest against excessive profits from monopoly facilities.

The primary legal instruments for PPPs are contracts. Stern (2009) highlights the fact that infrastructure services through PPPs are mostly supplied through sets of contracts, usually long-term ones that can successfully correspond to the issues of public policy and regulation. The basic contracts in PPPs are expensive, incomplete and, often, inefficient in allocating risks (Rui Cunha and Sanford, 2010); thus they constitute a major source of risks, of increases of costs, of renegotiations and of causes of failures (Garvin, 2010). Could rigid contracts, at least until the anticipated period of renegotiations, provide an efficient framework for achieving successful PPPs? Collins (1999) as cited in Stern (2009) suggests that contracts should be perceived as determinants of commercial collaboration and relationships between partners, rather than safeguards against deviations from agreements. While not abnegating their penal character in cases of serious breaches of trust, their primary objective should be to constitute a platform for working out solutions; therefore they should express at any given time the consent of all stakeholders to a course of action. How could this be achieved? Relational contracts have been considered as an option to facilitate or minimize renegotiations and, in general, better manage the partners' conflicting interests and policies during a PPP (de Brux, 2009). Relational contracts provide flexibility, in terms of legal binding and, conceptually, are appropriate for responding to organizational, social and political risks due to their dynamic nature, i.e. their evolution with time through incorporation to the partnering practices of the lessons learned from the dynamics of the partnership. However, while the use of relational contracts could, theoretically, reduce substantially the number of contracts between the several partners of a PPP, in practice, a long-period partnership on the provision of public services with substantial amounts at stake (i.e. loans, profits, tariffs, guarantees, etc.) could hardly be supported by so informal a type of contract.

Performance contracts could also be an option; however, they can be effective primarily for services provision and in countries with mature public administration agencies that can conduct the performance appraisals and decide upon the viability of the project. The adverse impact of performance contracts on PPPs for infrastructure facilities is very well highlighted by Garvin (2010) who reviewed thoroughly Grout (1997) and Hart (2003) and provided an insight to the effect of both bundling and unbundling on the trade-off between the investment in facilities and performance requirements. Garvin (2010) clearly states that unbundling construction from service provision seems more appropriate in the cases where it is easier to specify the quality of the infrastructure, rather than specifying the quality of the service to provide; furthermore, unbundling is advantageous in terms of operability and aesthetic appraisal of the infrastructure (Garvin, 2010). Therefore, performance-based contracts, which are more effective for services provision, are inefficient for PPPs whose primary goal is the provision of infrastructure facilities.

Considering that more detailed and complete contracts would be either infeasible due to the uncertainties and risks in the long period of the partnership, or ineffective because of the existence of strict provisions that would regulate in a definite and robust way the project's operation and affect participants' behaviours (Garvin, 2010), an alternative risk-response strategy would be the short-term contracts that lead to re-bidding. Klein (1998) refers to re-bidding and more specifically to the Chadwick-Demsetz auction as an option to regulate the adverse impact on the PPPs of the monopolistic nature of infrastructure developed in such context. Furthermore, Rey and Salanié (1990) suggest that short-term contracts are much more powerful tools, especially in the case of information asymmetry, which is normal for

PPPs. Therefore, well written short-term contracts may provide stronger guarantees than long-term ones for viable PPPs. A very important benefit would be with regard to the management of PPPs risks. The risks that are identified and managed in a contract may be identical, in terms of nature and number, regardless of the contractual period; however, it is the capacity of assessing these risks accurately that is enhanced in the case of short-term compared to long-term contracts, mainly because the assumptions and conditions required for risk assessment are, naturally, more valid and accurate for short-term estimates compared to long-term ones. A more effective assessment, especially of the discussed risks, which are volatile and complex, would facilitate proper and more direct risk allocation among partners. Compared to the much criticized practice of renegotiations that is inherent in long-term, incomplete contracts (de Brux, 2009), the alternative of systematic re-bidding is better suited to many of the CSF of PPPs:

- With regard to transparency, instead of ambiguous processes and (often dubious) internal agreements, a renewal of the partnership through re-bidding provides better administrative and public control, which is required for services normally provided through PPPs. Such a process, which would introduce all appropriate disclosure measures (e.g. those discussed in the case of Canada), could ensure public participation at a satisfactory level without the need to apply more demanding solutions (e.g. the Swiss paradigm).
- With regard to performance, shorter periods between audits would result in upgraded quality standards and an increase of the service level provided to the public. In particular, since the performance achieved by the private entity would inevitably constitute a criterion for renewal of the partnership, the re-evaluation through an open bidding process would add a further motive for the already contracted private entity to ensure high standards in the provision of services during the partnership period.
- With regard to financing, a re-bidding process in short terms would force unbundling of services in the partnership, which, in general, is less costly than the mostly preferred bundling rationale in PPPs, in terms of construction (Carmona, 2010) and financing costs.

Despite the above discussion, a short-term contracting and re-bidding strategy for PPPs could draw much scepticism, especially since current practice, generally, favours incomplete, long-lasting contracts (e.g. Build-Own-Operate-Transfer, Design-Build-Finance-Maintain(Operate), etc.). Several important issues could be raised, such as: a) the capability and willingness the public sector to run contractual processes in close time periods; b) the opportunity for discontinuities in services provision due to a change of private partner after the re-bidding process; c) the advantage held by incumbent partners in the re-bidding process; d) the attenuation of the incentivizing nature of bundling in PPPs; and perhaps most important of all: e) the potential change in the nature of PPPs from a partnership to an outsourcing infrastructure management scheme.

Starting from the last point, it should be stressed that PPPs' primary goal has changed through the years: from a tool of privatizing infrastructure or disguising public expenditure by excluding from the budget public services provided through PPPs to a tool that achieves 'net present value for money as measured against services the government could provide on its own' or 'optimal risk allocation between the public and private sector partners (rather than maximum risk transfer to the private sector)' (PPIAF and EASSD, 2007). These aims, together with the two fundamental characteristics of PPPs, namely: a) the scope, which is infrastructure and services provided normally by the public sector; and b) the duration, which is not indefinite, actually imply an outsourcing of public duties to the private sector for the public food. The fact that a PPP is a highly sophisticated method that involves long-term periods and complex procurement and reimbursement practices for the concessionaire, does not alter its fundamental nature, that of an outsourcing method. This is why Klein (1998), viewing the process from the position of the public sector, states: '*In a way, the process of choosing a concessionaire would then look more like that of choosing an important employee.*'

Based on the above, the nature of PPPs is not challenged by the use of short-term contracts, especially, since their duration remains undefined. It is a matter of use of the appropriate model to define the duration of such a contract; however, a ballpark estimate could place the maximum at around 25 years. This estimate is not arbitrary, but rather based on the empirical data drawn from one of the most successful programmes of PPPs, that of the Chilean concessions in the 1990s (Fischer, 2011 in IGC, 2011; FAD, 2004; Gómez-Lobo and Hinojosa, 2000). Table 16.8 summarizes data from Fischer (2011), as well as from IGC (2011) based on Fischer (2011), that present the average duration and renegotiations as a percentage of investment of concessions in Chile until 2007.

Table 16.8 clearly shows that the duration of the concessions reaches an average of 23 years; while in the case of airports the concessions' durations reach an average of 13 years. Gómez-Lobo and Hinojosa (2000) present a ten-year concession for the Route 5, Talca–Chillán highway project. The average of 24 per cent of renegotiations as a percentage of the total investment, although marked as being too high and as a major problem of the Chilean PPPs programme (IGC, 2011; FAD, 2004), in fact is considerably lower compared to the renegotiations of PPPs in Latin America as a whole. This figure is based on Guash (2007) who records: a) 69 per cent of renegotiations in the transportation sector, i.e. around 165 per cent an increase of compared to the respective propantion for highways PPPs in Chile; and b) 54 per cent of renegotiations in all sectors, i.e. around 125 per cent increased renegotiations compared to the respective proportion for all PPPs in Chile. The Chilean PPPs for infrastructure programme does not prove the appropriateness of short-term contracts for more viable and more successful PPPs, especially, since the duration of the concessions has never been explicitly linked to the programme's success and, of course, because it was not the only reason for the success; it indicates, however, that PPPs for infrastructure are viable for shorter concession periods.

What differentiated the Chilean from the Mexican example that was also based on short-term contracts but was a spectacular failure, was the necessary adjustments that were made in the first case, in order to ensure the private sector's incentives and the public sector's

Table 16.8 Duration and renegotiation as fraction of investment of PPPs in Chile until 2007

Project type	Number of projects	Average concession's duration (years)	Renegotiation as fraction of investment (%)
Highways	26	27.3	26
Airports	10	13.1	12
Gaols	3	22.5	26
Reservoirs	2	27.5	9
Transantiago	5	15.8	12
Public infrastructure	4	23.2	1
Overall average		22.7	24

protection of interests (Gómez-Lobo and Hinojosa, 2000). These adjustments could also respond to the reservations for short-term contracts with regard to: a) the potential disconti-nuities in services provision due to a change of the private partner after the re-bidding process; and b) the retention of incentives for private partners to participate in a short-term PPP. These adjustments included but were not limited to: a) the establishment of a tendering mechanism that linked bids with the concession's duration and profits; b) the introduction of fluctuating tolls and tariffs based on quality performance and demand; c) the establishment of a system of bonds (e.g. guarantee bonds, performance bonds) that provided a steady environ-ment for the PPPs during their whole life cycle.

What is clearly implied from the above is that a short-term duration of PPPs is neither unfeasible nor problematic. The burden for the public sector to run contractual processes in close time periods is in inverse proportion to the experience it gains with time. Furthermore, the fair treatment of bidders could be ensured by a bonus–malus point system for the incum-bent partner who has already proved his contribution to the viability of the partnership, in terms of achieving performance standards, raising profits, etc.

Reservations about short-term contracts for PPPs are, reasonably, based on the reality of current practice in PPPs. Instead of pursuing viable partnerships, both the public and the private sector, in most cases, pursue a viable project. As long as the public entity is more concerned about the provision of services itself, instead of the implications for providing these services, the partnership is unchallenged, unless the private entity asks for a raise in profits or is forced, for own reasons, to withdraw from the partnership. This is the reason why in many cases, the so-called viable PPPs are, in fact, concealed failures thanks to the public partner's excessive efforts and contribution (Hall, 2010; Hall, 2008; Guash, 2007 and others).

16.5 Conclusions

Public–private partnerships have evolved over the last 20 years to a mature infrastructure delivery scheme. Globally the implementation of PPPs these days is more efficient compared to the previous decade, at least in terms of achieving viable projects in the long run. However, despite the development of a great body of knowledge and of the extensive experience gained, it is evident that several issues still draw the attention of researchers and practitioners in the field. Beyond the traditional and extensively studied issues of financing and risk allocation, less explored topics require the attention of researchers; one of the most fundamental among them is the better management of social, political and organizational risks. These risks emanate from the inherent properties of PPPs, namely: a) the complex relationships between the key stakeholders in PPPs; and b) the strong dependence on the economic and social envi-ronment wherein they are developed. Whilst identifiable, they remain vague in content and this is the reason why various researchers classify them in different ways, in several risk taxonomies. However, a different perspective of the notion of legal risks could assist in their homogenization in a single group. In particular, considering that social, political and organi-zational risks: a) depend on the statutory and regulatory boundaries of the legal and contractual framework that governs a PPP; and b) are incorporated in both mentioned frameworks, it becomes evident that they can be considered as legal risks in a broad sense. In view of that, it is clear that the legal, regulatory and contractual frameworks require a systematic and in-depth investigation to foster further success of PPPs.

The current trend in PPPs implementation, both in theory and in practice, is to address more effectively the expectations and the incentives of the partners to the contractual framework of the partnership. In this way, the risks related to social, political, organizational and, partially, economic issues could be better allocated and treated in the long run reducing renegotiations, which most of the time indicate a malfunctioning partnership that is maintained at the expense of the public sector or the end users. Standardization of contracts, transparent clauses and disclosure processes are gaining more and more ground, not only in the literature, but especially and more important, in those countries with, historically, considerable impact on the development of this project delivery scheme. These policies should be additional to a legal context that needs to achieve a compromise between: a) clarity in relationships and allocation of risks between partners; b) stability that ensures an adequate level of security for the investment; c) flexibility, in order to, properly, address dynamic risks; and d) efficiency in the provision of services and in fulfilment and advancement of the quality standards for services. To achieve these objectives, it is proposed that the legal context should be based on a distinct law for PPPs and multilateral contracts among partners. The law should work as the contextual framework of the partnerships, i.e. it should define the boundary conditions for the setting of contracts. It should also serve as a regulatory tool from the procurement phase to the end of the partnership. The contracts should define the details of any specific partnership. Since the long contractual period has been identified as the main reason for incomplete contracts and renegotiations, instead of changing the type of contracts to relational or performance-based, short-term contracts should be considered as an alternative. Short-term contracts do not alter the nature of the partnership and include the same risks, which mostly are inherent to this project delivery scheme; however, by reducing the time of the contract's validity, these risks become easier to assess and manage. Moreover, short-term contracts can, reasonably, result in better performance, in terms of transparency in processes and provision of high-quality services.

Two steps are essential towards the implementation of the proposed legal and contractual frameworks, which can inherently respond to several hard to quantify risks. The first should be further research on critical details such as: the duration of the contracts, the standardization of their number and content, the level of unbundling, and the securing of attractiveness of the investment to funders. The second should be for the public and private partners to re-consider PPPs as a mutual commitment that serves primarily the society, instead of their own interests. Provided this shifting in priorities occurs, it is very likely that PPPs will become an even more successful infrastructure and services delivery scheme.

References

Abdel Aziz, A.M. (2007). 'Successful delivery of Public–Private Partnerships for infrastructure development'. *Journal of Construction Engineering and Management* 133(12), 918–31.

Alinaitwe, H. (2011). 'Contractors' perspective on critical factors for successful implementation of Private Public Partnerships in construction projects in Uganda'. In: Mwakali, J.A. and Alinaitwe, H.M. (eds) *Advances in Engineering and Technology, Contribution of Scientific Research in Development.* Kampala: Macmillan Uganda, 298–304.

Allard, G. and Trabant, A. (2008), 'Public–Private Partnerships in Spain: Lessons and Opportunities', *International Business & Economics Research Journal*, 7(2), 1–24.

Barbas, A. (2010). '*Correlation between critical socio-economic factors and implementation of PPP projects*', MSc Thesis (*in Greek*), Thessaloniki: Aristotle University of Thessaloniki, Greece.

Bing, L., Akintoye, A., Edwads, P.J. and Hardcastle, C. (2005). 'The allocation of risk in PPP/PFI construction projects in the UK', *International Journal of Project Management*, 23(1), 25–35.

Bryde, D. (2008). 'Perceptions of the impact of project sponsorship practices on project success', *International Journal of Project Management*, 26(8), 800–9.

Carmona, M. (2010). 'The regulatory function in public–private partnerships for the provision of transport infrastructure', *Research in Transportation Economics*, 30(1), 110–25.

Choi, J., Chung, J., Lee, D.-J. (2010). 'Risk perception analysis: Participation in China's water PPP market', *International Journal of Project Management*, 28(6), 580–92.

Cunha Marques, R. and Berg, S. (2011). 'Public–Private Partnership contracts: a tale of two cities with different contractual arrangements', *Public Administration*, 89(4), 1585–1603.

de Brux, J. (2009). *'The dark and bright side of renegotiations: an application to transport concession contracts'*, Discussion Paper Series, EPPP DP No. 2010-1. Chaire EPPP, IAE-Pantheon-Sorbonne.

de Los Angeles Baeza, M. and Vassallo, J.M. (2010), 'Private concession contracts for toll roads in Spain: analysis and recommendations', *Public Money & Management*, 30(5), 299–304.

El-Gohary, N.M., Osman, H. and El-Diraby, T.E. (2006). 'Stakeholder management for public private partnerships', *International Journal of Project Management*, 24(7), 595–604.

Essig, M. and Batran, A. (2006). 'Public–private partnership – Development of long-term relationships in public procurement in Germany', *Journal of Purchasing & Supply Management*, 11(5–6), 221–31.

Estache, A., Juan, E. and Trujillo, L. (2007). *'Public–Private Partnerships in transport'*, World Bank Policy Research Working Paper Series, WPS4436. The World Bank. Available at SSRN: http://ssrn.com/abstract=1072402.

Farlam, P. (2005). *'Assessing Public–Private-Partnerships in Africa'*, Nepad Policy Focus Report No.2, South Africa: The South African Institute of International Affairs (SAIIA).

Fiscal Affairs Department (FAD) (2004). *'Public–Private Partnerships'*, International Monetary Fund.

Fischer, R. (2011). *'Lessons from the Chilean PPP experience'*. [PowerPoint slides]. Presented at the International Growth Centre Conference in Rwanda.

Galilea, P. and Medda, F. (2010). 'Does the political and economic context influence the success of a transport project? An analysis of transport public–private-partnerships', *Research in Transportation Economics*, 30(1), 102–9.

Garvin, M.J. (2010). *'Governance of PPP projects through contract provisions'*, Working Paper, Blacksburg, Virginia: Virginia Tech.

Gómez-Lobo, A. and Hinojosa, S. (2000). *'Broad Roads in a Thin Country: Infrastructure Concessions in Chile'*. World Bank Policy Research Working Paper 2279, Washington: The World Bank.

Guash, J.L. (2007). *'Negotiating and renegotiating infrastructure PPPs and concessions: Key issues for policy makers'*. [PowerPoint slides]. Presented at the International Seminar on Strengthening Public Investment and Managing Fiscal Risks from Public–Private Partnerships, Budapest, Hungary.

Hall, D. (2008). *'PPPs in the EU – a critical appraisal'*, UK: Public Services International Research Unit (PSIRU), University of Greenwich.

Hall, D. (2010). *'More public rescues for more private finance failures – a critique of the EC Communication on PPPs'*, UK: Public Services International Research Unit (PSIRU), University of Greenwich.

Hammami, M., Ruhashyankiko, J.-F. and Yehoue, E.B. (2006). *'Determinants of Public–Private Partnerships in infrastructure'*, (WP/06/99). Washington: International Monetary Fund.

HM Treasury (2007). *'Standardisation of PFI contracts'*, Version 4, Norwich: The Stationery Office, 1.

International Growth Centre (IGC) (2011). *'The Promise and Peril of Public Private Partnerships: Lessons from the Chilean Experience'*, IGC Rwanda Policy Note Series No. 1, United Kingdom: International Growth Centre.

Jamali, D. (2004). 'Success and failure mechanisms of Public Private Partnerships (PPPs) in developing countries: Insights from the Lebanese context', *The International Journal of Public Sector Management*, 17(5), 414–30.

Jefferies, M., Gameson, R. and Rowlinson, S. (2002). 'Critical success factors of the BOOT procurement system: reflections from the Stadium Australia case study', *Engineering, Construction and Architectural Management*, 9(4), 352–61.

Klein, M. (1998). *'Bidding for concessions'*. World Bank Policy Research Working Paper no. 1957, Washington DC: The World Bank.

La Porta, R., Lopez-de-Silanes, F., Shleifer A. and Vishny, R.W. (1998). 'Law and Finance'. *Journal of Political Economy*, 106(6), 1113–55.

Levinson, D., Garcia, R. and Carlson, K. (2006). 'A framework for assessing Public Private Partnerships'. In: Rietveld, P. and Stough, R. (eds 2006) *Institutions and Regulatory Reform in Transportation*, Edward Elgar Publishers, Ch.13, 284–304.

Lienhard, A. (2006). 'Public Private Partnerships in Switzerland: experiences – risks – potentials', *International Review of Administrative Sciences*, 72(4), 547–63.

Mahalingam, A. (2010). 'PPP experiences in Indian cities: barriers, enablers and the way forward', *Journal of Construction Engineering and Management*, 136(4), 419–29.

Moszoro, M. and Gąsiorowski, P. (2008). *'Optimal capital structure of public-private-partnerships'*, (WP/08/1) International Monetary Fund.

Pangeran, M.H. and Wirahadikusumah, R.D. (2010). Challenges in Implementing the Public Sector Comparator for Bid Evaluation of PPP's Infrastructure Project Investment. In: *Proceedings of the First Makassar International Conference on Civil Engineering (MICE2010)*, March 9–10, Makassar, Indonesia, 1229–39.

Pohle, T. and Girmscheid, G. (2009). 'PPP-risk identification and allocation model: the critical success factor for PPPs'. In: Ghafoori, N. (ed.) *Challenges, Opportunities and Solutions in Structural Engineering and Construction*. CRC Press, 745–50.

Private Participation in Infrastructure Projects Database (2011). http://ppi.worldbank.org/explore/ppi_exploreSector.aspx?sectorID=2 The World Bank Group, Accessed 28/12/2011.

Public-Private Infrastructure Advisory Facility (PPIAF) and Infrastructure Consortium for Africa (ICA) (2008). *'Attracting Investors to African Public-Private Partnerships: A Project Preparation Guide'*, Washington DC: The World Bank.

Public–Private Infrastructure Advisory Facility (PPIAF) and East Asia and Pacific Sustainable Development Department (EASSD) of The World Bank (2007). *'Public–Private Partnership Units: Lessons for their Design and Use in Infrastructure'*, Washington DC: The World Bank.

Renda, A. and Schrefler, L. (2006). *'Public–Private Partnerships National Experiences in the European Union'*, Directorate A, DG Internal Policies of the Union, Brussels.

Rey, P. and Salanié, B. (1990). 'Long-Term, Short-Term and Renegotiation: On the Value of Commitment in Contracting', *Econometrica*, 58, 597–619.

Rui Cunha, M. and Sanford, B. (2010). 'Revisiting the Strengths and Limitations of Regulatory Contracts in Infrastructure Industries', *Journal of Infrastructure Systems*, 16(4), 334–42.

Shan, X., Hou, W., Ye, X. and Wu, C. (2011). 'Decision-Making Criteria of PPP Projects: Stakeholder Theoretic Perspective', *Engineering and Technology*, 77, 696–700.

Stern, J. (2009). *'Relationship between Regulation and Contract in Infrastructure Industries'*, CCRP Working Paper No: 14, London: City University.

Tang, L., Shen, Q. and Cheng, E.W.L. (2009). 'A review of studies on public–private partnership projects in the construction industry', *International Journal of Project Management*, 28(7), 683–94.

Tecco, N. (2008). 'Financially sustainable investments in developing countries water sectors: what conditions could promote private sector involvement?', *International Environmental Agreements: Politics, Law and Economics*, 8(2), 129–42.

Thomsen, S. (2005). *'Encouraging Public-Private Partnerships in the Utilities Sector: The Role of Development Assistance'*, Overview Study for the Roundtable 'Investment for African Development: Making it Happen', 25–7 May, Kama Hal, Entebbe, Uganda.

Thomson, C. and Goodwin, J. (2005). *'Evaluation of PPP projects financed by the EIB'*, Evaluation Report, European Investment Bank.

Walker, D.H.T., Bourne, L.M. and Shelley, A. (2008). 'Influence, stakeholder mapping and visualization', *Construction Management and Economics*, 26(6), 645–58.

Xenidis, Y. and Angelides, D.C. (2005). 'The Legal Risks in Build-Operate-Transfer projects', *Journal of Construction Research*, 6(2), 273–92.

Zhang, X. (2005). 'Financial viability analysis and capital structure optimization in privatized public infrastructure projects', *Journal of Construction Engineering and Management*, 131(6), 656–68.

Zhao, G. and Wang, S. (2007). 'Indicators of social impact assessment for BOT/PPP projects'. In: *Proceedings of the International Symposium on Social Management Systems (ISMS2007)*, March 9–11, Yichang, China, 64–72.

Zheng, S. and Tiong, R.L.K. (2010). 'First Public–Private-Partnership application in Taiwan's waste-water treatment sector: Case study of the Nanzih BOT wastewater treatment project'. *Journal of Construction Engineering and Management*, 136(8), 913–22.

Part VIII

Accountability, auditing and assessment of public–private partnerships

Accountability and accounting for public–private partnerships

Ron Hodges

17.1 Introduction

There are several distinct, but related, issues concerning the accountability of Public Private Partnerships (PPPs). First, there is desire to achieve *value for money* in PPP contracts through the establishment of rigorous processes designed to ensure an appropriate balance of cost incurred by and risk transferred from the public sector. Second, there is a demand for *political* accountability in that democratic states will normally provide some form of accountability of the executive through legislative bodies to citizens for public policy. This chapter concentrates on PPP accounting as a third element of accountability. There are two major and distinct approaches to accounting for national finances. The first, *national accounting*, is derived from a statistical approach to measuring macroeconomic performance, developed at a comparative international level (Jones 2003). The second, *financial accounting*, is based upon generally accepted accounting principles (GAAP) which derive from accounting professionals and is designed to measure the financial performance of individual entities, which may be consolidated into larger economic units, for example whole of government accounts (Chow *et al.* 2007). Both approaches will be described later in the chapter. The financial accounting process will be considered further because it should assist in providing transparency of the financial consequences for individual entities of entering into PPP projects. This process is linked to value for money concerns in that financial accounting may help to disclose, *ex-post*, the achievement or absence of value for money in PPP contracts. It is linked to political accountability in that financial reporting disclosure has the potential to promote transparency of PPP transactions, but cannot, in itself, guarantee that governance and political structures are adequate to ensure that appropriate lessons are learnt and best practices adopted in public policy development.

The first objective of this chapter is to provide the reader with an understanding of the importance of PPP accounting and some of the challenges to regulators in the development of PPP financial accounting rules. Particular attention is given to the UK and its Private Financial Initiative (PFI), as representing an example of the choppy waters of PPP accounting. The financial accounting of PFI schemes has been one element of this controversy in view of its potential to limit public sector financial accountability by off-balance-sheet financing and the impact of the mode of accounting on investment decisions.

The second objective of this chapter is to provide a reflection on current international developments in PPP accounting through an examination of recent proposals of the International Public Sector Accounting Standards Board (IPSASB). In February 2010 the IPSASB issued an Exposure Draft (ED) of a proposed international standard *ED43 Service Concession Arrangements: Grantor*. Written responses to the proposals in ED43, from a variety of national and international regulators, accounting bodies and professional firms, were released in September 2010. In October 2011, IPSASB published a new standard *IPSAS32 Service Concession Arrangements: Grantor*, which is due for implementation by 2014.

In this chapter PPPs are taken to be contractually driven arrangements in which private sector organizations are responsible for matters such as the design, building operating and financing of infrastructure assets used to provide public services. The cost of the arrangement is paid for by user charges or by contributions from taxation authorized by the public sector grantor or by some combination of both. For terminological clarity, the label PPP will be used in this chapter to reflect the general type of arrangement indicated above, except when referring to specific PFI accounting regulations, studies and guidance. A further term, Service Concession Arrangements (SCAs), will be introduced later in the chapter, in the context of international accounting regulations directed at some types of PPPs.

The remainder of the chapter is structured into six further sections. Section 17.2 sets the scene by considering why PPP accounting is important and outlining the major issues underlying the financial accounting of PPP projects. Section 17.3 introduces the principles and related institutions, such as the International Accounting Standards Board (IASB) and the IPSASB which, along with national regulators, make up the accounting regulatory 'jigsaw puzzle' of PPP accounting. Section 17.4 provides a description of the development of PPP accounting in the UK illustrating change and complexity over a period of almost 20 years. Section 17.5 provides an international perspective on PPP accounting regulations based upon the guidance and proposals of the IASB and IPSASB. Section 17.6 contains the empirical element of the chapter to provide an analysis of the responses to ED43 and leading to the publication of IPSAS32. Section 17.7 provides some concluding thoughts on PPP accounting, from the perspectives of academic, policy and practitioner communities.

17.2 Major issues in PPP accounting

The recent accounting literature on PPP is dominated by two themes. One is the question of whether they deliver value for money and the other, considered here, is how PPP projects should be accounted for. Governments in many countries promote PPPs on the basis of the former consideration, that they are capable of providing value for money as a result of a combination of perceived efficiencies within the private sector and through an effective allocation and management of the project risks between the public and private sectors. However, there is an added attraction for governments to support PPPs as it may enable assets to be brought on stream for the provision of public services without the capital costs being incurred or reported immediately against public borrowings. This second reasoning may become particularly attractive in recessionary periods, whether or not value for money impacts can be proven, while bodies such as the IMF continue to express concern about the fiscal risk of PPP in the wake of the financial crisis (Akitoby *et al.* 2007; Burger *et al.* 2009). This suggests that PPP accounting will continue to have a public policy importance beyond the technical issues that underlie its financial reporting.

The opportunity for governments to enter into PPP arrangements while avoiding the need to recognize the related assets and obligations in government financial reports, arises in two distinct circumstances. One is where the government uses a cash basis for its financial reporting; effectively this means that governments and other public sector entities report on the basis of their receipts and payments in any accounting period. This makes PPPs attractive as only amounts paid or payable in the short term are treated as government expenditure, there is no balance sheet[1] to reflect future contractual obligations. The other situation is where the public sector entity uses the accrual basis of financial reporting, under which income and expenditure is recognized as it occurs rather than when cash is paid or received (e.g. IPSASB 2006: par. 7). The accrual basis results in the construction of a balance sheet to reflect the assets and liabilities of a reporting entity. However, various arguments are used that PPPs do not give rise to the need to report assets and liabilities in public sector balance sheets. If these arguments are accepted, this results in an 'off-balance-sheet' treatment of PPP schemes in which, as with cash-based accounting systems, neither the assets nor future obligations to pay for them are recognized; instead payments under the scheme are reported as expenditure when they become due for payment.

The accounting treatment of PPP assets and obligations may seem to be a purely technical issue. Certainly, as this chapter will illustrate, there are some complex technical decisions that underlie PPP accounting. However, accounting treatments also have an influence on policy adoption and implementation. In particular, if PPP schemes create contractual obligations but are kept (artificially) off public sector balance sheets under an accruals-based accounting system or are excluded due to the absence of reporting liabilities under a cash-based accounting system, this may lead to hidden fiscal risks as a result of indebtedness being understated and unmanaged. Furthermore, the opportunity to use off-balance-sheet treatments may distort decision-making in favour of particular types of PPP arrangements, pushing out capital-based or other PPP forms that may represent stronger value for money. More generally, a view that PPP schemes are adopted for opportunistic accounting reasons damages the reputation of the whole PPP market and casts doubt on the validity of even the most robust *ex-ante* comparison with public funded alternatives (Heald and Georgiou 2010).

One of the objectives of accounting is to seek to determine classifications of transactions in order to develop consistency in the reporting of similar economic events across different entities and jurisdictions. This creates the need to determine criteria for such classifications. Such criteria might be based upon a set of (broad) principles or through the development of (detailed) rules of application (Benston *et al.* 2006); either approach may lead to difficulties in seeking consistency of accounting treatment. The application of broad principles may lead to inconsistent interpretations when applied to particular economic events. The creation of detailed rules of application may result in the development of contractual arrangements designed to push the resulting accounting treatment into one desired classification rather than another, irrespective of the underlying substance of the arrangements.[2] The development of PFI accounting in the UK, considered later in this chapter, is an example of such a conflict between, in that case, the principles-based standard of the Accounting Standards Board and the more rules-driven guidance issues by the UK Treasury.

The fundamental accounting issue revolves around the question of which party, the private-sector operator or the public-sector grantor, should recognize the assets and related financial obligations by their inclusion in its balance sheet.[3] Whose assets are they and how will they be paid for?

Intuitively, assets used in PPP arrangements might be expected to be recognized in the accounts of either the operator or the grantor, but not in both or neither. However, there is no guarantee of consistency of PPP accounting treatment between the private and public sectors as they may be subjected to different regulatory regimes and there may be no

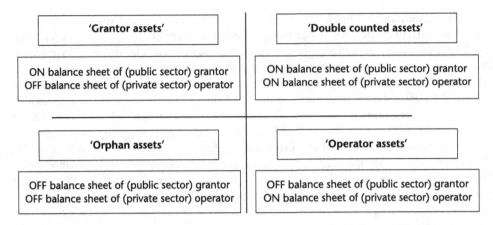

Figure 17.1   Alternative financial accounting treatments of PPP assets

Source: Adapted from Heald and Georgiou, 2011

requirement for such consistency to be agreed between the parties to a PPP scheme. This gives rise to four possible combinations of accounting treatment of PPP assets (and the related financial obligations) shown in Figure 17.1.

If there is consistency in application of the accounting treatment between the public sector grantor and the private sector operator then either the top left or bottom right quadrants in Figure 17.1 will apply; the top left-hand quadrant when the public sector grantor recognizes the asset and the bottom right quadrant when the asset is recognized by the private sector operator. If the private and public sector parties are subjected to different regulations, or they interpret their position differently to the other party, the top right or bottom left quadrants in Figure 17.1 may apply. The top right quadrant implies double counting, whereby the assets are recognized in both sets of financial statements; the bottom left quadrant implies the existence of orphan assets which appear in neither set of accounts.

So what is the basis for determining whether or not PPP assets, and related financial obligations, are recognized or not in the respective balance sheets? For accrual-based accounting[4] the definitions of assets and liabilities are based upon control (of an asset) and the likelihood of a flow of future economic benefit to or from the reporting entity. For example:

1   An asset is a resource controlled by the entity as a result of past events and from which future economic benefits are expected to flow to the entity.
2   A liability is a present obligation of the entity from past events, the settlement of which is expected to result in an outflow from the entity of resources embodying economic benefits.

(IASB 1989: par. 49)

Legal ownership of the asset is not necessarily the conclusive factor to determine the existence of assets or liabilities. Accounting has traditionally been based upon considering the substance of transactions rather than their legal form (e.g. IASB 1989: par. 35). In PPP transactions legal ownership during the contractual period may rest with either party, or even a third party; there may be a right or an obligation of the grantor to purchase the asset at the end of the contract and, in such cases, the basis of consideration on the transfer will vary from one contract to another. Rather than the issue of legal ownership, decisions concerning the recognition of assets in accounting are based upon one of two methodologies – the 'risk and rewards' method and the 'control' method.

The risk and rewards method seeks to analyse which party carries the greater risks attached to the assets and therefore is likely to benefit or suffer if such risks materialize into increased or reduced rewards. The control method is based upon an analysis of the extent to which each party is able to control or regulate the use of the asset during the PPP contract. The difficulties inherent in using either of these approaches will be considered later in the chapter in the context of the development of accounting for PPPs in the UK and more recent proposals for the development of an international public sector accounting standard for PPP accounting. Although intended to be distinct concepts, it is useful to appreciate that issues of risk/reward and control are not necessarily unrelated. For example, it is unlikely that risks in a PPP arrangement would be accepted without some expectation that such risks could be controlled or managed to reduce their significance or likelihood; indeed one of the underlying expectations of PPPs is that risks are allocated to the partner most able to manage (control) them.

17.3 The accounting regulatory jigsaw puzzle

A short description is provided here of the regulatory structure of PPP accounting. It is labelled as a 'jigsaw puzzle' because regulatory frameworks differ between countries and across regions and there are different levels of harmony between accounting regulations developed by international bodies and those of individual nation states. Furthermore, the regulatory structure may differ between public and private sectors and in different entities within each sector. For example the accounting rules in the private sector are likely to be more extensive for quoted companies than non-quoted businesses. In the public sector there may be different legislation applicable to central government, local government and other public sector bodies. The various regulatory bodies may be seen to compete for influence in the arena of 'regulatory space' (Hancher and Moran 1989; Young 1994) resulting in changes in the regulatory structure over time, for example, through a process of convergence of national regulation with international financial reporting standards (Fontes *et al.* 2005).

17.3.1 National accounts

The System of National Accounts (SNA) is developed through cooperation of the United Nations, the European Commission, the IMF, the OECD and the World Bank; the current version is the SNA 2008 (United Nations Statistical Division 2009). Under the SNA, institutional units resident in an economy are grouped together into five sectors covering non-financial corporations, financial corporations, government units, non-profit institutions and households (ibid: par. 1.10). These sectors are intended to be mutually exclusive, so that, for example, PPP accounting treatment in national accounts would seek explicitly to avoid the double counting or exclusion of assets and liabilities from measures of the national economy. The European System of Integrated Economic Accounts (ESA 95) is based upon similar principles, being derived from an earlier version of the SNA, for national accounting in the EU (Eurostat 1995).

National Accounts are structured to seek out consistency of reporting across economic sectors, whereas no such obligation is placed on the shoulders of accountants or auditors to ensure consistency of treatment of a particular PPP arrangement in the GAAP-based financial accounts of the operator and grantor (Jones 2003: 23). Under ESA95, the national accounts of member states are required to classify the assets of a particular PPP scheme as being either wholly government sector assets or wholly non-government assets; the assets cannot be split between the two sectors.

The classification is based upon the risk and rewards method (Eurostat 2004). If project construction risks and either asset availability risks or service demand risks are transferred to the private sector operator, then the PPP assets and the associated debt obligations are classified as part of the non-government sector. If these risks are judged not to be so transferred, the assets and associated debt are classified within the government sector. The initial capital expenditure is recorded as government capital formation, thereby increasing any public expenditure deficit and the imputed loan is added to government borrowing figures (EPEC 2010).

The treatment of PPP transactions under ESA 95/SNA 2008 has, in the past, been based largely upon the equivalent financial accounting treatment. However, as described in the next section, a change from the risk and rewards method to the control method of PPP accounting in GAAP-based accounts will create an inconsistency between national accounting and financial accounting. This suggests either that national statistical offices will need to determine a separate balance sheet classification of PPP schemes for national accounts or else that the national accounting rules will need to change to the control method of classification to harmonise national and financial accounting rules (EPEC 2010: 24–7). For example, in the UK, the national accounting framework is based currently upon different principles (i.e. risk and reward) to the financial accounting framework leading, potentially, to different balance sheet and budgeting treatments of PPP assets and obligations between the two systems.

In practice many PPP schemes are likely to transfer construction risk to the private sector operator. Construction risk covers events related to the initial state of the involved assets such as late delivery, significant additional costs and technical deficiencies (Eurostat 2004: 9). Such risks are likely to be managed most effectively by the private sector consortium, which is likely to include a construction company. Of the remaining two risks, it is likely that asset availability risk will be held and managed by the private sector operator in many PPP arrangements as the private sector would wish to ensure that the availability element of any service charges is recovered by them. In contrast, service demand risk is more likely to be retained by the public sector, particularly if it is influenced by public policy considerations; for example the demand for prison places will be influenced by government policies towards punishment of criminals and sentencing arrangements. The result is that the transfer of construction and availability risks to the private sector operator will be sufficient to enable the PPP scheme to be treated as a service arrangement and therefore avoid the need to book the capital cost of the arrangement within government borrowings under ESA 95.

It may be difficult for national regulators to ensure articulation between the accounts of entities in different sectors for national accounting purposes. For example in the UK, the ESA 95 treatment following Eurostat (2004) is likely to result in the majority of PPP assets and obligations being off the public sector balance sheet. However, such tangible assets are unlikely to be on the balance sheets of private sector operators. This is either because private sector operators do not consider that they carry the majority of risks or because they use contract debtor accounting, under which any asset is treated as a financial receivable rather than a tangible fixed asset (Heald and Georgiou 2011). Given the weak nature of the tests in Eurostat (2004) it seems likely, in the foreseeable future, that many PPP arrangements will be excluded from the determination of assets and borrowings in the national accounts of EU members. Indeed, given that private sector financial accounting regulation does not cover all PPP arrangements, there is a likelihood that the Eurostat test may result in neither government nor non-government recognition of PPP assets. Furthermore, there may be calls for reform of this approach, if this is seen to be inconsistent with approaches adopted by non-EU countries under SNA 2008.

17.3.2 Financial accounting in the private sector

The regulation of GAAP-based accounting standards is promoted at both international and national levels.[5] Accounting standards for application in the private sector, at an international level, are developed through the *International Accounting Standards Board* (IASB). The IASB is part of the *IFRS Foundation*,[6] which describes itself as 'an independent, not-for-profit private sector organization working in the public interest'. Its principal objectives include the development of 'a single set of high quality, understandable, enforceable and globally accepted international financial reporting standards (IFRSs) through its standard-setting body, the IASB'.

The IASB follows a system of due process (IASCF 2006) which includes the publication of documents such as consultation papers, exposure drafts of proposed accounting standards leading, after a comment period and review, to International Financial Reporting Standards (IFRSs). The *IFRS Interpretations Committee* acts as the interpretation body of the IASB. Its mandate is to review widespread accounting issues and to issue guidance (known as IFRICs) on the application of existing IFRSs to these issues.

The number of countries adopting IFRs as the basis for private sector accounting has expanded in recent years. The decision by the European Union to adopt IASB standards for accounting by EU quoted companies in 2005 and the decision by authorities in Australia and New Zealand to adapt their own national accounting standards from the same year are strong indications of the growing influence of the IASB. Furthermore, the IASB has sought to extend its influence beyond quoted companies by the issues of guidance for small and medium-sized enterprises (IASB 2009). Authorities in some jurisdictions interpose their own structures for the adoption and adaption of international standards to national or regional contexts. For, example the *European Financial Reporting Advisory Group*[7] (EFRAG) examines proposed international standards and interpretation guidance before making a recommendation to the European Commission on whether or not the proposals should be endorsed for adoption in the EU.

Accounting standards at the national level for application within the private sector have been developed in many countries. In the UK, the *Financial Reporting Council*[8] is responsible for promoting high-quality corporate governance, setting standards of corporate reporting and enforcing accounting and auditing standards. Its accounting standard setting arm is the UK *Accounting Standards Board*[9] (UKASB), which until 2005 was responsible for setting accounting standards for application by all companies in the UK and Ireland. Since the EU adoption of IFRS for quoted companies, the UKASB's standards have been applicable to those unquoted companies not adopting International GAAP.[10]

The influence of national private sector accounting standards setters in most countries has been reduced in recent years as the work and scope of the IASB has expanded. The one exception to this appears to be the Financial Accounting Standards Board[11] (FASB) in the USA. The FASB continues to work with the IASB in major projects with the purpose of reducing differences between their respective accounting standards.

17.3.3 Financial accounting in the public sector

In recent years the *International Public Sector Accounting Standards Board*[12] (IPSASB) has developed a suite of international public sector accounting standards (IPSASs) for use by public sector entities. IPSASB is part of the *International Federation of Accountants*[13] (IFAC), a Swiss-based organization of the world's professional accounting bodies. The development of international GAAP-based accounting standards in the public sector is less well-developed than its equivalent private sector structure. This reflects the desire of central governments in many countries to retain control over their own accounting policies as well as the limitations in the capacity of the IPSASB which, it has been suggested, 'is part-time, resource-constrained and yet to really develop its governance model and financial viability' (Stevenson 2010: 310). The IPSASBs approach is to base its own standards on those of the IASB where the requirements of IFRSs are applicable to the public sector, and to develop public sector specific standards for those issues not dealt with in IFRSs. IPSASB also promotes the convergence of international and national public sector accounting standards and the convergence of accounting and statistical bases of financial reporting (IPSASB 2007).

The application of public sector accounting standards in national jurisdictions is dependent upon the regulatory structure established in each country and there are many variations in the approach to the regulation of public sector accounting. Governments will wish to retain the right to make their own accounting regulation, but often do so with the help of an advisory body (Lüder and Jones 2003) and may base their own accounting policies on national standards or on the work of international bodies such as the IASB or the IPSASB. For example in the UK, the Treasury takes advice from the *Financial Reporting Advisory Board*[14] (FRAB) when considering financial reporting matters. Public sector accounting in the UK, up to 2009–10, was based upon UKASB standards but has now begun a transition to IASB standards.[15] The USA has established an independent private sector body, the *Government Accounting Standards Board*[16] (GASB) to develop accounting policies for state and local government. Australia has adopted an approach of developing a single set of accounting standards, based upon IFRS and applicable to all sectors, in which the *Australian Accounting Standards Board*[17] (AASB), a government agency with certain statutory functions, adapts international standards for application in Australia. In Europe there are relatively few countries that have formally adopted the IPSASB standards (Christiaens *et al.* 2010: 537). However, many of the requirements in IPSAS are derived from IFRS or are similar to some national standards, leading to high levels of disclosure compliance in many aspects of accounting. Pina and Torres (2003: 340) indicate high levels of compliance with IPSAS disclosure requirements from those countries which have integrated accruals-based methods into their public sector financial accounting systems.

17.4 Accounting for PPPs in the UK

The development of PPP accounting in the UK is a story of change and complexity. The early years of development of the PFI from 1992 to 1997 were accompanied by an absence of specific accounting guidance from either the UKASB, for the private sector, or from the Treasury to guide practice in the public sector, and there was little standardization in the disclosure of PFI development costs (Hodges and Mellett 1999).

Following the Treasury's PFI Taskforce *Technical Note 1* (TTN1) (Treasury Taskforce 1997: par. 13) public sector procuring entities should not recognize the underlying asset if the private sector operator's equity holders were exposed to 'real commercial risk' over the operating phase of the contract, demonstrated by there being the potential for significant variation in the return to the operator's equity holders. This illustrates an early use of the risk and rewards method to guide PFI accounting, although in a relatively restricted manner in that TTN1 did not use the variability of financial obligations of the public sector entity to determine whether or not assets and obligations should be recognized in public sector balance sheets.

In the same year, the UKASB issued an exposure draft to standardize private sector accounting for PFI schemes (ASB 1997). The exposure draft took a different starting point by requiring a consideration of whether the contract could be separated into elements for services and property that operated independently of each other (ASB 1997: par. F5). Where a contract could be separated the property-based element was treated as a lease for accounting purposes. Where contract payments could not be separated, the decision to capitalize an asset depended upon which party to the contract had access to the benefits of the property and exposure to related risks. These principles, based upon the risk and rewards method, were taken through to an amended financial reporting standard (FRS5A) applicable to private sector entities (ASB 1998) and led to a revision of the Treasury guidelines (TTN1R) to interpret the ASB standard for application in the public sector (Treasury Taskforce 1999).[18]

While TTN1R was intended as an interpretation of FRS5A, it became apparent that there were differences in the way that the two documents were structured and interpreted which created opportunities for regulatory arbitrage; effectively PFI contracts which might have been expected to be on the public sector balance sheet under FRS5A might be excluded under TTN1R. Heald and Georgiou (2011) suggest that several differences appear to have been influential in creating this ambiguity in the accounting treatment. First, FRS5A placed a particular emphasis on demand risk (the risk that demand for services provided through the asset might change) and residual value risk (the risk of changes in the value of the property at the end of the contract) whereas TTN1R encouraged the consideration of a wider range of risks in determining which party to the contract held the major risks and rewards in the arrangement. Second, the consulting firms of accountants provided different interpretations of the appropriate accounting treatment. For example, case studies provided to the 'big four' accounting firms had drawn out differences in the interpretation of PFI accounting rules which could result in varying responses to the on/off balance sheet decision (FRAB 2006c: 2). Studies have shown that the measurement of risk and its allocation are highly subjective and, at the margin, can switch the decision criteria of whether a PFI scheme is seen to be value for money compared to more traditional public sector capital expenditure (e.g. Froud 2003; Shaoul 2005; Broadbent et al. 2008). The public sector accounting treatment was determined often by a quantitative assessment of risk allocation between the public and private sector parties to the contract with that party which carried most of the total risk recognizing the assets and obligations on its balance sheet. However, the assessment of the nature and value of such risks, and their separate quantification by public and private sector partners, could lead to neither party recognizing those assets and obligations (Heald 2003: 351–8).

The next ten years witnessed widespread criticism of PFI accounting in the UK. The criticism reflected concern that the government's desire to keep PFI liabilities off public sector balance sheets was driving the development of capital projects towards a particular type of financing, using private finance on terms which would satisfy the accounting requirements, whether or not this was the most effective way of developing public services. During this period the Treasury's stated position was that the use of PPPs, and the form that they took, was on the basis of best value for money rather than a particular accounting treatment (e.g., Treasury 2004, 2006). However, this was at odds with a perception of managers and the media that, at least in some parts of the public sector, 'PFI is the only game in town'.

Related accounting concerns were the absence of the recognition of PPP assets and obligations in public sector balance sheets and the difficulty of assessing the operators' accounting treatment and results. The operator in many PFI deals is a shell company, set up as a special purpose vehicle with most of its operations and expenditure sub-contracted to members of the consortium (Treasury 2003: 37). It also became apparent that the accounting treatment of

PPPs was influenced heavily by the specific regulations applied in parts of the public sector; for example local government PFIs in the UK were invariably off-balance sheet because any 'PFI credits' needed by local government to fund the costs of a scheme required such costs to be recognized as annual charges rather than capital expenditure.

In March 2006, the Treasury, encouraged by the FRAB, established a PFI Working Group to examine how the accounting might be developed. A number of options were considered including the revision or withdrawal of TTN1R (FRAB 2006a). In the context of the national accounts, the Office of National Statistics also recommended the need for clarification and reform (FRAB 2006b: 4–5). The Working Group reported back to the FRAB in February 2007 and was in favour of withdrawing TTN1R (FRAB 2007a). The following month Gordon Brown, as the Chancellor of the Exchequer, announced in his budget that the UK would change its government accounting to an IFRS basis from 2008–9 (later postponed to 2009–10).

This decision effectively removed both FRS5A and TTN1R as the basis of PPP accounting in the UK public sector with effect from 2009–10. The FRAB minutes reflect the different views of members of this change of direction with one member regarding it as 'a major step forward both as regards accounting in general and PFI accounting in particular' while another suggested that 'the Treasury was using this adoption decision to kick PFI accounting back into the long grass' (FRAB 2007b: 3).

The position in the UK from 2009–10 is that both quoted and other large corporations and the public sector apply an IFRS basis of PPP accounting. This provides a stronger basis for consistency for accounting treatment within and between sectors in the future to avoid double counted or orphan assets described in Figure 17.1. It will also provide a more transparent record of the future obligations inherent in PFI schemes. For example, the Office for Budget Responsibility (OBR 2011: 42) reports that about £5.1 billion of PFI capital liability (0.4 per cent of GDP) was recorded on balance sheet in the National Accounts at March 2010, but that the total capital liability of all PFI contracts was closer to £40 billion (2.9 per cent of GDP) at that date.

17.5 International guidance on PPP accounting

The development of international guidance on PPP accounting is described here, first considering the interpretation statement *IFRIC12 Service Concession Arrangements* (IASB 2006) for the private sector and then the IPSASB proposals for public sector accounting in *ED43* and *IPSAS32 Service Concession Arrangement: Grantor.*

17.5.1 The development of IFRIC12

The Interpretations Committee (IFRIC) of the IASB first began consideration of the issues of SCAs in October 2003 and early in its deliberations determined that it would base it approach for the recognition of assets 'on who controls the infrastructure and that control may be separated from ownership' (IASB 2005: par. 29). In March 2005, three exposure drafts were issued that were later to be combined to form the basis of IFRIC12. There were particular concerns over the scope of the standard, the interpretation of the control method and the varying forms of accounting that resulted from its application. It is apparent that some of these concerns continued after the publication of IFRIC12 in November 2006. In Europe, for example, the EFRAG endorsed IFRIC12 in March 2007, although there were dissenting views from three of its members (EFRAG 2007: 16). The European Commission procured a questionnaire and effect study which reported in June 2008 so that the adoption of IFRIC12 in the European Union was not established formally until March 2009 (European Commission 2008, 2009).

In summary, IFRIC12 deals only with accounting by private sector operators involved in PPPs. The scope of the statement is restricted to what are described as public-to-private service concession arrangements (SCAs) where:

1 The grantor controls or regulates what services the operator must provide with the infrastructure, to whom it must provide them, and at what price; and
2 The grantor controls − through ownership, beneficial entitlements or otherwise − any significant residual interest in the infrastructure at the end of the term of the arrangement.

(IASB 2006: par. 5)

If both these conditions are satisfied, the operator is required, following IFRIC12, to avoid the recording the infrastructure as tangible assets and, instead, to adopt one of three accounting treatments.

First, a 'financial asset' model is required when the operator has an unconditional, contractual right to receive cash or other financial asset from or at the direction of the grantor (ibid: par. 16). For example, this might apply under a PPP contract in which the operator will receive contractual payments of a given amount (subject to compliance with the terms of the contract) from a public sector grantor or where users' charges will be topped up to a minimum level by the grantor. Under this model a capital amount receivable is recognized in the balance sheet of the operator. As cash is received by the operator over the term of the contract, the receipts are split between a 'capital' element, which reduces the amount receivable left in the balance sheet, and a 'revenue' element which may be seen as interest accruing from the financial investment of the operator in the PPP contract.

Second, an 'intangible asset' model is used if the operator has a contractual right to receive user charges from the provision of the infrastructure (ibid: par. 17); in effect the operator bears the demand risk without any guarantee of recovery from the grantor. In this model, income received from the operation of the infrastructure is recognized as revenue in the accounts of the operator. The expenses of the operator include a charge for amortization of the intangible asset.

Third, a 'mixed asset' model is required for those PPPs which represent a combination of the first two models (ibid: par. 18); for example if an operator is entitled to receive a fixed sum of cash from the grantor together with a variable amount from user charges depending upon demand for services. In this model the operator's original investment in the infrastructure would need to be split between a financial and an intangible asset, depending upon the extent to which future receipts are provided through the grantor or through expected recovery from user receipts.

The broad effect of IFRIC12 is that PPP operators will not recognize the assets used in the scheme as property, plant and equipment. Therefore the possibility of 'double-counted' tangible fixed assets as described in Figure 17.1 is very limited. However, there remain uncertainties arising from the definition of SCAs in IFRIC12. First, the meaning of 'controls or regulates' is subject to various interpretations. If the use of the asset is determined by the public sector, which pays regular service charges for its use, control would seem to be clearly with the grantor. However, infrastructure assets such as toll-roads, in which the operator may have control over the level of user charges, might be viewed to be outside the control of the grantor and therefore the application of IFRIC12 becomes determined by the extent of regulation imposed on the operator. The application guidance of IFRIC12 uses a broad definition to include not only regulation by the grantor itself but that:

> the grantor and any related parties shall be considered together. If the grantor is a public sector entity, the public sector as a whole, together with any regulators acting in the public interest, shall be regarded as related to the grantor for the purposes of this Interpretation.
>
> *(ibid: par. AG2)*

Second, the scope of IFRIC12 is narrowed by the requirement that grantor control is required both over the services provided and over any significant residual interest in the infrastructure; this leaves out of its scope arrangements which, *inter alia*, limit control to either the services or the residual interest but not both.

The accounting model applied by operators may be influenced by factors other than IFRIC12, such as taxation effects and the pattern of resulting profitability. The financial asset model may have important advantages to some operators (Heald and Georgiou 2011: 230–1). In some jurisdictions the financial asset model may help to ensure that tax relief is given in full for the up-front investment in the PPP contract, in contrast to an intangible asset model or recognition of property, plant and equipment which may limit relief to annual allowances on fixed assets. Second, the financial asset model, based upon identifying investment income, may give a regular pattern of profitability over the whole contract period. In contrast, the intangible asset model may result in losses being reported in the early years of the contract, particularly if the intangible asset is amortized using straight line or accelerated depreciation methods (IASB 2005: 11).

17.5.2 The development of ED43 and IPSAS32

It was always likely that the IPSASB proposals on PPP accounting would be linked closely to those of the IASB. The policy of IPSASB is to seek to base its own accrual-based standards on those of the IASB 'by developing IPSASs that are converged with IFRSs, adapting them to the public sector context' (IPSASB 2008a: 2). Early discussions in July 2006 with some national standard setters, the IASB, and an IMF task force led to an approved project brief later that year. The project resulted in the issue of a consultation paper in March 2008 (IPSASB 2008b). The IPSASB re-affirmed its support for the control method in February 2009 and, after further analysis of comments arising from the consultation, ED43 was published in February 2010.[19]

The proposals in ED43 are intended to 'mirror' IFRIC12 to provide a standard that addresses the accounting issues of PPPs from the perspective of the public sector grantor (ED43: par. AG3). The proposals relate only to those public sector bodies that adopt accrual accounting based upon or guided by IPSAS; therefore excluding those public sector bodies which base their financial reporting on cash-based methods. The scope of the proposals (ibid: par. 10) is prescribed in a near-identical way to that in IFRIC12 except that the word 'infrastructure' is replaced with the word 'asset'. The basis for conclusions in the exposure draft explains that the infrastructure label used in IFRIC12 appears to have a much wider meaning that is used in some jurisdictions (ibid: par. BC8). Effectively the scope appears to include any type of asset that could be the subject of a PPP arrangement. These include a) assets constructed or developed or purchased by an operator for use in the arrangement; b) existing assets of the operator to which the grantor is given access for the arrangement; c) existing assets of the grantor, which the operator upgrades for the purposes of the arrangement; and d) existing assets of the grantor for which the operator gains access for the arrangement and in which the grantor retains control of the asset (ibid: par. 8).

In summary, the accounting treatment for service concession assets in the accounts of the grantor is for those assets to be recognized as tangible fixed assets[20] to be accounted for in accordance with the relevant standard (IPSAS17) on accounting for property, plant or equipment. This is intended to result in a consistency of accounting treatment if applied by the public sector in a manner consistent with the application of IFRIC12 by the private sector. The tangible assets would be likely to appear only in the grantor's accounts, while the operator's accounts recognize a financial or an intangible asset representing the cash flows recoverable from the PPP arrangement.

The accounts of the grantor would recognize liabilities to match the initial value of the service concession asset. The exposure draft identifies two types of liability that may be recorded; a single method may be used or some combination of the two (ibid: par. 19).

A 'financial liability' is recognized when the grantor is required to compensate the operator for the service concession asset by making payments. The grantor is required to allocate its payments to the operator between an element that reduces the outstanding liability, a finance charge and a charge for services (ibid: par. 21). The latter two elements would be recognized as expenses in the year in which they are incurred.

A 'performance obligation' is recognized by the grantor when the operator has the right to collect fees from the users of the service concession asset or where the operator is granted access to another revenue-generating asset (ibid: par. 22). The accounting treatment by the grantor in subsequent years is to reduce the liability 'as access to the service concession asset is provided to the operator, ordinarily over the term of the service concession arrangement' (ibid: par. AG38). This results in income being recognized in the revenue statement of the grantor over the period of the arrangement.

In conceptual terms, the ED43 financial liability of the grantor would match the IFRIC12 financial asset of the operator. In other PPP schemes the ED43 performance obligation of the grantor would match the IFRIC12 intangible asset of the operator. However, the measurement of these items in the balance sheets would differ between the grantor and the operator as a result of the use of different accounting policies and estimates in their separate accounts. The next section considers the responses to the proposals of ED43 and the subsequent impact of IPSAS32.

17.6 The responses to ED43

ED43 was issued in February 2010 and the IPSASB gave until 30 June 2010 for the receipt of comments on the proposals. These comments provide an indication of the support (or lack of it) of the major features of the proposals. The comments received by the IPSASB were made available on its website[21] from September 2010. I undertook an analysis of these comment letters in January 2011. The analysis of responses to proposed regulation has been a regular element of studies of lobbying behaviour in the accounting literature (Walker and Robinson 1993; Hodges and Mellett 2004). The main objective in this instance was to identify those issues of concern or disagreement that had been raised in the comment letters and which might identify some of the challenges facing the IPSASB in the development of a definitive standard. Such matters may result in changes from the proposed regulation to the authoritative standard after their consideration by the standard setters. They may reflect issues that will continue to represent challenges in the application after the definitive standard has been published. For example, earlier studies of the development of PFI accounting in the UK reflect the disagreement amongst different categories of respondents regarding the fundamental on/off balance sheet treatment prescribed in regulation under UK GAAP (Broadbent and Laughlin 2002; Hodges and Mellett 2002; Khadaroo 2005).

All 33 comment letters were downloaded and printed. All comment letters were read for a first time to get a general indication of the scope and commonality of issues raised. In this case only one specific question was set by the IPSASB, so the rest of the analysis was carried out by relating issues in the comment letters to each major part of the proposals in ED43, rather than assuming pre-defined issues of importance. All letters were then read a second time to draw out those specific matters, and in some cases proposals for change, which were raised by the commentators. There was no attempt to classify the letters in terms of being broadly supportive, or not, of the IPSASB proposals as some respondents provided a statement of general support along with many detailed criticisms, while other comment letters dealt only with detailed issues without expressing an overall view. However, a summary is provided below of respondents' views on the mirroring principle which underlies the proposals.

The publication of *IPSAS32 Service Concession Arrangements: Grantor* in October 2011 has provided an opportunity to relate my original analysis to those changes made by IPSASB in developing its accounting standard. IPSAS32 is applicable from 2014, so an understanding of its full impact is still some years away.

17.6.1 The specific matter for comment: the 'mirror' principle

It is common for accounting standard setters to provide a number of specific questions for commentators to consider in their responses. However ED43 was accompanied by only one specific question.[22]

> This Exposure Draft addresses service concession arrangements from the grantor's perspective. It mirrors the principles set out in IFRIC12 for accounting by the operator. Do you agree with this approach?
>
> *(ED 43: 4)*

Most letters contained a specific response to this question. These responses are included in Table 17.1, analysed according to the type of respondent. The table shows that two-thirds of respondents were supportive of the concept of 'mirroring' the requirements of IFRIC12. Many gave reasons for this support, for example:

> Given the IPSASB's 'rules of the road' for developing its standards, we agree with the basic approach for the proposals of the ED to mirror the principles set out in IFRIC12 for accounting by the operator. We do not believe that the public sector environment necessitates differences in the approach to the financial reporting of service concession arrangements from private sector standards. Further, we expect that the mirrored approaches will result in consistency in the financial reporting of the public sector grantor and private sector operator to an individual service concession arrangement, particularly the recognition of the infrastructure assets underlying the arrangement.
>
> *(KPMG: 1–2)*

However, the support of many was qualified in the detail of their comment letter and some even expressed such qualification in the same paragraph as that stating overall support. This

Table 17.1 Analysis of responses to the specific matter for comment: Do you agree with the approach in ED43 to mirror the principles set out in IFRIC12?

Type of respondent	Support mirror principle	Against mirror principle	View not specified	Total
Government departments or agencies	4	5	0	9
Public sector auditors	4	0	1	5
Accounting standards setters	2	1	1	4
Accounting professional bodies	9	0	1	10
Accounting firms	2	1	0	3
Individuals	1	0	1	2
Total	22	7	4	33

List of respondents:
Government departments or agencies: CNOCP – Public Sector Accounting Standards Council (France); CSPCP – Public Sector Financial Reporting Advisory Committee (Switzerland); DGFB – Directorate General of Public Finance (France); ESV – National Financial Management Authority (Sweden); HOTARAC – Heads of Treasuries Accounting and Reporting Advisory Committee (Australia); MFBC – Ministry of Finance British Columbia (Canada); MFQ – Ministry of Finance Quebec (Canada); NZT – Treasury (New Zealand); TBC – Treasury Board (Canada).
Public sector auditors: ACAG – Council of Auditors-General (Australasia); ACUK – Audit Commission (UK); AGQ – Auditor General of Quebec (Canada); CdC – Cour des comptes (France); WAO – Audit Office (Wales).
Accounting standard setters: AASB – Accounting Standards Board (Australia); GASB – Governmental Accounting Standards Board (USA); SAASB – Accounting Standards Board (South Africa); UKASB – Accounting Standards Board (United Kingdom).
Accounting professional bodies: ACCA – Association of Chartered Certified Accountants (UK for International body); CIPFA – Chartered Institute of Public Finance & Accounting (UK); FACPCE – Federation of Economic Science Professionals (Argentina); FAR – Institute for the Accountancy Profession (Sweden); FEE – Federation of Accountants (Europe); ICAP – Institute of Chartered Accountants (Pakistan); ICAS – Institute of Chartered Accountants (Scotland); JAB – Joint Accounting Bodies (Australia); JICPA – Institute of Certified Public Accountants (Japan); PSAB – Public Sector Accounting Board (Canada).
Accounting firms: EY – Ernst & Young (Germany for International firm); KPMG (UK for International firm); Mazars (France).
Individuals: Hodges (UK); Maresca (Canada).

indicates a less than wholehearted endorsement of the proposals, even if the general approach is supported. Some commentators indicated that public sector accounting standards should be based on the needs of users of public sector accounts with regard being given to the wider extent of accountabilities in a public sector context rather than being driven by conformance with a standard (IFRIC12) designed for the private sector (e.g. WAO: 2). The international accounting firms and some of the national standard setters appeared to take the matter of consistency across sectors as being of particular importance. For example, the Australian Accounting Standards Board was critical of the narrow scope of IFRIC12/ED43, but nevertheless supportive of the proposals to mirror the two sets of regulations to develop consistency across sectors (AASB: 2). Standard setters from countries which have sector-neutral accounting regulations or closely aligned accounting between the public and private sectors appeared more likely to support the mirroring process than those from countries that maintain stronger accounting distinctions between the public and private sectors.

There were seven respondents who disagreed with ED43 mirroring the approach adopted in IFRIC12. The reasons given can be split between first, those who felt that the principle of mirroring was inappropriate, or at least questionable; and second, those who stated that the inadequacies of IFRIC12 made the mirror approach inadvisable.

In the first case, the mirror principle was criticized as not being based upon existing conceptual frameworks of accounting, along with recommendations that IPSASB should base its proposals upon existing practices (e.g. Mazars: 2) or that the proposals did not provide adequate justification to support the principle of mirroring:

We consider that the principle of the 'mirror' with the IFRS . . . is a shift with the IPSAS Board previous approach on setting public sector accounting standards. As the 'mirror' is not a known accounting principle, the IPSAS Board should at least have defined very clearly in the Exposure Draft what was the definition and impact of this innovative approach.

(CNCP, p.2)

[T]he 'mirror' effect seems to be limited as the grantor and the operator do not retire the same resource from the service concession asset: from the grantor's perspective, the service concession asset provides a potential service, from the operator's perspective, the service concession asset provides economic benefits. Furthermore, since the 'symmetry' accounting principle is not an acknowledged accounting principle, it should be more justified.

(DGF: 2)

Other commentators point to what they see as inadequacies in IFRIC12 which make it inadequate for mirroring, for example:

We disagree with the approach based solely on control as described in the exposure draft. Referring to the Canadian conceptual framework of the Public Sector Accounting Board, we are of the view that an asset has three essential features: (1) It represents a future benefit in that it may contribute to future cash flow or the supply of goods or services; (2) the government is in a position to control access to this benefit; (3) the transaction or fact at the source of the government's control over such benefit, has already occurred. Therefore, to recognize an asset, the government must also assume the risks and receive the benefits inherent in ownership of the good.

(MFQ: 2)

Overall, there was support for the IPSASB mirroring proposals and this approach and the standard confirms the use of the mirror approach (IPSAS32: 33). There are some differences in terminology reflecting that IFRIC12 and IPSAS32 represent accounting from the different contractual sides of an SCA. It is possible that the development of these proposals will result in the IPSASB to seeking to integrate the principle of mirroring within its wider conceptual framework project.

17.6.2 The scope of the standard

The scope of the ED43 was an issue that was raised by a large number of respondents. In some cases, this reflected disagreement with the limited coverage of those types of PPPs within the ED's rather narrow definition of SCAs; effectively this represents some discomfort with IFRIC12 as the basis for providing the mirror from which the ED is constructed. In other cases the comments reflect uncertainty of whether or not particular types of PPP will be covered by the proposed standard. If the scope of coverage of the standard is narrow, the opportunity for regulatory arbitrage is increased by the ability of organizations to design PPP arrangements that will fall just outside its boundaries. For example:

The service concession property could include: (a) grantor-controlled during and after the concession period; (b) operator-controlled during the concession period and grantor-controlled thereafter; (c) grantor-controlled during the concession period and operator-controlled thereafter; or (d) operator-controlled during and after the concession period. It is disappointing that the ED only considers one of these cases. This is unhelpful to grantors involved in other forms of service concession arrangement.

(HoTARAC: 1)

Other examples, questioning the scope of the proposed standard, included concerns as to whether BOOT (build-own-operate-transfer) arrangements would be covered by the proposed Standard (AASB: 3); whether SCAs with a government business enterprise as the grantor were included (JAB: 2); whether the proposals were intended to cover SCAs for which both grantor and operator were public sector entities (KPMG: 2); and the need to clarify the type of assets that fall within the scope of the Standard (SAASB: 2–3).

The limited coverage of ED43 seemed to represent a major limitation of the proposals to many commentators. The difficulty that the IPSASB faced was that extending the scope of the standard would destroy the principle of mirroring. IPSAS32 confirms the mirroring process and retains the limited scope of ED43; for example public-to-public arrangements are excluded because they are outside the scope of IFRIC12 and government business enterprises are excluded because they are outside the scope of IPSASs. This illustrates the limitation of deriving IPSASB standards directly from IASB work; to overcome this limitation may involve the IASB and IPSASB working together in the future to widen the scope of their respective standards. Furthermore the potential for widely differing arrangements within PPPs suggest that determining consistent and comparable accounting treatment across all PPPs will be a difficult and time-consuming project.

17.6.3 'Control' versus 'risk and rewards'

It was mentioned earlier that ED43 used the principle of control to determine which party should recognize the assets in a service concession arrangement, rather than basing its accounting treatment on the allocation of risks and rewards. The control basis was supported explicitly by many of the respondents. However, the separation of issues of control from those of risk and reward may not always be appropriate or feasible as the control of assets may partly be evidenced by the bearing of risk and having access to the benefit or detriment of differing levels of reward.

Some respondents gave specific reasons for supporting the control-based approach, such as that it was more likely to produce more consistent reporting than a risks/benefits approach (NZT: 1) and that it was consistent with international or national conceptual frameworks of accounting (CdC: 4). However, the determination of control was recognized by some respondents as having the potential to lead to a lack of symmetry between sectors. For example, respondents appeared generally to support a view that the term 'regulates' should be defined in a narrow sense, referring to specific regulation promoting control over PPP assets, and not a general power of a government to establish a regulatory environment. The IPSASB retained this approach and made some changes in its guidance (IPSAS32: 15). The ability to regulate may be an aspect in which interpretations will differ between countries and sectors and it seems likely to be an important feature in determining control of the asset, which in turn underlies the recognition decision.

17.6.4 Performance obligation issues

The proposed standard provides that the obligations of the grantor should be recognized as either a 'financial liability' or a 'performance obligation' or some combination of the two.

The recognition of the financial liability appears to raise few concerns of principle amongst respondents as it is based on the grantor's obligation to make future cash payments to the operator (although some measurement issues were raised).

In contrast the principle and measurement of the performance obligation resulted in a whole series of comments. Some comments questioned the underlying conceptual basis of these obligations and whether they were consistent with other IPSAS (e.g. ACAG: 3; CdC: 6) or asking for clarification of its meaning and scope of application (e.g. WAO: 4; CNCP: 6). One respondent suggested that the ED43 approach was both conceptually inappropriate and impracticable:

> The amount of consideration is not an obligation that is expected to be settled through repayment, and the Board is concerned that including the entirety of the amount as a liability may confuse readers who are trying to assess the magnitude of the claims against the Government's financial resources. While a transferor has an obligation to provide an operator with access to the facility, the *value* of the transferor's obligation to allow access does not vary according to the amount of consideration received. Therefore the fair value of a contributed asset or the present value of consideration received would not properly measure this obligation. The Board is not aware of a reasonable, practical proxy what would reliably measure the obligation to *allow access*.
>
> (GASB: 3)

This aspect of the proposals presents a number of difficulties for the IPSASB if it wishes to follow though the mirroring of IFRIC12. Some sort of liability is necessary to mirror the intangible asset of the operator in IFRIC12. However, such a liability is problematic in the extreme. The proposals appear to contradict existing standards that define liabilities more narrowly. The obligation itself is difficult to reconcile with anticipated outflows of resources of the public sector entity; recall that the intangible asset of the operator is based upon anticipated receipts from users, rather than from the grantor. This approach leads to accounting in which the income of the operator from users is reflected in the accounts of the grantor and is matched against the amortization of the SCA assets in the grantor's accounts. This creates potential conceptual difficulties if one entity (the grantor) is effectively recognizing the income of another (the operator) as well as the practical difficulties of measuring the remaining performance obligation at each balance sheet date. For example, GASB proposals for PPP accounting for state and local government bodies makes a nuanced argument that such consideration is 'applicable to future periods' rather than an 'obligation to sacrifice resource' (GASB 2010, par. 48).

In line with many of the comments from respondents, the IPSASB altered the approach in IPSAS32 by requiring the liability in the accounts of the grantor to represent deferred income rather than a performance obligation (IPSAS32: 10). This approach fits more easily with existing conceptual frameworks of accounting by recognizing income over the term of the arrangement. It also implies that grantor income recognition could be determined by spreading the value of the assets transferred to the operator, having regard to the economic substance of the SCA, rather than relying directly upon the revenue recognition policy of the operator.

17.6.5 Timing of initial recognition of the service concession asset

The allocation of risks relating to the SCA assets continues to play a role in determining the accounting treatment, despite the control approach underlying the proposals. One example of this relates to the proposal in ED43 that assets and the related obligations would not be recognized in the grantor's balance sheet until those assets came into use, in those cases where the operator bears the main construction risks. This proposal came in for considerable criticism. Some commentators felt that it did not reflect the risks of the grantor during the construction period, for example:

> We believe that, even if the operator bears the construction risk, the analysis of control criteria may lead to the conclusion that control is transferred to the grantor *continuously* during the construction period . . . in the case of breach of contract during the construction period, the arrangement may stipulate that the operator shall be compensated from the grantor for an amount corresponding to the financial investment in the service concession asset incurred by the operator.
>
> *(Mazars: 2)*

The absence of the recognition of SCA assets under construction could also create a difference in accounting treatment between operators' and grantors' financial statements and between SCAs and other financial arrangements:

> The deferral of recognition of the liability will inappropriately incentivise these types of transactions and provide financial engineering opportunities for Governments to report lower levels of debt in comparison to more direct financing transactions that have similar economic or present-value impact. The financial implications can be significant as these arrangements are for large amounts and often involve a construction period covering a number of years.
>
> *(NZT: 2)*

This illustrates the difficulty in practice of separating the determination of risk and rewards from the basis of control. If implemented, the practical implication of this proposal might have been that public sector obligations from those SCAs that had assets under construction would not have been recognized in the financial statements of grantors. The IPSASB provided additional guidance in the standard (IPSAS32: 17–18) to make it clear that the grantor's asset and liability would normally be accrued over the period of construction (IPSASB 2011: 26).

17.6.6 Transitional arrangements

There are two distinct proposals for application of the proposed standard (par. 29–30). Those entities that have recognized service concession assets and related liabilities, revenues and expenses are expected to apply the new standard retrospectively. This retrospective application is normally required to new or amended standards and accords with IPSAS3 'Accounting Policies, Changes in Accounting Estimate and Errors'. The ED also proposed that those entities that have not previously recognized service concessions assets should be allowed to apply the new standard prospectively, although they have the option of retrospective application. This proposal was the subject of a number of critical comments. One respondent did accept that there might be reason for allowing the prospective treatment:

> While it seems contrary to good practice to permit entities to apply standards prospectively, we accept this approach if it encourages the adoption of IPSASs. However, in relation to this standard specifically, it seems relatively harsh to permit an entity which

has not taken steps to bring service concession arrangements on balance sheet to avoid restating its accounts while requiring an entity which has done so to restate its accounts.

(*ICAS: 3*)

Some other respondents were more direct in their view that the IPSASB had got this wrong, for example:

> Allowing prospective application by some entities would permit the continued non-recognition of potentially significant service concession assets for many years into the future and defer the achievement of comparability.

(*AASB: 5*)

This prospective recognition for grantors which had not previously recognized SCA assets and liabilities would seem to allow the non-recognition of some PPP assets for many years ahead. The authoritative standard is more restrictive than ED43; requiring either retrospective recognition or that SCA assets and liabilities should be recognized, using an estimated cost measure, at the earliest period for which comparative figures are available and the standard should then be applied prospectively (IPSAS32: 12). Differences between retrospective and prospective application of IPSAS32 will remain for many years, although the quantitative effect of this is not possible to determine currently. More generally, prospective application of IPSAS32 weakens the efforts towards consistent treatment and presentation within public sector accounts and defeats the attempt to mirror fully the equivalent private sector accounting.

17.7 Summary and conclusions

This chapter has provided a description and analysis of the financial reporting of PPP arrangements. The chapter has focused on the accrual-based accounting systems, as cash-based accounting systems do not routinely reflect the assets and future obligations arising from PPP arrangements. In contrast, accrual-based accounting has the potential to do so even if that potential is not always realized. One of the major concerns of PPP financial accounting has been the lack of consistency, both within and between the public and private sectors. This has led to uncertainty over the recognition of PPP assets and the related obligations in financial statements. An underlying conceptual issue is whether PPP assets should be recognized on the 'Risk and Rewards' basis, dependent upon which party to the agreement carries the major risks and rewards relating to the property, or the 'Control' basis dependent upon whether the operator or the grantor is able to control and regulate the use of the property.

The treatment of PFI transactions in the UK was used as an example of the difficulties surrounding PPP accounting. The UK followed a 'Risk and Rewards' approach based upon UK-GAAP. This has led to inconsistency of PPP accounting between the public and private sectors with resulting 'orphan assets' and 'double counting'. The inconsistency was generated by the uncertainties inherent in identifying and measuring risks and the subjectivity involved in determining the balance of risk between the parties. These inconsistencies were aggravated by the possibility of arbitrage between the ASB approach in FRS5A and the Treasury's interpretation in TTN1R. The UK has, from 2009–10, switched its public sector financial accounting to be based on IASB standards resulting in increased recognition of PFI assets and obligations on public sector balance sheets.

This chapter provided an examination of the development of GAAP-based accounting guidance at an international level. The IASB, through its interpretation committee, has issued IFRIC12 for private sector operators and the IPSASB has developed the proposals in ED43 leading to the issue of IPSAS32, intended to mirror the IFRIC12 treatment in the accounts of public sector grantors. It remains to be seen whether the potential for improved consistency of PPP accounting between the public and private sectors in these regulations will be realized. Even if the mirroring is complete, there remain matters of uncertainty and judgement in PPP accounting that may result in differences in application between the two sectors and within each sector. Some of these issues are considered below, with particular examples from the UK experience.

First, the scope of IFRIC12 and IPSAS32 is quite narrow as currently defined. One of the possible consequences of this is that those entering into PPP arrangements will structure future PPP agreements deliberately to fall outside the scope of IFRIC12/IPSAS32 in order to retain flexibility of accounting treatment. PPP arrangements might be structured so that either grantor control is limited in some distinct, but not necessarily significant, way or a residual interest is retained by the operator rather than the grantor. In the UK, a number of schemes have been developed that might be interpreted as falling outside the scope of these standards, as a result of the operator retaining a significant residual interest in the assets or the managing body being regarded as outside public sector control.

Second, the control basis for determining recognition of PPP assets has brought most PFI scheme assets onto the UK public sector balance sheet for financial accounting purposes (Treasury 2011), but there remains uncertainty in how the meaning of 'regulate' will be interpreted from one sector or nation state to another. Contractual or regulatory arrangements might, at the margin, push the scheme on or off balance sheet as preferred or required to meet particular needs for project approval. This would be very similar in principle to the way in which the measurement of risk allocation has caused inconsistency in PFI accounting in the UK.

Third, there remains no direct requirement for the operator and grantor to agree mutually consistent accounting for any particular PPP arrangement. For example, it is likely that operators will be reluctant to follow any accounting treatment that has adverse taxation consequences for them. This might cause operators to wish to avoid the capitalization of tangible or intangible assets if it causes taxation allowances to be restricted. There may be a preference towards the financial asset treatment under IFRIC12 to gain full taxation recoverability of costs and to seek to spread the reported profitability of the PPP arrangements. Clearly, corporate taxation regulation in each country will have an influence here.

Fourth, it is unlikely that IFRIC12 and IPSAS32 will be applicable to all entities that are involved in PPP projects. For example, public and private sector business entities are excluded from IPSAS32 in the role of grantor. Some private sector operators are not subject to IFRS requirements; for example the operators in many PPP schemes in the UK are special purpose vehicles, which, due to their size or structure, are not required to apply international accounting standards. If the special purpose vehicle is controlled by an EU-listed parent company, a parallel set of accounts will be required, based upon IFRIC12, for consolidation into the parent company financial statements.

Although the underlying objective of PPP financial accounting may seek to provide information relevant to decisions relating to fiscal sustainability, it is notable that such issues are rarely raised explicitly within the comment letters on these accounting proposals. This reflects the largely technical aspects that dominate discussion at this stage of the development of accounting regulation. However, the outcome of these decisions may still have an impact on future decision of public policy and financing. For example, if PPP contracts are constructed so that their obligations fall outside the scope of IPSAS32, there may be continuing underreporting of these liabilities at the individual entity level under financial accounting regimes.

The potential for under-reporting is compounded if national accounting rules enable the reporting of these obligations to be circumvented at the national accounting level. On the other hand, the explicit recognition and disclosure of future PPP obligations in accounts may result in increased exposure of public sector entities to public authorities and the media, particularly if such arrangements are perceived as threatening the sustainability of public services. This suggests that accounting for PPPs will continue to have a high profile in the years ahead.

Notes

1 IASB terminology currently refers to the 'Statement of Financial Position' in place of 'balance sheet'; however, the latter term is used here because the PPP accounting is often associated with the concept of 'off-balance sheet finance'.
2 There is a continuing 'principles versus rules' debate which is concerned with whether accounting regulation, such as financial reporting standards, should be based upon the application of broad principles or detailed rules. The distinction between principles and rules is one of alternative perceptions, while accounting standard setters invariably promote their standards as being principles-based. Interested readers might enjoy the special edition of *Abacus*, July 2006 (vol. 42, no. 2).
3 This issue applies also to other financing arrangements such as leasing. For example, in the absence of internationally adopted standards for PPP accounting, most EU countries have relied upon the accounting standard used for leases to assess whether PPP assets belong in substance to the public sector, based upon economic risk and rewards assessment (EPEC, 2010, p. 6).
4 Although this chapter concentrates on accrual-based accounting methods prescribed by the IPSASB, it may be appreciated that a cash-based approach will create similar concerns of future fiscal sustainability because it results in the recognition of assets only when they are paid for and there is no balance sheet containing long-term assets and liabilities.
5 The differences between GAAP accounts, based upon international and various national regulations, are beyond the scope of this chapter. These differences in accounting regulations and practices are sometimes indicated by the use of labels such as International GAAP (based broadly upon International Standards) and those of different countries e.g. US-GAAP, UK-GAAP.
6 http://www.ifrs.org/Home.htm (accessed 31 October 2010).
7 http://www.efrag.org/homepage.asp (accessed 4 November 2010).
8 http://www.frc.org.uk/about/ (accessed 4 November 2010).
9 http://www.frc.org.uk/asb/ (accessed 4 November 2010).
10 Recent proposals of the UKASB point towards a future regime in which medium-sized companies will follow regulation based upon the IASB standard for medium entities with UK standards ceasing (ASB 2010).
11 http://www.fasb.org/home (accessed 12 February 2011).
12 http://www.ifac.org/PublicSector/ (accessed 5 November 2010).
13 http://www.ifac.org/ (accessed 5 November 2010).
14 http://www.hm-treasury.gov.uk/psr_frab_index.htm (accessed 5 November 2010).
15 http://www.hm-treasury.gov.uk/frem_index.htm (accessed 5 November 2010).
16 http://www.gasb.org/ (accessed 5 November 2010).
17 http://www.aasb.com.au/AASB-Board.aspx (accessed 5 November 2010).
18 Studies of the development of these regulations include Broadbent and Laughlin (2002, 2005), Hodges and Mellett (2002), Kirk and Wall (2001) and Rutherford (2003). Hodges and Mellett (2005) conclude that the compromise between the ASB, the Treasury and the accounting firms maintained the apparent integrity of the ASB's conceptual framework, enabled the Treasury to retain flexibility in its PFI guidelines and provided fee earning opportunities for accounting firms and other advisors.
19 IPSASB project history at http://www.ifac.org/PublicSector/ProjectHistory.php?ProjID=0064 (accessed 28 October 2010).
20 The ED also covers the possibility of such assets being recognized as intangible assets (par. 13).
21 See http://www.ifac.org/Guidance/EXD-Comments.php?EDID=0134&Group=All+Responses (accessed 28 October 2010).

22 The New Zealand Treasury criticized the absence of other specific questions on which comments were requested, stating

> Without the focus provided by specific questions, we believe that the IPSASB will have difficulty balancing the views and comments it receives. If only one or a small number of respondents raises a particular issue, the IPSASB will not have the benefit of knowing whether the concerns are widely held, or whether there is a wide awareness of the issue. To avoid accusations of due process failure, the Board may need to consider re-exposing its judgements on the comments it receives.
>
> (NZT, p. 2)

References

ASB – Accounting Standards Board (1997) *Exposure Draft: Amendment to FRS 5 Reporting the Substance of Transactions: The Private Finance Initiative*, London: Accounting Standards Board.

—— (1998) *Amendment to FRS 5 Reporting the Substance of Transactions: Private Finance Initiative and Similar Contracts*, London: Accounting Standards Board.

—— (2010) *FRED 43 and 44: The Future of Financial Reporting in the UK and the Republic of Ireland*, London: Accounting Standards Board.

Atikoby, B., Hemming, R. and Schwartz, G. (2007) 'Public investment and public-private partnerships', *Economic Issues*, 40, Washington DC: International Monetary Fund.

Benston, G.J., Bromwich, M. and Wagenhofer, A. (2006) 'Principles versus rules-based accounting standards: the FASB's standard setting strategy', *Abacus*, 42(2): 165–88.

Broadbent, J. and Laughlin, R. (2002) 'Accounting choices: technical and political trade-offs and the UK's private finance initiative', *Accounting, Auditing and Accountability Journal*, 15(5): 622–54.

—— (2005) 'Government concerns and tensions in accounting standard-setting: the case of accounting for the Private Finance Initiative in the UK', *Accounting and Business Research*, 35(3): 207–28.

Broadbent, J., Gill, J. and Laughlin, R. (2008) 'Identifying and controlling risk: the problem of uncertainty in the private finance initiative in the UK's National Health Service', *Critical Perspectives on Accounting*, 19(1): 40–78.

Burger, P., Tyson, J., Karpowicz, I. and Coelho, M. (2009) *The Effect of the Financial Crisis on Public–Private Partnerships*, working paper 09/144, Washington DC: International Monetary Fund.

Chow, D., Humphrey, C and Moll, J. (2007) 'Developing whole of government accounting in the UK: grand claims, research complexities and a suggested future research agenda', *Financial Accountability & Management*, 23(1): 27–54.

Christiaens, J., Reyniers, B. and Rolle, C. (2009) 'Impact of IPSAS on reforming governmental financial information systems: a comparative study', *International Review of Administrative Sciences*, 76(3): 537–54.

EFRAG – European Financial Reporting Advisory Group (2007) *Adoption of IFRIC 12 Service Concession Arrangements*, 23 March 2007, Brussels: EFRAG, available HTTP: <http://www.efrag.org/projects/detail.asp?id=29> (accessed 30 October 2010).

EPEC – European PPP Expertise Centre (2010), *Eurostat Treatment of Public–Private Partnerships: Purposes, Methodology and Recent Trends*, Luxembourg: European Investment Bank.

European Commission (2008) *Endorsement of IFRIC 12 Service Concession Arrangements, Effect Study – Report*. Brussels: 12 June 2008.

—— (2009) *Commission Regulation (EC) No. 254/2009*, Brussels: OJEC 26 March 2009.

Eurostat (1995) *European System of Accounts (ESA 95)*, Luxembourg, Eurostat. http://circa.europa.eu/irc/dsis/nfaccount/info/data/esa95/en/esa95en.htm (accessed 30 October 2010).

—— (2004) *Long Term Contracts between Government Units and Non-government Partners (Public–Private Partnerships)*, Luxembourg: Eurostat.

Fontes, A., Lima-Rodrigues, L. and Craig, R. (2005) 'Measuring convergence of national accounting standards with International Financial Reporting Standards', *Accounting Forum*, 29(4): 415–36.

FRAB – Financial Reporting Advisory Board (2006a) 'PFI update paper from HM Treasury', *Agenda Item (80)04 of the FRAB Meeting – 29 June 2006*, London: FRAB.

—— (2006b) ' "On-On" and "Off-Off" balance sheet PFI/PPP Capital Assets – issues and recommendations – Office for National Statistics'. *Agenda item 82(04) of the FRAB Meeting – 31 October 2006*, London: FRAB.

Ron Hodges

—— (2006c) 'PFI update paper from HM Treasury'. *Agenda Item (83)03 of the FRAB Meeting – 11 December 2006*, London: FRAB.

—— (2007a) 'FRAB meeting – 12 February 2007', *minutes item 2 (FRAB(85)01)*, London: FRAB.

—— (2007b) 'FRAB meeting – 19 March 2007', *minutes item 10 to 12 (FRAB(86)01)*, London: FRAB.

Froud, J. (2003) 'The Private Finance Initiative: risk, uncertainty and the state', *Accounting, Organizations and Society*, 28(6): 567–89.

GASB – Government Accounting Standards Board (2010) Exposure draft (revised): *Accounting and Financial Reporting for Service Concession Arrangements*, Norwalk, CT: GASB.

Hancher, L. and Moran, M. (1989), 'Organising regulatory space' in L. Hancher and M. Moran (eds), *Capitalism, Culture and Economic Regulation*, Oxford: Clarendon Press, 271–99.

Heald, D. (2003) 'Value for money tests and accounting treatment of PFI schemes', *Accounting, Auditing and Accountability Journal*, 16(3): 342–71.

Heald, D. and Georgiou, G. (2010) 'Accounting for PPPs in a converging world' in Hodge, G., Greve, C. and Boardman, A. (eds) *International Handbook on Public-Private Partnerships*, Cheltenham: Edward Elgar, 273–61.

—— (2011) 'The substance of accounting for public private partnerships', *Financial Accountability & Management*, 27(2): 217–47.

Hodges, R. and Mellett, H. (1999) 'Accounting for the Private Finance Initiative in the United Kingdom National Health Service', *Financial Accountability & Management*, 15(3/4): 275–90.

—— (2002) 'Investigating standard setting: accounting for the UK's Private Finance Initiative', *Accounting Forum*, 26(2): 126–51.

—— (2004) 'How accounting standards develop: Walker and Robinson revisited', *European Accounting Association Congress*, March 2004, Prague, Czech Republic.

—— (2005), 'Accounting for the UK's Private Finance Initiative: An interview-based investigation', *Abacus*, 41(2): 158–79.

IASB – International Accounting Standards Board (1989) *Framework for the Preparation and Presentation of Financial Statements*, London: IASCF Publications.

—— (2005) *IASB Project Update: Service Concessions*, London: IASCF Publications.

—— (2006) *IFRIC 12 Service Concession Arrangements*, London: IASCF Publications.

—— (2009) *International Financial Reporting Standard for Small and Medium-sized Entities*, London: IASCF Publications.

IASCF – International Accounting Standards Committee Foundation (2006) *Due Process Handbook for the IASB*, London: IASCF Publications.

IPSASB – International Public Sector Accounting Standards Board (2006) *IPSAS 1: Presentation of Financial Statements*, Toronto: IFAC.

—— (2007) *Strategy and Operational Plan, April 2007*, Toronto: IFAC.

—— (2008a) *Process for Reviewing and Modifying IASB Documents*, Toronto: IFAC.

—— (2008b) *Consultation Paper: Accounting and Financial Reporting for Service Concession Arrangements*, Toronto: IFAC.

—— (2011) *Service Concession Arrangements: Grantor*, IPSASB Meeting – June 2011 – Naples, Agenda Item 4, New York: IFAC.

Jones, R. (2003) 'Measuring and reporting the nation's finances: statistics and accounting', *Public Money & Management*, 23(1): 21–7.

Khadaroo, I. (2005) 'An institutional theory perspective on the UK's Private Finance Initiative accounting standard setting process', *Public Management Review*, 7(1), 69–94.

Kirk, R. and Wall, A. (2001) 'Substance, form and PFI contracts', *Public Money and Management*, 21(3): 41–6.

Lüder, K. and Jones, R. (2003) 'The diffusion of accrual accounting and budgeting in European governments – a cross-country analysis', in Lüder, K. and Jones, R. (eds), *Reforming governmental accounting and budgeting in Europe*, Frankfurt: Fachverlag Moderne Wirtschaft, 13–58.

Office for Budget Responsibility (2011) *Fiscal Sustainability Report*, July 2011, London: The Stationery Office.

Pina, V. and Torres, L. (2003) 'Reshaping public sector accounting: an international comparative view', *Canadian Journal of Administrative Sciences*, 20(4): 334–50.

Rutherford, B. (2003) 'The social construction of financial statement elements under Private Finance Initiative schemes', *Accounting, Auditing and Accountability Journal*, 16(3): 372–96.

Shaoul, J. (2005) 'A critical financial analysis of the PFI: selecting a financing method or allocating economic wealth?' *Critical Perspectives on Accounting*, 16(4): 441–71.

Stevenson, K.M. (2010) 'Commentary: IFRS and the domestic standard setter. Is the mourning period over?' *Australian Accounting Review*, 20(3): 308–12.

Treasury (2003) *PFI: Meeting the investment challenge*, London: HM Treasury.

—— (2004) *Value for Money Assessment Guidance*, London: HM Treasury.

—— (2006) *PFI: strengthening long-term partnerships*, London: HM Treasury.

—— (2011). *PFI Signed deals March 2011*. London: HM Treasury, available on the internet at www. hm-treasury.gov.uk/ppp_pfi_stats.htm. Accessed 9 August 2011.

Treasury Taskforce (1997) *Technical Note 1: How to Account for PFI Transactions*, London: HM Treasury.

—— (1999) *Technical Note 1 (revised): How to Account for PFI Transactions*, London: Office of Government Commerce.

United Nations Statistical Division (2009) *System of National Accounts 2008*, New York: United Nations. Available HTTP: <http://unstats.un.org/unsd/nationalaccount/sna2008.asp>. Accessed 28 October 2010.

Walker, R.G. and Robinson, P. (1993) 'A critical assessment of the literature on political activity and accounting regulation', *Research in Accounting Regulation*, 7: 3–40.

Young, J.J. (1994) 'Outlining regulatory space: agenda issues and the FASB'. *Accounting, Organizations and Society*, 19(1): 83–109.

Accountability and public–private partnership contracts: un mariage de convenance?

Istemi S. Demirag and Iqbal Khadaroo

18.1 Introduction

Accountability is often used to explain certain decisions, behaviours or actions whose outcome may not always be desirable to certain social groups. As it is a subjectively constructed concept, it changes with context. Thus the complex and multi-faceted notion of accountability is often interpreted as a form of stewardship and/or responsibility involving some forms of account giving. In this regard 'why', 'to whom', 'for what' and 'how' we give an account will have significant implications for the account receivers. While one set of groups may find the account giving satisfactory in terms of their expectations from the behaviour of the accountor, others may find this completely unsatisfactory. Giving an account of an action or behaviour may therefore involve a complex set of relationships addressed to a particular group of people often with conflicting expectations or needs. How then can we hide behind this complex term of accountability to resolve the conflicting expectations of groups of people? To understand accountability, we need to unpack the complex nature of the relations embedded in it and discuss their relevance in specific context. In this chapter we critically examine the concept of accountability in terms of its new types and forms within the public private partnership (PPP) system of New Public Management (NPM). It is argued that the expectation from accountability in PPPs as a way of improving value for money (VFM) by improving productivity, cost-cutting, contracting out, compartmentalizing and top-slicing is not as clear as one might think. Finally we provide some directions for further research in some of these areas of PPP accountability.

18.2 What is accountability?

Sinclair (1995) states that accountability is a complex, abstract and elusive concept that is difficult to understand particularly in the public sector where there are complex sets of requirements and expectations from stakeholders. It is difficult to situate accountability in a single framework of accounting rules, legal obligations or economic and managerial rationality. Sinclair argues that accountability is often interpreted from the context of execution of responsibilities and being answerable for them and that 'accountability is subjectively constructed and changes with context' (Sinclair 1995: 219). However, the changing nature of accountability creates difficulties in identifying its various forms, including but not limited to political, legal, public, managerial, professional, bureaucratic and personal (Sinclair 1995: 231). Stewart (1984: 17–18) argues that there are different levels of accountability and develops a 'ladder of account-ability' to differentiate between them. Accountability for 'probity' and 'legality' considers whether resources in the organization have been used properly and according to the rules and law. 'Process accountability' is the next level where the processes of actions of the agents are evaluated and considered. This is followed by 'performance accountability' and 'programme accountability' where an account of the detailed work of the 'agent' is considered (Stewart 1984: 17–18). In these entire forms and levels of accountability Stewart points out that one still needs to answer the basic question of 'to whom' the accountable individual is obliged, and 'for what' and in what form is the accountability discharged. This is quite pertinent to accountability in PPPs where user needs and accountability issues are somewhat different from industries involving either the public sector or the private sector. Although Stewart (1984) and others (Sinclair 1995; Mulgan 2000; Koppell 2005) have provided a comprehensive discussion of account giving in an institutional setting (that is, the conduct of accountability) and have engaged in debates of the relative merits of the different forms of accountability, they have largely ignored the behavioural and ethical dimensions of accountability (that is, the accountability for conduct). Iyoha and Oyerinde (2010: 361) argue that 'accountability in public expenditure can more easily be realized within the context of a sound accounting infra-structure and a robust accounting profession, not through laws and anti-corruption agencies which are reactive in nature'. They point out that policies, legislation and standards have failed mainly as a result of poor accounting and accountability in the public sector.

The assumed relationship between accountability and performance developed through established policies and programmes such as PPP provides two different perspectives on accountability. The first perspective is the one that highlights the institutional perspectives and responsibilities of accountable actors and the second stresses the functional and emergent characteristics of account giving behaviour of the individual (Dubnick 2005; Demirag and Khadaroo 2011). The central argument in the development of our accountability model is that both approaches require due attention for the useful conceptualization of accountability.

Definitions of accountability are evolving as the ideologies, accepted norms in society are changing for justifications, rationalizations and other forms of account-giving (Benoit 1995). Accountability is also seen as a mechanism for coping with demands for answerability (Lerner and Tetlock 1999). Others have argued that in functional terms, accountability can be regarded as a primary means for managing expectations where expectations are multiple, diverse and often conflicting (Dubnick and Romzek 1991, 1993). Dubnick (2005) points out that recently accountability has developed into an assumed universal solution for some of the most intractable problems in modern governance. In this respect, Messner (2009: 918) 'raises the question of whether more accountability is always and unambiguously desirable from an ethical point of view'. Messner (2009) argues that demands for accountability may become so perverse to be ethically desirable for the person or organization that is expected to give an account. This form of accountability, in the name of ethics, forces the accountor to account for something that is very difficult or even impossible to justify and in this respect does 'violence' to the accountor (Messner 2009: 918; Roberts 2009: 962). Messner (2009: 919) states that although in many situations, it is reasonable to demand more accountability, accountability itself may become a problematic practice, through the burden that account-ability may place on the accountable self who is expected to provide a convincing account even in situations where this is extremely difficult or even impossible.

The second report of the Nolan Committee on standards in public life in the UK has identified accountability as comprising seven principles (Nolan Committee 1996: ii). It states that holders of public office are accountable for the decisions and actions to the public and must submit themselves to whatever scrutiny is appropriate to their office. This definition of accountability is not helpful conceptually as it does not explain what the scrutiny is and how this is to be carried out. Moreover it fails to explain what actions should be taken if the people undertaking the scrutiny are not satisfied by the accountor. However, when taken together with the rest of the principles, accountability as part of the broader remit of principles of public life becomes more meaningful. The first three of these relate to ethical and moral issues: selflessness, integrity, and honesty. The principle of selflessness argues that decisions taken should be solely in the interest of the public, the holders of the public office should not seek to gain financial or other material benefits for themselves, their family or their friends. Similarly the principles of integrity suggest that the account givers should not place themselves under any financial or other obligation to outside individuals or organizations that might influence them in the performance of their duties. The honesty principle argues that people in accountable positions should declare any private interests relating to their public duties and take steps to resolve any conflicts arising in a way that protects the public interest. These three principles, taken together, form the ethical characteristics of accountability and concern the behavioural aspect, introduced above. Then there are the mechanical or more technical characteristics of accountability, which is the institutional aspect of accountability. These include objectivity and openness. By objectivity it is understood that in carrying out public business holders of public office should make choices on merit. The principle of openness recognizes the interest of broader stakeholders and the need for making decisions and actions transparent to them. The last principle of public life also takes accountability to a further level in that it states that holders of public office should have a leadership role in and should support these principles themselves by leading by example. Altogether, these principles of public life provide a better understanding of the principles of public sector accountability in practice.

18.3 PPP and accountability

18.3.1 An overview of PPP; definition and applications

To what extent do NPM and PPP have accountable mechanisms in order to enhance the public sector's ability to deliver more effective and efficient public goods and services? PPP provides a useful case for understanding accountability and the way in which accountability is delivered in practice, which we will call its mechanisms. Under PPP, capital funding for major infrastructure investments is provided by private investors such as banks and equity investors. PPPs therefore do not use large scale upfront public spending, instead the payments are made through instalments to a private consortium for buildings and services delivered throughout the life of the contract. The consortia known as Special Purpose Vehicle (SPV) usually consists of banks and large construction firms who are contracted to design, build, and in some cases manage new infrastructure projects which are typically for a specified duration. During the PPP contractual periods the building is leased by a public authority from the SPV. The private sector obtains finance for its investments in the underlying assets usually through a combination of a small amount of equity finance and a large amount of senior debt. At the end of the contractual period ownership returns to the public sector. Figure 18.1 shows the structure of a typical PPP contract.

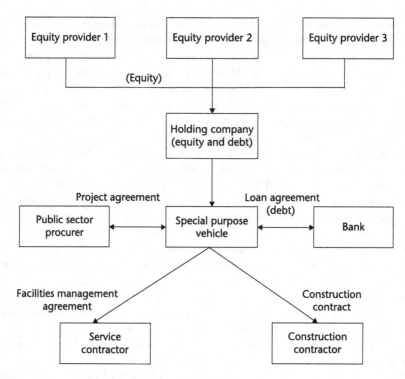

Figure 18.1   Structure of a typical PPP contract

Source: Adapted from Demirag *et al.* 2010

There is a growing interest globally in PPP type of infrastructure investment. For example in the last decade or so nearly 1,000 PPP contracts have been signed within the European Union with a total value of approximately 200 billion Euros (Demirag 2008: 54). The leading European countries with PPP infrastructure are the United Kingdom, Portugal and Spain where investment in infrastructure through PPP has become significant. In the UK over 630 PPP projects have been signed and of these 540 are now fully operational; representing over £63 billion infrastructure investments since 1992 (Demirag *et al.* 2010: 4).

In selecting a PPP method of investment over other traditional procurement methods, a procuring authority's choice is based on 'value for money' (VFM) considerations. The method chosen is often the one that provides the most VFM to the public sector. However, this does not always mean that the selected method of infrastructure investment is the cheapest of all the available options to the public authorities. Arguably, PPP projects transfer some of the design, building, and operational risks to the private sector and therefore the public sector may be willing to pay over and above the cost of traditional procurement methods.

The government argues that under PPP projects the 'private sector takes on the major project performance risks, like cost overruns and delay', and thus avoid wasting public resources when compared to traditionally procured projects which often result in spiraling costs and delays in completion (HM Treasury 2003: 4). One important question to ask here is whether the premium paid to the private sector for PPP projects is worth the amount of the risk transferred from the public sector to the private sector.

18.4 PPP and accountability: a theoretical model of the relationships

PPP consists of a set of governance relationships and mechanisms with 'meta' objectives of achieving certain political outcomes such as modernization. As in any other governance mechanism, it has accountability systems in addition to it being a NPM reform programme. PPP, at the micro level, is not only a contractual relationship but also has communal, political and managerial relationships. In addition it includes a whole set of accountability structures – both formal such as contracts and management, which may need to be renegotiated, and informal such as communal and political. These perspectives of PPP have been incorporated into a recent model developed by Demirag and Khadaroo (2011). This model of accountability developed specifically for the PPP process initially explores the question of whether there exists a viable empirical foundation to build a form of 'intelligent accountability' that meets the challenge posited in Onora O'Neill's critique of the 'new accountability' (see Onora O'Neill's 2002 BBC Reith Lectures). O'Neill (2002) posits that 'intelligent accountability' is based on good governance, independent inspection and careful reporting. Our accountability framework attempts to explore the socio-psychological and socio-cultural mechanisms that foster or obstruct the development and implementation of intelligent accountability processes in general and VFM attainment and measurement systems in particular.

The PPP accountability model adopted in this chapter is based on related work by Dubnick (2003, 2005), Demirag et al. (2004) and Demirag and Khadaroo (2011). The model of PPP accountability (see Figure 18.2) highlights accountability cultures and systems. The model introduces four accountability cultures developed by Dubnick (1996, 1998, 2003). Each of these cultures of accountability is characterized by a distinct orientation to account giving that impacts on the response of those being held to account to different accountability forms and technologies. *Answerability* cultures reflect hierarchical and other forms of structured social settings where individuals perceive themselves as responsible for reporting, justifying or explaining their actions to others. Answerability is a prerequisite for control. Mulgan (2000: 563) uses controllability terminology for answerability. For Mulgan controllability is also explored from a bureaucratic and organizational setting. Mulgan indicates that accountability is a vital mechanism of control and in this sense these two concepts are intimately linked with each other. Referring to public accountability, Mulgan argues that in democratic societies, people wish to control the actions of public officials and therefore make these officials answer, explain and accept sanctions. It is in this context we use answerability synonymously with controllability because both answerability and controllability enable subordinates to do the things that are desired by the principals. *Liability* culture represents settings where individuals regard themselves as subject to a system of rules and laws that carry the potential for sanctions (positive or negative). Dubnick argues that individuals and organizations should be held liable for their actions and/or rewarded for their good performance. Hence the liability dimension of accountability deals with both penalty and reward systems. In democratic systems, elected officials are held liable through the electoral process under which bureaucrats cannot be held liable. They are only held liable in the criminal sense for malfeasance. Koppell (2005: 97) argues that the mere revelations of performance and wrongdoings do not alone constitute accountability; consequences must also be faced. Mulgan (2000) does not identify liability as a distinct form of accountability, but refers to it under the accountability dimension of 'control'. He also uses the liability notion of accountability for bringing civil servants under control.

Dubnick and Justice (2002) argue that *blameworthiness* culture requires a shift in focus from standard and predictable roles and structures to one's relative social position or identification with a certain group. As Dubnick (1996, 1998, 2003) points out, one is held accountable

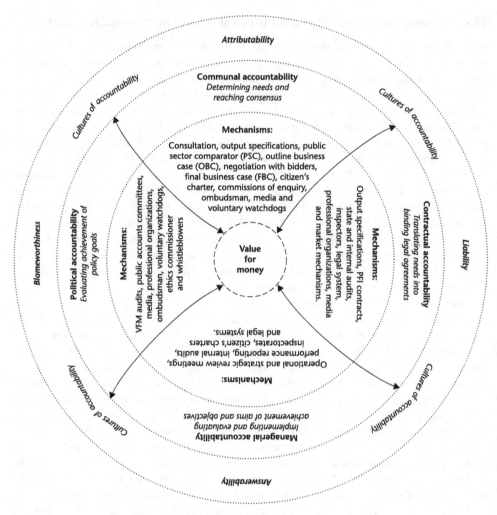

Figure 18.2 PPP accountability processes and VFM mechanisms

Source: Adapted from Demirag and Khadaroo 2011

because one is regarded as socially, if not organizationally, blameworthy. Hence this culture stresses the sense of responsibility within a moral community where expectations are generalized rather than specific to individuals or their roles in society (Demirag and Khadaroo 2011). Messner (2009) points out that the accountable self is an opaque, exposed and mediated self that is inherently limited in its ability to give an account of itself. Partly because of these limits, Messner argues that one cannot expect demands for accountability to be always fully met. Finally, *attributability* culture places attention on the individuals' roles and the expectations related to those roles. Dubnick (2003) refers to 'attributability' culture where non-work behaviour of a public worker affects his/her job not because of his/her accountability performance at work but because of his/her job in the public life and its associated expectations. The sources of such standards are people who 'attribute' an action or behaviour to an actor and would demand or expect an account, if they were in a position and able to do so

(Dubnick 2003, 2005). Attributability does not have to relate to work in public office and it sometimes can affect the lives of private individuals when it is regarded as grounds for adverse personal action. For example, day-to-day behaviour of an attorney at law to his neighbours may be expected to be law abiding and transparent because of his formal position in office. This is possible even when the action of the individual concerned has had nothing to do with their position in work (Dubnick and Justice 2002: 30).

Demirag and Khadaroo (2011) highlight four major accountability systems in PPPs: *Managerial accountability, Contractual accountability, Communal accountability* and *Political accountability*. They point out that PPP requires a kind of oversight system in place to ensure that the contract terms are adhered to during PPP implementation. *Managerial accountability systems* are therefore developed for the period of the contract mainly to monitor and assess the VFM from PPP contracts (Stewart 1984; Sinclair 1995). The authors argue that the ultimate VFM outcome of PPP will be largely determined by how PPP policies and guidance are formulated at the macro level by government policies and implemented at the micro organization level (see also, English and Guthrie 2003: 493). In this process performance monitoring and evaluation of PPP programmes, such as how contractors are paid or penalties implemented, are used to determine and assess the extent to which PPP projects are meeting the service standards agreed in the contracts. Demirag and Khadaroo (2011) argue that public sector managers and contractors should adopt 'customer-oriented' techniques to assess the extent to which needs of PPP users are satisfied. Moreover, adequate PPP monitoring mechanisms may be required to safeguard the public interest to ensure that PPP delivers the VFM benefits foreseen at the appraisal stage as well as monitoring the financial health of contractors as poor cash flows could put the viability of PPP contracts in danger. PPP contracts are designed to enable the public sector transfer risks associated with the design, construction and operation of a facility. This is expected to be formally achieved through a *contractual accountability system* that creates liabilities and obligations for the partners to comply with. Asenova and Beck (2010) argue that the prerequisite of obtaining capital from the private sector under PPP limits the extent to which the private sector can be held managerially accountable. Although they can be held accountable for the services contracted, the level of openness regarding crucial financial and project parameters including details of their financial models, their risk assessment allocation, mitigation procedures are not subject to public scrutiny. More generally, the managerial versus contractual accountability raises questions regarding the interrelatedness of the different accountability systems. For instance, it might be claimed that meeting the contractual accountability requisites renders the managerial accountability superfluous. Another issue in this respect, may indicate the interwoven nature of the concepts. For example, as will be identified below, the communal accountability may result in additional claims honoring the interests of a small group which may affect the VFM of the PPP project as a whole.

Demirag and Khadaroo (2011) argue that two additional accountability systems can be observed in PPP schemes. These are communal and political accountability systems respectively. A *communal accountability system* is concerned with meeting the demands and needs of stakeholders, users, clients and other interest groups. The spectrum of interest groups will have to be limited depending on the circumstances most appropriate. This system emerges (in formal or informal forms) from interactions with these various parties, mostly through the consultation process during PPP procurement and implementation. Demirag and Khadaroo (2011) argue that communal accountability involves seeking the legitimacy and consensus of stakeholder groups affected by a particular policy through their participation in the decision making process. They argue that accountability is both a moral and discursive practice; moral on grounds that it involves human agency and has consequences on people by affecting their lived experiences; and discursive because it requires an agreement between the accountor and accountee in terms of how the expectations of the accountee are to be met (Francis 1990; Lehman 2005). In the communal accountability dialogue with interest groups is an essential accountability mechanism for understanding and responding to the stakeholder needs (Behn 1998; Farrell 2000; Roberts 2002; Shearer 2002). This is because, as Demirag and Khadaroo (2011) point out, open and transparent public debate can positively contribute to achieving better VFM. Fowles (1993), for example, argues that citizen participation in public sector governance reduces power differentials between service providers and service users to promote better downward accountability and safeguard the longer-term interests of taxpayers and service consumers. Demirag and Khadaroo (2011) argue that although the UK's last Labour government has sought to promote more participation from community members it has failed to gain their political support. In this respect, the PPP policy has been criticized on grounds that the decision making process is not transparent and interest groups do not have the power to challenge the PPP policy (Edwards and Shaoul, 2003a, 2003b; Pollock *et al.* 2007). Demirag and Khadaroo (2011) argue that 'active' participation in the PPP decision-making process by stakeholders may be an important source of VFM where the various interest groups would be challenged to justify their opinions and course of actions such that the chosen alternative is acceptable and appeals to the common interest of all stakeholders. On the other hand, collective actions of interest groups may substantively raise the upfront investments of infrastructure projects. Frequently, these actions result in extensive additional provisions to meet the objections of a relatively small interest group. For instance, the one-billion-euro tunnel in the high-speed railway track through Holland is a result of landscape-protecting activism. From a broader, national perspective the tunnel raised quite some doubt about its VFM. Moreover, additional project claims might impede the contractual accountability, e.g. causing hold-up situations. Stakeholder dialogue in these circumstances can provide important accountability mechanism in that open dialogue among the interested parties would bring about different perspectives and interpretations of a particular issue and would lead to more accountable and transparent PPP policy making. However, Asenova and Beck (2010) argue that because of PPP's role as an investment opportunity to re-invigorate the private sector, it prioritizes the risk-return criteria of the private sector over the needs of the public sector client and its stakeholders, creating conflict of interests. They argue that the way PPPs are planned, structured and financed in order to meet private sector expectations together with statutory requirements for risk transfer challenges does not enable it to satisfy the accountability demands of other stakeholders. Bracci (2009) found that governance systems that foster autonomy and participation have the potential to create conflict with efficiency and effectiveness objectives and undermine public services and pointed to the need for less hierarchical (or bureaucratic) notions of accountability, giving more attention to the interplay between the formal and informal, and the lateral and vertical accountability connections. (See also Ezzamel *et al.* (2007: 168) who found a complex pattern of accountability relationships and 'tensions between new forms of regulatory financial accountability, imposed in the name of greater efficiency and effectiveness, and folk accountability'.) Ezzamel *et al.* (2007: 168–9) point out to the formal and informal 'discourses intertwining, overlaying and moving closer with one strand (the regulatory) seemingly proceeding to dominate' and suggest that this relationship is 'partly speculative and should form the object of future investigations'.

A *political accountability system* is rooted in the constitution of most Westminster democracies where parliamentary institutions may act as a check on the Executive government (the political party with the majority of seats in the House of Commons) by scrutinizing the policies pursued (Gendron *et al.* 2001; Broadbent and Laughlin 2003). Demirag and Khadaroo (2011) state that in Westminster democracies, powers are separated among the Executive government, the Parliament (representing public interest) and the public. In the UK, the National Audit Office (NAO) investigate individual PPP projects for VFM, and the Public Accounts Committee calls on the responsible public sector executives to account in cases where PPP contracts are experiencing difficulty. English and Guthrie (2006: 3) argue that 'Auditors-general have traditionally provided independent oversight of the activities of executive government and their agents, playing a key role in public accountability' and disclosing inefficient utilization of public funds. Through their VFM recommendations, best practices and lessons may be disseminated to other parts of the public sector (Leeuw 1996: 94). However, the power of public sector auditors in the UK may be limited in that they can only assess the way government policies are implemented in their VFM audits. They are 'independent of government' and can only question but not change government policies (NAO 2009: 11).

Gasmi *et al.* (2006) argue that international agencies and donors (e.g. the World Bank, the Department for International Development), have been relatively effective in supporting 'good' governance systems in the developing countries. However, 'politically accountable' systems of governance have still got a long way to go to achieve their objectives of developing accountability systems in developing countries. They argue that established regulatory agencies also need long-term support and objectives in order to improve regulatory practice. The short-termism displayed by these institutions over the last decade or so has resulted in undermining the human capital as well as the technical tools and instruments required by an efficient practice of regulation. The failures of the donor institutions, as argued by the authors, have been due to lack of long-term sustainable policies and as a result of assuming that newly established regulatory agencies will be self sustaining in five years. The need to explain and support these newly created institutions by their host environments is essential if these new governance structures are to work in the long term. A clear understanding of the political accountability systems is essential by ring fencing regulatory agencies from local political interference. In this context for public private partnership to work in developing countries, the latter will require specially developed PPP units run by state officials and protected from locally elected politicians who may steer its development to their own party advantages. These may involve technical assistance in developing an appropriate legal code of practice and ensuring that the PPP board establish and comply with approved international PPP procedures and regulations. At a broader governmental level legal changes necessary for the development of PPP policies can be undertaken in countries that are committed to improve their 'accountability' systems. In some of these countries accountability systems in general are not as well developed as those in developed countries and hence PPP would require installing good accountability and governance systems essential for the improvement of public services.

18.5 Conclusions and issues for further research

This chapter has discussed the elusive concept of accountability and developed a generic theoretical model of the relationships between accountability and PPP. The accountability mechanisms and cultures identified in Figure 18.2 may be used as a skeletal framework for conducting empirical research in a specific PPP context, such as health, education, transport, defence or prisons. It is acknowledged that the framework would need further refinements and empirical evidence gathered may lead to the identification of new accountability processes, mechanisms and cultures.

PPP contracts rely on long term and ongoing relationships with the private sector, which are difficult to specify contractually at the outset, and therefore require flexibility and renegotiations during their terms. The relationships between the private and public sectors are changing over time and there is some evidence to suggest that more flexibility is practised in interpreting contracts (Demirag and Burke 2010). These relationships are open systems and require more governance skills. However, even with this flexibility of governance systems it may not be possible for the governments to discharge the whole accountability associated with the provision of public services because of the inherent limits of accountability (Messner 2009). Another implication of these emerging network and governance arrangements has resulted in the private sector becoming part of the governance system in the provision of public services. But this may raise some constitutional problems as the government may not be contracting out its authority and legitimacy in the provision of public services.

PPP with its new emergent forms of networking and governance mechanisms is an elusive, dynamic and difficult public policy whose accountability systems may be unacceptable in different ways for different stakeholders. As discussed earlier there are many accountability systems in PPP arrangements with different objectives. Arguably the obvious system of accountability that can be identified is contractual accountability. But managing the contractual accountability process is difficult during the life of a PPP as many contracts are renegotiated while the other accountability processes such as political, managerial, communal, also play a significant part in the background and affect decision making. Moreover, these accountability processes are interwoven and may impact each other over the life of the contract. For example, failure to meet expectations of stakeholders and specify their requirements in a binding contract would adversely impact managerial and political accountability processes after the PPP contract is implemented. This may lead to increased cost and even the demise of the PPP contract (Edwards and Shaoul 2003a).

The relationship between accountability and performance has been explored and questioned in a number of recent studies (Perrin 1998; Behn 2002; Modell 2004; Cavalluzzo and Ittner 2004; Dubnick 2005; Demirag and Khadaroo 2011), leading to the question of what factors might underpin the assumed connection between the two. The role of cultural factors has not been addressed directly, although work by Hood (1998) provides a foundation for such an analysis.

In his seminal work Dubnick (2003) posits that cultures of accountability are concerned with how governments ought to or should behave as they try to steer their choice of accountability cultures from top to bottom in PPP systems. Therefore, if the 'right type and kind' of accountability systems are not used in the PPP system then perverse behaviour may result in much worse performance than intended. Dubnick therefore argues that these informal cultures of accountability in addition to the formal systems of accountability need to be examined. In the context of PPP systems we need to further explore the socio-cultural and social psychological mechanisms that foster or obstruct the development and implementation of intelligent accountability systems in general and PPP performance measurement systems in particular. Dubnick points out that given these variations in accountability cultures, an effort to impact on the performance of an individual or any group of individuals would be most effective if the appropriate forms of accountability mechanisms were applied to that individual or group. It follows that a misfit of accountability mechanisms and accountability cultures will result in less success in achieving improved performance through accountability or, worse still, what O'Neill terms 'counterproductive' performance (Demirag and Khadaroo 2011).

These are all theoretical conjectures and are speculative in nature without any strong empirical support. We suggest that some of these cultures may be more dominant in specific formal systems of accountability than in others. For example, under the contractual account-ability process, the liability culture may be prevalent. Communal cultures may be more appropriate with the attributability culture where competence of state officials may become an important consideration. Managerial accountability may be more consistent with an answerability culture and under political accountability systems the blameworthiness culture may dominate the other cultures as reflected in Figure 18.2.

References

Asenova, D. and Beck, M. (2010) 'Crucial silences: When accountability met PFI and finance capital', *Critical Perspectives on Accounting*, 21, 1: 1–13.

Behn, R. D. (1998) 'The new public management paradigm and the search for democratic account-ability', *International Public Management Journal*, 1, 2: 131–64.

—— (2002) 'The psychological barriers to performance management or why isn't everyone jumping on the performance-management bandwagon?', *Public Performance & Management Review*, 26, 1: 5–25.

Benoit, W. L. (1995) *Accounts, Excuses and Apologies: A theory of image restoration strategies*, Albany: State University of New York Press.

Broadbent, J. and Laughlin, R. (2003) 'Control and legitimation in government accountability processes: The private finance initiative in the UK', *Critical Perspectives on Accounting*, 14, 1/2: 23–48.

Cavalluzzo, K. S. and Ittner, C. D. (2004) 'Implementing performance measurement innovations: evidence from government', *Accounting, Organizations and Society*, 29, 3&4: 243–67.

Demirag, I. and Burke, R. (2010) 'Management of Demand Risk in Irish PPP Roads', The European Accounting Association Annual Conference, Istanbul, Turkey, 19–21 May 2010.

Demirag, I. (2008) Keeping PFI on course, *AgendaNi*, December: 54–5.

Demirag, I., Dubnick, M. and Khadaroo, I. (2004) 'A framework for examining accountability and value for money in the UK's Private Finance Initiative', *The Journal of Corporate Citizenship*, 15: 63–76.

Demirag, I. and Khadaroo, I. (2011) 'Accountability and value for money: A theoretical framework for the relationship in public–private partnerships', *Journal of Management & Governance*, 15, 2: 271–96.

Demirag, I., Khadaroo, I., Stapleton, P. and Stevenson, C. (2010) *Public Private Partnership Financiers' Perceptions of Risk, Research report*, Scotland: Institute of Chartered Accountants Scotland (ICAS).

Dubnick M. J. (1996) 'Public Service Ethics and the Cultures of Blame', Paper presented at the Fifth International Conference of Ethics in the Public Service, Brisbane, Queensland, Australia, August 5–9.

—— (1998) 'Clarifying Accountability: An ethical theory framework', in C. Sampford and N. Preston (eds), *Public sector ethics: Finding and implementing values*, London: Routledge.

—— (2003) 'Accountability and ethics: Reconsidering the relationships', *International Journal of Organization Theory and Behavior*, 6, 3: 405–41.

—— (2005) 'Accountability and the promise of performance: In search of the mechanisms', *Public Performance and Management Review*, 28, 3: 376–417.

Dubnick M. J. and Justice, J. B. (2002) 'But can you trust them to be ethical?', Paper presented to the 63rd annual conference of the American Society for Public Administration, Phoenix, AZ, 23 March.

Dubnick M. J. and Romzek, S. B. (1991) *American Public Administration, Politics and the Management of Expectations*, New York: Macmillan.

—— (1993) 'Accountability and the Centrality of Expectations in American Public Administration', in J. L. Perry (ed), *Research in Public Administration*, Greenwich CT: JAI Press.

Edwards, P. and Shaoul, J. (2003a) 'Controlling the PFI process in schools: A case study of the Pimlico project', *Policy and Politics*, 31, 3: 371–85.

—— (2003b) 'Partnerships: For better, for worse?', *Accounting, Auditing & Accountability Journal*, 16, 3: 397–421.

English, L., and Guthrie, J. (2003) 'Driving privately financed projects in Australia: What makes them tick?', *Accounting, Auditing & Accountability Journal*, 16, 3: 493–511.

—— (2006) 'State Audit of Public Private Partnerships in Australia: A Lack of Public Accountability?', European Accounting Association, March 2006, Dublin, Ireland.

Ezzamel, M., Robson, K., Stapleton, P. and McLean, C. (2007) 'Discourse and institutional change: "Giving accounts" and accountability', *Management Accounting Research*, 18, 2: 150–71.

Farrell, C. (2000) 'Citizen participation in governance', *Public Money and Management*, 20, 1: 31–7.

Fowles, A. J. (1993) 'Changing notions of accountability: A social policy review', *Accounting, Auditing & Accountability Journal*, 6, 3: 97–108.

Francis, J. R. (1990) 'After virtue? Accounting as a moral and discursive practice', *Accounting, Auditing & Accountability Journal*, 3, 3: 5–17.

Gasmi, F., Noumba Um, P. and Virto, L. R. (2006) 'Political accountability and regulatory performance in infrastructure industries: An empirical analysis', Policy, Research working paper; no. WPS 4101, The World Bank.

Gendron, Y., Cooper, D. and Townley, B. (2001), 'In the name of accountability: State auditing, independence and new public management', *Accounting, Auditing & Accountability Journal*, 14, 3: 278–310.

HM Treasury (2003) *PFI: Meeting the Investment Challenge*, London: HMSO.

Hood, C. (1998) *The Art of the State: Culture, Rhetoric and Public Management*, Oxford: Clarendon.

Iyoha, F. O. and Oyerinde, D. (2010) 'Accounting infrastructure and accountability in the management of public expenditure in developing countries: A focus on Nigeria', *Critical Perspectives on Accounting*, 21, 5: 361–3.

Koppell, J. (2005) 'Pathologies of Accountability: ICANN and the Challenge of "Multiple Accountabilities Disorder"', *Public Administration Review*, 65, 1: 94–108.

Leeuw, F. (1996) 'Performance auditing, new public management and performance improvement: Questions and answers', *Accounting, Auditing & Accountability Journal*, 9, 2: 92–102.

Lehman, G. (2005) 'A critical perspective on the harmonisation of accounting in a globalising world', *Critical Perspectives on Accounting*, 16, 7: 975–92.

Lerner, J. S. and Tetlock, P. E. (1999) 'Accounting for the Effects of Accountability', *Psychological Bulletin*, 125, 2: 255–75.

Messner, M. (2009) 'The limits of accountability', *Accounting, Organizations and Society*, 34, 8: 918–38.

Modell, S. (2004) 'Performance measurement myths in the public sector: A research note', *Financial Accountability & Management*, 20, 1: 39–55.

Mulgan, R. (2000) 'Accountability: An ever-expanding concept?', *Public Administration*, 78, 3: 555–73.

NAO (National Audit Office) (2009) *Annual Report*, London: HMSO.

Nolan Committee (1996) *Second Report – Seven Principles of Public Life* (available at http://www.archive.official-documents.co.uk/document/parlment/nolan/nolan.htm).

O'Neill, O. (2002) 'The philosophy of Trust', BBC Reith Lecture, available at: http://www.bbc.co.uk/radio4/reith2002/.

Perrin, B. (1998) 'Effective use and misuse of performance measurement', *American Journal of Evaluation*, 19, 3: 367–79.

Pollock, A., Price, D. and Player, S. (2007) 'An examination of the UK's Treasury's evidence base for cost and time overrun data in UK value for money policy and appraisal', *Public Money and Management*, 27, 2: 127–33.

Roberts, J. (2009) 'No one is perfect: The limits of transparency and an ethic for "intelligent" accountability', *Accounting, Organizations and Society*, 34, 8: 957–70.

Roberts, N. (2002) 'Keeping public officials accountable through dialogue: Resolving the accountability paradox', *Public Administration Review*, 62, 6: 658–69.

Shearer, T. (2002) 'Ethics and accountability: from the for-itself to the for-the-other', *Accounting, Organizations and Society*, 26, 7: 541–73.

Sinclair, A. (1995) 'The Chameleon of Accountability: Forms and Discourses', *Accounting, Organisations and Society*, 20, 2&3: 219–37.

Stewart, J. (1984) 'The role of information in public accountability', in A. G. Hopwood and C. R. Tomkins (eds), *Issues in Public Sector Accounting*, Oxford: Philip Allan.

19

Public–private partnerships: international audit findings

*Ineke Boers, Freek Hoek, Cor van Montfort and Jan Wieles**

19.1 Introduction

This chapter discusses the findings on PPPs set out in audits performed by various national (or 'supreme audit institutions', as they are also called)[1] and regional audit offices. Audit offices play a key role in auditing government accounts and operations, and in promoting sound financial management and overall accountability in their governments. Thanks to their tasks and independent status, audit offices are ideally placed to supply the world of PPPs with hard facts based on empirical research.

19.1.1 Audit offices and PPPs

There is no doubt about the potential relevance of PPP projects as a subject for audit office reports. Massive public interests are often at play in such projects, in terms both of the (quality of) public services they seek to supply and of the public money invested in them. Although PPPs generally are privately financed, it is ultimately either taxpayers or consumers who pay for the cost of PPP projects. Value for money, regularity (i.e. the regularity of the expenditure on PPP projects) and, equally importantly, the accountability of PPP projects are all highly relevant issues for audit offices.

Basically, audit offices perform two types of audits: financial and regularity audits on the one hand and value-for-money (VFM) audits on the other. The former are connected with government accounts and are in many instances directed at the issuing of financial statements. The latter are all about the efficiency and effectiveness of government, its policies and its institutions. All audit offices perform financial audits, but there are variations in the extent to which they also perform – or are entitled to perform – VFM audits. Audits are usually performed *ex post* (after the fact).

19.1.2. Scope of the study

This chapter is based on a study of audit office reports on PPPs that we carried out in 2010. Our study was restricted to audit office reports on DBFM(O) concessions and similar projects.

451

Design, Build, Finance and Maintain (Operate) Projects are concessions under which the DBFM(O) aspects of a project (often infrastructural or a public utility) are contracted out to private-sector partners, usually under 25–30-year contracts and paid for by user or availability fees. In other words, no account was taken of audits of other types of PPPs, such as public–private alliances and conventional contracts (for example, outsourcing contracts) between public-sector and private-sector parties.

The main objects of our study were separate reports on PPP projects, or reports in which the PPP aspect played a key role. This meant that most of the reports we examined were on VFM audits. For this reason, the attention given to PPPs in regularity audits or audits directed at issuing financial statements on accounts published by public bodies was largely left aside. The distinction between regularity audits and VFM audits does not mean that no regularity aspects can come up in VFM audits.

The focus of this study lies on reports published by audit offices on PPP projects performed by the *national* government. During our research, we encountered a number of interesting studies by audit offices operating at regional (provincial or state) level. Where relevant, we have included their findings in our report.

We did not beforehand limit our study to a given period of time. Most of the reports we traced were published between 2000 and 2010, with the bulk appearing in the years 2008 and 2009. Our study was concluded mid-November 2010.

19.1.3 Study method

The reports used for this study originate from three sources: some were sourced directly from our international contacts, others were found on websites maintained by the various audit offices and others were provided in response to a mailing we distributed asking for information on PPP audits. In total we looked at 58 audit offices this way.

In the end we collected 48 relevant reports published by 21 audit offices (including both national and regional audit offices) in 13 countries. The number of audit offices around the world to have published reports on PPPs is not particularly large. We limited our study to reports or summaries of reports published in Dutch, English, German, French or Spanish. Most audit offices have versions of their websites in one of these languages, mostly English. Our survey may not include all relevant audit office reports in relation to PPPs. But we do believe that the picture our study paints is fairly representative for the findings of audit offices on PPPs.

In this study we refer to 38 of the 48 reports we used. Not because the others are not relevant, but because they do not add new findings and conclusions to those we give in this chapter. Also, referring to a certain report in this chapter does not imply that the same topic is not raised in another report; the various citations are just meant to illustrate the topic. There is a great similarity in findings and a great unanimity in standards and conclusions of the various audit offices.

Our analysis of the reports we collected shows, not surprisingly given the nature of the role played by audit offices, that most audit offices took a fairly critical attitude to PPPs. Although some reports do contain positive findings on PPP projects (e.g. Australia, New South Wales 2006; Australia, Victoria 2008), as a consequence this study concentrates on areas in which there is scope for improvement. But our study does not mean to give conclusions or an opinion on the use or sense of PPPs.

19.1.4 Audit offices and reports on PPPs

Our study covers audit reports from the following audit offices.

Table 19.1 Audit offices and reports

Country (province or state)	Audit office	Website	Number of reports included in study
Austria	Österreichische Rechnungshof	www.rechnungshof.gv.at	1
Australia, New South Wales	The Audit Office of New South Wales	www.audit.nsw.gov.au	2
Australia, Victoria	Victorian Auditor-General's Office	www.audit.vic.gov.au	2
Belgium	Rekenhof – Cour des Comptes	www.ccrek.be	2
Canada, Alberta	Office of the Auditor General of Alberta	www.oag.ab.ca	3
Canada, Novia Scotia	Office of the Auditor General of Nova Scotia	www.oag-ns.ca	2
Canada, Ontario	Office of the Auditor General of Ontario	www.auditor.on.ca	1
Canada, Quebec	Vérificateur général du Québec	www.vgq.gouv.qc.ca	2
Czech Republic	Nejvyšší kontrolní úřad	www.nku.cz	1
Germany, Baden-Württemberg	Rechnungshof Baden-Württemberg	www.rechnungshof.baden-wuerttemberg.de	1
Germany, Bavaria	Bayerischer Oberster Rechnungshof	www.orh.bayern.de	1
Germany, federal level	Bundesrechnungshof	www.bundesrechnungshof.de	3
Hungary	Állami Számvevőszék	www.asz.hu	5
India	Comptroller and Auditor General of India	www.cag.gov.in	8
Ireland	Office of the Comptroller and Auditor General	www.audgen.gov.ie	2
Lithuania	Valstybės kontrolė	www.vkontrole.lt	1
The Netherlands	Algemene Rekenkamer	www.rekenkamer.nl	3
UK	National Audit Office	www.nao.gov.uk	2 (72)
USA, New York	Office of the State Comptroller, New York State	www.osc.state.ny.us	2
USA, Virginia	Auditor of Public Accounts, Commonwealth of Virginia.	www.apa.virginia.gov	1
USA, federal level	United States Government Accountability Office (GAO)	www.gao.gov	3

Most reports originate from Europe (22). Our list does not include any reports from South America or Africa. The UK's National Audit Office is by far the biggest producer of reports on PPPs, having published a total of 72 such reports on private finance initiatives, including a survey document of which we made extensive use for the purpose of our own study (UK 2009). Also several reports deal with more than one PPP project.

So what possible explanations can there be for the unavailability – or availability, as the case may be – of audit reports? Although this is not an aspect that we examined during our study the following factors – apart from the chosen method of stock-taking – may conceivably play a role:

- the national policy on PPPs: i.e. the number of PPP projects actually performed in the country in question;
- the mandate: certain audit offices may have mandates limited to perform only financial audits, or they may be subject to certain other restrictions in terms of their ability to perform VfM audits;
- priorities: audit offices may tend to focus on short-term public spending and, in parallel with this, assume that the degree of (financial) risk associated with PPP projects is relatively low;
- expertise: the complexity of PPP projects and the lack of specialist expertise available to the audit office in question.

19.1.5 Format of the chapter

This chapter sets out the findings of audit offices on:

- the pre-contract stage;
- financing and costs;
- contract management;
- political accountability;
- the evaluation of PPP projects;
- the policies and conditions that need to be fulfilled for PPPs to be successful.

The chapter ends with a number of concluding remarks on PPP and comments on the role played by audit offices in this connection.

19.2 The pre-contract stage

This section discusses the findings of audit offices on:

- the use of an added value test for assessing a PPP;
- the design of added value tests, and its inherent limitations;
- the way added value tests are used in practice, and the supporting evidence;
- the procurement phase.

19.2.1 Added value tests: not always used

Government policy in many countries is to ascertain whether carrying out projects, often of an infrastructural nature, as a PPP generates any added value compared with a situation in which the same project were to be performed by government. Despite this, a number of audit offices have found that such a comparison is not always made. In the Flanders region of Belgium, for example, the Belgian Court of Audit found that the public-sector contracting authority only very rarely performs an added value test to support its decision to have a given project performed either in PPP or traditional procurement (Belgium 2009: 12). The same applies to projects in India, Hungary, Canada and Lithuania examined by the relevant national audit offices: the decision to have the project performed by a PPP was not found to be supported by any hard evidence (India 2008a: 39, 2008b: 9; Hungary 2006: 2–3, 2007a: 1; Canada, Ontario 2008: 104; Lithuania 2008).

> It was the government of the day that decided to follow the public–private partnership approach. [. . .] The costs and benefits of alternative procurement approaches, including traditional procurement, were not adequately assessed.
>
> *(Canada, Ontario 2008: 104)*

One possible explanation for the absence of these added value tests may be a desire to ensure that the financing for the projects in question is kept off the balance sheets (see section 1.3). In that case, using a PPP or an alternative form of private-sector financing is no longer a question of choice, but a precondition for the project.

19.2.2 Added value tests: inherent limitations

In the majority of countries on which audit office reports were available, added value testing – often performed in the form of a Public Sector Comparator (PSC) – did appear to form part of the standard procedure. Although there is a broad consensus that added value tests are 'useful tools', many audit offices are critical about the way in which they are used, pointing to certain *inherent limitations* that decision-makers tend to ignore in practice.

First of all, the results of an added value test depend (in part) on certain arbitrary assumptions and estimates of a large number of parameters whose value is uncertain. Examples of these include the scale and monetary value of risks (see section 19.3.2) and the discount rate used. The latter is the rate of interest used to calculate the net present value of the costs and benefits of a long-term investment project. In many cases, audit offices found that the discount rate applied was either too high or too low. They also noted that, the higher the discount rate, the more preferable a PPP seemed as compared with a conventional public-sector alternative, and vice versa.

> It is recognized that the higher the discount rate used to convert to today's dollars of the cash flows associated with the two options, the more the PPP will appear preferable over a conventional public sector method, and conversely, because the PPP method permits for the spreading out of expenses over a longer period than does the conventional method.
>
> *(Canada, Quebec 2009: 16)*

This could result in a situation in which an excessively high discount rate is used without good reason (Canada, Quebec 2009: 16).

The same mechanism applies to the amount and rating of the transferred risk to the concessionaire. The higher this is and the higher the discount rate, the higher the added value of the PPP. The Austrian Court of Audit found in the PSC for a road project an inexplicable high transferred risk value compared to other countries and a consequently high added value for the PPP (Austria 2010: 33–7).

One of the problems in the choice of the discount rate is the absence of any sector-specific PSCs, which means that discount rates cannot be set with the specific circumstances of the sector in question in mind. The US Government Accountability Office notes in this connection that 'discount rates used in PSCs to calculate the present value of future streams of revenue may be arbitrarily chosen by the procuring authority if not mandated by the government' (USA 2008: 54).

Also, the long-term nature of PPPs (the contract periods are usually 25–30 years) does not add to the reliability of added value tests. This restriction is often neglected in administrative and political communications, and hence in the decision-making procedure. Also decisions are often based on a best-case scenario, without taking the worst case into account. For example, in a report on the construction of a high-speed rail link, the Netherlands Court of Audit claimed that ministers were acting too hastily in writing to parliament about the project's 'proven added value', and stressed that this 'added value' was merely 'the highly uncertain result of a theoretical exercise' (The Netherlands 2002: 62).

Second, an added value test may not take certain costs into account. Our analysis of audit reports shows, however, that only a relatively small number of audit offices we looked at took account of the extra cost resulting from the use of new types of outsourcing as compared with the cost of conventional forms of outsourcing. The UK's National Audit Office is one of the few audit offices to point to this additional cost, which it says includes the additional cost incurred in raising loans and risk capital (i.e. equity and subordinate debt), a risk premium, transaction costs, the cost of complex tendering procedures and contract management costs (UK 2009: 22). The Netherlands Court of Audit also refers to transaction and management costs that are not factored into the cost of PPPs (The Netherlands 2002: 23, 62).

Third (and this is a fundamental point), added value tests are economic models that offer hardly any scope for factors of a qualitative or strategic nature. The Auditor General of Quebec (Canada) states in this connection that 'other factors, which are hard or impossible to quantify from a financial standpoint, may have an impact on the value of the options, and these advantages and drawbacks must be reviewed' (Canada, Quebec 2009: 17).

> In the business cases of Montreal's University Health Centers, the qualitative analyses do not deal much with the drawbacks which the PPP method could entail (example: the uncertainty of the transfer of risks, the long-term survival of the private consortium, the flexibility to meet the needs) and the advantages of the conventional method.
>
> *(Canada, Quebec 2009: 17)*

In other words, the outcome of an added value test should not be the sole factor that is taken into consideration when deciding in principle whether or not to opt for a DBFM(O) contract. As the UK's National Audit Office points out:

> Like any financial model, they cannot be relied upon as a sole source of assurance. Strategic issues can outweigh considerations of pure cost efficiency, but are unconvincing if they appear as *post hoc* rationalizations. They need to be clearly stated at the outset and built into the procurement process. When assessing private finance projects, we expect the public authority to have considered carefully whether there are strategic advantages or disadvantages from using private finance, such as: the need for a development to be operational by a particular date; the ability to access scarce skills; the desire of supporting particular parts of industry; the need for flexibility; or the inability to commit to long term current spending.
>
> *(UK 2009: 21)*

19.2.3 Added value tests: often not enough supporting evidence

The UK's National Audit Office concludes that there is practical evidence to show that added value tests are prone to mistakes, manipulation and misuse (UK 2009: 20). Computational errors, inaccurate estimates of parameters and the lack of good benchmarks may sometimes result in a PSC painting an overly flattering picture (Ireland 2004: 11–12). Equally, certain costs may be wrongly included in the cost of a public-sector project approach, or they may be overestimated (Canada, Ontario 2008: 104–5). Also, for instance, the estimate for the future use made of a road may be too optimistic (Austria 2010: 48). Because projects generally have a long life, even very slight variations in estimates can have massive financial consequences.

Another important observation is that the advantages of a particular proposal are often stressed without actually comparing the proposal with an alternative option, such as a fully conventional procurement and construction process (Belgium 2009: 34; Germany 2009: 41). The German Court of Audit emphasizes the importance of such a comparison (Germany 2009: 17–18). In some cases, the private-sector performance of a project in the form of a DBFM(O) contract is compared with fully traditional public procurement, but not with other options such as DB or turn-key contracts (Canada, Quebec 2009: 16).

It is interesting to wonder *why* so much goes wrong when added value tests are used. In certain cases, the PSC was conducted amid an overriding impression that it had already been decided that the outcome would be positive. Clearly, such an atmosphere is not conducive to the reliability of the test. At the same time, one should acknowledge the extreme difficulty of making a careful comparison between DBFM(O) contracts and their more traditional procurement counterparts. This is because of the large number of unknowns, the long life of the project, the high cost of mitigating the risks involved, and the difficulty of making accurate projections of future market prices. The problem is compounded by the absence of comparative data. Reliable figures are needed in order to calculate the cost of maintaining conventional building projects, and these should be based on the cost of comparable projects. Unfortunately, data on the latter may not be transparent, or it may prove that the projects themselves are not comparable (Germany, Baden-Württemberg 2009: 6, 40; Austria 2010: 24–5).

Nonetheless, notwithstanding the many criticisms levelled at added value tests, there is no reason to conclude that DBFM(O) contracts are by definition based on flimsier arguments or less reliable data than other types of contract. There is, after all, a shortage of studies comparing the merits of DBFM(O) contracts with those of conventional contracts in this and other respects. As the UK's National Audit Office points out, 'public authorities generally undertake greater scrutiny of the costs and benefits of PPPs than they do for other types of projects. In part, this is because there is greater guidance on what they need to do' (UK 2009: 45).

19.2.4 Procurement

Audit offices have performed many audits of the procurement processes of DBFM(O) contracts. The UK's National Audit Office writes that an effective tendering procedure is 'vital because the initial commercial terms often last throughout the life of the project' (UK 2009: 52–3). The National Audit Office reckons that the greatest threat to the 'value for money' arises 'during the final stage of negotiations, when negotiation is with a single preferred (or final bidder) and competitive tension is at its weakest' (UK 2009: 52–3).

Although a number of reports conclude that the procurement was 'fair and open' (Belgium 2009: 14, 63–4; Canada, Alberta 2010: 13), things sometimes go wrong. For instance, insufficient account may have been taken of the prevailing market conditions (Belgium 2009: 13, 47), or there may not have been enough competition for the contract (Lithuania 2008; The Netherlands 1993: 3).

> The Court of Audit believes that the selection procedure used for raising finance for the Wijker Tunnel [. . .] did not provide sufficient guarantees that the outcome would be as beneficial as possible to the State. [. . .] The Court of Audit feels that the minister should have prevented a situation from arising in which she entered into a contract on the basis of a single tender without having any alternatives from which to choose.
>
> *(The Netherlands 1993: 3)*

A frequently signalled problem in the audit reports we examined was the inadequate nature of the internal and external controls applied, particularly during the procurement stage. In some cases, the use of such controls would appear to conflict with the need for preserving the confidentiality of the projects in question. In expressing a positive opinion on the role of the special 'fairness auditor', the Auditor General of Alberta in Canada shows that controls and confidentiality are not necessarily in conflict with each other.

(Canada, Alberta 2010)

> A Fairness Auditor was engaged to observe procurement processes and report on adherence to the fairness principles contained in the Management Framework: Procurement Process. The Fairness Auditor's interim and final reports concluded that the fairness principles were complied with. We tested conclusions contained in the Fairness Auditor's report. [. . .] Based on our work, we concur with the Fairness Auditor's conclusions.
>
> *(Canada, Alberta 2010: 27)*

19.2.5 Summing up

Generally speaking, audit offices adopt a neutral stance on the *potential* for added value of DBFM(O) contracts. Audit offices tend, however, to be critical about the *use* of added value tests in calculating a contract's added value. For example, not all relevant costs are included in a PSC, there is often little scope for qualitative arguments and no full comparison may have been made with the alternative options. Audit offices also stress the importance of the procurement procedure, which should involve a sufficient number of competitive tenders and should be subject to adequate internal and external controls.

19.3 Financing and costs

The way in which PPP projects are financed, their costs calculated and the associated risks appraised are all common topics of audits, as are the issues of financial cost-benefit analyses and financial reporting. This section discusses a number of findings in relation to:

- off-balance sheet financing;
- risk appraisal and allocation;
- long-term financial obligations;
- costs of refinancing;
- asset values and ownership rights at the end of the project;
- competition and effects of the credit crunch.

19.3.1 Off-balance sheet financing: a spurious incentive

Governments have an incentive to design public-sector projects in such a way that the financing is kept off the governments' balance sheet, which means that obligations are not capitalized in the accounts. Not only can this incentive result in the added value test being biased towards a PPP approach, as we have already pointed out, it can also lead to terms of PPP contracts being less than ideal.

The UK's National Audit Office described the pressure to keep projects off the balance sheet in its summary report published in 2009, in which it reported that 78 per cent of the PFIs (Private Finance Initiative) in the UK were financed by off-balance sheet methods (UK 2009: 35–6).

> Public authorities often have no alternative source of funding and feel pressured to use private finance because its treatment in financial accounts and budgets make it seem more affordable from the public authority's perspective.
>
> *(UK 2009: 20)*

> Seventy eight per cent (£22 billion) of operational PFIs in England by capital value are not recorded on the balance sheet of public sector financial accounts and thus excluded from the Public Sector Net Debt statistics part of the National Accounts. Only 22 per cent (£6 billion) are on-balance sheet.
>
> *(UK 2009: 35–6)*

> Yet many public authority project and programme managers have continued to tell us that they feel pressure to shape projects so that they are off-balance sheet.
>
> *(UK 2009: 40)*

The Hungarian State Audit Office found that 'choosing a PPP method has been justified by the high level of indebtedness, the attempts to decrease the deficit of the public finances and that in the course of the investments the Government would have liked to ensure also the advantages expected from PPP projects' (Hungary 2009: 1-2).

Off-balance sheet financing is attractive for EU member states as it makes it easier for them to comply with the EU's financial criteria. In the case of Spain, for example, off-balance sheet financing helped it to comply with the criteria for accession to the European Monetary Union (USA 2008: 20).

> By keeping the capital costs off the public budget, Spain mitigated budgetary challenges and met macroeconomic criteria for membership in the European Union's Economic and Monetary Union.
>
> *(USA 2008: 20)*

The same applies to the Flemish regional government in Belgium, which sees a clear link between PPPs and the financial requirements laid down by the EU (Belgium 2009: 25).

> In this context, the Flemish Government regards alternative forms of financing, including PPPs, not just as an option, but as an indispensable tool in achieving its investment goals in an European System of Accounts-neutral manner.
>
> *(Belgium 2009: 25)*

A number of audit offices report on the off-balance sheet financing of PPP projects by getting a separate legal entity to act as the contracting authority (e.g. Austria 2010; Belgium 2007). One example is the ASFINAG (*Autobahnen- und Schnellstraßen-Finanzierungs-Aktiengesellschaft,* the 'Motorways Financing Limited Company') in Austria (Austria 2010: 14), where the State retains the legal title and the separate legal entity becomes the beneficial owner of the infrastructure, over which it has a right of usufruct. This means that the present and future costs of the PPP infrastructure are not visible on the government's balance sheet.

The UK's National Audit Office concludes that the desire to keep PPP contracts off the State balance sheet may create a risk that such contracts are drafted primarily with this in mind rather than with the primary aim of delivering the maximum VfM. This leads to less than ideal solutions such as limited public ownership, relatively low percentages of debt finance, relatively long-lasting projects and inefficient transfers of risk to private-sector parties (e.g. the transfer of inflation and residual risks) (UK 2009: 40–1).

The Belgian Court of Audit also concluded that there were not many occasions on which the government sought to achieve an optimum distribution of risks for the purpose of effective risk management. According to the Belgian Court of Audit, risks were allocated virtually for the exclusive purpose of keeping the financing off the government's balance sheet. More specifically, although the construction and availability risks were transferred to the private-sector partner, in certain cases, the risk associated with the volume of investment was also transferred to the private-sector partner, even though this is a risk that the Flemish regional government is best placed to manage (Belgium 2009: 13).

Financial reporting standards clearly play a role in deciding whether PPP projects should appear on the government's balance sheet and, if so, how. The UK's National Audit Office points out that the adoption of the International Financial Reporting Standards (IFRS) means that PPPs are now more likely to appear more regularly and more clearly on the government's balance sheet (UK 2009: 42). This should put an end to the spurious incentives to keep them off the balance sheet.

IFRS replaces UK GAAP's focus on the balance of risk with a focus on the balance of control. This means that a public authority's accounts will record the asset and liability of a PFI project on a balance sheet where it:

1 controls or regulates what services the contractor must provide with the PFI asset, to whom it must provide them and at what price; and
2 controls any significant residual value interest in the fixed asset at the end of the arrangements (e.g. the public authority can control the use of the asset at the end of the contract, perhaps by an option to purchase it at a set price).

In practice, we expect that nearly all PFI projects will be on the published balance sheets of the individual public bodies after the implementation of IFRS.

(UK 2009: 42)

A problem, however, is that the IFRS are not based on the same principles as those underlying the EU's reporting standards, the European System of Accounts (ESA 95). This means that the information on the risks and obligations pertaining to PPPs distributed at a European level continues to be incomplete.

ESA 95 is produced by the European Commission to standardize economic statistics between EU Member States. ESA 95 is in turn consistent with the System of National Accounts, which was prepared under the auspices of the United Nations and is used globally. [. . .] ESA 95 determines the treatment of PFI projects on the basis of the balance of risk. [. . .] We expect that, whilst nearly all PFI projects will be recorded on the balance sheets of their public client's accounts, the majority will not be included in statistics of Public Sector Net Debt. This removes the incentive to shape projects against the detailed financial reporting standards to ensure that they are off-balance sheet in the accounts.

(UK 2009: 42)

19.3.2 Risk appraisal and allocation

A clear specification, appraisal and allocation of the risks associated with a PPP project are absolutely vital for its success and added value. Many of the audit office reports on PPPs devote a considerable amount of space to this aspect. One of the few audit offices to take a positive view is the Office of the Auditor General in Alberta:

> The systems demonstrated that risks were transferred to, or retained by, the party who could most cost-effectively manage the risk. Risk was appropriately allocated between the province (departments or school jurisdictions) and contractors.
>
> (Canada, Alberta 2010: 20)

The majority of audit office reports we used in our study, however, contain critical comments on the way in which risks are appraised and apportioned. A number of these risks are discussed in more detail below.

19.3.2.1 Risks are not clearly defined

The Belgian Court of Audit concluded, for example, that the government did not perform full risk analyses in relation to the majority of PPP projects. As a result, the Court believed that the government departments in question were also not well placed to negotiate on the terms of the contract (Belgium 2009: 13). A failure to clearly define the risks involved may induce parties to try and foist their responsibility onto others or to offer non-standard prices. The Auditor General of Quebec came to a similar conclusion (Canada, Quebec 2010: 4). In two reports on toll tunnels published in the early 1990s, the Netherlands Court of Audit concluded that only a limited amount of the risk involved had been transferred to the private sector. The State still bore responsibility for the bulk of the risk associated with larger traffic flows (The Netherlands 1990: 1993).

19.3.2.2 Risks are dependent on other parties

In a report on a high-speed rail link, the Netherlands Court of Audit found that, although the government was responsible for only two significant types of risk (the risk of traffic flows being lower than projected, and the risk of policies and legislation being amended), in certain cases the government would still foot the bill even if the private-sector party in question failed to discharge its contractual obligations. This is because the private-sector party is dependent on the performance of other parties (The Netherlands 2002: 71). This is known as the 'interface risk'.

19.3.2.3 Subcontracts cause risks to transfer back to the government

In some cases, subcontracts have the effect of causing certain risks to transfer back to the government, even though the government continues to pay for their mitigation. This was a finding of the Auditor General of Nova Scotia, Canada, for example, in an audit he performed of service contracts for schools:

> Two developers subcontracted their responsibilities under their service contracts for certain schools to the regional school boards. These subcontracts effectively transfer the risks for the operation and maintenance of the schools assumed by the developers in the service contracts back to government.
>
> (*Canada, Nova Scotia 2010: 27*)

19.3.2.4 No advantages compared with conventional contracts

The Bavarian Supreme Court of Audit analysed the way in which the risks had been appraised and managed in a road construction PPP project that was intended to act as a pilot scheme for future projects. It concluded not only that the way in which risks are appraised and managed in a PPP contract does not offer any advantages over a conventional contract, but also that risks such as those pertaining to cost rises or project management could easily be managed by smart conventional types of contract (Germany, Bavaria 2006: 7, 53, 61).

19.3.3 Long-term budget inflexibility

A number of the audit offices whose reports we studied also cited the long-term nature of the project funding as a risk. The Bavarian Supreme Court of Audit describes as one of the drawbacks of PPPs the fact that they create certain long-term financial obligations which severely curtail the government's room for manoeuvre:

> Every PPP project is based on a direct loan and creates long-term financial obligations for the future, thus restricting the government's future freedom of movement accordingly.
>
> (*Germany, Bavaria 2006: 62*)

The Court of Audit in Baden-Württemberg also referred to the risk of saddling future generations with high costs due to the fact that PPP projects have a long lifespan (Germany, Baden-Württemberg 2009: 46–7).

> The Court of Audit [also] warns about the increasing strain that is placed on future budgets by PPP projects governed by contracts usually lasting between 20 and 30 years (known as 'grey debt'). Therefore, the state budget needs to be made more transparent by including clear information on this point.
>
> (*Germany, Baden-Württemberg 2009 press release: 4*)

19.3.4 Costs of refinancing

The UK's National Audit Office warns that the government must be careful not to lose money when refinancing loans or attracting new investors (UK 2009: 57):

> The NAO recommended in its review of refinancing that authorities assess the impact of refinancing proposals on the future of the project. Factors to consider are particularly service delivery incentives, increased termination liabilities, and the impact of receiving the gain over time if the contract is terminated. [. . .] New sharing arrangements appear to

be working well, but there have been exceptions. We criticized one of the early refinancings, the Norfolk and Norwich PFI Hospital, for only securing the NHS Trust 29 per cent of the £116 million refinancing gain, whilst increasing the contract's termination costs.

(UK 2009: 57)

The investors may change during the course of the project, and the government must be alert to the motives attracting investors to the project:

The development of the secondary market was described in an NAO report on refinancing and the equity market. [. . .] In terms of managing PFI contracts, public authorities need to be aware that investors in their projects may change. The authorities should make sure they understand the business drivers of any new investors.

(UK 2009: 58)

19.3.5 Asset values and ownership rights upon completion of the project

A number of audit offices also discuss the transfer of projects to the government at the end of the contract period. For example, they highlight the importance, in a situation where the government is planning to acquire the ownership of a project at the end of the contract period, of reaching a clear agreement beforehand on the state of the facility to be handed back and on the valuation principles used (Australia, New South Wales 2009: 4; Canada, Nova Scotia 2010: 40, 45). There may be a risk that, if the principles on which the appraisal is based turn out to work against the government's interests, thus resulting in an excessively high purchase price, the government has in fact no choice other than to extend the contract or terminate and vacate the project (Canada, Nova Scotia 2010: 40).

19.3.6 Effects of competition and credit crunch on PPPs' VfM

Innovative forms of outsourcing such as DBFM(O) contracts generate value for money only in a competitive market. The UK's National Audit Office points out that markets, including financial markets, are by no means always competitive: 'Since the credit crisis, there have been particular difficulties in achieving competitive financing' (UK 2009: 20). Similarly, the recent downturn in global financial markets sometimes created uncertainty about the receipt of promised donations by private sector parties (Australia, Victoria 2009: 52).

The credit crunch has also resulted in a relative rise in the cost of borrowing for private-sector parties, thus making PPP contracts more expensive. The UK's National Audit Office claims that, in order to generate value for money during the credit crisis, it may sometimes be necessary to look for both additional sources of finance and potential savings, or else to reappraise the risks involved in the project (UK 2009: 31–4).

This fall in the swap rate has offset some of the increased margins. The NAO does not hold data on the finance costs of projects it is not auditing. It is thus difficult for us to be precise on what the overall effect has been. However, based on our talks with stakeholders, we estimate that the absolute nominal cost of private finance is (roughly) in the region of 30 to 130 basis points higher in 2009 than it was before 2008. This has decreased the affordability of projects.

(UK 2009: 32)

19.3.7 Summing up

With one or two exceptions, the audit office reports we studied are all highly critical of the financing and the cost aspects of PPP projects. Both the costs and the risks are kept off balance sheets; cost calculations are not complete; alternative options are not examined on an equivalent basis; and the government still bears an excessive proportion of the risks involved and hence all too frequently ends up footing too much of the bill.

19.4 Contract management

This section looks at the audit findings on the management of PPP contracts. The following issues are addressed:

- the importance of good contract management;
- performance monitoring;
- staff competence;
- contract changes.

19.4.1 The importance of good contract management

No matter how good a contractual deal is, it is highly unlikely to achieve value for money if it is poorly managed. According to the Auditor-General of New South Wales, Australia, it is becoming increasingly evident that in order to maximise effectiveness, PPPs need to be well managed throughout every phase from establishment of the project deed, through operation and finally to handback (Australia, New South Wales 2009: Foreword; Australia, Victoria 2008: 3). The UK's National Audit Office reports, however, that contract management is not a high-priority issue in relation to PPP projects (UK 2009: 9, 59).

> But a culture continues to exist across much of the public sector of exclusive focus on making the deal. This is in part because much of the VFM of a PPP is established in the planning, tendering and commercial terms embedded in the contract. It is also due to the influence of bringing in technical, legal and commercial advisors whose role it is to ensure that the contract is based on the right commercial terms, and the pressures of negotiation. [. . .] The culture of making the deal has led to the neglect of contract management issues.
>
> (UK 2009: 58–9)

That project management is a recurring problem is clearly illustrated by the delays affecting DBFM(O) projects in practice and by the failure of certain projects to comply with the relevant technical specifications (India 2008a: 39; Czech Republic 2008 press release; UK 2009: 10).

19.4.2 Shortcomings in performance monitoring

Monitoring is a key aspect of good contract management. Monitoring enables the contracting authority to ascertain whether the preset targets have been met and whether the PPP is delivering the agreed goods and services, i.e. whether it is performing in accordance with the agreed contract terms. The audit offices involved in our study regularly encountered shortcomings in both the planning and the execution of monitoring activities.

In some cases audit offices found that the underlying contract gives the government the tools it needs to monitor the degree to which the PPP is complying with the contract terms (e.g. The Netherlands 2002: 71). In many cases, however, they found that the underlying contract either does not contain any monitoring clauses or contains monitoring clauses that are inadequate (e.g. Canada, Nova Scotia: 38; USA, New York State 2002: 14–15). As a consequence, the public authority may not have access to important information it requires to ensure compliance with contract terms (e.g. Canada, Quebec 2010: 38).

> Comprehensive contract terms and management processes and procedures which ensure services paid for are received are essential to protecting the public interest. Our audit identified significant weaknesses in both of these areas. As a result, we cannot conclude on whether key calculations supporting contract payments are correct or whether many services paid for are received.
>
> (*Canada, Nova Scotia 2010: 27*)

Audit offices also found that, even when contracts do contain clauses on performance management and monitoring, the systems are not always well designed (e.g. Hungary 2007a: 2). The UK's National Audit Office points out in this connection that:

> [performance management systems] are difficult to get right, needing to be both well calibrated and managed. Whether services meet an operating specification can involve subjective judgements, such as the meaning of 'clean' in a hospital or the acceptable level of incidents of self-harm in a prison. [. . .] In other situations performance indicators may be misleading or lack objectivity.
>
> (*UK 2009: 55*)

Furthermore, audit offices sometimes conclude that, even where the underlying contract contains effective monitoring clauses and a well-designed system of performance management, the monitoring activities and internal controls may not actually work or work properly in practice (e.g. USA, New York State 2002: 5, 14; Ireland 2006: 95).

> The responses to the audit questionnaire, and the subsequent discussions with the principals of the project schools, raised some doubt as to the extent to which the required maintenance and management services are fully provided. That gives rise to the issue of whether the verification procedures, currently followed by the Department, provide adequate assurance regarding the full delivery of contract services. [. . .] There would appear to be insufficient communication between the Department and the project schools with regard to performance issues.
>
> (*Ireland 2006: 95*)

One of the main problems is that the public authority may not be sufficiently reliant on receiving negative feedback. This may be the case, for example, if staff fail to report faults (UK 2009: 55) or if it is wrongly assumed that the standard of performance must be right as long as users do not complain, even though the users are not actually aware of the detailed service level requirements specified in the contracts (Canada, Nova Scotia 2010: 27–33).

Another interesting finding in this connection is that the government may undermine the success of performance management not just by being *too remote* from the project, but actually by being *too close* to it. For example, the Hungarian State Audit Office found that local authorities were so heavily involved in the operational management of a PPP that it was difficult for them to hold the private-sector partners to account for any non-compliance:

> In practice, however an operational practice has taken place, contrary to the original operation contracts in the course of which the local governments representing the public sector and/or their economic companies have mostly taken over the operational tasks or part of them from the private sector. Their taking a direct or indirect role in the operation (via their economic companies) has decreased the possibility of calling the private partners to account for the level of providing public tasks.
>
> (*Hungary 2009: 1–2*)

Performance regimes (i.e. payment schedules) that outline service levels and apply penalties to providers if they fail to live up to them are potentially powerful tools for controlling contract performance. However, audit offices observe that authorities in practice fail to impose penalties for deficient/non-performance despite the fact that there are relevant clauses in the concession agreements (India 2008b: 30; UK 2009: 28).

> One reason for few penalties is that public clients do not always enforce the contract. Sometimes penalties are offset for other services rendered or suspended as part of a plan to work together to improve performance. Sometimes public clients fear that applying penalties will harm their relationship with the contractors and cause further performance degradation. [. . .] The NAO does believe that public authorities should only waive a penalty where this achieves a higher benefit than the penalty, and after consideration of any moral hazard. [. . .] The main reason for few penalties, however, is likely to be that most project managers report satisfaction with operational performance. [. . .] High levels of satisfaction are also normally reflected in our reports and surveys of users. There may be a risk of bias in project managers self-reporting their satisfaction level. Their views, however, remain an important barometer of performance.
>
> (*UK 2009: 56*)

19.4.3 Shortage of competent staff

One of the risks inherent in good project management and performance monitoring is that there may not be enough competent staff working for the public authority in question, and also that there may be a lack of continuity in this connection. This aspect is regularly stressed in the UK's National Audit Office publications, according to which:

> a lack of staff continuity from the tendering to the contract management stages makes it harder to achieve a high standard of contract management, and causes a loss of technical and commercial knowledge. A change in staff makes it harder to establish effective relationships between the public authority and the contractors. [. . .] Some public authorities do not employ a full-time contract manager, leaving key risks unmonitored and unmanaged. There is a shortage of the commercial and project management skills needed to manage private finance and other major complex projects across government. There is insufficient training for contract managers across government, and limited career structures.
>
> (*UK 2009: 59*)

One popular means of compensating for the lack of expertise and continuity is the use of external consultants. The 'effective use of advisors brings many benefits, including the spread of skills between projects and the provision of key skills at specific points. But it can lead to higher project staff costs; departmental staff not taking responsibility for commercial decisions; and commercial knowledge of projects being lost when they leave' (UK 2009: 55).

Other audit offices in addition to the UK's National Audit Office also point out that, in order to effectively monitor performance and contract compliance, the executive agency that the public authority needs to maintain during the life of the contract has to meet extremely high standards in terms of organisation, expertise and continuity. For example, the Netherlands Court of Audit concludes that, in the case of a high speed rail link project, the government was in fact dependent on external expertise for the effective management, monitoring and control of the project's operational stage (The Netherlands 2002: 45, 76). Other audit reports suggest that proper tendering procedures are not consistently used for recruiting external consultants and that the (often high) cost of engaging external consultants is not always included in price comparisons (Canada, Ontario 2008: 105).

19.4.4 Changes place pressure on added value

Audit offices found that amending a PPP project after the contract has been signed often creates problems and in many cases raises the cost of the project so much as to jeopardize its added value. This may be due to deficiencies in planning. As the Office of the Auditor General of Ontario in Canada reports, 'part of the cost involved in modifying the facilities for the installation of equipment could have been avoided with better planning' (Canada, Ontario 2008: 105). But at the same time, the long life of projects means that changes during the operational or maintenance stage are often unavoidable. Nonetheless, it is clear from audit reports that the government does not always get value for money from such changes. For example, the government sometimes wrongly decides not to follow public procurement procedures in the case of major changes and, in many cases, the private-sector party in question charges an additional management fee which 'may not be justified by the work needed to process the changes' (UK 2009: 56). Finally, it is often difficult to work out how the costs of certain changes have been calculated, and hence whether they are realistic. For this reason, there is a greater risk of legal proceedings in relation to such changes (Austria 2010: 13–14).

19.4.5 Summing up

Audit offices found shortcomings in both the planning and execution of contract management. One of the problems in this connection is the difficulty of formulating good performance indicators. In some cases, the underlying contract does not contain adequate monitoring clauses. However, there are also instances in which, even though a good system of performance management has been put in place, monitoring and internal controls still prove inadequate in practice. The shortage of competent staff employed by public authorities is a factor here. Audit offices also found that changes made during the course of a project place the value for money under pressure. It emerges from the analysis that enforcing all the elements of PPP contracts is essential. Also, monitoring of the execution of contracts with full access by the public sector to relevant information is crucial for the success of PPPs.

19.5 Political accountability

Parliaments can be involved in PPP projects at different times and in different ways. Their role may take the form, for example, of a decision in principle on whether or not to perform the project in question as a PPP, a 'go or no go' decision during the contract negotiations, or as the recipient of progress reports. This section examines the findings of audit offices in relation to the role played by parliament. The following issues are addressed:

- the influence exerted by parliament on the contract terms and negotiations;
- the transparency of budgetary information;
- the progress reports submitted to parliament.

19.5.1 Lack of parliamentary influence on contract terms and negotiations

Not much research has been performed into the role played by parliaments during the preliminary stages and the contract negotiations. The Netherlands Court of Audit is an exception to the rule, having concluded in an audit report on a high-speed rail link – a € 2.3 billion contract – that the Dutch parliament was not sufficiently informed on financial analyses, risks, changes in scope and the claimed efficiency gains of the contract (The Netherlands 2002: 80–1). In its audit the Court also found that the relevant policy documents did not contain arrangements on the negotiating mandate of the responsible minister, or on the explicit right of the House of Representatives to approve the draft contract (The Netherlands 2002: 36–7). This had the effect, the Court concluded, of undermining the House of Representatives' supervisory function and right to amend and approve the government's budget.

In responding to these conclusions, the government said that the State's negotiating position would have been seriously undermined if the House had been informed on certain aspects of the contract and be able to alter the outcome of the negotiations (The Netherlands 2002: 81–2). The Court of Audit stated that it is possible to involve and inform parliament in a smart, effective manner, without becoming embroiled in technical, legal or financial details, and without undermining the State's negotiating position (The Netherlands 2002: 82).

19.5.2 Limited transparency of budgetary information

A number of audit offices, the Dutch and Belgian audit offices in particular, criticized the lack of transparency in the budgetary information on PPP projects. For example, the Netherlands Court of Audit claimed that the way in which the cost of PPPs was budgeted and the risks were allocated was at odds with conventional budgetary methods (The Netherlands 2002: 25):

> The budget is limited to investment periods of five years, whereas PPP projects last 30 years and are priced on the basis of the life-cycle cost. Moreover, PPP projects involve the transfer to private-sector parties of certain risks for which the government would not make any charge were it to retain responsibility for them.
>
> (*The Netherlands 2002: 25*)

The Belgian Court of Audit made a similar comment in 2009, when it said that the budgetary information on PPP projects was 'insufficiently complete and clear'. According to the Court, the reports did not provide sufficient clarity about the extent to which 'the payment obligations – which last beyond the end of the present legislature and also extend beyond the horizon of the multiannual budget – are already restricting the government's future room for manoeuvre in terms of policy-making. Insufficient information is provided on government shareholdings' (Belgium 2009: 15).

19.5.3 Incomplete progress reports to parliament

In certain cases, parliaments receive regular progress reports from the government, including a list of current PPP projects. For example, the British government reports to parliament twice a year on the long-term obligations arising from PFI projects. Acting in collaboration with the UK's National Audit Office, the Treasury (the UK's Finance Ministry) has drawn up guidelines for reporting to parliament (source: PPP, The government's approach, 2000: 33, in: The Netherlands 2002: 25).

PPP contracts are long-term contracts generating payment obligations over a number of years. In Belgium, although the Flemish regional government's long-term obligations are authorized in the form of budget decrees, a large number of PPP-based obligations are incurred by independent agencies and hence are not authorized by budget decrees (Belgium 2009: 15).

A number of audit reports claim that the information given in progress reports is at times incomplete and does not go into specific problems affecting the project in question (The Netherlands 2002: 37; Belgium 2009: 15). The Belgian Court of Audit concluded, for example, that the information in the first two reports that the Flemish regional government presented to the Flemish parliament (situation as in 2009) on current PPP projects and other programmes funded by alternative finance initiatives was not entirely complete:

> For example, the reports do not contain any information on PPP initiatives that have either been terminated or refocused. Moreover, basic terms such as the 'sum invested' are interpreted differently in the various project forms and no accurate explanation is given of the differences between a 'planned decision', a 'decision that has already been taken' and 'a decision that has been put into effect'. The information has not been adjusted to the budgetary documents: it does not contain any clear multi-year table showing all future annual costs accruing from all commitments. No clear distinction is made between basic information and recent developments. Although the Flemish regional government provided more streamlined information on the various projects in the third report, published in December 2008, the information was not entirely up to date.
>
> *(Belgium 2009: 15)*

19.5.4 Summing up

We found that most audit reports published on PPPs by audit offices did not look at the way in which parliament is kept informed, nor at the opportunities open to parliament for influencing the terms of PPP contracts. But the audit offices that looked at this matter found that there is scope for improving the way in which budgetary and reporting procedures are used for informing parliament about PPPs. They were very critical: a great deal of financial information remains outside the routine budgetary and reporting procedures.

19.6 The evaluation of PPP projects

Reliable, thorough evaluations during and after the project are crucial if governments are to learn from PPP projects and improve their policies. Evaluations can be performed at various stages of a project and may relate to certain discrete project stages. For example, they may cover the procurement procedure, the operational stage or the entire process. This section discusses the following topics:

- practical and methodological difficulties encountered in performing evaluations of DBFM(O) projects;
- providing evidence of the added value inherent to DBFM(O) projects.

19.6.1 Government evaluations and analyses often absent or incomplete

The reports published by audit offices show that, in practice, the evaluations produced are often not good enough to provide a basis for support or as input for learning.

First of all, the performance of a project evaluation is not always part of the standard project procedure. This is a missed opportunity for governments to learn from their mistakes. The UK's National Audit Office does not mince its words, concluding that 'a lack of systematic evaluation of operational projects results in missed lessons and means that the costs and benefits commonly assumed in business cases remain largely unproved' (UK 2009: 20).

A second problem is the absence of measurable project objectives or policy aims, which makes it difficult to perform good evaluations in practice. This is just as much a problem for the audit offices themselves, which do not have any objectives they can use as reference points for their audits.

> The documents supporting the decisions in principle taken by the Flemish regional government refer to the policy objectives the PPP projects are supposed to help achieve. However, the specific objectives formulated for the projects in question are not sufficiently SMART to enable a policy review to be performed after the completion of the projects.
>
> *(Belgium 2009: 33)*

A third problem for both evaluators and auditors alike is the absence of relevant data and reference material (see subsection 19.1.2). For example, there is still a shortage of good cost analyses at present, because data are often not collected in a systematic way. This means that it is not possible to make a good comparison between different types of contract or different methods of government procurement. The UK's National Audit Office reports that:

> the main reason that we have not seen such costs comparisons is because departments do not collect data on whole-life costs of projects in a systematic way: central government rarely collects data from local government-funded projects or a devolved funding; PPP costs are rarely collated centrally and, where they are, they are hardly ever updated for contract variations; the costs of ongoing services for conventionally procured buildings are rarely monitored, making whole-life costs very difficult to compare; different procurement routes collect data on different bases
>
> *(UK 2009: 49–50)*

19.6.2 Too little hard evidence of added value generated by PPPs

Partly because of the absence of sufficiently robust evaluations, there is still no hard evidence to show that DBFM(O) projects represent the most efficient form of government procurement. Not surprisingly, many audit offices are critical of the promises made about DBFM(O) projects. The tone of many reports is that, whilst there are clearly potential benefits to be gained from using PPPs, there is no reason, in the light of the practical problems, to assume that these benefits will automatically accrue.

> We find that using private finance brings benefits, but these cannot be counted on. Our reports assess VFM at a particular point in time. That may be after contract letting or at some stage during the contract's operation. Based on these snapshots, we have found some projects which have the potential to be VFM, some where the VFM is uncertain, and some where the project has failed to achieve VFM, normally because it was tendered or managed poorly. [. . .] It is easier to count the failures: a fifth of the projects we have examined have clearly failed to achieve VFM, normally due to poor tendering or contract management.
>
> (UK 2009: 19)

Various audit offices have attempted to ascertain whether PPPs are in effect cheaper than a public-sector alternative. Some reached a cautiously positive conclusion. For instance the Hungarian State Audit Office, which performed an audit of a PPP formed to provide student accommodation, concluded that the use of a PPP had resulted in any event in lower maintenance costs (Hungary 2007b: 1–2).

> Per-unit maintenance costs are lower at the newly constructed dormitories and the reconstructed residence halls than at the traditionally run residence halls.
>
> (Hungary 2007b: 2)

On the other hand, the UK's National Audit Office claims there is no evidence to support the assertion that the whole-life cost of PPPs is lower than that of conventional contracts:

> PFI provides a contractual guarantee that the public client will fund the ongoing maintenance of the building. This has generally meant higher annual maintenance costs than previously and less budgetary flexibility. [. . .] Whether it will lead to an overall reduction in whole-life costs would be very difficult to prove.
>
> (UK 2009: 27)

The Bavarian Supreme Court of Audit even concludes that PPP road construction projects did not actually generate any efficiency gains that could not have been obtained with conventional procurement methods:

> The Bavarian Supreme Court of Audit summarizes the results of its audits as follows: a realistic cost comparison cannot identify any benefits of a PPP over a conventional solution. Cost savings arise if construction work proceeds without any delays. This would also have been possible if the conventional method had been used. The same applies to the cost advantages in using a general contractor as compared with breaking the project down into separate components in accordance with the procurement guidelines.
>
> (Germany, Bavaria 2006: 62)

Although PPPs are expected to improve the manageability of costs and reduce the risk of budget overshoots, a number of audit offices did identify instances of overspending and higher-than-estimated project costs (e.g. Czech Republic 2008 and Canada, Quebec 2010). These may be the result of changes in criteria or conditions, but equally they may be due to a failure to take account of all relevant costs in advance.

19.6.3 Summing up

It is clear from the audit reports we examined that good DBFM(O) evaluations are few. Methodological problems and a lack of willingness to undertake critical evaluations are the main contributory factors. At the same time, the few evaluations that were included in the audits did not show clear evidence that DBFM(O) projects are more efficient than the traditional forms of procurement.

19.7 Policies and conditions for successful PPPs

Audit offices pinpoint a number of vital requirements that both government policy and government organizations need to meet in order to ensure that PPPs are successful. These are:

- a clear definition of the public interest that is at stake;
- the use of a programme-based approach;
- the use of standardized contracts and manuals;
- the creation of knowledge resource centres.

19.7.1 A clear definition of the public interest that is at stake in the PPP

Audit offices attach great value to a clear definition of the public interests that are at stake in the PPP in question (e.g. ISSAI 5220: 18; ISSAI 5240: 8; USA 2008: 9)

> Governments in some countries, including Australia and the UK, have developed systematic approaches to identifying and evaluating public interest before agreements are entered into, including the use of public interest criteria, as well as assessment tools, and require their use when considering private investments in public infrastructure. For example, a state government in Australia uses a public interest test to determine how the public interest would be affected in eight specific areas, including whether the views and rights of affected communities have been heard and protected and whether the process is sufficiently transparent.
>
> (USA 2008: 9)

19.7.2 Programme-based approach

Audit offices often recommend that government departments and agencies adopt a programme-based approach to PPPs (e.g. Hungary 2009: 3). The UK's National Audit Office claims that:

> greater support for public authorities is provided by those departments managing their PPPs as part of a structured programme, such as the Waste Infrastructure Development Programme and the Building Schools for the Future programme. These departments provide an overall aim of the programme, develop the private-sector supply side, evaluate projects and disseminate good practice. Our reports on these programmes have highlighted the benefits that such an approach can bring to a portfolio of projects.
>
> (UK 2009: 60)

However, some audit offices also levelled criticisms at such structured programmes or PPP resource centres. For example, the Netherlands Court of Audit criticized the measurability of the objectives set for the Dutch PPP Knowledge Resource Centre (i.e. no targets and no quality definition; The Netherlands 2000: 14, 19–20). In its report *National Maritime Development Programme*, the Office of the Comptroller and Auditor General of India wrote that PPPs had not yet got off the ground, partly because no clear time schedule for all stages of schemes was formulated and 'that concerted efforts should be made to implement these schemes in a time-bound manner' and also that 'while framing BOT agreements performance benchmarks need to be fixed as per identified best practices' (India 2010: 86, 93).

19.7.3 Standardized contracts and manuals

In their audit findings and recommendations, the audit offices stress the importance of using standardized contracts and procurement procedures, and of producing guidelines and manuals for these. The UK's National Audit Office believes that these should offer great advantages in that 'standardized contracts generally provide a sound basis for the allocation of generic risk in a PFI project' (UK 2009: 23). 'Standardisation enables private finance contracts to achieve greater consistency in best practice' (UK 2009: 29). As the Belgian Court of Audit sees it, standardization leads to lower transaction costs, less complexity and greater transparency (Belgium 2009: 14). The Auditor General of Nova Scotia points to another benefit: 'a contract management manual, for instance, would provide guidance to current and new staff, helping to ensure there are adequate and consistent contract management processes followed when staff responsibilities change or new staff are hired' (Canada, Nova Scotia 2010: 37).

Whereas many audit offices (e.g. USA 2009: 38–9; Canada, Nova Scotia 2010: 37; Hungary 2007b: 1; Belgium 2009: 14) found that no manuals on PPPs were available, in those countries in which manuals had been produced, these sometimes displayed shortcomings. For example, the Netherlands Court of Audit found in 2002 that the manual produced by the Ministry of Finance for the financial management of PPP and DBFM(O) projects did not discuss the aspects of integrity of staff (The Netherlands 2002: 77).

19.7.4 Knowledge resource centres

Audit offices found that, as a consequence of the lack of standardization, the transfer of knowledge all too often took place on an *ad-hoc* basis (e.g. Belgium 2009: 14). They emphasized the importance of PPP resource centres and support units (e.g. Lithuania 2008: 4; Canada, Alberta 2007: 38).

> cooperation between the public and private sector hides high risks as long as there is [. . .] no organization responsible for the coordination, evaluation and auditing tasks.
>
> (*Hungary 2005: 3*)

A number of audit offices recommended setting up national knowledge resource centres to support local and regional authorities, as well as individual organizations such as schools (e.g. USA 2009: 38–9). As far as they are concerned, these resource centres and support units do not necessarily need to be public-sector organizations. The US Government Accountability Office points out, for example, that:

some countries have further protected the public interest in transit projects that use alternative approaches by establishing quasi-governmental entities to assist project sponsors in implementing these arrangements. Entities such as Partnerships UK, Partnerships Victoria, and Partnerships BC are often fee-for-service and associated with Treasury Departments on the provincial and national levels.

(USA 2009: 37)

The US Government Accountability Office goes on to say that:

according to officials in the UK and Canada, these entities create a consistent approach to considering public-private partnerships, such as understanding a project's main risks, which can reduce the time and costs incurred when negotiating a contract. Further, by using standardized contracts developed by these entities, project sponsors can reduce transaction costs – such as legal, financial, and administrative fees – of implementing transit projects that use alternative approaches. Moreover, project sponsors and consultants told us that entities like Partnerships UK and Partnerships BC can foster good public-private partnerships and help further protect the public interest by ensuring consistency in contracts and serving as a repository of institutional knowledge.

(USA 2009: 37)

19.7.5 Summing up

It is remarkable to read so frequently in audit reports that governments have failed to take basic action such as drafting standardized contracts and producing PPP manuals. Governments would also appear to be bad at institutionalizing their own knowledge. In this sense, a programme-based approach coupled with a clear definition of the nature of the public interest that is or should be addressed by the PPP in question is crucially important. Audit offices stress the importance of standardization as allowing governments to lower the transaction costs and mitigate the lack of expertise and the degree of continuity. The latter is a particular problem for governments as compared with private-sector parties, who are generally able to offer better pay.

19.8 General conclusions and lessons learned

A number of summary conclusions may be drawn, and lessons learned, from our analysis of the audit reports. Broadly speaking, we conclude that audit offices are fairly critical with regard to PPPs. As might be expected, audit office reports tend to focus more on those aspects where there is scope for improvement than on things that go well. The main conclusions and lessons regarding PPPs – which also can be read as a list of do's and don'ts – are the following:

19.8.1 Added value test

A number of audit offices found that no added value tests had been performed to corroborate the financial and economic benefits ascribed to PPP projects. At the same time, various audit reports pointed out that, even where such tests were used, certain limitations were inherent in them and their use by decision-makers. The same applies to the conclusions drawn on the basis of the results of added value tests: there is often insufficient evidence to support such conclusions. The claims made about the efficiency gains generated by PPPs on the basis of the outcome of these tests are debatable at the very least.

19.8.2 Procurement

The procurement procedures on which PPP contracts are based are a recurring topic in audit reports. According to the audit offices in question, the tender procedures followed are generally – albeit not always – adequate, with problems arising for example where insufficient account is taken of market conditions or where not enough competitive bids are received. One problem frequently identified by audit offices is the absence of sufficient internal and external controls. These controls would sometimes appear to conflict with the need for preserving the confidentiality of sensitive business information in relation to the projects in question.

19.8.3 Financing and costs

Apart from one or two exceptions, the findings of audits of the financing and costs of PPP projects are all very critical: cost calculations are not complete, alternatives are not compared on a comparable basis, and the government still bears a disproportionate degree of the risk and hence ends up footing too much of the bill. The incentive to keep the cost of the project off the balance sheet may result not only in the added value test being biased towards a PPP approach, but also in the terms of PPP contracts being less than ideal.

19.8.4 Contract management

Many audit offices also found shortcomings in both the planning and execution of contract management, pointing in this connection to the difficulty of formulating good performance indicators. In some cases, contracts do not contain effective monitoring clauses. In other cases, even where there is a well-designed system of performance management, the monitoring activities and internal controls do not actually work properly in practice. The fact that government officials do not possess the necessary expertise is a problem in this respect. Audit offices also found that amendments made to contracts after they have been signed tend to jeopardize their added value.

19.8.5 Political accountability

Broadly speaking, we found that most audit reports did not look at the way in which parliament is kept informed, nor at the opportunities open to parliament for influencing the terms of PPP contracts. In addition to reporting to parliament on specific projects and submitting progress reports on policy, there is also scope for using routine budgetary and reporting procedures to inform parliament about PPPs. This is a point about which audit offices that looked into the information of parliament are very critical: a great deal of financial information remains outside the regular budgetary and reporting procedures.

19.8.6 Evaluations

Good DBFM(O) evaluations are few and far between. In part, this is due to methodological problems and a lack of willingness to undertake critical evaluations. This is a missed opportunity for the public sector to learn from past mistakes. At the same time, we also found that the value for money and added value of PPP projects are aspects that can be computed only in the long term, on the basis of the whole life of the contract in question, which often extends to a period of over 30 years. Hardly any PPP projects have reached this point yet.

19.8.7 Organization and prerequisites

A number of audit offices argue in favour of a policy on PPP and the adoption of a programme-based approach to PPP projects. These are often absent. A PPP policy should include a clear definition of the nature of the public interest that is at stake in the projects in question, as well as a thorough analysis of the added value of using a PPP as compared with a public-sector alternative. This policy should be underpinned by facilities for collecting and sharing knowledge and experience in the form of knowledge resource centres, and by the development of standardized contracts and manuals. In those cases where governments have formulated a policy on PPPs, it is not always fully adopted in practice.

To sum up, huge public interests are often at stake in PPP projects, in terms of the nature and quality of the public services and facilities delivered by them, and the amount of public money invested in them. Audit offices can have an important contribution in this field, not only by issuing audit reports on the subject but also by publishing best practices and guidelines for (the audit of) PPP projects.[2] Public accountability is a key aspect of PPP projects, and improving accountability can help to improve both the decision-making on these projects and the value for money they generate.

Notes

* This chapter does not necessarily reflect the opinion of the Netherlands Court of Audit.
1 The worldwide association of national audit offices, INTOSAI, has 188 members in 193 officially existing countries. National audit offices are a relatively new phenomenon in some countries, such as the new democracies in Africa and Eastern Europe. In many other countries, however, they have been around for many centuries.
2 The UK's National Audit Office is a particularly keen exponent of this. INTOSAI, the international organization of supreme audit institutions, published several guidelines for the audit of PPPs (ISSAI 5220, 5240). The Office of the Comptroller and Auditor General of India has also formulated guidelines for auditing PPP projects (e.g. India 2009).

References

Australia, New South Wales (2006). The Audit Office of New South Wales. Auditor General's report. Performance Audit. *The New Schools Privately Financed Project.* Sydney, March 2006.

Australia, New South Wales (2009). The Audit Office of New South Wales. Auditor General's report. Performance Audit. *Handback of the M4 Toll Way. Roads and Traffic Authority of NSW.* Sydney, October 2009.

Australia, Victoria (2008). Victorian Auditor General. *The New Royal Women's Hospital – a public private partnership.* June 2008.

Australia, Victoria (2009). Victorian Auditor General. *The New Royal Children's Hospital – a public private partnership.* May 2009.

Austria (2010). Österreichische Rechnungshof. *Umsetzung des PPP–Konzessionsmodells Ostregion, Paket 1.* Berichte Bund 2010/2, 10 February 2010.

Belgium (2007). Rekenhof. *Besluitvorming Oosterweelverbinding.* Verslag van het Rekenhof aan het Vlaams Parlement. Stuk 40 (2007–2008) – Nr. 1. Zitting 2007–2008, 30 October 2007.

Belgium (2009). Rekenhof. *Publiek-private samenwerking bij de Vlaamse overheid.* Verslag van het Rekenhof aan het Vlaams Parlement. Brussel, February 2009. Stuk 37-A (2008–2009) – Nr. 1. Zitting 2007–2008, 25 February 2009.

Canada, Alberta (2007). Auditor General Alberta. Annual report of the Auditor General of Alberta 2006–2007, Volume 1 of 2, pp. 29–61. *Assessing and prioritizing Alberta's infrastructure needs.* 19 September 2007.

Canada, Alberta (2010). Auditor General Alberta. Report of the Auditor General of Alberta, pp. 13–30. *Alberta Schools Alternative Procurement.* April 2010.

Canada, Nova Scotia (2010). Office of the Auditor General. Report of the Auditor General, pp. 27–49. *Chapter 3. Education: Contract Management of Public–Private Partnership Schools.* February 2010.

Canada, Ontario (2008). Office of the Auditor General of Ontario; 2008 Annual Report, pp. 102–24. *Chapter 3, Section 3.03. Brampton Civic Hospital Public-private Partnership Project.* Fall 2008.

Canada, Quebec (2009). Auditor General of Quebec. Report of the Auditor General of Quebec to the National Assembly for 2009–2010. Volume II. Highlights, pp. 15–18. *Watch over the projects to modernize Montréal's University Health Centers.* November 2009.

Canada, Quebec (2010). Auditor General of Quebec. Report of the Auditor General of Québec to the National Assembly for 2010–2011. *Special report on the projects to modernize Montreal's University Health Centers.* Highlights.

Czech Republic (2008). Nejvyšší kontrolní úřad (Supreme Audit Office). Informace z kontrolní akce č. 08/16; *Projekt partnerství veřejného a soukromého sektoru Výstavba justičního areálu v Ústí nad Labem.* 2 December 2008. Supreme Audit Office, The Czech Republic. *Efficiency of the public-private partnership project in Ústí nad Labem unguaranteed.* Press Release – 2 December 2008.

Germany (2009a). Der Präsident des Bundesrechnungshofes als Bundesbeauftragter für Wirtschaftlichkeit in der Verwaltung. *Chancen zur Entlastung und Modernisierung des Bundeshaushalts.* Bonn, 23 November 2009.

Germany (2009b). Der Präsident des Bundesrechnungshofes als Bundesbeauftragter für Wirtschaftlichkeit in der Verwaltung. Gutachten des Bundesbeauftragten für Wirtschaftlichkeit in der Verwaltung. *Zu Öffentlich Privaten Partnerschaften (ÖPP) im Bundesfernstraßenbau.* Gz.: V 3 – 2006 – 0201 vom 05.01.2009.

Germany, Baden-Württemberg (2009). Rechnungshof Baden-Württemberg; *Wirtschaftlichkeitsanalyse von ÖPP-Projekten der ersten und zweiten Generation bei Hochbaumaßnahmen des Landes.* Az.: V-1208HB-0602.14. Beratende Äußerung nach § 88 Abs. 2 Landeshaushaltsordnung. March 2009.

Germany, Bavaria (2006). Bayerischer Oberster Rechnungshof. Jahresbericht 2006, pp. 53–62. TNr. 18. *Öffentlich Private Partnerschaften im Staatsstraßenbau.* October 2006.

Hungary (2005). *Summary of the audit of the operation of the financial management of the Ministry of Justice,* Report no. 0567, December 2005.

Hungary (2006). *Summary of the comparative audit on the funding arrangements for motorway development projects,* Report no. 0645, December 2006.

Hungary (2007a). *Summary of the audit of the building and financial operation of the Palace of Arts,* Report no. 0660, January 2007.

Hungary (2007b). *Summary of the higher education investment programme for residence halls,* Report no. 0741, October 2007.

Hungary (2009). *Summary of the Audit on the Implementation of PPP Development Projects of Local Governments Supported in the Framework of the Sport XXI Facility Development Programme and on the Projects' Impact on the Services Provided by Local Governments,* Report no. 0919, July 2009.

India (2008a). Comptroller and Auditor General of India. Audit Report (Civil), Uttarakhand for the Year 2007–2008, Chapter III, Section 3.1. *Public Private Partnership Project: Uttaranchal Bamboo Foundation.*

India (2008b). Comptroller and Auditor General of India. *Public Private Partnership in Implementation of Road Project by National Highways Authority of India (PSU).* Performance Audit – Report 16 of 2008.

India (2009). Comptroller and Auditor General of India. *Public Private Partnerships (PPP) in Infrastructure Project.* Public Auditing Guidelines.

India (2010). Comptroller and Auditor General of India. Report No. 3 – *Performance Audit of Functioning of Major Port Trust in India – Ministry of Shipping. Section 6.1 National Maritime Development Programme.* Report No. 3 of 2009–2010, pp. 80–93.

ISSAI 5220. International Standards of Supreme Audit Institutions. INTOSAI Professional Standards Committee. ISSAI 5220. *Guidelines on Best Practice for the Audit of Public/Private Finance and Concessions (revised).*

ISSAI 5240. International Standards of Supreme Audit Institutions. INTOSAI Professional Standards Committee. ISSAI 5240. *Guideline on Best Practice for the Audit of Risk in Public/Private Partnership (PPP).*

Ireland (2004). Comptroller and Auditor General. Report on Value for Money Examination Department of Education and Science. *The Grouped Schools Pilot Partnership Project.* June 2004.

Ireland (2006). Comptroller and Auditor General. Annual Report 2006. Presented pursuant to Section 3(11) of the Comptroller and Auditor. General (Amendment) Act, 1993 – Dublin. *The Public Private Partnership Pilot Schools Project – Follow Up,* pp. 94–102.

Lithuania (2008). Press Release *Private capital has a little potential to provide public services*, issued in connection with Performance Audit Report 'Private Public Partnerships', 2008-01-15. *Valstybino Audito Ataskaita, Viešojo, Ir Privatus Sektoriaus Bendradarbiavimus*, 2008 m. sausio 15 d. Nr. VA-P-30-5-1.

The Netherlands (1990). Verslag van de Algemene Rekenkamer over 1989. *Private financiering en exploitatie van de Noordtunnel.* Tweede Kamer, vergaderjaar 1989–1990, 21 481, nr. 2, pp. 285–98.

The Netherlands (1993). Algemene Rekenkamer. *Private Financiering Wijkertunnel.* Tweede Kamer, vergaderjaar 1992–1993, 23 205, nr. 1.

The Netherlands (2002). Algemene Rekenkamer. *Nieuwe financiële instrumenten in publiek-private samenwerking.* Tweede Kamer, vergaderjaar 2001–2002, 28 472, nrs. 1–2.

United Kingdom (2001). National Audit Office. *Managing the relationship to secure a successful partnership in PFI projects.* National Audit Office (HC 375, 2001-02).

United Kingdom (2009). National Audit Office. *Private Finance Project.* A paper for the Lords' Economic Affairs Committee. October 2009.

United States of America (2008). United States Government Accountability Office. Report to Congressional Requesters. *Highway Public–Private Partnerships; More Rigorous Up-front Analysis Could Better Secure Potential Benefits and Protect the Public Interest.* GAO-08-44. February 2008.

United States of America (2009). United States Government Accountability Office. Report to Congressional Committees. *Public Transportation; Federal Project Approval Process Remains a Barrier to Greater Private Sector Role and DOT Could Enhance Efforts to Assist Project Sponsors Process, and Options Exist to Expedite Project Development.* GAO-10-19. October 2009.

United States of America, New York (2002). New York State. Office of the State Comptroller. *New York City Department of Parks and Recreation. Ooversight of Public-Private Partnerships.* 2000–N-16. June 2002.

United States of America, Virginia (2005). Auditor of Public Accounts, Commonwealth of Virginia. *Review of the Public Private Education and Infrastructure Act.* November 2005.

Index

Abadie, Richard 327
ABC analysis of risk 256
Abdel Aziz, A.M. 401, 402, 403
ABN AMRO 101, 103, 122
Abrahamse, J.E. 12
accountability 6, 413, 439, 447–9: anti-corruption policy 218, 219, 220, 221–2; auditing 468–9, 475, 476; democratic accountability risk 41, 44, 47, 50, 51; financial crisis 360; legal framework 60; legal risks 402; modern public–private dichotomy 11; nature of 439–41; overview 441–2; partnership arrangements 380, 384, 385; public sector comparator 218; theoretical model of PPP relationships 443–7
accounting 6, 413–14, 432–4: accountability 440; auditing 460–1; financial crisis 332, 338, 343; international guidance 422–3; major issues 414–17; regulatory structure 417–20; responses to ED43 425–32; UK 420–2; *see also* national accounting
Accounting Standards Board (ASB) 415, 421, 432, 434n. 10
accrual accounting 415, 416, 420, 432: public budget norms 307, 318, 319
Acemoglu, Daron 31, 51n. 1
act of God (*force majeure*) 239, 242, 243
added value tests in auditing 454–7, 458, 474
administration policy implications, and game theory 188–9
A4 PPP, the Netherlands 380
Africa 32, 164
African Development Bank (AfDB) 360, 366
agency partnerships, Ireland 377, 378
Aghion, P. 128, 131, 145n. 5
Agranoff, R. 379
Ahadzi, M. 145n. 4
Ahmed, S.M. 99
air traffic control 152
Akintoye, A. 250
Akitoby, Bernardin 45, 310, 312, 414
Albano, G.L. 215
Albert, W. 14

Alberta, Canada: auditing 453, 457, 458, 461, 473; financial crisis 341
Aldrete, R. 59
Alinaitwe, H. 392, 396, 397, 398, 400
Allais, Maurice 21
Allard, G. 403
Allen, Douglas W. 11
Allen Consulting Group 24
Allens Arthur Robinson (AAR) 102
Alonso-Condo 132
Ameden, H. 140, 141
Amorelli, Lara 53
amortization 293–4
Amos, Paul 48, 55
Amsterdam 12, 13
Anderson, E. 112
Andres, Luis A. 164
Angelides, Demos C. 346n. 12, 399, 400
annual debt-service cover ratio (ADSCR) 241–2
answerability cultures, and accountability 443, 449
anti-corruption policy 218–22
Araújo, S. 134, 137
Argentina: anti-corruption policy 219; financial crisis (2001–2) 172. 16; geographical concentration of PPPs 158; Integrity Pact 219; water and sanitation 156
Arndt, R. 98, 99
AS/NZS 98
Asenova, A. 373, 379, 381, 383
Asenova, D. 445, 446
Asia Pacific 337
Asian Development Bank (ADB) 73n. 7, 360, 366
Asian financial crisis 170n. 16, 338, 351
assessment of PPPs 6, 158–60
asset classes 360–1
asset/profit risk (APR) model 251, 281–9
asset specificity 304: risk allocation 112–14, 119, 124; transaction cost economics 108, 110, 112–14
asset utilization model 63, 65
asset values, auditing 463
Athias, L. 134, 137, 379, 382
attributability cultures, and accountability 444–5, 449

479

salary levels, anti-corruption policy 220
Salzmann 397
Samii 397, 398
Sanford, B. 402, 404
sanitation *see* water and sanitation
Sao Paulo Stock Exchange (BOVESPA) 53
Saussier, Stéphane 133, 134, 137, 145n. 2, 159, 379, 382
Savedoff, William 159, 161
Schermer-polder 13, 19
Schierenbeck, H. 250
Schrefler, L. 395
screening strategies 192–4, 195, 196, 197, 203
SCT, General Directorate of Road Development 65
Secretary of Communications and Transport (SCT), Mexico 61, 62, 63, 65
selflessness and accountability 441
separating equilibrium, game theory 179, 180
Serbia 46
Service Concession Arrangements (SCAs) 414, 422, 423, 428, 429, 430–1, 432: IFRIC 12 guidance 312
sewerage *see* water and sanitation
shadow tolls (revenue enhancement) 306: financial crisis 344; legal frameworks for successful PPPs 58, 59; project finance 236
Shan, X. 392
Shaoul, J. 373, 379, 383, 421, 446, 448
Shearer, T. 446
Shirley, Mary 159, 165, 170n. 5
Shleifer, A. 21
shocks: anti-corruption policy 220; corruption 216, 217, 218; incomplete contracts 127, 137–8, 141, 142, 143, 144; research PPPs 141
short-term contracts 404–5, 406–7, 408
shortcomings of PPPs 3, 149–51: challenging nature of PPPs 160–8; double alignment problem 152–5; future of PPPs 168–9; slow and uneven spread of PPPs 155–60
signalling strategies 179, 189–91, 195, 197, 203
Silver, A. 10
Simon, Herbert A. 21
Sinclair, A. 439–40, 445
Singapore 220, 357
site risks 235
Skelcher, C. 379
Slywotsky, A. 138
Smith, A.J. 181, 192
Smith, Adam 10, 11, 31
Smith, M. 378, 379
Smith, Nigel J. 332
Smyth, H. 379, 383
social environment 393–5, 407
social risks 395, 396, 407–8
social welfare 209–10
Société d'Exploitation des Eaux de Guinée (SEEG) 162

Société Nationale des Eau de Guinée (SONEG) 162
Søreide, T. 214
South Africa: capital value of PPPs 345n. 2; financial crisis 339–40; legal frameworks for successful PPPs 50, 54; Public Sector Comparator 50; unsolicited proposals 54
South Asia 337, 352, 353, 362, 363
South Holland 13
South Korea *see* Korea, Republic of
Southern Cross Station (SCS) redevelopment project, Melbourne 100: construction risks 102–3; financial risks 101–2; market risks 103; planning and design risks 102
sovereign debt crisis 5, 350, 367–9
Spackman 397
Spagnolo, G. 222n. 8
Spain: auditing 459; financial crisis 340; geographical concentration of PPPs 158; legal framework 47, 58, 166, 403; market for PPPs 442; minimum traffic/revenue guarantees 58; obstacles and shortcomings of PPPs 166; partnership arrangements 383, 384, 386; project finance 232; value of PPP transactions 23
special purpose companies/vehicles (SPCs/SPVs) 304: accountability 441; accounting 421, 433; bankruptcy 263–4; Dutch Republic 13, 21; legal risks 393; partnership arrangements 373, 374, 375, 377–80, 381–4; project finance 228; risk allocation model 256–2, 263–4, 286, 288, 289–99, 305–6, 311; trends and features of PPPs 25
'Specific Circumstances' clauses 215, 216
Spence, A.M. 179, 180, 192
Spielman, D. 139
Spiller, Pablo T. 159, 161, 165, 169
Spotless Services Australia Ltd 122
Stability and Growth Pact (SGP), European Monetary Union 317
staffing problems, auditing 466–7
stakeholders in PPPs 374–5: Irish roads 376–7; risk profile of PPPs 392–3
Standard & Poor's (S&P) 55, 233, 289, 326
standardized contracts: anti-corruption policy 219–20, 222; auditing 473, 474, 476; legal risks 401–2, 408
state guarantees 306: financial crisis 330, 339, 340, 341; Korea 341; legal frameworks for successful PPPs 58; public budget norms 309, 310, 311, 312; trends and features of PPPs 23, 25
state-owned banks 340
static games 176: complete information 176–7; incomplete information 178–9
step-in rights 342
Stern, J. 403–4
Stevens, R. 139, 140, 141, 142, 144, 403
Stevenson, K.M. 420
Stewart, J. 440, 445
Stiglitz, J. 192

Printed in the United States
by Baker & Taylor Publisher Services